THE GREAT DESTROYER

BARACK OBAMA'S WAR ON THE REPUBLIC

DAVID LIMBAUGH

THRESHOLD EDITIONS

New York   London   Toronto   Sydney   New Delhi

Threshold Editions
A Division of Simon & Schuster, Inc.
1230 Avenue of the Americas
New York, NY 10020

Copyright © 2012 by David Limbaugh
Previously published in 2012 by Regnery Publishing, Inc.

First Threshold Editions trade paperback edition October 2014

THRESHOLD EDITIONS and colophon are trademarks of Simon & Schuster, Inc.

For information about special discounts for bulk purchases, please contact Simon & Schuster Special Sales at 1-866-506-1949 or business@simonandschuster.com.

The Simon & Schuster Speakers Bureau can bring authors to your live event. For more information or to book an event, contact the Simon & Schuster Speakers Bureau at 1-866-248-3049 or visit our website at www.simonspeakers.com.

Cover design by Ariana Grabec-Dingman
Cover art by Pool/Getty Images

Manufactured in the United States of America

10 9 8 7 6 5 4 3 2 1

Library of Congress Cataloging-in-Publication Data

Limbaugh, David.
 The great destroyer / by David Limbaugh.
 p. cm.
1. Obama, Barack. 2. United States—Politics and government—2009–
I. Title.
 E907.L56 2012
 973.932—dc23
                        2012016263
ISBN 978-1-4767-7442-8

To my good friends in the conservative community on Twitter—
a patriotic group of warriors fighting to save the Republic—
and to the tea party movement, which has proven
that the torch of freedom still burns brightly in America

CONTENTS

Introduction to the Paperback Edition...............................ix

Introduction 1

Chapter One
The War on America 13

Chapter Two
The War on the Right.. 37

Chapter Three
The War on the Disobedient 75

Chapter Four
The War on Our Culture and Values................................. 93

Chapter Five
The War on the Economy... 133

Chapter Six
The War on Our Future 167

Chapter Seven
The War on Oil 207

Chapter Eight
The War on Other Energy Sources 237

Chapter Nine
The War on Business 263

Chapter Ten
The War on America's National Security 305

Chapter Eleven
The War on Guns: Operation Fast & Furious 345

Chapter Twelve
The War on the Dignity of His Office 369

Conclusion 399

Acknowledgments 405

Notes 409

Index 481

INTRODUCTION TO THE
PAPERBACK EDITION

When the hardcover version of this book was released in the summer of 2012, I truly didn't expect President Obama to be reelected in November, but he was, and rather handily.

I can't remember any other instance in my lifetime in which a president with such a manifestly poor first-term record was elected to a second term. The election results caused many to wonder whether the American electoral landscape had permanently changed. Had the demographics shifted so dramatically in favor of the Democratic Party? Or have we created such an enormous dependency class that Democrats will have an unchallenged claim on national politics for the foreseeable future?

Though I felt mightily dejected at the election results, I didn't believe at the time, and I believe even less today, that the Republican Party will forever be relegated to minority status. Indeed, as I write these words, the Democrats are expected to receive a major "shellacking" in the November 2014 presidential elections. Though President Obama won't technically be on the ballot, this election is shaping up to be a clear referendum on him and his policies, especially Obamacare. He is currently in denial about this and is struggling to change the narrative to read that Obamacare is a success. He's desperately trying to convince his party's congressional candidates not to disavow his "signature legislative achievement," and to run on Obamacare, instead of running *from* it. But if they know what's politically good for them they'll ignore him, and even then, they'll be fighting an uphill battle.

So, no, I refuse to accept that the Democrats own America from this point forward, for if I accept that premise then I have effectively given up on America, and I'm not about to do that. On the other hand, if Republicans don't quit rolling over for Obama and the Democrats in certain important areas, they will continue to have difficulty appealing to a broad base of voters. If the Republican establishment continues to push "comprehensive immigration reform," if it otherwise emulates Democrats instead of pursuing an agenda based on conservative principles, and if it demonizes and ostracizes tea partiers and other Reagan conservatives, then it very well might be accelerating its own demise.

We're not there yet, and I'm praying we never will be.

At this point, despite the infighting among Republicans, Obama is imploding. Recent polls show his approval ratings at an all-time low. A Fox News poll found that 61 percent of Americans believe he "lies" about important public issues either "most of the time" or "some of the time." How far he has fallen in five short years.

Obama is making many Americans—far more than Beltway denizens might imagine—very nervous. Obama set out to fundamentally change America. He told us he would do it and he has certainly lived up to that promise. From the time he made that commitment, people have been apologizing for him, saying he really didn't mean that. He wasn't really a socialist. He didn't actually have a grudge against America. He wasn't really a race-baiter. He didn't truly subscribe to the venom his preacher,

Rev. Jeremiah Wright, disseminated. He was only speaking in broad figurative terms when he told Joe the Plumber he wanted to spread the wealth around. He believed in making America prosperous, but just wanted to go about it in a different way. He wanted to bring the parties together. He wanted to work toward uniting America and restoring economic growth.

Well, those paying attention knew better. There was no mystery here. Obama did have a grudge against America. He did agree with Rev. Wright's sermons, which he *did* listen to and embrace. Domestic terrorist turned English professor Bill Ayers was indeed a colleague of Obama's, not just some guy he knew in the neighborhood. Obama was determined to fundamentally change America and has proceeded to do so in the following ways:

- by greatly expanding the welfare state,
- by using federal taxing and spending to significantly redistribute wealth,
- by further growing the federal regulatory superstructure,
- by empowering labor unions,
- by radically restructuring America's healthcare,
- by permanently changing the demographic landscape of America and American culture,
- by opening the floodgates to immigration without assimilation,
- by diminishing America's military power and influence in the world,
- by turning traditional values on their head,
- by selectively shrinking religious liberty,
- by assaulting America's conventional energy industry while subsidizing impractical and recklessly wasteful green-energy alternatives,
- by diluting the Second Amendment, and
- by unilaterally abandoning the war on terror and treating it as a law enforcement matter.

On top of all this he has stubbornly pursued reckless spending policies, cynically dismissed the enormousness of the debt, and obstructed
policies aimed at restructuring our entitlement system, which is guaranteed to bankrupt us in its current form. Obama defenders and
garden-variety liberals insist that gargantuan deficit spending was
necessary to stimulate the economy because of the major recession
Obama inherited from President George W. Bush. In fact, the housing
and financial crises leading to this recession were largely a result of
policies that Obama and his fellow liberals pursued and which George
W. Bush tried to prevent, as I documented in the hardcover edition.
Those issues aside, however, this reckless spending not only drove
us further into dangerous debt, but did not grow the economy. This
ongoing deficit spending continued to constitute an enormous drain
on the economy and prevented it from recovering. As of early May
2014, the economy is arguably stalled and possibly back in recession.
Obama still has no answers except to promise malaise in perpetuity,
mitigated only for some by ratcheting up his covetous transfer payments.

Obama has been touting the steady reduction of the nominal unemployment rate, but that figure is particularly misleading in his economy.
It conveniently ignores the fact that we have the lowest labor participation
rate since 1978—meaning more people have literally quit looking for
work and removed themselves from the labor market, which is not
reflected in the unemployment rate. On top of that, some 50 million
people are on food stamps. Indeed, twenty five percent of Americans are
on government food assistance. This is Obama's America. This is the
necessary consequence of overtaxing, over-regulating, and excessive
redistribution.

Obama says we have "the lowest unemployment rate in over five
years," conveniently ignoring that we have the lowest labor participation
rate in decades and that some 50 million people are on food stamps! His
spending, taxing and regulations are killing the job market.

In addition to draining the private sector of our economy and drown-
ing us in debt and regulations, Obama has also continued his pattern of
abusing his executive authority. Repeatedly, he has threatened to use his

"pen" and "phone" to circumvent congressional opposition and the constitutional balance of power that ensures our liberties. But he doesn't just issue executive orders to get around the legislative branch as he did when Congress refused to pass the Dream Act; he literally rewrites laws on the fly by granting exemptions and delaying enforcement and implementation dates, most notably with the Obamacare employer mandate. He also sometimes ignores Congress altogether when he so chooses, as we saw in his decision to use military force in Libya. As of this writing, he is considering changing the nation's deportation policies on his own initiative, simply because Congress won't yield to his demands on the issue.

Obama is also still exhibiting his thin-skinned propensities as he bristles at any criticism, as though there should be an inverse relationship between the frequency of his dishing out insults and that of his being the recipient of criticism. We recently learned that after Dr. Ben Carson criticized the direction America was moving (without mentioning Obama by name) during his keynote address at the 2013 National Prayer Breakfast, the White House was offended and asked that Carson call Obama to apologize. Similarly, famed Watergate journalist Bob Woodward reported that a "very senior person" at the White House warned him in an email that he would "regret doing this," when he criticized Obama over the looming budget cuts involved in the "sequester." When Jake Tapper, then at ABC, asked Obama why he was bringing up the issue of gun violence in the wake of the Sandy Hook Elementary School shootings when he had not raised the issue during previous incidents of gun violence over the last four years, Obama was annoyed. Obama shot back defensively, "Well, here's where I've been, Jake. I've been President of the United States dealing with the worst economic crisis since the Great Depression, an auto industry on the verge of collapse, two wars. I don't think I've been on vacation."

Hmm—he could have fooled us.

When the Republicans try to rein in Obama's spending and bring him to the table over entitlement reforms, he vilifies them as partisan hacks who lack compassion and protect the rich at the expense of the poor and the middle class. He continues to manipulate the race issue with demagoguery, implying that the Republicans are race-driven when they support voter ID laws to safeguard the integrity of our elections, when they insist on border enforcement, when they oppose endless unemployment benefits and increases in the minimum wage, when they try to reduce rather than expand the welfare rolls, and when they are determined to reduce spending and reform entitlements.

The Obama-liberal mind-set goes even further in implying that merely being a conservative is racist.

Obama is not doing all the work toward fundamentally transforming America on his own. He has established a climate conducive to such changes by other like-minded leftists. Militant homosexual activists apparently believe they have a green light to punish those who still believe in traditional marriage, as witnessed by the boycotts of various business establishments owned by Christians, the pressure on Brendan Eich to resign as CEO of Mozilla because it was publicized that he had donated a thousand dollars to support Proposition 8, the California ballot measure to ban same-sex marriage, and the badgering of a baker to force him to cater a same-sex wedding. In Obama's America (and elsewhere), the left excoriated actress Kirsten Dunst for affirming traditional roles for men and women, though she uttered not one syllable against the feminist movement. In Obama's America, Democrats continue to exploit their fraudulently manufactured war on women by the GOP.

The foreign policy front is no better. Obama promised that he would make America respected again on the world stage, but he has made a mess of foreign policy across the board. Russian President Vladimir Putin has negotiated circles around (and mocked) Obama, the Middle East is in constant turmoil. Afghanistan and Iraq are in far more precarious straits than before, Saudi Arabia openly distrusts Obama, and China is on the verge of replacing the United States as the world's largest economy. In the meantime, Secretary of State John Kerry is doing Obama's bidding in mistreating our loyal and able ally, Israel, accusing her of apartheid during a closed-door meeting of the Trilateral Commission. When caught, Kerry protested that he misspoke, but it strains credulity to suggest that such a term is the result of a slip of the tongue. It's notable, also, that

Obama has not reprimanded Kerry for his remarks, much less asked for his resignation.

In the past eighteen months there has been no letup in the Obama scandals. Obama and Attorney General Eric Holder continued to stonewall Congress on Fast and Furious, never having offered the public any kind of satisfactory explanation for the outrage and making no one in the administration accountable. On Benghazi, Obama and his cohorts, including Hillary Clinton, have so far escaped responsibility, despite all the unanswered questions and despite deliberately misleading the public into believing the attack on our consulate was caused by an anti-Islamic video, when they knew that was not the case. After the administration's stonewalling the investigation for more than a year, a lawsuit filed by Judicial Watch resulted in the administration's being forced to turn over documents concerning Benghazi. One of those—an email from Ben Rhodes, an assistant to the president and deputy national security adviser for strategic communications, dated September 14, 2012—turned out to be a veritable smoking gun. It was sent to about a dozen members of Obama's inner circle, including press secretary Jay Carney, and contained talking points to prepare then UN Ambassador Susan Rice for the Sunday talk shows.

Three of the four main bullet points Rhodes was advising Rice to communicate were patently false. They were "to convey that the United States is doing everything that we can to protect our people and facilities abroad"; to underscore that these protests are rooted in an Internet video, and not a broader failure of policy; and "to show that we will be resolute in bringing people who harm Americans to justice, and standing steadfast through these protests." The United States under the Obama administration clearly did not do everything it could to protect our people and facilities. They did not (and still have not as of this writing) do anything to bring to justice those responsible for the attacks. But most outrageous, the attack was not the result of a spontaneous protest to an anti-Islamic video, but "pre-planned" by al-Qaeda and "complex," and the administration knew that because the CIA had made that very clear. The administration manufactured this canard in order to insulate Obama from criticism some two months before the November 2012 election. Obama had boasted that he had al-Qaeda on the run, and this attack, which was a coordinated attack instigated by al-Qaeda, proved his policies in this regard had failed and put the lie to his claim. It revealed that Obama might have acted precipitously in participating militarily to overthrow the Libyan regime, without even consulting Congress, and against warnings that more-radical forces might emerge in the vacuum created by a regime change.

In the wake of being caught red-handed, the administration continued to deny having concocted the video story to protect Obama at the expense of America's interests. Press secretary Jay Carney's circumlocutions on the matter were so transparently dishonest that his former mainstream media colleagues were visibly appalled. Obama still has not apologized, and Susan Rice has so far refused to retract her obviously false story, much less apologize for it. The administration has never answered why changes were made to the talking points memo to blame the video for the attack. Nor have there been any explanations forthcoming from the White House on why the administration failed to protect the Benghazi mission or on what President Obama was doing the night of the attack.

Every month more news seeps out that further incriminates the Internal Revenue Service and points to a conspiracy involving the White House to target conservative and pro-Israel groups for discriminatory treatment in acquiring tax exemptions prior to the 2012 election (and continuing). Released emails show questionable behavior by this agency, with direct knowledge and probable participation by the White House, far more than ever occurred under President Richard Nixon.

The Justice Department under Obama and Holder remains under a cloud, not only with Fast and Furious, but also concerning scandals involving the Justice Department's massive culling of Associated Press reporters' phone records concerning a leak investigation, the department's slandering of Fox News reporter James Rosen over classified information, and its monitoring of Rosen's phone calls and emails.

But nothing has damaged Obama's reputation more than his handling of Obamacare, which exposed who Obama really is. In turn, nothing has damaged America more than this horrible law. From the beginning of

Obama's push for Obamacare to the present, he has shown himself to be relentlessly inflexible and dictatorial, a partisan bully, a remorseless deceiver, and an arrogant practitioner of lawlessness. He was caught flat-out in specific lies such as "If you like your plan or your doctor, you can keep them," and "Health care premiums for an average family of four will decrease by $2,500."

The disastrous rollout of Obamacare showcased Obama's utter incompetence as a manager and his callousness over the damage he caused to people. He flippantly waved off any suggestion that people were being hurt by Obamacare—although millions were losing their coverage under a program billed as protecting people's insurance coverage.

While Obama tried to make us believe that the problems were solely computer-related, those paying attention understood that if anything, the website debacle, ironically, might have provided him cover for the law's substantive failures. Obama remained unrepentant, however, and as soon as he could get away with it, he began making frequent trips to the presidential podium to boast about having reached his goal of seven million new enrollees—the magic number supposedly needed for the bill's funding to work.

Here again, Obama was engaged in flagrant deceit. While seven million people may have signed up, this number alone was staggeringly misleading. Millions of new enrollees already had other coverage, far too few were in the necessary "young and healthy" category necessary to make the numbers work, 15 to 20 percent of enrollees hadn't secured coverage because they hadn't paid their premiums, and an estimated one million more people lost their insurance and couldn't afford to replace it because Obamacare's mandated coverage provisions caused premiums to increase. As astonishingly bad as these numbers were, how much worse would it have been for Obama's sign-up efforts if uninsured Americans hadn't had a gun put to their heads to force them to acquire insurance?

Obama's latest obsession, while waiting for another shot at comprehensive immigration reform, has been his crusade against alleged income inequality in America. This is but another propaganda offering he is using to transform America. After all, he has been in office for more than five years and has only exacerbated these "inequalities," and not because he didn't get his way on policy. His stimulus package, taxes, spending, entitlements and Obamacare were all implemented, and there are still major earnings gaps between the poor and middle class and between the middle class and the wealthy, as there always will be in a free society.

Obama can't abide that capitalism and freedom result in some people's prospering more than others economically, even though far more people prosper overall, and the poor and middle classes do better than under any other system.

America was built on the ideas of freedom and equal opportunity for all. Every day, Obama is taking a sledgehammer to those principles and is hurting the middle class and the poor. Should leaders of a supposedly free society be focusing on how much each person has relative to the next person or on policies designed to give everyone a better chance at prosperity, as only capitalism and free markets do?

Obama ought to be trying to inspire all people to prosper, instead of inciting everyone to covetousness and resentment over whether the other guy has more. His policies have not only swallowed our individual liberties, they have actually harmed the very people he pretends to help. In the long run, it hurts people to become wards of the state. Policies that discourage work and incentivize any kind of welfare impoverish society as a whole and impede growth.

But for all Obama's hype against income inequality in this country, people still move in and out of income groups with surprising frequency. *National Review*'s Kevin Williamson observes that more than half of adult Americans will be at or near the poverty line sometime in their lives. Seventy-three percent of the people will at some point be in the top 20 percent; 39 percent will achieve the top 5 percent for at least a year; and 12 percent will make the top 1 percent for at least a year.

The upshot is that Obama is shooting at a moving target. These income groups are *not* fixed; the middle class and poor are *not* forever consigned to their respective income levels.

If Obama would just quit meddling with our free market, we would see not only vastly more economic growth but also less poverty and greater income mobility. Isn't that what we should aspire to, rather than a government that controls all economic results and, in the process, spreads economic misery?

In keeping with his charmed political career, Obama will not be held electorally accountable personally. He will probably drag down his party—possibly to catastrophic losses—in the 2014 midterm elections. In the end, he might have delivered liberalism damaging blows from which it will have to labor to recover.

If the Republican Party can unite and begin to champion conservative ideas as if they believe in them, they can not only turn things around in the upcoming elections in 2014 and 2016 (and beyond), but they can also institute policies that will begin to reverse the immeasurable damage Obama has done to our economy and our standing in the world.

David Limbaugh
May 2014

INTRODUCTION

This book chronicles the destructive policies and actions of the Obama administration since my last book, *Crimes Against Liberty,* was published in August 2010. The two books together are intended to provide an encyclopedic account of President Obama's broad-based assault on the American republic. In the pages that follow, I chronicle his war on our Constitution and our political and economic liberties, and recount his assault on America's economic, social, cultural, national security, business, and industrial institutions.

While informed readers will be familiar with many of the events detailed in this book, I dare say they won't find a comparable one-stop shop for this contemporary history we've all experienced. It is my hope that the sheer volume and nature of Obama's misdeeds documented herein will shock the conscience of fair readers and demonstrate the gravity of the condition in which America now finds itself after nearly four years of his socialistic and lawless behavior, and underscore the

1

urgency that he be defeated in 2012. In addition, I trust that along with
Crimes Against Liberty, *The Great Destroyer* will in future years serve
as a reminder of how close America came during these years to losing
finally, forever, its freedom tradition and its rightful place as the greatest,
freest, noblest, and most prosperous nation in the history of mankind.

As we'll see in this introduction and in the following chapters, President Obama has repeatedly revealed his impatience with our Constitution's separation of powers and its checks and balances, lamenting that
democracy is sometimes "messy" and frustrating. He just wants the other
branches to get out of his way, because he can't allow a silly inconvenience like the Constitution to obstruct his utopian vision for America.

Obama and his allies have repeatedly broadcast their intentions in
this regard. His former chief of staff, Rahm Emanuel, promised that
Obama would govern through "executive orders and directives to get the
job done across a front of issues."[1] Obama told NBC News anchor Brian
Williams in August 2010 that his "next two years" as president would
be much more about "implementation" and "management" than "constant legislation."[2] "What I'm not gonna do is wait for Congress," he
baldly proclaimed in an interview on *60 Minutes*.[3] And in January 2012,
frustrated with a GOP Congress that properly refused to rubber-stamp
his destructive agenda, he said, "But when Congress refuses to act, and
as a result, hurts our economy and puts our people at risk, then I have
an obligation as President to do what I can without them. I've got an
obligation to act on behalf of the American people. And I'm not going
to stand by while a minority in the Senate puts party ideology ahead of
the people that we were elected to serve."[4]

Obama implements his power-grabs through administrative usurpations of legislative power, executive overreaches, and unconstitutional
legislation, assisted by the many radical, unaccountable czars he has
appointed. In his failed jobs bill (the "American Jobs Act"), he sought to
create a new group of czars (the American Infrastructure Financing
Authority) to manage more than a trillion dollars of taxpayer money for
infrastructure improvements—authority that already resides with the
Department of Transportation, the Department of Energy, and the U.S.
General Services Administration.[5] Columnist Lurita Doan notes that the

White House has also assembled an expansive new cadre of unaccountable White House liaison officers who "seem to be the critical players in so many of the scandals now erupting." Working under the authority of Obama senior advisor Valerie Jarrett, these officers are largely "unqualified and inexperienced" and are "embedded into every single federal agency." Obama reportedly didn't have contact with a half dozen cabinet members during his first two years in office,[6] he rarely meets with his real, Senate-confirmed cabinet members, and increasingly relies on his czars and junior staffers who insulate him from contact with the public.[7]

Conservatives have been exercised over Obamacare, but Obama's Dodd-Frank financial bill is arguably every bit as illegitimate. The bill created the Consumer Financial Protection Bureau (CFPB), to be headed by a five-year presidential appointee whose power, according to one legal expert, would be "so significant it may be unconstitutional." "I am not familiar with an institution that gives so much power to one person," says Todd Zywicki, a law professor at George Mason University. This person, Zywicki explains, does not even have to consult Congress on the agency's budget, which every other agency is required to do. He just has to submit his budget to the Federal Reserve, and as long as it is less than 12 percent of the Fed's revenue, it will be approved. "Basically," notes Zywicki, "this director can do whatever he or she wants with only limited review."[8]

Obama didn't want to wait on the Senate to confirm his appointee to run the CFPB, so he carved out a "special advisory role" at the bureau and appointed the anti-capitalist Harvard professor Elizabeth Warren to lead a team of thirty to forty people at the Department of Treasury.[9] "This legalistic gambit serves as a fig leaf for a very different reality: Mr. Geithner will never reject any of Ms. Warren's 'advice,'" observes Yale Professor Bruce Ackerman. "The simple truth is that the Treasury secretary is being transformed into a rubber stamp for a White House staffer."[10]

Once Warren had served her purposes, Obama nominated former Ohio attorney general Richard Cordray to head the CFPB, because he had established a record in his state as a fierce opponent of banks' mortgage foreclosure practices.[11] Obama circumvented the Senate's refusal to confirm Cordray through his recess appointments power, taking the unprecedented step of exercising it when the Senate was technically still in session.[12]

GOP opposition to Cordray was based more on the outrageous power he would acquire under the statute than on any particular objections to Cordray himself. Under the act, the Federal Reserve, rather than Congress or the Treasury Department, will control the CFPB's funding and budget, thus diminishing its accountability. In December 2011, forty-five senators sent a letter to President Obama objecting to the enormous power Cordray would have as head of the CFPB. "The Director of the CFPB, by design, is set to lead one of the least accountable and most powerful agencies in Washington," Senator Mitch McConnell declared on the Senate floor. "What we're saying is no single person who's unaccountable to the American people should have that much power. We are asking for the same structure as the SEC, the CFTC, and the FDIC, the FTC, the NLRB, and the Consumer Product Safety Commission—the same structure we use anytime we give unelected bureaucrats new powers that need to be checked to protect against abuse.... We don't need any more unelected, unaccountable czars in Washington."[13]

Democrats masterminded the Dodd-Frank bill under the pretense that it would prevent future financial crises such as we experienced in 2008, but as explained in *Crimes Against Liberty*, it will likely cause more problems than it solves. C. Boyden Gray, White House counsel for the George H. W. Bush administration, in December 2010 wrote that the bill "create[s] a structure of almost unlimited, unreviewable and sometimes secret bureaucratic discretion, with no constraints on concentration—a breakdown of the separation of powers, which were created to guard against the exercise of arbitrary authority."[14]

Under the act, the Treasury can petition federal district courts to seize banks that receive government support and non-bank financial institutions the government believes could pose a risk to national financial stability—those "too big to fail." If the entity refuses to comply, the court will decide, sometimes in secret, whether to proceed with receivership. The court, noted Gray, "can eliminate all judicial review simply by doing nothing for 24 hours, after which the petition is granted automatically and liquidation proceeds.... This means the U.S. Treasury and Federal

Deposit Insurance Corp. are acting as a sometimes secret legislative appropriator, executive and judiciary all in one."[15]

As for the bill's constitutionality, Gray said, "It is hard to believe that the Supreme Court would not throw out parts of this scheme as violations of either the Article III judicial powers, due process or even the First Amendment, assuming the justices do not find all of it a violation of the basic constitutional structure." Furthermore, the CFPB and the Financial Stability Oversight Council are also vulnerable to constitutional attack.[16]

More recently, others have begun drawing attention to the threat of Dodd-Frank. In April 2012, Peter J. Wallison of the American Enterprise Institute echoed and expanded on Gray's concerns. After detailing the act's multitudinous defects, he asked, "Does this sound like America? How can this have happened without most people knowing about it? The answer is found in Rahm Emanuel's iconic remark, 'You never want a serious crisis to go to waste.'" Dodd-Frank, Wallison says, was hatched in that crisis atmosphere and rushed through Congress with almost no Republican votes. "It is every bit the ideological sibling of Obamacare," he says, "and if it survives will have as profound an effect on the future of the U.S. financial system as Obamacare will have on health care."[17]

But Obama is quite proud of Dodd-Frank. While denouncing banks for charging debit card fees, he said, "You don't have some inherent right just to get a certain amount of profit if your customers are being mistreated.... This is exactly why we need this [CFPB]. We need somebody whose sole job is to prevent stuff like this."[18] Indeed, Dodd-Frank and Obamacare typify Obama's America: extraordinary power is granted to small groups, bureaus, agencies, and entities to make crucial decisions about the most important aspects of our lives, from our personal health to our finances—in secret and with little accountability—and through structures and processes wholly inimical to our Constitution and our republican form of government.

Sometimes, instead of allocating power to unaccountable agencies and individuals, Obama simply circumvents the law altogether. In chapter seven, we'll see how his renegade Department of Interior wholly defied a federal court order invalidating his ban on deepwater drilling in the Gulf of Mexico. But that is hardly an isolated case. When a federal judge struck down Obama's executive order forcing taxpayers to fund embryonic stem cell research, the administration didn't just appeal the decision; the National Institutes of Health, while saying new grants would be temporarily discontinued, issued guidelines for researchers who had already received such funding, suggesting they could essentially disregard the court's ruling.[19]

Similarly, Interior Secretary Ken Salazar took advantage of a lame duck session of Congress to announce he had directed the Bureau of Land Management to survey its holdings with the goal of designating millions of acres of public land wilderness areas off-limits to development. Outraged, Republican Congressman Don Young responded, "The extreme environmentalist groups couldn't get their wilderness bill past Congress and so now they are circumventing this country's legislative body and having the agencies do their dirty work."[20]

On her website, columnist and blogger Michelle Malkin regularly chronicles the administration's ongoing "stealth land grabs." In one post she describes the administration's "'Great Outdoors Initiative' to lock up more open spaces through executive order," a program that complements a "separate, property-usurping initiative" whereby "17 energy-rich areas in 11 states" have been selected as sites for possible federal "monuments." Malkin also writes about Salazar's elevation of the National Landscape Conservation System (NLCS)—some 27 million acres of wilderness, conservation areas, rivers, and monuments—to a "directorate" within the Bureau of Land Management to manage the lands and protect their values, meaning to safeguard them from evil energy producing activities. The Interior Department inspector general, according to Malkin, has singled out the NLCS for illegal lobbying and coordination with environmental groups that oppose human use of these public lands.[21] In sum, it appears enviro-liberal groups have been acting in concert with the administration to turn federal lands—the federal government owns approximately a third of the land in the United States—into a radical environmentalist project.

Obama made good on his promise to sidestep Congress via executive fiat in his immigration policy as well. For example, the director of

U.S. Immigration and Customs Enforcement issued an immigration enforcement memo directing ICE agents, attorneys, and directors to exercise "prosecutorial discretion," which meant to ease up on deportation actions for illegal aliens who have been students in this country, have lived here since childhood, or have served in the American military—a policy proposed in the DREAM Act that had been spurned by Congress. "This is outright lawlessness on the part of the administration," exclaimed columnist Charles Krauthammer. "The Dream Act was rejected by Congress. It is now being enacted by the executive, despite the express will of the Congress. That is lawless. It may not be an explicit executive order; it's an implicit one."[22] Interestingly, Obama had just told the amnesty-supporting La Raza organization a month before, "I can't change immigration laws on my own," though it "is very tempting."[23]

Then in March 2012, after the Senate had again defeated Obama's beloved Dream Act the previous December, the Obama Department of Homeland Security proposed a new rule to make it easier for illegal immigrants who are immediate family members of American citizens to apply for permanent residency, which experts say could affect more than one million illegal immigrants. Republicans accused Obama of bypassing Congress again. "President Obama and his administration are bending long-established rules to grant backdoor amnesty to potentially millions of illegal immigrants," observed Congressman Lamar Smith.[24]

When Congress refused to pass Obama's $447 billion jobs bill, including one of its provisions to create a $1.5 billion summer jobs fund, Obama would not be denied, and launched a summer jobs initiative to create 110,000 unpaid "volunteer jobs" that would supposedly help create 180,000 "work opportunities" in 2012. The administration also plans to create a "jobs bank" to facilitate more hiring of youth for summer jobs. Heralding the initiative, the White House declared, "Today's announcement is the latest in a series of executive actions the Obama administration is taking to strengthen the economy and move the country forward because we can't wait for Congress to act."[25]

The Obama administration's federal interventionism and lawlessness knows no bounds. Consider these further examples:

- According to columnist Debra J. Saunders, Obama may have begun an undeclared war on states that are imposing the death penalty, using the Food and Drug Administration to withhold approval of drugs used to execute convicted killers.[26]

- Obama plans to boost "gun safety" via executive order. He is exploring potential changes in gun laws that can be secured through executive action and has directed the attorney general to form working groups with "key stakeholders" to identify common-sense gun control measures "fully respecting Second Amendment rights."[27]

- Four-star general William Shelton testified at a classified congressional hearing that the White House pressured him into changing a political briefing to reflect support for a wireless project by Virginia satellite broadband company LightSquared, a Democrat-backed firm, despite the Pentagon's concerns that the project could interfere with GPS.[28] LightSquared is owned by the Harbinger Capital hedge fund, which is led by billionaire investor Phil Falcone. According to the National Legal and Policy Center, after Falcone visited the White House and made large donations to the Democratic Senatorial Campaign Committee, the FCC granted LightSquared "a highly unusual waiver that allows the company to build out a national 4G wireless network on the cheap."[29]

- The administration unilaterally implemented a new waiver plan that makes major changes to the No Child Left Behind Act, flagrantly thwarting the intent of the law and Congress.[30] The administration will grant waivers to states from the law's requirement that schools become proficient in math and reading by 2014, provided they adopt education policy changes the administration deems necessary.[31] Heritage expert Mike Brownfield says Obama's fiat amounts to "NCLB on steroids—ballooning the federal role in education."[32]

- At a "Jobs Council" meeting in October 2011, Obama pushed his advisors to approve stimulus projects "without additional congressional authorization." He ordered them to "scour this report, identify all those areas in which we can act administratively without additional congressional authorization and just get it done."[33]
- Obama "recess-appointed"—when the Senate wasn't actually in recess—three new members for his controversial National Labor Relations Board, ignoring pleas from Republicans that he respect the NLRB's traditional bipartisanship.[34]
- In the crucial swing state of Nevada, Obama announced one of his many schemes to help "responsible underwater homeowners" refinance their mortgages. This time, they won't need an appraisal or a new full credit check, and "risk-based fees" will be eliminated. He had already announced up to one-year forbearance for homeowners who had lost their jobs.[35]
- Obama announced a plan to initiate a taxpayer-funded stimulus through the student loan program he had earlier commandeered on behalf of the federal government. Loan repayment rules would be severely relaxed on the absurd theory that students would spend the money they saved and thereby stimulate the economy. In making this move, Obama ignored the staggering potential losses on individual loans that taxpayers will eat, as well as economists' warnings of an impending college debt bubble that is pushing up tuition rates and jeopardizing credit markets.[36]
- Obama's senior appointees at the U.S. Office of Management and Budget ignored a document subpoena from the House Subcommittee on Oversight and Investigations related to the Solyndra debacle.[37] This was part of a pattern of the administration defying congressional oversight; Obama's attorney later told congressional investigators that the administration would

not cooperate with a document subpoena on Solyndra because the request was allegedly driven by partisanship.[38] The Department of Homeland Security similarly snubbed GOP Oversight Committee Chairman Darrell Issa's document demand concerning allegations of political interference with FOIA requests to the agency. Issa claims the DHS also instructed career employees not to search for the requested documents.[39]

- Although federal employees are banned from soliciting money for an election while in any room or building occupied in the discharge of official duties, the White House produced a fundraising video, apparently in the Map Room, to offer Obama and Vice President Joe Biden as dinner guests for a raffle winner.[40]

- Big Brother Obama approved a federal "anti-bullying" policy wherein Education Department officials have threatened school officials with legal action unless they monitor students' lunchtime chat and even their Facebook posts for ideas and words deemed to be harassing of certain students.[41]

- The pro-Israel group Z Street alleges in a lawsuit that an IRS agent said it might not be granted 501(c)(3) tax-exempt status because its position on Israel differs from the Obama administration's official policies.[42]

- Despite Obama's repeated denunciations of the Bush administration for awarding no-bid contracts in the Middle East, under Obama's watch the U.S. Agency for International Development awarded a no-bid, $266 million contract for a lucrative electricity project in southern Afghanistan.[43]

- Obama's closest allies have politicized completely inappropriate venues, such as the denunciation by Obama advisor Valerie Jarrett—with nary a peep from the left-wing ideologues of church/state separation—of congressional Republicans for blocking Obama's jobs bill during a church service in Atlanta honoring Martin Luther King Jr. Day.[44]

- Obama's EPA imposed an oppressive $75,000-per-day fine on an Idaho couple after designating their property as "wetlands." The Supreme Court rebuked the agency in a 9–0 decision for its high-handed and erroneous edict that the couple was not entitled to judicial review of the EPA's compliance order, and allowed the suit to proceed.[45]

Additionally, attorneys general from numerous states issued a memo detailing twenty-one violations of law committed by the Obama administration. The list includes, among others detailed in this book:

- The FCC's regulation of the internet in defiance of a court order;
- Obamacare's individual mandate;
- The EPA's failure to comply with its own data standards, as revealed by the EPA inspector general;
- Without giving the state time to respond to the charge, the EPA included Texas in a regulation alleging that its air pollution affected a single air-quality monitor all the way in Granite City, Illinois;
- By enacting costly federal regulations, the EPA usurped Oklahoma's authority in the Clean Air Act to determine its own plan for addressing emissions.[46]

Crimes Against Liberty set forth President Obama's essential contempt for and rejection of America's founding principles and much of its history preceding his presidency. While he professes allegiance to our Constitution, our free market economy, our military, and many of our cultural institutions, in office he has demonstrated an unmistakable disdain for all of them. While he holds himself out as a bipartisan conciliator willing to entertain all ideas, he has been more ideologically dogmatic, polarizing, and intentionally divisive than any president in history. While he wants the American people to regard him as a polished statesman who has brought dignity to his office, he has behaved as bully who, in the spirit of his community organizing mentor, Saul Alinsky, isolates, freezes, and demonizes his opponents rather than building a consensus with them. He has refused to accept accountability for his actions and still, preposterously, blames his predecessor George W. Bush for the havoc Obama has wrought on America.

While he would have us believe he is a quasi-messianic figure who will deliver us from despair, he has, in fact, brought America to the brink of financial collapse. Instead of offering constructive solutions to our impending national bankruptcy, he goes back to the same, destructive tactics of scapegoating the so-called wealthy, and not only refuses to exercise leadership to navigate us out of our difficulties, but deliberately obstructs those who offer solutions that will work. While America's financial house burns, Obama doesn't merely fiddle, he pours on accelerants.

Unless we radically turn things around, stop our fiscal bleeding, implement policies to grow the economy and restructure entitlements, halt the systematic gutting of our military and national defenses, and stop attacks on our culture, our social fabric, and our religious liberties, America will indeed cease to be a shining city on a hill. But I am confident that the American people, as ardent lovers of liberty and of their country, will make their voices heard in November and replace President Obama with a president who can once again unshackle the American people and help lead us back to financial soundness, economic prosperity, and reliable national security, and restore a climate of liberty, including religious liberty, to this great and wonderful land.

CHAPTER ONE

THE WAR ON AMERICA

President Obama has shown in both word and deed that he rejects America's founding ideals, which is why he promised to fundamentally change this nation, and why he has embarked on a disturbing course to fulfill his promise. America's greatness, for Obama, is not found in our freedom tradition and our protection of private property, rugged individualism, equal opportunity, merit based achievement, and entrepreneurship. Instead, it depends on a hyperactive, benevolent government to stimulate the economy, initiate and control business activity, and distribute benefits and wealth to strive toward equality of outcome rather than of opportunity.

Obama has repeatedly laid out his vision for stimulating the economy, including in a Denver speech in October 2011 when he was promoting his latest "jobs bill." He said, "So the truth is, the only way we can attack our economic challenges on the scale that's necessary—the only way we can put hundreds of thousands of people, millions of people, back to work—is if Congress is willing to cooperate with the executive branch and we are able to do some bold action, like passing the jobs bill." The same day, in Washington, D.C., Congressman Paul Ryan articulated a competing vision, declaring, "The American Idea belongs to all of us.... What makes America exceptional—what gives life to the American Idea—is our dedication to the self-evident truth that we are all created equal, giving us equal rights to life, liberty and the pursuit of happiness. And that means opportunity."[1]

That outlook was once dominant in this nation. And it is still dominant among the people—but not in the Oval Office.

I'M SO SORRY

President Obama has continued to indulge his fondness for apologizing to foreigners for the United States. When coalition forces inadvertently burned copies of the Koran—which had apparently been defaced by prisoners using them to convey messages to each other— Taliban insurgents called on Afghans to kill foreign troops in revenge. The Koran burnings led to seven straight days of violent protest in which at least forty people were killed, including two American soldiers.

Obama then outraged Americans by sending a letter to Afghan president Hamid Karzai apologizing for the incident—without uttering any objection to the killing of the U.S. soldiers. As Republican presidential candidate Newt Gingrich said, "It is Hamid Karzai who owes the American people an apology, not the other way around."[2] Obama, unfazed by the criticism, bragged that his apology "calmed things down," but lamented, "We're not out of the woods yet," as if it were incumbent on America to continue to grovel.[3]

This was part of a pattern. The *Japan Times* reported, based on a WikiLeaks cable, that in the fall of 2009, Obama sought to visit Hiroshima or Nagasaki personally, to apologize for the nuclear bombings of those cities. This was too much even for the Japanese; their vice foreign minister, Mitoji Yabunaka, dismissed the idea as a "non-starter," insisting that "both governments must temper the public's expectations on such issues" and that if such gestures are to be made, they should be done "without fanfare."[4]

But Obama—peculiarly—was hell-bent on showing contrition whether Japan wanted it or not. After the Japanese rejected the idea of Obama himself visiting Hiroshima, the administration reached a notch down the government chain and in August 2010 sent Ambassador John V. Roos to the annual atomic bombing commemoration in Hiroshima. Never before had the United States sent an official to the ceremony,[5] having always defended the bombings because they shortened a war that Japan launched against the United States with a sneak attack on Pearl Harbor, and because the bombings ultimately saved thousands of American and Japanese lives by obviating an American invasion of Japan.[6]

Obama seems to think it's customary diplomatic practice to apologize for his own country or belittle her in front of foreign audiences, even though his foreign counterparts seldom feel the need to reciprocate. On Veterans Day 2010, instead of extolling America and our armed services, Obama was in Indonesia celebrating its "Heroes Day," lauding its veterans "who have sacrificed on behalf of this great country," and criticizing Americans for distrusting Islam. While Obama often seems alienated from America, he took pains to show that his connection to Indonesia is deeply personal, telling his audience, "When my stepfather was a boy, he watched his own father and older brother leave home to fight and die in the struggle for Indonesian independence."[7]

In March 2011, Obama claimed that Republicans are heartlessly blocking "comprehensive immigration reform." There was nothing new in his statement, except for one thing: he made it on foreign soil, in El Salvador, which has over two million people who live and work in the United States, 30 percent of whom do so illegally.[8] Salvadoran officials declined to return the favor by apologizing for running their country so poorly that hundreds of thousands of their citizens have illegally moved to America.

Obama's habit of smacking America in front of foreign audiences has apparently rubbed off on his confidants. One of his spiritual advisors, Jim Wallis, chose Britain as his venue to attack American greed and nationalism. At the Hope Forum UK, Wallis unleashed a vicious class-warfare attack on Fox News and the "right-wing media in America," which he denounced as "a media that has an ideological point of view, that America is best and the rest of you don't even count, that the rich are our salvation, and that when I say the 1% of the country has more wealth than the bottom 90 percent they say, 'That's a good thing, that's a good thing, just keep feeding the rich and the poor with their little tin cups hoping the rich are good tippers—that's a good thing for the economy.'"[9] With his spiritual counselor harboring this worldview, is it any wonder Obama has openly identified with the Occupy Wall Street Movement and its bogus "99 percent" mantra?

Of course, Obama's prodigious criticism of America is by no means confined to foreign settings. On July 4, 2010, at a White House cookout attended by military personnel, he deviated from the ordinary presidential practice of celebrating our founding principles and instead delivered a mini-diatribe with class warfare and racial themes. He said, "We celebrate the principles that are timeless, tenets first declared by men of property and wealth but which gave rise to what Lincoln called a new birth of freedom in America—civil rights and voting rights, workers' rights and women's rights, and the rights of every American."[10] There's Obama's view of the Founding Fathers: a group of rich and privileged elitists.

Obama's comments, it should be noted, sound relatively mild compared to the views of Michelle Obama. In a 2010 speech to the NAACP, the first lady portrayed America as though it's still dominated by Jim Crow-style inequality. "When so many of our children still attend crumbling schools, and a black child is still far more likely to go to prison than a white child ... when African-American communities are still hit harder than just about anywhere by this economic downturn and so many families are just barely scraping by, I think the founders [of the NAACP] would tell us that now is not the time to rest on our laurels. When stubborn inequality still persists in education and health, in income and wealth, I think those founders would urge us to increase our intensity and to increase our discipline and our focus and keep fighting for a better future for our children and our grandchildren."[11]

President Obama doesn't let the facts get in the way of his ideological pronouncements. In a speech to the Hispanic Caucus in September 2010, he was delighted to tell his audience that "Mexicans" were here in

America long before the United States was even an idea—he was apparently unaware that Mexico gained independence decades after the United States did. Praising all those who have inhabited this "land of plenty" over the years—including the British, French, Dutch, Spanish, Mexicans, and "countless Indian tribes"—he declared that what eventually bound us together was "faith and fidelity to the shared values we all hold so dear." He then began reciting the Declaration of Independence, but he conspicuously omitted the Declaration's identification of who endowed men with unalienable rights—that is, "their Creator."[12] Perhaps Obama considers the idea of a Creator to be insufficiently inclusive.

Obama sometimes seems incapable of restraining his urge to take irreverent swipes at America and American history. Even his picture book for children, *Of Thee I Sing: A Letter to My Daughters*, contained an implied slap at America; in his choice of "13 famous Americans," he included Sitting Bull, the Indian chief who defeated U.S. general George Custer at the Battle of the Little Bighorn.[13]

"ILL-CONCEIVED, ILL-CONCEALED CONTEMPT"

Obama's presidency has seen its share of bad economic news. While immodestly taking credit for the occasional positive development, Obama tends to deflect negative economic news by blaming American business or the American people themselves.

In June 2011, apparently attempting to avoid responsibility for new and dismal unemployment numbers, he told an audience in Iowa that American manufacturers needed to "up [their] game" if we are going to successfully compete in global markets.[14]

At a September fundraiser in San Francisco, Obama shifted the blame to the entire American people, saying, "We have lost our ambition, our imagination, and our willingness to do the things that built the Golden Gate Bridge."[15] Two days later, he declared that the United States "had gotten a little soft and we didn't have that same competitive edge that we needed over the last couple of decades. We need to get back on track."[16] As if to prove he hadn't misspoken, he used the occasion of the

Asia-Pacific Economic Cooperation summit in Hawaii to take another dig at Americans and American businesses. "We've been a little bit lazy, I think, over the last couple of decades," he mused. "We've kind of taken for granted, well, people will want to come here and we aren't out there hungry, selling America and trying to attract new business into America."

Not only did this demonstrate Obama's reflexive inclination to blame America; it was just plain false, illustrating that our president is woefully out of touch with American businesspeople. U.S. small businesses have made valiant efforts to attract foreign businesses to their communities throughout the United States. To the extent they've had difficulty, it is not their lack of industriousness, but the tax and regulatory obstacles that big government liberals have placed in their path, putting America at a comparative disadvantage, as described in chapter nine.

Columnist and Fox News contributor Charles Krauthammer took exception to Obama's gratuitous criticism, saying, "No one is asking him to go out there and to be a jingoistic cheerleader. But when you call your own country 'lazy' when you are abroad, and call it 'unambitious and soft' when you are home, I think what you are showing is not tough love, but ill-conceived, ill-concealed contempt." Krauthammer also faulted the anti-business climate in the United States, rather than American laziness. "Look: Why are people reluctant to invest?" he asked. "We have the highest corporate tax rate in the world—in the industrialized world." Krauthammer observed that the National Labor Relations Board tried "to shut down a $1 billion plant that was constructed as a favor to Obama union allies.... People look abroad and say, 'This isn't a place I want to do business.' It's his issues, his overregulation, over-taxation and all the red tape he has added. And now he blames Americans' laziness? I think it's unseemly."[17]

At a campaign event in November, Obama displayed his brand of "bipartisanship," telling his supporters that Republican leaders, if left to their own devices, would ruin the United States as a land of opportunity— but that his daughters would thrive anyway. "Our kids are going to be fine. And I always tell Malia and Sasha, look, you guys, I don't worry about you ... they're on a path that is going to be successful, even if the country as a whole is not successful."[18] Uplifting sentiments for his children, perhaps, but for the nation he is supposed to lead?

ANTI-AMERICAN PROPAGANDA? YES, PLEASE!

The Arab-based Al Jazeera network is notoriously loaded with anti-American and anti-Semitic propaganda and was the preferred outlet for Osama bin Laden's public communiqués. Yet Obama appointee for assistant secretary at the Department of Homeland Security, Juliette Kayyem, openly encouraged U.S. cable companies to begin broadcasting Al Jazeera. In an op-ed in the *Boston Globe,* Kayyem wrote, "With rare exceptions the largest American cable and satellite providers simply do not provide viewers access to Al Jazeera English, the cousin to the powerful Qatar-based world news network.... Not carrying the network sends a message to the Arab world about America's willingness to accept information, unfiltered, from the very region we spend so much time talking about."[19]

"Unfiltered"? Al Jazeera is little more than a propaganda tool for the Emir of Qatar, who established and funds the network. Kayyem also took the opportunity to dutifully attack the Bush administration for trying to establish an alternative station to counter Al Jazeera "on the false assumption that the Arab world had little access to information from the outside world." Kayyem whined that "then-Secretary of Defense Donald Rumsfeld used to verbally accost Al Jazeera's war coverage as 'vicious, inaccurate, and inexcusable.'"

"Verbally accost"? Whose side is this lady on? Kayyem bewailed that Arabs believe U.S. cable companies reject Al Jazeera because America doesn't want to hear from the Arab world. But her entire op-ed reinforced that very view, undermining her professed concern.[20] Regardless, our overarching concern should not be what kind of signals we are sending to the Arab world, but the accuracy of the news that is disseminated to the American people. As Ed Lasky wrote in the *American Thinker*, "We have enough terror apologists in the media already without an entire station devoted to obscuring the truth being beamed into America's homes."[21]

STICKING IT TO THE UNITED STATES
SO THE UN DOESN'T HAVE TO

President Obama's impulse to disparage America is intrinsic to his hard-left worldview. Consider, for example, the United States' report to the United Nations Human Rights Council (HRC), which was America's first such submission. While the document reads as an indictment of this nation's record by the anti-American Human Rights Council itself, it's sobering to recognize that it was produced by the Obama administration, which handed the rogue nations on this council the gift they've been waiting for—a validation of their ongoing denunciation of our country. The report sounds more like leftist revisionist history than an objective statement of the United States' record and position on civil rights.

Under the section "Freedom of Political Participation," the report boasts of efforts of "several members of Congress and other policymakers and advocates" to "establish a national mandate for universal voter registration."[22] This is an extremely controversial proposal by Democrats ostensibly to ensure that *all* eligible citizens are registered to vote. In reality, it is a political ploy to increase voting among Democrat-leaning groups such as welfare recipients—and possibly illegal aliens and convicted felons—and a recipe for increasing voter fraud.[23] This highly charged partisan scheme should not be passed off as a corporate statement of the United States in an official report to the UN. Our reports should reflect the existing policy of the United States, not a leftist policy wish list.

Tellingly, the report reflects Obama's view that pre-Obama America was egregiously discriminatory and that he is earnestly striving to correct our past sins. "Work remains," the report says, "to meet our goal of ensuring equality before the law for all." Seeing as equal opportunity and equal protection are already enshrined in our Constitution and in our statutory and common law, it's not immediately clear to what the report is referring. But its meaning becomes clear with its repeated insinuations that our society discriminates against gays and lesbians, and that higher unemployment among African Americans and Hispanics is due to disparities in opportunity (as opposed to, say, welfare programs that might provide a disincentive to work).

Indeed, the report editorializes extensively about America's alleged discrimination against homosexuals. "In each era of our history," it intones, there is "a group whose experience of discrimination illustrates the continuing debate of how we can build a more fair society. In this era, one such group is LGBT Americans." It then discusses same-sex marriage: "Debate continues over equal rights to marriage for LGBT Americans at the federal and state levels, and several states have reformed their laws to provide for same-sex marriages, civil unions, or domestic partnerships." This is but a thinly veiled argument that the refusal to sanctify same-sex marriage in most U.S. states—a policy ratified by the people in dozens of referenda—is tantamount to a human rights violation.[24]

In the report, the administration also boasts about having introduced Obamacare, which it suggests will end our allegedly discriminatory medical system.[25] The report seems anxious to confess, for example, that a disproportionate number of Asian-American men suffer from stomach cancer—as if that is the system's fault, or worse, the result of some malicious, racist mindset. Indeed, the report employs civil rights language in impugning the present system, saying Obamacare will help "reduce disparities and discrimination in access to care."

The report further laments that "U.S. courts have defined our federal constitutional obligations narrowly and primarily by focusing on procedural rights to due process and equal protection of the law." Not to worry, though, because "as a matter of public policy, our citizens have taken action through their elected representatives to help create a society in which prosperity is shared, including social benefits provided by law, so that all citizens can live what [Franklin] Roosevelt called 'a healthy peacetime life.'" It states that Obamacare and the administration's other social initiatives have "reflected a popular sense that the society in which we want to live is one in which each person has the opportunity to live a full and fulfilling life." Though it's unclear what this happy rhetoric means, it can hardly be stated that the American public favors Obamacare.

The report also articulates the administration's partisan views on the War on Terror and Obama's opposition to enhanced interrogation techniques. It details a number of executive orders he signed upon taking office, including the one reiterating his promise—still unfulfilled—to close the Guantanamo Bay detention facilities. It also discusses his creation of a task force to review the "appropriate disposition of each detainee held at Guantanamo." It practically constitutes an apology from the United States for its detention and interrogation policies.

By far the most objectionable part of the report is its submission of U.S. laws and policies for UN review. Encompassing both state and federal legislation, the submission includes Arizona's immigration law (which, incidentally, Obama officials also denounced as a form of American "racial discrimination" during a self-flagellating discussion with officials from Communist China, one of the world's worst human rights offenders.)[26] In its report, the Obama administration offers an update on its attempts to block the Arizona law: "A recent Arizona law, S.B. 1070, has generated significant attention and debate at home and around the world. The issue is being addressed in a court action that argues that the federal government has the authority to set and enforce immigration law. That action is ongoing; parts of the law are currently enjoined."

In a blistering letter to Secretary of State Clinton expressing her "concern and indignation," Arizona Governor Jan Brewer declared,

> Simply put, it is downright offensive that the U.S. State Department included the State of Arizona and S.B. 1070 in a report to the United Nations Council on Human Rights, whose members include such renowned human rights "champions" as Cuba and Libya. Apparently, the federal government is trying to make an international human rights case out of S.B. 1070 on the heels of already filing a federal court case against the State of Arizona. The idea of our own government submitting the duly enacted laws of a State of the United States to "review" by the United Nations is internationalism run amok and unconstitutional. Human rights as guaranteed by the United States and Arizona Constitutions are expressly protected in S.B. 1070 and defended vigorously by my Administration.

Demanding that the administration withdraw the reference to S.B. 1070 from its report, Brewer warned that her state would "fight any attempt by the U.S. Department of State and the United Nations to interfere with the duly enacted laws of the State of Arizona in accordance with the U.S. Constitution."[27]

The administration's suit against Arizona is wholly indefensible. That Obama would take the issue to the UN speaks volumes about his antipathy for American sovereignty.

FUNDING THE UN: A FOOL AND HIS MONEY ARE SOON PARTED

The United States gives the Palestinians $600 million every year, $225 million of which is funneled directly to the Palestinian Authority, in violation of U.S. law. This aid is exceedingly controversial, considering that the PA has abandoned the Oslo Accords' framework for peace, eschewed negotiations with Israel, and is instead seeking direct UN recognition as an independent state. In addition, Palestinian Media Watch reported that the PA used U.S. funds to pay salaries to some 5,500 Palestinian terrorist prisoners in Israeli jails, some of whom murdered Americans.[28]

The U.S. State Department is also paying money to the UN Development Program, which in turn funds the Inter Press Service (IPS)—an organization that purports to be "a communication channel that privileges the voices and the concerns of the poorest." What this means, according to Michael Rubin, an American Enterprise Institute scholar, is that we are indirectly funding a group that is "shilling for Venezuela, Zimbabwe, the Islamic Republic of Iran, Hamas, and Hezbollah."[29] It would appear, based on IPS publications, that the group is also promoting a Palestinian uprising against Israel.[30]

This is all unsurprising; the UN is a notoriously corrupt and dysfunctional organization that lacks accountability. UN peacekeeping troops have been implicated in "a string of sex scandals from Bosnia to the Democratic Republic of Congo to Haiti," the *New York Times* reports. The scandals range from sex trafficking to rape to pedophilia, yet abusive UN soldiers are often simply sent home without punishment. According to the *Times*, "In April, 16 peacekeepers from Benin were sent home from Ivory Coast—more than a year after Save the Children U.K. found that the soldiers traded food for sex with poor, underage girls. More than 100 troops from Sri Lanka were sent home from Haiti in 2007 because of widespread accusations of sex with minors."[31]

The Obama administration seems untroubled by the UN's warped values and irresponsibility, and by its obvious hostility toward the United States. In fact, Secretary of State Hillary Clinton, in a speech to the Council on Foreign Relations in September 2010, called the UN "the single most important global institution," adding that "we are constantly reminded of its value."[32] Indeed, sometimes Obama defers more to UN institutions than to the legislative branch of his own government—that was clearly the case when he sought the UN's approval to intervene in Libya but not the approval of the U.S. Congress.

Republicans such as Congresswoman Ileana Ros-Lehtinen have long pressed for reforms to the UN, but the administration resists their efforts. It ignores critics who argue for America's withdrawal from the UN Human Rights Council, and who have a long list of arguments for such action:

- The majority of its forty-seven member nations are not free countries, according to democracy watchdog Freedom House. Many of these regimes are notorious human rights abusers, such as China, Cuba, Libya, Saudi Arabia, Pakistan, and Russia.
- Eighteen HRC members are part of the Organization of the Islamic Conference, which has leveraged its membership in the HRC to promote its "defamation of religion" campaign aimed at outlawing criticism or mockery of Islam.
- The HRC has never passed resolutions on behalf of civil rights victims of China, Cuba, Iran, Saudi Arabia, or Zimbabwe.
- It has targeted Israel in six out of ten of its "special sessions" involving issues with countries and has named Israel in

70 percent of its condemnatory resolutions.[33] Indeed, the unfair scapegoating of Israel was a major reason cited by the Bush administration for refusing to participate in the HRC.

- The HRC appointed as an "expert" Richard Falk, an international law professor at Princeton who has endorsed 9/11 conspiracy theories blaming the U.S. government for the attacks.[34]

The United States pays some 22 percent of the UN's regular budget and 25 to 27 percent of its peacekeeping budget. Our exact donations to the UN aren't even known, because there are so many UN-affiliated organizations that it's difficult to accurately track our total contributions. Whatever our contributions may be, it's clear the Obama administration has incompetently monitored them; in 2011, it was discovered that we overpaid our share of the peacekeeping budget for 2010–2011 by a whopping $286.7 million, more than three-quarters of the entire $377 million in "cuts" that Congress adopted in the 2011 budget negotiations.[35] The non-partisan watchdog Citizens Against Government Waste (CAGW) argues that the United States should reduce its UN contributions by one-quarter. "As the U.S. attempts to grapple with mounting deficits and debt, organizations like the U.N. should not be spared the knife when it comes to trimming budget fat," says CAGW president Tom Schatz.[36]

Especially in these difficult economic times, it's hard to justify funding the UN at all, much less making a disproportionate contribution.

THE INTERNATIONAL GREEN DREAM

It sometimes seems that to President Obama, there is no cause too controversial or fantastic to be denied taxpayer funding. A case in point: the administration has joined the new Arab-based International Renewable Energy Agency (IRENA), which was "formed in 2009 in response to growing international interest in the adoption of renewable energy technologies to meet the challenges of sustained economic growth, energy security and climate change."[37]

It's not enough that millions of taxpayer dollars are already funneled toward renewable energy worldwide through the United Nations. Now, Obama plans to donate some $5 million to IRENA,[38] whose charter demands mandatory contributions from its members based on the level of their UN contributions.[39] In other words, once again, the United States will bear a disproportionate share of the costs—as if the Middle East's petro-states couldn't spend a pittance of our oil money on developing their own alternative energy.

"THIS IS ABSOLUTELY BACKWARDS"

Obama talks a good game about bringing American businesses home, while his oppressive regulatory and tax policies send them overseas. In his zeal for green energy development, he also casually extends loan guarantees to foreign businesses that have yielded little domestic fruit. In August 2011, Energy Secretary Steven Chu said that the Department of Energy (DOE) had offered a $133.9 million loan guaranty to Abengoa Bioenergy Biomass of Kansas LLC, a subsidiary of a multi-billion-dollar Spanish company. Abengoa aims to use the funds to develop a cellulosic ethanol plant in Hugoton, Kansas, that would convert hundreds of thousands of corn stalks and leaves into some 23 million gallons of ethanol per year. The Department of Energy estimates that with our loan guaranty and others, totaling some $2.6 billion, the project should create 195 permanent jobs.[40]

President Obama presented his jobs plan in Apex, North Carolina, at the headquarters of WestStar Precision, a specialty manufacturer that had just opened a new facility in San Jose, Costa Rica, creating many jobs in that country, but few, if any, in the United States. Republicans were amazed that Obama could be so tone deaf as to promote his American Jobs Act there. GOP spokesman Rob Lockwood said, "Well, the president is coming here to apparently tout how to create jobs in America, and the location he's chosen has just apparently opened up a new manufacturing plant in Costa Rica. So we are curious how a plant in Costa Rica creates American jobs."[41]

Well, American jobs are important, but so is campaign cash, and Obama's choice of speech venue is understandable once you know that the company's owner, Ervin Portman, is a local Democrat on the Wake County, North Carolina, Board of Commissioners and a donor to Obama's 2008 presidential campaign.

This wasn't the first time Obama spoke at a North Carolina-based company with overseas employees. The previous June he spoke at Cree LED light company, also to discuss job creation, despite that company's outsourcing of many jobs to China.[42] Making matters worse, Cree was a major recipient of Obama stimulus funds—$39 million as an Advanced Energy Manufacturing Tax Credit—and apparently used at least a portion of those funds to send jobs overseas. The company's CEO, Chuck Swoboda, has openly indicated his intention to use American taxpayer dollars in China, bragging that more than 50 percent of his company's employees live and work there. He told a Chinese audience that although Cree is an American firm, "Cree management never runs this company as a U.S. company."[43]

The Department of Energy has acknowledged that up to 80 percent of some of the green programs related to the stimulus bill, which involved $2.3 billion of manufacturing tax credits, went to foreign firms that employed workers in China, South Korea, and Spain. These vaunted green jobs continue to enrich foreign producers, said Peter Morici, a University of Maryland business professor, because of those nations' state subsidies and their abundant pool of cheap labor—a fact that has upset Obama's union constituencies.[44]

Obama's allies, like the man himself, sometimes fail to match their rhetoric with their actions. The president appointed Ursula Burns, CEO of Xerox, as vice chairwoman of the President's Export Council, a panel seeking ways to increase U.S. exports and thus domestic jobs. In a recent interview, Burns warned about outsourcing, arguing, "The work has to be done, so we send the work to people in other places that can get it done. This is absolutely backwards." Perhaps Burns' concerns over outsourcing would be more credible if, shortly after she expressed them, Xerox had not informed its product engineering employees that the company was negotiating to outsource jobs to India-based HCL Technologies.[45] Along the same lines, the administration expediently launched a Buy American campaign, seeking to "ensure that transportation infrastructure projects are built with American-made products," just two months before U.S. Transportation Secretary Ray LaHood boasted that he'd advised his daughter to buy a Toyota.[46]

It's one thing for a private American company to choose, for business reasons, to outsource jobs overseas; it's another for a president who has created an unfriendly business climate at home to complain about it. But it's a whole different matter for this president to guarantee a $2.1 billion loan to a foreign-owned company, as he did with German-owned joint-venture Solar Trust of America.

That guaranty arose from an ill-considered 2005 energy bill that empowered the Department of Energy to guarantee private bank loans for "innovative energy technologies." Obama took it to the next level, expanding the project's scope and relieving debtor companies from having to make a down payment. This needlessly increased the exposure of the American taxpayer when we could least afford it. The program has been poorly run since its inception, having widespread gaps in loan documentation.[47] As we will see in chapter eight, the Solyndra scandal was the logical consequence of such negligence.

In a separate example, from the seemingly endless stash of EPA funds used for outlandish green schemes, the Obama administration, through the Arizona Department of Environmental Quality, paid for replacement mufflers for dozens of Mexican trucks to reduce their exhaust emissions, with more to be upgraded in the future.[48] It was apparently unthinkable to suggest that Mexico should pay to upgrade its own vehicles.

Indeed, it seems this administration will support *any* progressive cause, foreign or domestic. For example, federal funding of left-leaning National Public Radio is already controversial, but not only has the Obama administration increased this funding,[49] it's even gearing up to distribute a "significant" sum of money to a foreign state-owned news service. The money is meant to assist the BBC World Service in preventing the suppression of the internet in closed societies such as Iran and China.

Although this may sound like a good cause, one should note that Britain's Foreign Service decided to cut World Service's funding by 16 percent. If the British are scaling back their own service, why is the Obama administration anxious to step into the breach?[50]

AMERICAN CULTURE? THAT'S INTOLERANT!

It's not just for raw political reasons that Obama and the Democrats pander to ethnic identity groups and block serious attempts to secure our borders. Their attitude also flows from their enthusiasm for multiculturalism, which often amounts to an indictment of American and Western culture rather than a mere tolerance of other cultures. They reject American exceptionalism and the very idea of a unique American culture, and this mindset seems to be eating away at the national spirit. Not too long ago, 60 percent of Americans believed American culture was superior to other cultures, but today fewer than 50 percent do.[51] This statistic will not trouble the cultural relativists, but it is troubling to those who still believe that America is the greatest nation in the world and must continue to lead free people and free nations.

This helps to explain the Left's reluctance to promote the assimilation of immigrants into our culture, their mastery of the English language for their own and society's benefit, and their learning of rudimentary civics lessons to instill a sense of pride in their new nation. This is why Americans are now bombarded with foreign-language appeals from everyday businesses—political correctness demands it.

Sadly, the Obama administration is promoting the fracturing of our culture. Obama's Education Department recently supported a first-ever national Spanish spelling bee for students from fourth through eighth grade in New Mexico at the National Hispanic Cultural Center. The event was held in Albuquerque and featured eleven students from four states.[52]

Liberals insist that America's greatness lies in her diversity, but that misses the point. It is wonderful that Americans descend from many ethnicities and nationalities, but without a common bond based on the cultural unity that *e pluribus unum* implies, we will become an increasingly balkanized country. America is unique in the history of nations precisely because it is united around principles, ideals, values, and a specific and unique form of constitutional governance. As the Investors.com editors eloquently wrote, "No other nation in history has been as committed to freeing men, delivering justice and, as the capital of capitalism, advancing prosperity and social mobility as the U.S. has been. None has ever been so humane, so charitable, so inclusive, so overflowing with optimism. It shouldn't be up to the political class to set the tone of the culture. But in our current environment, a change at the top would help restore the faith we've lost in ourselves."[53]

"WE DON'T WANT TO DRINK WATER FROM A WHITE WATER FOUNTAIN"

With immigration, as with many other items on his agenda, Obama thumbs his nose at those who advocate the rule of law in our approach to the knotty problem. He's expressed his support for illegal alien sanctuary cities and for suspending deportations of non-criminal illegal immigrants.[54] His administration has also produced a memo detailing a strategy to circumvent Congress administratively in pursuit of amnesty for illegals.[55]

Obama has gone so far as to embrace the National Council of La Raza, a Hispanic activist organization that advocates open borders and impunity for lawlessness. During the 2008 presidential race Obama courted the group, and in July 2011 he addressed their annual conference in Washington, D.C., expressing his solidarity with them and their goals. Obama bragged that he had "poached quite a few of [their] alumni to work in [his] administration." He also sent La Raza a clear message that Democrats were their friends and Republicans their enemies, declaring, "But here's the only thing you should know. The Democrats and your President are with you. Don't get confused about that. Remember who it is that we need to move in order to actually change the laws."[56]

During his address, Obama also reiterated his support for the DREAM Act, a small-scale amnesty that would grant permanent residency to illegal alien high school graduates who meet conditions such as attending college or joining the military. When Congress refused to approve the DREAM Act amid popular opposition, Obama officials bypassed the people's representatives and simply implemented many of the bill's provisions administratively. As Mark Krikorian from the Center for Immigration Studies remarked, "When the president spoke to La Raza recently and said he couldn't just go around Congress and enact an amnesty, the assembly started chanting, 'Yes, you can! Yes, you can!' Well, he did."[57]

La Raza is a decidedly race-based organization, as its name suggests: La Raza means "The Race." It supports discounted tuition and driver's licenses for illegal aliens as well as illegal alien sanctuary cities. Some believe it serves as the public relations front group for the militant Mexican Reconquista movement, which seeks Mexico's re-conquest of the American southwest.[58] La Raza has also funded a Mexican separatist charter school, Academia Semillas Del Pueblo, whose principal articulated these "educational" objectives:

> We don't necessarily want to go to White schools. What we want to do is teach ourselves, teach our children the way we have of teaching. We don't want to drink from a White water fountain, we have our own wells and our natural reservoirs and our way of collecting rain in our aqueducts.... Ultimately the White way, the American way, the neo liberal, capitalist way of life will eventually lead to our own destruction.[59]

The school provides this description for its 8th grade "United States History and Geography" class: "A People's history of Expansion and Conflict – A thematic survey of American politics, society, culture and political economy; Emphasis throughout on the nations the U.S. usurped, invaded and dominated; Connections between historical rise of capitalism and imperialism with modern political economy and global social relations."[60]

The administration has almost tripled the amount of taxpayer funds (from $4.1 million to $11 million) distributed to La Raza since one of the group's former top officials, Cecilia Muñoz, began serving as Obama's Director of Intergovernmental Affairs. The government watchdog Judicial Watch disclosed that the money came from various sources, with a major portion—60 percent—coming from the Department of Labor, whose head honcho, Hilda Solis, has close ties to La Raza and has begun a national campaign to protect illegal immigrant workers in the United States. Other funding came from the Department of Housing and Urban Development ($2.5 million for housing counseling), the Department of Education ($800,000), and the Centers for Disease Control ($250,000). In addition, the Justice Department granted $600,000 in 2009 and $548,000 in 2010 to Ayuda Inc., a social service and legal assistance organization that provides immigration law services to illegal aliens along with a guarantee to protect their identities.[61]

ASSERTIONS "UNACCOMPANIED BY PERSUASIVE LEGAL CLAIMS"

It's hard to say if it was Obama's ethnic pandering, his multicultural bent, or his reflexive liberalism that led his administration to petition the United States Supreme Court for a stay of execution for a Mexican man convicted of abducting, raping, and murdering—by bludgeoning with a rock—a sixteen-year-old Texan girl, Adria Sauceda. Humberto Leal Jr. apologized and virtually confessed to the murder as he was strapped to the gurney in the death chamber, saying, "I have hurt a lot of people. Let this be final and be done. I take the full blame for this. I am sorry and forgive me, I am truly sorry."[62]

Leal was convicted in 1995, but arresting authorities allegedly didn't advise him of his right to contact his nation's consulate, an oversight that supposedly violated the UN's Vienna Convention on Consular Relations. Liberals inside and outside the administration wanted a stay of execution to provide time for passage of a pending bill offered by Senator Patrick Leahy that would have mandated federal review of the case. While the administration complained about the importance of the United States demonstrating respect for international law, it did not exhibit much respect for American law, given the jury's conviction of Leal based on compelling evidence.[63]

The media focused on the diplomatic implications of the case while offering scant details of the heinous crime.[64] They seemed untroubled by the savagery of the murder or the damning evidence against Leal, such as bite marks found on Sauceda's neck that matched Leal's teeth; blood discovered on the underwear Leal wore the night of the murder; blood stains found on the passenger door and seat of Leal's car; and the fact that thirty minutes after Leal and Sauceda left a party together, Leal's brother arrived at the party and revealed that Leal had come home with blood on him and admitted he'd killed a girl.[65]

The Supreme Court refused to grant the stay, proclaiming, "Our task is to rule on what the law is, not what it might eventually be." Nor was the Court impressed by the administration's extra-legal arguments about possible diplomatic fall-out from the execution. The Court declared, "We have no authority to stay an execution in light of 'an appeal of the president' presenting free-ranging assertions of foreign policy consequences, when those assertions are unaccompanied by persuasive legal claims."[66]

PRAISING COMRADE CHE

Based on the administration's leftist internationalism, it was no surprise when Alec Ross, the State Department's senior advisor on innovation, paid homage to Che Guevara as an exemplar of freedom. At the Innovate Conference in London in June 2011, Ross said, "One thesis statement I want to emphasize is how [the internet] disrupt[s] the exercise of power. They devolve power from the nation state—from governments and large institutions—to individuals ... the Internet has become the Che Guevara of the 21st Century."[67] Che Guevara, of course, was a mass-murdering communist who declared just after the Cuban Missile Crisis, "If the [nuclear] missiles had remained, we would have fired them against the very heart of the U.S., including New York. The victory of socialism is well worth millions of atomic victims."[68]

Along these lines, the U.S. Navy officially named its new cargo ship the USNS *Cesar Chavez*, after the controversial labor leader. Congressman Duncan D. Hunter criticized the choice, arguing that Chavez was a

Communist who hated the Navy. "This decision shows the direction the
Navy is heading," said Hunter. "Naming a ship after Cesar Chavez goes
right along with other recent decisions by the Navy that appear to be
more about making a political statement than upholding the Navy's
history and tradition. If this decision were about recognizing the Hispanic
community's contribution to our nation, many other names come to
mind, including Marine Corps Sgt. Rafael Peralta, who was nominated
for the Medal of Honor for action in Iraq."[69]

TAXES AND REGULATIONS GO GLOBAL

Obama's rejection of American exceptionalism proceeds from his
leftist affinity for globalism and for transnationalism—the notion that
U.S. law should be subordinate to international law. Obama appointed
Yale Law School dean Harold Koh—the United States' leading advocate
for transnationalism—as the State Department's legal advisor, and he
appointed for commerce secretary John Bryson, who some believe,
partially based on a video, favors a world government. In the video,
Bryson speaks favorably of the 2009 UN climate negotiations in
Copenhagen as "the closest thing we have to a world governance
organization," hinting that it provides the best model for imposing global
climate regulations. Colin Hanna, president of Let Freedom Ring, says
that Bryson's statements prove he supports a more powerful United
Nations that can impose its will on climate change policies.[70]

Climate change is not the only issue on which Obama wants to
empower the UN. In September 2010, in preparation for the UN Summit
on the Millennium Development Goals (MDGs), Obama endorsed
"innovative finance mechanisms"—a euphemism for global taxes. The
revenue generated from these "mechanisms" would be over and above
our foreign aid spending and would provide another avenue for Obama's
grand goal of wealth redistribution, this time on a global scale. One
related proposal calls for "small global taxes," such as one scheme
advocated by Cuban dictator Fidel Castro, to tax international currency
transactions to the tune of $35 billion a year. Alarmed by these plans,
Senator David Vitter introduced Senate Resolution 461, "expressing the

sense of the Senate that Congress should reject any proposal for the creation of a system of global taxation and regulation." Predictably, the Democrat-controlled Senate Finance Committee refused to take action on the resolution.[71]

President Obama's fingerprints are all over these developments. It's no secret he has been a strong supporter of the UN since he was in the Senate and that he even sponsored the Global Poverty Act, a failed attempt to force the United States' compliance with these MDGs.

Perhaps of even greater concern is the "Monterrey Consensus" contained in an outcome document for the UN Summit on MDGs. The document, which has been approved by the UN General Assembly, expresses participating nations' commitment to spend 0.7 percent of their Gross National Product on foreign aid for developing nations. In 2009, Obama fully embraced the so-called Millennium Development Goals which, if implemented earlier, would have imposed staggering costs on the United States. As Accuracy in Media reported, "Over a 13-year period, from 2002, when the U.N.'s Financing for Development conference was held, to the target year of 2015, when the U.S. is expected to meet the Millennium Development Goals, this amounts to $845 billion from the U.S. alone, according to Jeffrey Sachs of the U.N.'s Millennium Project."[72]

Liberals sometimes complain that Obama's critics portray him as not fully American—an "other" who doesn't relate to American values. However widespread this impression may be, Obama himself is mostly responsible. With his incessant belittling of America, both at home and abroad, and his obsequious flattering of foreign governments—many of whom are hardly friends of America—our own president constantly betrays his deep unease about our nation, our history, and our founding ideals. These expressions cannot be dismissed as mere verbal miscues since his administration's policies—from its advocacy of Al Jazeera to its enthrallment with the United Nations—reflect the same worldview. If Obama really believes in American exceptionalism, if he really is proud of his country, if he really thinks we are the rightful leader of the free world, then he only needs to do one thing to convince us: act like it.

CHAPTER TWO

THE WAR ON THE RIGHT

President Obama campaigned on bringing a new style of politics to Washington, vowing to give us a new tone and a bipartisan, post-racial approach that would bring the parties together for the good of the nation. In his Grant Park speech, where he addressed the nation for the first time as president-elect, Obama proclaimed, "Young and old, rich and poor, Democrat and Republican, black, white, Hispanic, Asian, Native American, gay, straight, disabled and not disabled, Americans have sent a message to the world that we have never been just a collection of red states and blue states. We have been and always will be the United States of America."[1]

But from the beginning he has been one of the most partisan and divisive presidents in our history. Because his extremist liberal agenda has been unpopular with the electorate, he has demonized his opponents as a means of diverting attention from the substance of the legislation or policy in question and making it a contest about personalities. As I showed in *Crimes Against Liberty*, he has always picked out one or more groups to target with each initiative ("Fat-cat Bankers," "the Wealthy," big insurance companies with their "obscene profits," "Big Oil," etc.), but on all proposals he also demonizes Republicans who, obviously, he regards as his main adversaries.

He said he didn't want Republicans to do a lot of talking; he'd prefer they "sit in back."[2] He chided the tea party for protesting his reckless spending, saying, "You would think they'd be saying thank you."[3] He denounced Republicans in Congress as "hostage takers"—with the American people as their hostages—for opposing his tax policies.[4] He told Latinos that people who believed in protecting America's borders "aren't the kinds of folks who represent our core American values."[5] Even at a back-to-school speech to high school students in Washington, D.C., Obama couldn't leave politics out of the mix. The *Los Angeles Times* admitted that Obama used his supposedly uplifting message to students as a means to stump for his jobs bill.[6]

In recent years, "hope and change" has given way to another motto. As Republican National Committee Chairman Rence Priebus noted, "With this president it's all politics, all the time."[7]

"THE EMPIRE IS STRIKING BACK"

Throughout the 2010 campaign, Obama harped on a theme that has been a hallmark of his entire presidency—do-nothing Republicans are solely responsible for the poor economy, deceitfully obstructing Obama's herculean efforts to spark economic growth. At a Democratic fundraiser in Atlanta in August 2010, Obama claimed Republican leaders "have not come up with a single, solitary, new idea to address the challenges of the American people. They don't have a single idea that's different from George Bush's ideas—not one. Instead, they're betting on amnesia. That's what they're counting on. They're counting on that you all forgot. They think that they can run the okey-doke on you. Bamboozle you."[8] In fact, Republicans had consistently offered new ideas only to be peremptorily rejected by Obama. It was Obama who was stuck on the same failed ideas. His promised panacea—his grandiose stimulus package—had already fallen flat, and yet he offered no new economic policies, only more spending.

As the 2010 elections drew near, Obama began deriding Republicans as lazy Slurpee sippers who stand around doing nothing while Democrats struggle valiantly to improve the economy. At a Democratic rally at Bowie State University in Maryland, he said, "We're down there. It's hot. We were sweating. Bugs everywhere. We're down there pushing, pushing on the car. Every once in a while we'd look up and see the Republicans standing there. They're just standing there fanning themselves—slipping on a Slurpee."[9] Castigating Republicans for not helping to get a car moving was an odd metaphor considering just a few months before, Obama had blamed Republicans for driving "the car into the ditch" and yet wanting "the keys back." "You can't have the keys back," said Obama. "You don't know how to drive."[10]

In a rally in Philadelphia, Obama boasted that three million Americans were back at work because of "the economic plan Joe and I put in place, that's the truth.... The hole we're climbing out of is so deep. The Republicans messed up so bad, left such a big mess, that there is [sic] still millions of Americans without work."[11] At a campaign stop in Ohio, he portrayed Republicans as the villains from Star Wars. "They're fighting back," he warned. "The empire is striking back. To win this election, they are plowing tens of millions of dollars into front groups. They are running misleading negative ads all across the country."[12]

In Los Angeles, Obama painted the Republican Party as so extreme that Abraham Lincoln would lose the GOP nomination today. Again, he accused Republicans of standing on the sidelines while he saved the economy from a second Great Depression, and of wanting to bring back the kind of deregulated economy that ostensibly led to the financial crisis. Republicans are "clinging to the same worn-out, tired, snake-oil ideas that they were peddling before," he intoned.[13]

Despite all *his* bellicosity, Obama said that if Republicans won the congressional elections, they would have to learn to get along with him and "work with me in a serious way."[14] A few days later, he told radio host Steve Harvey that he needed people in Congress "who want to cooperate, and that's not Republicans.... Their whole agenda is to spend the next two years trying to defeat me, as opposed to trying to move the country forward."[15]

"IT'S A SUBSTANCE PROBLEM"

All of Obama's heated rhetoric failed to avert electoral catastrophe for the Democrats. But just as he had failed to see Scott Brown's upset election to the U.S. Senate in January 2010 as a direct repudiation of his agenda, particularly Obamacare, he misread this monumental, personal defeat as well. In anticipating his defeat a month earlier, Obama had already begun to rationalize the inevitable, passing it off as a failure to get his message out. He said he'd focused so much on policy that he'd not spent enough time making his case to the electorate. Former Bush White House press secretary Ari Fleischer, incredulous at Obama's obtuseness, remarked, "I think he's more out of touch than anybody ever thought if he believes the problems are from marketing and not substance. Cap and trade is not a communication problem, it's a substance problem."[16]

But Obama still didn't grasp how unpopular his policies were (or simply pretended not to), for after the defeat in November, he defended his positions—those that had just been resoundingly rejected by the American people—as "tough" but "right." After demonizing Republicans for two years, he appealed for "common ground," while still signaling he had no intention of backing off his agenda.

The day after the election, an angry, defiant Obama let his hair down during a conference call with his leftist friends at MoveOn.org. "We always knew that bringing about change wasn't going to be easy," he argued. "And, it might get tougher in the days ahead, but the message I take away from these elections is very simple. The American people are still frustrated and they still want change and we just gotta work harder to deliver the change the American people want.... Sometimes I know this is exhausting, but we didn't sign up for doing what was easy, we signed up for doing what was right."[17]

In a different setting he declared, "Yesterday's vote confirmed what I've heard from folks all across America. People are frustrated, they're deeply frustrated with the pace of our economic recovery."[18] Yes, but they were even more frustrated—and genuinely outraged—at his radical leftist agenda and his ruinous spending. As House Republican Leader John Boehner observed, "The American people spoke, and I think this is pretty clear that the Obama-Pelosi agenda is being rejected by the American people. They want the president to change course."[19]

CIVILITY FOR THEE, NOT FOR ME

For years, Democrats have demonized conservative opinion as hateful, bigoted, and homophobic, and at least as early as the Clinton years they began to suggest that it could lead to violence. This was President Clinton's angle when he sought to link Timothy McVeigh's Oklahoma City bombing to conservative talk radio. Since then, Democrats have consistently used this intimidation tactic to chill or discredit conservative speech.

Despite Obama's campaign promise to usher in a "new tone," one of the earliest references to this phrase being used during his term appeared in a much different context in a *Politico* piece. In early February 2009, Josh Gerstein wrote, "With his economic stimulus plan facing serious resistance on Capitol Hill, President Obama struck a combative new tone Thursday, publicly chastising 'some in Congress' for trying to make major changes to the near-trillion-dollar legislation now in the Senate." Obama insisted, "We can't go back to the same worn-out ideas that led us here in the first place. You've been hearing 'em for the last 10 years, maybe longer."[20]

The Democrats' passive-aggressive attitude toward civility was brought into stark relief in January 2011 after Jared Loughner, a mentally ill malcontent, opened fire outside a Safeway supermarket in Tucson, Arizona, killing six people and wounding fourteen others, including Congresswoman Gabrielle Giffords. President Obama delivered the memorial address for the victims at the University of Arizona in Tucson. In the speech, he called for what the *New York Times* described as a "new era of civility," urging that if the "tragedy prompts reflection and debate... let's make sure it is worthy of those we have lost. Let's make sure it's not on the usual plane of politics and point scoring and pettiness that drifts away with the next news cycle." Obama added, "If, as has been discussed in recent days, their deaths help usher in more civility in our public discourse, let us remember that it is not because a simple lack of civility caused this tragedy—it did not—but rather because only a more civil and honest public discourse can help us face up to our challenges as a nation, in a way that would make them proud."[21]

Obama's plea for civility would have seemed more sincere if his allies weren't announcing from every conceivable media forum that the shootings were the fault of "violent" conservative rhetoric. They especially sought to tie the murders to Sarah Palin—simply because her PAC displayed a map that placed targets over districts where it was trying to unseat Democrats. Although "targeting" a political opponent is a commonly used metaphor across the political aisle, the map—whose targets were decried by the Left as "gun sights"—suddenly emerged as the prime example of the Right's supposed descent into murderous extremism.

Two days after Giffords' shooting, the Atlantic Wire, a website associated with the *Atlantic*, ran an article asking, "Did Sarah Palin's Target Map Play [a] Role in Giffords Shooting?" The article quoted *Atlantic* blogger Andrew Sullivan, a vociferous Obama supporter, professing, "No one is saying Sarah Palin should be viewed as an accomplice to murder"—and then he seemingly proceeded to do just that: "Many are merely saying that [Palin's] recklessly violent and inflammatory rhetoric has poisoned the discourse and has long run the risk of empowering the deranged. We are saying it's about time someone took responsibility for this kind of rhetorical extremism, because it can and has led to violence and murder."[22]

A Democrat operative later admitted that the Democrats plotted to blame another right-leaning group for the shootings. "They need to deftly pin this on the tea partiers," said the unnamed Democrat. "Just like the Clinton White House deftly pinned the Oklahoma bombing on the militia and anti-government people." Another Democrat strategist argued that there was a similarity between Tucson and Oklahoma City because both "took place in a climate of bitter and virulent rhetoric against the government and Democrats."[23]

Meanwhile, Obama was content to issue vague calls for civility from both sides, never once calling out his own supporters and allies for their over-the-top accusations. Of course, these accusations assumed, without a shred of proof, that the shooter was conservative or at least influenced by conservative rhetoric. So it didn't help their cause when investigators revealed the shooter was mentally deranged, with no connection to any conservative cause, group, or public figure.

I'VE BEEN DOING BIN LADEN

After the Giffords shooting, Obama abandoned his call for a political truce and returned to his usual truculence. In his various budget standoffs with Republicans—who were seeking to rein in Obama's outlandish federal spending that has saddled us with unsustainable deficits and a record national debt—Obama had long since opted, in lieu of reaching across the aisle, for the "if they bring a knife, we'll bring a gun" approach. He opened his press conference on June 29, 2011, with unmasked partisan stridency, implying Republicans were shirking their responsibilities while he was magnanimously becoming involved in the budget debate despite his earth-shattering obligations elsewhere. "I've been doing Afghanistan, bin Laden and the Greek crisis. You need to be here. I've been here. Let's get it done."

Conveniently forgetting his own record-setting pace for presidential golf, he returned to his tried-and-true meme of lazy Republicans. "These are bills that Congress ran up," he claimed. "They took the vacation, they bought the car, and now they are saying maybe we don't have to pay. At a certain point they need to do their job."[24] His chutzpah in portraying himself as an innocent bystander amid the spiraling national debt was breathtaking. But he wasn't through. When asked if he would sign on to a compromise involving tax breaks, he replied, "I've said to Republican leaders, 'You go talk to your constituents and ask them: Are you willing to compromise your kids' safety so some corporate jet owner can get a tax break.'" After pulling the work ethic and class warfare cards, he couldn't resist throwing in a little scaremongering, claiming the Republicans wanted to "pay the Chinese, but not seniors."[25]

An exchange between a reporter and White House press secretary Jay Carney over the budget battles during the summer of 2011 revealed the administration's bizarre view of bipartisanship. The reporter asked Carney how the president's rallying people to call on Republican

congressmen to compromise promoted "an atmosphere of bipartisanship."
The reported asked, "Does that foster a sense of cooperation?" Carney
responded, "What the President has called for is for those Americans who
believe that we need compromise in Washington to communicate that to
their members of Congress. That can be Democrats or Republicans. That
is hardly a partisan message. It is explicitly a bipartisan message." When
the reporter reminded Carney that only Republican congressmen were
being called out, he responded, "Well, I think the problem we've seen
here is a lack of willingness to compromise by Republicans."[26] In other
words, the failure of both sides to agree to Obama's plan was a result of
Republican partisanship; Obama's refusal to compromise did not
constitute partisanship because his proposals were eminently reasonable.

Over and over, by refusing to condemn rancorous language from
Democrats, Obama proved his calls for civility were insincere and politically motivated. Obama was silent amid reports that Congressman Mike
Doyle, a Pennsylvania Democrat, said in a closed-door meeting in reference to tea party Republicans, "We have negotiated with terrorists. This
small group of terrorists have made it impossible to spend any money."
Biden reportedly responded, "They have acted like terrorists."[27] Biden
later denied saying this, though there was no denying his comment to
Senate Democrats earlier in the day that Republican leaders have "guns
to their heads" in the budget negotiations, and that the deal would
remove the tea party's "weapon of mass destruction"—referring to the
threat of defaulting on U.S. debt obligations, which was an unlikely
scenario anyway, as explained in chapter six. Continuing to employ the
precise kind of martial language the Left had denounced after the Giffords
shooting, Doyle told *Politico* that Republicans "have no compunction
about blowing up the economy to get what they want."[28]

DEFLECTION: A VALUED SKILL FOR TEAM OBAMA

Obama pressed his attacks on conservatives even during press conferences with foreign leaders. During a joint presser at the White House
with the German chancellor Angela Merkel, he once again blamed
President George W. Bush for the poor economy, declaring, "It is just

very important for folks to remember how close we came to complete disaster. The world economy took a severe blow two and a half years ago, and in part that is because of a whole set of policy decisions that had been made, and challenges that have been unaddressed over the course of the previous decade."[29]

Vice President Biden found a trip to China to be a suitable occasion for attacking the tea party. When asked about the administration's efforts to reduce the deficit following the Standard & Poor's downgrade, Biden blamed everything on conservative opposition to Obama's agenda. Biden said that Medicare (and other entitlements) would be easy to fix, "but there is a group within the Republican Party that is a very strong voice now that wanted different changes, and so the deal fell through at the very end." As Britain's Nile Gardiner observed, Biden was saying the administration had a perfect plan to deal with the deficit but the tea party ruined it: "What he doesn't mention, of course, is that his own administration is responsible for an unprecedented increase in government spending, and running the largest deficits since World War II."[30] But Obama was in sync with Biden, calling the credit downgrade "a self-inflicted wound" by Republicans. He added, "That's why people are frustrated. You can hear it in my voice; that's why I'm frustrated."[31]

Obama did not make these comments simply in the heat of the moment; he keeps up his attack on Republicans, rain or shine. While stumping for his jobs bill in Michigan, he blasted the GOP Congress for "the worst part of partisanship, the worst part of gridlock." "There are some in Congress right now," charged Obama, "who would rather see their opponents lose than Americans win, and that's got to stop. We're supposed to all be on the same team, especially during tough times." Once again, he urged his audience to write members of Congress (meaning Republicans) to urge them to pass his jobs bill.[32]

Still trying to divert attention from his own record, his own hyper-partisanship, and his own stubborn aversion to compromise, he kept trying to leverage Congress' poor public approval ratings (Congress, it should be noted, almost always rates poorly, no matter which party is in control) to push his agenda. In his weekly radio address a few days later, he lashed out at "partisan gridlock." As if he were wholly outside the political process, he said, "You've got a right to be frustrated. I am. Because you deserve better. I don't think it's too much for you to expect that the people you send to this town start delivering." He then urged Americans—yet again—to contact members of Congress.[33] Months later, in October, he was still at it. "The question then is, will Congress do something?" he intoned. "If Congress does something, then I can't run against a do-nothing Congress. If Congress does nothing, then it's not a matter of me running against them, I think the American people will run them out of town. Because they are frustrated."

No matter how he spun it, though, the Republican Congress had passed Paul Ryan's reform plan, the "cut, cap and balance bill," and countless other reforms only to have them die in the Democrat-controlled Senate or at the threat of a presidential veto. Try as he might, he could not explain away the fact that he was the one who had spurned the recommendations of his own Bipartisan Budget Commission, who had failed to present any good faith legislation aimed at curbing entitlement spending, whose budget deficits were in excess of a trillion dollars as far as the eye could see, whose stimulus packages were bankrupting us, and whose Senate hadn't submitted a budget for some nine hundred days.

That same month, at a private fundraiser in Tampa, Florida, First Lady Michelle Obama engaged in some old-fashioned scaremongering, reminding her audience that Obama's Supreme Court nominees would help craft decisions whose impact would be felt "for decades to come—on our privacy and security, on whether we speak freely, worship openly, and love whomever we choose. That is what's at stake here."[34] Apparently, a Republican president would install justices who would prevent us from speaking, worshiping, and loving freely. In the Obamas' eyes, the GOP boogeyman knows no bounds.

"THEY GOT A WAR WITH US"

Obama's closest allies regularly hurl the most belligerent accusations at Republicans as Obama stands on the sidelines, pretending to be above it all. Consider the introduction Obama received from Jimmy Hoffa during a Labor Day address to union members in Detroit. Urging his audience to vote out Republican lawmakers who were blocking Obama's agenda, the Teamster president unleashed a bellicose speech full of allusions to war and violence. He declared,

> We got to keep an eye on the battle that we face: The war on workers. And you see it everywhere, it is the Tea Party. And you know, there is only one way to beat and win that war. The one thing about working people is we like a good fight. And you know what? They've got a war, they got a war with us and there's only going to be one winner. It's going to be the workers of Michigan, and America. We're going to win that war. President Obama, this is your army. We are ready to march.... Everybody here's got a vote.... Let's take these sons of bitches out and give America back to an America where we belong.[35]

After those incendiary remarks, Obama bounced up to the podium, grinning widely, and proceeded to shower Hoffa with accolades. During his speech, Obama's tone was less violent, but no less partisan. He said, "We're going to see if congressional Republicans will put country before party. You say you're the party of tax cuts? Well then, prove you'll fight just as hard for tax cuts for middle-class families as you do for oil companies and the most affluent Americans. Show us what you got."[36]

Obama later professed not to have heard Hoffa's war-like comments. Some observers found this explanation improbable, but it was certainly unsurprising, considering Obama claims never to have heard Jeremiah Wright's rantings though he sat through twenty years of his reverend's "G— D— America" sermons. As criticism of Hoffa intensified over the ensuing week, Obama seemed to absolve himself of any responsibility to condemn uncivil speech from his allies; his communications chief Dan Pfeiffer defiantly declared Obama would not "serve as the speech police for the Democratic Party."[37]

On September 8, the day of his vaunted jobs speech, Obama demonstrated his "bipartisanship" by circulating advance talking points to liberal media and Democratic legislators. It wasn't just his selective release of speech highlights that reeked of partisanship, however; the talking points themselves were chock full of it. They telegraphed that Obama would depict the economy as a casualty of President George W. Bush— this was *two and a half years* into Obama's term, mind you—and that Republicans were, in the words of the Daily Caller, "unpatriotic and greedy partisans," while Obama himself was "an optimistic, fair-minded, reformist, bipartisan, fiscal moderate."[38]

"WE DON'T BELIEVE IN A SMALL AMERICA"

Once again contradicting Obama's calls for a "new tone" in politics, Team Obama developed a plan to harshly attack Mitt Romney after he emerged in 2011 as the frontrunner for the GOP's presidential nomination. In August, under the headline, "Obama Plan: Destroy Romney," *Politico* revealed that "Barack Obama's aides and advisers are preparing to center the president's reelection campaign on a ferocious personal assault on Mitt Romney's character and business background." The story quoted a prominent Democratic strategist closely tied to the White House, who said bluntly, "Unless things change and Obama can run on accomplishments, he will have to kill Romney."[39] As *NewsBusters*' Tim Graham quipped, "There was no, 'I mean, politically,' in that sentence. Should the Secret Service be calling Politico for leads?"[40]

While Obama's advisers denied it, the *Politico* piece also suggested the Obama camp would try to paint Romney as a weird person who just happens to be a Mormon. As *Politico* noted, "The step from casting Romney as a bit off to raising questions about religion may not be a large step for some of the incumbent's supporters."

The focus on Romney by no means left other GOP presidential candidates immune from the Left's attacks. Actress Janeane Garofalo voiced suspicions that Herman Cain had been paid by an unknown entity to enter the presidential contest solely to deflect attention from the party's racism.[41] And Tim Pawlenty received an ungracious kick just after dropping out of the race, with Democratic National Committee Communications Director Brad Woodhouse announcing, "While protecting tax breaks for the wealthy and big oil while proposing to end Medicare, slash

Social Security and pile additional burdens on the middle class might win plaudits with the Tea Party, it's not remotely what the American people are looking for."[42]

The whole slate of GOP presidential candidates came under fire after they failed to immediately denounce one or two audience members at a GOP debate in Orlando who booed for about one second when a gay soldier asked a question about the military's policies toward gays. Some of the candidates later said they didn't hear the booing; others thought it was directed at the solder's challenging question, not at him personally. Nevertheless, despite his refusal to condemn the inflammatory remarks of Hoffa—a close political ally who made his comments in the act of introducing Obama himself—Obama wasn't about to pass up an opportunity to denounce the entire GOP field.

At the Human Rights Campaign's annual dinner, Obama attributed the incident in Orlando to Republicans' fundamental lack of morality, compassion, or tolerance, which supposedly drives their entire agenda and their opposition to his own. His speech frequently decried "small America," which he depicted as a cruel, dystopian place where roads and schools are allowed to crumble, teachers are laid off, and where the government irresponsibly cuts social services while handing out tax breaks for the rich. In case it wasn't already clear that "small America" was code for the Republican agenda, Obama clarified the point by invoking the Orlando debate: "We don't believe in the kind of smallness that says it's okay for a stage full of political leaders—one of whom could end up being the President of the United States—being silent when an American soldier is booed. We don't believe in that. We don't believe in standing silent when that happens. We don't believe in them being silent since."[43]

That was a sweeping indictment of Republicans, but Obama's swipes can also be exceedingly petty, such as his scheduling of a joint session of Congress to unveil his jobs bill at the same time Republicans would be debating at the Reagan Presidential Library. When questioned about the timing, White House press secretary Jay Carney said the Republican debate was "not enough of a reason" to change the timing of the president's speech.

So here we had Obama, insisting that Republican leaders dutifully serve as public props for another presidential re-election campaign speech in the guise of a new jobs bill, and at the same time telling Republicans he didn't respect their ideas enough to avoid a scheduling conflict that would force Americans to choose between listening to the president or his Republican opponents.[44] But GOP leaders in Congress resisted Obama's scheduling demand, forcing him to reschedule his bipartisan jobs harangue. After all, the president, according to Carney, was only interested in "speaking to people, speaking to Congress about the need to do things, to create jobs to get the economy going. Americans," said Carney, "are sick and tired of the bickering, the gridlock."[45]

"THEY'D LOVE TO SEE [US] HANGING ON A TREE"

As the GOP contest wore on, the White House kept up its attacks. Seemingly oblivious to the manifest unpopularity of the president's agenda, White House communications director Dan Pfeiffer said that the only reason Obama was struggling against potential GOP presidential candidates in the polls was that the American people weren't familiar enough with their ideas to understand how bad they were. Pfeiffer said that once Americans learned, for example, that Mitt Romney's economic plan would "essentially end Medicare, end Social Security"—a crass distortion if not an outright lie—they would come around.[46]

The Democrats' attacks on the GOP reached farcical extremes. Vice President Biden told an audience in Toledo, Ohio, "This is a different kind of fight. This is a fight for the heart and soul of the labor movement. This is a fight for the existence of organized labor. You are the only folks keeping the barbarians at the gate."[47] In perhaps the single most incendiary remark of the campaign, Congressional Black Caucus whip Andre Carson told the crowd at a CBC town hall meeting in Miami, "Some of these folks in Congress right now would love to see us as second-class citizens. Some of them in Congress right now with this tea party movement would love to see you and me—I'm sorry, Tamron—hanging on a tree."[48]

Meanwhile, Obama continued urging his supporters to give his congressional opponents an earful, but he didn't take kindly when the tables were turned on him. At a public meeting, Iowa tea party member Ryan Rhodes confronted Obama about Biden's alleged characterization of tea partiers as terrorists. Obama said Biden had denied making the statement, but then assumed a defensive posture, saying, "Now, in fairness, since I've been called a socialist who wasn't born in this country, who is destroying America and taking away its freedoms because I passed a health care bill, I'm all for lowering the rhetoric."[49]

Obama may be all for ratcheting down the rhetoric when he's the target, but like clockwork, within days, he was slamming Republicans again. Vacationing in Martha's Vineyard, he pointedly said, "The only thing preventing us from passing these bills is the refusal by some in Congress to put country ahead of party. That's the problem right now. That's what's holding this country back."[50]

"REPUBLICAN LEADERS IN WASHINGTON JUST DON'T GET IT"

When Obama delivered his vaunted "jobs speech" at his rescheduled joint session of Congress, it turned out to be little more than a demand for another stimulus package inside a glorified campaign speech for his re-election. After scandal, waste, and failure had discredited his first stimulus plan, he was insisting that we do more of the same. Obama knew Republicans would never go along with his jobs plan, so his purpose in proposing it was to set Republicans up as obstructionists, hoping to use this as a campaign Hail Mary to distract the electorate's attention from his record.

Obama's speech was standard fare for his left-wing base. After excoriating Republicans—whom he'd summoned to sit still for this diatribe—for wanting to "wipe out basic protections that Americans have counted on for decades," he suggested the GOP is dragging America into "a race to the bottom where we try to offer the cheapest labor and the worst pollution standards."[51] As for substantive job-creating proposals, Obama offered little besides his typical vague, Keynesian promises to make them magically appear through more government spending.

After his petty speech, Obama acted as though Republican opposition to the bill was all that was preventing a robust economic rebound. He had used the same ploy a year earlier during a weekly radio address in which he had plugged another so-called jobs bill that would extend unemployment benefits and give states billions in fiscal relief. Obama said then, "Republican leaders in Washington just don't get it. While a majority of Senators support taking these steps to help the American people, some are playing the same old Washington games and using their power to hold this relief hostage—a move that only ends up holding back our recovery. It doesn't make sense."[52]

Obama's political strategy is really pretty simple: his policies don't work, so he blames his opponents for blocking him from adopting more of them.

YOU WANT TO REDUCE THE NATIONAL DEBT? THAT'S RACIST!

"Lazy, obstructionist Republicans" is just one meme in the White House's extensive arsenal of insults hurled at Obama's political opponents. Republicans are also heartless and cruel, homophobic, sexist, proudly ignorant, and inherently violent. But more than anything else, according to the administration and its allies, Republicans are irredeemably, rabidly racist. Of course, Democrats have been reflexively accusing Republican public figures of racism for decades; what's new under the Obama administration is that with the birth of the tea party, those accusations are now routinely flung at ordinary Americans who primarily criticize the president's spending policies.

Democrats and their media enablers like to go hunting for racism among tea partiers. They often don't even hide their assumptions, as was evident when NBC News reporter Kelly O'Donnell remarked to a black protestor, Darryl Postell, at an April 2010 tea party event in Washington, "There aren't a lot of African-American men at these events. Have you ever felt … uncomfortable?" Postell shot back, "No, no, these are my people, Americans."[53]

Failing to find any racism to support their accusations, Democrats seem willing to manufacture racist incidents. The most famous of these may have been Congressman John Lewis's allegation in March 2010 that tea party protesters yelled racial slurs at black congressmen entering the Capitol building. Unfortunately for Lewis, copious film footage taken at the scene and uploaded onto the internet utterly failed to reveal a single slur.[54]

The NAACP, a major Obama supporter, has been a prime proponent of the "tea party is racist" smear, adopting a resolution at its 2010 convention in Kansas City condemning "racist elements" in the tea party movement and demanding its leaders denounce their bigotry. NAACP president Benjamin Todd Jealous denounced "the Tea Party's continued tolerance for bigotry and bigoted statements," insisting, "The time has come for them to accept the responsibility that comes with influence and make clear there is no place for racism and anti-Semitism, homophobia and other forms of bigotry in their movement." First Lady Michelle Obama spoke at the convention but saw no need to condemn the baseless attacks on the tea party—attacks which provoked vehement protests from tea party groups.[55]

Though President Obama once sneeringly referred to tea partiers with the obscene term "teabaggers," he generally refrains from engaging in the most inflammatory attacks on the tea party. Instead, he delegates that job to his supporters, whose diatribes go without presidential condemnation, even when they're made in Obama's presence. At a private White House dinner in May 2010, when a guest suggested that tea partiers were motivated by angst over having a black president, Obama didn't lift a finger in protest, instead agreeing there was a "subterranean agenda" afoot that was racially based.[56]

One of Obama's principal "spiritual advisors," Reverend Jim Wallis, is known for demanding a new tone from Republicans while rejecting civil discourse himself. During a British radio interview, he attributed the entire tea party movement to racism, declaring, "Fox News has been the assassin of Obama's religion.... What they're trying to do is disconnect him and his values from the American people. And to be blunt, there wouldn't be a Tea Party if there wasn't a black man in the White House."[57]

Attorney General Eric Holder also got into the mix just as he came under fire over the gunwalking scandal Operation Fast and Furious. In a *New York Times* interview, while acknowledging that many of his opponents were offended by his policies, Holder suggested that racism, too, motivated some of his critics. "The more extreme segment," said Holder, alluding in part to the tea party, viewed the attacks on him as "a way to get at the president because of the way I can be identified with him, both due to the nature of our relationship, and, you know, the fact that we're both African American."[58] Georgia Democratic congressman Hank Johnson made the connection to the tea party explicit, having earlier called Fast and Furious "another manufactured controversy by the Second Amendment, NRA Republican tea party movement." He asked, "How many firearms are sold to al-Qaeda terrorists, to other convicted felons, to domestic violence perpetrators, to convicted felons, to white supremacists?"[59]

It seems the administration's antipathy for the tea party has even trickled down to the IRS. In early March 2012, David French of the American Center for Law and Justice reported on National Review Online that his colleagues had been in contact with "literally dozens of tea party organizations that have received intrusive information demands from the IRS" in response to tea-party requests for tax-exempt status, which French says seriously impinge on their First Amendment rights. These information requests concern who the groups are associating with and whether they are in contact or have relationships with legislative bodies or political candidates. Significantly, these demands have not been in response to allegations of wrongdoing against the parties, but simply in response to their applications for tax exemptions.

Is the Obama IRS "using the routine process of seeking and granting tax exemptions to undertake a sweeping, top-down review of the internal workings of the tea party movement in the United States," as French suggested?[60] Before answering that question, recall that Obama's own campaign organization, Organizing for America, once labeled tea party opponents of Obamacare "right-wing domestic terrorists."[61] If Team Obama views tea partiers as a dangerous threat, would it really be surprising to learn that it treats them as such?

DIVIDE AND CONQUER: OBAMA'S IDENTITY POLITICS

Team Obama traffics in racism accusations and identity politics as a natural part of its left-wing worldview, but there is also a crass political motive for it all; Obama's empowerment depends on maintaining a certain level of support among specific demographic and ethnic groups, to whom he presents himself as a protector against racist, malevolent Republicans. He referred to these constituencies in a Democratic National Committee video in spring 2010, when he urged "young people, African Americans, Latinos and women ... to stand together once again."[62]

Leading up to the 2010 congressional elections, as it became clear that the Democrats were going to lose, they ratcheted up their demagogic, race-based overtures. In October 2010 Obama said on the Latino network Univision, "If Latinos sit out the election instead of saying, 'We're going to punish our enemies and we're going to reward our friends who stand with us on issues that are important to us,' if they don't see that kind of upsurge in voting in this election, then I think it's going to be harder."

There could be no mistaking whom Obama was identifying as the enemy. When the host complained that Obama was not doing enough and asked what Latinos could do to advance immigration reform, Obama replied, "Look, the steps are very clear. Pressure has to be put on the Republican Party." Obama then made the baseless, inflammatory accusation that Republicans are engaged in a "cynical attempt to discourage Latinos from voting."[63]

Michelle Obama followed this same theme in an interview with Univision in February 2011, when she called on Latinos to help persuade Republicans to support the Dream Act mini-amnesty. The first lady said, "So I urge the Latino community, he needs help, he's got to have Republicans and Democrats in Congress who are going to step up. If a sound immigration bill gets put on the President's desk he is going to sign it. But it's got to get through Congress. He can't do it alone."[64]

In the final weeks of the congressional election campaign, Obama engaged in a black radio blitz in Chicago, Philadelphia, Milwaukee, Florida, and Ohio, making overt racial appeals for votes. Addressing blacks directly and specifically identifying with them as a group, he said, "Two years ago you voted in record numbers and we won a victory few deemed possible.... But now ... the same Republicans who fought against change are pushing the same plan that crashed our economy.... We can't afford to go back. On November 2nd, I need you to stand with me, and vote!"[65] Furthermore, during an interview with Michael Baisden, Obama suggested Republicans were "trying to hijack democracy."[66] "The reason we won in [2008] is because young people, African Americans, Latinos—people who traditionally don't vote in high numbers—voted in record numbers. We've got to have that same kind of turnout in this election." If Republicans were to take back Congress, said Obama, "they've already said they're going to go back to the same policies that were in place during the Bush administration. That means that we are going to have just hand-to-hand combat up here on Capitol Hill."[67]

In an interview with Reverend Al Sharpton, Obama fully agreed with Sharpton's suggestion that, while Obama wasn't on the ballot, blacks needed to vote like he was because this was about his agenda.[68] Continuing in this vein, Vice President Joe Biden, further demonstrating his unique gift for civility and understatement, warned a few days later, "This is not your father's Republican party. This is a different brand.... If we lose, we're going to play hell."[69]

Just a few weeks before the 2010 congressional elections, Obama said to his Philadelphia audience that Republicans "are counting on young people ... and union members ... and black folks staying home."[70] Then he made an inflammatory, race-based appeal to Latino voters in a radio interview on KVEG in Las Vegas a few days before the election, suggesting Republicans were trying to gin up hatred for immigrants. He said, "The Latino vote is crucial and obviously, you know, when you look at some of the stuff that's been going on during this election campaign that has tried to fan anti-immigrant sentiment. I note that a lot of Latinos, you know, feel under assault."[71]

In order to cement its political coalition, the administration champions itself as the defender not just of minorities, but of women, too. Vice President Biden, in his inimitable way, showcased the Obama team's appeals to women at a fundraiser in Philadelphia, where he despicably compared Republicans to those who excuse rapists by blaming their victims. He said that before the adoption of the Violence Against Women Act, which he had promoted,

There was this attitude in our society of blaming the victim. When a woman got raped, blame her because she was wearing a skirt too short, she looked the wrong way or she wasn't home in time to make dinner.... But it's amazing how these Republicans, the right wing of this party—whose philosophy threw us into this God-awful hole we're in, gave us the tremendous deficit we've inherited—that they're now using, now attempting to use, the very economic condition they have created to blame the victim—whether it's organized labor or ordinary middle-class working men and women. It's bizarre. It's bizarre.[72]

Unsurprisingly, the administration's identity politics have not been well-received by the American people at large. A *Washington Post*-ABC News poll in mid-2010 showed that only four in ten respondents believed Obama's presidency had improved racial relations, compared to six in ten who had expected relations to improve at the time of his inauguration. As time passed it only got worse. In January 2011, only 35 percent said Obama had helped race relations. Only 19 percent of blacks believed they enjoyed a level playing field with whites, and close to half of them believed racial equality either wouldn't be achieved in their lifetimes or never would be.[73] The actor Morgan Freeman seemed to agree, telling CNN's Piers Morgan that Obama's presidency had made racism *worse* in the United States—though predictably for a Hollywood liberal, he blamed tea party members, describing their outlook as "Screw the country.... We're going to do whatever we can to get this black man outta here."[74]

As columnist Jeff Kuhner wrote, "In recent memory, no president has so deliberately and publicly sought to pit racial and gender groups against each other. The president is not simply the titular head of a party or the leader of government. He is the head of state and embodies the collective will of the American people. He is the president of all Americans—not just certain segments of his electoral coalition. Mr. Obama's rhetoric is reckless. It is fostering civil strife and racial animosity."[75]

Despite portraying himself as a veritable guardian angel for minorities, Obama's economy is hitting the African-American middle class the hardest. As Fox News' John Roberts reported, "The unemployment situation across America is bad, no doubt. But for African-Americans in some cities, this is not the great recession. It's the Great Depression. The

Economic Policy Institute reported that the black unemployment rate, as of July 2011, was 19.2 percent, and if you include those who had quit looking for work, it would exceed 20—which equates to a depression."[76]

"WE'RE BETTER THAN THAT"

When the contentious debate erupted over a Muslim developer's plans to build a mosque next to Ground Zero in Manhattan, Democrats found yet another issue to manipulate in their endless campaign against alleged Republican prejudice. As Americans expressed opposition to the mosque and to Obama's vague support for the project, Obama's former White House communications director Anita Dunn, who had previously choreographed the administration's war on Fox News and other perceived opponents, "launched," according to a Daily Caller report, "a furious attack against Republicans who have criticized President Obama's remarks on the Ground Zero mosque, labeling the GOP as the party of intolerance."[77]

Appearing on MSNBC, Dunn invoked the familiar trope that Republicans are intolerant toward "almost any kind of difference in American society." She denied speculation that she had coordinated her attack with Obama advisors David Axelrod and Dan Pfeiffer, saying they "did not know, approve, or suggest" her comments. Coordinated or not, her ugly and divisive statements were entirely consistent with the administration's position and doubtlessly enjoyed its full blessing.

After all, Obama said Republicans were engaged in a "race to the bottom," promoting the worst things in the American character. Exploiting that theme, Dunn depicted the Ground Zero mosque debate as a contest between champions of religious liberty and Republican bigots who are "labeling all Muslims in this country as terrorists" and whose party has practically "decided to update itself as the Know-nothing version 2.0."

According to Dunn—and by inference, to Obama—you can't oppose a provocative, in-your-face mosque next to the very site of the 9/11 attacks without being a bigot. "We're better than that," insisted Dunn. "And that's what the president was trying to take this argument to. I think to a much higher level."[78]

"DISSEMINATING PUSHBACK"

The administration has prided itself on using social media tools like Facebook and Twitter to get its message out. And in typical form, it has used these media as vehicles for attacking the Right.

Obama has said "more and more people, especially young people, are getting their information through different media. And, historically, part of what makes for healthy democracy, what is good politics, is when you've got citizens who are informed, who are engaged." That's true—but the White House seems to make an exception when citizens become informed about things it doesn't want them to know.

The White House exploits social media not just to "cognitively infiltrate" its critics, as Obama regulatory czar Cass Sunstein called it,[79] but to bully them, urging supporters to use the social networks to pressure Congress to roll over for Obama's agenda. "Tweet at your Republican legislators and urge them to support a bipartisan compromise to the debt crisis," pleaded a post on Obama's Twitter feed. To up the pressure, Obama said he would "post the Twitter handles of GOP lawmakers in each state." Similarly, Obama's staff also uses his Facebook page as a campaign tool.[80]

The White House takes social media so seriously that it assigned a person—Jesse Lee—to be its "director of progressive media and online response," a position dedicated to refuting criticism of Obama on social media. Lee came well-prepared for an aggressive, partisan job, having cut his teeth with the Democratic National Committee, former House Speaker Nancy Pelosi, and under Rahm Emanuel's direction at the Democratic Congressional Campaign Committee. Obviously, the administration's targets are not limited to professional politicians or reporters, but include anyone who dares to challenge it, even private citizens on social media. During a one-month period in 2011, instead of promoting the national interest, Lee, on the taxpayer's dime, used 15 percent of his tweets on Twitter to debate Obama's partisan positions with conservative Kevin Eder.[81]

Commentator Ed Morrissey said he'd originally defended the right of the White House to respond to its critics on social media, though recognizing it would "make the Obama administration look petty and thin-skinned, and would diminish the seriousness and dignity of the

Presidency." But, he added, he hadn't realized "just how far below their weight the White House would punch."[82] Nor can we overlook that this lowbrow propaganda campaign is at taxpayer expense.

The administration's deployment of Lee as its social media point man was not part of some innocuous plan to connect with the public. Two months prior to Lee's Twitter skirmish with Eder, the *Huffington Post* had reported that the White House "is now making moves to integrate an online rapid response team inside the White House communications office." An internal memo from White House Communications Director Dan Pfeiffer said that Lee had been working in the new media and "serving as the White House's liaison with the progressive media and the online community," but now he would "take on the second role full time working on outreach, strategy and response."

Notice the glaring admission that the White House works with "the progressive media"—that is, the liberal media, favorable to its policy agenda. The new role the White House carved out for Lee signaled, according to the *Huffington Post*, that the White House was "adopting a more aggressive engagement in the online world in the months ahead." Nor was the White House's choice of Lee accidental. Lee had overseen the truculent White House blog that got in a flame war with Glenn Beck, in which Lee accused Beck of lying about the administration on his show. Apparently, Lee got high marks from the boss, because he was promoted to the Twitter position for "the purposes of disseminating pushback."[83]

Some say the White House makes use of another reliable ally for attacking its critics—Media Matters, a fiercely partisan left-wing group that promotes boycotts of non-liberal media figures. In February 2012, the Daily Caller website published an exposé revealing close coordination between the White House and Media Matters. The Daily Caller reported,

> A group with the ability to shape news coverage is of incalculable value to the politicians it supports, so it's no surprise that Media Matters has been in regular contact with political operatives in the Obama administration. According to visitor logs, on June 16, 2010, {MM founder David} Brock and then-

Media Matters president Eric Burns traveled to the White House for a meeting with Valerie Jarrett, arguably the president's closest adviser. Recently departed Obama communications director Anita Dunn returned to the White House for the meeting as well.

It's not clear what the four spoke about—no one in the meeting returned repeated calls for comment—but the apparent coordination continued. "Anita Dunn became a regular presence at the office," says someone who worked there. Then-president of Media Matters, Eric Burns, "lunched with her, met with her and chatted with her frequently on any number of matters."

Media Matters also began a weekly strategy call with the White House, which continues, joined by the liberal Center for American Progress think tank. Jen Psaki, Obama's deputy communications director, was a frequent participant before she left for the private sector in October 2011.

Every Tuesday evening, meanwhile, a representative from Media Matters attends the Common Purpose Project meeting at the Capitol Hilton on 16th Street in Washington, where dozens of progressive organizations formulate strategy, often with a representative from the Obama White House.[84]

It may surprise some that a president who promised us bipartisanship and who claims to promote political civility would team up so closely with an attack group whose staffers boast that they got news anchor Lou Dobbs fired from CNN. But the Obama administration recognizes a valuable ally when it sees one, and it is Media Matters' take-no-prisoners approach to politics that makes it so effective. "We were pretty much writing their prime time," a former Media Matters operative remarked about MSNBC. "But then virtually all the mainstream media was using our stuff."[85]

As the Daily Caller noted, the group's campaigns—campaigns that obviously endeared it to the White House—can be downright ruthless, with no compunction about attacking local reporters who don't toe Obama's line: "Reporters who weren't cooperative might feel the sting of a Media Matters campaign against them. 'If you hit a reporter, say a beat reporter at a regional newspaper,' a Media Matters source said, 'all of a sudden they'd get a thousand hostile emails. Sometimes they'd melt down. It had a real effect on reporters who weren't used to that kind of scrutiny.'"[86]

ANTI-LIFE REPUBLICANS?

As described above, throughout his first term, Obama often delegates the harshest attacks on Republicans to his supporters while presenting himself as being above the fray. This strategy descended into self-parody in October 2011 when Obama cited Reverend Martin Luther King's admonition that Americans should be slow to question each other's love of country—the same day his deputy press secretary Josh Earnest demanded that Republicans "put country before party" and vote for Obama's jobs bill.

When Obama said, "If [Martin Luther King] were alive today... he would want us to know we can argue fiercely about the proper size and role of government without questioning each other's love for this country,"[87] apparently he meant "without questioning *his* love of country," not that of Republicans. And in typical form, the next day Obama followed up his call for civility with another jab at those Republicans whose plan, he said, boiled down to "dirtier air, dirtier water, less people with health insurance."[88]

Even *Politico*, hardly a conservative publication, featured an op-ed by Keith Koffler arguing that while conservatives often accuse Obama of waging class warfare, his "reelection strategy is about more than the haves and have-nots. It appears he is seeking to stir up full-blown cultural warfare against a large and diverse segment of society known as Republicans." Unable to run on his economic record, Obama "and his advisers seem to have decided instead to mount a deeply polarizing campaign based on 'values'—suggesting his vision for America is correct even if the economy is not right yet." And, Koffler noted, "in waging this battle, Obama is saying nasty and dangerous things. He is promoting his own principles—not just by touting their goodness, but by suggesting that

Republicans hold to an offensive, even un-American philosophy. By painting his opposition as not just wrong but evil, Obama risks dividing the nation in a profound and unnecessary way."[89]

Obama indeed was characterizing Republicans as full-blown evil. In his disingenuous remarks on the GOP's debate in Orlando, he also described conservative audiences as "cheering at the prospect of somebody dying because they don't have health insurance." As Koffler wrote, "Allegations that Republicans want sick people to die and hate homosexuals are caricatures you might expect of an extreme House member or a raving partisan running for local office. That a president would say—or even believe—such things is deeply disturbing."[90] To be sure, no reasonable person, especially not a United States president, could actually believe audience members were hoping people would die—as opposed to registering their vocal opposition to Obama's socialized medicine scheme.

Obama's remarks established a bizarre theme—Republicans promoting mass death—that trickled down beyond his inner circle. USAID administrator Rajiv Shah testified to the House Appropriations State and Foreign Ops Subcommittee that the Republican budget plan, which contained $61 billion in baseline budget cuts—as opposed to actual cuts— would necessitate scaling back a malaria control program and lead to the deaths of thirty thousand children. It would also allegedly cause twenty-four thousand deaths due to immunization shortages and another sixteen thousand deaths from a lack of skilled attendants to oversee childbirths.[91]

ALL-OUT CLASS WARFARE

From the beginning of his splash onto the national stage, Obama has been a class warrior seeking to stoke envy and pitting people in different income groups against each other. He continually demonized big businesses, corporations, and "the wealthy," always hinting they had somehow gamed the system to achieve their success. In his view, of course, the free market system is inherently corrupt, and absent stringent federal regulations, it inevitably leads to unacceptable disparities in income and wealth.

He used class warfare as a bludgeon in virtually every policy initiative he promoted, from his stimulus bill, to cap and trade, to Obamacare, to his jobs plan, to his budget and tax proposals, to his support for the Occupy Wall Street movement. It was always about the "rich" not paying their fair share. Obama's treasury secretary Tim Geithner, speaking on CNBC, suggested the "wealthy" should pay higher taxes because "the most fortunate Americans ... [should] bear a slightly larger burden of the privilege of being an American."[92]

Well into his third year, even Obama's media friends had to concede how intentionally confrontational and divisive he was. In October 2011 the *Washington Post* reported, "There is a noticeably more aggressive, confrontational President Obama roaming the country these days, selling his jobs plan and attacking Republicans for standing in the way of progress by standing up only for the rich."[93]

This self-professed uniter began to call out leading congressional Republicans by name. Obama accused House Speaker John Boehner of having "walked away from a balanced package." Then, speaking from a bridge connecting the states of Boehner (Ohio) and Senate Minority Leader Mitch McConnell (Kentucky), Obama singled out the two Republican leaders for blocking job creation. He mocked GOP presidential candidate Rick Perry as "a governor whose state is on fire, denying climate change."[94] Blasting House Majority Leader Eric Cantor for opposing his jobs bill, Obama demanded, "Does he not believe in rebuilding America's roads and bridges? Does he not believe in tax breaks for small businesses or efforts to help our veterans?"[95]

Of course, Obama knew precisely why Cantor and the Republicans opposed his jobs bill: because it was no such thing. His bill called for some $447 billion in borrowed federal money that would neither create jobs nor stimulate the economy any more than his first failed stimulus bill of nearly twice that amount, but it would accelerate our path to national bankruptcy. Obama's clear implication was that Republican opposition to his agenda was purely partisan, putting the GOP's selfish interests above the nation's, and especially those who are most in need.

As always, Obama wasn't merely trying to divide the American people; he was also aiming to shore up support from his militant leftist base, which was upset with him for not being radical enough. As the *Post* reported, "The emergence of this more pugnacious Obama has heartened Democrats, especially the most liberal ones, who spent the past few months dejected by what they saw as the president's unwillingness to engage his opponents in political combat."[96]

ACT "LIKE GROWNUPS"

There is perhaps no better example of Obama's petulant intolerance for opposition and his disdainful attitude toward his Republican opponents than his posturing during the budget battles of mid-2011. As those skirmishes heated up in April, Obama called a White House press conference. But instead of laying out his side's position on the debate, he made it personal, as usual, demonizing his opponents, suggesting they weren't opposing him on principle—responsible fiscal stewardship—but for purely partisan gain. "We don't have time for games," said a "visibly irritated" Obama. "The only question," he continued, "is whether politics or ideology is going to get in the way of preventing a shutdown."[97] And after having sat out of the budget talks until then, he had the audacity to demand that congressional leaders act "like grownups,"[98] end the impasse, and reach an agreement, as if his own refusal to agree to crucial, meaningful budget cuts weren't the primary cause of the deadlock.[99]

At one point during the budget debates, Obama peevishly decided to take his ball home when House Republicans refused to yield to his dictatorial edicts, abruptly ending a tense budget meeting and walking out of the room. He also threatened Eric Cantor, "Eric, don't call my bluff. I'm going to take this to the American people." If anyone was bluffing, it was probably Obama, who must have been aware that at the time more voters opposed raising the debt ceiling (45 percent) than supported it (32 percent).[100]

At no time did Obama register similar disgust for the failure of the Democrat-controlled Senate to pass a budget for almost a thousand days. Like a tyrant who had usurped complete authority over the legislative branch, Obama condescendingly proclaimed, "If they can't sort it out, then I want them back here tomorrow."[101] Accusing Obama and Democrats of creating the false appearance of budget cuts with "smoke and mirrors," House Speaker John Boehner responded, "The president is certainly entitled to disagree with our budget, but what exactly is his alternative? If he wants to have an 'adult conversation' about solving our fiscal challenges, he needs to lead instead of sitting on the sidelines."[102]

Notably, during this round of budget negotiations, after expressing his frustration that his congressional children couldn't break their impasse, Obama vowed to personally get on the case, saying, "I want a meeting again tomorrow here at the White House … and if that doesn't work, we'll invite them again the day after that." The very next day Obama spent a total of three minutes on the phone with House Speaker John Boehner and then jetted off to Philadelphia for a campaign event billed as a town hall meeting on "winning the future." Following that meeting he flew to New York City for an event with Reverend Al Sharpton.[103]

Hedging its bets, the administration started lining up the pieces to place the blame on Republicans should a deal not be reached. Treasury Secretary Timothy Geithner said that Republican lawmakers would be responsible not just if the country defaulted on its debt obligations, but if through protracted negotiations, it came close to defaulting and spooked the markets. "Lawmakers," said Geithner, "will say there's leverage in it, we can advance it. But that would be deeply irresponsible and they will own the risk. It won't happen in the end, but if they take it too close to the edge, they will own responsibility for that miscalculation."[104]

THE MEDICARE SCARE

As far as the Democrats were concerned, during the budget debates there weren't any depths to which the Republicans would not sink. Vice President Biden said the Republicans were asking those who are struggling to bear the burden and letting the most fortunate off the hook, which Biden said bordered on being immoral. When CBS News' Chip Reid asked White House press secretary Jay Carney, "Does the president agree with that?" Carney replied, "Why, I think he does. Yes."[105]

Biden said it was wrong to ask senior citizens receiving Medicare to pay more in taxes when people earning more than $1 million a year receive a substantial tax cut. Of course, that was a complete distortion, since Republicans were proposing neither an increase in taxes for lower income groups or seniors nor a tax cut for those earning more than $1 million per year. They were merely standing their ground in refusing to allow the years-old Bush tax cuts to expire for the highest income bracket—for individuals making $200,000 per year and households $250,000 a year—not $1 million and above as Biden misrepresented. Republicans were not demanding further cuts, but only that the existing rates for all income brackets remain the same.

At a speech in mid-April ostensibly to unveil his own budget plan, Obama concentrated largely on denouncing Republicans, some of whom were attending the event at Obama's invitation. According to the *Washington Post*, Obama "repeatedly attacked the budget released by the House GOP last week in a sharp, partisan tone.... In the speech, he used as many words to attack the GOP proposal as to lay out his own." Obama said, "A 70 percent cut in clean energy, a 25 percent cut in education, a 30 percent cut in transportation, cuts in college Pell Grants that will grow to more than $1,000 per year. That's the proposal. These aren't the kinds of cuts you make when you're trying to get rid of some waste or find extra savings in the budget. These aren't the kinds of cuts that the fiscal commission proposed. These are the kinds of cuts that tell us we can't afford the America that I believe in and, I think, you believe in."[106]

Though Obama had offered no plan to reform Medicare, and the GOP-backed Ryan Plan was geared precisely toward saving the program, Obama declared that the Republicans' plan would "end Medicare as we know it." It was vintage Obama, excoriating a Republican proposal but offering nothing of his own, and using Republicans as props and the event as a campaign stunt, just as he did in the fraudulently labeled "Bipartisan Health Care Summit." Obama continued, "Their vision is less about reducing the deficit than it is about changing the basic social compact in America." Then came the inevitable class warfare: "There's nothing serious about a plan that claims to reduce the deficit by spending a trillion dollars on tax cuts for millionaires and billionaires. And I don't think there's anything courageous about asking for sacrifice from those who can least afford it and don't have any clout on Capitol Hill."[107]

The *Washington Post* could not ignore Obama's lack of substance and absence of details, observing, "Even as he savaged the GOP proposal, Obama was less than specific about his own. He did not say exactly how he would reform how corporations are taxed, what he would do to achieve a simpler tax system or which defense programs he would cut. On Social Security, he not only didn't announce a proposal but would not say whether one was likely to be included in the final legislation."[108]

Congressman Paul Ryan responded with disbelief, disappointment, and uncharacteristic albeit righteous anger to Obama's pugnacious tone. "I am very disappointed in the president," Ryan declared:

> I was excited when we got invited to attend his speech today. I thought the president's invitation … was an olive branch. Instead, what we got was a speech that was excessively partisan, dramatically inaccurate, and hopelessly inadequate to addressing our country's pressing fiscal challenges. What we heard today was not fiscal leadership from our commander in chief. What we heard today was a political broadside from our campaigner in chief…. Rather than building bridges, he's poisoning wells. By failing seriously to confront the most predictable economic crisis in our nation's history, the president's policies are committing us and our children to a diminished future. We are looking to bipartisan solutions not to partisan rhetoric…. Exploiting people's emotions of fear, envy and anxiety is not hope, it's not change; it's partisanship. We don't need partisanship, we don't need demagoguery, we need solutions.[109]

"A SUGAR-COATED SATAN SANDWICH"

In the days that followed, Obama only sharpened his attacks, accusing Republicans of wanting to turn the United States into a "Third World" country because they were not willing to "invest" in infrastructure improvements. "Under their vision," said Obama, "we can't invest in roads and bridges and broadband and high-speed rail. I mean, we would be a nation of potholes, and our airports would be worse than places that we thought—that we used to call the Third World, but who are now investing in infrastructure."[110] With all his haughty criticism, Obama never has explained what happened to that $862 billion of borrowed money he spent for "shovel-ready" jobs to rebuild our infrastructure. He just laughed about his epiphany that shovel-ready jobs don't actually exist.

In the end, after all of Obama's whining about GOP obstructionism and its refusal to compromise or even negotiate in good faith, once a debt-ceiling deal was reached, the White House bragged that it had strong-armed Republicans into capitulating. It boasted on its blog, "The president stood firm and forced Republicans to back down, preventing them from using the prospect of default as leverage again in six months by ensuring that any additional debt-limit increases will not be needed until 2012."[111]

Far from appreciative of the compromise, Obama called Republican opposition to his plan "a manufactured crisis." As if to suggest that all efforts by Republicans to rein in his spending orgy were solely geared toward harming the economy—never mind that none of his grandiose spending sprees had done anything to stimulate economic growth—Obama said, "Voters may have chosen divided government but they sure didn't vote for dysfunctional government. They want us to solve problems, they want us to get this economy growing and adding jobs."[112]

Obama conspicuously declined to object to querulous reactions to the deal from fellow Democrats. Congressman Emanuel Cleaver, chairman of the Congressional Black Caucus, described the agreement as "a sugar-coated Satan sandwich" and "a shady bill."[113] Congressman Luis Gutierrez proclaimed, "The Tea Partiers and the GOP have made their slash and burn lunacy clear, and while I do not love this compromise, my vote is a hose to stop the burning. The arsonists must be stopped."[114] Congresswoman Maxine Waters declared, "As far as I'm concerned—the tea party can go straight to hell."[115]

When difficult negotiations yield an agreement, leaders often praise the other side and express hope for more cooperation in the future. But after repeatedly describing Obama's counterparts as callous, heartless barbarians, Team Obama had gone so far out on the rhetorical ledge that it probably couldn't climb down even had it wanted to.

"THEIR VISION IS RADICAL"

Indeed, Obama used the budget agreement as a launching pad to step up his attacks on the GOP. Just a few days after the agreement was struck, speaking about Republican proposals for entitlement reform at the headquarters of Facebook in Palo Alto, California, he declared, "I think it is fair to say that their vision is radical." He continued, "I don't think it's particularly courageous. Nothing is easier than solving a problem on the backs of people who are poor, or people who are powerless, or don't have lobbyists, or don't have clout."[116]

At his next campaign stop, in San Francisco, Obama mocked Republicans as "climate change deniers." Referring to rising oil prices, with no hint that his own policies were partly to blame, he said that curbing our reliance on foreign oil is a "national security imperative." As usual, he also said nothing of his bitter resistance to increasing domestic oil production. At the home of SalesForce.com CEO Marc Benioff, he said, "And then there's the environmental aspect of it. There are climate change deniers in Congress and when the economy gets tough, sometimes environmental issues drop from people's radar screens."[117]

Switching gears, Obama used the tenth anniversary of the 9/11 attacks to offer Republicans another phony olive branch. In an op-ed in *USA Today*, he exhorted Americans to reclaim "the true spirit of America" that united us after the attacks—the "ordinary goodness and patriotism of the American people and the unity that we needed to move forward together, as one nation." It was odd, given his recent history, to read Obama's words: "Let's never forget the lesson we learned anew 10 years ago—that our differences pale beside what unites us and that when we choose to move forward together, as one American family, the United States doesn't just endure, we can emerge from our tests and trials stronger than before."[118]

His declared truce was as ephemeral as the "saved or created" jobs he attributes to his stimulus bill. The very day after the 9/11 anniversary, Obama told NBC News that the "vast majority" of Americans reject the "extreme" ideas of the tea party movement. "I do think that the extreme position that you hear that says government has no role to play in growing our economy, that the federal government has no function to play in building a strong middle class, is absolutely wrong. I reject that view. And I think the vast majority of Americans reject that view."[119]

Not missing a beat, the next day Obama again accused Republicans of playing political games in opposing his jobs bill. But what Republican would have supported a proposal to spend another $447 billion to "stimulate" the economy when the first "stimulus" bill was such an abject failure and when we are so inundated by debt? Again, he urged his audience to bombard congressmen with tweets and emails to pressure them into further bankrupting the nation. The ongoing irony was that it was Obama who was *always* political, *always* partisan. As Republican National Committee chairman Rence Priebus said, "We all get the joke. He's in Virginia, Ohio, and North Carolina. Doing what? Selling to the American people for his re-election effort."[120]

"A STRATEGY OF RUINING THE COUNTRY TO RULE THE COUNTRY"

Polarization and divisiveness come as easy to Obama as falling off a log, but, tellingly, at a certain point he made a conscious effort to dial up his militancy as a matter of strategy. David Plouffe, who joined the White House team in January 2011, has been described as "the chief choreographer for the president's performance." Plouffe, under heat from the base for not being combative enough—as ludicrous as that charge was—reportedly pushed Obama to adopt a more strident tone. Plouffe had been advising Obama to stay above the fray for fear of alienating independents, but he allegedly yielded to the pressure and "answered the appeals of his party and finally set the president on a more partisan… course."[121]

The suggestion that Obama's default position was anything other than hyper-partisan was patently absurd. But his advisors and the media would have had us believe otherwise, obviously assuming we'd been living in a vacuum the past three years, oblivious to Obama's militant partisanship. So the liberal media persisted in portraying Obama as a veritable pacifist toward his political opponents, as when the *New York Times* wrote, "To the relief of many Democrats, Mr. Obama has become more assertive lately in attacking Republicans and drawing contrasts with them."[122] Similarly, *The Hill* portrayed Obama's cheap shots at Governor Rick Perry as "some of the most direct and combative for Obama so far,"[123] as if he hadn't been that petty for years.

Not that Obama's fellow Democratic strategists needed the prompting, but Obama clearly created a vitriolic climate. Veteran Democratic strategist Bob Shrum said, "It's certainly obvious Republicans have established a strategy of ruining the country to rule the country," adding that Obama should convince voters "that he was a warrior for ordinary people." Translated, Obama's charge was to recast "Obama, the reasonable man, as a reasonably angry man."[124] It would be interesting to know if that's how Shrum would have characterized Obama's unscripted comments at a private dinner with supporters in Chicago a few months prior. Captured on a hot mic, Obama said, "You want to repeal healthcare? Go at it. We'll have that debate. You're not going to be able to do that by nickel-and-diming me in the budget. You think we're stupid?"[125]

This is quite odd and markedly distinct from other presidents. President George W. Bush, for all the unfair partisan arrows he took, always represented himself as leader of all the American people and of the United States. By contrast, Obama deliberately set out on a course to cast himself as a president not of all the people, but only of those whose cause he championed or who had the good sense to side with him. Political commentator Peter Wehner, who worked in the George W. Bush White House, wrote, "Obama has become the most intentionally divisive president we've seen in quite some time." It's not unusual for a president's policies to be divisive, admitted Wehner, but Obama "now belongs in a separate category. Each day, it seems, he and/or his supporters are seeking to divide us. The rhetoric employed by the president and his allies is meant to fan the flames of resentment, to turn Americans against one another, and to stoke feelings of envy, grievances, and rage."[126]

Thus, if anyone was expecting Obama to change course to a more harmonious path, they would be disappointed. David Plouffe continued to reinforce Obama's proclivities toward bullying and community organizing against his opponents, as well as his flair for ridicule. To demonize and diminish the tea party in the midst of yet another political standoff over the budget and a potential government shutdown, Plouffe said in late September 2011, "We're not going to make progress on the deficit, on things we can do right now for jobs, on tax cuts, unless those 30 or 40 Tea Party members of the Republican House stop being the focal point of our discussion." Plouffe further accused Republicans of "playing politics with disasters," referring to the claim that the Federal Emergency Agency's Disaster Relief Fund would be insolvent unless a continuing resolution were passed.

Obama, for his part, was ridiculing accusations that he stoked class warfare even as he stridently did so. He told a crowd in Ohio, "If asking a billionaire to pay the same tax rate as a plumber or teacher makes me a warrior for the middle class, I'll wear that charge as a badge of honor. Because the only class warfare I've seen is the battle that's been waged against the middle class in this country for a decade."[127]

The next day, in California campaigning again, Obama said that the Republican vision of government would "fundamentally cripple America in meeting the challenges of the 21st century." Lavishing his militant leftist base with the choicest of red meats, he declared, "From the moment I took office what we've seen is a constant ideological pushback against any kind of sensible reforms that would make our economy work better and give people more opportunity."[128]

At the end of Obama's second year in office, CNN asked, "Which president, in recent history, had the most polarizing second year in office?

The answer," wrote CNN political producer Shannon Travis, "President Obama, according to a fresh analysis." Travis cited a Gallup poll comparing Obama's second year approval numbers—from January 2010 to January 2011—to those of other presidents, reporting that some 81 percent of Democrats approved while only 13 percent of Republicans did, representing a 68 percent gap, higher than any other president in his second year. George W. Bush had a higher gap during the most contentious periods of the Iraq War, but Obama was clearly trending toward record-setting territory in just his second year, in stark contrast to the conciliatory image on which he'd campaigned.[129]

This is the inevitable result of Obama's brawling, ends-justify-the-means attitude toward his opponents. Portraying Republicans and tea partiers as advocates of everything from racism to mass death, Obama and his allies don't engage with conservatives, but seek to thoroughly discredit them as honorable human beings. For this administration, the personal is indeed political—and it will resort to any means necessary to win.

CHAPTER THREE

THE WAR ON THE DISOBEDIENT

Throughout his entire presidency, President Obama has not only habitually bullied his political opponents, he's harassed any person, organization, or industry he perceives as hindering his agenda. Disrespecting the separation of powers doctrine, Obama even threw his weight around the Supreme Court, warning the "unelected" justices that it would be "extraordinary" and "unprecedented" for them to overturn Obamacare—though, since the individual mandate is manifestly unconstitutional, striking it down would hardly be unprecedented at all; it would just be a big blow to Obama's agenda. What *was* unprecedented was for a sitting president to directly comment on a case pending before the Court in an effort either to intimidate the justices into ruling his way, or to lay a foundation to politicize the decision if they didn't.[1]

It doesn't matter that his domineering approach is inconsistent with his professed bipartisanship or his calls for a new tone in politics. Nor does it seem to matter when others call attention to his intimidation tactics. He was raised in Chicago's mean streets of "community organizing," and that is all he knows. His vaunted rhetorical powers that served him so well on the campaign trail have yielded him no fruit since he took office; he has failed to persuade the American people to buy into his agenda no matter how many speeches he has delivered on Obamacare, his Jobs Bill, or any other initiative. And whenever he encounters resistance to one of his transformative government schemes, he always falls back on the same thing: his legacy of political brawling.

"HOW MANY OTHER PAPERS HAVE GOTTEN CALLS LIKE THIS?"

No criticism, no matter how small or insignificant, seems to escape the notice of this thin-skinned president. When the *Pleasanton Weekly*, a small weekly newspaper in California, ran a feature on the presidential helicopter Marine One, the White House bristled that the story reflected poorly on Michelle Obama—because it included one sentence indicating that the first lady acted dismissively toward the pilots. One would think the White House has more pressing concerns than a slightly unfavorable story in a small local paper, but *Pleasanton Weekly* president Gina Channell-Allen said a White House official asked her to cut that reference from the article. While the first lady's press secretary, Katie McCormick, denied contact with the paper, Allen stuck by her story, saying she "complied" with the request "because it was not worth making a fuss over."[2] HotAir.com raised an interesting question: "How many other papers have gotten calls like this?"[3]

The administration tries to browbeat bigger newspapers as well, such as its banishment of the *Boston Herald* from an Obama event in Boston as punishment for its printing a front-page op-ed by GOP presidential candidate Mitt Romney. White House spokesman Matt Lehrich unapologetically pronounced, "I think that raises a fair question about whether the paper is unbiased in its coverage of the President's visits." Moreover, White House press secretary Jay Carney personally called MSNBC to object to comments political analyst Mark Halperin had made about Obama. According to the Daily Caller, MSNBC immediately suspended Halperin indefinitely.[4]

The White House also blacklisted *San Francisco Chronicle* reporter Carla Marinucci because she had the audacity to record, via cellphone, a video of protesters at an Obama fundraiser in the Bay Area and post it on the internet. True to form, the White House denied it had threatened Marinucci's banishment, but the *Chronicle*'s editor, Ward Bushee, stood his ground. "Sadly, we expected the White House to respond in this manner based on our experiences yesterday," he said. "It is not a truthful response. It follows a day of off-the-record exchanges with key people in the White House communications office who told us they would remove our reporter, then threatened retaliation to Chronicle and Hearst reporters if we reported on the ban, and then recanted to say our reporter might not be removed at all." Phil Bronstein, another *Chronicle* reporter, corroborated Bushee's story, saying "The Chronicle's report is accurate.... I was on some of those calls and can confirm Ward's statement." Making matters worse, numerous journalists confirmed that the White House had issued implied threats of additional punishment if the story of its banishment of Marinucci became public.[5]

Bronstein noted that the blacklisting "affects the newsgathering of our largest regional paper (and sfgate) and how local citizens get their information," adding that "Carla cannot do her job to the best of her ability if she can't use all the tools available to her as a journalist." Bronstein concluded, "The President's practice not just with transparency but in other dealings with the press has not been tracking his words, despite the cool glamour and easy conversation that makes him seem so much more open than the last guy.... Barack Obama sold himself successfully as a fresh wind for the 21st century. In important matters of communication, technology, openness and the press, it's not too late for him to demonstrate that."[6]

Clearly, intimidating the press has become standard fare for a president who, ironically, vowed to make his administration "the most open and transparent in history."[7] As blogger Keith Koffler observed, "The

Obama White House has long practiced the tactic of bullying reporters who write what it doesn't like."[8]

"IT'S GOING TO COST YOU"

Consistent with their penchant for class warfare, Obama and his administration have demonized entire industries. As I document in chapter seven, they have launched a sustained assault on oil companies, threatening a criminal investigation into British Petroleum over the Gulf oil spill and vowing to punish the whole industry with higher taxes.[9] With no place for oil producers in his utopian dreams, Obama has given the Department of the Interior the green light to harass them. Upping the pressure, in 2010 the department created the Office of Natural Resources Revenue, an office exclusively dedicated to extracting royalties from energy companies. The agency's zealous chief, Gregory J. Gould, issued a threat to oil companies that ran afoul of the department's edicts, announcing, "We're sending a message to the industry that if you do cut corners, it's going to cost you. You could quickly take care of the federal deficit if you use the maximum [penalties]."[10]

The industry is well aware that the administration views it as the enemy. Allison Nyholm, a royalty expert with American Petroleum Institute, remarked, "We are worried about an adversarial process. There is huge discretion in the fines. That is where the rub is going to occur."[11] As a big-spending liberal, Obama really ought to be thankful for oil companies, which contribute royalties from thousands of offshore oil and gas leases to the tune of some $10 billion to $13 billion a year, reportedly constituting the government's second biggest source of revenue after federal taxes.[12]

Aside from oil firms, the administration has also turned investment companies into a favorite whipping boy. Vice President Joe Biden denounced hedge fund managers as people who "play with other people's money," and "get taxed at 15 percent because they call it capital gains."[13] This was a cheap shot, meant to imply that hedge fund managers enjoy special tax treatment when in fact they are subject to the same capital gains tax rate as everyone else. Capital gains are always subject to a lower rate than ordinary income because they are based on income derived from the sale of assets. The White House consistently conflates the two types of taxes as part of its class war strategy to demonize the "wealthy."

BUSINESS: THE NEW PUBLIC ENEMY #1

When President Obama nominated M. Patricia Smith for solicitor of the Department of Labor on March 20, 2009, Republicans were concerned by her track record as New York State commissioner of labor, including her cozy relationship with unions. In that position, she created a first-of-its-kind program that involved the deputizing of unions and advocacy groups as watchdogs against private-sector businesses, with an eye especially to reporting wage violations. Employing typical liberal euphemisms, Smith insisted the unions and advocacy groups were merely helping the Labor Commission with "education," but an internal memo revealed that the commission referred to the groups as "enforcers." Republicans and businesses regarded this program as an "unprecedented and unwarranted" intrusion on private companies that would not only have a chilling effect on business, but could empower unions to pressure companies into accepting union contract terms or into unionizing their firms. Within weeks of her initiation of the "wage watch" program, numerous trade groups representing restaurants, retail outlets, convenience stores, and other types of business in New York drafted a letter to Smith complaining that the program "steps well over the boundaries of even the most constructive collaboration with community groups and advocates."

Some GOP lawmakers called on Obama to withdraw Smith's nomination, saying she misled the Senate Health, Education, Labor and Pensions Committee about the function of the "wage watch" program. Senator Mike Enzi wrote Obama, "If it was her intention to mislead the Senate, then I must oppose her nomination. If she unintentionally gave inaccurate statements to the Senate, then I question her ability to manage a large corporation, since she does not have a clear understanding of what is taking place in her own department in New York." When pressed at her confirmation hearing, Smith said she had no plans to consider this type of program at the federal level.[14]

As it turns out, the Republicans' concerns were vindicated. Perhaps Smith didn't recreate a "wage watch" program at the federal level per se, but she went further; under her direction, the Department of Labor staff issued a draft "operating plan" to significantly increase enforcement measures against private sector employers suspected of committing unfair labor practices, a move the National Legal and Policy Center described as a "plan to bully employers." The think tank, having examined the plan, concluded that its details "indicate Smith, like her boss, Labor Secretary Hilda Solis, views the department's relationship with business as necessarily highly adversarial."[15]

Smith showcased her anti-business animus in her draft "operating plan," which was reportedly adopted by the Labor Department. Rife with presuppositions about the inherent improprieties of private-sector employers, the plan effectively aimed to turn the department into a menacing enemy of businesses. The plan called for "identifying a public affairs liaison in each regional office to send stronger, clearer messages to the regulated community about DOL's emphasis on litigation." One tactic would be for the department's Occupational Safety and Health Administration (OSHA) to "deter (employers) through shaming." As the *Wall Street Journal*'s John Fund observed, "Whatever it might involve, it doesn't sound appropriate for an agency charged with carrying out the law in an even-handed fashion." The National Policy Center noted, "These liaisons can't be expected to be even-handed, as their very job depends on threatening employers with lawsuits. They will give working with (as opposed to working against) employers secondary priority."[16]

The plan also directed the department to "engage in enterprise-wide enforcement," meaning they would target multiple work sites of a single company. It further advocated "imposing shorter deadlines for implementing remedial measures in conciliation agreements and consent decrees."[17]

It also called for the department to "engage in greater use of injunctive relief," which was practically a mandate for compliance enforcement lawsuits, and would surely involve court-imposed penalties that might exceed heavy administrative fines.

Perhaps the most disturbing provision of the plan is one that called for the department to "identify and pursue test cases" to stretch the meaning of the law. This is an extremely aggressive use of the judicial system to expand the law's parameters, effectively transforming the department into a vehicle that seeks out trouble rather than trying to quell it. The department has over four hundred lawyers throughout the United States who could systematically harass private companies, all as a means of imperiously forcing changes in the employer-employee relationship that conform to the liberal ideological vision.

This decidedly anti-business attitude is in stark contrast to that shown by the Bush Labor Department under Labor Secretary Elaine Chao, who argued that "the best way to protect workers is to help employers understand their legal obligations and promote collaborative working relationships between employers and workers on safety and other issues." In other words, the Republican approach has not been to deny the role of government altogether, but it certainly hasn't identified employers as the government's number one enemy. Bush's approach worked: workplace injuries and illnesses declined some 21 percent beginning in 2002 and reached record lows at the end of Bush's second term.[18]

The Obama administration's anti-business bias is even more offensive in light of how favorably it treats unions. It has reversed Bush administration policies requiring greater union transparency, promoted a card-check policy to intimidate employees from opting out of union representation, and the Obama Labor Department rescinded its Form T-1, which, in order to promote transparency, required unions to disclose information on strike funds and other accounts under their authority. In addition, the Labor Department intended to shift whistleblowing oversight authority from OSHA to the Office of Labor-Management Standards—conveniently, just as the administration has gutted that office's staff and funding.[19]

The bottom line is this: the Obama administration encouraged and funded transparency, enforcement, and even litigation against private companies while decreasing all those things with respect to unions—all of which reveals not just the administration's micromanaging approach to governance, but its bitter determination to empower unions and emasculate private firms.

A "TEA PARTY DOWNGRADE"

Credit rating agencies must strenuously safeguard their independence if they are to protect their reputation for unbiased analysis—and that's a problem for the Obama administration. When Standard & Poor's decided to downgrade the United States' credit rating in 2011, the White House and the U.S. Treasury launched a coordinated attack on the agency's credibility. The campaign first appeared in a memo posted on the Treasury's website by one of its senior officials, John Bellows. Charging that the downgrade was based on a $2 trillion error, the post said, "Independent of this error, there is no justifiable rationale for downgrading the debt of the United States.... The magnitude of this mistake—and the haste with which S&P changed its principal rationale for action when presented with this error—raise fundamental questions about the credibility and integrity of S&P's ratings action."[20] Gene Sperling, head of the White House Council of Economic Advisers, leveled a similar attack on S&P, while a senior administration official declared, "This is a facts-be-damned decision. Their analysis is way off, but they wouldn't budge."[21]

In defense of its actions, S&P president Deven Sharma said the government's angry response was "the same you would get from any other country or company." Sharma told the *Wall Street Journal*, "We are supposed to be objective, and others are always trying to convince us why the risk is less than we think it is."[22]

While the Obama administration tried to blame the downgrade on the agency itself or on Republican brinksmanship during budget negotiations, the real problem was the government's failure to devise a plan to restructure long-term entitlements—and that failure can be laid squarely at the feet of President Obama and the Democrats. S&P official John Chambers said the impasse was a factor in the downgrade—without assessing more fault on either the president or Congress—but indicated this problem has been long in the making and centers on entitlements.

Moreover, he admitted to the mistake the administration had highlighted, but explained it made no material difference in the long-term debt-to-GDP ratio, which was a tacit admission that the budget impasse was not the cause of the downgrade—it was our overwhelming debt, driven by entitlements.[23]

But the White House would not back off. On *Face the Nation*, Bob Schieffer pressed White House advisor David Axelrod on his claim that Republicans were to blame for the downgrade. Schieffer asked, "Are you saying the President bears no responsibility for this, that this was all the fault of the other side?" Axelrod replied, "Listen Bob, what I'm saying is review the history of what happened here ... this is essentially a Tea Party downgrade. The Tea Party brought us to the brink of a default."[24]

As S&P stood its ground, the administration increased the pressure. The Securities and Exchange Commission asked S&P to disclose all its associates who were aware of the decision to downgrade the U.S. debt before it was announced, ostensibly to examine the possibility of insider trading. This inquiry was initiated even though the SEC admitted it was not aware of any leak from an S&P insider, nor had it heard of any suspicious trading in connection with the downgrade or its announcement.[25]

Shortly after the SEC began its probe, S&P president Deven Sharma suddenly announced he would resign. An observer might easily conclude he was forced out under government pressure, though Vice President Biden, while claiming to have no direct knowledge of the matter, said his "instinct" was that disgruntled businesses may have influenced the resignation.[26]

"A CREEPY, AUTHORITARIAN NUTJOB"

In *Crimes Against Liberty* I discussed how the White House established an official email address and a website dedicated to encouraging people to snitch on their neighbors who criticize the administration. Although their campaign died within a few weeks amid a public outcry, they never gave up.

In September 2011, in a similar spirit, Obama's re-election campaign launched AttackWatch.com, whereby Obama supporters are encouraged to report all attacks against the administration—meaning any expressions of criticism, no matter how warranted. As one critic noted, "Wow, not only are Obama & Co. incredibly thin-skinned; they're paranoid."[27]

Obama for America national field director Jeremy Bird said that the site, which features Orwellian slogans encouraging people to "support the truth," aims to provide "resources to fight back" against attacks. Even President Obama himself, never hesitating to avail himself of opportunities to demean the dignity of his office, personally entered the fray, tweeting, "We've launched a new way to track and respond to attacks. President Obama: #AttackWatch. Check it out: attackwatch.com."

The site doesn't seem to have improved Obama's standing among the American people, but its associated Twitter account has provided conservatives with a convenient forum for ridiculing the AttackWatch campaign. As one critic tweeted, "There's a new Twitter account making President Obama look like a creepy, authoritarian nutjob."[28]

THE CRUSADE AGAINST VOTER ID LAWS: "AN AFFRONT TO CIVIC ORDER"

The Obama administration may think it's worthwhile to engage enemy nations in dialogue, but it has found one target deserving of an all-out assault: American states that defy Obama's will.

This campaign features a concerted attack on states that commit the cardinal sin of passing voter ID laws. Take Arizona, against which the Obama-Holder Justice Department filed a brief in a Ninth U.S. Circuit Court of Appeals case arguing that the state's law requiring proof of citizenship to register to vote preempted federal law. Arizona attorney general Tom Horne said the administration was trying to thwart Arizona's voter ID laws in an effort to boost the vote among illegal immigrants, who would most likely vote Democrat. "Nobody that I've talked to, regardless of political persuasion, can understand how a court can tell us that we can't make sure that people who vote are citizens," Horne declared, citing evidence proving that illegal immigrants had indeed registered to vote.[29]

The campaign against Arizona is no isolated act. The Obama DOJ has overturned South Carolina's voter ID law, rejected a similar law in

Texas, and blocked Georgia's voter ID law before capitulating when the
state fought back in court. These laws generally require voters simply to
show one of many possible forms of ID to verify their identity, and some
oblige the government to provide free ID to those who request it. Yet
Obama's officials baselessly claim that asking someone to show ID to
vote—a mundane act, *National Review*'s Jonah Goldberg noted, typically required to fly on a plane, rent a car, ride Amtrak, or stay at a
hotel—is racially discriminatory.[30]

The DOJ objects to other anti-voter fraud measures as well. When a
tea party group in a district of Harris County, Texas, recruited poll
watchers to help root out voting fraud, the Justice Department moved
against them as fast as a high-speed train. Poll watchers had credible
reasons for concern; there were some 24,000 addresses with more than
six registered voters each, more than ten times the number of such houses
in most districts. Furthermore, many people registered from vacant lots,
numerous people were registered in a seven-bed halfway house, and there
were registrations by self-admitted non-citizens, along with other pecu-
liarities. Lo and behold, it was later found that tens of thousands of these
fraudulent registrations had been manufactured by a union-connected
group called Houston Votes.[31]

The Texas Democratic Party was the moving complainant against
the tea partiers, but that apparently did not raise the suspicions of the
hyper-politicized Department of Justice; instead of focusing on the voter
fraud allegations, the DOJ launched an investigation into the poll watchers for allegedly intimidating voters.[32] Of course, the DOJ didn't show
the same concern about voter intimidation when it famously dismissed
nearly all the charges against the New Black Panther Party, whose members were filmed during the 2008 presidential elections patrolling a
Philadelphia voting precinct, one with a nightstick, while taunting white
voters that they were about to be ruled by a black man.[33]

If the DOJ's activities end up increasing voter fraud, the votes of all
legal voters will be devalued. But there are certain groups whose voting
rights are zealously defended by the DOJ—for example, non-English
speakers. Citing anecdotal evidence that people had been discouraged
from voting, DOJ officials in 2010 compelled Ohio's Cuyahoga County

to print bilingual voting ballots under threat of a lawsuit. To make sure the county got the message, DOJ officials also forced it to agree to hire more bilingual poll workers, create a "community-based Spanish-language advisory committee," and allow federal observers to monitor the county's elections.[34]

While the DOJ found bilingual ballots to be a top priority in Ohio, it didn't take an interest in press reports that 5,800 dead people still appeared on the state's voter registration rolls. It had shown the same apathy toward voter fraud the previous year when it abandoned a case against Missouri for failing to clean up its voter rolls, even though a third of the state's counties reported more registered voters than voting-age residents.[35]

Meanwhile, where was the DOJ when immigration officials informed an illegal alien in Tennessee he could still become a U.S. citizen even though he had voted illegally? The government merely required him to "submit a letter of explanation of … when you discovered that you were not a United States Citizen"—as if, opined the *Washington Times* editors, "he hadn't known." They concluded, "The Obama administration and liberal bureaucrats are working to help everybody vote, whether or not they are eligible (or even alive). This undermines the rights of legal Americans whose votes are improperly diluted of value by fraud. The scandals are an affront to civic order."[36]

With the 2012 presidential elections approaching, we can expect the Justice Department to continue attacking states that pass voter ID laws and other anti-voter fraud measures, citing the preposterous pretext that such precautions harm minorities. Though a strong majority of Americans—even Democrats—support these laws, Obama and Holder seem anxious to press the matter to pander to their leftist base.[37]

The DOJ's antipathy toward states that enforce voter fraud laws or fail to meet its demands for multicultural accommodations reflects the department's aggressive, politicized law enforcement under the tenure of Attorney General Eric Holder. As J. Christian Adams, a former lawyer for the DOJ's Voting Rights Division, reported in his whistleblower book *Injustice*, "Holder's term has been marked by racially discriminatory law enforcement, politicized and ideological hiring, court-imposed sanctions on DOJ lawyers, and corrupt decisions to allow American voter rolls to overflow with deceased citizens and ineligible felons."[38]

ILLEGAL IMMIGRATION: "OUR OWN GOVERNMENT HAS BECOME OUR ENEMY"

The Obama administration has also crusaded against states that attempt to stem the inflow of illegal immigrants. States are forced to adopt their own enforcement measures due to Obama's manifest refusal to secure the border. But in the face of all evidence, Obama declared in Texas in May 2011 that he's done everything necessary for border security, and that now it's time to drop the issue and begin advancing his thinly veiled plans for a massive illegal alien amnesty. Obama's comments were hard to take seriously considering, as Texas congressman Michael McCaul observed, that up to 90 percent of the border in the state where Obama was speaking is still not under operational control.[39]

As documented in *Crimes Against Liberty*, a primary target of the administration's campaign has been Arizona and its immigration law, S.B. 1070. The DOJ's lawsuit against the state received a major setback in April 2012 when most of the law was upheld by a U.S. appeals court. Nevertheless, the administration continues to argue that the law allows for racial profiling, even though the bill expressly prohibits the practice. Obama officials further allege that S.B. 1070 preempts federal law, an accusation dismissed by Arizona senator Jon Kyl, who notes, "It's simply the state of Arizona providing some additional law enforcement assistance for the federal government."[40]

But the administration doesn't want this assistance, because it doesn't want a secure border at all. Sheriff Paul Babeu of Pinal County, Arizona, whose department patrols a portion of the U.S.-Mexico border, said the federal government was not only failing to assist his state with border patrol efforts, but was actually impeding them. "What is very troubling is the fact that at a time when we in law enforcement and our state need help from the federal government, instead of sending help they put up billboard-size signs warning our citizens to stay out of the desert in my county because of dangerous drug and human smuggling and weapons and bandits and all these other things and then, behind that, they drag us into court with the ACLU," said Babeu, who described the administration's cooperation with the ACLU against Arizona as "simply outrageous." He declared, "Our own government has become our enemy and is taking us to court at a time when we need help."[41]

Continuing its assault on the states, in August 2011 the Justice Department filed a lawsuit against Alabama over its new immigration law, alleging it impinges on the federal government's constitutional authority over immigration. "Setting immigration policy and enforcing immigration laws is a national responsibility that cannot be addressed through a patchwork of state immigration laws," claimed Eric Holder.[42] But why should the federal government mind if border states pass laws to aid the enforcement of existing federal laws, so long as they are not in conflict with them? The reason, as noted, is that the Obama administration doesn't want any state to protect its borders more vigorously than is consistent with the administration's lax policies, so it speciously invokes the Constitution, in an attempt to elevate a disagreement over policy into a constitutional issue.

House Oversight Committee ranking member Darrell Issa had previously exposed the flaws in the administration's constitutional argument in discussing the Arizona law. "The administration can't have it both ways," he said. "They can't have e-verify, they can't have these programs where they're supposed to take criminals and pass them over to the federal government if they're illegally in the country and then say, 'but if you do it wholesale where it actually works, we're going to come after you.'" Issa also noted that Arizona (like other states with similar laws) "is not incarcerating people for being illegally in the country, they're offering them up to the federal government to take their responsibility."[43]

The administration's attacks on the Alabama immigration law provide a textbook example of false rhetoric and disingenuousness. For example, the DOJ claimed Alabama's law would be "highly likely to expose persons lawfully in the United States, including school children, to new difficulties in routine dealings."[44] To the contrary, in addition to permitting officials to check the immigration status of students in public schools, the law simply allows authorities to question people suspected of being in the country illegally, which is no different than the routine police procedure of detaining people they have probable cause to believe committed a crime. There is, of course, a chance that some innocents might be detained and later released, but that is the case in any enforcement action, and is hardly a good reason to forego enforcement altogether. The DOJ also blasted the law for "attempt[ing] to drive aliens off the grid," which is rather like criticizing drug laws for forcing drug dealers to conceal their illegal activities.[45]

The DOJ even argued that the Alabama law could impact U.S. diplomatic relations with foreign countries, warning that "Alabama is not in a position to answer to other nations for the consequences of its policy." In the upside-down world of the Obama administration, a U.S. state must not take legal actions against illegal aliens if the actions risk offending the government of the illegals' home country.

And in perhaps its most ludicrous assertion, the DOJ claimed the law's requirement that officers report suspects to federal immigration officials "unnecessarily diverts resources from federal enforcement priorities and precludes state and local officials from working in true cooperation with federal officials."[46]

Of course, the "priority" the administration is really defending is its policy not to enforce federal immigration laws.

The DOJ train next pulled into South Carolina, which the administration sued in November 2011 to block its new immigration law. The law does not allow police to go hunting for immigration violators, but only to check the status of someone who the police have detained for another reason. The law specifically forbids officers from holding someone solely on suspicion of being an illegal immigrant, but that didn't impress the DOJ, which claimed the law is unconstitutional. South Carolinian Rob Godfrey said, "If the feds were doing their job, we wouldn't have had to address illegal immigration reform at the state level. But, until they do, we're going to keep fighting in South Carolina to be able to enforce our laws."[47]

These state laws are widely popular; two Rasmussen surveys from 2011 found that 67 percent of Americans approve of states such as

Alabama and Arizona passing immigration laws when the federal government fails to act, and that 60 percent of Americans think the federal government actually encourages illegal immigration.[48] But overturning these laws remains a major priority for Holder. "The department is committed to evaluating each state immigration law and making decisions based on the facts and the law," he proclaimed. "To the extent we find state laws that interfere with the federal government's enforcement of immigration law, we are prepared to bring suit, as we did in Arizona."[49] A top DOJ official was even dispatched to Alabama to hunt for evidence the administration could use to strike down the state's immigration law, thus betraying that the DOJ predetermines its position on these laws.[50] Perhaps Holder should have said that his DOJ was prepared to enjoin any state that interfered with the federal government's *non-enforcement* of immigration law.

Aside from its ideological zeal, the administration, as noted, has a cynical political motivation for this campaign: it helps gin up support from the administration's leftist base. The move is said to complement Obama's 2012 campaign game plan to boost turnout among Hispanics in swing states like Florida, Virginia, and North Carolina. As Mark Krikorian of the Center for Immigration Studies said, the administration "sees every Alabaman as having a Bull Connor on the inside waiting to come out.... They're attacking Alabama to motivate left-wing voters in other states."[51]

Despite the administration's hostility, some thirty states have adopted their own immigration enforcement laws since Arizona passed S.B. 1070 in April 2010. While Obama officials would have us believe this is all motivated by bigotry and other sinister factors, illegal immigration is a major law enforcement and public safety concern that drains state budgets nationwide in the areas of education, healthcare, and other public services. But none of this matters to the Obama administration.

We can surmise that a major reason the administration finds these laws so threatening is that they are working. Since Arizona approved S.B. 1070 in April 2010, even though some of its provisions were enjoined by a federal judge, crime in Phoenix plunged to a thirty-year low. Just two years ago the city ranked second only to Mexico City for incidents of kidnapping.[52]

TARGETING RED STATES: "COULDN'T HE PRETEND HE'S PRESIDENT ... OF ALL THE PEOPLE?"

Unsurprisingly, the Obama administration's war against the states focuses disproportionately on red states—including its jealous approach to immigration enforcement. For example, people have asked why Holder hasn't taken action against Rhode Island, which has reportedly undertaken local immigration enforcement for years. As the *Boston Globe* revealed, "From Woonsocket to Westerly, the troopers patrolling the nation's smallest state are reporting all illegal immigrants they encounter, even on routine stops such as speeding, to U.S. Immigration and Customs Enforcement, known as ICE." The article also indicated that ICE agents, as opposed to their superiors in the Obama administration, actually appreciate state assistance in immigration enforcement: "ICE has repeatedly urged police departments to take advantage of its Law Enforcement Center in Vermont," the *Globe* reported.[53]

The administration also has a habit of denying requested federal aid to red states—a strange practice in light of Obama's propensity toward budget-busting federal spending. The White House repeatedly denied requests from Texas for disaster relief for destructive wildfires, and it also refused Oklahoma's request for disaster assistance for record flooding in 2010. As Edmond, Oklahoma, resident Rick Machaceck remarked, "It's not good. They spend money on everything else. Then, when somebody does need help, we don't get it." The White House declined to explain why it denied Oklahoma's request.[54]

Wisconsin may not be a red state per se, but with a Republican governor and Republican legislature, it drew Obama's attention; specifically, he saw fit to take sides in the 2011 dispute between public sector unions and Wisconsin governor Scott Walker over the state's collective bargaining practices. The legislature's approval of Walker's collective bargaining reform was a strictly intrastate issue in which the president had no reasonable grounds for intervening, but he just couldn't refrain. Employing his familiar Alinskite tactics, Obama vigorously supported the unions as tens of thousands of union members flooded the state capitol in a failed effort to pressure legislators to reject Walker's bill. The unions became increasingly militant, and the president refused to call for restraint even when they began threatening Republican officials and their families, some of whom stopped sleeping in their own houses due to safety concerns. As *National Review*'s Jay Nordlinger wondered, "Couldn't Obama say something? Couldn't he pretend he's president—president of all the people—and say, 'We have political disagreements, but we're going to work them out peacefully and democratically. For example, massing at lawmakers' homes, to shout and threaten, is out of bounds.'"[55]

Obama's team apparently gave the Wisconsin unions more than just rhetorical support, bringing Obama's experience at community organization from the streets of Chicago to Pennsylvania Avenue. When Wisconsin Democrats fled the state in a vain attempt to stop the legislature from approving collective bargaining reform, Wisconsin Senate majority leader Scott Fitzgerald said that people clearly believed state Democrats were engaged in a stalling tactic in order to give Obama's Chicago team time to organize an effort to recall Republican legislators. Just four months earlier, the people of the state had democratically elected the Republican officials Obama and Wisconsin Democrats were seeking to recall.[56]

During his 2008 presidential campaign, Barack Obama portrayed himself as a transformative figure who would usher America—and the world—into a shining new future of international peace, racial harmony, and environmental improvement. With this immodest view of his own historical importance, it makes perfect sense that, as president, he and his team would show little tolerance for dissent or for those who won't fall in line behind his agenda; after all, these recalcitrants are impeding his glorious vision where the oceans stop rising and the planet begins healing. Surely no one of good will could possibly want to delay that day's arrival. No, in the Obama administration's view, those who stand in Obama's way cannot be reasoned with and certainly don't deserve an audience. Whether local reporters or the president of Standard & Poor's, they are the enemy, and are treated as such.

CHAPTER FOUR

THE WAR ON OUR CULTURE AND VALUES

President Obama has sought to pass himself off as a social moderate since bursting onto the national scene. He downplayed his liberal views on abortion—even misrepresenting his opposition to a bill to protect babies born as a result of failed abortions—and pretended he opposed same-sex marriage. Why, he's a married man with young children; he's a traditional values guy.

In fact, President Obama is by far the most socially liberal president in the nation's history, a man who has reignited the nation's culture wars and brought them to a fever pitch. A fierce abortion advocate, he holds radical views on a full range of social and cultural issues. From same-sex marriage and gays in the military, to federal funding for embryonic stem cell research, to abstinence education, to racial preferences, his administration reliably sides with the extreme left wing of the Democratic Party.

Illustrating this administration's broken moral compass, Vice President Joe Biden, on a trip to China, suggested he sympathized with that country's authoritarian one-child policy. In prepared remarks, no less, he said,

"Your policy has been one which I fully understand—I'm not second-guessing—of one child per family." Biden was implying that our nation has no moral objection to a policy that involves forced abortions, sterilizations, and other major human rights abuses. Under this policy, according to Tom McCluskey of the Family Research Council, "hundreds of millions of Chinese women have been forced to have abortions. China's unborn children who are tested and found to be female are at special risk. Nor is this heinous policy limited to the unborn. Female infanticide is routine in rural China."[1] Amid widespread criticism of Biden's remarks, the White House issued a statement saying, "The Obama administration strongly opposes all aspects of China's coercive birth limitation policies, including forced abortion and sterilization."[2]

But does it really? Maybe Biden's statement wasn't out of school at all; perhaps he was speaking for President Obama too. Indeed, when Congressman Dana Rohrabacher pressed Secretary of State Hillary Clinton to say whether Obama had confronted Chinese President Hu on the one-child policy during Hu's visit to Washington, Clinton simply replied that "we" regularly raise the issue with the Chinese. She was unable to say whether Obama personally had discussed the issue with Hu—ever.[3]

A SECRET, "OPEN EXCHANGE" ON GAY ISSUES

As president, Obama has used gay rights as a wedge issue to divide Americans. He paints conservatives and Republicans as intolerant homophobes who favor a "small America," as opposed to the inclusive "big America" he purports to embrace.[4]

Under Obama, the Department of Education refused to allow reporters into break-out sessions at its first Lesbian, Gay, Bisexual, Transgender (LGBT) Youth Summit, even though it was a a taxpayer-funded event attended by teenagers. CNS News pressed Education Department public affairs specialist Jo Ann Webb to explain the secrecy, and she said, "Every summit we've had has been this way. It's to promote an open exchange and that's just the rule, okay?" When the reporter protested that it was a tax-sponsored event, Webb repeated her answer. CNS News also sought an explanation from Obama's "Safe-Schools Czar," Assistant Deputy

Education Secretary Kevin Jennings, who claimed the media's presence "has a silencing effect" on participants.[5]

Speaking by video at the summit, Education Secretary Arne Duncan announced that his department would be warning school districts across the country against blocking students from forming gay-themed organizations in their schools.[6] In fact, the entire summit seemed tailored to identity politics, appealing to the attendees exclusively as gays. What's more, many of the appeals were barely disguised pleas to support the Obama administration. For example, a homosexual staff member for Health and Human Services Secretary Kathleen Sebelius told students that Sebelius "gets us" and is "tireless" in her support of lesbian, gay, bi-sexual and transgender youth." HHS administrator Pam Hyde declared, "Your federal government has finally come out of the closet in support of LGBT youth." Sebelius herself said, "I want to tell you, you have a friend in this administration, who will stand beside you each and every step along the way."[7]

Sebelius also discussed statistics indicating that gay youths are more likely to experience depression, have thoughts of suicide, suffer other emotional problems, or abuse drugs or alcohol—problems she and the administration presume are solely related to the students' victimization by "homophobes." As Sebelius said, "We know these behaviors are not the result of who these young people are. They are the result of what's happening to them."[8]

During his term Obama also signed a hate crimes bill into law that adds "sexual orientation" as a protected class, and even extended his gay rights policy to America's foreign affairs, introducing a gay rights declaration at the United Nations, marking the first time the United States had endorsed such policies in that forum.[9] He further mandated that U.S. foreign aid would be conditioned on the recipient country's policy toward gay, lesbian, and transgender bias, and required all government agencies involved in foreign affairs to promote LGBT rights globally.[10]

"EVOLVING"

Obama has tweaked and massaged his position on same-sex marriage as his term has unfolded, continuing his years-long pattern of disingenuousness on the issue. Although he claims to oppose same-sex marriage, he signed a questionnaire in 1996 indicating his support for it. He originally denied it was his signature on the form, but years later, his press secretary Jay Carney admitted it was his after all.[11]

Obviously, that means Obama supported same-sex marriage back then. But Carney defiantly said that what was important was that from the time of his presidential campaign to the present, Obama's position has been consistent: he has opposed same-sex marriage, but his view "is evolving."[12] Recently, Obama has continued claiming his views on the issue are "evolving," saying there is "no doubt" his opinion is being affected by seeing friends, families, and children of gay couples "thriving."[13]

The upshot is that Obama was for gay marriage in 1996, though he later denied it, has been openly against it since 2008, and is now warming to it again, though he's still opposed to it. That's more like spinning than evolving. What we obviously have with Obama is a politician who supports same-sex marriage but is unwilling to pay the political price of admitting it (at least before the 2012 election), especially among his core black constituency, which strongly opposes same-sex marriage.

But the administration's support for same-sex marriage on various legal fronts reveals Obama's deceit. While still claiming to oppose gay marriage, Obama strongly supports the Respect for Marriage Act, which would repeal the federal Defense of Marriage Act (DOMA). DOMA defines marriage for federal law purposes as being between one man and one woman; provides that states may refuse to recognize the validity of same-sex marriages sanctioned in other states or territories; and prohibits the federal government from recognizing same-sex marriages.

In fact, the administration broke normal constitutional procedures by denouncing DOMA as unconstitutional and by indicating it would not enforce the law or defend it in court.[14] House Speaker John Boehner responded, "In practice they can just look the other way. But this is not the way our government was intended to work. Our government is intended that Congress would pass the laws, the president would decide whether he wanted to sign them or veto them."[15]

Obama's decision to shirk his constitutional obligation to enforce the law produced immediate consequences. Mere hours after Attorney

General Eric Holder announced the new policy, litigants cited Holder's position in a court filing in their case to strike down California's statutory definition of traditional marriage.[16]

The administration shrouded its decision-making process in its usual secrecy. When the Family Research Council sued the Justice Department for internal documents related to the decision, the DOJ withheld twenty-seven pages of emails, provoking Judicial Watch to file a Freedom of Information Request lawsuit. Judicial Watch president Tom Fitton commented, "Once again the Obama administration is playing politics with the Freedom of Information Act to avoid telling the American people the truth about one of its indefensible positions. The evidence suggests the nation's highest law enforcement is refusing to enforce the law to appease another special interest group."[17]

Obama extended his assault on traditional marriage to the state level in March 2012, less than two months before North Carolina residents would vote on a state constitutional amendment defining marriage as a union of a man and a woman. Obama's campaign spokesman Cameron French issued a statement saying the amendment "would single out and discriminate against committed gay and lesbian couples—and that's why the president does not support it." Bishops Michael Burbidge of Raleigh and Peter Jugis of Charlotte responded that Obama's "stated opposition to the referendum... is a grave disappointment, as it is reported to be the first time that the President has entered into this issue on the state level, further escalating the increasing confusion on the part of some in our society to the very nature of marriage itself."[18]

All of this is troubling because the administration, by waging war against traditional marriage, is placing the imprimatur of government on the view that supporters of traditional marriage are somehow morally flawed and bigoted. As Archbishop Dolan, president of the U.S. Conference of Catholic Bishops, said, "Our federal government should not be presuming ill intent or moral blindness on the part of the overwhelming majority of its citizens, millions of whom have gone to the polls to directly support DOMAs in their states and have thereby endorsed marriage as the union of man and woman." Indeed, the DOJ argued in its brief in a recent lawsuit that federal courts should rule that treating same-sex couples differently from married heterosexual couples should be the legal equivalent of racial discrimination. Dolan observed that the federal government has no business treating a policy disagreement concerning the meaning of marriage as a federal offense, but that's exactly where this is all headed.[19]

Obama's assault on traditional marriage is also reflected in federal administrative regulations. An official at the Department of Education's LGBT summit announced that the administration is actively recruiting LGBT parents to adopt children and become foster parents, and a White House spokesman indicated Obama wants a federal mandate to guarantee adoption rights for same-sex couples.[20] Meanwhile, the Agriculture Department implemented a sensitivity training program on "heterosexism," and the Office of Navy Chaplains issued, then rescinded, a directive requiring Navy chapels to allow same-sex wedding ceremonies.[21]

A THREAT TO RELIGIOUS LIBERTY

Advocates of traditional marriage have long contended that the government has a compelling interest in protecting the institution of marriage as the union of one man and one woman because, among other reasons, men and women each make unique and important contributions to parenting. As Maggie Gallagher, president of the Institute for Marriage and Public Policy, testified in a House Committee hearing on marriage, "Marriage is the union of a husband and wife for a reason. These are the only unions that can create new life and connect those children in love to their mother and father."[22] Similarly, a recent action alert posted on the website for the U.S. Conference of Catholic Bishops said, "Protecting marriage as the faithful and lifelong union of one man and one woman is critical to the common good." The bishops emphasized how critical DOMA is to protecting marriage.[23]

Archbishop Dolan wrote a letter to Obama warning that unless he ended his administration's "campaign against DOMA, the institution of marriage it protects, and religious freedom," the president would "precipitate a national conflict between church and state of enormous proportions." According to CNS News, "Dolan indicated that the only 'response' he and his colleagues had received from their previous communications was a stepped up attack on marriage by the administration."[24]

As Dolan intimated, the assault on traditional marriage poses a threat to religious freedom. According to scholar Thomas Messner, if enough people come to believe that support for traditional marriage is tantamount to bigotry—which is the precise argument the Left often makes—then belief in traditional marriage could "come to be viewed as an unacceptable form of discrimination that should be purged from public life through legal, cultural, and economic pressure."[25]

This concern is neither imagined nor exaggerated. Messner describes three principal ways religious liberty could be suppressed:

1. Entities holding to the traditional marriage view could be denied equal access to various government benefits, and public sector employees could be subject to censorship, disciplinary action, and even termination.
2. Individuals could be subject to greater civil liability under nondiscrimination laws that include sexual orientation and marital status as protected categories.
3. Proponents of traditional marriage could be subject to private forms of discrimination and a climate of contempt for the expression of their views.[26]

Some of these threats are already evident today. For example, Cisco Systems terminated its business relationship with consultant Dr. Frank Turek, who had been conducting leadership and team building programs with them for years, after they discovered, based on an employee's complaint, that he had written a book years ago arguing against same-sex marriage. Shortly thereafter, Bank of America fired Turek as well. Turek said, "I get a lot of flak for just actually agreeing with what a majority of Americans agree on and that is that marriage is between one man and one woman."[27] As another example, the New Mexico Civil Rights Commission prosecuted a local photography business that turned down an opportunity to film a same-sex commitment ceremony because of the owners' religious convictions.[28]

Messner has described another already-occurring form of discrimination against religious groups. Certain independent or nontraditional religious groups, called "parachurches," which hire those who subscribe to the same religious views, could face civil liability for religious discrimination for firing those they discover do not hold to their views.[29] In just such a situation, two former employees sued World Vision, a Christian charity, after being fired for no longer following the group's religious commitments. While a federal appellate court ruled against the former employees, one judge indicated he would deem it discrimination for a prospective employer to prefer his coreligionists over others.[30]

These are not isolated examples; after studying some one thousand state laws that prohibit discrimination based on sexual orientation, gender, or marital status, the Becket Fund for Religious Liberty concluded that more than "350 separate state anti-discrimination provisions would likely be triggered by recognition of same-sex marriage."[31]

"EXTREME," "UNTENABLE," AND "REMARKABLE"

There are other signs of this administration's lack of commitment to religious liberty. In October 2011, Obama's Justice Department asked the Supreme Court to approve a lawsuit that would force a parochial Lutheran school to violate its long-held, religiously based policy not to hire teachers who had violated its rule against resorting to lawsuits to resolve disputes. Hosanna-Tabor Evangelical School, a K-8 school in Redford, Michigan, replaced a teacher, Cheryl Perich, after she was diagnosed with narcolepsy and was unable to teach for two semesters. In January 2005, Perich threatened to sue unless she was reinstated. The church told Perich that such a lawsuit would violate its conflict resolution policy that forbids "called" employees resolving disputes in secular court. When Perich allegedly repeated her threat to sue, the congregation voted to rescind her call.

The Equal Employment Opportunity Commission stepped in and filed a complaint against the church under the Americans with Disabilities Act, alleging the church "retaliated" against Perich for pursuing a lawsuit. The church, however, insisted its decision was simply based on beliefs held by orthodox Lutherans for centuries. The Obama Justice Department then weighed in on Perich's behalf, as did Americans United for Separation of Church and State and American Atheists Inc., which filed amicus briefs siding with the administration against the church.[32]

The DOJ's position contradicted forty years of precedent in lower courts, which have generally recognized a ministerial exception to job-discrimination laws that protects the religious freedom of entities to hire and fire their own leaders.[33] The exception allows religious entities to give "preference in employment to individuals of a particular religion" and to "require that all applicants and employees conform to the religious tenets of such organization."[34]

So what about this case warranted the DOJ's involvement? The intervention of the two atheist organizations is instructive; their goal clearly was not to protect a single aggrieved employee, but to attack the church's policy against resorting to courts to resolve disputes, a policy based on the New Testament book of First Corinthians.

In oral arguments before the Supreme Court, even liberal Justice Elena Kagan seemed incredulous when the DOJ's lawyer, Leondra Kruger, said she thought neither of the First Amendment's two religion clauses—the Establishment Clause or the Free Exercise Clause—applied to this case, and that it was the First Amendment's freedom of association that was at issue. Kagan said she found that argument "amazing." In response to a question from Chief Justice John Roberts, Kruger said it would make "no difference whether the entity was a religious group, a labor group, or any other association of individuals." This prompted Justice Antonin Scalia to exclaim, "That's extraordinary. That is extraordinary. We are talking about the free exercise clause and about the establishment clause and you say they have no special application?"[35]

In January, the Supreme Court, in what the Becket Fund for Religious Liberty called "its most important religious liberty case in twenty years," ruled against the Obama administration in a unanimous 9–0 decision, holding that the view of religious liberty it presented was "extreme," "untenable," and "remarkable." The Court unambiguously declared that religious groups should be allowed to choose their leaders free from government interference. Luke Goodrich, Deputy National Litigation

Director at the Becket Fund, proclaimed, "This is a huge victory for religious freedom and a rebuke to the government, which was trying to regulate how churches select their ministers."[36]

A PREDETERMINED CONCLUSION
ON GAYS IN THE MILITARY

When Obama began his push to repeal the "Don't Ask, Don't Tell" policy on gays in the military, the liberal media dutifully reported that the armed forces' top brass fully endorsed his policy. In reality, while some officers such as Admiral Mike Mullen, chairman of the Joint Chiefs of Staff, did publicly support the repeal, others from the Army, Air Force, and Marines clearly did not. "We sometimes ask Marines what is their preference and I can tell you that an overwhelming majority would like not to be roomed with a person that is openly homosexual," said former Marine Corps Commandant General James Conway.[37] Similarly, then-Army Chief of Staff General George Casey said, "I do have serious concerns about the impact of a repeal of the law on a force that is fully engaged in two wars. We just don't know the impacts on readiness and military effectiveness."[38]

The administration buttressed its case for repealing Don't Ask, Don't Tell via the Comprehensive Review Working Group (CRWG)—a large-scale survey of military members that found repealing the policy was unlikely to harm military effectiveness or cause disruptions. However, the inspector general of the Department of Defense concluded that an executive summary of the group's findings was prepared *before* the soldiers were even questioned on the matter. Elaine Donnelly of the Center for Military Readiness said that Congress "was deceived, probably deliberately, by those with a pro-repeal agenda." The CRWG's purpose, said Donnelly, "was to circumvent and neutralize military opposition to repeal of the law."[39]

She said the inspector general's investigation concluded that the CRWG study was "a publicly-funded, pre-scripted production put on just for show" to create "an illusion of support" for repealing Don't Ask,

Don't Tell. The IG report also found that a person with "a strongly emotional attachment to the issue" and "likely a pro-repeal agenda" leaked misleading information to the *Washington Post* in violation of security rules. Following that alleged leak, the *Post* reported that the survey had found that 70 percent of active-duty and reserve troops were not troubled by repeal. Partly as a result of this apparent fabrication, Congress rushed through the vote on repeal during its lame-duck session in December 2010, and Obama quickly signed it into law, though delaying its implementation for one year. The Obama administration, said Donnelly, "misused military personnel, funds, and facilities to help President Obama to deliver on political promises to gay activists at the expense of trusting troops who became unknowing props in the pro-repeal campaign."[40]

In his statement celebrating the Repeal Act, Obama said that ending the policy "would enhance our national security [and] increase our military readiness." This hardly reflected a consensus view. Marine Corps Commandant James Amos warned that the change could impact discipline, erode unit cohesiveness, and ultimately cost lives. As Family Research Council president Tony Perkins noted, "The American military exists for one purpose—to fight and win wars. Yet, today, the U.S. military became a tool in reshaping social attitudes regarding human sexuality. Using the military to advance a liberal social agenda will only do harm to the military's ability to fulfill its mission."[41]

THE *REAL* ANTI-SCIENCE PRESIDENT

President Obama has aggressively supported embryonic stem cell research—a controversial process that involves destroying human embryos. Pro-life advocates oppose the procedure on various grounds including moral ones, citing reports that companies have used aborted fetal cell lines—human embryonic kidney cells taken from an electively aborted baby—to test their products.[42] President George W. Bush limited federal funding of such research to a small number of cell lines created before August 9, 2001. Any cell lines created since then were off-limits to federal funds, which in no way precluded privately funded research.

In keeping with his campaign promise, President Obama, through executive order, lifted the ban on federal funding of embryonic stem cell research, publicly affirming his well-known affinity for active government intervention in science. Urging him to re-evaluate his decision, Congressman John Boehner said, "The president has rolled back important protections for innocent life," while Congressman Eric Cantor warned that "federal funding on embryonic stem cell research can bring on embryo harvesting, perhaps even human cloning."[43]

A coalition filed a lawsuit seeking to nullify Obama's executive order and enjoin federally funded research. On August 23, 2010, a U.S. District Judge granted a preliminary injunction to the coalition,[44] but it was lifted about a month later by a three-judge panel of the U.S. Court of Appeals for the D.C. Circuit. The panel bought the Justice Department's argument that enjoining these activities would cause irreparable harm to this kind of research, even though privately funded research could continue freely. The panel also seemed to ignore the demonstrably poor scientific track record at issue: reportedly, no human being has ever been cured of a disease using embryonic stem cells,[45] and the research is fraught with problems when used to treat animals.[46]

Adult stem cell research, which should be less controversial because it does not involve destroying human embryos, has been much more effective, being used to treat more than a hundred diseases and medical conditions.[47] But so militant is Obama's anti-life agenda that on the same day he lifted President Bush's ban on federal funding of embryonic research, he also rescinded Bush's executive order to fund adult stem cell research. Bioethics attorney Wesley J. Smith said Obama's action showed that he, not his predecessor, is the anti-science president, "Of course, the administration didn't have the candor or courage to publicize this part of his nasty work," said Smith. "But the now dead order explicitly required funding for alternative methods such as the new IPSCs, which offer so much promise without the ethical contentiousness." Smith continued, "I can think of only two reasons for this action, for which I saw no advocacy either in the election or during the first weeks of the Administration. First, vindictiveness against all things 'Bush' or policies considered by the Left to be 'pro-life' and second, a desire to get the public to see unborn human life as a mere corn crop ripe for the harvest."[48]

MAKING ABORTION RARE? HARDLY

Obama has often repeated the mantra, common among Democrats, that he wants to make abortion "safe, legal, and rare."[49] His silver-tongued assurances even persuaded such staunch pro-life advocates as former Reagan Justice Department official Doug Kmiec that Obama would be more pro-life in practice than many outspoken pro-life politicians. Kmiec was apparently unmoved that Obama told Planned Parenthood in 2007, "The first thing I'd do as president is sign the Freedom of Choice Act"—a bill that would eliminate federal, state, and local restrictions on abortion. Of course, Obama's position often changes, depending on his audience. In the weeks leading up to his vaunted commencement address at Notre Dame, where he sought to portray himself as a reasonable moderate on the abortion issue, he said the Freedom of Choice Act "is not the highest legislative priority."[50] Little did his audience know his administration would later deny a government grant to the Catholic Church for helping human trafficking victims, a move widely attributed to the Church's anti-abortion position.[51]

Indeed, many of Obama's subsequent actions would show just how immoderate he is on the abortion issue. Not only does he not apologize for abortion, he proudly celebrates it as a woman's sacred right. While many Christians and others of faith consider abortion in America to be a stain on our nation's moral record, Obama publicly commemorated the thirty-ninth anniversary of *Roe v. Wade* as a "historic anniversary." He said, "We must remember that this Supreme Court decision not only protects a woman's health and reproductive freedom, but also affirms a broader principle: that government should not intrude on private family matters."[52]

Some pro-life advocates contend that Obama's policies show he is actually promoting *more* abortions. He has undoubtedly spread his pro-abortion leanings throughout the government by consistently nominating or appointing ardent pro-abortion officials and advisors. These include:

- His former chief of staff Rahm Emanuel, who had a 0 percent pro-life voting record from the National Right to Life;
- Former senator Tom Daschle, Obama's failed nominee as Health and Human Services secretary, whose pro-abortion voting record was well established;
- Former NARAL legal director Dawn Johnsen, who served on his Department of Justice Review Team, and later as assistant attorney general for the Office of the Legal Counsel;
- Ellen Moran, former director of the pro-abortion outfit Emily's List, as White House communications director (Emily's List only supports candidates who favor taxpayer-funded abortions and oppose a partial-birth abortion ban);
- Pro-abortionist Jeanne Lambrew as deputy director of the White House Office of Health Reform, a choice that "excited" Planned Parenthood;
- Melody Barnes, another Emily's List board member, as director of the Domestic Policy Council;
- Secretary of State Hillary Clinton, who has a perfect pro-abortion voting record and even supported making unlimited abortions an international right.[53]

Between his election and inauguration, Obama's in-your-face pro-abortion transition team published a 55-page memo from numerous pro-abortion groups listing their demands. The memo's publication apparently surprised these groups, which thought Obama would initially be more discreet about his pro-abortion proclivities, and which feared that news of Obama's work on their behalf would block progress on their militant agenda. But Obama's zeal for the cause hardly surprised pro-life activists, who remembered his July 2007 pledge that he would be Planned Parenthood's fierce advocate.[54]

Calling for more funding for Planned Parenthood and other abortion groups, the memo also urged Obama to lobby Congress to pass the Freedom of Choice Act, as Obama had already pledged to do, which would legalize unlimited abortions through all stages of pregnancy and nullify hundreds of pro-life laws in all fifty states, ranging from partial-birth abortion bans to parental involvement laws. Further, the memo advocated striking all limits on taxpayer-funded abortion in various circumstances, the appointment of pro-abortion judges, repeal of the Hyde Amendment, and including an abortion mandate in Obama's healthcare reform program. The memo also pushed for restoration of funding for the United Nations Population Fund (UNFPA), even though that organization has supported China's oppressive one-child policy, which includes forced abortions and sterilizations. Finally, the memo urged Obama to reverse the so-called Mexico City Policy, whose reversal would effectively restore taxpayer funding for groups that promote or perform abortions in other nations.[55]

As president, Obama quickly acted on the agenda outlined in the memo. In his first week in office, he signed an executive order reversing the Mexico City Policy.[56] By 2013, this will likely result in hundreds of millions of dollars being distributed to groups that promote or perform abortions throughout the world, such as the International Planned Parenthood Federation—an organization that endorses abortion on demand as a universal birth control method. With the Mexico City rule reversed, two major abortion providers, U.S.-based Planned Parenthood and Marie Stopes International, both became eligible for taxpayer funding without discontinuing their performance or advocacy of abortion.[57]

The administration also cooperated with pro-abortion advocacy groups at the United Nations during the March 2009 Commission of the Status of Women meeting, where they worked on a document that included language that could be used to promote an international right to abortion. The administration called for a review of all national laws to ensure they comply with international human rights instruments, which some fear could be misused to force countries to remove restrictions on abortion.

In addition, the administration created a new foreign policy advisory post inside the State Department that would focus on global women's issues, immediately appointing pro-abortionist Malanne Verveer to lead it as ambassador-at-large. Verveer has been a staunch advocate of the UN's Committee on the Elimination of Discrimination Against Women (CEDAW), a radical international agreement that seeks to enforce "abortion rights" internationally and to reduce or negate parental rights, among other things. Were the United States to approve the convention, it would be legally bound to take all appropriate measures to eliminate discrimination against women in the field of healthcare in order to ensure, on the basis of gender equality, access to healthcare services, including those related to family planning. Though CEDAW doesn't include the word "abortion," the CEDAW committee interprets Article 12 to include abortion as a part of family planning. Under it, countries that restrict or outlaw abortion are reprimanded and instructed to change their laws.[58]

Approving CEDAW would require a 67-vote majority in the Senate. With Secretary of State Hillary Clinton having indicated that ratification is a major priority of the Obama administration, Verveer is working on Capitol Hill to get this accomplished,[59] and she appeared before the U.S. Senate Foreign Relations Committee's hearing on Women and the Arab Spring in November 2011 to tout the importance of ratifying the convention.[60]

OBAMA'S BROKEN ABORTION FUNDING PROMISE

Further violating his pledge to make abortion rare, President Obama and congressional Democrats enabled the District of Columbia to fund abortions with taxpayer dollars, resulting in some three hundred abortions being performed with public funds. Associated Press files showed that the District expended $185,000 for elective abortions for any reason and at any point in the pregnancy for women below the poverty level. Douglas Johnson, legislative director for the National Right to Life Committee, said, "The responsibility for these 300 government-funded abortions rests squarely with President Obama, who urged Congress to lift the longstanding ban in 2009, and with Democratic leaders Nancy Pelosi and Harry Reid, who rammed through the repeal without allowing roll call votes on the issue in either house of Congress. Some of these unborn children would be alive today, if it had not been for the Obama-dictated change in policy."[61]

In his healthcare reform speech to a joint session of Congress on September 9, 2010, Obama said, "One more misunderstanding I want to clear up—under our plan, no federal dollars will be used to fund abortions." But in fact, the Obamacare bill did provide that federal dollars would pay for elective abortions and explicitly authorized federal subsidies for private abortion insurance. As a result, in order to secure the vote of Congressman Bart Stupak for the bill, Obama had to promise Stupak he would issue an executive order reaffirming a ban on the federal funding of abortion.[62] As Tony Perkins, president of Family Research Council, noted, "By offering an executive order as a so-called solution, President Obama is finally admitting there is a problem with a bill that would force taxpayers to pay for elective abortions for the first time in over three decades." Perkins also observed that an executive order would not likely have much legal effect.[63]

Many doubted Obama's sincerity in following through with this commitment. Sure, he issued an executive order as he promised, but it didn't keep him from planning to fund abortions through high-risk insurance programs to be created by his Obamacare bill in states such as Pennsylvania, New Mexico, and Maryland.

On July 13, 2010, three months after the bill was signed, the Obama administration approved the allocation of $160 million in federal funds to Pennsylvania for a high-risk pool of people with pre-existing conditions. The administration claimed the Pennsylvania legislation would pay for abortions only in cases of rape, incest, or to save the mother's life, yet the statutory language omitted those restrictions. The solicitation describing the plan said it would include "only abortions and contraceptives that satisfy the requirements" of certain Pennsylvania statutes. One of those statutes specified that abortions could be provided by physicians who would determine whether in their "best clinical judgment, the abortion is necessary... in light of all factors (physical, emotional, psychological, familial and the woman's age) relevant to the well-being of the woman. No abortion which is sought solely because of the sex of the unborn child shall be deemed a necessary abortion."

Doug Johnson, legislative director for the National Right to Life Committee, said this language means that "federal funds will subsidize coverage of abortion performed for any reason, except sex selection. The Pennsylvania proposal conspicuously lacks language that would prevent funding of abortions performed as a method of birth control for any other reason, except sex selection—and the Obama administration has now approved this."[64]

The administration also authorized federal funding for abortions in the state of New Mexico. National Review Online reported that the state's new, $37 million high-risk pool would begin receiving benefits in August, including elective abortion services, and this was corroborated by the state insurance department's website. House minority leader John Boehner said, "In just the past 24 hours, we've learned of two states in which the new federal high-risk insurance programs created under Obamacare and approved by the Obama administration will use federal funds to pay for abortion, despite promises by the White House and Democratic leaders that no such funding would occur under Obamacare. These developments provide stark confirmation that President Obama's executive order last spring was little more than a political ploy to ensure passage of Obamacare by circumventing the will of the American people, who are clearly opposed to taxpayer-funded abortion."[65] A few days later, it was announced that Maryland, too, would receive federal funds for high-risk insurance programs created under Obamacare that would include coverage for abortion.[66]

Despite its aggressive record of federal funding for abortion, the administration still misrepresents its position. In early 2011 Health and Human Services Secretary Kathleen Sebelius declared, "There is no taxpayer funding for abortion. Not at community health centers, not as part of the new bill, not as any part of any services that we deliver."[67]

HAVING "SURROGATES DO ITS DIRTY WORK"

Further demonstrating its pro-abortion zeal, the Obama administration lobbied and contributed funds to convince the people of Kenya to approve a new constitution that would loosen restrictions on abortion. The administration denied it had lobbied for the proposed constitution, but our ambassador to Kenya revealed that the United States had given $2 million for "civil education" about the constitution and was committed to giving more. When the constitution was approved, Obama exulted, "My administration has been pleased to support Kenya's democratic development and the Kenyan people."[68]

The Government Accountability Office (GAO) investigated the administration's spending in Kenya and discovered that at least one grantee of the funds openly pushed to expand abortion—notwithstanding the Siljander Amendment, a law that prohibits federal tax dollars from being used to lobby for or against abortion in other nations. Further, the GAO reported that a key Obama official stonewalled investigators. Congressman Chris Smith said, "The Obama administration basically hired surrogates to do its dirty work of abortion promotion in Kenya. U.S. policy on international constitutional reform is, by law, supposed to be abortion-neutral." Instead, it actively lobbied for abortion with taxpayer dollars.[69] The GAO called for an internal review of the expenditure of these funds. It also suggested that the State Department develop "specific guidance" to comply with restrictions on funding for abortion laws overseas, a suggestion the State Department rejected.[70]

HARASSING A PEACEFUL, PRAYERFUL MAN

Obama's Justice Department definitely got "the memo"—not the one instructing his administration to make abortion "rare," which was never sent, but the one promoting the work of pro-abortionists. In deference to Obama's soulmates at Planned Parenthood, the DOJ sued an elderly pro-life "sidewalk counselor" for his ministry on behalf of young pregnant ladies outside the Planned Parenthood facility in Washington, D.C. Dick Retta, described as a "peaceful, prayerful man," conducts training sessions to empower fellow pro-life advocates to offer words of encouragement to young women who enter and leave the abortion center. He insists he does not seek to block access to the facility, but to remind women that they have a choice—something self-styled pro-choice proponents would have no objection to if they were really "pro-choice," and if abortion were not a highly profitable industry. Retta and his associates also offer post-abortion healing for women, based on their belief, supported by peer-reviewed research, that significant numbers of women who undergo an abortion suffer emotional or mental health problems.[71]

Despite Obama's insincere call for us to "work together to reduce the number of women seeking abortions," his administration doesn't take kindly to people actually trying to achieve that goal. His Justice Department doesn't regard Retta as an innocuous champion of life, but rather "among the most vocal and aggressive anti-abortion protesters outside the Clinic." So the DOJ's Civil Rights Division sued Retta for $25,000 in fines, alleging that he has obstructed entrance to the clinic and that he walks "very closely beside patients" and yells at them, allegations that reportedly shocked Retta.[72]

Thus, Obama's Justice Department looks the other way when New Black Panther Party members brandish nightsticks outside election places to intimidate voters, but seeks to punish a harmless man reciting the Lord's Prayer and passing out brochures outside an abortion clinic. Retta's loving words cautioning against abortion are verboten, while the Panthers' intimidating threats are ignored.

By contrast, the administration showed surprising leniency toward a woman who assaulted Retta. After the woman pepper-sprayed him when he offered her pro-life literature, the government granted her a generous plea deal in which it would drop charges after just six months' probation. There were reportedly no fines, community service, or any other probationary conditions except that she avoid re-arrest for six months.[73]

"THE MOST PRO-ABORTION PRESIDENT IN OUR COUNTRY'S HISTORY"

Barack Obama has been a strong ally of Planned Parenthood, the abortion factory that performed, in 2009, some 910 abortions a day.[74] His administration has shown its allegiance in many ways: while pro-life groups were largely shut out of Obama's healthcare summit, Planned Parenthood was invited, along with other pro-abortion groups; the White House website serve.gov at one point promoted the organization's abortion business by recruiting pro-abortion volunteers on its behalf;[75] Obama threatened to veto bills that would de-fund the Planned Parenthood abortion business;[76] and the Obama Justice Department filed legal papers to support Planned Parenthood in a lawsuit challenging the state of Indiana's legislation that cut off funding for abortions.[77]

During one of the many congressional budget skirmishes, the administration refused to relent on funding for Planned Parenthood. It had no problem eliminating $600 million in funding for Community Health Centers, which provide health services to the poor, including mammograms and pre- and post-natal care. But it insisted that Planned Parenthood's work was indispensable in providing women's healthcare. Frank Cannon, president of the American Principles Project, said that in 2010 Community Health Centers performed 320,000 mammograms while Planned Parenthood performed none. Cannon said, "Coating its ideology in flowery language about women's health and alleged Republican mean-spiritedness, liberal Democrats refused to cut one dime out of Planned Parenthood's plump federal purse during the budget debate. All the while a sharp knife was being taken to community health centers that actually perform full-scale exams for the needy."[78]

It came as no surprise, then, when Obama's administration ignored undercover sting videos showing Planned Parenthood centers appearing to assist supposed sex traffickers in arranging abortions and STD testing for their underage prostitutes. In light of the videos, Congress approved a bill to defund Planned Parenthood. But the group was protected by its Democratic supporters in the Senate, who defended its funding, and by the Obama Justice Department, which refused to prosecute anyone involved. Lila Rose, head of the Live Action organization, the group that released the videos, said, "An untold number of women, and possibly underage girls, are being exploited and likely in danger and the Justice Department is looking the other way."[79]

These sordid events have not dampened the administration's support for Planned Parenthood in the slightest. In June 2011, New Hampshire's Executive Council voted not to renew its $1.8 million contract with Planned Parenthood clinics in the state because of their provision of abortions. Just as with Indiana, the administration would not take no for an answer; the Health and Human Services Department argued that New Hampshire broke federal rules because de-funding Planned Parenthood might deny low-income women access to "family planning"—even though assistance is available from other agencies. New Hampshire Health and Human Services commissioner Nick Toumpas worried that the state could lose federal Medicaid funding if it didn't bend to the administration's demands. Daniel St. Hilaire, a member of the New Hampshire Executive Council, said that the state's contract should go to an organization that does not perform abortions. Republican David K. Wheeler said, "It is wrong to require taxpayers who believe that abortion is murder to have to pay for (abortions)."[80]

The administration ended up circumventing the Executive Council and contracting directly with the Planned Parenthood clinics, a move that prompted Susan B. Anthony List president Marjorie Dannenfelser to complain, "President Obama has proven time and time again that he will do whatever it takes to ensure that Planned Parenthood continues to receive taxpayer subsidies, even if that means going around a state's elected representatives. Obama is the most pro-abortion President in our country's history and his allegiance to Planned Parenthood is unwavering."[81]

The public got a firsthand view of the militant politics of Planned Parenthood when Susan G. Komen for the Cure, an organization committed to fighting breast cancer, decided to cut funding for the group because it does not do mammograms. But after Planned Parenthood, Democratic congressional leaders, and the liberal media publicly attacked Komen, it decided it would still allow the organization to submit grant requests. The coordinated assault was so vicious that Karen Handel, a top Komen official who was influential in the initial decision to defund, resigned from her position with the group. Kristan Hawkins of Students for Life was outraged at these developments, saying "Handel's resignation only furthers Planned Parenthood's status as a bully who shakes down whomever they need to in order to get their way.... Komen had good reason to defund Planned Parenthood and is now paying the price for doing business with thugs."[82]

Indeed, scandal surrounds this organization Obama seems to revere. Karen Reynolds, a long-time employee of Planned Parenthood Gulf Coast, in Texas, has filed a legal action alleging that twelve Planned Parenthood mills in Texas and Louisiana defrauded the government by billing medical agencies for unnecessary services and for services that were never provided.[83]

Planned Parenthood also showed its radical pro-abortion colors when it joined with other pro-abortionists such as NARAL to promote a Washington state law that would require health insurance coverage for abortion if a health plan covers maternity care—a law that would compel everyone who wants to buy insurance coverage for maternity, including those morally opposed to abortion, to purchase policies that would cover elective abortions.[84] While Planned Parenthood claims to be about much more than abortions, some of its critics say that it "continually lobbies for and in fact promotes abortion on demand, unrestricted, and unregulated," and is even "promoting abortion for underage minors without any parental involvement or consent."[85]

"DIMINISHING THE CIVIL RIGHTS" OF HEALTHCARE PROVIDERS

In 1973, Congress passed the Church Amendment, which barred any entity that "receives a grant, contract, loan or loan guaranty" under certain federal titles from "discriminating in the employment, promotion, or termination of employment of any physician or other health care personnel" because that person refuses to perform or assist in a "service or activity" that "would be contrary to his religious beliefs or moral convictions."[86] Because the law did not specify how aggrieved parties would seek remedies, the Bush administration in 2008 issued clarifying regulations establishing a complaint procedure. But in March 2009, the Obama administration suspended these regulations, once again thwarting the intent of Congress.

Without specified legal remedies, the injured parties may be left without recourse. Catherine Cenzon-DeCarlo, a nurse working at Mount Sinai Hospital in New York, a recipient of federal funds, filed an administrative complaint with the Office of Civil Rights (OCR) at the U.S. Department of Health and Human Services (HHS) as well as a federal lawsuit alleging she had been forced to participate in an elective second-trimester abortion. While the OCR/HHS opened an investigation, a federal appeals court shot down her lawsuit, saying the Church Amendment didn't confer a cause of action for injured parties. The fate of Cenzon-DeCarlo's administrative complaint was unclear because of the administration's suspension of the 2008 Bush regulations. As Chuck Donovan of the Heritage Foundation observed, "A civil rights law without an enforcement mechanism is just a noble sentiment."[87]

In his speech at Notre Dame on May 17, 2009, Obama said, "Let's honor the conscience of those who disagree with abortion, and draft a sensible conscience clause, and make sure that all of our health care policies are grounded not only in sound science, but also in clear ethics, as well as respect for the equality of women."[88] The remarks were particularly cynical, considering that a few months earlier the White House had quietly announced that Obama had started the process of overturning protections President Bush had put in place to make sure medical staff and centers are not forced to do abortions.[89] In March 2009, while administration officials were telling the media that they were merely trying to clarify the existing rules,[90] in fact, they had just published in the Federal Register a proposal to rescind the pro-life protections entirely.[91]

At least two congressmen were not fooled by Obama's dissembling. Jim Sensenbrenner of Wisconsin and Chris Smith of New Jersey held a press conference following Obama's Notre Dame remarks, calling on Obama to stop his effort to overturn the Bush protections. In a letter to Obama, they wrote, "You indicated that you wanted to 'honor the conscience of those who disagree with abortion.' Given our agreement in regard to a conscience clause, we respectfully request that you put an end to your Administration's review of the Bush administration rule that enforces existing conscience protection laws and completely forego the rescinding of this rule."[92]

But Obama continued to deceive the public on these policies. Despite the fact that his administration was in the process of repealing the Bush regulations, in September 2009, in one of his many healthcare speeches, Obama said, "One more misunderstanding I want to clear up—under our plan … federal conscience laws will remain in place."

On March 22, 2010, true to form, Obama signed Obamacare into law, a bill that contains no conscience protections. Meanwhile, his administration was still working hard to cancel the Bush conscience rights protections. In a lawsuit that the state of Connecticut filed to overturn the Bush-era protections, Obama administration attorneys admitted in papers filed with the court that the administration was seeking to finalize a rescision of the conscience rules.[93]

In February 2011, the HHS scrapped a portion of the 2008 Bush rule, calling it "unclear and potentially overbroad in scope." Officials then adopted a new rule that retained protections for conscientious objectors to abortion, but provided no protection for medical workers who have moral or religious objections to dispensing abortifacients such as Plan B, Ella, or other emergency contraception that could cause an abortion in some cases.

The HHS released a statement emphasizing that the new rule supported the conscience protections on abortions, but without mentioning the detrimental impact it would have on conscience rights concerning abortifacients. Dr. J. Scott Ries, on behalf of the Christian Medical Association, charged that the new rule would "weaken the only federal regulation protecting the exercise of conscience in health care." Accusing the administration of using a specious argument (ensuring access to contraception) to justify abandoning conscience protections for dispensing abortion drugs, Ries argued that "absolutely no evidence is presented to justify any such concern. In the process, the administration blatantly ignores the scientific evidence that certain controversial prescriptions that abortion advocates promote as contraception are actually potential abortifacients, ending the life of a living, developing human embryo. This is a critical concern for pro-life patients, healthcare professionals and institutions."[94]

The rule change, Ries maintained, diminishes the civil rights of physicians[95] and will result in losing conscience-oriented healthcare professionals and faith-based institutions, which will imperil the poor and patients in medically underserved areas. National surveys have shown that 90 percent of faith-based physicians say they would leave the medical profession before performing procedures that violate their consciences. A similar deterrent effect is occurring with faith-based medical students, 20 percent of whom say they are "not pursuing a career in

Obstetrics or Gynecology" because of what they perceive to be discrimination and coercion in that specialty. Dr. Ries pointed out that this means fewer physicians in a field that is already facing critical shortages.[96]

"PREGNANCY IS NOT A DISEASE"

The administration further eroded conscience rights in August 2011 when the HHS categorized birth control and certain drugs that can cause abortions as "preventive care," thus requiring insurance companies to cover them. This decision violates the conscience rights of Catholics and other religious and pro-life individuals who have moral objections to paying for insurance that covers birth control and abortion drugs.[97]

The U.S. Conference of Catholic Bishops strongly criticized the administration for the preventive services mandate that "requires health plans to cover female surgical sterilization and all drugs and devices approved by the FDA as contraceptives, including drugs that can attack a developing unborn child before and after implantation in the mother's womb."[98] The new HHS guidelines would also force Catholic colleges to choose between violating the law or violating the Catholic faith, according to Patrick Reilly, president of the Cardinal Newman Society, because they would force Catholic colleges to help students and employees obtain free contraceptives and sterilization. "Our religious freedom is under attack," said Reilly.

Showing the administration's cynicism toward the life issue, HHS Secretary Kathleen Sebelius argues that the preventing services mandate pays for itself because fewer babies are born—babies that would otherwise need healthcare. "The reduction in the number of pregnancies compensates for the cost of contraception," she says, which is similar to President Obama's contention that "the overall cost of healthcare is lower when women have access to contraceptive services."[99] The HHS said its preventive services mandate aims to "help stop health problems before they start." But as Cardinal DiNardo, archbishop of Galveston-Houston and chairman of the USCCB Committee on Pro-Life Activities, said, "Pregnancy is not a disease, and children are not a health problem—they are the next generation of Americans. It's now more vital than ever that

... employers and employees alike ... have the freedom to choose health plans in accordance with their deeply held moral and religious beliefs."[100]

The administration's relentless attack on conscience rights repeatedly pushed the issue into the spotlight. On November 2, 2011, the House Energy and Commerce Subcommittee on Health held a hearing in which numerous panelists argued that the Obamacare mandates threaten conscience rights and access to care. Furthermore, many employers with moral objections to such mandatory coverage were not mollified by the mandate's narrowly drawn religious exemption, which can be invoked only by organizations which primary mission is to inculcate religious belief and which hire and serve co-religionists. The U.S. Conference of Catholic Bishops said that under this exemption "even the ministry of Jesus and early Christian Church would not qualify as religious." Indeed, Janet Belford, chancellor and general counsel for the Washington Archdiocese, said, "HHS has drafted a religious exemption that is so narrow that it excludes virtually all Catholic hospitals, elementary and secondary schools, colleges and universities, and charitable organizations, none of which impose a litmus test on those they serve, as the HHS mandate would have them do." Others worried that the rule could reduce access to care because some employers would have no choice but to drop coverage to avoid violating their convictions.[101]

In January 2012, the HHS issued a statement reiterating its position that Obamacare requires health insurance plans to cover abortion-inducing drugs. Religious organizations that requested conscience exceptions were thwarted, as expected, as the administration gave them a year to comply with the requirement. This HHS rule would require religious entities to provide insurance plans that, in effect, cover abortions, which means that organizations grounded in the pro-life principle would have to cover their employees' abortions.[102] In its typical high-handed fashion, the administration prohibited a Catholic Army chaplain from reading a letter by Timothy Broglio—archbishop of the Military Services, USA—criticizing the mandate.

This mandate sparked such a backlash that Obama devised a "compromise": he would require insurance companies, rather than employers, to pay for birth control and abortifacients. In fact, this was no compromise at all, but a sham. As a group of prominent law professors and academics noted in a jointly written letter,

> This so-called "accommodation" changes nothing of moral substance and fails to remove the assault on religious liberty and the rights of conscience which gave rise to the controversy. It is certainly no compromise. The reason for the original bipartisan uproar was the administration's insistence that religious employers, be they institutions or individuals, provide insurance that covered services they regard as gravely immoral and unjust. Under the new rule, the government still coerces religious institutions and individuals to purchase insurance policies that include the very same services.

The argument that religious employers will not be paying for the coverage is specious, the authors noted, because insurance companies will pass the costs of these services on to the purchasers. Nor, they said, was it any compromise that the insurance company would be the one explaining the insurance coverage to the employee.[103] But with his signature imperiousness, Obama said there would be no further discussion of the matter.

Outraged pro-life groups and individuals saw through the ruse. Alleging that the Catholic Church is being "despoiled of her institutions," an influential Catholic cardinal, Francis George of Chicago, warned that Catholic hospitals in the United States may close in two years under this new mandate.[104] Activists organized a protest at federal buildings in more than fifty cities throughout the United States with the theme "Stand Up for Religious Freedom—Stop the HHS Mandate!"[105]

CHILDREN AS "SEXUAL BEINGS"

There are two main approaches to sex education. The so-called "safe-sex" or "comprehensive" approach focuses on the physical risk of sexually transmitted diseases and pregnancy, and emphasizes contraception, especially condoms. Most supporters of this approach regard sex and sexuality as matters of personal choice that ought not be dictated by religious or political strictures.[106] In contrast, the abstinence approach centers on the social and psychological aspects of sexual activity. It teaches young adults to delay engaging in sexual activity, warns of the dangers of casual sex, and encourages students to consider sexuality as part of a process of developing intimacy and lifelong commitment.[107]

President George W. Bush's administration strongly promoted the abstinence approach, with the 2007 budget alone including approximately $204 million for such education programs.[108] President Obama, being reliably liberal across the board, predictably replaced Bush's program with a comprehensive teen pregnancy prevention program.[109] More than 176 abstinence education programs would lose funding under Obama's change.[110]

Proponents of the abstinence approach worried that the elimination of funding midstream in a five-year grant award would deprive some two million students of key skill-building lessons.[111] However, Melody Barnes, a White House domestic aide, said the change "reflects the research.... In any area where Americans want to confront a problem, they want solutions they know will work, as opposed to programming they know hasn't proven to be successful."[112] Congresswoman Carolyn Maloney boasted, "It's about time that evidence-based management—and sanity—return to family planning programs."[113]

While critics of so-called abstinence-only characterize it as a moralistic, head-in-the-sand approach, in reality it is abstinence-centered, but is not solely about abstinence; it does not preclude teaching about contraception. It teaches abstinence from sexual activity outside marriage as the standard for all school-age children while emphasizing related social, psychological, and health benefits. It teaches kids life skills, how to make decisions that are grounded in personal responsibility, and how to develop healthy relationships and marriages.

Proponents of abstinence programs deny critics' claims that the weight of the evidence discredits the abstinence method. To the contrary, a number of studies cited by the National Abstinence Education Association demonstrate the program's effectiveness.[114] Heritage Foundation scholars Robert Rector and Christine Kim cite studies showing that young adults who receive abstinence education exhibit greater psychological health and perform better academically. Abstinence can also decrease teenagers' rates of contracting STDs, having children out of wedlock, and experiencing psychological harm. Rector and Kim found that twelve out of sixteen studies of abstinence education reported positive findings, as did five out of six studies of virginity pledges. The authors concluded, "Genuine abstinence education is therefore crucial to the physical and psycho-emotional well-being of the nation's youth.... When considering effective prevention programs aimed at changing teen sexual behavior, lawmakers should consider *all* of the available empirical evidence and restore funding for abstinence education.[115]

Another recent study showed that abstinence education programs are effective and are strongly supported by parents, many of whom believe recent sex education programs do not reflect their values. Embarrassed that this study had been funded by its own Health and Human Services Department, the Obama administration initially refused to publicize the results and even denied Freedom of Information Requests to release it, though it finally relented amid grassroots pressure. The study found that 70 percent of parents believe that sexual relations should be postponed until marriage.[116]

On the other hand, comprehensive sex education programs, such as those the administration supports, are sometimes used as vehicles to promote values that many parents oppose. The "comprehensive" approach is often not comprehensive at all, and it can put kids at greater risk of pregnancy because it de-emphasizes abstinence—the most effective way to reduce teenage pregnancy—and promotes the use of condoms while downplaying their failure rates and related health risks. Indeed, some refer to this approach as "condom-based sex education."

A Heritage Foundation study found that comprehensive sex-ed curricula often provide no standards about when students should begin sexual activity. Though an overwhelming majority of adults (94 percent) and of teens (92 percent) believe it is important that society sends a "strong message" that young people "should not have sex until they are, at least, out of high school," few, if any, comprehensive sex-ed programs promote or even include that message. In this study, the authors examined nine separate curricula consisting in total of 942 pages, and found fewer than ten sentences urging young people to defer sexual activity until a later age—and most of these sentences lacked force.[117]

Consider one "comprehensive" sex-ed program that was contemplated in the Helena, Montana, public school system. The program would teach fifth graders that "sexual intercourse includes, but is not limited to vaginal, oral or anal penetration." It would teach kindergarteners about "basic reproductive body parts (penis, vagina, breast, nipples, testicles, and scrotum)." It would teach all grades that marriage is a "commitment by two people." It would teach first graders that "human beings can love people of the same gender and people of another gender." It would teach that sexual orientation refers to a "person's physical and/or romantic attraction to an individual of the same and/or different gender." And, it would teach sixth graders that sexual intercourse includes "using the penis, fingers, tongue or objects."[118]

Irrespective of whether one supports an abstinence-centered approach, there are serious objections to so-called comprehensive programs, which would likely be even more unpopular if more parents were aware of their contents. In fact, many parents would be shocked to learn what the HHS once taught on its own website. In a post titled "Questions and Answers About Sex" the HHS instructed, "Children are human beings and therefore sexual beings.... It's hard for parents to acknowledge this, just as it's hard for kids to think of their parents as sexually active. But even infants have curiosity about their own bodies, which is healthy and normal." The post further related that teens may "experiment" with homosexuality as part of "exploring their own sexuality." None of this is surprising considering that President Obama has declared his support for "age-appropriate" sex education for kindergarteners.[119]

AT WAR WITH THE TRADITIONAL FAMILY

President Obama's Fiscal Year 2010 Omnibus Appropriations bill contained numerous items that should concern traditional values voters.[120] Aside from defunding abstinence education and funding "comprehensive" sex education, it included:

- A 30 percent increase from President Bush's 2008 budget on means-tested welfare programs, including housing, food stamps, and healthcare. Studies have shown these programs perpetuate dependency and that expanding them harms individuals in the long run and is detrimental to the economy and jobs.

- An allowance of federal taxpayer money for "needle exchange" programs for drug addicts. Aimed at impeding the spread of infection rather than eradicating addiction, these programs exacerbate the underlying problem by focusing on symptoms instead of causes, similar to the condom-based approach to sex education.

- Substantial increases in Title X family planning funding, the main recipient of which was Planned Parenthood.

- An increase of $5 million to the UN Population Fund, some of which is allocated in support of China's draconian one-child policy.

- As noted, an increase of $103 million for overseas family planning groups that promote or perform abortions— groups that were denied federal funding entirely until Obama cancelled the "Mexico City policy."

- A removal of the ban on federal funding for enforcing the "Fairness Doctrine," through which the Left aspired to emasculate conservative talk radio. Under Republican pressure, the FCC abolished the rule in 2011.

- Changes affecting funding for the District of Columbia, including: a) the elimination of a scholarship program allowing some poor D.C. parents to send their children to private school; b) lifting a ban on the District using local funds to promote and finance abortions for residents; c) removing the prohibition on federal tax money being used for healthcare benefits for domestic partners of D.C. employees; d) allowing D.C. to use local funds to begin and operate a medical marijuana program; and e) removing the restriction on using local funds for a needle exchange program for drug addicts in the District. Even a clause prohibiting such programs from operating within 1,000 feet of schools, day care centers, or youth centers was removed from the bill.[121]

"A NATION OF COWARDS ON RACE"

In light of all the painful racial crises our nation has experienced, color blindness has become a deeply rooted American value. As famously proclaimed by Martin Luther King Jr. in his iconic "I Have a Dream" speech, we should be judged on the content of our character, not the color of our skin. The broadest swath of the American people agrees on this simple, fundamental principle; unfortunately, our president's statements, appointments, and policies testify that he belongs to the small, radical fringe that does not.

Obama has obviously harbored deeply rooted racial baggage in his life. He admitted as much in his book *Dreams from My Father*, writing, "I ceased to advertise my mother's race at the age of 12 or 13, when I began to suspect that by doing so I was ingratiating myself to whites." And of course, for twenty years Obama attended a church pastored by the racist Reverend Jeremiah Wright, who preached the militant, racially centered creed of Black Liberation Theology.

In 2012, the late Andrew Breitbart's websites released video clips showing Obama's connection to racist academic Derrick Bell, the first black Harvard Law School professor. It turns out Obama, while a Harvard Law student, strongly supported and warmly embraced Bell after the professor initiated a high-profile campaign to pressure Harvard into hiring a black female law professor. As explained by author and economist Thomas Sowell, who was interviewed about the incident at the time, Bell wasn't referring only to black skin color, but a black woman who also *thought* black. That is, Bell wasn't merely insisting that Harvard's hiring be based on race, but on ideology. Sowell also revealed that Bell, who had an "ideological intolerance" and a "totalitarian mindset," launched a despicable attack against a young black professor who objected to Bell's agenda.[122]

Calling Derrick Bell "the Jeremiah Wright of academia," Joel Pollak of Breitbart.com explained that Bell was the originator of critical race theory, "which holds that the civil rights movement was a sham and that white supremacy is the order and it must be overthrown."[123] Bell, who argued that "racism is an integral, permanent and indestructible component of this society,"[124] was indeed a racial militant extraordinaire, which is why it's unsettling to see video of future President Barack Obama urging Harvard students to "open up your hearts and your minds to the words of Professor Derrick Bell."[125]

Some might dismiss these signals as old attitudes that Obama has since outgrown. But if Obama is now committed to race-blindness, it's strange that his administration is shot through with high-ranking officials who obviously oppose him on that score.

For example, Obama's nominee for assistant attorney general of the Justice Department's Civil Rights Division, Thomas Perez, is a strong proponent of racial preferences in admissions to schools that train healthcare professionals. He has advocated that medical schools drop standards for black applicants, arguing they are more likely to work in "underserved" communities than whites.[126] Similarly, in August 2009 the U.S. Commission on Civil Rights expressed concern that Obama's healthcare legislation included racially discriminatory provisions such as according minority students preferential treatment for scholarships and favoring medical schools deemed more likely to send graduates to underserved areas.[127]

Obama's former green jobs czar, Van Jones, was decidedly radical, including on race issues. In September 2009 he declared, "You've never seen a Columbine done by a black child. Never. They always say, 'We can't believe it happened here. We can't believe it was these suburban white kids.' It's only them. Now a black kid might shoot another black kid. He's not going to shoot up the whole school." Military analyst Ralph Peters responded, "It's symptomatic of the extreme leftward lurch of this administration. It's the farthest left administration we've ever had in American history. Obama makes FDR look like Barry Goldwater."[128]

Van Jones' bizarre declarations became well known, leading to his resignation. What is less well-known is that the same month Jones spit out his racial analysis of Columbine, Obama's "diversity czar" (the FCC's Chief Diversity Officer), Mark Lloyd, was caught on video saying, "There are few things, I think, more frightening in the American mind than dark-skinned black men." A few years earlier Lloyd had complained that whites owned and controlled 98 percent of all federal broadcast licenses and urged white media executives to "step down" so that "more people of color, gays," and "other people" "can have power." Lloyd also panned the First Amendment, saying the freedoms it guarantees are "too often an exaggeration.... The purpose of free speech is warped to protect global corporations and block rules that would promote democratic governance."[129]

In May 2009, amid debate over Obama's nomination of Sonia Sotomayor as a Supreme Court justice, White House press secretary Robert Gibbs pointedly admonished "anybody involved in this debate to be exceedingly careful with the way in which they've decided to describe different aspects of this impending confirmation." The remark was a clear insinuation that Sotomayor's critics were motivated by racism. And in fact, race *had* entered the discussion—but only because Obama's nominee herself viewed the legal system through the prism of race and group identity, once having said that a "wise Latina woman" like herself should be more capable of adjudicating certain kinds of cases than a white male.[130]

DIVERSITY UBER ALLES

Contradicting candidate Obama's post-racial appeals, the Obama administration has zealously promoted race-based policies and preferences—under the euphemism of "diversity"—inside and outside the government. The Obama administration used federal "stimulus" funds for such politically correct projects as purchasing manuals for every Omaha public school teacher, administrator, and staff instructing them on how to become more culturally sensitive.[131] And according to *The Hill*, the Obama Agriculture Department has implemented numerous diversity initiatives and even hired a consulting firm to advise on diversity issues.[132] Department Secretary Tom Vilsack said the agency would also adopt most of the recommendations from a two-year study that examined USDA's alleged history of discrimination and its alleged civil rights failings, which is all in line with the administration's goal of bringing "transformational change" to a department that has been guilty of "egregious cases of discrimination." One recommendation was that the USDA's rural development department should be made more accessible to women and that a "chief diversity officer" should be appointed in each of the agency's state offices.[133]

But spreading "diversity" through just one department is not nearly ambitious enough for Obama. In August 2011, he issued an executive order called "Establishing a Coordinated Government-Wide Initiative to Promote Diversity and Inclusion in the Federal Workforce." The order calls for all agencies in the federal government to "develop and issue" a "diversity and inclusion strategic plan." Though vague, the order reflects the administration's obsession with race and the inclusion of race-based factors for employment. While these types of initiatives are often billed as efforts to prevent discrimination, they promote it by their very terms, compelling government agencies to factor in race and ethnicity in their employment decisions rather than to factor them out, encouraging them to discriminate rather than to aspire toward a policy of non-discrimination.[134]

Not content with making the entire federal government subject to its race-conscious "diversity" initiatives, the administration does what it can to impose them on the private sphere as well. For example, an inspector general report on the government's takeover of GM and Chrysler contained a little-known finding: "Dealerships were retained because they were recently appointed, were key wholesale parts dealers, or were minority- or woman-owned dealerships." This seems to mean that in order to meet the Obama administration's unilaterally imposed race- and gender-based strictures, the big auto companies were forced to close potentially stronger dealerships because their owners were the wrong race or the wrong sex.[135]

In July 2011, Attorney General Eric Holder gave banks a good dose of diversity, ordering them to relax their mortgage underwriting standards and approve loans for minorities with poor credit as part of a new crackdown on discrimination, according to *Investors Business Daily*.

Prosecutions, said *IBD*, had "already generated $20 million in loan set-asides and other subsidies from banks that have settled out of court rather than battle the federal government and risk being branded as racist." A Department of Justice spokeswoman admitted that another sixty banks were under investigation.[136] It's hard to imagine more striking proof that the administration learned nothing from the nation's housing and financial crisis.

The expansion of race preferences in school admissions is a key goal of the Left, and this administration has worked hard to further it as well. In March 2010, the Obama administration filed an amicus brief in the U.S. Court of Appeals for the Fifth Circuit, supporting the University of Texas's use of racial preferences in undergraduate admissions. In the brief, the administration advocated preferences not just at the university level but also from kindergarten through high school: "In view of the importance of diversity in educational institutions, the United States, through the Departments of Education and Justice, supports the efforts of school systems and post-secondary educational institutions that wish to develop admissions policies that endeavor to achieve the educational benefits of diversity in accordance with [the Supreme Court's 2003 decision upholding the use of preferences by the University of Michigan law school]."[137]

The administration, even in its presentation of budget proposals, couches its marketing materials in terms of identity politics—what the plan will do for specific minorities and other groups, as if it strives to end once and for all the notion of *e pluribus unum* and the very idea of the melting pot. Its byword, instead, should be "balkanization." The administration's list of "fact sheets" for the 2012 budget included, among other items: Expanding Opportunities for the LGBT Community, Expanding Opportunities for Latino Families, Fighting the HIV/AIDS Epidemic and Supporting People Living with HIV/AIDS, Helping Women and Girls Win the Future, Standing with Indian Country, Winning the Future for African-American Families, Winning the Future for Asian-American and Pacific Islander Families, and Winning the Future for People with Disabilities.[138]

Eventually, Obama began to describe his legislation in terms of the benefits it would provide for blacks. The administration described an unemployment benefits renewal and tax bill as "a major win for African-American families." The White House sent out an email outlining the specific ways the bill would benefit black families, which was not only interesting for its racial focus, but also as an illustration that Obama had no answer other than extending government benefits to reverse the devastating effects of his economic and regulatory policies on black families. There was no eye to growth and no incentives, only more income and wealth redistribution to perpetuate and deepen the dependency cycle. Despite his enormous transfer payments and other leftist policies, 15.8 percent of adult African Americans were unemployed in December 2010, more than twice the rate of whites and also dwarfing the national average of 9.8 percent. Obama's email bragged that 2.2 million African-American families would benefit from the expansion of the Earned Income Tax Credit and Child Tax Credit in the bill, while the unemployment extension, it said, would benefit 1.1 million African Americans.[139]

OBAMA'S DEPARTMENT OF INJUSTICE

If Obama really wanted to run a post-racial administration, it's hard to explain why he would appoint Eric Holder as his attorney general. This, after all, is a man who, just a month into Obama's presidency, publicly denounced the American people as a "nation of cowards" on racial issues—even though at the time we had a black president, a black attorney general, and black men leading both political parties. As multiple former Justice Department employees have testified, under Holder's direction, the DOJ has become the government's premier employer of racial militants. It's hard to believe this has escaped Obama's notice, and it certainly hasn't shaken his complete confidence in his attorney general.

A few months after Holder called Americans cowards, the DOJ dismissed voter intimidation charges against New Black Panther Party members, even though the government had already won a default judgment against the defendants a month earlier when they had failed even to appear in court.[140] It was later revealed that in March 2007 then-candidate Barack Obama, during a campaign stop in Selma, Alabama, had shared a podium with members of the New Black Panther Party, received a personal greeting from the wife of Panther chief Malik Zulu Shabazz, and walked next to Panther members in a civil rights march.[141] Notably, Malik Zulu Shabazz, who was one of the Panthers who marched near Obama, was also one of the party members charged in the voter intimidation case that the DOJ dismissed. As Andrew McCarthy wrote at National Review Online, "This is a shocking story, and a breathtaking indictment of the mainstream media which went out of its way to avoid vetting Obama as a candidate—and to make sure anyone who tried to do due diligence got no sunshine. A candidate who chose to appear in the company, of say, the KKK, would have provoked relentlessly hostile media coverage, and, in short order, have been marginalized as disqualified to hold responsible elective office."[142]

Scandalously, on February 11, 2011, the U.S. Commission on Civil Rights, with the help of Obama's newly appointed commissioners, voted to shut down its investigation of the DOJ's dismissal of the Panther case. This was a sweet reward for Eric Holder, who had been trying to suppress the investigation for eighteen months by stonewalling document requests and forbidding his subordinates from being deposed or interviewed. Writing for Pajamas Media, former FCC commissioner Hans A. von Spakovsky said he "couldn't believe how the Commission's Democratic appointees abandoned their duty as civil rights commissioners in order to defend the administration's stonewalling." He claimed some commissioners had "acted as the virtual defense counsel for the Obama administration, trying to stop the investigation and obscure and obfuscate the Commission's findings."[143]

The inexplicable dismissal of the New Black Panther case reflected deeply disturbing trends at the Obama-Holder DOJ. In his book *Injustice*, J. Christian Adams, a former DOJ attorney who had worked on the New Black Panther case, gave a firsthand account of how the DOJ, under Obama's presidency, has been staffed top-to-bottom with radical racialists who believe civil rights laws should not be enforced in cases involving black offenders and white victims. Adams further recounted how numerous aspects of the DOJ's expansive authority—from voting rights to business regulations to employment and housing rules—now serve a fringe racial agenda that would repulse the vast majority of Americans.[144] Adams and others also alleged that those at the Justice Department fighting for race-neutral application of the civil rights laws were subjected to harassment and intimidation.[145]

Testifying before the U.S. Commission on Civil Rights, Christopher Coates, a DOJ Voting Section veteran with extensive civil rights credentials, said the election of President Obama "brought to positions of influence and power with the Civil Rights Division many of the very people who had demonstrated hostility to the concept of equal enforcement of the Voting Rights Act." Coates provided specific examples of how the division refused to enforce civil rights laws to protect white victims against black perpetrators. He averred that his supervisor, Loretta King, who was then acting assistant attorney general, expressly forbade him from even asking prospective DOJ employees if they would be willing to commit to race-neutral law enforcement. Moreover, Coates testified that the DOJ is refusing to enforce federal laws requiring states to remove ineligible voters from their rolls, including dead people and incarcerated felons—laws that DOJ radicals believe somehow to be racist.[146]

After more than three years of Obama's presidency, it is hard to deny that his administration is engaged in a sustained attack on Americans' most cherished values. This makes perfect sense when you consider how Obama and his officials view a large segment of the American people: we are unenlightened cowards, bitterly clinging to guns and religion, brimming with xenophobia and racism, a people with a history that demands a lot of apologies. To improve our condition, Obama and his allies seek to enlighten us, putting us on the righteous path of federally funded abortion and racial preferences. That is their vision—and if we don't share it, then they'll use all the coercive power of government to make us see the light.

CHAPTER FIVE

THE WAR ON THE ECONOMY

On July 3, 2008, campaigning in Fargo, North Dakota, Obama told us who he thinks is responsible for the government's deficit spending and the national debt: "The problem is, is that the way Bush has done it over the last eight years is to take a credit card from the Bank of China in the name of our children, driving up our national debt from $5 trillion dollars for the first 42 presidents—number 43 added $4 trillion dollars by his lonesome, so that we now have over $9 trillion dollars of debt that we are going to have to pay back—$30,000 for every man, woman and child." He then added a striking accusation: "That's irresponsible. It's unpatriotic."[1]

After years of President Obama's unprecedented scapegoating of his predecessor for every imaginable problem facing the United States while refusing to acknowledge his own culpability in our current economic troubles and debt crisis, people tend to forget what the economy was actually like under most of President George W. Bush's tenure. Like

President Obama, he inherited a recession. Following passage of his unfairly maligned tax cut package, we experienced six consecutive years of economic growth, from the fourth quarter of 2001 until the fourth quarter of 2007. Real GDP grew more than 17 percent between 2000 and 2007, and labor productivity gains averaged 2.5 percent after 2001, which exceeded the averages of the three preceding decades. Furthermore, real after-tax income per capita increased by more than 11 percent, and there was a 4.7 percent increase in the number of new businesses formed.

Contrary to Obama's propaganda, the tax cuts did not only benefit the "wealthy." All income groups received a cut as tax relief reached 116 million Americans. Nor did the tax cuts starve the federal Treasury. Just as with the Kennedy and Reagan tax cuts, revenues grew—tax receipts rose $542 billion between 2000 and 2007.[2] And while President Bush undoubtedly spent way too much money, his deficits have been dwarfed by Obama's. In the first four years of the Bush tax cuts, the deficit shrank 57.3 percent, and in 2007, the last year before the onset of the financial crisis, the deficit shrank to $161 billion, a mere fraction of Obama's deficit for fiscal year 2011.[3]

JOBS "SAVED OR CREATED"? TRY "DESTROYED"

President Obama has repeatedly acknowledged that he expects to be judged on his economic performance, and that if he does poorly the people will not reelect him.[4] So let's take a look at his record. On February 17, 2009, Obama signed into law his $868 billion stimulus bill, promising it would "save or create"—a ludicrous, immeasurable metric—3 to 3.5 million jobs by the end of 2010 and keep employment below 8 percent. In fact, unemployment greatly exceeded that the entire time, often surging past 9 percent.[5]

How about those 3.5 million jobs? Well, J. D. Foster of the Heritage Foundation reports that at the end of 2010, Obama had amassed a 7.6 million jobs deficit. When he made his promise there were 135.1 million jobs in the economy, so to reach his target we would have needed

138.6 million jobs by the end of December 2010. As it turned out, there were only 131 million jobs.[6] Not only did Obama fail to reach his goal, but we had much fewer jobs than we had when he started and much fewer than we would have had if he'd just left things alone.

The following charts show the disparity between Obama's promises on jobs and actual employment trends. The first chart, from the House Budget Committee, shows the unemployment percentages he promised with his stimulus against both those he delivered, and what would have occurred with no stimulus. Not only did he fail to come close to his projections, but he made matters worse than they would have been without the stimulus. The second, from the Heritage Foundation, shows the net jobs deficit between what Obama promised (to save or create 3.5 million jobs) and the actual results (a net loss of 7.3 million jobs; this chart was prepared before revised calculations showed the net deficit was actually slightly higher—7.6 million jobs).

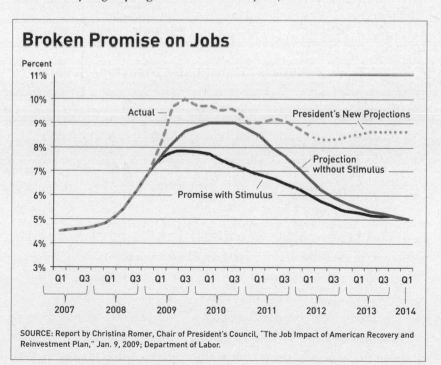

Broken Promise on Jobs

Percent

SOURCE: Report by Christina Romer, Chair of President's Council, "The Job Impact of American Recovery and Reinvestment Plan," Jan. 9, 2009; Department of Labor.

Obama Jobs Deficit: 7.3 Million Jobs

President Obama pledged to create 3.5 million
new jobs by 2010, which would place total U.S.
employment at 137.8 million. Using that figure as
a target, Obama's jobs deficit currently stands at
7.3 million.

Total U.S. Employment, Targeted and Actual,
in Millions of Jobs

Dec. 2010:
137.8

**Obama's
Jobs
Target**

134.3

Jobs Deficit
(based on November 2010
employment figures):
7.3 million

Actual

130.5

```
D J F MAM J J A S OND J FMAM J J A S OND
2008 2009                 2010
```

139
138
137
136
135
134
133
132
131
130
129
128

Note: Figures have been rounded.

Source: Heritage Foundation calculations and U.S. Department of
Labor, Bureau of Labor Statistics, "The Employment
Situation—November 2010," Table B-1, at
http://www.bls.gov/news.release/pdf/empsit.pdf (November 3, 2010).

☎ heritage.org

Economists Timothy Conley and Bill Dupor conducted a separate
study on the effects of the stimulus and came to different conclusions,

but still very unfavorable to Obama. In their paper, "The American Recovery and Reinvestment Act: Public Sector Jobs Saved, Private Sector Jobs Forestalled," they reported, "Our benchmark results suggest that the ARRA [the "stimulus"] created/saved approximately 450 thousand state and local government jobs and destroyed/forestalled roughly one million private sector jobs. State and local government jobs were saved because ARRA funds were largely used to offset state revenue shortfalls and Medicaid increases rather than boost private sector employment. The majority of destroyed/forestalled jobs were in growth industries including health, education, professional and business services."[7]

Shortly after the release of this report, the administration's own figures revealed that the stimulus was a stunningly inefficient catalyst for job growth. The White House's Council of Economic Advisers reported that using "mainstream estimates of economic multipliers for the effects of fiscal stimulus," the stimulus had added or saved nearly 2.4 million jobs at a cost of $666 billion. That translates to $278,000 per job—and that's accepting the absurd assumption that 2.4 million net jobs were "created or saved" using some mythical multiplier effect. The report also revealed that as of just six months before the report was issued, the stimulus had created or saved just under 2.7 million jobs, which meant that in that half-year period it had *cost* the economy almost three hundred thousand jobs.[8] Even CBO director Douglas Elmendorf told the Senate Budget Committee that the stimulus had a "negative effect on the growth of GDP over 10 years."[9]

"THE LONGEST STRETCH OF HIGH UNEMPLOYMENT SINCE THE GREAT DEPRESSION"

Three years after the stimulus bill passed, the Congressional Budget Office released a devastating report card on its effect on unemployment—though that is not quite how the report was presented. The report said,

The rate of unemployment in the United States has exceeded 8 percent since February 2009, making the past three years the longest stretch of high unemployment in this country since the Great Depression. Moreover, the Congressional Budget Office (CBO) projected that the unemployment rate would remain above 8 percent until 2014. The official unemployment rate, of course, excludes those individuals who would like to work but have not searched for a job in the past four weeks as well as those who are working part-time but would prefer full-time work; if those people were counted among the unemployed, the unemployment rate in January 2012 would have been about 15 percent.... Compounding the problem of high unemployment, the share of unemployed people looking for work for more than six months—referred to as the long-term unemployed—topped 40 percent in December 2009 for the first time since 1948, when such data began to be collected; it has remained above that level ever since.[10]

While the economy has finally begun to show some signs of recovery, it has been too little, too late. Proponents of Keynesian stimulus spending would have us believe that the government, almost like magic, can quickly create economic activity and jobs by injecting borrowed money into the economy. Some Keynesians even claim the spending elixir is so powerful that jobs will appear almost regardless of how or where the money is spent. So, in essence, unemployed workers can be paid to dig and refill ditches, and that will stimulate the economy.

History has proved otherwise, as with FDR's New Deal spending designed to deliver the nation from the Great Depression. In 1939, when a doubling of federal spending failed to boost economic growth, FDR's Treasury secretary Henry Morgenthau said something that the die-hard Obama ideologues would never concede. Morgenthau lamented, "We have tried spending money. We are spending more than we have ever spent before and it does not work.... After eight years of this administration we have just as much unemployment as when we started… and an enormous debt to boot!"

The Keynesian model—which also failed quite spectacularly when tried in Japan during the 1990s[11]—does not acknowledge that money spent by the government has to come from somewhere. Thus, whenever money is artificially allocated to government spending, it reduces spending, savings, or investment elsewhere—specifically, in the private sector. The net stimulative effect is often zero—or it can be worse, since the government's top-down decisions on where to spend money are rarely as economically efficient as money spent in response to market signals. The more sobering reality, though, is that even if stimulus packages worked, we could hardly afford the addition of this reckless deficit spending to our already crippling national debt.

In his January 2012 State of the Union speech, Obama bragged that he'd presided over twenty-two consecutive months of private-sector job growth—the greatest growth since 2005, he said. James Sherk of the Heritage Foundation conceded that the labor market was stronger than a year before, but noted that Obama cited his statistics out of context. The recession technically ended in June 2009, and the unemployment rate, after skyrocketing above 10 percent and remaining above 9 percent for a few years, had finally fallen below 8.5 percent.[12]

Historically, said Sherk, job creation surges after a deep recession. Unemployment rose to 10.8 percent in 1981–1982 before Reagan's tax cuts had kicked in. After the recession ended, "hiring boomed…. Millions of formerly unemployed workers found new jobs and unemployment rapidly returned to pre-recession levels." But this has not happened in President Obama's recovery—"the weakest recovery in more than half a century." In fact, in every previous recovery following World War II, employment had completely recovered inside of four years. But in December 2011, some four years after the recession began, payroll employment was 4.0 percent below its level in December 2007. As of December 2011, private-sector employment was 4.5 percent below its pre-recession level. In all, there were 5.6 million net fewer jobs, the lion's share—5.2 million—being private-sector jobs. In the fourth quarter of 2011, net hiring was 40 percent less than during the recovery in 1983. Job creation, then, was significantly below the normal pace following a major recession and even below 2005 levels. The following U.S. Department of Labor chart illustrates the relative sluggishness of Obama's "recovery."[13]

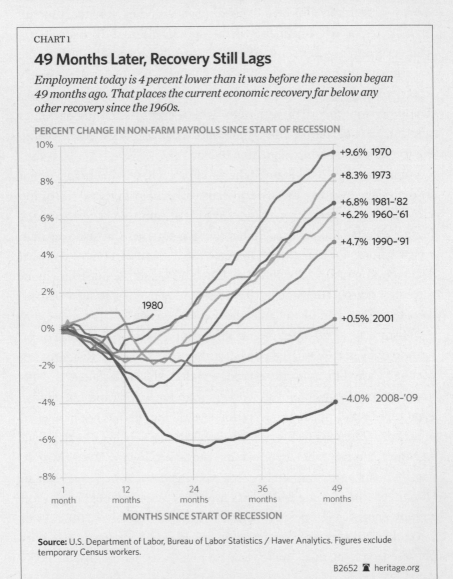

CHART 1

49 Months Later, Recovery Still Lags

Employment today is 4 percent lower than it was before the recession began 49 months ago. That places the current economic recovery far below any other recovery since the 1960s.

PERCENT CHANGE IN NON-FARM PAYROLLS SINCE START OF RECESSION

+9.6% 1970
+8.3% 1973
+6.8% 1981–'82
+6.2% 1960–'61
+4.7% 1990–'91
1980
+0.5% 2001
−4.0% 2008–'09

MONTHS SINCE START OF RECESSION

Source: U.S. Department of Labor, Bureau of Labor Statistics / Haver Analytics. Figures exclude temporary Census workers.

B2652 ☎ heritage.org

Even though joblessness has fallen to 8.3 percent, that's still extraordinarily high based on historical standards, and especially based on the Democrats' blistering critique of the George W. Bush years, when unemployment was often below 5 percent and averaged 5.3 percent. Not since the recession of the early 1980s has unemployment been so high. And while the January 2012 job growth numbers—243,000 net jobs added—were encouraging, they weren't good enough. Even at this steady growth rate, which is hardly certain, unemployment would still be 7.3 percent at the end of 2012 and not down to what economists consider the natural rate of unemployment—around 5.2 percent—before April 2015. This Heritage Foundation chart shows the jobs picture:

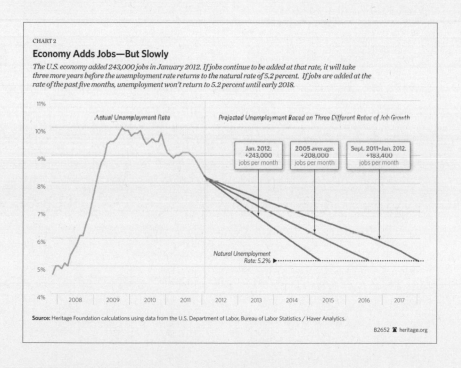

CHART 2

Economy Adds Jobs—But Slowly

The U.S. economy added 243,000 jobs in January 2012. If jobs continue to be added at that rate, it will take three more years before the unemployment rate returns to the natural rate of 5.2 percent. If jobs are added at the rate of the past five months, unemployment won't return to 5.2 percent until early 2018.

Actual Unemployment Rate

Projected Unemployment Based on Three Different Rates of Job Growth

Jan. 2012: +243,000 jobs per month

2005 average: +208,000 jobs per month

Sept. 2011–Jan. 2012: +183,400 jobs per month

Natural Unemployment Rate: 5.2%

Source: Heritage Foundation calculations using data from the U.S. Department of Labor, Bureau of Labor Statistics / Haver Analytics.

B2652 heritage.org

And there's more bad news. In addition to unemployment among blacks reaching a 27-year high,[14] Obama's term has seen the largest drop in income ever for the poorest Americans—the bottom 20 percent. Obama's broken promises to produce economic growth and upward mobility, especially for the lowest income groups, might be an additional reason—beyond class warfare politics—he incessantly demands more income redistribution. He gets to blame the "rich," deflecting his own responsibility, and compensate for his policy failures by shifting more of their money to the lower income groups, rather than helping to make them part of an opportunity society. In the process, he even gets to invoke Christian principles, telling his audiences, "I am my brother's keeper."[15] This chart, based on Census Bureau data, tells the story:[16]

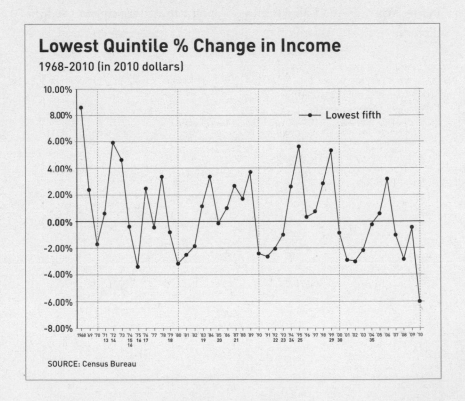

SOURCE: Census Bureau

LABOR PARTICIPATION: EVEN WORSE THAN IT SEEMS

As noted, although unemployment was marginally improving, the figures being reported were misleading because they failed to factor in the falling labor force participation, i.e, those people who were no longer seeking employment. The actual labor force—the combined number of those employed and those still looking for a job—was at its lowest percentage since 1983. Only 63.7 percent of adult Americans were in the labor force at the beginning of 2012 compared to 66.2 percent at the beginning of 2008, a drop of 2.5 percentage points.[17]

Some of this was attributable to demographic factors such as the retirement of baby boomers. But there was more to the story. Since the recession began, participation rates plunged by two percentage points, unrelated to demographic factors. The Congressional Budget Office estimates that the jobless rate would be 1.25 points higher if labor force participation had not decreased; the CBO, as noted above, says it would be even higher than that.

Unfortunately, the "recovery" has not resulted in the participation rate climbing back up.[18] The chart below shows the dramatic decline in labor force participation:

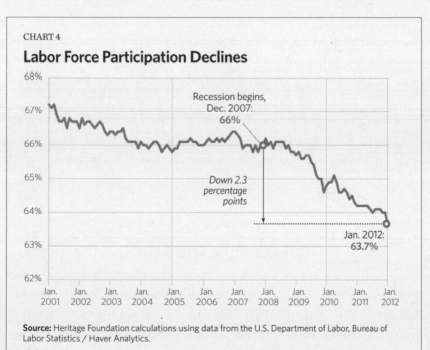

CHART 4

Labor Force Participation Declines

Recession begins, Dec. 2007: 66%

Down 2.3 percentage points

Jan. 2012: 63.7%

Source: Heritage Foundation calculations using data from the U.S. Department of Labor, Bureau of Labor Statistics / Haver Analytics.

B2652 ☎ heritage.org

The standard unemployment figures also downplay another unsettling trend: private-sector job creation is at near record lows. Fewer existing businesses are hiring and fewer entrepreneurs are starting new businesses, meaning fewer jobs are available for the unemployed. Prior to the recession, more than five million new employees were hired each month, but this figure fell to 3.6 million by June 2009. By February 2012 it had only slightly improved to four million.[19] While fewer employees are being laid off since the start of the recession, unemployment remains high because of these sluggish job creation figures, as the following chart demonstrates:

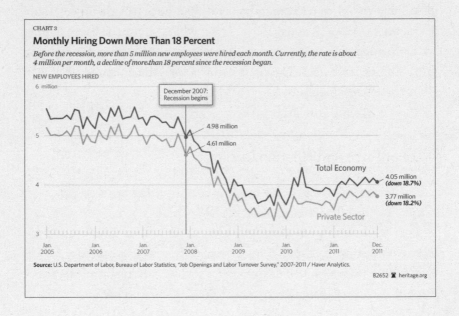

CHART 3

Monthly Hiring Down More Than 18 Percent

Before the recession, more than 5 million new employees were hired each month. Currently, the rate is about 4 million per month, a decline of more than 18 percent since the recession began.

NEW EMPLOYEES HIRED

December 2007: Recession begins

4.98 million

4.61 million

Total Economy

4.05 million (down 18.7%)

3.77 million (down 18.2%)

Private Sector

Jan. 2005 Jan. 2006 Jan. 2007 Jan. 2008 Jan. 2009 Jan. 2010 Jan. 2011 Dec. 2011

Source: U.S. Department of Labor, Bureau of Labor Statistics, "Job Openings and Labor Turnover Survey," 2007–2011 / Haver Analytics.

B2652 heritage.org

CORRUPTION AND WASTE

The Obama administration's extravagant spending schemes inevitably involve enormous amounts of waste and corruption. Take the stimulus: the Government Accountability Office found that the federal government awarded $24 billion in stimulus funds to some 3,700 contractors and vendors—5 percent of all stimulus recipients—who owed a combined three-quarters of a billion in unpaid federal taxes. Senator Tom Coburn remarked, "That such a huge amount of the stimulus money went to known tax cheats should be a wakeup call for Congress."[20]

Senators Coburn and John McCain issued a report, called "Summertime Blues," on the one hundred most wasteful projects funded in President Obama's $868 billion stimulus bill. Here are just a few blood-boiling examples:

- The U.S. Forest Service was set to spend $554,763 to replace windows at a visitors center on Mount St. Helens in Washington state that was closed in 2007.
- The government gave $762,372 to the University of North Carolina to develop a computerized choreography program that could lead to a YouTube-like "Dance Tube" online application.
- An abandoned train station in Glassboro, New Jersey, was converted into a museum with $1.2 million in federal stimulus funds.[21]
- The GOP research team also analyzed stimulus waste, state by state, citing such examples as a $15 million grant to construct an airport in an Alaskan village with 165 residents, a $950,000 study on the genetic makeup of ants, and $4.3 billion to build high-speed rail between two sparsely populated rural towns.[22]

In November, the Treasury Department revised its loss estimate for the GM bailout from $14.33 billion to $23.6 billion, racking up another confirmed failure for Obama's economic record. The $23.6 billion amounted to a 25 percent loss for the federal government on its $60 billion "investment" in GM. In addition, according to Shikha Dalmia of *Reason*, taxpayers would also take a hit because the administration allowed GM to write off $45 billion in losses, which could amount to $15 billion in lost revenues. The total hit to taxpayers could amount to $38.6 billion.[23]

Astronomical losses were also uncovered at Fannie Mae and Freddie Mac. While the administration claimed the actual cost of the federal government's guarantees to the mortgage giants was $130 billion, the CBO put the real cost at almost 2.5 times that: $317 billion.[24]

The administration received a couple more failing grades—this time from a surprising source, its former economic advisor Austan Goolsbee—for its Cash for Clunkers program and the home buyer tax credit passed in 2009, which Goolsbee said he would not back "if given a second chance." Admitting the administration had misjudged how long it would take the economy to recover, Goolsbee explained that Obama was hedging his bets to cover either a long or short recovery. These two programs, he said, "were geared to trying to shift" the recovery from 2010 into 2009. "Given it's taken this long [to recover], I don't think you would do that short-run stuff."[25]

INFRASTRUCTURE BOONDOGGLES

President Obama remains unchastened by his failed promises to jumpstart the economy or contain unemployment with his stimulus program. He just demands more of the same, as we saw with his push for a $50 billion high-speed rail project and his $447 billion jobs bill.

Obama's disregard for empirical data on high-speed rail is remarkable. The experience of other countries with high-speed rail, available for all to review, is that it is an expensive undertaking, with relatively low public demand, high ticket prices, and a need for ample government subsidies. America's own experience with such projects is no better. In 2011, planners of a California high-speed rail project tripled its projected costs (voters were told it would cost $33.6 billion when they voted to approve the project, and estimates later rose to $98.5 billion) and announced trains would not be running for twenty-two years. But this didn't keep Vice President Joe Biden from heartily supporting the project, which received an infusion of $2.25 billion from the federal stimulus.[26]

Obama's initial stimulus bill allocated only a small percentage of monies to infrastructure improvements, despite his assurances that boundless shovel-ready jobs awaited. But his FY2013 budget seeks $50 billion to "jumpstart" transportation projects and $476 billion over six years for "surface transportation projects," including high-speed rail. How would Obama pay for what would amount to a $135 billion spending increase? Simple: with phantom savings from the wars in Afghanistan and Iraq.

The administration, of course, continues to peddle the specious Keynesian claim that these stimulus dollars are not wasteful because they create jobs, exerting a multiplier effect as they ripple through the economy. As noted above, that would only be the case if this stimulus money appeared out of nowhere. But it has to come from somewhere, which means instead of stimulating the economy, we are just shifting resources.[27] Forcing so much federal spending leads to inefficiencies and often suppresses private-sector growth, which, along with other factors, could cause a net negative effect on the economy.

A recent European Central Bank international study showed just that. Examining data from 108 national economies, the study concluded that "government consumption is consistently detrimental to growth," and that this was true "irrespective of the country sample considered." The ECB study found that while government spending can sometimes help, in excess it reduces economic growth through "government inefficiencies, crowding-out effects, excess burdens of taxation, distortion of the incentives systems, and interventions to free markets." Economist Veronique de Rugy has also cited domestic studies concluding that "federal spending in states caused local businesses to cut back rather than grow."[28]

BUSH CREATED THIS MESS, SO I'LL MAKE IT WORSE—MUCH WORSE

Obama and his fellow Democrats still blame President Bush for Obama's disastrous economic record and the enormous, unprecedented deficits and national debt Obama has accumulated. Given their position, based on such obviously distorted spin, one might reasonably assume their argument would be, "President Bush permitted staggering debt to accrue. We are going to initiate policies to radically reverse this trend, balance the budget, and begin to retire our crippling debt." Instead, they say, essentially, "We will continue to blame Bush for creating too much debt, but in fact we don't care about the debt, and we'll prove it to you by creating deficits and debt that dwarf anything Bush could have imagined in his most destructive fantasies. We will not only refuse to reduce the debt, we will continue to grow it to the point of unsustainability." There is no better argument for attributing this view to Team Obama than its actual record: in February 2012, Obama racked up the worst one-month deficit in United States history—$229 billion, bringing the accumulated deficit for the first five months of fiscal year 2012 to $631 billion.[29]

Is there anything to Obama's claim that Bush created this mess, that it was much worse than Obama had imagined before he took office, and that Obama has worked hard to dig us out of the mess and reduce our deficits and debt? After Obama presented his FY2012 budget, which isn't appreciably different from his FY2013 budget in terms of its projected spending and deficits, the Heritage Foundation prepared charts comparing deficits under Obama and Bush. The picture tells a grim story—one that Obama would prefer you not hear (or see)—and it does not lie:

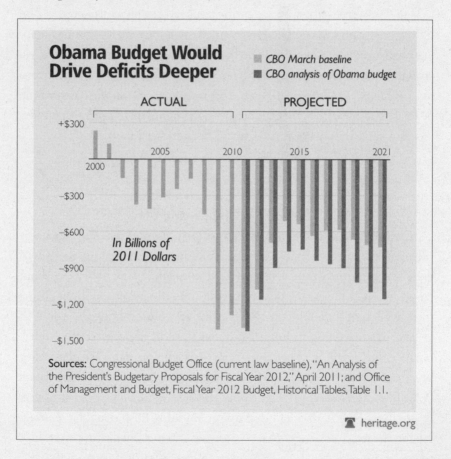

A House Budget Committee chart also shows that Obama's deficits dwarfed Bush's (though experts have argued over who should be blamed for FY2009). It further shows how Obama makes no real effort to curb the long-term deficit, and that it even begins to climb again in the out years—and this is best case scenario. We must be mindful that these are *projected* figures—showing Obama doesn't even aspire on his budgetary blackboard to control spending.

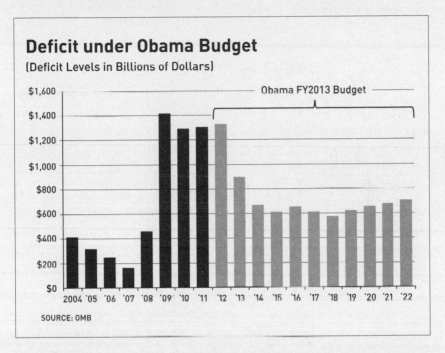

Deficit under Obama Budget
(Deficit Levels in Billions of Dollars)

As noted above, the Bush deficit in 2007, when both the Iraq and Afghanistan wars were proceeding with full force, was a fraction of Obama's 2011 deficit—putting the lie to the Democrats' claim that the wars created our bankrupting deficits. As Heritage's Mike Brownfield and Emily Goff explain,

> Without a doubt, deficits during the Bush Administration were too high, especially in the early years. More could and should have been done to restrain spending. But, without a doubt, the Bush deficits were puny compared to what Obama and his congressional allies have inflicted. For Obama's apologists to seek cover in the Bush deficits is shameless. To use these diversions to now take attention away from the real problem to which Obama has added is outrageous.... So next time Obama or his allies in the press go back to the well and recite the well-worn verse that spending is all the other guy's

fault, take a look at the facts. President Obama has steered a fiscal course that will lead to more spending and deeper deficits and ultimately to vastly higher taxes.[30]

"A BUDGET WORTHY OF GREECE"

Considering Obama's domestic record to date—the utter failure of his economic programs, the dismal state of the economy and jobs, the looming debt placing the United States within a stone's throw of a Grecian-style financial collapse—rational observers might have expected the president, in his fourth and final try prior to the November elections, to present a fiscally responsible budget. But his addiction to profligacy, his obsessive desire to remake America in his image and advance his radical agenda for economic redistribution, and pressure from his leftist base must have been too much to resist—his fiscal year 2013 budget, presented in February 2012, was as reckless as its three predecessors.

Obama's budget was so bereft of sensible stewardship that he knew it could never pass Congress. So his strategy was obviously to leverage it to curry favor with his base and use it as further ammunition to blame Republicans for his economy and debt. In the words of syndicated columnist Charles Krauthammer, "This administration is so used to blaming everything on Republicans—earthquakes, hailstorms, who knows, the rising of the ocean.... The president knows that we are headed over a cliff. He just wants to get past Election Day as he does on everything—on Keystone, on debt ceiling limits, on everything. But this is a budget worthy of Greece and for the president of the United States to offer it knowing how dire our situation is, is truly scandalous."[31]

In this budget Obama demonstrated that he'd learned nothing from his failed policies; if anything, he doubled down on the worst of them. His budget amounted to an unimaginative recycling of his inaptly named "Winning the Future" and "An America Built to Last" campaigns. The budget not only didn't propose spending reductions; it called for substantial increases of $227 billion, and added $329 billion to the projected deficit. It called for $315 billion more "stimulus" spending—completely disregarding the failures of his previous stimuli—and included $2.7 trillion more spending over the next ten years than the Congressional

Budget Office's baseline projections. While Obama glibly proclaimed he was cutting deficits by $4 trillion over the next decade, more than $2 trillion of this illusory $4 trillion in "savings" were already in law— not added with this budget—including almost $1 trillion for money that had neither been requested nor spent in Iraq and Afghanistan.[32] More damningly, his budget would in fact add $7 trillion in deficits over the next ten years.[33]

This FY2013 budget was the fourth straight in which Obama called for a deficit exceeding $1 trillion, flagrantly disgracing his promise to cut the deficit in half in four years. This House Budget Committee chart juxtaposes the actual deficit figures against Obama's February 23, 2009, promise, "Today I am pledging to cut the deficit we inherited by half by the end of my first term in office":

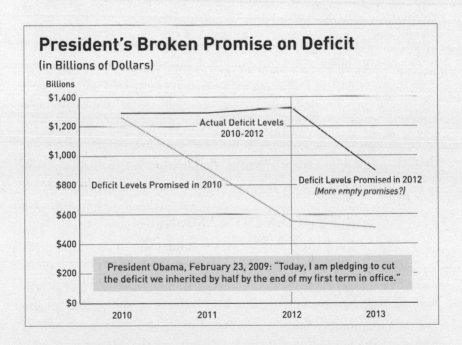

Obama's budget calls for spending $47 trillion and raising taxes by $1.9 trillion over the next decade—an increase over current projections when what we need is a radical decrease. It also foresees spending $3.8 trillion in the next fiscal year and increasing it incrementally—yet substantially—to $4.3 trillion in 2016 and to a staggering $5.8 trillion in 2022.[34]

Clearly, Obama isn't even attempting to bring the budget, the deficit, or the national debt under control. When he took office the national debt was $10.626 trillion. By March 20, 2012, after just just three years and two months, it had increased by almost $5 trillion to $15.583 trillion, which was about the same amount it increased during George W. Bush's entire eight-year tenure.[35] And Obama's latest budget projects will add almost another $1 trillion to the debt this year—and these are optimistic forecasts—meaning he will have increased the national debt by a staggering $6 trillion in his first term.

Even if it's unfair to attribute this entire amount to Obama because some of the spending was set in place when he took office, he is responsible for the lion's share of it, and he has not made a good faith effort to reverse the problem. Indeed, according to the House Budget Committee and Senate Budget Committee Republican Summary of President's FY2013 Budget, the total national debt by the end of FY2022 under Obama's latest budget would be almost $26 trillion, at which time annual interest payments on the debt would be almost $1 trillion.[36]

Putting all this in perspective, the Heritage Foundation reports that Obama's projected budget foresees spending in excess of 22 percent of GDP "throughout the decade... more than twice the New Deal's share of the economy in its peak years. In constant dollars, outlays are more than three times the peak of World War II."[37]

ENTITLEMENTS TO CONSUME
ALL TAX REVENUES BY 2052

Obama has relentlessly pushed for high-speed rail and other "stimulus" construction jobs such as repairing and rebuilding roads, bridges, and schools. Not once in arguing his case has he apologized for the failure and corruption of his first stimulus bill or his cynical, callous misrepresentation that shovel-ready jobs awaited the infusion of federal money. In a meeting with his Jobs and Competitiveness Council in Durham, North Carolina in June 2011, Obama wise-cracked, "Shovel-ready was not as shovel-ready as we expected."[38]

But he just demands more. Even with his proposed tax increases, which he scores statically—as if increasing tax rates on producers won't dampen economic growth—and his proclaimed savings based on money that was never allocated in the first place (e.g., Afghanistan and Iraq), his projected deficits never come in under $575 billion—the low point in his projections in 2018. But then his projected deficits soar back to $704 billion in 2022. Note that our average post-World War II publicly held debt has been 43 percent of GDP; today it is 74.2 percent and will increase to 76.5 percent by 2022 under Obama's budget.

On top of all this, Obama has not even taken a run at entitlement reform for Medicare, Medicaid, and Social Security, though they are the principal drivers of our deficits and debt. To illustrate what a farce and scandal this omission is: by 2050, these three entitlements plus Obamacare are projected to gobble up 18 percent of GDP, which is around the historical average of federal tax revenue. Other than retreading the tired proposals of top-down cuts to medical providers, Obama refuses to acknowledge that, fiscally speaking, we are doomed unless we restructure entitlements.[39] This Heritage Foundation chart, based on the 2010 budget figures—and matters are much worse now—illustrates this sobering reality:

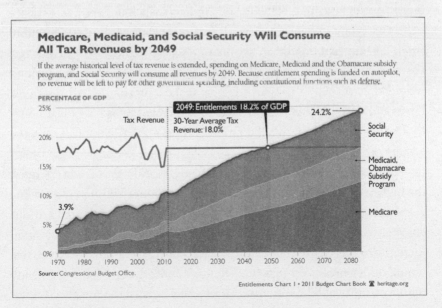

Medicare, Medicaid, and Social Security Will Consume All Tax Revenues by 2049

If the average historical level of tax revenue is extended, spending on Medicare, Medicaid and the Obamacare subsidy program, and Social Security will consume all revenues by 2049. Because entitlement spending is funded on autopilot, no revenue will be left to pay for other government spending, including constitutional functions such as defense.

PERCENTAGE OF GDP

2049: Entitlements 18.2% of GDP

Tax Revenue

30-Year Average Tax Revenue: 18.0%

24.2%

Social Security

Medicaid, Obamacare Subsidy Program

Medicare

3.9%

1970 1980 1990 2000 2010 2020 2030 2040 2050 2060 2070 2080

Source: Congressional Budget Office.

Entitlements Chart 1 • 2011 Budget Chart Book ♞ heritage.org

Obama claims ramped up education spending is a key to economic growth, believing jobs will magically appear if central planners create job-training partnerships between academia and the private sector. So he proposed a 3.5 percent increase (above 2012 levels) to $69.8 billion for the Department of Education, with $850 million in new grants for his Race to the Top program and $80 million in federal funding for teacher training in science, technology, engineering, and mathematics. As for higher education, he would authorize $8 billion in new spending for the Community College Career Fund to expand certification programs and job training at community colleges. His budget also increases the maximum Pell Grant award.[40]

His budget forbids any of this money from funding for-profit colleges—the dreaded private sector. This is consistent with his previous policy targeting for-profit universities, exemplified by the Department of Education's new restrictions on these institutions. These include restrictions on student loan access for students attending for-profit institutions whose average debt-to-earnings ratio exceeds 12 percent of a graduate's income.[41]

As noted, Obama's budget calls for $1.9 trillion in new taxes over the next decade, and when you subtract his $88 billion in tax cuts—mainly incentives for pursuing behavior he approves, such as green activities— he's proposing a net increase of $1.8 trillion. Projected revenues would equal 20.1 percent of GDP in ten years, well above the historical average. He would raise taxes on families making above $250,000 per year and would knife through their existing personal exemptions and deductions. He would increase capital gains taxes to 20 percent (which would amount to 23.8 percent if the new Obamacare surtax applies) and also raise the estate tax.

Stunningly, he proposed to tax dividends at ordinary income tax rates, the highest of which, in some cases, would amount to 43.4 percent when combining the 39.6 percent rate with the 3.8 percent Obamacare surcharge, when applicable. In that dividends are already double taxed (being taxed at 35 percent at the business level), the new effective rate would approximate 63 percent. Obama's budget also includes a rough outline to replace the Alternative Minimum Tax with the so-called Buffett

Rule, which would impose a new minimum tax of 30 percent on millionaires, just to further gouge higher income earners. On top of that, as another punitive tweak, he would eliminate deductions for families earning more than $1 million per year—including deductions for mortgage interest, retirement savings, and healthcare expenses.[42]

These tax increases would cripple an already sluggish economy and stalled job market, inevitabilities Obama doesn't factor into his projections, making them look more optimistic than is warranted.

ROSY PROJECTIONS

The Heritage Foundation's economic experts tell us that all administrations are accorded some license in adopting optimistic growth projections for their budgets, but that their forecasts rarely deviate substantially from the Blue Chip forecasts, which is an average of selected private sector prognosticators. The January Blue Chip forecast projects real output in 2012 at 2.2 percent, as does the Congressional Budget Office's forecast. Well, the administration chose to use a 2.7 percent growth figure—for 2012, the most important year because, obviously, all other years included in the calculation follow, and their projected growth accrues to that higher first-year budget figure.

According to Heritage, the net effect of these assumptions is that the administration shows 3.9 percent more cumulative growth than the Blue Chip forecast. Heritage's J. D. Foster observes, "In economic terms, that's like adding an extra year of growth—an extra *very good* year of growth." In real terms, this means, for example, that with the more realistic Blue Chip assumptions, the projected deficit for 2016 would be $844 billion instead of the $649 billion foreseen by the administration.[43]

"NOTHING COULD BE FURTHER FROM THE TRUTH"

Perhaps no part of Obama's budget is more myopic and brings about more senseless waste than his "green energy" projects. Even Department of Energy inspector general Gregory Friedman admitted that the Obama administration's goal of stimulating the economy with "shovel-ready" energy jobs was unrealistic. "The concept of shovel-ready projects was not realized, nor, as we now have confirmed, was it a realistic expectation," Friedman told the House Oversight Committee.[44]

With his FY2013 budget he continues on that path, notwithstanding his scandalous failures with Solyndra and other green energy boondoggles, as discussed in chapter eight. To mention just one example, he called for $310 million for the SunShot initiative, which seeks to make solar energy competitive and subsidy free by 2020. Instead of allowing consumers and the energy industry to make their own choices, Obama prefers his Department of Energy to act as commissar in making those decisions irrespective of market forces. His budget also allocates funds for development of other green sources, including wind, geothermal, and biofuels.

Obama is impervious to the notion that these energy sources will naturally develop if global demand warrants it, and if not, they'll likely fail anyway, as has been the case with his forced projects so far. He can't understand that businesses and investors make their own decisions about the wisdom of investing their dollars, taking into account market signals and other factors.

When government interposes itself and manipulates those factors, including by injecting taxpayer subsidies into a president's pet projects, it skews market signals and virtually builds in failure. But Obama is compelled to dicker with industry, and so his budget gives the Department of Energy some $290 million for R&D to boost energy efficiency in manufacturing processes.[45]

All these policies stem from Obama's core belief that government, not the private sector, is the main source of societal advancement and technological progress. Consider natural gas; after Obama attributed America's current natural gas boom to public funding, Heritage expert Nicolas Loris retorted that "nothing could be further from the truth." Yet Obama "wants to unnecessarily dump money into an already-booming industry," so his budget proposes $421 million in fossil energy R&D, which includes $12 million to advance technology to develop natural gas resources. Much of the rest of this money is carved out for the development of other green technologies. In the meantime, while subsidizing these energy sources, Obama is seeking to punish reliable domestic energy sources via measures such as eliminating tax deductions for the oil industry.[46]

THE ON-GOING OBAMACARE DEBACLE

Obama continues to dissemble about his signature "accomplishment," the Patient Protection and Affordable Care Act, or Obamacare, which is making healthcare neither more affordable nor more accessible, and whose fate awaits the ruling of the Supreme Court. In fact, in September 2011, Gallup reported that the percentage of American adults who were without health insurance has increased during Obama's presidency and has continued rising since the passage of Obamacare.[47]

In his FY2013 budget, Obama once again made the false assertion that Obamacare would bend the healthcare cost curve down, even claiming it would reduce the deficit by $1 trillion over the next ten years. Brazenly, he continued to make these claims after the double counting (Medicare) and other fraudulent accounting tricks (e.g., the "Doc Fix") had long since been exposed as a "shell game."[48] Moreover, shortly after he presented his budget, it was revealed that Obamacare's gross cost during the next decade was expected to be almost double the $940 billion estimate Obama represented to the American people. The mathematical gyrations the Democrats used to conjure the $940 billion figure were nothing short of deceitful; the Congressional Budget Office, long after it had favorably scored the bill in time to validate it for enactment into law, announced on March 14, 2012 that the costs would be closer to $1.76 trillion.[49]

In another egregious misrepresentation, Obama had claimed that under Obamacare, Americans could keep their own insurance plans if they liked them. But the CBO now estimates that as Obamacare kicks in, many more Americans will lose their private coverage—and will be subject to fines—than we were originally told. The CBO estimates that the government will fine individuals $45 billion, instead of $34 billion, for not having coverage, and businesses will pay closer to $96 billion, some $15 billion more than the initial projections.[50] According to this CBO report, Obamacare could cause up to twenty million people to lose their coverage.[51] Along the same lines, a *McKinsey Quarterly* survey from June 2011 found that nearly one-third of employers say they will "definitely or probably" stop offering their employees healthcare coverage under Obamacare.[52]

According to a survey by the insurer Willis Group, the situation is even worse than that. Willis reports, "Survey respondents indicate into the second year of Health Care Reform implementation, less than 30 percent of employers were able to maintain grandfathered status of their health care plans." Willis notes that the "rapid loss of grandfathered status far outpaces The Department of Health & Human Services' expectations." HHS projected that 78 percent of employers would retain their grandfathered status by the end of 2011, that 62 percent would by the end of 2012, and that 49 percent would by the end of 2013. Willis says the accelerated loss of grandfathered status "suggests that employers have had to make many plan changes to offset cost increases," and that employers have likely chosen to forfeit their grandfathered status to control costs. When Obamacare opponents had warned this would happen, the bill's supporters ridiculed them as partisan fear-mongers. But the facts are sometimes a disturbing inconvenience.[53]

Time has revealed even more deceit in the administration's cost projections for Obamacare. The administration, in its budget request in early 2012, asked for an increase of $111 billion in subsidies to help poor people buy insurance. House Ways and Means chairman Dave Camp said, "This staggering increase in health insurance exchange subsidy spending cannot be explained by legislative changes or new economic assumptions, and therefore must reflect substantial changes in underlying assumptions regarding the program's utilization and cost."[54]

Even before it has fully taken effect, Obamacare is having other negative effects that undermine the administration's assorted justifications for the bill. For example, Gallup has found:

- Nearly half of small businesses aren't hiring due to healthcare costs and government regulation.
- The cost of health insurance for many Americans climbed more sharply this year than in previous years, outstripping

any increases in workers' wages and showing Obamacare is actually making healthcare less affordable.

- The lack of clarity about the cost implications of Obamacare is an impediment for companies to begin hiring.
- Obamacare regulations are preventing small businesses from expanding, with 74 percent of small business owners blaming Obamacare for hurting job creation.[55]

In addition, the *New York Times* confirms that doctors are leaving small private practices in droves, and that small insurance firms are disappearing.[56] According to one survey, nine out of ten physicians are unwilling to recommend healthcare as a profession now that Obamacare has been enacted. That survey also shows that 60 percent of doctors believe Obamacare will negatively affect patient care, and 51.4 percent believe it could compromise the doctor-patient relationship. In addition, some 43 percent of physicians are contemplating retirement within the next five years because of Obamacare.[57]

Additionally, when some groups recommended less screening for prostate, breast, and cervical cancer—stressing that such screenings can be harmful,[58] an argument we never seemed to hear before—many observers attributed the proposal to new cost concerns created by Obamacare.[59]

Obamacare also unleashed some seventeen new taxes (some say twenty),[60] which would cost $502 billion between 2010 and 2019, including a tax on "Cadillac" employer health plans, individual and employer mandate penalties, a health insurance premium tax, and a web of tax implementation rules to take effect in 2013 that are harming private industry.[61]

A punitive 2.3 percent medical device excise tax will be particularly damaging, resulting in higher costs and job losses in the medical device industry. Stephen Ferguson, chairman of Cook Medical, says new taxes and regulations will "consume 15 percent more of our earnings." Another company, Stryker, which makes artificial hips and knees, announced that Obamacare's burdens were causing it to cut 5 percent of its global workforce, or about 1,000 workers. Many other companies will be similarly affected.[62]

Obamacare also imposes an additional 3.8 percent "sales" tax on a certain portion of the gain (in excess of $500,000 for married couples or $250,000 for singles) on certain home sales (and other unearned income) for couples whose adjusted gross income exceeds $250,000 ($200,000 for singles).[63] Grover Norquist, president of Americans for Tax Reform, says that five of these new taxes will fall most directly on seniors.[64] The following chart illustrates the extent of these seventeen new taxes:

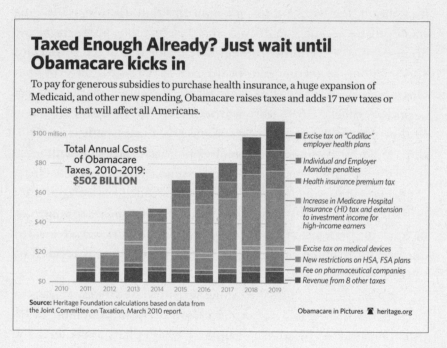

FURTHER EMPOWERING THE IPAB: "A RADICAL AND COUNTERPRODUCTIVE PLAN"

Obama's budget merely nibbles around the edges of Medicare and Medicaid which, along with Social Security—as noted—are the main drivers of our impending financial crisis. Moreover, his initial bill created the Independent Payment Advisory Board (IPAB), which will be a frighteningly powerful bureaucratic entity comprised of fifteen appointees who will make one-size-fits-all command decisions on healthcare accessibility, treatment, and fees. Despite justifiable fears that it could limit our freedoms and medical choices, including end-of-life decisions, Obama's budget has proposed to expand the board's powers. He and his experts and propagandists can characterize it in creative ways, but this board, among other things, will be a glorified rationing body, and if it does exercise cost-savings, it will do so at considerable cost to our freedoms and our access to and quality of care.[65]

Essentially, the IPAB—which Obamacare entrusts with overseeing Medicare—could only cut medical costs overall and/or Medicare spending by assuming the power to unilaterally enforce spending caps via payment cuts to service providers. By law, the IPAB is required to keep total Medicare spending below a specified legal cap that will increase at a marginally faster pace than the growth rate of the nation's economy. Since the IPAB will have no jurisdiction to affect how beneficiaries interact with Medicare, virtually its only option to reduce costs will be to impose arbitrary spending caps, which is what Medicare has been doing for decades. Such categorical reductions in reimbursement rates have failed to restrain Medicare costs and have reduced access of seniors to essential healthcare. Congressional Republicans unsuccessfully moved to repeal IPAB, knowing it can only be effective if it's granted arbitrary and draconian authority.[66]

Obamacare and IPAB double down on this failed Medicare model—and according to many experts, this will result in more and more medical professionals refusing to accept Medicare patients, thus reducing seniors' access to care. This is not a moderate approach by reasonable reformers. In the words of economics expert J. D. Foster, "It is a radical and counterproductive plan to hand over immense power to an unelected board to reduce payment rates by fiat and implicitly to ration services for seniors."[67]

In addition to all this, the Obama administration also created a $6 billion network of nonprofit "CO-OPs" that will "compete" with private insurers, according to columnist Michelle Malkin, which she calls "socialized medicine through the side door." While Republicans sliced $2 billion from this "slush fund," Malkin says the program is still alive and well, with some $700 million in taxpayer-funded low-interest loans being recently parceled out to seven such CO-OPs in eight states with more to come the next year. More scandalous, Kaiser Health is reporting that the Obamacare CO-OP overseers are already predicting a nearly 40 percent default rate for these loans[68]—in keeping with Obama's practice of ignoring accountability when it serves his cause. It should come as no surprise that a number of these loan recipients are left-wing groups and, in some cases, friends of Obama.[69]

At one time, when Obamacare was new and fresh, Obama insisted that it was a crucial part of his economic agenda, but by the time of its second anniversary, he had begun retreating from that position.[70] The Obamacare legislation is a whopping 2,700 pages, containing 425,116 words, but the regulations promulgated to implement it contain over two million words.[71]

"CRONY CAPITALISM, BAILOUT FAVORITISM, AND GANGSTER GOVERNMENT"

Obamacare is already so damaging that the administration arbitrarily issued more than a thousand waivers to various groups and companies in order to defer their pain and further deceive the public about the bill's actual costs—at least until after the 2012 election. At issue is Obamacare's requirement that health insurers raise their annual benefit limits gradually until 2014, when all such limits would become illegal.[72] In March 2011, the administration granted 128 new, one-year waivers to this rule, bringing the total number of recipients to 1,168 businesses, insurers, unions, and other groups, involving around three million people. Congressman Fred Upton stated the obvious: "The fact that over 1,000 waivers have been granted is a tacit admission that the healthcare law is fundamentally flawed."[73]

Looking at these numbers, columnist Michael Barone raised a separate question: "Why are more than half of those 3,095,593 in plans run by labor unions, which were among Obamacare's biggest political supporters? Union members are only 12 percent of all employees but have gotten 50.3 percent of Obamacare waivers." Barone noted that when coupled with the administration's NLRB action against Boeing and the IRS's attempt to levy a gift tax on donors to certain groups "that just happen to have spent money on Republicans," it appears the administration is "punishing enemies and rewarding friends—politics Chicago style." To Barone, it smelled of "crony capitalism, bailout favoritism and gangster government."[74] That stench grew stronger when it came to light that some 20 percent of the 204 waivers granted in April 2011 were given to gourmet restaurants, nightclubs, and fancy hotels in Nancy Pelosi's congressional district.[75] In January 2012, amid growing accusations of corruption, the HHS announced an end to the waiver program. By that time some 1,231 companies had received waivers, covering almost four million people.[76]

"SITUATIONAL TRUTH"

The financial centerpiece of Obamacare is the individual mandate, which forces people to buy healthcare insurance. In March 2012 the Supreme Court heard arguments surrounding the mandate's dubious constitutionality. The administration's lawyer told the justices that the government-imposed charge for violating the individual mandate is a tax—as opposed to a fine or penalty—and thus Congress has the authority to impose it.[77] Interestingly, when ABC's George Stephanopoulos asked Obama in September 2009 if the individual mandate was a tax increase, Obama replied, "I absolutely reject that notion."[78] But when it was necessary for his administration to argue otherwise, it did.

The administration showed its slipperiness on this question in February 2012 during the testimony of Obama's director of the Office of Management and Budget, Jeffrey Zients, before the House Budget Committee. Congressman Scott Garrett tried to get Zients to admit that the individual mandate is a tax, and would thus violate Obama's repeated promise not to impose new taxes on middle- and lower-income groups. "Wouldn't this be a tax on people who make less than $250,000 a year?" asked Garrett. Finally, after bumbling about, Zients said, "No"—a direct contradiction of the argument the administration put to the Supreme Court.[79]

Obama used similar deceit on the Medicare issue. Despite promising Obamacare would "put Medicare on a sounder financial footing." Obama warned during the budget negotiations around a year later that Medicare could go insolvent. Charles Krauthammer commented, "You've heard of situational ethics? This is situational truth."[80]

GUTTING NATIONAL DEFENSE

How do Obama's budgets handle national security, a realm Obama constantly promises he won't shortchange? Well, his assertions might fly if you accept his naïve beliefs that we don't need to be prepared to fight two wars at once, that rivals such as China, Russia, and Iran aren't increasing their military budgets and readiness, and that Islamic terrorism isn't a major threat. But most people understand that our national security will be imperiled by systematic military downgrading—and that is what Obama's budgets do.

Although national security is one of the few clearly constitutionally prescribed areas of federal expenditures, it is the one area in which Obama pushes for major spending cuts. Specifically, he seeks to reduce our total defense spending from $721.3 billion in FY2010 to $601.3 billion in FY2017. Obama's FY2013 budget would decrease the Department of Defense budget 1 percent below the 2012 level,[81] which has already proved to be insufficient, given the military's expanded commitments.

If his budget proposals are adopted, the Navy, for example, might be rendered impotent to stave off Iranian military action in the Strait of Hormuz while simultaneously attending to its other interests at sea. The Coast Guard may have to choose between defending the sea or our borders. Our Air Force might be forced to pursue missions without any certainty that it will be able to control the airspace. The Marines would be short of ships necessary to make their force deployments. And the Army's resources would be dangerously downscaled.[82]

Nor does Obama's budget account for further defense cuts, totaling half a trillion dollars over the next nine years, that will be imposed by the Budget Control Act of 2011—provisions that kicked in when the vaunted congressional "Supercommittee" was unable to agree to budget cuts. Secretary of Defense Leon Panetta said the cuts would be devastating, but Obama has offered no assurances that he would support their repeal. To the contrary, he has promised he would veto any effort to forestall or thwart this "sequestration." Through this ill-conceived sequestration, defense would bear half the automatic cuts, though it accounts for less than 20 percent of the federal budget—a recklessly disproportionate result.[83]

One major problem with Obama's economic stewardship is that he doesn't learn from his failures. This is doubtlessly due to his ideological zeal for a comprehensive array of leftist causes and pressure from his progressive base. Every failed stimulus program, green energy boondoggle, and debt-laden budget proposal is followed up with demands for more of the same. More than three years into his presidency, he continues to blame President Bush for all our economic troubles, disregarding the fact that his own federal spending on Cash for Clunkers, windmills, high-speed rail lines, and other so-called economic stimuli and redistributionist schemes, along with his failure to tackle entitlement reform, have blown up the deficit while failing to improve the economy.

Now, in this election season, we are supposed to believe that these policies will work if only we try them for four more years.

CHAPTER SIX

THE WAR ON OUR FUTURE

Congressman Paul Ryan has been the national leader in offering an alternative vision to President Obama's reckless, bank-busting spending agenda. Ryan's updated Path to Prosperity (2.0) plan, recently passed by the GOP Congress and rejected by the Democratic Senate, is a balanced approach to our budgetary and systemic entitlement problems. It would preserve the existing Medicare program for those currently enrolled or becoming eligible in the next ten years (those fifty-five and older today), but would provide new options for those under age fifty-five, with extra support for those who have greater medical needs. It includes Medical Savings Accounts that are fully funded for low-income beneficiaries and wholly available to those above that income category.

Ryan's plan would strengthen the healthcare safety net by making Medicare permanently solvent—a claim validated for an earlier version of the plan by CBO estimates and consultations with the Office of the Actuary of the Centers for Medicare and Medicaid Services.[1] It would also modernize Medicaid by reforming high-risk pools and giving states maximum flexibility to tailor their own Medicaid programs to the needs of their citizens.

Ryan's Roadmap plan, as distinguished from his Path to Prosperity plan, also contains specific and concrete reform measures for Social Security, analogous to the Path's Medicare proposals. It would preserve existing benefits for those at or approaching retirement age and provide new options for those under fifty-five, including personal retirement accounts for more than a third of their Social Security taxes. But because not enough GOP Congress members would support this Social Security component of Ryan's Roadmap plan, his Path to Prosperity, which Congress did approve, instead just calls for bipartisan action to restore Social Security to solvency.

Obama and the Democrats have responded to Ryan's Path to Prosperity, both the original version and the updated one, with insult, ridicule, demagoguery, demonization, and fear-mongering. Obama has repeatedly misrepresented the plan as robbing Americans of their Social Security, Medicare, and Medicaid, all of which it expressly preserves.

Without addressing the unfunded liabilities from these entitlements, the long-term budget can never be balanced and the United States will become insolvent. But Obama has continually kicked the entitlements issue down the road, virtually ignoring the looming crises in his current budget and even exacerbating the problem by approving Obamacare, a monstrous new entitlement. Because he refuses to tackle entitlements or to make any appreciable dent in discretionary spending (other than for our vital national defense needs), he can't balance the budget—even in the long-term and even using his ultra-rosy economic forecasts.

This was evident in February 2012 when Obama's Office of Management and Budget director Jeffrey Zients testified before the House Budget Committee about Obama's FY2013 budget proposal. Congressman Scott Garrett asked Zients a simple question: "If we pass this budget tomorrow, when does the budget balance in this country under your proposal?" Zients began his reply, "We achieve significant progress..." Garrett cut him off and demanded to know "just the year." After floundering around further, Zients stammered, "That's not a year question." Incredulous, Garrett asked, "Is it your answer that this budget never balances?" Committee Chairman Paul Ryan then interceded, saying, "Time for the gentleman is expired. Witness is obviously not going to answer the question."[2]

There was a reason Zients wouldn't respond to the question—because the true answer would be, "President Obama's budget will never balance."

THE ECONOMY "SHUTS DOWN IN 2027"

Treasury Secretary Timothy Geithner's testimony before Congress two days later was no more reassuring. Paul Ryan asked him, "Do you think this budget averts the deterioration of our fiscal problem?" Geithner responded, "We're not claiming this solves all the problems facing the country. But it does meet the critical essential test ... of restoring our deficits to a more sustainable position for the next ten years."

Ryan then produced the following chart of the projected results of Obama's budget:[3]

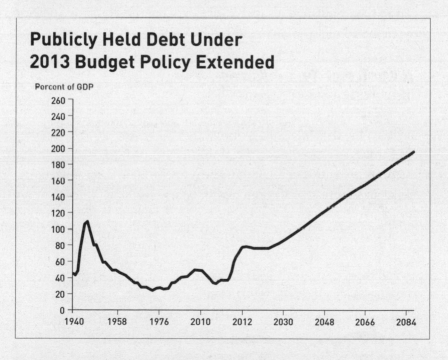

Publicly Held Debt Under 2013 Budget Policy Extended

Percent of GDP

Holding up the chart, Ryan said, "I just don't see the rhetoric matching the results.... Out of your budget ... you say that—this is your budget—says that the government's position gradually deteriorates, that our fiscal condition deteriorates. These are *your* numbers.... This is *your* deficit path."

Geithner claimed the chart showed "just exactly what I said, which is if you look at 2012, for the next 10 years, it stabilizes that debt burden as a share of the economy."

Amazed, Ryan asked, "And so we'll just allow it to take off after that?"

Geithner replied, "No, no. No. And then … and then you're right, and as millions of Americans more retire, then those costs in Medicare and Medicaid start to increase again. And that's why we're saying openly and directly to you, that we're gonna have some work to do."

Geithner then criticized Ryan's Path to Prosperity budget plan, saying, "You would lower that path—in ways that would substantially increase the burden of health care costs on middle-income seniors. And although we agree with you we're gonna have more work to do, but we're not gonna adopt an approach that would undermine that basic benefit…"

Ryan then presented his own chart showing the dramatic contrast between the administration's plan and his own:

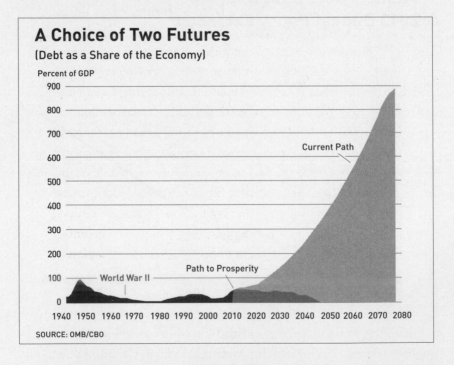

Ryan pointed out that under the administration's current approach of ignoring entitlement reform and continuing to accrue trillion-dollar deficits, the CBO tells us that the economy "shuts down in 2027."

Geithner implied that what follows after 2020 is largely irrelevant, that all we should be focusing on today is what happens between 2010 and 2020, and that there is a "pretty small gap" between the two approaches during those years. In other words, the administration's budget only addresses the next ten years and we'll deal with what comes after that later.

Ryan would have none of it, saying,

> Here's the point: leaders are supposed to fix problems. We have a $99.4 trillion unfunded liability. Our government is making promises to Americans that it has no way of accounting for them. And so you're saying, yeah, we're stabilizing it but we're not fixing it in the long run. That means we're just gonna keep lying to people. We're gonna keep all these empty promises going. And so what we're saying is, in order to avert a debt crisis, I mean, you're the treasury secretary... if we can't make good on our bonds in the future, who's gonna invest in our country?
>
> We do not want to have a debt crisis. And so it comes down to confidence and trajectory. Do we have confidence that we're getting our fiscal situation under control and we're preventing the debt from getting at these catastrophic levels?... You're showing that you have no plan to get this debt under control. You're saying we'll stabilize it but then it's just gonna shoot back up. And so my argument is, that's Europe. That is bringing us toward a European debt crisis because we're showing the world, the credit markets, future seniors, people who are organizing their lives around the promises that are being made to them today, we don't have a plan to make good on this.[4]

Notably, Geithner did not deny Ryan's point that the administration's budget is nothing more than a band-aid—if that—to make the fiscal situation slightly less catastrophic over the next ten years, and does nothing to address the years thereafter, when the unfunded liabilities will come due and place the United States in an immediate crisis. "Maybe we're not disagreeing in a sense that I made it absolutely clear that what our budget does is get our deficits down to a sustainable path over the budget window," said Geithner.

Ryan then interjected, "And then they take back off."

Geithner responded,

> And ... let's talk to ourselves why do they take off again? Why do they do that? Because we have millions of Americans retiring every day and that will drive a substantial growth in health care costs. And so you were right to say we're not coming before you today to say we have a definitive solution to that long-term problem. But what we do know is we don't like yours because ... what yours would do is put an undue burden on middle-income seniors and substantially raise the burden on them for rising health care costs.[5]

Ryan shot back, "We're fine that you don't like our path. That's what politics and Republicans and Democrats and difference of opinions are all about. But if we don't come up with a plan for this country we're gonna pull the rug out from under people who are relying on these benefits."

Ryan also refuted Geithner's glib argument that Ryan's plan would allow seniors to wither on the vine, saying, "Now, we don't agree with your interpretation of our plan because we provide more for the poor and the middle-income and less for the wealthy. And we think that's the smart way to go on funding these important guaranteed programs."[6]

"IT'S DEEPLY DISTRESSING THAT THE CUTS WE AGREED TO ... YOU HAVE ELIMINATED IN THIS BUDGET"

In a separate budgetary meeting before the Senate Committee on the Budget, Geithner was forced by Senator Jeff Sessions to admit that the administration has no plan to address the nation's unsustainable long-term fiscal path. "Even if Congress were to enact this budget, we would still be left with—in the outer decades as millions of Americans retire—what are still unsustainable commitments in Medicare and Medicaid," said Geithner. "And we are going to have to find ways to come together and make progress on those commitments." He claimed that the administration's plan would make the budget sustainable for the next ten years and "give us some time to figure out how we resolve our major differences and how to make sure we reform Medicare and Medicaid in a responsible way."[7]

But time is just an excuse. Ryan produced his "roadmap" for restructuring entitlements in 2008, his original Path to Prosperity budget plan in April 2011, and his updated Path to Prosperity 2.0 plan in March 2012, while the administration still has presented no plan to reform entitlements. Obama's team doesn't even dispute that Ryan's plan would restore America's long-term solvency, but Obama refuses to endorse it because he would apparently prefer to bankrupt the nation before agreeing to a sound, fair Republican plan to restructure entitlements.

Sessions then strongly criticized the administration for having already breached its recent promises regarding budget cuts—which illustrates the futility in compromising with Democrats. Sessions commented, "It's deeply distressing that the cuts we agreed to six months ago you have eliminated in this budget. And you're not marking to them, and you increased spending. And even when you count the war savings [billions in illusory savings from withdrawing troops from Iraq and Afghanistan], which are bogus, the CBO will technically agree with that, but we know the other committees haven't counted those, you will have an increase in spending."[8]

"THIS WOULD CAUSE U.S. INDEBTEDNESS TO EXPLODE"

Ryan's warnings to Geithner about the U.S. bond markets deserve attention. James Pethokoukis, the Money and Politics columnist for Reuters, reported that the White House often quotes the outside economic-analysis firm "Macroeconomic Advisers." But back in July 2011, shortly after Congressman Ryan unveiled his first Path to Prosperity budget, the firm seemed to validate Ryan's concerns. It issued a statement declaring,

> Assuming current fiscal policies remain in force, our economic model suggests that interest rates will rise considerably over the next decade, with the yield on the 10-year Treasury note

reaching nearly 9% by 2021. Private interest rates will rise as federal borrowing competes for savings that might otherwise finance private investment. In addition, yields could rise if there is growing risk associated with current fiscal policy. If such risk is systemic, it raises yields generally. If it reflects a growing probability of sovereign default, it raises Treasury yields relative to private yields. Rising rates would be a precursor to something worse: a full-fledged fiscal crisis with further sharp increases in yields, declines in stock prices, and a plummeting dollar.

Pethokoukis then noted,

This is bad. Really bad. The official budget forecasts one typically hears about in the media are from the Congressional Budget Office. And those forecasts assume Uncle Sam can borrow at low interest rates, like, forever. The super-cautious CBO baseline predicts the U.S. government will add an additional $6.8 trillion in debt over the next decade, bringing cumulative debt held by the public to $18.2 trillion. Debt as a share of the economy would be 76.7 percent. The forecast also assumes short-term interest rates 3.3 percent, long-term 4.8 percent.

But, said Pethokoukis, Macroeconomic Advisers thinks long-term rates will reach 9 percent. "This," he argued, "would cause U.S. indebtedness to explode."

To confirm all this, Pethokoukis reported, Ryan asked the CBO to forecast how various interest rate scenarios would affect U.S. debt. The results were startling. If interest rates rose to 9 percent, it would add an additional $5 trillion to the national debt by 2021. But even this may understate the problem because the calculations were based on the CBO's baseline forecast. Many analysts believe that's way too optimistic and that the debt-to-GDP ratio will already be 101 percent in 2021, even with low interest rates. Furthermore, these static calculations did not factor in the possibility that this astronomical debt would depress economic growth.

In response to Ryan's questions, the CBO conceded that economic variables would have a dramatic impact on the forecasts. It said that a rise in interest rates of just 1 percent a year could increase deficits by $1.3 trillion over ten years. Likewise, reduced economic growth of just 0.1 percent each year could increase deficits by $310 billion over ten years, and a 1 percent annual rise in inflation could add nearly $900 billion to deficits. The result of this "alternative fiscal scenario" is that our debt-to-GDP ratio could reach 250 percent.[9] Here is the CBO's chart illustrating these nightmare scenarios:

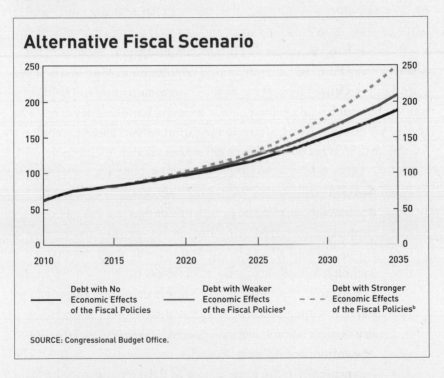

Alternative Fiscal Scenario

| | Debt with No Economic Effects of the Fiscal Policies | Debt with Weaker Economic Effects of the Fiscal Policies[a] | Debt with Stronger Economic Effects of the Fiscal Policies[b] |

SOURCE: Congressional Budget Office.

Contrary to what Team Obama would have you believe, our current deficits do not stem from unduly low tax rates on the wealthy or anyone else; our current taxes are no lower, and in some cases are higher, than under President George W. Bush—and Bush's deficits were dramatically lower. These deficits largely arise from Obama's profligate spending—

though, it's important to note, that is not the sole cause. Another important factor, which accounts for hundreds of billions of dollars in budgetary shortfalls, is the sluggishness of the economy, which is contributing to a constricted economic base that generates less productivity and income and thus less tax revenue. Obama's oppressive tax and regulatory policies across the board are devastating to jobs, to economic growth, and ultimately to the budget as well.

To address the problem, we don't necessarily have to adopt every jot and tittle of Ryan's plan. But it is specific and warrants serious consideration. We must either implement Ryan's plan or another that does just as good a job stimulating economic growth, slashing domestic spending, preserving our vital national defenses, and restructuring entitlements while preserving benefits for seniors and others most dependent on them.

Ryan's Path to Prosperity—both its original and revised versions—deserves more than the administration's contemptuous dismissals. It is a sound and sensible strategy for stabilizing the economy, stimulating economic growth, and eliminating our looming national debt crisis. The revised version 2.0, which is largely the same as the original except for a few important tweaks such as with Medicare, would:

- Cut $5.3 trillion in government spending over the next decade compared to the president's budget.
- Eliminate hundreds of duplicative programs, ban earmarks, and aim to bring non-security discretionary spending to levels below those of 2008.
- Reduce government spending to lower than 20 percent of GDP, as distinguished from President Obama's budgets, in which spending sometimes exceeds 22 percent and even 23 percent over the next decade.
- Dramatically reduce the national deficits and put the budget on the path to balance and actually pay off the national debt.
- Reject Obama's proposed tax increases and simplify the tax code by substituting two personal income tax rates (10 percent and 25 percent) for the six current rates and

by reducing the corporate income tax rate from 35 percent to 25 percent.

- End corporate welfare by stopping taxpayer bailouts of failed financial institutions, reforming Fannie Mae and Freddie Mac, and preventing Washington from picking the winners and losers across sectors of the economy.

- Repeal and defund Obamacare, thus eliminating some $800 billion in tax increases and the budget-busting spending increases it imposes, which have turned out to be much higher than Obama originally projected.

- Reject Obama's proposals for across-the-board cuts in national defense funding and provide $554 billion for national defense spending in FY2013, which is a realistic amount to achieve America's military goals and strategies. This plan allows for future real growth in defense spending to modernize our armed forces. Because of the sequester imposed by the Budget Control Act, our defense budget is in line to be cut by $55 billion in January 2013, pursuant to Obama's budget. Ryan's plan would eliminate these additional cuts and replace them with other spending cuts.

- End Obama's war on domestic energy and remove regulatory and tax barriers on the energy industry.

- Reform Medicaid by converting the federal share of Medicaid spending into a block grant, giving states the flexibility to tailor their own programs to fit their citizens' needs.

- Restructure Medicare by protecting those in and near retirement and giving younger Americans choices such as a traditional fee-for-service Medicare plan or other options that are currently enjoyed by Congress members.

- Call for bipartisan action to restore Social Security to solvency.[10]

The first of the following three charts shows the stark contrast between Ryan's Path to Prosperity 2.0 and President Obama's FY2013 budget.[11] The second contrasts government spending as a share of the economy under the president's budget over the next decade with that under the Path to Prosperity 2.0,[12] and the third contrasts the respective spending trajectories of Ryan's Roadmap and our current spending path over the long term:[13]

A Contrast in Visions

	The President's Budget	The Path to Prosperity
Spending	Net $1.5 trillion increase to current policy	Cuts spending by $5 trillion relative to President's budget
Taxes	Imposes a $1.9 trillion tax increase; Adds new complexity and new hurdles for hard-working taxpayers, making it more difficult to expand opportunity	Prevents President's tax increase; Reforms broken tax code to make it simple, fair and competitive; Clears out special interest loopholes and lowers everybody's tax rates to promote growth
Deficits	Four straight trillion-dollar deficits; Breaks promise to cut deficit in half by end of first term; Budget never balances	Brings deficits below 3 percent of GDP by 2015; Reduces deficits by over $3 trillion relative to President's budget; Puts budget on path to balance
Debt	Adds $11 trillion to the debt—increasing debt as a share of the economy—over the next decade; Imposes $200,000 debt burden per household; Debt skyrockets in the years ahead	Reduces debt as a share of the economy over the next decade; Charts a sustainable trajectory by reforming the drivers of the debt; Pays off the debt over time
Size of Government	Size of government never falls below 23 percent of the economy, making it more difficult to expand opportunity	Brings size of government to 20 percent of economy by 2015, allowing the private sector to grow and create jobs
National Security	Slashes defense spending by nearly $500 billion; Threatens additional cuts by refusing to specify plan of action to address the sequester; Forces troops and military families to pay the price for Washington's refusal to address drivers of debt	Prioritizes national security by preventing deep indiscriminate cuts to defense; Identifies strategy-driven savings, while funding defense at levels that keep Americans safe by providing $544 billion for the next fiscal year for national defense spending
Health Security	Doubles down on health care law, allowing government bureaucrats to interfere with patient care; Empowers an unaccountable board of 15 unelected bureaucrats to cut Medicare in ways that result in restricted access and denied care for current seniors, and a bankrupt future for the next generation	Repeals President's health care law; Advances bipartisan solutions that take power away from government bureaucrats and put patients in control; No disruption for those in or near retirement; Ensures a strengthened Medicare program for future generations, with less support given to the wealthy and more assistance for the poor and sick

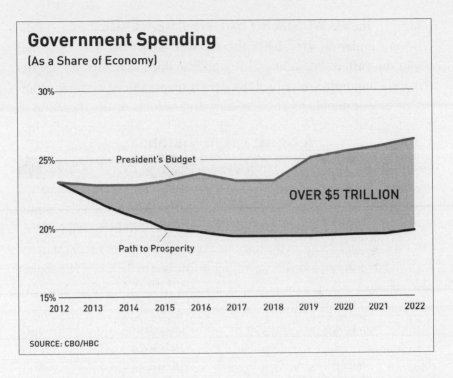

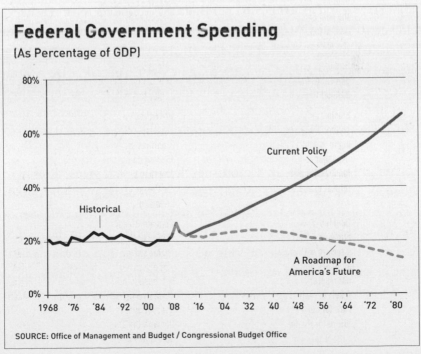

"NO WONDER THAT WE ARE HEADED FOR THE LARGEST DEFICIT EVER"

In contrast to the Ryan and Republican approach, Obama has not seriously attempted to reduce the deficit or debt since he took office, because these problems are necessary byproducts of his addiction to spending and redistribution, as well as his slavish attachment to tired Keynesian economic theories holding that the best way to promote economic growth is through government spending. Even CBO Director Douglas Elmendorf, following a report that the 2011 budget came in at more than $1.5 trillion, in testimony before the Senate Budget Committee in January 2011, admitted what Obama and Timothy Geithner either can't see or can't admit: if we want to avert a debt-driven fiscal calamity, we will have to bring deficit spending under control soon. "The longer that you wait to make those policy changes … the greater the negative consequences [of the national debt] will be," he said.

Echoing Paul Ryan, Elmendorf said that waiting too long to curb spending and reduce the debt could make investors anxious about the government's ability to finance its debt, resulting in higher interest rates, higher taxes, and governmental paralysis in responding to emergencies. Elmendorf warned—and this was in January 2011—that if our current policies continue, the deficit could reach almost 100 percent of GDP by the end of the decade. Committee Chair Kent Conrad, a Democrat, observed, "Spending as a share of our national income is at the highest level in 60 years. Revenue as a share of our national income is at its lowest level in 60 years. No wonder that we are headed for the largest deficit ever."[14]

Yet in his State of the Union speech earlier that week, President Obama's words on the deficits and debt were, as usual, painfully unserious. He called for a five-year freeze on non-mandatory domestic spending (whatever happened to that?) and waxed eloquent about the need to reform entitlements while offering no specifics (and more than a year later, he had still offered no specifics). In fact, in his speech Obama called for *new* government spending on infrastructure, education, and research to help boost job creation—funding he would call for again, unimaginatively, in his next State of the Union speech.[15] Far from pleas for austerity, Obama was demanding more profligacy and merely paying lip service to a domestic spending freeze and entitlement reform.

Unveiled a few weeks later, Obama's FY2012 budget contained the same disappointing features he signaled in his State of the Union speech. Illustrating that the deficit and debt problems were low priorities, Obama didn't mention the word "debt" until thirty-five minutes into his remarks.[16] He again called for the five-year domestic-spending freeze, which Paul Ryan had warned would not be enough to solve the debt crisis. Indeed, Obama's budget would have reduced budget deficits over the next decade by $1.1 trillion, only a quarter of the amount proposed by his own Bipartisan Debt Commission ($4 trillion),[17] whose recommendations he mostly ignored despite having promised he would be "standing with them."

Obama touted budget "cuts" that were mere smoke and mirrors and gimmicks. First, he redefined Pell grants as mandatory spending instead of discretionary spending, thus taking it "off budget" for the manipulative purpose of selling his plan. Without this bogus re-categorization, discretionary spending would have increased by $14 billion. He similarly reclassified $54 billion of surface transportation from discretionary to mandatory spending, and he resorted to his all-purpose gimmick of touting "savings" from Iraq and Afghanistan. Obama's sham accounting on these three items alone made discretionary spending appear to be $106.2 billion lower than it actually was. An honest rendering showed that his budget didn't cut discretionary spending at all, but increased it by $31 billion.[18]

Considering the nation's financial straits, Obama's FY2012 budget was disgraceful. He proposed $3.73 trillion total spending for the fiscal year (25 percent of GDP, the highest levels since World War II); $46 trillion in spending over the next decade, including $8.7 trillion of new spending; and $26.3 trillion in total new debt by 2021,[19] including entitlement obligations, which he made no effort to reduce. All in all, as our financial condition became more dire, his approach stayed exactly the same—as it would the following year.

"WE WILL NOT BE ADDING MORE TO THE NATIONAL DEBT"

Grossly mischaracterizing his FY2012 budget as a prescription for austerity, Obama declared that his plan "puts us on a path to pay for what we spend by the middle of the decade." The statement clearly implied he would balance the budget within four or five years, though as ABC News' Jake Tapper correctly noted, "At no point in the president's 10-year projection would the U.S. government spend less than it's taking in."[20] But Obama claimed, "We will not be adding more to the national debt.... We're not going to be running up the credit card any more." I responded in my syndicated column,

> Now juxtapose that sentence with the facts, even as he presents them. He has pledged to freeze—at already unacceptably high levels—domestic spending for five years. What cuts he would make over the next 10 years would only total $1.1 trillion—an average of just over $100 billion a year. Look at Obama's own budget deficit projections for the next decade, beginning with 2012. 2012: $1.101 trillion, 2013: $768 billion, 2014: $645 billion, 2015: $607 billion, 2016: $649 billion, 2017: $627 billion, 2018: $619 billion, 2019: $681 billion, 2020: $735 billion, 2021: $774 billion. Total for 10 years: $7.205 trillion—an average deficit of $720 billion per year.
>
> You simply cannot square these numbers with Obama's statement that he wouldn't be adding to the debt, unless he's actually confused about the difference between "deficits" and "debt," and that's almost as scary a thought as the numbers themselves. That is, when you operate at staggering deficits

that will add almost three-quarters of a trillion dollars to the debt each year, you are adding to the national debt; you are continuing to run up the national credit card. A third-grader could understand that. So tell me: What do you make of a man who presents a projected 10-year budget that, best case, would add $7.205 trillion to the national debt but simultaneously tells you he won't add to the debt?[21]

The president's refusal to address the deficit, debt, and entitlement problems is astonishing given his declaration early in his term, "I didn't come here to pass our problems to the next President or the next generation— I'm here to solve them." The administration's own summary budget tables, comparing budgeted receipts to budgeted outlays year by year, made the point strikingly clear:

2010: Receipts: 2,163 [Billion Dollars] / Outlays: 3,456 [Billion Dollars]
2011: Receipts: 2,174 [Billion Dollars] / Outlays: 3,819 [Billion Dollars]
2012: Receipts: 2,627 [Billion Dollars] / Outlays: 3,729 [Billion Dollars]
2013: Receipts: 3,003 [Billion Dollars] / Outlays: 3,771 [Billion Dollars]
2014. Receipts: 3,333 [Billion Dollars] / Outlays: 3,977 [Billion Dollars]
2015: Receipts: 3,583 [Billion Dollars] / Outlays: 4,190 [Billion Dollars]
2016: Receipts: 3,819 [Billion Dollars] / Outlays: 4,468 [Billion Dollars]
2017: Receipts: 4,042 [Billion Dollars] / Outlays: 4,669 [Billion Dollars]
2018: Receipts: 4,257 [Billion Dollars] / Outlays: 4,876 [Billion Dollars]
2019: Receipts: 4,473 [Billion Dollars] / Outlays: 5,154 [Billion Dollars]
2020: Receipts: 4,686 [Billion Dollars] / Outlays: 5,422 [Billion Dollars]
2021: Receipts: 4,923 [Billion Dollars] / Outlays: 5,697 [Billion Dollars][22]

AN ADDITIONAL $80,000 OF DEBT PER HOUSEHOLD

On top of this already depressing news, the Congressional Budget Office found that Obama's budget request had significantly understated costs and deficits. Obama projected that his budget would generate

$7.2 trillion in deficits—which would have been reckless enough—but the CBO calculated deficits of $9.5 trillion—a staggering figure that exceeds the entire accumulated federal debt from the beginning of the Republic through 2010. While Obama routinely eviscerated President George W. Bush for his annual deficits, Obama's deficits have dwarfed Bush's. When Bush implemented his tax cuts, his FY2003 budget deficit was $377 billion, and within four years it had shrunk to $161 billion.[23] Obama's deficits for the first four years have exceeded or will exceed $1 trillion, and there appears to be no end in sight. Looking at the next decade, based on Obama's FY2012 budget proposal (FY2013 would show little, if any improvement), the CBO indicated that his deficits would never fall short of $748 billion and will start skyrocketing again in the out years, reaching as high as $1.2 trillion by 2021—and this assumed there would be no major military conflicts to finance.

This merely confirmed the obvious: that revenues from Obama's tax increases—he would raise taxes by 1.3 percent of GDP—could never keep up with his spending hikes of 4 percent of GDP, even assuming a static analysis with no suppression of growth based on these tax hikes. As long as he refuses to tackle entitlements, the deficit simply cannot be controlled. Over the next ten years, according to these numbers, Obama would pile an additional $80,000 per household of debt onto American families.[24]

Try as they might, Obama's team could not defend his deficits. During her Senate confirmation hearing on March 17, 2011, Heather Higginbottom, Obama's nominee for deputy director of OMB, was told by Senator Jeff Sessions, "In years 8, 9 and 10 it [Obama's budget proposal] goes up every year and reaches approximately $900 billion from $600 billion, as a low point in the entire 10 years." He continued, "The highest debt Bush ever had was $450 billion. You don't have a single year when the budget falls below $600 billion do you?"[25]

Higginbottom replied, "That's correct, and Senator, both the president and the director have talked repeatedly about these being the first steps we need to take, and we need to come together in a bipartisan fashion as the chairman and some of his other colleagues are doing to look at these long-term issues. So this isn't the end of the road." She insisted, "The president's budget is the first step in the budget process."

While Higginbottom attempted to deflect equal responsibility for these deficits onto Republicans, the figures in question came directly from Obama's budget. His own proposals out of the gate showed these enormous deficits, so even had Republicans sprinted across the aisle and embraced them in toto, the deficits would remain at these unsustainable levels.

Sessions also asked Higginbottom about assertions by Obama and his budget director, Jacob Lew, that Obama's budget wouldn't add to the debt. When Higginbottom began an evasive response, Sessions pressed, "No, I asked you, heard by the American people, is that a true statement or not?" Higginbottom replied, "I can't express how the American people would hear that. What I can say is of course the interest payments on the debt will add to the debt."

Higginbottom later tried to deflect this question through a Clintonian parsing of the meaning of words. "I'd like to explain what they are referring to," she explained. "Both the president and the director are referring to an effort to pay for the programs the government's operating costs as they're proposed. That's a concept of primary balance, which I know you and the director have discussed. That notion doesn't speak to the interest payments. When the president came to office it was a $1.3 trillion deficit. We have to borrow money to pay on that deficit."

Sessions responded, "Did Mr. Lew or the president of the United States, when they made that statement, we will not be adding to the debt, did they say, by the way American people, what we really meant is some arcane idea about not counting interest payments that the United States must make as part of our debt? Did they say that?" Higginbottom answered, "I'm not sure exactly what they did say."[26]

So we were left with Obama's nominee for this crucial position telling us that when Obama said he wouldn't add to the national debt, he really meant that he wouldn't add to the "primary balance"—a manufactured, meaningless term obviously designed to deceive the public by ignoring interest payments that must be made with the very same green-backs as primary debts or principal payments.

"BLISTERING PARTISANSHIP AND
MULTIPLE DISTORTIONS"

For those who believed claims by Barack Obama and his top officials that they sought a bipartisan solution to our fiscal problems, the administration's venomous response to the unveiling of Paul Ryan's original Path to Prosperity plan must have been a real eye-opener.

In a speech at George Washington University on April 13, 2011, Obama neither soberly considered Ryan's plan nor presented an alternative one; he just engaged in Chicago-style attacks and insults, actually disparaging Ryan's and the Republicans' human decency. "Their vision is less about reducing the deficit than it is about changing the basic social compact in America," Obama proclaimed. He accused Republicans of pitting "children with autism or Down's syndrome" against "every millionaire and billionaire in our society." Claiming the plan would "end Medicare as we know it," he bitterly remarked, "There's nothing courageous about asking for sacrifice from those who can least afford it and don't have any clout on Capitol Hill." He continued,

> They paint a vision of our future that's deeply pessimistic. It's a vision that says if our roads crumble and our bridges collapse, we can't afford to fix them. If there are bright young Americans who have the drive and the will but not the money to go to college, we can't afford to send them.... It's a vision that says America can't afford to keep the promise we've made to care for our seniors.... This is a vision that says up to 50 million Americans have to lose their health insurance in order for us to reduce the deficit.... Worst of all, this is a vision that says even though America can't afford to invest in education or clean energy; even though we can't afford to care for seniors and poor children, we can somehow afford more than $1 trillion in new tax breaks for the wealthy.[27]

Obama then outlined his own "plan," which was no plan at all—there were no specifics, just his usual empty promises, platitudes, and misrepresentations.

In the speech, Obama once again blamed America's fiscal problems on President George W. Bush and his "two wars." He also faulted Bush's prescription drug entitlement, even though the Democrats' alternative plan at the time was projected to cost far more than Bush's.[28]

Obama also had the audacity to acknowledge that "around two-thirds of our budget is spent on Medicare, Medicaid, Social Security, and national security," yet he showed no real willingness to tackle any of those, save national security. After those categories and interest on the debt, he said, all that's left is 12 percent of the budget, and that so far the cuts proposed by Washington politicians "have focused almost exclusively on that 12%." Note that Obama made this charge in response to Paul Ryan's plan, which comprehensively addresses the other 88 percent and was shrilly denounced by Democrats for that very reason.

The *Wall Street Journal*'s editorial board called Obama's jeremiad "extraordinary," with "its blistering partisanship and multiple distortions ... the kind Presidents usually outsource to some junior lieutenant." They noted that Obama's initial political goal was to defuse criticism about his unseriousness on the debt—unseriousness shown by his $3.73 trillion budget and his dismissal of the fiscal commission's recommendations, even while reports were confirming that his deficit for the preceding year was at an all-time high.[29]

When Congressional Budget Office director Doug Elmendorf was asked in congressional hearings how Obama's spending blueprint—as laid out in his speech at George Washington University—would affect the budget framework, Elmendorf replied, "We don't estimate speeches," which served as a fitting and devastating metaphor for Obama's approach to the budget.[30]

In the end, although Obama may have made progress in demonizing Paul Ryan, he was less successful in advocating his own budget plans; despite all his posturing, he couldn't get even one member of his own party in the Senate to vote for his FY2012 budget proposal, which went down in an embarrassing 97–0 defeat in May 2011.[31] This kind of unanimity is becoming a habit for Obama's budgets—less than a year later, the House rejected his FY2013 budget proposal by a perfect 414–0 margin.[32] That alone, in saner times, would have been enough to ensure Obama's defeat in 2012.

A SHEEP IN HAWK'S CLOTHING

In his budget battles, Obama consistently masquerades as a deficit hawk even as he resists budget cuts and demands more spending. On July 15, 2011, Paul Ryan, referring to yet another of Obama's feints toward frugality, summarized what Obama had actually done since taking office in 2009. Ryan noted that Obama had initiated a 24 percent increase in non-discretionary spending, which would add $734 billion in spending over the next ten years. Under his budgets, the government was spending some 24 percent of GDP when it had historically averaged slightly above 20 percent. Under his FY2012 budget, according to the CBO, he would never spend less than 23 percent of GDP in ten years, and at the end of the ten years it would climb back to 24 percent. This pattern, it should be noted, would be repeated in his FY2013 budget: applying temporary fiscal band-aids and letting the debt gush out later, after he will be long gone from office.

Ryan provided a table from the CBO to illustrate the reckless allocations Obama has made to increase the base budgets for major government agencies. People tend to forget that while Obama pretends Republicans are demanding extreme austerity and want to cut off essential services, Obama had increased the base budgets for his pet agencies both in his stimulus bill, which should have had nothing to do with such expenditures, and in his yearly budgets. Most of this new spending was special interest spending for domestic government agencies. One "egregious" example, noted Ryan, was that the EPA's budget increased by 36 percent in just two years, and if you include the $7 billion stimulus injection, it enjoyed a two-year increase of 131 percent. These spending increases are shown in the following CBO table.[33]

Table 2: Discretionary Spending by Government Agency
Scored Non-Emergency BA (in Millions of Dollars)

	2008	2009	Stimulus	2010	2011	Base Budget Growth 08-10	Total with Stimulus 08-10	Base Budget Growth 10-11
Agency								
Agriculture	20,853	23,149	12,480	26,080	22,214	25.1%	84.9%	-14.8%
Commerce	6,827	9,252	7,936	13,852	5,762	102.9%	219.1%	-58.4%
Corps of Engineers	5,600	5,403	4,600	5,445	4,868	-2.8%	79.4%	-10.6%
Defense	479,203	511,070	7,435	530,690	528,997	10.7%	12.3%	-0.3%
Education	57,412	57,745	97,407	63,715	67,401	11.0%	180.6%	5.8%
Energy	24,149	26,459	38,735	26,634	25,585	10.3%	170.7%	-3.9%
EPA	7,590	7,645	7,220	10,298	8,699	35.7%	130.8%	-15.5%
Health & Human Services	72,976	77,393	22,397	83,656	72,956	14.6%	45.3%	-12.8%
Homeland Security	34,851	41,746	2,755	40,963	41,769	17.5%	25.4%	2.0%
Housing Urban Dev	37,671	41,291	13,625	46,049	41,177	22.2%	58.4%	-10.6%
Interior	11,150	11,195	3,005	12,069	11,643	8.2%	35.2%	-3.5%
International Assistance	21,323	15,647	38	21,885	21,866	2.6%	2.8%	-0.1%
Judicial Branch	5,812	6,070	0	6,428	6,487	10.6%	10.6%	0.9%
Justice	21,102	23,351	4,002	23,924	21,468	13.4%	32.3%	-10.3%
Labor	11,508	12,328	4,806	13,532	12,486	17.6%	59.4%	-7.7%
Legislative Branch	4,035	4,466	25	4,735	4,615	17.3%	18.0%	-2.5%
NASA	17,110	17,702	1,002	18,723	18,404	9.4%	15.2%	-1.3%
NSF	6,032	6,490	3,002	6,927	6,874	14.8%	64.6%	-0.8%
Indep. Agencies & Allowances	5,884	10,378	6,984	11,766	7,898	100.0%	218.7%	-32.9%
Social Security	8,168	8,530	1,002	9,284	9,035	13.7%	25.9%	-2.7%
State Department	11,357	20,562	564	26,371	26,164	132.2%	137.2%	-0.8%
Transportation	10,733	13,390	48,120	21,382	13,780	99.2%	547.6%	-35.6%
Treasury	11,997	12,690	187	13,463	13,105	12.2%	13.8%	-2.7%
Veterans	39,416	47,606	1,401	53,040	56,449	34.6%	38.1%	6.4%
Total	932,767	1,011,638	288,728	1,090,911	1,049,782	17.0%	47.9%	-3.8%

Source: Congressional Budget Office Score of Enacted Appropriations

"THERE'S STILL NOTHING OUT THERE.
WHY NOT JUST RELEASE THE PLAN?"

Obama repeatedly claimed that Republicans had offered no plan to reduce the deficit and debt and were only criticizing his plans, which was an extraordinary display of projection, even for Obama. In fact, the GOP-controlled House had advanced numerous substantive proposals, including Ryan's Path to Prosperity and the Cut, Cap, and Balance Act, both of which Obama and his Democratic colleagues roundly rejected.

When pressed during the budget negotiations, White House press secretary Jay Carney floundered when trying to explain why Obama hadn't produced a detailed plan to tackle the debt. One reporter asked, "There's still nothing out there. Why not just release the plan?"

Carney replied, "You need something printed for you, you can't write it down?"

The questioner retorted, "It's not a plan. No, it's not a plan.... It wasn't a plan the same way that we're getting a plan on the House side or that we're getting a plan on the Senate side. It's not."[34]

The House passed Ryan's plan 235–189 on April 15, 2011, with no Democrats supporting the measure and only four Republicans voting against it.[35] The Senate voted down Ryan's plan on May 25, 2011, by a 57–40 vote, with five Republicans voting with Democrats, though one of those, Senator Rand Paul, voted no because he didn't believe the spending cuts went far enough. Paul Ryan later responded that the Senate's action represented an "irresponsible abdication of leadership."[36]

During the acrimonious debt-ceiling debates, the Republican House made certain demands as a condition to agreeing, yet again, to increase the debt ceiling. Democrats argued this was petty partisan politics, but in fact the Republicans, having no majority in the Senate and facing a recalcitrant Democratic president, had limited options to press for fiscal responsibility. Obama and the Democrats bitterly resisted major spending cuts and insisted only on tax hikes on the "wealthy," which wouldn't have made a dent in the deficit and would have been devastating to an ailing economy. Among the Republicans' demands was that the president agree to their cut, cap, and balance proposal. The plan was to *cut* the deficit in half the next year through discretionary and mandatory spending reductions; implement statutory enforceable *caps* to align federal spending with average revenues at 18 percent of GDP with automatic spending reductions to be triggered if the caps are violated; and to send the states a *balanced budget amendment*, which would include protections against tax increases and a spending limitation amendment that would align spending with average revenues.[37]

Rejecting all the GOP proposals on sight, Obama, in a *Today Show* interview in June, found a creative scapegoat for the sluggish economy: ATMs. Speaking as if the machines had just materialized since his inauguration, Obama declared, "There are some structural issues with our economy, where a lot of businesses have learned to become much more efficient with a lot fewer workers. You see it when you go to a bank and you use an ATM, you don't go to a bank teller… or you go to the airport and you use a kiosk instead of checking in at the gate. So all these things have created changes."[38] A few months later, the *IBD* editorial page listed all the things which Obama had blamed for his economic failures, including President Bush, ATMs, Republicans, gridlock, the media, businesses, and "misfortune."[39] The editors omitted a few others, such as the Gulf oil spill and the Japanese tsunami.

During a presidential press conference on June 29, Obama condescendingly chided Congress for not working out a compromise on the debt ceiling as punctually as his children do their homework, though he had been AWOL for much of the process, and when he wasn't, he was actually obstructing a reasonably responsible agreement to cut spending. Showing a remarkable degree of self-absorption, Obama detailed how hard he was working to reach a deal, saying he had met Republican leaders and had put Vice President Biden in charge of the effort. Predictably, he concluded that it was all the fault of Republicans; referencing GOP leaders, he exclaimed, "At a certain point, they need to do their job."[40]

"HE IMPERIOUSLY SUMMONED CONGRESSIONAL LEADERS"

On July 15, 2011, Obama strutted out to a press conference to make an indignant announcement that he opposed the Cut, Cap, and Balance Act as well as a balanced budget amendment to the Constitution. As a counterpoint, he focused on raising taxes, saying, "The American people are sold [on tax increases]. The problem is members of Congress are dug in ideologically." He said "poll after poll" showed Republican and Democratic voters want "a balanced approach," including both tax hikes and spending cuts, and warned that the country was "running out of time" to avoid fiscal "Armageddon." As if he'd not been alternatively obstructing and abdicating any leadership role throughout the process, Obama added, "We should not even be this close on a deadline. This is something we should have accomplished earlier."[41]

Unable to get anywhere with Obama, House Republicans passed Cut, Cap, and Balance on July 19 by an almost straight party-line vote, 234–190. Paul Ryan noted that the bill "cuts $5.8 trillion in spending over the next decade, locks in those savings with enforceable caps on spending, and forces Washington to finally live within its means with a Balanced Budget Amendment." Ryan charged that the White House refused to cooperate with Republicans or offer a credible plan of its own and that Senate Democrats had not passed a budget for over eight hundred days (and hundreds more days have passed since then—the last time they passed a budget was April 29, 2009). He warned, "The coming debt crisis is the single most predictable economic disaster in the history of the nation."[42]

Obama had vowed to veto the bill,[43] but that proved unnecessary because the Democratic Senate voted on July 22, by a strict party-line 51–46 vote, to table it. Majority Leader Harry Reid spectacularly denounced the plan as "one of the worst pieces of legislation to ever be placed on the floor of the United States Senate."[44]

Increasingly frustrated that Republicans wouldn't bend to his dictates, Obama, in the words of columnist George Will, "imperiously summoned congressional leaders to his presence: 'I've told them I want them here at 11 a.m.'.... upon what meat doth this our current Caesar feed that he has grown so great that he presumes to command leaders of a coequal branch of government?" Will argued, "The current occupant's vanity and naiveté—a dangerous amalgam—are causing the modern presidency to buckle beneath the weight of its pretenses."

Will also provided a trenchant summary of the debt-ceiling negotiations, praising the "87 House Republican freshman" whose "inflexibility astonishes and scandalizes Washington because it reflects the rarity of serene fidelity to campaign promises" and who, by refusing to roll over to Obama's dictates, had vindicated the separation of powers doctrine and "rescued the nation from Obama's preference for a 'clean' debt-ceiling increase that would ignore the onrushing debt tsunami." Obama said he wondered whether Republicans "can say yes to anything." Will answered this too: "Well, House Republicans said yes to 'cut, cap and balance.' Senate Democrats, who have not produced a budget in more than 800 days, vowed to work all weekend debating this. But Friday they voted to table it, thereby ducking a straightforward vote on the only debt-reduction plan on paper, the only plan debated, the only plan to receive Democratic votes."[45]

"I CANNOT GUARANTEE THAT THOSE CHECKS GO OUT"

The administration constantly resorted to demagoguery to cloak its obstruction of Republican proposals to reduce the deficits and national debt. This was all the more appalling considering Obama's castigation of President George W. Bush for "challenges that have been unaddressed over the previous decade."[46] As the government approached the debt ceiling, Obama began fear-mongering about the United States defaulting on its principal obligations. This was always an unlikely occurrence because even with the ceiling reached, enough revenues would still come in to satisfy our primary obligations. Nevertheless, Obama ratcheted up his rhetoric, threatening to withhold Social Security checks. "I cannot guarantee that those checks go out on August 3rd if we haven't resolved this issue," he warned, "because there may simply not be the money in the coffers to do it."

This was more deception. The government would receive $2.174 trillion in revenues during the year, with Social Security outlays totaling $727 billion, and it had already borrowed money to supplement that $2.174 trillion. So Obama undoubtedly knew there would be plenty of money to service our primary obligations and Social Security benefits.[47]

Meanwhile, Obama invoked class warfare against private jet owners, as if to imply that we couldn't balance the budget as long as we allowed these "tax breaks for the wealthy." But this was another red herring, as eliminating the deduction, even assuming no negative impact on private usage, would yield only about $3 billion in additional revenue, which is 0.075 percent of the $4 trillion in deficit reduction that Obama was allegedly seeking—a statistically insignificant figure.[48]

In typical fashion, Obama, his demagoguery in full tilt, declared, "It's my hope that everybody is gonna leave their ultimatums at the door, that we'll all leave our political rhetoric at the door."[49] Columnist Charles Krauthammer pointedly highlighted Obama's hypocrisy, writing, "And then, from the miasma of gridlock, rises our president, calling upon those unruly congressional children to quit squabbling, stop kicking the can down the road, and get serious about debt."[50]

Incongruously, White House press secretary Jay Carney took time out from the administration's doom-mongering over the debt ceiling to brag about the wonderful state of the economy. In July 2011, he said, "Well, two things remain uncontestably true. The economy is vastly improved from what it was when Barack Obama was sworn into office as president. We were in economic free-fall. There were predictions that we were headed to the second Great Depression."[51] Illustrating the administration's poor record of economic analysis, weeks after Carney's comments, former White House economic advisor Jared Bernstein, who had co-authored the administration's famous report predicting the stimulus would keep unemployment below 8 percent, admitted he was wrong and forecast that unemployment would not fall below 8 percent before the end of 2012.[52]

Meanwhile, as noted previously, our ever-rising national debt led Standard & Poor's to downgrade the United States' credit rating for the first time in ninety-four years, a move Obama promptly blamed on Republican opposition to increasing the debt ceiling. America had retained its credit rating through two world wars, the Great Depression, FDR's New Deal, LBJ's Great Society, and the military buildup of the Cold War, yet S&P found that America's new, unprecedented debt levels warranted a downgrade.[53] Obama responded that when it came to domestic spending and defense, "there's not much further we can cut."[54]

The defense issue aside, it was a revealing look at his worldview. By merely curbing the rate of increase in domestic spending, he believed he had gone way beyond the bounds of reason.

"I MAKE NO APOLOGIES FOR BEING REASONABLE"

Even after the parties agreed to a deal to resolve the budget ceiling impasse, Obama was still champing at the bit to hike spending. As soon as the Budget Control Act of 2011 was passed, Obama announced new spending proposals—under the euphemism "key investments"—which included higher taxes, extended unemployment benefits, and a "national infrastructure bank." As columnist Michelle Malkin observed, "The infrastructure banks would borrow more money the government doesn't have to dole out grants that wouldn't be paid back and don't require interest payments."[55] Essentially, Obama was looking to create an entirely new financial structure to facilitate his profligacy.

Indeed, the debt-ceiling agreement only seemed to make Obama more partisan and combative. On a campaign blitz through Minnesota, Iowa, and Illinois, a frustrated Obama sought to re-fight the just-finished debt battle. He lashed out at all his GOP presidential rivals, saying, "That's just not common sense. You've got to be willing to compromise to move the country forward." He added, "I make no apologies for being reasonable."

Obama failed to mention that the GOP's resistance to his pleas for a tax hike was a perfectly reasonable position, since higher taxes would hinder economic growth and make it even harder to balance the budget. In fact, to agree to *his* plan, which he had demanded because his stubborn ideology required punishing the "rich," was *not* reasonable if the goal was to improve the nation's fiscal position.[56]

At any rate, after the debt-ceiling agreement, Obama demanded yet more spending, this time for his proposed $447 billion jobs bill. The administration claimed the bill would "support"—another meaningless, immeasurable metric—four hundred thousand education jobs via grants to the states. As Hot Air's Ed Morrissey pointed out, the administration used a similar rationale when arguing about all the jobs its original stimulus bill "saved or created." But, he noted, many of the "saved" jobs were bureaucratic ones—not just the teachers, police officers, and fire fighters continually touted by Team Obama—and the stimulus simply enabled the states to delay painful but necessary cost-cutting measures. Morrissey also pointed out that Obama had a calculated political motive for subsidizing these particular employees—many of them belong to Obama-supporting public employee unions such as the SEIU and AFCSME.[57]

In fact, the entire jobs bill was a farce. Obama knew it couldn't pass the GOP-controlled House, but he pushed for it anyway to stoke his leftist base and to position himself to blame Republicans for obstructing his "recovery." Sam Youngman, in *The Hill*, likened the American Jobs Act to Elvis: "The King made $60 million last year even though he died in 1977. The lesson: Just 'cause something is dead doesn't mean it can't be effective. And so it is with President Obama and his jobs bill. It's dead as is." Republican as well as some Democratic leaders had made that clear but, wrote Youngman, "that will not stop Obama from talking about the jobs bill and nothing else. That's because the White House hopes the president's steady drumbeat of 'pass the bill' can become a rallying cry for his supporters even if it doesn't create a single job."

One Democratic strategist noted cynically, "He has to keep this up so long that after people stop thinking it has a chance, they start thinking that he is some sort of crazy for creating jobs. Repetition, repetition, repetition."[58] This charade reached the pinnacle of absurdity when Senate Democrats changed Senate rules in part to avoid a symbolic vote on the jobs bill.[59] Even after Democrats obstructed the vote on his own bill, Obama continued to hammer *Republicans* for obstruction.

"THE FOOD STAMP PRESIDENT"

As documented in *Crimes Against Liberty*, Obama repeatedly breached his promise not to raise taxes of any kind on families making $250,000 or less. He has also flirted with implementing a value-added tax (VAT), which would necessarily obliterate his tax pledge. In an interview with CNBC's John Harwood in April 2010, Obama refused to rule out imposing a VAT, as had his economic advisor Austan Goolsbee.[60] Some have speculated Obama has racked up so much debt, at least in part, to justify enacting a VAT as a desperate deficit-reducing measure—even though a VAT would utterly fail in that role, as seen throughout Europe. On the *Journal Editorial Report* on Fox News Channel, *Wall Street Journal* editorial page editor Paul Gigot mused, "I think the strategy is—has been all along—increase spending, then ultimately, you will have to raise taxes to pay for it. And in a second term, the idea is, try to get a value-added tax, if possible, or a major energy tax. Because they know they can't pay for this spending just by taxing the rich."[61]

Obama's redistributionist philosophy is reflected not only in his tax plans, but in his drastic expansion of welfare programs. Republican presidential candidate Newt Gingrich took heat for calling Barack Obama the "food stamp president," but the evidence supports Gingrich. Judicial Watch reported that the Obama administration rewarded the state of Oregon a $5 million bonus for its efficiency in adding foodstamp recipients to already bulging rolls. This was under the government's Supplemental Nutrition Assistance Program (SNAP) to reduce "food insecure households" by increasing access to food stamps. According to Judicial Watch, the Department of Agriculture has recently launched a multi-million dollar initiative to recruit more food-stamp participants.[62]

Some claim these types of awards date back to the Bush administration.[63] That may be partially true, but the Heritage Foundation reports that between FY2008, the last of President George W. Bush's fiscal years, and FY2011, the average per capita benefit of SNAP almost doubled from $39.3 billion to $75.3 billion (in constant 2011 dollars).[64] The *Wall Street Journal* reported in November 2011 that nearly 15 percent of the U.S. population—45.8 million—received food stamp assistance in the month of August and that food stamp rolls had risen 8.1 percent over the preceding year, according to the Department of Agriculture.[65]

The number of Americans who receive some form of federal government aid has skyrocketed just in the past five years to 67.3 million people, or 21.8 percent (excluding government employees). The following charts show how the percentage was about half that in the 1960s, before President Lyndon Johnson launched his War on Poverty and Great Society programs. The numbers then rose until the mid-1990s, fell slightly, and then rose slightly again during the George W. Bush administration. But during President Obama's term the trajectory has been nearly vertical:[66]

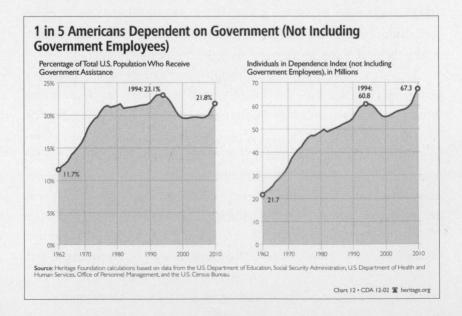

1 in 5 Americans Dependent on Government (Not Including Government Employees)

Percentage of Total U.S. Population Who Receive Government Assistance

Individuals in Dependence Index (not Including Government Employees), in Millions

Source: Heritage Foundation calculations based on data from the U.S. Department of Education, Social Security Administration, U.S. Department of Health and Human Services, Office of Personnel Management, and the U.S. Census Bureau.

Chart 12 • CDA 12-02 ☎ heritage.org

A shocking 70.5 percent of federal spending is now dedicated to dependence programs of one kind or another, and this percentage has grown sharply during Obama's term as well, as shown in the following chart:[67]

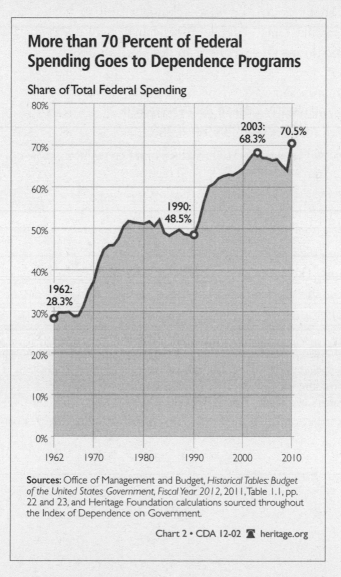

More than 70 Percent of Federal Spending Goes to Dependence Programs

Share of Total Federal Spending

2003: 68.3%

70.5%

1990: 48.5%

1962: 28.3%

Sources: Office of Management and Budget, *Historical Tables: Budget of the United States Government, Fiscal Year 2012*, 2011, Table 1.1, pp. 22 and 23, and Heritage Foundation calculations sourced throughout the Index of Dependence on Government.

Chart 2 • CDA 12-02 ☎ heritage.org

In addition, under President Obama, an even greater percentage of Americans—49.5 percent—is not paying income taxes. Thus, we have more and more Americans depending on federal transfer payments, set against a dwindling number of taxpayers. This trend imperils our national destiny, for the electoral power grows ever stronger among those whose vested interest is in receiving transfer payments from others rather than contributing to society's productivity and wealth. Again, this number has been steadily rising, with intermittent dips, since the 1960s, but it has exploded during Obama's term, as this chart shows:[68]

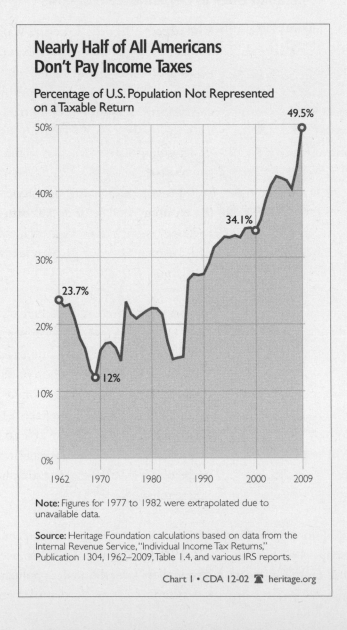

Nearly Half of All Americans Don't Pay Income Taxes

Percentage of U.S. Population Not Represented on a Taxable Return

49.5%

34.1%

23.7%

12%

Note: Figures for 1977 to 1982 were extrapolated due to unavailable data.

Source: Heritage Foundation calculations based on data from the Internal Revenue Service, "Individual Income Tax Returns," Publication 1304, 1962–2009, Table 1.4, and various IRS reports.

Chart 1 • CDA 12-02 ☎ heritage.org

This trend reflects the administration's redistributionist philosophy, but also its nonsensical belief that welfare payments stimulate jobs. When the *Wall Street Journal*'s Laura Meckler asked White House press secretary Jay Carney how exactly extending unemployment insurance creates jobs, Carney issued a reply that sounded like a *Saturday Night Live* parody of Keynesian theory:

> Oh, uh, it is by, uh, I would expect a reporter from the Wall Street Journal would know this as part of the entrance exam. There are few other ways that can directly put money into the economy than applying unemployment insurance. It is one of the most direct ways to infuse money directly into the economy because people who are unemployed and obviously aren't running a paycheck are going to spend the money that they get. They're not going to save it; they're going to spend it. And with unemployment insurance, that way, the money goes directly back into the economy, dollar for dollar virtually. Every place that, that money is spent has added business and that creates growth and income for businesses that leads them to decisions about jobs, more hiring.

Carney estimated that unemployment benefits alone could create up to one million jobs.[69] Unsurprisingly, Obama's Agriculture secretary, Tom Vilsack, just a week later argued that food stamps are a stimulus as well. "I should point out, when you talk about the SNAP program or the food stamp program, you have to recognize that it's also an economic stimulus," Vilsack declared. "Every dollar of SNAP benefits generates $1.84 in the economy in terms of economic activity. If people are able to buy a little more in the grocery store, someone has to stock it, package it, shelve it, process it, ship it. All of those are jobs. It's the most direct stimulus you can get in the economy during these tough times."[70]

OSAWATOMIE PROGRESSIVISM

If there had been any expectation that Obama would set politics aside and begin working toward a bipartisan solution to our entitlement and debt problems, he emphatically removed it in a speech in Osawatomie, Kansas, in December 2011. According to his aides, he chose the location because Teddy Roosevelt had delivered his "New Nationalism" speech there in 1910.

In the speech, Obama invoked Teddy Roosevelt's memory in support of Obama's belief that capitalism just can't work without a beneficent federal government keeping it in check and restraining capitalist predators. He wholly distorted American history to imply that our free market system, which has produced the most economically successful society in history, only worked when progressives had tweaked it. But America's economic problems, especially the ones we are currently facing, have not been caused by unregulated capitalism, but by profligate federal spending, excessive taxation, and overregulation by unaccountable officials and bureaucrats. The problem hasn't been unfettered robber baron capitalists, but an overreaching, over-intrusive federal government that won't let the market breathe.

But Obama needed to allege there were inherent flaws in capitalism itself, in order to support his claim that without his intervention, the system, and its capitalist (read: Republican) exploiters, would gobble up all the wealth for themselves and leave the rest of the American people— Obama's constituents—with nothing. So he doubled down on class warfare, telling some of his fellow Americans just how unfair other Americans are. "Some billionaires have a tax rate as low as one percent," Obama intoned. "One percent. That is the height of unfairness. It is wrong. It's wrong that in the United States of America, a teacher or a nurse or a construction worker, maybe earns $50,000 a year, should pay a higher tax rate than somebody raking in $50 million."

It didn't matter to Obama that what he was saying was untrue—as *Washington Post* fact-checker Glenn Kessler verified when he coaxed an admission from an administration official that the White House had no data to support Obama's claim.[71] What mattered was that it was inflammatory enough to divert attention from our real financial crises. This would be critically important as Obama headed into the final year of his term to face off with Congressman Paul Ryan, once again, on the budget.

REPUBLICANS PASS RYAN BUDGET;
OBAMA GOES BALLISTIC

In February 2012, before Obama submitted his FY2013 budget, Paul Ryan predicted the president would "duck the tough decisions, he's not going to offer a solution to our fiscal problems to our coming debt crisis and he'll probably have sprinkled throughout his budget some of the kind of themes he threw out in the fall and the State of the Union address for his campaign." While pledging that he and the Republicans would present a plan, like they had the year before, to tackle entitlements and reform the tax code, Ryan warned that this would be Obama's fourth budget that failed to offer a solution to the nation's fiscal problems and coming debt crisis. Ryan's words were prophetic.

On March 29, 2012, the House approved Ryan's plan on a 228–191 vote, mostly along party lines. White House spokesman Jay Carney immediately attempted to discredit the bill, claiming it would create "a segmented replacement for Medicare that would burden seniors and end the program as we know it." House Speaker John Boehner shot back that it would set "a course that's sustainable not just for our generation, but for our kids and our grandkids."[72]

In a speech to news executives a few days later, Obama ripped into Republicans and their budget plan, saying they were so radical that even Ronald Reagan wouldn't be able to win the GOP primary today. Decrying Republicans' bleak, backward, "radical vision," Obama denounced the proposal as "thinly veiled social Darwinism." "It is antithetical to our entire history as a land of opportunity and upward mobility for everybody who's willing to work for it," Obama proclaimed, adding that "it's a prescription for decline." He cavalierly instructed the media to report that the parties were not equally to blame, for it was Republicans who were unwilling to compromise.[73]

Meanwhile, as Ryan had predicted, Obama continued steering the economy toward fiscal oblivion, offering no plan of his own to restructure our entitlement programs, which hang like the sword of Damocles over our country.

★ ★ ★

Obama's demagogic response to Ryan's budget had it completely backward, as usual. *He* is the one thwarting equal opportunity and upward mobility; *he* is the one offering a bleak, radical vision that is antithetical to our history; *he* is the one discouraging people from contributing to our society and working, and punishing those who are successful; *he* is the one who has been unwilling to compromise and has ensured our national decline. He and his party are at fault for our economic and financial crises, not Republicans, who have tried in vain to correct our national course.

At a time when attentive Americans are horrified over our nation's fiscal condition and imminent national bankruptcy, Paul Ryan has shown true leadership with a mastery of the budgetary material and a bold, innovative, and realistic plan to restore us on the road not just to fiscal solvency, but to economic growth. His plan is the primary antidote for Obama's destructive vision and agenda. Ryan has made clear that our problems become more intractable with every day we wait to address them. Each day more people reach retirement age, and every year our unfunded liabilities grow at an alarming rate. Experts have warned that we have two or three years at most to get our fiscal house in order. After that, our bond markets will go south and we will end up like Greece and other economic basket cases.

Our choice is either to design the solution ourselves, whereby we limit and manage the pain, or continue to kick the can down the road and eventually suffer a financial collapse, when far worse pain will be forced upon us.

The Obama administration's approach of putting its finger in the dike today and holding it there for ten years while we forever ruminate and posture about possible solutions is reckless and immoral. The president and his economic advisors must be aware of that. Yet all they do is obstruct and demonize those, like Paul Ryan, who are trying to save the nation. The only cuts they can abide are those that ensure the "wealthy" enjoy much less of their own money, and those that slash our defense budget and endanger our national security.

You may or may not support Ryan's proposals, which the Republican Congress has largely embraced, but at least he has presented a serious, comprehensive reform plan. By contrast, Obama has offered no plan to solve or even to address our nation's monumental debt problems.

Obama once proclaimed that he believes in American exceptionalism just as "the Greeks believe in Greek exceptionalism." Well, if America continues on our current fiscal path, we're going to learn firsthand what "Greek exceptionalism" really feels like.

CHAPTER SEVEN

THE WAR ON OIL

O n the campaign trail in 2008, Barack Obama offered a telling glimpse of his outlook on oil. After complaining to CNBC's John Harwood that "we've been consuming energy as if it's infinite," Obama was asked, "So, could these high prices help us?" Without batting an eye, he replied, "I think that I would have preferred a gradual adjustment."[1] So Obama didn't object to high prices per se; he just favored a longer process of price increases.

He had once laid out a similar, gradualist strategy for healthcare reform, telling a group of fellow leftists that he supported a single-payer health insurance system—that is, a government-run system—but cautioning that it might take time to lay the political groundwork for such a change.[2] This is sophisticated, strategic thinking from a central planner determined to bring "fundamental change" to our nation.

Obama's support for higher gas prices reflects his statist, ideological hostility to oil. He dreams of transforming the economy into one that runs on windmills, algae, solar panels, and other forms of alternative energy, with plentiful "green-collar jobs" for all. Although oil is the essential mainstay of U.S. industry, to Obama it's just a dirty fossil fuel that obstructs our transition into a "clean energy" economy. The more expensive and rare oil becomes, the more we will be forced to cultivate other energy sources—or so he believes.

Affecting this transition has become a fundamental goal of Obama's presidency, with tens of billions of taxpayer dollars and countless onerous energy regulations being dedicated to the cause. But it has created political problems for Obama, since Americans don't want higher gas prices and would rather drill for more oil in America than place our faith in windmills and algae—not to mention Middle Eastern tyrants. Nevertheless, by disguising his plans when he must and ramming them through when he can, Obama has greatly hindered U.S. oil production, setting our economy further back at a time we can least afford it.

BOOSTING PRICES TO EUROPE'S LEVELS

One of the core problems of Obama's energy policy is that alternative fuels are nowhere near ready to replace petroleum. "Green" energy sources won't be practical for decades, if ever, and recklessly pursuing them to oil's detriment guarantees energy scarcity, austerity, and malaise for the United States. As columnist Victor Davis Hanson wrote, "So much of this Administration's talk about energy sounds similar to a bull session in the faculty lounge, or what we would expect from lifelong bureaucrats and public functionaries who have never experienced long commutes or struggles in the harsher, profit-driven private workplace."[3]

Obama's energy agenda is spearheaded by Energy Secretary Steven Chu, who said in 2008 that higher gas prices would be useful for coaxing Americans into energy efficient cars and for encouraging them to move closer to their workplaces. "Somehow we have to figure out how to boost the price of gasoline to levels in Europe," Chu said, at a time when gas prices in Europe averaged $8 a gallon.[4]

Chu's statement, issued before he became energy secretary, is not something administration officials are supposed to say in public. So

Obama later declined to publicly endorse Chu's remarks, and Chu himself, after his appointment, claimed he no longer holds that view. But the duo's governing record speaks for itself. Under Obama and Chu, the Energy Advisory Board does not include a single executive from an oil company, nor, for that matter, from a natural gas, coal, or nuclear company, though 92 percent of the energy consumed in the United States is from these fuels. The board also lacked representatives from electrical utilities, which are the single greatest source of the nation's power consumption, at 40 percent.[5]

Other cabinet members are working from the same playbook. As I documented in *Crimes Against Liberty*, Obama's secretary of transportation, Ray LaHood, said he wanted to "coerce people out of their cars" and onto public transportation and bicycles, an utterance that prompted columnist George Will to lampoon him as the Secretary of Behavior Modification.[6] Similarly, Secretary of the Interior Ken Salazar said in 2008, when he was a U.S. senator, that he would oppose all offshore drilling irrespective of rising gas prices, even if they were to reach $10 a gallon.[7]

"COMPLETELY UNINFORMED ABOUT THE OIL AND GAS INDUSTRY"

Since taking office, Obama has fought a relentless battle against our own oil companies. In September 2010, the Department of the Interior issued an edict requiring oil and gas companies to permanently plug thousands of Gulf wells that had been idle for five years or more. Mark Kaiser, director of Research and Development at the Center for Energy Studies at Louisiana State University, estimated that this could cost between $1.4 billion and $3.5 billion, and that companies would lose between $6 billion and $18 billion in revenues from future production, with smaller oil producers to be hardest hit.[8]

One constant theme in Obama's energy rhetoric is his demand that Congress raise taxes on oil companies, which he often phrases as a plea to end "subsidies" for these firms. By presenting this as a matter of simple fairness, Obama avoids discussing the damaging ramifications of such a policy. These were detailed by Democratic congressman Dan Boren, who noted that ending the "percentage depletion" and "intangible drilling costs (IDCs)" tax incentives will drive up the costs of oil production and increase our dependence on foreign oil.

Describing the existing tax incentives as "absolutely critical for domestic oil and gas production for thousands of independent producers across the nation," Boren said Obama "is completely uninformed about the oil and gas industry," which "is not made up of just major companies," but "of small independent firms ... that produce a vast majority of our domestic production." Stunningly, Boren declared, "It is estimated that eliminating percentage depletion and IDCs for domestic independents would reduce U.S. drilling by 30-40 percent." Boren further noted that these legal changes would not affect the major oil companies that Obama constantly flays, since they are barred by law from receiving percentage depletion.[9]

Boren's only mistake was to assume Obama was uninformed about the consequences of his proposals. To the contrary, it appeared Obama had completely given up fighting higher gas prices when he commented in April 2011, as gas prices approached $4 a gallon, "I'm just going to be honest with you. There's not much we can do next week or two weeks from now."[10] Most Americans believe increasing our own oil production will lower gas prices, but Obama willfully obstructs that path in favor of pouring billions into untested "clean-energy" projects that are compiling an impressive record of failure.

When a man asked Obama during an April 2011 town hall meeting about high gas prices, the president laughed and replied, "If you're complaining about the price of gas and you're only getting 8 miles a gallon, you know, you might want to think about a trade-in."[11] There could be no better display of the president's callous disregard of everyday Americans and their energy concerns.

"A FEDERAL RESPONSE EFFORT DOOMED TO FAIL"

On April 20, 2010, the Deepwater Horizon drilling rig exploded and caught fire some forty-two miles southeast of Venice, Louisiana, while completing the drilling process for a BP well, killing eleven workers. A few days later a second explosion occurred, and the vessel sank. Within days, officials discovered that oil was leaking from drilling pipe five thousand feet below the surface at a rate of one thousand barrels a day. Inside of a week, the leak caused an oil sheen and emulsified crude slick to form, covering 28,600 miles.[12]

The White House was late to comment on the oil spill, but on May 2, 2010, in one of his early remarks on the accident, Obama sounded calm and measured. "I am going to spare no effort to respond to this crisis for as long as it continues," he announced. "And we'll spare no resource to clean up whatever damage is caused. And while there will be time to fully investigate what happened on that rig and hold responsible parties accountable, our focus now is on a fully coordinated, relentless response effort to stop the leak and prevent more damage to the Gulf."[13] But in reviewing the administration's response to the spill, one could reasonably conclude that it was more focused on exploiting the incident to punish "big oil" and hinder oil production than on clean-up and assistance efforts.

On May 27, 2010, while reporting to the nation on the oil spill— which he was now referring to, accusatorily, as the "BP oil spill"— President Obama summarily pronounced judgment on BP: "As far as I'm concerned, BP is responsible for this horrific disaster, and we will hold them fully accountable on behalf of the United States as well as the people and communities victimized by this tragedy. We will demand that they pay every dime they owe for the damage they've done and the painful losses they've caused." It's always important for Obama to have a villain to blame to ensure that he is blamed for nothing—and BP certainly seemed to fit the bill. After acting as its judge and jury, Obama declared that BP would be using its "unique technology and expertise" to stop the leak. "But make no mistake," he intoned, "BP is operating at our direction. Every key decision and action they take must be approved by us in advance."[14]

A few weeks before the spill, when rising gas prices had produced a public clamor to allow more oil drilling, Obama had proposed expanding offshore oil exploration. But in his remarks on May 27, he announced a dramatic policy change: he would suspend the planned exploration in the Chukchi and Beaufort seas off the coast of Alaska, cancel the pending lease sale in the Gulf of Mexico and the proposed lease sale off the coast of Virginia, suspend action on thirty-three deepwater exploratory wells being drilled in the Gulf of Mexico, and most notably, impose a six-month moratorium on the issuance of new deepwater drilling permits in the Gulf. He conceded oil production is important, but argued that "we can't do this stuff if we don't have confidence that we can prevent crises like this from happening again."[15]

In a June address to the American people, Obama shamelessly capitalized on the spill to politicize the energy issue and stump for his proposed energy tax legislation. He also vowed to do "whatever's necessary to help the Gulf Coast and its people recover from this tragedy," which was insincere, since he initially refused to waive the Jones Act, a law that barred foreign ships from assisting the clean-up efforts. Thus, Belgian and other foreign companies with advanced technology were prevented from assisting for months, possibly because Obama's union backers viewed them as competition.[16]

In his speech, Obama also blithely acknowledged that his six-month moratorium on deepwater drilling "creates difficulty for the people who work on these rigs." That was quite the understatement, considering that some were estimating the ban could potentially cost 120,000 jobs and put another 46,200 jobs on hold during one of the toughest economic times in our history.[17]

Congressman Darrell Issa, the top Republican on the House Oversight and Government Reform Committee, issued an investigative report debunking the administration's claim that it aggressively and competently took charge of the clean-up effort. According to the report,

> Parish officials maintain that the federal government has not been in control since day one. In four separate interviews, senior-ranking Parish officials described how, until the President's visit on May 28, 2010, BP was running the operation. According to one official, "until two weeks ago [after the President's May 28, 2010, visit], BP was in charge and the Coast Guard looked to them for direction." Furthermore,

"Coast Guard asks BP," not vice-versa. When specifically asked to agree or disagree with the assertion that the federal government had been in control since day one, another official firmly disagreed.[18]

The committee's findings were astonishing. Disputing administration claims about the number and timeliness of assets it deployed in the Gulf, local officials claimed the administration was more focused on avoiding bad press than on addressing the disaster. The White House, they noted, "waited until Day 70 of the oil spill to accept critical offers of international assistance." It also inhibited the assistance of local workers and boats by not providing them with needed supplies and equipment.

Though the White House attributed its early silence on the spill to an initial failure to find a visible leak, official documents from the scene from Transocean officials and the Coast Guard revealed "clear and early indications of a substantial oil leak days earlier than White House accounts." Furthermore, local officials "strongly believe the President's call for a drilling moratorium will significantly compound the economic damage caused by the oil spill and will actually increase risk associated with future offshore drilling projects."[19] Issa concluded, "The evidence on the ground suggests that the White House has been more focused on the public relations of this crisis than with providing local officials the resources they need to deal with it."[20]

A later oversight report by Senator James Inhofe, ranking member of the Senate Committee on Environment and Public Works, confirmed the administration's egregious mishandling of the oil spill response. The Committee stated,

President Obama and members of his Administration clearly failed in their responsibility to exhibit decisive leadership during the BP disaster. Instead of removing red tape, bureaucracy, and onerous regulations, the Obama administration kept them in place, and refused to exercise available legal authorities to remove impediments blocking the most effective

and efficient courses of action. President Obama treated the
BP disaster as if it were business as usual, rather than a crisis
of national significance. The result was a federal response
effort that was doomed to fail from the very beginning.[21]

HOLDER "HAS COME CLOSE" TO CROSSING THE LINE

Further demonstrating the administration's fixation on public relations and its contempt for oil companies, Attorney General Eric Holder
made an unprecedented announcement that there would be a criminal
probe of the Gulf oil spill. "Given the extraordinary nature of what our
nation is facing there, we thought it was appropriate to let the American
people know that the federal government was understanding what was
going on here, and that we were using the full panoply of our powers to
open both a criminal investigation and a civil inquiry to ensure that the
American people don't pay a cent for the clean up," Holder declared on
CBS's *Face the Nation*. In other words, because Obama and Holder
wanted to impress the public that they were going all out, they decided
to violate long-standing rules in the U.S. Attorneys' Manual against making such disclosures.[22]

The *Washington Post* editorial board strongly criticized the administration's action which, it observed, "sent BP's stock price tumbling." It
rejected Holder's assertion of extraordinary circumstances, noting that
just a week before, an assistant attorney had demurred to Senator Barbara
Boxer's request for a criminal investigation, saying, "Consistent with
long-standing policy, we neither confirm nor deny the existence of such
an investigation." The board said that decisions to indict must be made
free of political influence and that "the attorney general must take great
care to avoid even the appearance of conflict. Mr. Holder may not have
crossed that line in the gulf oil matter, but he has come close."[23] For his
part, Holder refused to acknowledge any culpability and, with his typical
sophistry, speciously denied that his statement identified BP as the target
of the criminal investigation.[24]

Concerned about Obama's re-election prospects, the White House
quietly kicked off a new PR effort to mitigate the political backlash

against its egregious mismanagement of the oil spill and its assault on the Gulf economy. It sent political and communication aides to Alabama, Mississippi, and Louisiana, as well as to the swing state of Florida, which was a particular focus of these efforts.

Predictably, White House press secretary Robert Gibbs claimed the White House had dispatched officials to the region to ensure an effective response to the spill, not to do political damage control.[25] Yet in the end, Louisianans, according to one poll, by a 54 to 33 percent margin, think George W. Bush did a better job handling Hurricane Katrina than Obama did addressing the Gulf oil spill.[26]

But unlike President Bush, who rarely defended himself, Obama would not countenance such criticism. When NBC's Brian Williams asked him whether the spill was "Obama's Katrina," he shot back, "That is just not accurate. We've got a lot more work to do, but because of the sturdiness and swiftness of the response, there's a lot less oil hitting these shores and these beaches than anybody would have anticipated given the volume that was coming out of the BP oil well."[27] Even as everyone from local fishermen to the governor of Louisiana was blasting his moratorium for crushing the local economy, in a speech at Xavier University, Obama declared that New Orleans was making a comeback under his administration—that with its "rising achievement," it was "becoming a model for the nation."[28]

THEY "DON'T HAVE THE FOGGIEST IDEA WHAT'S GOING ON DOWN HERE"

On June 22, U.S. district judge Martin L. C. Feldman overturned Obama's deepwater drilling ban, stating that the administration had failed to justify a "blanket, generic, indeed punitive moratorium." The Fifth Circuit Court of Appeals later rejected the administration's request to stay Feldman's order.[29]

Irreversibly committed to the moratorium, Obama essentially refused to accept the ruling. Interior Secretary Ken Salazar said he would issue an order to effectively reinstate the moratorium, which he insisted was "needed to protect the communities and the environment of the Gulf

Coast."[30] In other words, this administration would not allow a silly federal court order to interfere with its singular determination to shut down domestic oil production. It would just write a new order and dare the court to overturn that one as well.

Indeed, nothing could break the administration's commitment to the moratorium, no matter how damaging it was. Even the departure of deepwater drilling rigs to other countries seemed inconsequential. White House advisor David Axelrod dismissively declared on *Fox News Sunday*, "These are rented rigs, and they go from place to place. It's not an optimal situation, but obviously we're dealing with the greatest environmental catastrophe of all time.... It's been a tremendous tragedy for that region. We don't want a repeat of it because we're imprudent."[31]

Yet according to industry experts, these drilling rigs are part of long-term contracts, and once they leave the area it is difficult to secure their return for years. Axelrod, in Obama fashion, deflected suggestions that the administration's moratorium was primarily responsible for ongoing economic losses, citing instead spill-caused disruptions in fishing, tourism, and related activities. Unconvincingly, Axelrod claimed that Obama wasn't opposed to new deepwater drilling, provided it can be done safely.[32]

As promised, on July 12, notwithstanding Judge Feldman's decision, Interior Secretary Ken Salazar effectively reinstated the moratorium on deepwater oil drilling in the Gulf, which would only allow drilling rigs to resume operating if they jumped through onerous bureaucratic hoops. The Department of the Interior didn't even deny it was seeking to reimpose the overturned moratorium, insisting the new moratorium was a refinement of the earlier one, not a retreat from it.[33]

So the moratorium continued to inflict damage. Although it ostensibly applied only to deepwater drilling, in fact the ban was accompanied by a de facto moratorium (via permit delays) on shallow-water projects, thus bringing nearly all oil exploration in the Gulf to a halt. The Louisiana Department of National Resources reported that shallow-water drilling permits in the Gulf have "dropped significantly since the federal moratorium"—only four such permits had been issued since that time. In the eleven months preceding the moratorium, an average of fourteen permits were issued per month. Noting that shallow-water drilling projects account for thousands of Louisiana jobs, the state's governor, Bobby Jindal, warned that obstacles to shallow-water drilling could inflict damage on the local economy on top of the harm being done by the deepwater drilling moratorium.[34]

Even Democratic operative James Carville, a Louisiana native, denounced the administration. "People here have been so let down," he exclaimed. "The government comes in ... and say[s] ... just blanket stop everything out there. And they're killing the economy here.... People in the Interior Department that issue these things don't have the foggiest idea about life here; they don't have the foggiest idea what's going on down here.... The federal government is just about to kill us ... with their regulatory tactics."[35]

Supporting Carville's claims, LSU finance professor Dr. Joe Mason released a study estimating that the effect of the six-month moratorium on offshore oil and natural gas production would result in the loss of thousands of jobs and $2.1 billion, including $500 million in wages and nearly $100 million in forfeited state tax revenues in Gulf states. Mason said, "A surprising number of jobs are among professionals—doctors and teachers who are supported by the communities whose economic base is oil and gas from the Gulf. If the communities can't afford to pay their teachers, they are going to lose those teachers."[36]

Other loss estimates were more dramatic. Jack Gerard, president of the American Petroleum Institute, which represents some four hundred oil and natural gas companies, estimated that "the administration's moratorium, if continued indefinitely—or similar legislative proposals which would make the deep water unavailable or uneconomic—would cost this country 175,000 jobs every year between now and 2035, according to our latest analysis." Gerard said that the Gulf accounts for 30 percent of our domestic oil production and 13 percent of our natural gas, with the deepwater portion alone producing 80 percent of the Gulf's oil and 45 percent of its natural gas. The oil and natural gas industry, according to Gerard, supports 9.2 million workers and 7.5 percent of all U.S. gross domestic product, and thus even a minor decline in the industry could make a tremendous impact on the economy.[37]

8,000-12,000 JOB LOSSES: GOOD NEWS!

Notwithstanding the administration's hype about the dangers of drilling, a government report revealed that as of July or August, three-quarters of the oil from the Deepwater Horizon spill had "already evaporated, dispersed, been captured or otherwise eliminated—and that much of the rest is so diluted that it does not seem to pose much additional risk of harm." Only about 26 percent of the oil released from the BP spill was still in the water or onshore in a form that could cause problems.[38] So much for David Axelrod's claim that this was "the greatest environmental catastrophe of all time."[39]

It later emerged, however, that the White House may have been responsible for the release of this report. Whereas the administration previously had an interest in playing up the enormity of the disaster in order to kill domestic oil production, after Obama officials came under fire for ineptly handling the cleanup, it suddenly had an interest in downplaying the spill's effects. Dr. Bill Lehr, a National Oceanic and Atmospheric Administration scientist, told congressional investigators it was White House officials who released the information about the oil's rapid dispersal, not scientists at NOAA. According to Lehr, the data to support that claim were not yet available nor was the peer review of the report complete. Congressman Darrell Issa commented,

> This is yet another in a long line of examples where the White House's pre-occupation with the public relations of the oil spill has superseded the realities on the ground. It is deeply troubling that White House officials apparently preempted the completion and review of a scientific study on the oil spill by NOAA scientists in order to tout conclusions that many experts believe may be deeply flawed.... This irresponsible action only adds to the perception that the Obama White House is more concerned about appearing competent than actually making sure the massive oil spill in the Gulf gets cleaned-up as quickly as possible.[40]

The national press, ever protective of Obama, began relegating news of the spill, the clean-up problems, and the continuing de facto moratorium to the back pages. Meanwhile, the administration sought to rebut criticism by releasing a Department of Commerce report in September showing that the moratorium had cost between eight thousand and twelve thousand jobs, a lower figure than some previous estimates. Of course, the report failed to account for certain important factors: it was still too early to tell whether the graver predictions would materialize; some of the potential losses were mitigated by the magnanimous decision of some large companies to retain their employees (meaning they inevitably absorbed some of these losses themselves); and some of the net job losses were offset by temporary clean-up work.

The administration's spinning of this report as "good" news angered the usually unflappable Louisiana governor Bobby Jindal, who said, "It is stunning that the Obama Administration explained today that the loss of up to 12,000 Gulf Coast jobs and $1.8 billion in total spending by drilling operators due to their six-month deepwater drilling moratorium was somehow good news because it was less than expected." He further declared, "It is even more unbelievable that an administration official testified about these anticipated job losses after admitting that the administration did not consider the economic impact of their deepwater drilling moratorium at all before implementing it."[41]

But just a week after the administration released its self-serving report, the American Energy Alliance released a new study identifying 19,536 job losses from the moratorium, indicating the administration had underestimated the figure by as much as 60 percent. But it was later revealed that the administration really hadn't underestimated the figure—before approving the moratorium, it had conducted internal studies concluding that the moratorium would cost twenty-three thousand jobs—and yet it proceeded anyway.[42]

Regardless of the precise numbers of jobs lost, the administration's cavalier approval of the devastating drilling moratorium, after experts repeatedly warned it would not enhance safety, was unconscionable and indefensible.

Amid all this failure, Obama triumphantly claimed credit when the leaking well was finally sealed. "Today," he said, "we achieved an important milestone in our response to the BP oil spill." In his two-paragraph statement, he conspicuously omitted words of praise or even acknowledgment for the BP oil drillers and relief workers who performed the capping and sealing. As the *Los Angeles Times'* Andrew Malcolm noted, "Instead, Obama praised—actually he commended—several members of his own cabinet and administration." He boasted, as if he had been the primary causal agent in the clean-up, "My administration will see our communities, our businesses and our fragile ecosystems through this difficult time."[43]

"ENCOURAGING OTHER COUNTRIES TO CREATE THE JOBS THAT WE NEED"

Even as Obama was crusading against domestic oil production, he was—appallingly—supporting oil production abroad. The U.S. government, via the U.S. Export-Import Bank, an independent federal agency, loaned more than $1 billion to the Mexican state oil company PEMEX in 2009 to support the company's oil drilling in the southern Gulf of Mexico and had $1 billion more planned for 2010.[44]

Similarly, on a trip to Latin America, Obama told Brazilian officials he wanted to help Brazil produce oil from newly discovered offshore sites. "We want to help with technology and support to develop these oil reserves safely, and when you're ready to start selling, we want to be one of your best customers," Obama declared, adding that "the United States could not be happier with the potential for a new, stable source of energy."[45]

Disgusted, Senator David Vitter exclaimed, "We have abundant energy resources off Louisiana's coast, but this administration has virtually shut down our offshore industry and instead is using Americans' tax dollars to support drilling off the coast of Brazil. It's ridiculous to ignore our own resources and continue going hat-in-hand to countries like Saudi Arabia and Brazil to beg them to produce more oil."[46]

It wasn't just ridiculous; it revealed Obama's callousness toward American businesses and workers, his cynicism toward his professed goal of curbing oil production throughout the world, and his insincerity in claiming he wants to lower our dependence on foreign oil. As Gulf Oil CEO Joe Petrowsky said, "It seems a double standard and it seems somewhat hypocritical to a country that desperately needs jobs ... that we're encouraging other countries to create the jobs that we need."[47]

As if further evidence were needed of the ludicrous futility of the administration's war on deepwater drilling, Cuba announced plans to drill five deepwater oil wells in the Gulf of Mexico between 2011 and 2013.[48]

"A CHILLING EXAMPLE OF THIS ADMINISTRATION'S MISGUIDED APPROACH"

At the end of September 2010, shortly before the revised moratorium expired, the Department of the Interior unveiled complex new drilling regulations, provoking the oil industry to warn of further drilling delays. "Operators will need to comply with tougher requirements for everything from well design and cementing practices to blowout preventers and employee training," Secretary Salazar announced. "They will also need to develop comprehensive plans to manage risks and hazards at every step of the drilling process so as to reduce the risk of human error."[49]

Karen A. Harbert, president of the U.S. Chamber of Commerce's Institute for 21st Century Energy, alleged that the new rules would create a de facto drilling moratorium to replace the expiring one. "The fact that BOEMRE [the administration's offshore drilling regulator] has not considered how the new regulations will affect the industry is a chilling example of this administration's misguided approach that will have unintended consequences such as increased imports and fewer American jobs," she warned.[50]

Indeed, while oil production from the Gulf was, as of April 2011, down more than 10 percent since Obama implemented the moratorium, our imports of foreign oil had greatly increased, pushing up gas prices and effectively increasing U.S. dependence on foreign oil by around

$1.8 billion just in the fourth quarter of 2010.[51] David Holt, president of the Consumer Energy Alliance in Houston, said Americans needed a message of hope rather than more economy-stifling regulations. "Instead, the timeline for this job-killing moratorium is blurred more than ever as it creates tremendous uncertainty for American consumers and those hard-working individuals whose livelihoods are tied to off-shore energy activity."[52]

The administration was aware that its new rules would dramatically increase drilling costs and therefore destroy jobs. The Department of the Interior estimated the regulations would raise operating costs by an estimated $1.42 million for each new deepwater well drilled with a floating rig, by $170,000 for each one drilled with a platform rig, and by $90,000 for each new shallow well. Ken Salazar—indifferent to the pain he was causing—claimed the increased costs were justified because the rules would reduce the likelihood of another spill.[53]

In rules issued by BOEMRE, the administration buried a disgraceful rationalization of the negative effects of the new regulations: "Currently there is sufficient spare capacity in OPEC to offset a decrease in GOM deepwater production that could occur as a result of this rule." Red State's Steve Maley translated the sentence into plain English: "It's OK if we lose domestic production capacity, because OPEC has plenty of oil."[54]

MANIPULATING SCIENCE

Eventually, indications arose that the administration's politicized, ideological response to the oil spill had spawned excessive secrecy and the crass manipulation of data. A report by Oil Spill Commission staff suggested that White House officials may have blocked the release of "a more accurate and dramatic estimate" of the oil spill's effects. The report indicated that the White House Office of Management and Budget had rejected an attempt by the National Oceanic and Atmospheric Administration to publicize some of its worst-case scenarios. "By initially underestimating the amount of oil flow and then, at the end of the summer, appearing to underestimate the amount of oil remaining in the Gulf, the federal government created the impression that it was either not fully competent to handle the spill or not fully candid with the American people about the scope of the problem," the commission report asserted.[55] The administration, of course, denied any wrongdoing.[56]

More damning, seven experts from the National Academy of Engineers claimed the Department of the Interior had misrepresented their views in its report that recommended the offshore drilling moratorium. While the report had suggested the experts endorsed the moratorium, the experts in fact argued that a drilling ban "will not measurably reduce risk further and it will have a lasting impact on the nation's economy which may be greater than that of the oil spill."[57]

The Department of the Interior's inspector general found that a staff member of White House energy advisor Carol Browner had indeed edited the report's executive summary to imply the experts endorsed the moratorium. However, the IG found the administration had not violated federal rules because it had offered a formal apology and publicly clarified the report. The Competitive Enterprise Institute, a free market think tank, called on President Obama to fire Browner for this "manipulation of science."[58]

A MINIMUM SEVEN-YEAR BAN

On October 12, the administration finally lifted the revised moratorium on deepwater oil drilling in the Gulf, with Interior Secretary Ken Salazar cynically announcing, "We're open for business." The effect was hardly dramatic, since oil companies had to comply with the "permitorium"—the new regulations that severely slowed the permitting process. Noting that a de facto drilling ban would remain in place, the Heritage Foundation's Rory Cooper observed that behind the rhetoric, President Obama had completely shut down the nation's oil drilling infrastructure, and at least 103 permits were awaiting review by BOEMRE. Experts expected the de facto ban to continue until the second half of 2011 and possibly into 2012. Notably, as of February 2011, the administration hadn't approved a single new exploratory drilling plan in the Gulf since Obama had supposedly lifted the ban.[59]

In fact, in December the Obama administration revoked its promise to expand offshore oil exploration into the eastern Gulf of Mexico and along the Atlantic coast. Using the Gulf oil spill as an excuse, Salazar approved an official moratorium on exploration in those areas for at least seven years. As the *New York Times* commented, "The move puts off limits millions of acres of the Outer Continental Shelf that hold potentially billions of barrels of oil and trillions of cubic feet of natural gas."[60]

Jack Gerard of the American Petroleum Institute warned the decision could result in the loss of tens of thousands of jobs, billions in government revenues, and greater dependence on foreign energy. Others noted that the policy would have negative rippling effects throughout the economy.[61] The seven-year moratorium, according to University of Illinois professor John W. Kindt, "is a ridiculous decision" that would devastate businesses.

Some found a deeper, unsettling problem. "The real issue," said Gerard, "is the Interior Department, which is the most scandal-ridden agency in American history. Along with an inability to regulate, the entire department is rife with conflicts of interest." Kindt agreed, noting that the administration was just as culpable for the gulf disaster as BP but has avoided public scrutiny. "The regulators at Interior didn't just have a cozy relationship with the people they're supposed to be regulating," said Kindt, "they had outright conflicts of interest."[62] The administration's excuse was that it was "adjusting [its] strategy in areas where there are no active leases" to "focus and expand [its] critical resources on areas that are currently active."

It seemed that instead of finding innovative ways to allow the industry to compensate for lost revenues and jobs from the Gulf spill, the administration was capitalizing on hyped-up environmental hysteria over it to further smother the industry. Rory Cooper reported that with all the reductions in drilling, the Energy Information Administration estimated that the government would lose $3.7 million in revenue per day from foregone royalties, amounting to $1.35 billion in 2011 alone. According to the U.S. Chamber of Commerce's Karen Harbert, "The Administration is sending a message to America's oil and gas industry: take your capital, technology, and jobs somewhere else."[63]

Unsurprisingly, amid all these moratoriums and regulations, energy companies such as Seahawk Drilling of Houston began going out of business. "The decision by regulators to arbitrarily construct unnecessary barriers to obtaining permits they had traditionally authorized has had an adverse impact not only on Seahawk, but on the sector as a whole," former Seahawk CEO Randy Stilley said.[64] In addition, Reuters reported that many of the more than thirty deepwater rigs in the Gulf, each of which employs some two hundred people, had "moved to other markets, first because of a U.S. halt last May after BP Plc's well blowout, and then because of the lack of permits once the moratorium was lifted."[65]

Sure enough, more than two months after the administration had nominally lifted its ban on deepwater drilling in the Gulf of Mexico, oil companies were still stymied from obtaining drilling permits. Even former president Bill Clinton called the drilling permit delays "ridiculous" at a time when the economy was struggling to rebuild.[66]

In March 2011, Obama reacted to the criticism in his usual manner, indignantly blaming the oil companies for their own lack of drilling. In a press conference, he suggested that the industry holds leases on tens of millions of acres that "aren't producing a thing" and announced that he had directed the Department of the Interior to investigate and report back to him so "we can encourage companies to develop the leases they hold and produce American energy." With amazing chutzpah he added, "People deserve to know that the energy they depend on is being developed in a timely manner." As *Investors Business Daily* observed, Obama was arguing that the companies were foregoing drilling and profit-making for no discernible reason. "It's a bizarro-world inversion of the usual complaint against oil companies—that they are reckless and all-too eager to despoil pristine lands in search of black gold."[67]

After greatly contributing to rising gas prices through his systematic assault on domestic energy, Obama, in June 2011, decided to release thirty million barrels of oil from U.S. emergency stockpiles—the Strategic Petroleum Reserve—to bolster the economy. It was striking how casually Obama chose to designate a non-emergency as an emergency to release just a few days' worth of the nation's total oil and petroleum consumption.[68] Treasury Secretary Timothy Geithner denied the decision was a political move, claiming it was designed to meet a shortfall caused by the crisis in Libya and other unrest in the Middle East.[69] In little more than a week it was clear that the move had no appreciable, lasting impact, for oil prices quickly climbed back to their previous levels.[70]

"HUNDREDS OF THOUSANDS OF LOST JOBS"

Eleven months after the Gulf drilling ban was technically lifted, drilling there was still negligible. The duplicitous White House wanted both to eat and keep its cake, reaping the PR benefits of pretending to encourage drilling, while in fact impeding it in every conceivable way. A study commissioned by the Gulf Economic Survival Team reported that the industry had signaled its intent to return its drilling operations to full capacity and had invested billions of dollars in well-containment technology, which effectively robbed the administration of safety as an excuse for its obstruction. The study also revealed that the failure of Department of the Interior regulators to understand complex new regulations— crafted by the administration's politically appointed bureaucrats—was a major contributor to the delays. The study concluded that the failure to safely restore oil and natural gas exploration levels in the Gulf would take a major toll on jobs and would reduce energy security.

According to the study, the 2012 "activity gap"—the losses stemming from the administration's delayed permit process—could total 230,000 American jobs, more than $44 billion of U.S. GDP, nearly $12 billion in tax and royalty revenues to state and federal treasuries, U.S. oil production of more than 400,000 barrels of oil per day (150 million barrels for the year), and a potential reduction of the amount that the United States spends on imported oil of around $15 billion.

Detailing the permitting hold-ups, the study found that in the six months following the lifting of the moratorium in October 2010, there was a 250 percent increase in the backlog of deepwater plans pending government approval, an 86 percent drop in the pace of regulatory approvals for plans, a 60 percent drop in all Gulf of Mexico drilling permits, and a 38 percent increase in the time required to reach each regulatory approval.[71] James Diffey, senior director of IHS Global

Insight's U.S. Regional Economic Group, said the study found that "an increase in oil and gas activity reverberates throughout the broader economy. Each new hire (in the Gulf) results, on average, in more than three additional jobs in an array of industries around the country"—not just in the Gulf region.[72]

A separate study by Quest Offshore Resources concluded that if the administration had really lifted its moratorium in October 2010, 190,000 more jobs, including 8,500 in California alone, would have been created in the United States over three years. The upshot of these avoidable delays was hundreds of thousands of lost jobs, billions of dollars of foregone federal and state tax revenues, and an increased dependence on foreign energy.[73]

Providing further proof of Obama's drilling obstructionism, Greater New Orleans Inc. reported in November 2011 that the administration had approved only 35 percent of the drilling plans for the Gulf of Mexico so far in 2011, and that it took an average of almost four months to get approval from BOEMRE. In previous years the approval rate had been 73.4 percent, more than double Obama's record, and the approval time had historically averaged sixty-one days, almost twice as fast.[74] Equally troubling, these lags were damaging beyond Louisiana, because one deepwater rig alone can create seven hundred local jobs. As Heritage's energy expert Nick Loris wrote, "Allowing access for exploration and creating an efficient regulatory process that allows energy projects to move forward in a timely manner will not only increase revenue through more royalties, leases and rent. It will also create jobs and help lower energy prices in the process."[75]

In January 2012, a report commissioned by the American Petroleum Institute concluded that the combined effect of the administration's moratorium and "permitorium" could cost the United States more than $24 billion in lost oil and natural gas investment in the next several years. As a result of these delays, the study found, capital and operating expenditures fell over the two preceding years by $18.3 billion. The region was responsible for about 6 percent of global investments in crude oil and natural gas, but it would have been nearly 12 percent for 2011 had the delays not been imposed. The report stated, "As a result of decreases in investment due to the moratorium, total U.S. employment is estimated to have been reduced by 72,000 jobs in 2010 and approximately 90,000 jobs in 2011."[76]

OTHER ASSAULTS ON DRILLING

Ken Salazar fights the administration's war on oil far beyond the Gulf. After issuing his revised offshore drilling moratorium in July 2010, Salazar scrapped seventy-seven oil lease sales in Utah approved by the Bush administration. Though the inspector general had found no evidence to support Salazar's claims that the Bush administration had rushed the sales, Salazar said he wanted to take a "fresh look" at the parcels before deciding whether to release them.[77]

In fact, these leases had not been approved casually, but after some seven years of scrutiny and debate. This is part of a larger pattern of the federal government blocking energy leases that have been the subject of environmental protests, despite the nation's current economic difficulties. The federal government at the time was reportedly holding $100 million for energy leases in the Rocky Mountains that have been delayed.[78] As if this weren't enough, *Investors Business Daily* reported that Salazar also blocked the leases of oil shale rights in five Western states "estimated to hold between 1 trillion and 2 trillion barrels of recoverable oil." The Energy Department's Argonne National Laboratory says that 800 billion of these are recoverable with current technology. In addition, a 2008 Utah Mining Association report states that the West's oil shale gives America the "potential to be completely energy self-sufficient with no demands on external resources." As the *IBD* editors noted, "If we could drill in places like that, maybe oil wouldn't be gushing a mile under the Gulf of Mexico."[79]

The campaign against drilling also reached Ohio, where Obama's Department of Agriculture decided to delay shale gas drilling for up to six months by cancelling a mineral lease auction for Wayne National Forest, a move that could cost up to 200,000 jobs and impede access to affordable energy. The delay was sought by environmentalists who ideologically oppose the process of hydraulic fracturing, known as "fracking."[80]

This process involves injecting high-pressure fluids to fracture the porous shale rock, enabling the extraction of the oil and gas trapped inside. Environmental activists claim fracking uses chemical additives that contaminate groundwater. This is a dubious assertion, since the shale formations used in fracking are thousands of feet deeper than the drinking water aquifers they allegedly contaminate and are separated from them by solid rock. As EPA chief Lisa Jackson admitted to a House Oversight Committee, "I'm not aware of any proven case where the fracking process itself has affected water."[81] Even in cases where problems arose from gas extraction during fracking, they were not due to the fracking process, but to drilling operations that weren't performed correctly, according to a study by the Energy Institute at the University of Texas at Austin.[82]

Nevertheless, the Obama administration is erecting regulatory impediments to fracking, apparently unconcerned that they risk destroying the economic boom fracking has brought to parts of Ohio, North Dakota, Pennsylvania, and elsewhere. The Ohio Oil and Gas Energy Education Program estimated that drilling in the Utica Shale, which would be suspended, would produce up to 204,500 jobs by 2015—though the USDA estimated the delay would only affect up to two hundred jobs. House Natural Resources Committee chairman Doc Hastings remarked, "The President's plan is to simply say 'no' to new energy production. It's a plan that is sending American jobs overseas, forfeiting new revenue, and denying access to American energy that would lessen our dependence on hostile Middle Eastern oil."[83]

Interestingly, while Obama vigorously fights fracking, he still boasts that his beloved government was instrumental in developing fracking technology, which he believes bolsters his case for government support for new energy projects. In fact, according to Nicolas Loris of the Heritage Foundation, this is just another of Obama's whoppers, because long before the government became involved, the private sector established the process.[84] Inaccurate or not, President Obama better be careful not to boast too much, for his perpetual gaffe-making vice president, Joe Biden, recently warned that fracking causes earthquakes.[85]

"MY WARNING IS NOT JUST SPECIFIC TO KEYSTONE"

In November 2011, under pressure from environmental activists and certain Nebraska officials, the Obama administration announced it would delay until after the 2012 presidential election the construction of the Keystone XL pipeline, a $7 billion project that would transport more than seven hundred thousand barrels of oil daily from Alberta, Canada to Oklahoma and the Gulf Coast in Texas. The State Department said it was ordering a review of alternative routes in lieu of the environmentally sensitive Sand Hills region of Nebraska.

According to the *New York Times*, this was just one in a series of administration decisions to push back difficult environmental issues past the November 2012 presidential election. The *Times* pointed to similar delays in reviewing the nation's smog standards, in conducting offshore oil lease sales in the Arctic, and in issuing new regulations for coal ash power plants.[86]

Even though the pipeline would decrease America's foreign energy dependence, create thousands of jobs at a time when 14 million Americans were unemployed, and generate a projected $5.2 billion in property tax revenues for the states the pipeline traversed—Montana, South Dakota, Kansas, Oklahoma, Nebraska, and Texas[87]—Obama yielded to environmental activists who threatened to withdraw their support for his reelection.

Obama seemed unconcerned by a warning from Canadian prime minister Stephen Harper that delaying the pipeline's approval would force Canada to ship its oil to Asia instead of to the U.S. "This highlights why Canada must increase its efforts to ensure it can supply its energy outside the U.S. and into Asia in particular," Harper had said, referring to the prospect of Obama delaying approval. "Canada will step up its efforts in that regard and I communicated that clearly to the president."[88]

Just as he has tried to distance himself from controversial actions of his Justice Department, the EPA, and other agencies, Obama pretended that the delay was a purely administrative matter within the State Department. "I support the State Department's announcement today regarding the need to seek additional information about the Keystone XL pipeline proposal," he declared.[89]

However, this was obviously a political decision coming straight from the top, as the State Department itself had found that the pipeline would not pose substantial environmental risks.[90] In fact, Obama personally intervened in a Senate fight over the pipeline, lobbying Democrats to reject an amendment calling for its construction.[91] Jack N. Gerard, president of the American Petroleum Institute, said Obama's decision was "all about politics and keeping a radical constituency, opposed to any and all oil and gas development, in the president's camp in 2012. Whether it will help the president retain his job is unclear but it will cost thousands of shovel-ready opportunities for American workers."[92]

Obama's stated concern about the pipeline's environmental impact was sorely misplaced. Indeed, there are already fifty thousand miles of oil pipeline in the United States that provide enormous economic benefits with very little environmental damage.[93] Moreover, as the Heritage Foundation's David Kreutzer observed, blocking the pipeline will actually *increase* the risk of environmental damage. As Kreutzer wrote,

> Let's acknowledge that blocking the XL pipeline won't stop development of the oil sands. It will slow some of the development, which will increase the world price of petroleum. However, the major impact of blocking the pipeline would be a significant diversion of the oil to non-U.S. consumers.... [Canadian oil will travel] an extra 6,000 miles across the Pacific in oil-consuming super tankers and then [be refined] in less-regulated Chinese refineries. In addition, be aware that replacing the Canadian oil means the U.S. also must import more oil by tankers, which are less efficient than pipelines.[94]

As there is no pleasing leftists, even when they win, some environmentalists were dissatisfied that Obama didn't summarily kill the pipeline. One such activist, Glenn Hurowitz, a senior fellow at the Center for International Policy, feared that Keystone XL could still be approved by a future Republican president. "I'm a little dismayed at suggestions that this kick-the-can decision means environmentalists will enthusiastically back President

Obama in 2012," Hurowitz said. "Is the price of an environmentalist's vote a year's delay on environmental catastrophe? Excuse me, no."[95]

But others focused on the economic costs of Obama's decision. The Heritage Foundation's Nicolas Loris argued that the delay was blocking new oil imports from Canada and preventing the creation of thousands of private-sector jobs. "Building the pipeline," said Loris, "would directly create 20,000 truly shovel-ready jobs; the Canadian Energy Research Institute estimates that current pipeline operations and the addition of the Keystone XL pipeline would create 179,000 American jobs by 2035."[96] In a bizarre attempt to deflect these kinds of charges, Obama declared, "However many jobs might be generated by a Keystone pipeline, they're going to be a lot fewer than the jobs that are created by extending the payroll tax cut and extending unemployment insurance."[97]

Despite his view of the payroll tax cut and unemployment insurance as crucial tools for job creation, he threatened to veto a bill including these measures, as well as others he favored, if the Keystone pipeline were included in the legislation. In his imperious style he threatened, "My warning is not just specific to Keystone. Efforts to tie a whole bunch of other issues to something that they should be doing anyway will be rejected by me."[98]

Outraged by the needless delay, Congress passed a bill forcing Obama to decide on Keystone XL. He knew the American people overwhelmingly supported the pipeline, but in the end, still afraid of alienating his left-wing base, Obama rejected the project. The economic consequences of his decision are still playing out, and in fact, had kicked in with his original decision to delay a decision. Welspun Tubular Company, a steel pipe manufacturer in Little Rock, Arkansas, which had five hundred miles of pipe waiting to be shipped out for Keystone XL, laid off sixty employees after the delay was announced.[99] Obama's decision was obviously wrongheaded, and editorial pages across the nation criticized it.[100]

Obama's opposition to oil drilling, fracking, and other domestic energy production comes at great cost to the American economy. Wood Mackenzie, an energy research firm, issued a report in September 2011 finding that the development of new and existing resources could increase domestic oil and natural gas production by the equivalent of over 10 million barrels of oil per day, support an additional 1.4 million jobs, and raise more than $800 billion of cumulative government revenue by 2030. By contrast, continuing on the current path of policies that delay lease and drilling permits, increase the cost of hydraulic fracturing, and delay the construction of pipelines such as Keystone XL will detrimentally impact production, jobs, and government revenues.[101]

OBAMA'S TWO FAVORITE ENERGY LIES

To defuse accusations that he is hostile to oil production, Obama frequently tells us that under his administration, U.S. oil production is higher than it's been in eight years. In addition, in his tireless effort to persuade us that we need to replace oil with alternative energy sources, he says we consume an alarming amount of oil in relation to the amount we have in reserve. Both claims are false on multiple levels.

As for the first claim, nonpartisan energy observers say Obama does not deserve credit for increased domestic energy production. Any increase in domestic drilling during his tenure has been almost entirely in areas over which the Obama administration exercises no authority. According to a study by the Institute on Energy Research (IER), oil production on federal land—over which the president has control—declined by 11 percent in fiscal year 2011, while oil production on state lands increased that year by 14 percent, and on private lands by 12 percent. "A lot of the wells that were supposed to be drilled weren't because of the moratorium," says the IER's Dan Kish. "Drilling is up in the U.S. on lands he has no say over. On lands he has all the say over, drilling is down."[102]

According to another analysis—by the Heritage Foundation—oil and gas production on federal land is down by 40 percent under Obama's presidency. In fact, in 2010, there were fewer onshore leases than during any year since 1984, and the administration held only one offshore lease sale in 2011.[103] The vast majority of today's oil production—for which Obama disingenuously claims credit—occurs on private land in North Dakota, Texas, and Alaska. Indeed, in North Dakota, oil production is booming and unemployment is at 3.1 percent—the lowest rate in the nation.[104]

Additionally, regardless of what statistics Obama cites, experts, including EIA administrator Richard Newell, say it takes around one to three years for any major federal policy action concerning oil production—such as issuing leases—to affect domestic oil production. Oil production was significantly higher in 2009 than in prior years, and while Obama was in office for most of that year, most of the production increase was due to action during the Bush years. The same is true for 2010.[105]

Obama's real attitude toward oil drilling was seen in August 2011, when a federal judge threw out administration rules that were slowing down expedited environmental review of oil and gas drilling on federal land. Ruling in favor of Western Energy Alliance against the federal government and Interior Secretary Ken Salazar, U.S. district judge Nancy Freudenthal reinstated the Bush-era rules that expedited these reviews. After the ruling, a defiant government attorney complained that the judge "completely discounted the government's argument that the harm was speculative."[106] Here, we see the cavalier attitude of this administration, decidedly at war with the industry and apparently unconcerned with the damage its policies were causing to the industry, to American workers, and to the American economy overall, as it implemented its reckless policies and then demanded the injured parties substantiate the damages beyond the level that satisfied the court. This is not the way a government of, for, and by the people is supposed to work.

Concerning his over-consumption claim, Obama argues, "Even if we drilled every drop of oil out of every single one of the reserves that we possess—offshore and onshore—it still wouldn't be enough to meet our long-term needs. We consume about 25 percent of the world's oil. We only have 2 percent of the reserves. Even if we doubled U.S. oil production, we're still really short."[107]

The United States has some 20 billion barrels of oil in reserves; "reserves" refers to "proven" reserves that are certain to be recoverable in future years from known reservoirs under existing economic and operating conditions. That is, we have 20 billion barrels that are recoverable *at current prices and under lands currently available for development*.[108]

That definition would exclude many oil reserves that Obama has declared off-limits. According to the Institute for Energy Research, we have more than 1.4 trillion barrels of oil that are technically recoverable in the United States with existing technology. The largest deposits are located offshore, in portions of Alaska and in shale deposits in the Rocky Mountain West. This means the United States has more recoverable oil than the rest of the world combined, outside of North America. The Heritage Foundation says this is enough to fuel every passenger car in the nation for 430 years. Therefore, "it is merely semantics—not a scientific assessment of what America has the capacity to produce—that allows critics to claim repeatedly that America is running out of energy."[109]

When you add in recoverable resources from Canada and Mexico, the total recoverable oil in North America exceeds 1.7 trillion barrels. "To put this in context, Saudi Arabia has about 260 billion barrels of oil in proved reserves."[110]

Even by the restrictive definition of reserves Obama is using, the 20 billion barrels figure is misleading, because he is clearly implying it is a fixed, or static, number—as though with every barrel of oil we consume, we are approaching our last available barrel. In fact, the number is not static, but is constantly changing.

The Institute tells us that in 1980, for example, the United States had 30 billion barrels of oil in reserves. But over the next thirty years— through 2010—we produced 77 billion barrels.[111] Now, how can it be that we produced two and a half times more oil than we had available, consumed a great deal, and still ended up with plenty left over?

Obama's own Energy Information Administration is predicting a steady increase in reserves on land *currently available for exploration*. Heritage's David Kreutzer says, "It projects that improvements in technology and the economics of extraction, production, and sales actually will lead to a 23.7 percent increase in U.S. reserves even after extracting billions of barrels of oil in the interim."

Further, Obama's formulation conflates two different measures. We might have only between 2 and 3 percent of the world's recoverable reserves, as narrowly and misleadingly defined, but we don't consume 25 percent of the world's oil reserves, which is what Obama wants us to believe. We consume closer to 22 percent—but it's not of reserves, it's of the world's oil *production*. And, as Heritage notes, "we consume about 22 percent of the world's production of everything," not just oil. Consumption is determined by income, not by available resources, and we also produce about 22 percent of the world's total output of all goods and services. Admittedly, we don't produce 22 percent of the world's total oil output; more like 6 to 10 percent. But experts say this number will increase in the future even without accessing the other abundant sources mentioned above.[112]

President Obama's war on oil is doing incredible damage to America, costing jobs, depressing economic growth, and hindering our national security by keeping us dependent on oil from Saudi Arabia, Venezuela, and other repugnant regimes. He claims to support more drilling alongside "green energy," but don't believe him—through all his rhetorical attacks on oil companies, through all his moratoriums and damaging regulations, through all his resistance to Keystone XL and fracking, it's clear that he views oil as an obstacle, not a complement, to his alternative energy schemes. By developing more of our own, bountiful supply of oil, we could lower unemployment, reduce gas prices, create more government revenues to help balance the budget, and reduce our dependence on foreign oil. But Obama has different priorities; instead of producing more oil, he wants to reduce and—in his utopian fantasies—ultimately eliminate it.

CHAPTER EIGHT

THE WAR ON OTHER ENERGY SOURCES

B arack Obama's mania for green energy exceeds all bounds of reason or prudence. He has dedicated tens of billions of dollars to a wide assortment of fantastic green projects, often falsely advertising them as being geared toward creating jobs and sparking economic growth. But jobs and growth, not to mention our public finances, end up the victims of his schemes, as he recklessly wastes federal money, distorts the economy by propping up uncompetitive companies and technologies, and suppresses tried and true sources of energy.

SHUTTING DOWN NUCLEAR ENERGY
IN THE NAME OF EXPANDING IT

President Obama has paid lip service to promoting nuclear energy while doing his best to kill it. In July 2010 the Department of Energy asked the Nuclear Regulatory Commission to reconsider its ruling that

the administration could not stop the licensing process for the Yucca
Mountain nuclear waste storage project without Congress' approval. The
government had already spent more than $12 billion to provide a safe
nuclear storage facility for ten thousand years at Yucca, but the administration, early in 2010, unilaterally defunded the project and requested
that the NRC rescind the facility's license request.

Obama had claimed to support nuclear power, and with great fanfare
had announced his intention to offer $36 billion in loan guarantees for
two new nuclear reactors in Georgia. But by impeding the Yucca project,
Obama jeopardized the future of the entire U.S. nuclear power industry,
which needs a reliable, long-term method of waste disposal along with a
more efficient regulatory scheme.[1] Congressional Democrats, always
eager to help the administration's efforts to stifle most traditional domestic energy projects, blocked a Republican bill to provide temporary funding of $100 million for Yucca for 2011. And while the administration
convened a commission to make recommendations for nuclear waste
disposal, Energy Secretary Steven Chu instructed the commission's members not even to consider Yucca or any other specific site. Thus, the Yucca
project was effectively killed. As the *Washington Times* editors said,
"Sentence first—verdict afterward."[2]

A year later, the Government Accountability Office reported that the
Obama administration's rush to shut down Yucca could delay the opening of a nuclear waste facility by more than twenty years and cost billions
of additional dollars. According to the report, several Energy Department
officials said they'd never seen such a large program come under so much
pressure to end that quickly. The administration, in its zealous haste, did
not provide a technical or scientific basis to justify the cancellation, nor
did it bother to identify possible risks attendant to the closure process.

The GAO report confirmed that Secretary Chu's decision to shut
down the facility was based solely on policy grounds, not safety concerns. Congressman Fred Upton, chairman of the House Energy and
Commerce Committee, commented, "It is alarming for this administration to discard 30 years of research and billions of taxpayer dollars spent,
not for technical or safety reasons, but rather to satisfy temporary
political calculations."[3]

While environmental extremists cite the nuclear accident in Fuku-shima, Japan, in arguing against the use of nuclear power, the accident really underscores the importance of addressing safety issues such as nuclear waste storage, not ignoring them and pretending they will go away.

CAFE STANDARDS: "A WILLFUL REJECTION OF REALITY"

In November 2011, the Obama administration settled on a proposal to require car manufacturers to nearly double the average fuel economy for passenger cars from 30.2 to 55.4 miles per gallon by 2025. Some analysts said the draconian proposal would effectively require most new vehicles sold in the United States to be battery-powered—and not coin-cidentally, boosting sales of battery-powered cars is one of Obama's pet causes. But the rule, a joint brainchild of the Department of Transporta-tion and the Environmental Protection Agency that would go into effect in 2017, was approved anyway, with short shrift given to its likely impact on automakers and the economy.[4]

Some research showed the plan stands to raise vehicle prices by more than $6,000, though the National Highway Traffic Safety Administration and the EPA would only admit to an average increase of $2,000 for each new passenger vehicle sold by 2025, at a total cost of up to $157 billion.[5] A study released by the nonprofit Center for Automotive Research in Ann Arbor, Michigan, however, estimated the new standards could increase vehicle prices by $10,000. The White House, impervious to economic laws and market forces, claimed the rule would reduce U.S. dependence on foreign oil and would save consumers more than $8,000 per vehicle in fuel costs by 2025.[6]

During its deliberations, the administration shrouded the new stan-dards in its usual secrecy, prompting a rebuke from Congressman Darrell Issa. "Beyond jobs that would be lost as a result of this rule," said Issa, "there are concerns that these new regulations were crafted in a manner inconsistent with laws and basic standards of transparency that had the effect of hiding special interest agendas."[7]

Whereas previous administrations customarily factored in greater costs to consumers, job losses, and negative effects on safety and vehicle utility to arrive at a target miles-per-gallon figure, it appeared the administration was issuing dictates with much less concern for those consequences.[8] But there *will be* consequences. Aside from higher prices, the new rule could force automakers to lighten their cars by dumping spare tires and through other means.

As critics noted, the fact that some carmakers have already jettisoned spare tires in the name of fuel economy undermines environmentalists' claims that, thanks to new technology, carmakers no longer have to downsize vehicles to increase their fuel economy. Smaller, lighter vehicles pose a problem because they suffer more damage during crashes, resulting in thousands of additional traffic deaths per year—which clarifies the shifting priorities of environmental activists.[9]

The *Wall Street Journal*'s Holman Jenkins wrote a devastating critique of the administration's zeal for raising CAFE standards, arguing it ignores engineering, the law of diminishing returns, the scarcity of materials needed for ultra-high-mileage vehicles, the likelihood that higher standards will cause Americans to drive their old cars longer, and the standards' non-existent impact on global carbon dioxide levels. All of this, he wrote, "is a willful rejection of reality.... In the end, only a psychiatrist might explain this urge to pile up new policy excesses, destined someday to blow up in our faces, in an age when history clearly calls us to confront past excesses. But Mr. Obama is not deep. His presidency has been a presidency of shibboleths, of endless boasts that he's delivering on the bien-pensant slogans that others just mouth."[10]

FEEDING THE MOUTH THAT BITES YOU

The Environmental Protection Agency has found a novel way to adopt unpopular policies—it funds environmental groups that sue the agency to force it to do so. This collusive jurisprudence, as one might call it, was revealed in a study by Budd-Falen Law Offices that found a dozen environmental groups have filed more than three thousand "sweetheart" lawsuits against the EPA and other agencies in the last decade. "Often the suits involve things the EPA wants to do anyway," said Jeff Holmstead, a Bush-era EPA official. "By inviting a lawsuit and then signing a consent decree, the agency gets legal cover from political heat." Congressman Ed Whitfield, head of the Energy and Commerce Committee's energy and power panel, says that more and more environmental policy is being directed with absolutely no input from elected representatives, but by private lawsuits that are settled with monetary payoffs.[11]

WATER POLLUTION REGULATIONS

The Obama administration announced in April 2011 that it would impose stricter pollution controls pursuant to the Clean Water Act on millions of acres of wetlands and tens of thousands of miles of streams. The rules were designed to prevent the intrusion of mining waste and the discharge of industrial pollutants into the waters used for swimming holes and drinking. Republicans and others objected, among other reasons, because the affected waters were under state jurisdiction, meaning this was simply another federal power grab by this administration.

The Clean Water Act was passed in 1972 to protect the "navigable waters of the United States." But over time, as with so many other areas of our law, it has been expanded to allow regulation of matters far beyond its intended scope. Now, bureaucrats use the law to justify regulation of any pool of water that is capable of accommodating a minuscule toy boat. The term "navigable" has been inflated to include such waters that collect into a "wetland" after a storm. Thus, we have an unaccountable administrative agency that is imposing these rules, which opponents say will substantially harm the economy.[12]

$57,000 PER HOME AND
"NO MATERIAL IMPACT ON JOBS"

While Obama's opposition to conventional domestic energy sources seems unbounded, it hardly exceeds his support for frivolous, wasteful green energy projects. In his 2011 State of the Union speech, he tried to characterize his green energy fantasies as a grandiose vision on par with John F. Kennedy's goal to get us to the moon before the end of the sixties. Obama called it "our generation's Sputnik moment" and, as is typical of specious liberal rhetoric, argued that our newfound commitment to green energy would be the key to our national security, not to mention saving the planet. "Already," he boasted, "we're seeing the promise of renewable energy."[13] Before the year ended, Obama's boasts had fallen flat and his plans had degenerated into monumental waste and scandal, including the notorious Solyndra project.

From the outset of his term, Obama showed an almost singular obsession with green energy development. Oddly, he wasn't pursuing this technology only because of his environmental extremism; his ideology also informs him that its development is the key to the nation's future economic prosperity and creating "countless jobs."

The *Washington Post* reported in June 2011 that Obama had "devoted more than half of his out-of-town private-business visits to promoting a single industry: clean technology." He toured twenty-two clean-energy companies in an amazing nineteen trips, where the ostensible purpose was to promote economic recovery and energy independence. He visited a lighting company in Wisconsin, an electric car battery manufacturer in Reno, and a company that produces "energy-efficient lighting" in Durham, North Carolina, repeatedly praising these types of firms in his radio addresses and speeches.[14]

There was a stench of crony capitalism in these trips, as many of the companies Obama visited had connections to his 2008 presidential campaign. The White House dismissed these ties as purely coincidental, but there was no escaping that these appearances also served as campaign opportunities. The *Washington Post* acknowledged that some of his "factory appearances have had a distinctly political feel," and that they were in states favorable to Obama in 2008.[15]

Obama had laid out his full vision for alternative energy in a seminal speech following the Gulf oil spill. Americans for Tax Reform critiqued his remarks, highlighting the many evasions and mistruths underlying his energy agenda. For example, Obama lamented, "Countries like China are investing in clean energy jobs and industries that should be here in America." What he didn't mention was that a staggering 80 percent of the first $1 billion of grants to wind energy firms in the 2009 stimulus bill was given to foreign companies to build turbines overseas.[16] The next

$2.1 billion of grants was hardly better, with 79 percent going to foreign-based companies.[17]

Obama bragged that "old factories" were reopening to produce wind turbines and that small businesses were making solar panels. But, as ATR pointed out, these were all jobs created by the infusion of taxpayer stimulus money stoking artificial supply with no corresponding market demand. As an example, Obama billed the DeSoto Solar Center in Florida as the "largest solar power plant in the United States." But it had received $150,000 of stimulus money and employed four hundred construction workers to build the site, only to end up with just two employees working for the firm—a textbook example of Obama's concept of sustainability.[18]

In his speech, Obama touted jobs his stimulus had created for weatherizing homes. In fact, $5 billion of stimulus money was appropriated and, as of the speech, fewer than 10,000 of the 593,000 designated homes had actually been weatherized. The inspector general concluded that this project had no material impact on jobs, and the Government Accountability Office reported that the Davis-Bacon wage laws translated to the project's expenditure of $57,000 per home involved.[19]

Take Seattle; in 2010, Mayor Mike McGinn learned that his city had received a $20 million federal grant to invest in weatherization. Amid great acclaim, on the eve of Earth Day—the secular holy day for environmentalists—McGinn traveled to the White House to make the announcement with Vice President Joe Biden. The two proclaimed the project's ambitious goals: creating two thousand living-wage jobs in Seattle and retrofitting two thousand homes in poorer neighborhoods. More than a year later, only three homes had been retrofitted and fourteen jobs had been created, many of which were administrative positions, not jobs for low-income workers. Michael Woo, director of the Seattle environmental group Got Green, observed, "It's been a very slow and tedious process. It's almost painful, the number of meetings people have gone to. Those are the people who got jobs. There's been no real investment for the broader public."

Moreover, the federal money mostly did not benefit lower-income homeowners, but went to the Washington Athletic Club and a few hospitals. "Who's benefitting from this program right now—it doesn't square with what the aspiration was," said Howard Greenwich of Puget Sound Sage. "I think what it boils down to is who's got the money."[20]

Also in his address, Obama casually conceded, "Now, there are costs associated with this transition [to his cap-and-trade scheme]. And some believe we can't afford those costs right now. I say we can't afford not to." But what were these costs? The ATR ticked off the items: gasoline prices would rise 58 percent, natural gas prices by 55 percent, heating oil prices by 56 percent, and electricity by 90 percent; annual energy costs for a family of four would increase $1,241; aggregate GDP losses would be $9.4 trillion, aggregate cap-and-trade energy taxes would be $5.7 trillion; job losses would be almost 2.5 million; the national debt would increase by $12,803 per person and $51,212 per a family of four; GDP losses for a single year would reach $400 billion by 2025 and would exceed $700 billion by 2012; net job losses would reach nearly 1.9 million by 2012 and perhaps as high as 2.5 million by 2035, and we could lose 1.4 million manufacturing jobs by 2035.[21]

FROM $1.3 MILLION TO $24.2 MILLION PER "PERMANENT" JOB

The green jobs component of the stimulus failed to improve the economy, but Obama would not relent. A month after his energy speech—in July 2010—reports showed that the economy had created private-sector jobs for six months in a row. Emboldened, Obama announced he was "accelerating the transition to a clean-energy economy and doubling our use of renewable energy sources like wind and solar power—steps that have the potential to create whole new industries and hundreds of thousands of new jobs in America."

Specifically, Obama said that his Department of Energy was awarding almost $2 billion in "conditional commitments"—meaning loan guarantees—to solar companies Abengoa Solar and Abound Solar Manufacturing, claiming Abengoa would create 1,600 construction jobs in Arizona and Abound would support 2,000 construction jobs and 1,500 permanent jobs in Colorado and Indiana. With these government loan guarantees, the money is loaned by the Treasury bank—not private lenders—pursuant to congressional authorization, so federal money is at risk from the beginning.[22] Blogger Ed Morrissey quantified how much the government was putting on the line in exchange for the relatively small number of jobs that might be created, finding we were placing $2 billion at risk to create a total of 5,100 jobs. That yields a potential cost of $392,156 per job—and only 1,500 of those would be permanent jobs, with the rest to end as soon as construction is complete. Morrissey concluded, "That means we will spend over $1.3 million per 'permanent' job in building this 'green economy,' which looks more like a red-ink economy with even a cursory check of the numbers."[23] So far, the government has forked out $70 million for Abound, and the company recently announced it would lay off 70 percent of its work force.[24]

Over two years the DOE ended up awarding Abengoa three separate loan guarantees totaling $2.78 billion for solar and ethanol plants. This is especially troubling, considering the concern didn't even seem to need U.S. government backed loan guarantees because in 2010 it qualified for private bank loans worth $161 million in eleven countries.[25] A $1.45 billion loan guaranty would "create or save" sixty permanent jobs at its Solana solar plant—amounting to $24.2 million per job; a $1.2 billion loan guaranty to a solar facility in the Mojave desert would produce seventy permanent jobs at $17.1 million a pop; and a $132 million guaranty to Abengoa Bioenergy Biomass of Kansas for a Dodge City ethanol plant would create sixty-five permanent jobs at $2 million each.[26]

SOLYNDRA: "INFUSED WITH POLITICS AT EVERY LEVEL"

The *Titanic* of Obama's green energy program was Solyndra, a California-based solar panel manufacturing company the Obama administration propped up with $535 million in federal loan guarantees, with taxpayers on the hook in the event of a default. The Treasury Department facilitated the loan with the support of the Energy Department, and the terms of the loan were approved by the White House Office of Management and Budget.[27]

This was unbridled liberalism, with the best of ostensibly good intentions and nary a concern for whether it was a viable enterprise that had the slightest prospect for success—a microcosm of the administration's grander failure, the $868 billion stimulus bill. In fact, Solyndra received the administration's first loan guaranty under the stimulus bill.[28]

Obama showed not the least reticence about his support for the project or any concern that its possible failure would dent the credibility of his clean energy pursuits, obviously having lived a political life mostly sheltered from accountability. Accordingly, he and his energy secretary Steven Chu made celebratory visits to the company's headquarters in the Silicon Valley. The cautionary warnings of House Republicans and government auditors that this wasn't a good investment didn't impress the administration.

Showing zero humility, the administration continually showcased Solyndra as a model project for America's future. Much fanfare accompanied the groundbreaking ceremony with Secretary Chu in attendance and Vice President Biden's image proudly on display through a video feed. "The announcement today is part of the unprecedented investment this administration is making in renewable energy and exactly what the Recovery Act is all about," Biden triumphantly declared. "By investing in the infrastructure and technology of the future, we are not only creating jobs today, but laying the foundation for long-term growth in the 21st-century economy."[29] During Obama's visit to Solyndra, he enthusiastically told its employees that his administration's financial support for the project was creating hundreds of jobs.[30] "We can see the positive impacts [of the stimulus] right here at Solyndra," he boasted.

Not everyone believed the rhetoric, however. Skeptics of the company's viability included not only Republicans, but apparently the firm's own employees, with one former worker later declaring, "Everyone knew that the plant wouldn't work."[31] Indeed, in April 2010, even before Obama's visit, auditor PricewaterhouseCoopers said that Solyndra's losses and negative cash flow raise "substantial doubt about its ability to continue as a going concern." As the *New York Times* reported, "Behind the pomp and pageantry, Solyndra was rotting inside, hemorrhaging cash so quickly that within weeks of Mr. Obama's visit, the company canceled plans to offer shares to the public."[32]

We later learned that despite the administration's public braggadocio, it had internally discussed Solyndra's potential collapse for quite some time. As early as 2009, Brad Jones of Redpoint Ventures sent an email warning Larry Summers, director of the National Economic Council, that Solyndra was a bad bet. Arguing that the Energy Department did not seem "well-equipped to decide which companies should get the money and how much," Jones said that while his own firm was backing Solyndra, the company had received its loan even though it had no profits and revenue short of $100 million. "While that is good for us, I can't imagine it's a good way for the government to use taxpayer money," Jones observed. Summers candidly replied, "I relate to your view that gov is a crappy vc [venture capitalist] and if u were closer to it you'd feel more strongly. What should we do?"[33]

In a *Washington Post* exposé based on "an analysis of thousands of memos, company records and internal e-mails," the paper found that Summers was not the only Obama official concerned about Solyndra and about Obama's larger green energy agenda. The communications uncovered by the *Post* showed "vigorous debate within the Obama White House about whether the solar-panel manufacturer was a smart bet. They also highlight the angst inside the West Wing about whether the president's initiative to support clean energy was ill-equipped to live up to its promises, or could, as some hoped, help validate Obama's use of $80 billion in stimulus to build a clean-energy industry."[34]

The *Post* further discovered that Obama's "green-technology program was infused with politics at every level." According to the paper, "political considerations were raised repeatedly by company investors, Energy Department bureaucrats and White House officials." What's more, the government's backing of Solyndra was supported by an extensive lobbying campaign, including "high-level maneuvering by politically connected clean-technology investors."[35]

When Solyndra was on the brink of collapse, what commanded the administration's attention was not so much the fate of the employees—

"rarely, if ever was there discussion of the impact that Solyndra's collapse would have on laid-off workers"—but the "political fallout" and the "optics" of the company's failure, and its possible effect on Obama's prospects for reelection. Ryan Alexander, president of the nonpartisan Taxpayers for Common Sense, said, "What's so troubling is that politics seems to be the dominant factor. They're not talking about what the taxpayers are losing; they're not talking about the failure of the technology, whether we bet on the wrong horse. What they are talking about is 'How are we going to manage this politically?'"[36]

A typical example is a January 31, 2011, email in which OMB staff members discuss how a Solyndra default, if timed correctly, could be spun to the administration's benefit. According to the staffer, "If Solyndra defaults down the road, the optics will arguably be worse later than they would be today.... In addition, the timing will likely coincide with the 2012 campaign season heating up, whereas a default today could be put in the context of (and perhaps even get some credit for) fiscal discipline/ good government because the Administration would be limiting further taxpayer exposure letting bad projects go, and could make public steps it is taking to learn lessons and improve/limit future lending."[37]

Adding scandal to injury, we later learned the administration had granted ready access to venture capitalists with stakes in administration-backed companies. Many of these individuals were Obama donors, and a number of them were given jobs in the administration overseeing its clean-energy program. Compounding this corrupt morass, there were revelations that senior administration officials pressured bureaucrats to fast-track approval of the loan in time to allow the administration to gain maximum political advantage through Biden's public unveiling of the project during a visit to California.[38]

"IT WAS AN INSANE BUSINESS MODEL"

Obama made his high-profile visit to Solyndra in May 2010 despite increasing signs of the firm's impending collapse. We later learned that administration officials and Obama fundraisers, fearing the firm would not survive, had urged him not to visit Solyndra and risk political embarrassment. But arrogant DOE officials gave Obama just enough assurances to allow him to proceed.[39]

In June 2010, the month following Obama's visit, the firm's CEO, Brian Harrison, boasted to the *Washington Post* about Solyndra's improving performance, saying that the company "doubled our production from 2009 to 2010, and we'll double it again from 2010 to 2011." To the contrary, one solar industry expert, Peter Lynch, revealed that Solyndra had experienced serious difficulties from the beginning and that it had always had an imbalanced financial model. "You make something in a factory and it costs $6, you sell it for $3, but you really, really need to sell it for $1.50 to be competitive," he said. "It was an insane business model. The numbers just don't work, and they never did."[40]

In November 2010 Solyndra announced it would lay off nearly 20 percent of its workers. Less than a year later, the company let go its remaining workers and filed for bankruptcy. Shortly after that, its offices were raided by the FBI and DOE. Top Solyndra executives later pleaded the Fifth Amendment and refused to testify before a congressional hearing.[41]

What was so recently heralded as the future of green energy and of a larger, thriving green economy ended in ignominious failure and as the target of a federal criminal investigation. It was a tale of an ideologically driven administration that rigged the system and cut corners to loan enormous amounts of money to a company manufacturing a politically correct product for which there was little public demand.[42]

LIBERALISM MEANS NEVER HAVING TO SAY YOU'RE SORRY

The Obama administration took pains to emphasize that the mere collapse of its flagship clean-energy project would not diminish its enthusiasm for funding similar concerns. They were not the least bit repentant, acting as though the half-billion-dollar loss was just the ordinary course of business, to be expected in the pursuit of a noble cause, and that they would soldier on, with taxpayer money, experimenting with more such wasteful projects. "The president will continue to support these initiatives and highlight the American ingenuity, the people and the private-sector companies that are helping to generate jobs and foster our nation's 21st-century clean-energy economy," said White House spokesman Clark Stevens. The White House released an unapologetic statement declaring, "While we are disappointed by this particular outcome, we continue to believe the clean energy jobs race is one that America can, must and will win. The Department of Energy's overall portfolio of investments—which includes dozens of other companies—continues to perform well and is on pace to create thousands of jobs."[43]

In fact, these companies were not providing permanent jobs, and the jobs they did offer were created only through government infusions of cash. The inability of these companies to compete in the market was all the more remarkable given the free advertising Obama gave them with his incessant promotions and visits. Brendan Doherty, an assistant professor at the U.S. Naval Academy, observed, "You couldn't get that kind of publicity if you devoted all your advertising budget to it."[44]

Obama himself was unapologetic. "Now there are going to be some failures. Hindsight is always 20/20," he said in an interview with ABC News and Yahoo! online television. "It went through the normal process and people thought this was a good bet."[45] We know that neither of those statements was true: it was an expedited process rife with conflicts of interest and favoritism, and many of his closest advisors thought Solyndra was far from "a good bet." Whether the federal government should be making these kinds of bets in the first place is another question.

Energy Department spokesman Dan Leistikow was equally unrepentant, saying, "We have always recognized that not every one of the innovative companies supported by our loans and loan guarantees would succeed. But we can't stop investing in game-changing technologies that are key to America's leadership in the global economy."[46] Being a "well-intentioned" liberal means never having to say you're sorry.

Unsurprisingly, even as the administration sought to justify the Solyndra investment, some officials blamed the entire mess on the Bush administration, saying the Bush DOE was the first to consider Solyndra's application. That allegation was true, but it left out one important detail—the Bush DOE *rejected* Solyndra's bid.[47]

Proving that the Solyndra denouement would not affect its energy policy one iota, just days before Solyndra shut down, the Department of Energy finalized a partial loan guaranty for $852 million to yet another solar energy company—Genesis Solar Energy Project, of California—with the promise that it would support eight hundred construction jobs and forty-seven operating jobs. "This project creates jobs, avoids greenhouse gas emissions and helps strengthen our nation's renewable energy future," Secretary Chu announced.[48]

But the administration's headlong rush to force-feed these green projects to the nation have led to other unanticipated problems—and from an unlikely source. In order to qualify for the loan, Genesis had to meet certain deadlines, but they've run into opposition from Native Americans, who are trying to delay or even scuttle the project because they say the accelerated approval process fails to protect wildlife and cultural resources.[49]

"THEY DID PUSH VERY HARD FOR US TO HOLD OUR ANNOUNCEMENT"

There was a good reason the administration was uncooperative with congressional investigators looking into the Solyndra affair. The House Committee on Energy and Commerce opened its investigation on February 17, 2011, requesting documents and a briefing on Solyndra. Four months later, the White House's Office of Management and Budget was stonewalling, failing to produce "a single page of its communications or analyses" pertaining to the Solyndra loan guaranty. Committee Democrats continually refused to cooperate and protested investigative efforts at every turn. On a strict party line vote, the Committee voted 14–8 to subpoena the OMB for these documents.

Upon Solyndra's declaration of bankruptcy in August 2011, House Energy and Commerce Committee chairman Fred Upton issued a joint

statement with the chairman of the investigations subcommittee, Cliff
Stearns, saying, "We smelled a rat from the onset. For an administration
that parades around the banner of transparency, they fought us tooth and
nail all summer long in turning over relevant documents related to the
credit approval. And today we found out why."[50]

Upton's committee concluded that the DOE and OMB did not take
adequate steps to protect taxpayer dollars, as emails and other communications showed that their staff repeatedly questioned whether Solyndra
had financial resources sufficient to warrant the loan guaranty. These
communications confirmed that the administration pressured the OMB
staff to expedite and complete its loan review prior to the groundbreaking ceremony at the company's facilities, which was being orchestrated
by the administration. These exchanges "clearly demonstrate that OMB
felt pressure to complete its review ahead of the September 4 event." They
also revealed that the White House jumped the gun, treating the loan
approval as a foregone conclusion, as they scheduled Vice President
Biden's and Secretary Chu's appearance before the DOE had even made
its final presentation to the OMB for the loan.[51]

The *Washington Post* too found that the Obama White House tried
to rush federal reviewers for a decision on the Solyndra loan guaranty.
Released emails from August 2009 showed that White House officials
repeatedly pestered OMB reviewers as to when they would decide on the
loan. OMB officials expressed concern they were being pressured to
approve the deal without adequate time to assess the risk to taxpayers.[52]
There were also reports that the DOE pressured Solyndra investors to
quickly increase their investment to justify the government's loan guaranty.

Tainting the ordeal further, Solyndra company representatives made
numerous visits to the White House to meet with administration officials—between March 12, 2009, and April 14, 2011, according to White
House visitor logs, Solyndra officials and investors made at least twenty
White House visits, including four meetings alone the week before the
loan guaranty was awarded.[53]

More bad news emerged surrounding a Solyndra restructuring deal
that the government had approved in February 2011, as the company

ran short of cash. The agreement, it was revealed, was crafted to give Solyndra's private investors priority ahead of the government—in other words, ahead of the taxpayers—on the first $75 million to be recouped in case of bankruptcy.

According to the committee, this subordination of taxpayer money to private creditors, one of whom was an Obama financial supporter, "appears to be in direct violation of the Energy Policy Act of 2005, which states that 'the obligation shall be subject to the condition that the obligation is not subordinate to other financing.'" Despite this clear language, DOE counsel issued a legal opinion approving the legality of the government's loan subordination under the Energy Policy Act.

Two Treasury Department officials told a House Energy and Commerce subcommittee they were unaware of any previous subordination of taxpayers to private investors in a government loan repayment.[54] The restructuring agreement was indeed unprecedented, but it was perfectly consistent with the administration's practice of ignoring customs, practices, and traditions as well as the law. It was eerily reminiscent of Obama's lawless subordination of secured creditors in favor of his union allies in the Chrysler restructuring scandal, as detailed in *Crimes Against Liberty*.

In the end, the DOE's subordination cost the taxpayers dearly. As part of its bankruptcy, the company agreed to auction off thousands of items from its California production facility, all to the benefit of the firm's private investors, not the taxpayers.[55] More maddening still, we learned the restructuring agreement was approved despite warnings from OMB staff that restructuring could cost taxpayers $168 million more than simply liquidating the company.[56]

In a final scandalous revelation, the *Washington Post* reported in November 2011 that the Obama administration had urged Solyndra executives to delay announcing its initial round of layoffs until after the November 2, 2010, midterm elections. "DOE continues to be cooperative and have indicated that they will fund the November draw on our loan (app. $40 million) but have not committed to December yet," wrote a Solyndra investor advisor on October 30. "They did push very hard for us to hold our announcement of the consolidation to employees and vendors to Nov. 3rd—oddly they didn't give a reason for that date."[57]

As HotAir's Ed Morrissey wrote, "This means that the DoE knew that Solyndra had begun to fail, and that the case they provided as part of Barack Obama's job stimulus wouldn't actually create jobs. In fact, it wasn't even going to *save* jobs. And yet the DoE not only succeeded in pressuring Solyndra into hiding the fact from the public and their investors, this sequence makes it look as though the Obama administration used the $40 million in loans as a bribe to keep Solyndra from making its layoff announcement in a timely manner." According to Morrissey, it also appeared that this thread led directly to the White House.[58]

"SOLYNDRA WAS JUST THE BEGINNING"

Like Solyndra, at least four other companies that received stimulus money have failed. Two of these were green energy firms: Evergreen Solar and SpectraWatt, both of which said they couldn't compete with Chinese competitors.[59] Various experts are now predicting hundreds of bankruptcies of U.S. solar companies when the market for solar panels, artificially inflated by government support, cools down. "Solyndra was just the beginning," says Jessie Pichel, chief of clean-energy research at the investment bank Jefferies & Co. "We're going to see a lot of companies go bankrupt." Mark Bachman, a renewables analyst at Avian Securities, predicts that only twenty to forty of the few hundred solar panel manufacturers in the world will survive the next few years.[60]

Undeterred by all these failures, Obama's DOE approved two more solar project loan guarantees just days before the federal deadline. The projects totaled more than $1 billion: a $737 million guaranty to Solar Reserve for a solar tower on federal land in Nevada, and $337 million to Arizona's Mesquite Solar 1. As experts note, these guarantees are virtually destined to fail, having been given to firms that could not make it on their own. Even Treasury Secretary Timothy Geithner's warning that these guarantees were too risky did not faze Obama, who never met a budget he felt compelled to balance or a risk of taxpayer money he believed he needed to justify.[61]

As with Solyndra, political connections appear to have been an important factor in the Solar Reserve loan; one of the company's business partners, PCG Clean Energy and Technology Fund (East) LLC, has Nancy Pelosi's brother-in-law, Ronald Pelosi, as an executive. Another of its investment partners, Argonaut Private Equity, employs Steve Mitchell, who was a member of Solyndra's Board of Directors.[62]

Indeed, Obama's green energy initiative has provided a tremendous outlet for cronyism. In *Throw Them All Out*, the Hoover Institution's Peter Schweizer revealed that 80 percent of the renewable energy companies backed by Obama's DOE are operated by or mostly owned by Obama donors. These companies' political largesse, says Schweizer, "is probably the best investment they ever made in alternative energy. It brought them returns many times over." Schweizer found that in the so-called "1705 Loan Guarantee Program alone ... $16.4 billion of the $20.5 billion in loans granted as of September 15 went to companies either run by or primarily owned by Obama financial backers—individuals who were bundlers, members of Obama's National Finance Committee, or large donors to the Democratic Party."

The administration's clean energy cronyism was also detailed in a 2010 Government Accountability Office report, which found that the Department of Energy "treated applicants inconsistently, favoring some and disadvantaging others." DOE inspector general Gregory Friedman testified that contracts had been steered to "friends and family."[63] GAO auditors also reported in 2010 that the DOE had given favorable treatment to certain loan guaranty applicants and had waived some of the required steps for five loan applicants to receive funding, one of which was Solyndra. The government fast-tracked these loan guarantees before receiving final reports that the risks were warranted.[64]

The GAO, upon examining the first eighteen government-guaranteed loans that the DOE approved, found that not one of them was properly documented.[65] "There's a consequence if you don't follow a rigorous process that's transparent," said Franklin Rusco, a GAO analyst. "It makes the agency more susceptible to outside pressures, potentially." And in fact, Solyndra benefitted a company whose financial backers include George Kaiser, an Oklahoma oil billionaire who functioned as a "bundler" of campaign donations and raised some $50,000 for Obama's 2008 campaign.[66]

In addition, the DOE inspector general called the DOE to task for not saving email communications discussing the selection of loan guaranty recipients. Based on this deplorable series of events, auditors were concerned that defaults of other similarly situated companies might be imminent if the department, in its haste to expedite these types of loans, exercised similar negligence in requiring the normal reviews.[67]

Shortly before this book went to press, we learned about more clean-energy debacles. First, there is A123 Systems in Massachusetts. Scott Heiss, who bought stock in the company, which manufactures large lithium batteries for automakers, filed a federal lawsuit against the firm alleging it hid problems at its plant that, if disclosed, would lower its stock price. The company, a beneficiary of $300 million of stimulus funding, laid off 125 workers in December 2011 and has announced a recall of malfunctioning battery packs that will cost it more than $55 million. And second, a company ludicrously named "Solar Trust of America" just filed for bankruptcy. As observers noted, its failure could be blamed on the demise of Solar Millennium AG, its German parent company. This was a close call for taxpayers, since the Energy Department approved a mammoth $2.1 billion loan guaranty for the doomed company. Luckily—no thanks to the DOE—the firm's CEO turned down the offer, saying it was too risky.[68]

GREEN JOBS—THE RECORD

Clean energy is not living up to its grandiose hype. President Obama at one point promised to create five million green jobs in ten years, while

California governor Jerry Brown said he envisioned half a million clean-technology jobs in his state by 2020. But even the *New York Times* conceded that "the results so far suggest such numbers are a pipe dream."[69] The green-tech program that included Solyndra involved a staggering $38.6 billion loan program that Obama claimed would create or save sixty-five thousand jobs. But two years after it began, the program had created only 3,545 new, permanent jobs, according to Energy Department figures.[70]

Eventually, even key Democrats began to publicly criticize Obama's green schemes. "You know, the green jobs have been about a lot of talk and not a lot has been happening on that," observed Congresswoman Maxine Waters. "All of this talk about the green jobs never materialized." Other influential members of the Congressional Black Caucus agreed. Congressman Emanuel Cleaver said, "African-Americans out there were saying, 'What do we have in common with this new, green technology?'"

A July 2011 *Washington Post*-ABC poll showed that rank-and-file liberal Democrats were losing faith in the program as well. "The number of liberal Democrats who strongly support Obama's record on jobs plunged 22 points from 53 percent last year to 31 percent," according to the *Post*. But Obama is deaf to the feedback, continuing his showpiece visits to renewable energy firms. One of them was Johnson Controls, Inc., a Michigan firm upon which the government bestowed $300 million to create 150 green jobs, or $2 million per job.[71]

When Obama talks about jobs, he invariably emphasizes green jobs.[72] And yet, the signs are everywhere that green jobs are a bust. The Brookings Institution released a study showing that clean-technology jobs constituted only 2 percent of the nation's jobs and only slightly more— 2.2 percent—in the Silicon Valley. Overall, federal and state efforts to stimulate job creation, according to the *New York Times*, "have largely failed, government records show."[73]

Consider a typical Obama stimulus project: $186 million was allocated to weatherize homes, with the result that California, as of August 2011, had spent only half the money and created some 538 full-time jobs in the preceding quarter. What accounted for the delay in the project's implementation? Another liberal requirement: the federal Department of Labor had to determine the prevailing wage standards. Even after the postponement, however, "the program never really caught on." Sheeraz Haji, a market research firm's chief executive, said, "Companies and public policy officials really overestimated how much consumers care about energy efficiency. People care about their wallet and the comfort of their home, but it's not a sexy thing."[74]

Typical of such high-minded liberal projects, clean-energy job training programs have also failed miserably. California's Economic Development Department records show that $59 million of government and private funds assigned to green jobs training and apprenticeship have yielded only 719 jobs, a staggering $82,000 per job. Of course, liberals cannot concede that government is unable to artificially create demand where it doesn't exist. "The demand's just not there to take this to scale," exclaimed the project manager at one of the companies that received cash infusions. Other activists complain that these green jobs would take hold if only Washington would do a better job of stacking the deck against conventional energy.

The *Wall Street Journal* likewise reported that while the solar industry has long been viewed by some as a remedy to our dependence on fossil fuels, those aspirations are rapidly disappearing as solar panel manufacturers continue to suffer through bankruptcies, cratering stock values, and mountains of debt. Ironically, part of the blame lies in a surfeit of supply, much of it generated by government subsidies facilitated by "well-intentioned" environmentalist liberals who apparently believed the power of their beneficence could overcome market forces.

While Solyndra's collapse captured the headlines in the last few months of 2011, at least five other solar panel makers filed for bankruptcy or insolvency around the same time. Nine of the ten largest publicly traded solar companies took a hit in 2011, and many others were experiencing difficulties as stock prices fell some 57 percent in the sector.[75] These reckless experiments are more evidence that even tens of millions of federal and state dollars thrown at pet liberal projects don't create jobs or stimulate the economy. Liberals may refuse to acknowledge the invisible hand of the market, but they are subject to it nonetheless.

REGULATING COAL OUT OF BUSINESS

A key energy source to be replaced by green energy, at least in the liberal imagination, is coal. Obama came to office vowing to adopt regulations that would bankrupt companies which build new coal plants,[76] and as president he has done his best in this regard, pressuring the coal industry from every which way, seemingly determined to drive the industry out of his green energy Neverland.

When the EPA adopted a new policy that tightened water quality standards for valley fills at surface coalmines in West Virginia, Kentucky, Pennsylvania, Ohio, Virginia, and Tennessee, the coal industry filed a lawsuit to challenge the rules. Arguing the move would eliminate tens of thousands of jobs and raise electricity prices, hundreds of coal miners traveled to Capitol Hill to protest the administration, claiming it was trying to wipe out the entire coal industry.

It's hard not to conclude that at the very least, the EPA was trying to wipe out mountain-top removal mining. After all, EPA administrator Lisa Jackson admitted the goal was to enforce a standard so strict that few, if any, permits would be issued for valley fills. West Virginia's senior state senator, Democrat John D. Rockefeller IV, bluntly declared that Jackson "doesn't understand the sensitivities economically of what unemployment means. Her job is relatively simple: clean everything up, keep it clean, don't do anything to disturb perfection. Well, you can't do coal and do that at the same time. God didn't make coal to be an easy thing to work with."

The EPA denied these regulations would either weaken the economy or cause unemployment. But U.S. senator Jim Webb, Virginia Democrat, supported Rockefeller. "We are not going to let the EPA regulate coal out of business," he proclaimed. Also attending the rally was Senate Minority Leader Mitch McConnell, who said that the Obama administration and the current Congress are the most anti-coal executive and legislative bodies in the nation's history.[77]

"AN UNWARRANTED POWER GRAB"

In July 2011, the EPA launched the next round of its assault against coal plants, announcing its Clean Air Transport Rule, ostensibly aimed at curbing smog and soot at power plants in thirty-plus states. The rule—whose compliance costs were estimated as high as $1 trillion over ten years, and which even the EPA admitted could cost the economy as much as $90 billion annually by 2020—outraged businesses.[78] John Engler, president of the Business Roundtable, called the proposal "the single most expensive environmental regulation in U.S. history, a job-killing rule it is under no obligation to impose on the struggling economy."[79]

In September 2011, as Obama moved into reelection mode and the public showed little support for another job-killing, economy-crushing EPA regulation, Obama shelved the proposal—though EPA administrator Lisa Jackson noted her agency will revisit the issue in 2013, after the election.[80] "Even President Obama recognizes that his administration's environmental agenda, with all its new rules and regulations, is a massive job killer and is destroying the economy," said Myron Ebell of the Competitive Enterprise Institute. "What is shameful about the President's decision to delay the new ozone rule is that it's all about improving his chances of being re-elected and has nothing to do with the economic damage that the rule would do. The fact that the President still wants to go ahead after he gets re-elected with a regulation that has been estimated to cost $1 trillion a year shows that he could care less about the U.S. economy and the millions of people who have lost their jobs."[81]

But the smog rule was hardly the EPA's sole job-destroying scheme. The agency has developed six other rules that together would entail an annual cost to the economy of $35 billion, according to the EPA's own figures. One of these proposed regulations is the area source rule, which would regulate mercury emission from boilers that provide heat and power for buildings throughout the nation. The Small Business Administration warned that the rule would "impose significant new regulatory costs" on businesses, cities, and other entities, but the EPA was unmoved. As the Heritage Foundation's Diane Katz observed, "The agency has long been a hyperactive regulator, but the rate at which it is now imposing ever-costlier rules had accelerated dramatically. Congress must act to curb the agency's unwarranted power grab if it hopes to see any meaningful economic recovery."[82]

Another costly new regulation, the cross-state air pollution rule, forces twenty-seven states to cut air pollution that is supposedly pushed across state lines by wind. Luminant, a Texas energy company, said the rule is forcing it to close several of its facilities, costing five hundred jobs. "We have hundreds of employees who have spent their entire professional careers at Luminant and its predecessor companies," said Luminant CEO David Campbell. "At every step of this process, we have tried to minimize these impacts, and it truly saddens me that we are being compelled to take the actions we've announced today. We have filed suit to try to avoid these consequences."[83] The administration appeared to have no interest in granting a reprieve from these rigorous deadlines, the importance of American jobs paling in its eyes next to the goal of a pristine environment.

In March 2012, the EPA proposed a new rule that, if implemented, could represent the *coup de grace* to the coal industry. The regulation would require any new power plant to emit less than one thousand pounds of carbon dioxide per megawatt hour of electricity produced. Because coal plants average 1,768 pounds of carbon dioxide per megawatt hour, new plants are highly unlikely to meet the revised standard. "This standard effectively bans new coal plants," observed Joseph Stanko, a lawyer who represents utility companies. "So I don't see how that is an 'all of the above' energy policy." Michael Brune, executive director of the Sierra Club, exulted that the new rule "captures the end of an era"—yet, displaying the group's trademark extremism, he argued that even this draconian regulation is "not sufficient."[84]

There can be no doubt about the intent of this rule, which EPA administrator Lisa Jackson revealed during an interview in November 2011. When asked about EPA regulations that are forcing the closure of coal-fired power plants, she replied, "First off, EPA doesn't require shutting down of any plant.... Some businesses are investing in nuclear; some are looking at natural gas. There are states that are leading the way on solar or wind.... What EPA's role is to do is to level the playing field so that pollution costs are not exported to the population but rather companies have to look at the pollution potential of any fuel or any process or any plant or any utility when they're making investment decisions."[85]

Or, stated another way, the administration fully intends, as Obama announced long ago, to bankrupt the coal industry.

Barack Obama said he wanted a transformational presidency, and this grandiosity is on full display in his energy agenda. Using every available method, from EPA regulations to unilaterally canceling the Yucca Mountain project, Obama is putting relentless pressure on certain disfavored industries, with coal and nuclear power topping the list alongside oil. Because nothing is available to replace the output of these firms, he seeks to advance technological progress on untested green energy projects through the sheer force of government. Blinded by his own ideology, he discounts the mounting costs of his program, pressuring his agencies to rush through billions of dollars in loan guarantees for firms like Solyndra that many observers, even among his own team, view as risky if not outright reckless.

Perhaps the most troubling aspect of the Solyndra affair—more troubling than the cronyism, the self-deluding economic analyses, the high-pressure rush to approve the loan guaranty, and the last-ditch restructuring attempt that cost the taxpayers tens of millions—is the administration's dogmatic refusal to rethink its approach in light of the company's collapse. If something that wasteful and that politically embarrassing cannot force some introspection, then in all likelihood nothing can—meaning we can expect to see a lot more Solyndras in the near future.

CHAPTER NINE

THE WAR ON BUSINESS

Despite claiming to be a "fierce advocate of the free market," Obama has consistently revealed his contempt for free enterprise and the private sector. He has compiled the most anti-business record of any modern president, vilifying the "wealthy" and the profit motive, while promoting major tax increases on small businesses, dividends, and capital gains. He has opposed, until this election year, corporate income tax reductions and has burdened businesses with stifling regulations. He has also betrayed an alarming ignorance of basic economics, cajoling businesses to step up and hire more people, as if their hiring decisions are purely a matter of personal whim and their failure to create jobs stems from just plain selfishness.[1]

Business doesn't seem to get much of a hearing in the deliberations of the Obama administration. This is unsurprising, considering most of Obama's appointments are academics who lack business experience. In describing Obama's original cabinet, *Politico* wrote, "This constellation of talent ... has something of a black hole. There is virtually no one on Obama's team with outsized achievements or a high-profile reputation earned in the world of business. There are no former CEOs in the Obama Cabinet. And among the people who make up his daily inner circle, there is only a dollop or two of top-level private sector experience."[2]

Even as it says it has streamlined and softened the regulatory climate, the administration has accelerated the pace and scope of regulations across the board, both with existing laws and with major new ones such as Obamacare and the Dodd-Frank financial regulation bill, which both create new regulatory labyrinths. Meanwhile, in its zeal to *appear* to be on the cutting edge of ethical rule-making—as opposed to actually operating ethically—the administration has proposed new ethics rules that are either irrelevant or actually harmful, such as a rule that would ban government employees from attending conferences and trade shows.[3]

While exuding hostility to business, Obama is beholden to Big Labor, which provides the financing and on-the-ground muscle for his political campaigns. In return, Obama consistently advances Big Labor's interests, most notably in protecting the unions above all others during the government take-over of GM and Chrysler, as described in *Crimes Against Liberty*.

Obama's favoritism toward labor unions typically comes at the expense of employers and non-union workers, such as his support for card-check legislation that would eliminate secret ballot voting on whether to form a union. Other examples include the countless pro-union actions of his NLRB, such as its rule requiring employers to place posters at the workplace informing employees of their right to organize;[4] its rules making it much more difficult for employees to rid themselves of unwanted unions through decertification;[5] and its legal actions against states that have opted for secret ballots instead of card check for unionization.[6]

Obama's NLRB also abandoned its longstanding precedent and adopted a new rule making it much easier for unionists to organize by allowing small groups of workers to form micro-unions when a majority of all employees wouldn't support unionizing.[7] Further, the NLRB approved the unions' ability to negotiate pre-recognition agreements in exchange for card check, thereby undermining the employees' rights through these "sweetheart deals";[8] and, as discussed later, it sued Boeing to prevent it from opening a plant in a right-to-work state.[9] In one telling maneuver, the administration, despite its stated commitment to increasing exports and bolstering free trade, delayed for three years sending to Congress trade agreements with South Korea, Panama, and Colombia—agreements Big Labor just happened to oppose.

The White House is aware of the widespread perception that it is anti-business, which is why in the summer of 2010, Obama launched a PR offensive with major corporations. Although Treasury Secretary Tim Geithner was all over the talk shows touting the administration's "pro-growth agenda,"[10] American businesses know better; a recent Gallup poll revealed that the top concern of small-business owners throughout America is the burden of "complying with government regulations."[11]

"AT HIS CORE, ANTI-BUSINESS"

Newsweek's Fareed Zakaria reported that he interviewed numerous business leaders, most of whom had voted for Obama, and that every one of them believe he is "at his core, anti-business." The businessmen griped that Obama has no business executives in his cabinet, that he rarely consults with CEOs other than for photo-ops, that he has no private-sector experience, that he clearly prefers government and non-profit work to that of private business, and that his tax and regulatory policies are uncertain.[12] As *Washington Post* business columnist Steven Pearlstein wrote, "There is no denying it—bad blood has developed between big business and the Obama administration, and that's not a good thing. Business executives dislike the uncertainty created by health-care reform and financial regulation.... They see a wave of new regulation heading their way after years of writing their own rules."[13]

New York Daily News owner and publisher Mortimer Zuckerman said that he detects in the Obama White House "hostility to the very kinds of [business] culture that have made this the great country that it is and was. I think we have to find some way of dealing with that or else we will do great damage to this country with a public policy that could ruin everything."[14]

Likewise, Verizon CEO Ivan Seidenberg issued a blistering indictment of the administration's anti-business posture. "By reaching into virtually every sector of economic life," said Seidenberg, "government is injecting uncertainty into the marketplace and making it harder to raise capital and create new businesses." This denunciation was especially noteworthy because Seidenberg has strongly supported Obama and tried to cooperate with the administration on all its major agenda items, including healthcare, finance reform, and energy. Nevertheless, Seidenberg admitted he was "troubled" by Obama's agenda and had "reached a point where the negative effects of these policies are simply too significant to ignore."[15]

George Buckley, CEO of 3M, is even more blunt about Obama. "We know what his instincts are," says Buckley. "He is anti-business." Calling the president's policies "Robin Hood–esque," he suggests manufacturers like 3M might have to move production abroad in order to stay competitive.[16] "Politicians forget that business has [a] choice," Buckley adds. "If it's hostile, incrementally, things will slip away. We've got a real choice between manufacturing in Canada and Mexico—which tend to be pro-business—or America."[17] Indeed, Obama's anti-business animus, not unexpectedly, has severely affected the economy. Former Federal Reserve governor Kevin Warsh noted, "Owing to a less-than-assured economic outlook and broad uncertainty about public policy, employers appear quite reluctant to add to payrolls."[18]

"EVERYBODY'S AFRAID OF THE GOVERNMENT"

Perhaps the most brutal criticism of Obama's anti-business agenda came from Steve Wynn, CEO of Wynn Resorts. During a company conference call, Wynn declared,

> And I'm saying it bluntly, that this administration is the greatest wet blanket to business, and progress and job creation in my lifetime. And I can prove it and I could spend the next 3 hours giving you examples of all of us in this market place that are frightened to death about all the new regulations, our

healthcare costs escalate, regulations coming from left and right. A President that seems, that keeps using that word redistribution. Well, my customers and the companies that provide the vitality for the hospitality and restaurant industry in the United States of America, they are frightened of this administration. And it makes you slow down and not invest your money. Everybody complains about how much money is on the side in America.[19]

Continuing his tirade, Wynn, himself a Democrat who supports Democratic Senate majority leader Harry Reid, claimed we haven't heard the kind of talk Obama employs "except from pure socialists.... Everybody's afraid of the government and there's no need soft peddling it. It's the truth.... And I'm telling you that the business community in this country is frightened to death of the weird political philosophy of the President of the United States. And until he's gone, everybody's going to be sitting on their thumbs."[20] Even liberal columnist Al Hunt conceded that, though he doesn't think the president is anti-business, "Obama should realize that's what he too often conveys."[21]

Yes, he does—but he sure doesn't seem hostile when it comes to the government sector. Consider, for example, remarks Obama made during a public appearance after a woman told him she'd been laid off from her government job. "Let me just first of all say that workers like you, for the federal, state and local governments, are so important for our vital services," the president said. "And it frustrates me sometimes when people talk about 'government jobs' as if somehow those are worth less than private sector jobs. I think there is nothing more important than working on behalf of the American people."[22] A month later, Obama's treasury secretary Timothy Geithner told the House Small Business Committee that the administration believes it has to raise taxes on small businesses so it can avoid having to "shrink the overall size of government programs."[23]

Obama has even asked Congress to allow private debt collectors to call the private cell phones of people who owe money to the federal government.[24] This proposal didn't sit well with consumer groups or many Democrats, but even privacy concerns will not prevent this president from ensuring the government doesn't have to go on a diet.

Meanwhile, the tone-deaf administration defiantly denies the truth before our eyes. Jared Bernstein, a top White House economic advisor, hilariously proclaimed, "President Obama is obviously deeply pro-business, pro-markets."[25]

THE OSAWATOMIE SPEECH

In chapter six we briefly discussed Obama's December 2011 speech at Osawatomie, Kansas. The president's comments there so thoroughly revealed his true views on business, and offered such a penetrating gaze into his attitude toward the entire free enterprise system, that they deserve closer scrutiny here.

Co-opting the memory of Teddy Roosevelt, Obama criticized the view that "the market will take care of everything"—in other words, he blasted supporters of a totally unregulated market. This was an obvious straw man, since even the purest conservatives don't advocate it, but Obama suggested that not only do conservatives support it, they actually implemented it. "It doesn't work. It has never worked," Obama insisted. "It didn't work when we tried it during the last decade. I mean, understand, it's not as if we haven't tried this theory.... We simply cannot return to this brand of 'you're on your own' economics if we're serious about rebuilding the middle class in this country.... It results in a prosperity that's enjoyed by fewer and fewer of our citizens."[26]

Obama was disingenuously implying that conservatives favor abject economic anarchy, an economy utterly free of laws, regulations, and fairness, as if believing in a free market means you oppose antitrust rules and other laws that prevent unfair business practices.

At the same time, Obama, perhaps unwittingly, revealed he has little faith in free markets at all. To him, only the strong arm of government can achieve equal opportunity, more equitable income distribution, and economic growth. Only if the government provides a college education for everyone can we compete in the global market. Only if the federal government steps in and prevents the wealthy from earning too much money will we be able to revive the economy.

Nowhere in his speech did Obama evince any awareness that over-regulation, not underregulation, is smothering the economy. Nowhere did he discuss the disastrous effects of his own policies or of the unfairness inherent in government, rather than the market, choosing the winners and losers by fiat, with all the attendant cronyism and corruption that inevitably follows.

Obama views the market as a place of brutal class struggle, where the government is duty-bound to intervene and support the weak against the predations of the strong. But class struggle is not what the American idea is about. "There are no class distinctions in America," noted Matthew Spalding of the Heritage Foundation in response to Obama's speech. "That's why Steve Jobs could start [as] an adopted child in a broken home, start Apple in a garage and become a billionaire eight times over. The real distinction here is caused by the rise of a new governing class of experts, bureaucrats and political elites who insist on ruling us to enforce 'fairness' rather than letting us govern ourselves under the rule of law."[27]

THE "BUFFETT RULE"

In his Osawatomie speech, Obama railed against the tax structure, saying the exploitation by the rich of middle- and lower-income earners is not only unfair, but is a primary cause of the economic downturn because it has suppressed opportunity. This was shameless, as Obama must be aware that the top income earners pay the lion's share of income taxes while the bottom half pays virtually none. The Tax Foundation reported that in 2009, the top 1 percent paid 40 percent of all federal taxes, the top 5 percent paid 59 percent, and the top 10 percent paid 70 percent.[28]

Obama also resurrected his populist anecdote that Warren Buffett's secretary pays a higher tax rate than Buffett does. After repeating this gross distortion, he segued into his call for adopting the "Buffett Rule," which would require those making $1 million or more per year to pay at least 30 percent of their income in taxes. The *Wall Street Journal* eviscerated the proposal, declaring that "the entire Buffett Rule premise is false."[29] Similarly, Jamie Dimon, CEO of JPMorgan Chase, said he was mystified that successful people are being demonized. "I just don't get it.... Most of us wage earners are paying 39.6 percent in taxes and another 12 percent in New York state and city taxes and we're paying 50 percent of our income in taxes."[30]

Obama's argument is the height of sophistry. CBO figures indicate that the top 1 percent of income earners already pay nearly 30 percent of their income in federal taxes.[31] In addition, in the rare case where wealthy people pay a lower effective income tax rate, it's a result either of lawful deductions (often charitable—not every deduction, as Obama would have you believe, is a loophole known only to silk-stocking lawyers),[32] income derived from tax-free municipal bonds, or capital gains and dividends on property they've acquired with money that has already been taxed.

Additionally, before the wealthy realize many of these gains, the businesses that produce them have already paid a corporate income tax rate of 35 percent (the second highest and soon to be the highest rate in the world). This means that Buffett, on much of this income, pays an effective rate of 50 percent (35 percent corporate plus 15 percent capital gains), which far exceeds what secretaries pay. Indeed, 99.4 percent of millionaires and billionaires pay far more in taxes in actual and relative terms than middle- and low-income earners, and for Obama to suggest otherwise is not only deeply deceitful but also damaging—because of the class envy he stokes—to the social fabric of this country. And if Obama is so eager for the rich to pay a 30 percent tax rate, he should accept John Boehner's suggestion that he make a voluntary contribution to the Treasury, since he only paid a 20.5 percent tax rate on his 2011 household income of $789,674.[33]

A recent analysis by the Congressional Joint Committee on Taxation reports that the Buffett Rule would only raise an additional $47 billion in revenues over ten years—about one half of 1 percent of the amount Obama's budget is projected to add to the national debt over that period of time.[34] Nonetheless, if Mr. Buffett wants to pay higher income taxes (though his current battle with the IRS seems to imply otherwise), he is free to restructure his investments, expenses, and contributions to do so. Easier yet, he can just make voluntary payments to the federal Treasury.

The following chart, based on IRS data for 2009 (the most recent available figures), shows that those who earn (in terms of adjusted gross income) above $10 million paid an average of 26.3 percent of their income in federal taxes, and those who earned between $1 million and $10 million averaged over 29 percent. By contrast, those earning between $50,000 and $75,000 paid 11.6 percent.[35]

Adjusted Gross Income, 2009	Average Federal Income Tax Rate
$10,000 to $15,000	6.80%
$15,000 to $20,000	6.60%
$20,000 to $25,000	8.70%
$25,000 to $30,000	9.70%
$30,000 to $40,000	10.00%
$40,000 to $50,000	10.60%
$50,000 to $75,000	11.60%
$75,000 to $100,000	12.30%
$100,000 to $200,000	16.30%
$200,000 to $500,000	24.60%
$500,000 to $1,000,000	28.80%
$1,000,000 to $1,500,000	29.40%
$1,500,000 to $2,000,000	29.60%
$2,000,000 to $5,000,000	29.70%
$5,000,000 to $10,000,000	29.10%
$10,000,000 or more	26.30%
Average	**17.80%**

Source: IRS Publication 1304, Table 1.1

Only 1,470 households in America with earnings of $1 million or more paid no federal income tax,[36] but that is surely because they took legal deductions including charitable donations. Obama, incidentally, has repeatedly called for severely curtailing the charitable deduction,[37] presumably to empower the government to play an even greater role in deciding who receives "philanthropic" redistributions.

At Osawatomie, Obama also falsely asserted that the tax cuts of 2001 and 2003 were "the most expensive tax cuts for the wealthy in history." The Bush tax cuts were not only for the rich; they were progressive, with the lower and middle income brackets getting deeper cuts than the highest income brackets. Note that Obama did not denounce the Reagan tax cuts of the early eighties, which were not only bigger cuts, but entailed an unprogressive 25 percent cut for all income brackets; that's because Obama can't blame Reagan for the failure of his policies the way he blames Bush.

Numerous liberal commentators thought Obama had recovered some of his messianic magic at Osawatomie. "This was Obama's best speech in a very, very long time, and it showed that he and his political people have finally figured out how to express the new, quasi-populist mood in this country in a way that sounds utterly majoritarian and unthreatening—and that backs the GOP into the corner of defending things that most Americans find indefensible," raved the *Daily Beast*'s Michael Tomasky.[38] Ron Fournier of the *National Journal* commented, "President Obama's 'fair shot' address Tuesday may be remembered as one of his best, a searing and historically poignant account of the greatest challenge of the American experiment: How do we give every citizen, rich or poor, a path to the good life?"[39]

Yet despite their best hopes, many liberals realized that even if Obama recaptured some of his rhetorical rhythm with his pugilistic speech, he offered no new solutions. *USA Today* admitted that "Obama's middle-class speech falls short of a cure,"[40] and the *Washington Post* conceded, "His policy prescriptions, at least so far, don't match the gravity of the problem he describes."[41]

BOEING: "RIDICULOUS" AND "LEGALLY FRIVOLOUS"

Having received orders for nearly a thousand 787 Dreamliner aircraft, Boeing Corporation began building a new plant in Charleston, South

Carolina, to assemble the planes. The company poured millions of dollars
into the facility, which was nearing completion in March 2011 when
the National Labor Relations Board (NLRB) filed a complaint against
Boeing alleging it had chosen to build the plant in South Carolina—a
right-to-work state where employees cannot be forced to join a union
or pay union dues—to retaliate against union employees in its plant in
Everett, Washington.

The Everett workers had gone on strike at least five times since the
1970s, including twice in the last five years, causing Boeing to miss orders
and costing it billions in lost business. Nevertheless, Boeing initially tried
to locate the new plant in Washington, only opting for South Carolina
after the International Association of Machinists refused to execute a
long-term no-strike contract. South Carolina would not only solve that
problem, it also had a friendlier business and tax climate.[42]

This would be a new plant—a new investment—and no workers in
Washington would lose their jobs because of it. That, apparently, was
irrelevant to the Obama administration, which injected the federal
government into a private business matter within a state jurisdiction,
and in so doing, risked destroying job creation when it was sorely
needed—all because it favors unions above American workers and the
economy.

The White House tried to distance itself from the Boeing affair,
attributing the decision solely to the NLRB. But South Carolina governor
Nikki Haley knew better, demanding an explanation why Obama "is
allowing unelected bureaucrats to come in and do the unions' dirty work
on the backs of businesses.... It's hurting the jobs in South Carolina and
every other right-to-work state. He owes us an answer."[43] The government's case was "ridiculous" and "legally frivolous," said Haley, who
accused the administration of "bullying" and "kick[ing] around a private
company, picking and choosing where it operates."[44] Congressional
Republicans weren't buying Obama's phony denials either, claiming the
decision was a ploy to appeal to his union base.

Although the NLRB is an independent agency, Obama has helped to
stack it with pro-union recess appointees, including Craig Becker, the

associate general counsel of the Service Employees International Union, and acting NLRB general counsel and career NLRB attorney Lafe Solomon. "It is very important to President Obama because unions and their workers comprise a big piece of the volunteer core of the Democratic Party and a lot of money besides," noted University of Virginia political science professor Larry Sabato. "The stronger unions are, the more workers and the more money they're going to put into Obama's campaign and all the Democratic campaigns."

Numerous Senate and House Republicans wrote a letter to Obama demanding he withdraw Solomon's nomination. They also pointed out that Obama's militant, pro-union policies, including the Boeing incident, were contradicting his smiley-faced "win the future" campaign. "If the NLRB prevails, it will only encourage companies to make their investments in foreign nations, moving jobs and economic growth overseas," they wrote. "America will not win the future if Washington penalizes workers in states that have discovered winning economic strategies."[45]

Senator Jim DeMint was outraged by the administration's assault on Boeing, saying, "It's clearly outside of the authority of this federal government to be threatening and bullying and trying to intimidate companies like Boeing who should have the freedom to locate their plants anywhere they want. It's intimidation."[46]

After months of harassing the company and wasting untold sums of money, the NLRB dropped the case upon the request of the machinist union, which won major concessions from Boeing. Company spokesman Tim Neal declared, "We have maintained from the outset that the complaint was without merit and that the best course of action would be for it to be dropped. Today that happened. Boeing is grateful for the overwhelming support we received from across the country to vigorously contest this complaint and support the legitimate rights of businesses to make business decisions."

But tenacious House Oversight Committee chairman Darrell Issa, who had issued subpoenas to the NLRB for documents related to its Boeing complaint, was not going to go softly into the night. "NLRB's decision to end its action against Boeing does not end the Oversight Committee's investigation into the agency," he announced. "NLRB's record of rogue action and lack of transparency with the public and Congress in this case—and in others—has raised serious questions that remain unanswered." Issa stated that he was pursuing the inquiry because "businesses must be free to conduct operations wherever in this country they can be most competitive."[47]

NLRB attorneys had stonewalled on the documents request, asserting they couldn't release the papers because the matter was under judicial review. But now that the NLRB had dismissed the action, Issa said, he expected "full compliance from the NLRB."[48] He realized that absent oversight and accountability, the administration would continue intimidating businesses on behalf of its union friends with impunity.

THE CARD CHECK AMBUSH

Where the Obama administration cannot empower unions legislatively, it is trying to do so administratively.

Congressional Democrats tried and failed to pass the "Employee Free Choice Act," an Orwellian euphemism for a law (also called card check) that would intimidate workers into joining unions by eliminating secret ballot voting for unionization.[49] So the NLRB is trying to achieve the same result through a rule allowing for "ambush" elections. These would stack the deck in votes on union membership by giving employers only ten days to make their case to employees against forming a union.[50] Also by administrative fiat, as previously noted, the agency is considering the establishment of micro-unions, called "mini-unions," that would balkanize companies and force employers to negotiate with numerous groups, which would both weaken their negotiating position and impose additional economic and manpower burdens.

In addition, the National Mediation Board is pursuing a rule change mandating that a vote for unionization would succeed on a simple majority of employees voting, whereas the old rule required an actual majority of all employees whether they voted or not. This change would greatly benefit Big Labor in its campaign to unionize Delta, the only remaining non-union holdout among the big airlines.

All these initiatives, as well as those documented earlier in this chapter, have helped Obama shore up his base; but they all, if put into effect, would have a chilling effect on job creation—and individual liberty.[51]

"THE NEXT THING YOU KNOW, OSHA'S AT YOUR DOOR"

The NLRB circulated an internal memorandum on May 10 outlining yet another scheme that would significantly enhance the power of unions over employers. The agency was seeking to change the existing rule that allows businesses to make major business decisions, such as relocating their facilities, without having to confer with the union, provided the changes aren't implemented for the main purpose of reducing labor costs.

Companies are not required to negotiate with unions on their business strategies, but the memo recommends changing that. Richard Siegel, the NLRB's associate general counsel, requested in the memo that the agency's regional directors flag business-relocation cases. The board, he said, was considering "whether to propose a new standard" in such cases to compel businesses to produce detailed economic justifications for their decisions to relocate and allow unions to bargain on them as a condition of relocating.

Scholars James Sherk and Hans A. von Spakovsky argued that such a rule change would raise business costs enormously. Unions could force protracted negotiations and delay the employer's decision to relocate (or otherwise) until the bargaining had reached an "impasse." The authors concluded, "The NLRB's goal is not just to prevent companies from investing in right-to-work states. The board apparently also wants to force employers to make unions 'an equal partner in the running of the business enterprise.'"[52]

Disturbingly, such a goal was neither contemplated nor required by the National Labor Relations Act and is clearly an administrative over-reach in pursuit of a policy goal. But, said Sherk and von Spakovsky, "the board wants business decisions made to benefit unions, not the shareholders, owners and other employees of a business, or the overall economy. The Boeing charges are evidently just a first step toward that goal."[53]

There are copious other examples of the administration tilting the playing field in favor of unions. Don Todd, a former Department of Labor chief, says the White House is intent on shaming companies into unionizing. "In a worst-case scenario, your union organizer comes to you, offers you a deal to unionize, you say, 'no,' and the next thing you know, OSHA's at your door," he explains. "Then Wage and Hour show up, and they want to publicize it. They always find something wrong—

it's like with bed-checks in boot camp in the army." Indeed, the admin-istration's solicitor of labor, M. Patricia Smith, reportedly engaged in similar corporate intimidation practices when she worked at New York's Department of Labor, where she "set up a neighborhood watch-style system for monitoring and investigating wage and hour violations by companies."[54]

The administration has also marshaled the cooperation of the EPA to swell union ranks by tightening "green" emission standards to push independent truckers into the Teamsters Union, which happened to have donated more than $2 million to Democratic candidates in the 2008 and 2010 elections. The truckers could technically still operate under the old standards because the new ones were not yet formal rules, but if the major port authorities won't admit them unless they meet the new green standards, they would be forced to join a union unless they could some-how afford to buy new green trucks.[55] There was little doubt the union was behind these stricter standards. Teamsters president James P. Hoffa wrote in a blog for the *Huffington Post*, "Right now, my union, envi-ronmental groups and L.A. Mayor Antonio Villaraigosa are battling industry polluters to protect a truck replacement program at the Port of Los Angeles that has reduced deadly emissions by close to 80 percent."[56]

"TECHNICAL" CHANGES THAT DON'T "MAKE ANY IMPACT"

Even as he piles more and more suffocating rules on American busi-ness, Obama pretends to recognize the depressing effect of excessive regulation. "Rules have gotten out of balance, placing unreasonable burdens on business—burdens that have stifled innovation and have had a chilling effect on growth and jobs," he declared in early 2011.[57] Osten-sibly to address these concerns, Obama went to great lengths to publicize a new initiative to streamline regulations and eliminate unneeded rules. In January 2011, he announced in the *Wall Street Journal* that he was signing an executive order requiring "that federal agencies ensure that regulations protect our safety, health and environment while promoting economic growth." He was ordering "a government-wide review of the rules already on the books to remove outdated regulations that stifle job creation and make our economy less competitive."[58]

Looking beneath the hype, however, Obama's initiative wasn't aimed at the real culprits. House Majority leader Eric Cantor described it as "underwhelming" because it didn't address major items such as the Dodd-Frank financial reform regulatory boondoggle, Obamacare, or endless new environmental regulations.[59] Bill Kovacs of the U.S. Chamber of Commerce dismissed Obama's changes as "technical," the kinds that don't "make any impact on the overall regulatory burdens that exist on the business community."[60] He noted that meaningful regulatory reform would make the permitting process more transparent by identifying which permits are being delayed and for what reasons.[61]

Obama congratulated himself for identifying and rescinding certain onerous regulations as part of his review, but he didn't explain what led to some of the more ludicrous rules in the first place. Should the administration be applauded for repealing the absurd EPA rule that defined milk as an "oil" that had to be treated as hazardous when spilled? Should it be praised for repealing a redundant rule forcing gas stations to maintain gas recovery systems?

Besides, as quickly as the administration was repealing some of these foolish rules, it was passing more and costlier ones. Moreover, certain important independent agencies were excluded from the initial review process, including the Federal Communications Commission, the Securities and Exchange Commission, and the Consumer Financial Protection Bureau.[62]

"NO OTHER PRESIDENT HAS BURDENED BUSINESSES AND INDIVIDUALS" MORE

Notwithstanding the administration's vaunted streamlining effort and claims by regulatory czar Cass Sunstein that annual regulatory costs "are not out of line by historical standards,"[63] regulatory costs have actually skyrocketed under Obama. Federal regulators during George W. Bush's two terms added a shocking $60 billion in annual regulatory costs,[64] but the Obama administration through March 2011 had already added some $40 billion in annual costs,[65] more than doubling the Bush rate.[66] Fiscal year 2010 alone saw a $26.5 billion increase in new costs, setting an annual record.[67] Also in 2010, according to the nonpartisan Congressional Research Service, the Obama administration issued one hundred major rules, the most since the Government Accountability Office began accumulating data in 1997.[68]

A recent study by Heritage Foundation experts James Gattuso and Diane Katz unveils the administration's regulatory zeal. During the first three years of the Obama administration, 106 new major federal regulations added more than $46 billion per year in new costs for Americans, and almost $11 billion in one-time implementation costs. This, say the experts, "is almost four times the number—and more than five times the cost—of the major regulations issued by George W. Bush during his first three years." And again, hundreds more regulations are on the way with finance, healthcare, and various environmental rules.[69] In 2011 alone, even after Obama's pledge to streamline the regulatory climate, his administration added thirty-two major new regulations, which increased annual regulatory costs by almost $10 billion and involved another $6.6 billion in one-time implementation costs.[70]

Apart from comparisons between administrations, the size of the regulatory behemoth, in actual terms, is staggering. Today, the expected paperwork burden for businesses is 119.4 million hours per year.[71] There are more than 281,000 people working in federal agencies, up 13 percent since 2008, while private-sector jobs fell by 5.6 percent, and 27 million Americans are now either unemployed, under-employed, or have taken themselves out of the job market altogether. Regulatory budgets during this period have ballooned by 16 percent. The Federal Register's eighty-thousand pages swelled another 18 percent in 2010, and thousands of new rules await approval.[72]

In 2011, through August, the administration proposed more than 340 regulations costing $65 billion to businesses that are struggling to create jobs.[73] In the month of July alone, the Obama administration added $9.5 billion in new regulatory costs with 229 proposed new rules and 379 finalized rules.[74] These figures, it should be noted, are typically underestimated, and don't account for hundreds of regulations the administration did not review because they are "non-major" rules—ones believed unlikely to cost at least $100 million per year. These include fuel economy and emission standards for cars, light-duty trucks, and medium-duty passenger vehicles with an estimated cost of $10.8 billion per year, new light bulb energy standards to cost $700 million, and restrictions on "short sales" securities to cost $1.2 billion, as well as a raft of other expensive rules imposed by the Dodd-Frank financial bill.[75] As Heritage expert Diane Katz wrote, "No other president has burdened businesses and individuals with a higher number and larger cost of regulations in a comparable time period."[76]

"WHEN DOES IT END?"

On top of all the damaging regulations already approved during Obama's short presidency, this nation is in for a regulatory tsunami once Obamacare is fully implemented.[77] For example, Obamacare will require major fast-food franchises to post calorie data on their menus and menu signs, an expensive, needless rule that will cost jobs. Domino's Pizza chain might have to spend $5 million to include this information, which is already available on its website and on nutritional pamphlets available in its stores. The CEO of CKE Restaurants, which owns Hardee's and Carl's Jr., told the House Oversight Committee the rule could cost his company $1.5 million, an amount sufficient to build one and a half new restaurants.

Ironically, but par for the course for nanny-state interventions, the law will end up depriving the customer of information that is now accessible. Every Hardee's and Carl's Jr. store currently has wall posters that provide information on fat, sodium, cholesterol, protein, carbohydrate content, and other data. Those posters will probably have to be removed for space considerations once the new law kicks in.[78] So the law of unintended consequences (and that's giving its authors the benefit of the doubt) will result in this rule not only addressing a non-existent problem, but creating a new one, e.g., for customers who might be measuring their fat, carb, or protein intake. It will also result in prohibitive costs each time a restaurant wants to change its menu items. "There are so many different things that I have to do right now that are just completely unnecessary that take away from our profits," said Charlie Malament, owner of four Domino's stores in Maryland. "When does it end? When does this stuff end? Just give a small business guy a break and let me take care of my customers and take care of my people."[79]

REGULATION NATION

In September 2011, Coca-Cola CEO Muhtar Kent made a remarkable statement. "In many respects, it is easier doing business in China, because of America's antiquated tax structure and political gridlock," he declared. "If you talk about an American company doing business in the world today with its Chinese, Russian, European or Japanese counterparts, of course we're disadvantaged. A Chinese or Swiss company can do whatever it wants with those funds [earned overseas]. When we want to bring them back, we are faced with a very large tax burden."[80]

Other CEOs share Kent's dismay at the state of the U.S. business climate. Clarence Otis Jr., CEO of Darden Restaurants, the parent of Olive Garden, Red Lobster, and LongHorn Steakhouse, said that the mountains of new regulations make it "increasingly difficult for businesses to see why and where creating new jobs makes sense." Otis said it was particularly difficult for businesses with low profit margins to survive in such an overregulated environment. In an op-ed for CNN, Otis argued that excessive regulations are killing job creation. He cited "regulatory mandates flowing from federal health care reform," as well as mandated paid leave and employee meal and rest break provisions in the law. Otis said that neither his shareholders nor customers could "afford the cost of the unbridled increase in regulation we're experiencing." Businesses like his want to expand, he said, but "a regulatory 'perfect storm' is forming that causes even the most well-intentioned business leaders to pause."[81]

The compliance costs for private-sector businesses are overwhelming. According to a Small Business Administration study, as of 2008, even before Obama's regulatory blizzard, cumulative compliance costs of federal rules and regulations for American businesses were more than $1.75 trillion a year. Small businesses—those which can least afford it and which create most of America's new jobs—were hardest hit. The SBA study found that small companies spend 36 percent more per employee for regulatory compliance costs than larger companies.[82]

Similarly, the Fraser Institute, which ranks nations based on their comparative economic liberty, dropped the United States to tenth place, based on 2009 data, placing us, for the first time, behind Canada. "Much of this decline is a result of higher government spending and borrowing and lower scores for the legal structure and property rights components."[83] This staggering $1.75 trillion annual cost of regulation is twice the amount of individual income taxes collected in the United States in 2010.[84]

A group of Republican Congress members led by Congresswoman Cathy McMorris Rodgers released a striking chart showing the dramatic impact on jobs likely to stem from just five of the Obama administration's proposed regulations.[85]

📎 REGULATION NATION

FIVE JOB-DESTROYING REGULATIONS PROPOSED BY THE OBAMA ADMINISTRATION

1   UTILITY PLANTS MACT & CSAPR
-1.4 MILLION JOBS

CEMENT MACT
-19,000 JOBS   **2**

3   COAL ASH REGULATIONS
-316,000 JOBS

GREENHOUSE GAS EMISSIONS
-1.4 MILLION JOBS   **4**

5   BOILER MACT REGULATIONS
-224,000 JOBS

COURTESY OF @GOPLABS

SOURCES:
(1) Utah AH Shurtleff, Congressional Testimony, 9/15/2011
(2) Portland Cement Assoc., The Monitor, Flash Report, January 2011
(3) EnergyFairness.org: Veritas Study, 6/20/211
(4) Affordable Power Alliance Study, March 2011
(5) CIBO Boiler MACT Jobs Study, 9/7/2011

It's increasingly clear that one of the best things—if not *the* best thing—we can do to spark economic growth is to ease the regulatory burden on business. The Phoenix Center for Advanced Legal and Economic Public Policy Studies found that a mere 5 percent reduction in the regulatory budget, amounting to $2.8 billion, could result in some $75 billion in private-sector growth in the GDP and add 1.2 million jobs per year. The paper concluded that to eliminate just one regulator would grow the economy an average of $6.2 million and create 100 private sector jobs annually. On the other hand, for every million-dollar jump in regulatory budget costs, the economy can be expected to lose 420 private sector jobs. The paper's authors thus suggest that Congress begin its budget cutting with the regulatory budget.[86]

"THERE'S MORE THAN ONE WAY OF SKINNING THE CAT"

An incomprehensible amount of legislative power has been delegated to or usurped by the federal administrative monster controlling much of our country. The Constitution gives Congress legislative authority, but over the years it has increasingly abdicated its legislative duties through delegation to virtually unaccountable, independent administrative agencies (most of which are in the executive branch). The judicial branch bears some responsibility for this pattern of extra-constitutional delegation as well, having long since abdicated its role as a constitutional watchdog and having routinely approved such transfers of power.

As a result, Congress can delegate some its tough decisions to theoretically impartial agencies and avoid hard work and political heat. This transfer of power further removes the people from the governing process, as these agencies answer to no one except the courts, which in the absence of something akin to gross error, rubber stamp their decisions. This is one of the insidious ways that our brilliantly crafted constitutional republic has been subverted in favor of rule by a soulless administrative state.

A perfect example of this phenomenon is seen in an incident that occurred following the 2010 congressional elections, when the people resoundingly rejected Obama's big government agenda. After the newly elected Republican majority said "no" to the administration's relentless march toward socialism with such legislative nightmares as cap-and-trade, Team Obama just regrouped and negotiated an end-run through administrative rules and regulations. Obama broadcast his intentions by responding to the failure of cap-and-trade with the arrogant, defiant proclamation, "There's more than one way of skinning the cat."

This is part of a pattern seen throughout the administration: although the FCC is ostensibly independent, under the leadership of Obama-appointed directors, it seeks to regulate the internet when legislation fails; the EPA exerts ever more authority over wetlands on its own initiative; and the administration capriciously grants thousands of waivers to exempt chosen companies and other concerns from some of the onerous costs of Obamacare—all without congressional authority, accountability, or oversight.

Congressional Republicans tried to rein in this regulatory madness. In December 2011, the House passed the Regulations from the Executive in Need of Scrutiny Act (REINS Act). The bill—which Obama has vowed to veto and which, in any case, is not expected to pass the Democrat-controlled Senate—would require that Congress approve every new "major" rule (any rule that the OMB determines will result in a $100 million annual effect on the economy) adopted by the executive branch.[87] This would make Congress more accountable and would certainly give the public more recourse than it has now, being subject to a pantheon of administrative agencies with little direct accountability. If Congress were required to approve every major administrative rule, the rule-makers would doubtless draft them less cavalierly. Senator Marco Rubio, a cosponsor of the bill, said, "It's time for Senate Democrats to stop standing in the way of another commonsense bill passed by the House of Representatives that will bring greater accountability and transparency to an archaic regulatory system that is actively impeding desperately needed private-sector job creation."[88]

FINED $15,000 FOR HIRING TOO MANY BROKERS

Peter Schiff, chief executive officer of Euro Pacific Capital, Inc., testified before the House Oversight and Government Reform Subcommittee on Regulatory Affairs on his firsthand experience with the stifling impact of government regulations on hiring and economic growth. Regulations have "substantially increased the costs and risks associated with job creation," Schiff explained. "Employers are subjected to all sorts of onerous regulations, taxes and legal liability." He said that in his business, securities regulations have prohibited him from hiring brokers for more than three years. "I was even fined fifteen thousand dollars expressly for hiring too many brokers in 2008," he said. "In the process I incurred more than $500,000 in legal bills to mitigate a more severe regulatory outcome as a result of hiring too many workers. I have also been prohibited from opening up additional offices. I had a major expansion plan that would have resulted in my creating hundreds of additional jobs. Regulations have forced me to put those jobs on hold."[89]

Oblivious to such testimony, Democratic Senate majority leader Harry Reid argued in a floor speech on November 15, 2011, that it's a "myth" that regulations cost jobs. "Only a tiny fraction of layoffs" have anything at all to do with tighter regulation, says Reid, who also claims there isn't "a single shred of evidence" that regulations cause major economic harm.[90]

Reid was relying on data from the Bureau of Labor Statistics, which reported that for the third quarter of 2011, only 0.3 percent of respondents polled cited governmental regulations and intervention as the reason for mass layoffs—defined as fifty or more workers being laid off for thirty-one days or more. But Heritage scholar James Gattuso explains that just looking at mass layoffs can be misleading. While those kinds of layoffs get the most media attention, they are just a portion of the job-loss equation. Many layoffs, says Gattuso, involve fewer than fifty employees at a time; indeed most small businesses don't even have fifty employees.

More important, as previously explained, job losses are *not* the main problem; a bigger one is the lack of job *creation*. Unemployment has remained high despite the fact that gross job losses have been relatively low; that's because job creation has been very low. The administration can spout the false metric of "jobs saved" all it wants, but until the economy starts creating new jobs, unemployment will remain high. The surveys cited by Reid are thoroughly deceptive, since employers aren't asked why they did not expand, only why they laid off employees.[91]

"DON'T ALWAYS BELIEVE WHAT YOU HEAR"

Obama's EPA takes Reid's argument one step further, claiming that increased regulations actually boost employment. The EPA wrote in February 2011 that "in periods of high unemployment, an increase in labor demand due to regulation may have a stimulative effect that results in a net increase in overall employment."[92]

This perverse belief comes from the top, for Obama is equally obtuse about the smothering effect of regulations. At a town hall meeting in Atkinson, Illinois, a farmer told him, "We enjoy growing corn and soybeans and we feel we do this as safely and efficiently as we possibly can, and mother nature has really challenged us this growing season.... Please don't challenge us with more rules and regulations from Washington, D.C. that hinder us from doing that. We would prefer to start our day in a tractor cab or combine cab, rather than filling out forms and permits to do what we like to do." After Obama asked him to cite a specific rule, the farmer discussed rumors of impending rules on noise pollution, dust pollution, and water runoff. Obama glibly responded, "Don't always believe what you hear," adding that he suspected if the farmer talked to the USDA, he'd find "that some of your fears are unfounded." Without ever addressing the meat of the concern, Obama assured the farmer that he was very concerned about farming problems because he comes from a farm state.[93]

Well, if the farmer's fears were unfounded, how does Obama explain the EPA's ludicrous proposed regulation on farm dust? The agency is seeking to revise the National Ambient Air Quality Standards (NAAQS) concerning "coarse particulate matter," otherwise known as dust. The current NAAQS regulate such things as soot, and now it's interested in that ubiquitous, evil substance, dirt.

The EPA's own scientific panel hasn't even determined that further regulation would be helpful, but that is no barrier to the agency, which apparently has little concern for the extra costs and time burdens this would place on farmers, resulting in higher food prices for the rest of us. Tightening the regulations could require farmers to undertake dust-control activities such as watering down dirt and gravel roads. Congress-woman Kristi Noem, to prevent or at least delay this nonsense, introduced the Farm Dust Regulation Prevention Act of 2011, which would bar the EPA from effectively revising the NAAQS for at least a year following passage of the act.[94] "The proposal to regulate farm dust is one of the most absurd ideas to come out of the EPA in a long time," said Congressman Tom Cole, a cosponsor of the bill. Cole insisted that farmers are fully capable of implementing common-sense measures to control their own dust and don't need further job-killing regulations. None of these arguments made any impression on Obama, who threatened to veto the bill.[95]

"BUREAUCRATS WHO KNOW NOTHING ABOUT RUNNING A BUSINESS"

The administration also heard an earful when White House chief of staff William M. Daley met with hundreds of manufacturing executives, who weren't buying Daley's claims that the administration was their friend. When Massachusetts manufacturing executive Doug Starrett claimed the administration was blocking construction on his company's facilities in order to protect fish, the group of businessmen "erupted in applause." Admitting that "sometimes you can't defend the indefensible," Daley conceded that the number of rules and regulations "that come out of agencies is overwhelming."[96] Yet the administration never changes its approach, which is to meet with business representatives and give speeches, never meaningfully reducing the smothering constellation of regulations.

One businessman perfectly captured the administration's obtuseness about the business world. Bernie Marcus, cofounder of Home Depot, said his company would never have succeeded had it launched today with these "impossible" regulations. "Every day," he explained, "you see rules and regulations from a group of Washington bureaucrats who know nothing about running a business. And I mean every day. It's become stifling." Asked about Obama's promise to streamline and eliminate regulations, he replied, "His speeches are wonderful. His output is absolutely, incredibly bad. As he speaks about cutting out regulations, they are now producing thousands of pages of new ones." Asked if he could sit down with Obama and talk to him about job creation, he replied, "I'm not sure Obama would understand anything that I'd say, because he's never really worked a day outside the political or legal arena. He doesn't know how to make a payroll, he doesn't understand the problems businesses face."[97]

Consumer Electronics Association president Gary Shapiro had equally sharp criticism for the administration's regulatory straightjacket. "I challenge anyone, and no one's ever answered me, to come up with a more anti-business administration," said Shapiro. "They're doing things that are very harmful to the economy. They're not bad people. They just have no experience with business." He argued that Obama is fostering a mindset that "business is evil," and which tells businesses that "there's not a sympathetic ear at all" in the White House. "It's the 'business is the enemy' thinking. I don't think that's a healthy thing to do."[98]

While the administration is smothering the private sector, it is growing the public sector at an unprecedented rate. One study showed that between 2009 and 2010, the regulatory staff at federal agencies increased about 3 percent, with indications it would grow by another 4 percent in 2011. In fact, if the federal government's regulatory operation were considered a business, it would be among the nation's fifty largest revenue producers and the third largest employer.[99]

"WE CAN CREATE A VIRTUOUS CYCLE"

Obama has been openly hostile to the pro-business U.S. Chamber of Commerce since early in his term.[100] Finally, presumably tired of being walked on, the Chamber rejected a last-minute request from White House advisor Valerie Jarrett to speak at a "Jobs for America Summit" in July 2010.[101] The administration, it should be noted, had deliberately excluded the Chamber from its jobs summit at the end of 2009—a meeting that was a mere photo-op, and which excluded many free market advocates besides the Chamber.

In February 2011, in a supposed overture to the Chamber, Obama couldn't help lecturing them, and railing against the free market again, about the heartlessness of its invisible hand. In a speech to the Chamber, he paraphrased John F. Kennedy, urging business leaders "to ask yourselves what you can do for America. Ask yourselves what you can do to hire American workers, to support the American economy, and to invest in this nation."

These remarks reiterated Obama's economically illiterate belief that businesses can make expansion and hiring decisions in a vacuum, irrespective of demand or a company's financial situation. To him, the profit motive is actually counterproductive to job creation because it increases overhead. He wholly discounts the economic reality that businesses cannot succeed if they make their hiring and expansion decisions for purely altruistic motives. As if anticipating his Osawatomie speech, he declared, "The benefits can't just translate into greater profits and bonuses for those at the top. They should be shared by American workers, who need to know that expanding trade and opening markets will lift their standard of living as well as your bottom line. We cannot go back to the kind of economy—and culture—we saw in the years leading up to the recession, where growth and gains in productivity just didn't translate into rising incomes and opportunity for the middle class."[102] In other words, "quit being so selfish and spread the wealth around, unlike you did during the Bush years."

Further betraying his ignorance of economics, he told the group, "I want to encourage you to get in the game.... And as you hire, you know that more Americans working means more sales, greater demand, and higher profits for your companies. We can create a virtuous cycle"[103]—as if by just hiring people regardless of the demand for them, *presto chango*, these companies can automatically make more sales and increase profits. Presumably, it's only their lack of virtue and compassion that keeps them from hiring now.

That was not a mere throwaway argument for Obama. In Maryland a month earlier, he had given another pep talk to businesses, sharing his belief that a business's decision to hire more workers and expand was purely a function of its own wishes, irrespective of external factors. "Now is the time to act," he instructed his audience at a window manufacturer. "If you are planning or thinking about making investments sometime in the future, make those investments now, and you're going to save money. And that will help us grow the economy. It will help you grow your business."[104]

HE STILL RECEIVES A FAILING GRADE IN BUSINESS

In his February speech to the Chamber of Commerce, Obama told them, as he had declared many times before, that he had assembled a group of business leaders to meet and advise him about how to get the economy moving—as if all the intricacies of the complex American economy could be divined and set aright if our experts would just break into study groups. "I've asked Jeff Immelt of GE to lead a new council of business leaders and outside experts so that we're getting the best advice on what you're facing out there," announced Obama. "I am confident that we can win the competition for new jobs and industries.... I know you love this country and want America to succeed just as badly as I do."[105]

Obama's many half-hearted overtures to business didn't yield much fruit. When he was stumping for his stimulus, he made a speech at Caterpillar boasting that the bill would directly prevent the company from having to lay off employees. Caterpillar CEO Jim Owens famously contradicted Obama as soon as he'd left the event. As to whether the bill would prevent layoffs, he said, "I think realistically no. The truth is we're going to have more layoffs before we start hiring again."[106] More than two years later, Obama hadn't done much to improve his reputation with that company. Its new CEO, Doug Oberhelman, maintains that Obama's relations with business have improved, but he still receives a failing grade—a 5 or 6 out of 10.[107]

"WE CANNOT ALLOW THE CORPORATE
TAKEOVER OF OUR DEMOCRACY"

In his weekly radio and internet address of August 21, 2010, Obama couldn't contain his frustration at his perceived business opponents who, along with the Supreme Court, reject his insistence on curtailing free speech through campaign finance reform legislation. He railed against "a flood of attack ads run by shadowy groups with harmless-sounding names. We don't know who's behind these ads and we don't know who's paying for them." He blamed this situation on the Supreme Court's ruling in the *Citizens United* case—"a decision that now allows big corporations

to spend unlimited amounts of money to influence our elections...."
He further proclaimed, "We cannot allow the corporate takeover of
our democracy."

Obama then took an obligatory shot at Republicans who killed his
proposed "Disclose Act," which would have circumvented the *Citizens
United* decision. "This can only mean that the leaders of the other party
want to keep the public in the dark," Obama insisted. "They don't want
you to know which interests are paying for the ads. The only people who
don't want to disclose the truth are people with something to hide."[108]

In fact, the Disclose Act, ostensibly designed to force most organizations to disclose their funding sources for political ads, was not about
promoting transparency but, in the words of Senate Minority Leader
Mitch McConnell, "about protecting incumbent Democrats from criticism ahead of November." While masquerading as practitioners of
transparency, the Democratic leadership brought the bill directly to the
Senate floor "without hearings, without testimony, without studies, [and]
without a [committee] markup."[109]

The following month, Obama ratcheted up his anti-corporate rhetoric
at a Democratic fundraiser in Connecticut. Complaining again about
Citizens United and Republican opposition to his Disclose Act, he
declared, "We tried to fix this, but the leaders of the other party wouldn't
even allow it to come up for a vote. We are not about to allow a corporate
takeover of our democracy." Democrats admitted Obama's rhetoric was
aimed at picking up congressional seats in the November elections.[110]
But as the election results showed, Americans didn't buy his assault on
business.

PROVING A NEGATIVE

Amping up his attack, Obama suggested that in light of *Citizens
United*, Republicans might even be receiving money via the Chamber of
Commerce from "foreign-controlled" corporations.[111] Enraging Republicans as well as the Chamber, Obama's charge was utterly misleading
because the Supreme Court expressly indicated that its *Citizens United*
ruling did not address foreign political contributions. As the Chamber's

top lobbyist, Bruce Josten, noted, "Federal law bans all foreign nationals from contributing either directly or indirectly to any candidate or political party 'in connection with a federal, state, or local election.'"[112]

The Chamber's intransigence only seemed to embolden Obama's community organizing team. When CBS's Bob Schieffer on *Face the Nation* pressed White House senior advisor David Axelrod for proof of the administration's allegation that the Chamber was funneling foreign money to Republican campaigns, Axelrod doubled down on the accusation, even while essentially admitting he had no evidence. "Do you have any evidence that it's not, Bob?" Axelrod demanded. "The fact is that the Chamber has asserted that, but they won't release any information about where their campaign money is coming from. And that's at the core of the problem." Schieffer dismissively replied that the charge about foreign money "appears to be peanuts." When Axelrod still refused to back off the allegation, Schieffer commented, "If the only charge three weeks into the election that the Democrats can make is that somehow this may or may not be foreign money coming into the campaign, is that the best you can do?"[113]

Clearly, this administration feels it can lodge scandalous charges without producing a scintilla of evidence, and unless the accused can prove a negative, it is presumed guilty. In fact, the Democratic National Committee produced a new ad accusing the Chamber of "benefitting from secret foreign money" and, along with the Republican Party, of "stealing our democracy." Former RNC chairman Ed Gillespie, one of those singled out in the DNC ad, said the Democrats' claim represented "an unbelievable mentality."

But it wasn't so much a "mentality" as a coordinated effort to accuse the Chamber and the GOP of undermining democracy with foreign assistance. Axelrod made this clear in his *Face the Nation* interview. "It's never happened before that organizations are spending this kind of money," he alleged. "And the American people need to ask, 'Why is the oil industry, Wall Street and others spending this kind of money to defeat candidates and elect others in this sort of secretive way?' You know, that is a threat to our democracy."[114]

Obama repeated the allegations in two campaign speeches that same week. In Chicago he claimed to have a specific example. "Just this week, we learned that one of the largest groups paying for these ads regularly takes in money from foreign corporations," he announced. "So groups that receive foreign money are spending huge sums to influence American elections."[115]

Amazingly, even the liberal press refused to play along this time. "A closer examination shows that there is little evidence that what the chamber does in collecting overseas dues is improper or even unusual, according to both liberal and conservative election-law lawyers and campaign finance documents," wrote the *New York Times*.[116] But that smack-down did not stop Vice President Joe Biden from joining the charade. "I challenge the Chamber of Commerce to tell us how much of the money they're investing is from foreign sources," he declared. "I challenge them. If I'm wrong, I will stand corrected." The Chamber responded in a press release, "We accept the vice president's challenge here and now, and are happy to provide our answer.... Zero. As in, 'Not a single cent.'"[117]

Of course, as they were hurling baseless charges at Republicans, the Democrats were silent on the copious amounts of foreign money funneled into their own campaigns over the years. In her blog, Michelle Malkin cited numerous examples, including convicted criminals and top Democratic fundraisers Norman Hsu and Hasan Nemazee, both connected with the Clintons; Obama's commerce secretary and Buddhist temple cash collector Gary Locke; the Senate Democrats' fundraising activities in Canada; and the Obama presidential campaign's overt solicitation of foreign contributions on its website. The Associated Press concluded that Obama had raised at least $2 million abroad, dwarfing the $229,000 raised by John McCain's campaign.[118]

In December 2010, the *Los Angeles Times* revealed a new element in the administration's offensive against the Chamber of Commerce. Throughout 2010, the White House hosted business leaders, ostensibly to discuss policy, but in a number of those meetings urged the executives to lobby the Chamber to cancel TV spots targeted against Obamacare.

One business lobbyist accused Obama senior advisor Valerie Jarrett of urging executives to withdraw from the Chamber. Jarrett denied the charge, though an Apple spokeswoman, suspiciously, would neither confirm nor deny that the White House had asked it to leave the Chamber. And notably, when some major companies quit the Chamber over disagreements on its positions on global warming, Energy Secretary Steven Chu responded, "I think it's wonderful."[119]

TARGETING THE PRIVATE JET INDUSTRY: "WORDS HAVE CONSEQUENCES"

For a time, Obama's crusade against business focused on scapegoating private jet owners. At a press conference in late June 2011, Obama mentioned "corporate jets" six times, as if they were a satanic emblem. "I think it's only fair to ask an oil company or a corporate jet owner that has done so well to give up that tax break that no other business enjoys," he proclaimed, with his typical dash of class warfare.

With this attack, Obama deliberately conflated two tax issues and the groups of people they affect: recipients of the Bush tax "cuts" for those making $250,000 or more a year on the one hand, and recipients of the tax deduction for corporate jet purchases on the other. A person typically has to make far more than $250,000 a year to afford to buy and maintain a private jet, yet Obama falsely implied that those earning $250,000 were part of the same group who travel in private jets. His singling out private jet owners was also disingenuous considering that the tax break they enjoy is not much different in principle from the one extended to the wealthy buyers of certain luxury electric cars. Purchasers of $100,000 electric-powered Tesla sports cars, for example, were entitled to a $7,500 tax credit, yet they were spared Obama's censure, as their credit is motivated by Obama's pet green project.[120]

Obama also failed to mention that the corporate jet tax break, "accelerated depreciation," was reauthorized by his own stimulus package and in the Small Business Lending Fund Act, which he signed. Its purpose wasn't to give the rich a gift, but to encourage purchases of expensive planes (and other large manufacturing products) to revitalize the ailing aviation industry and to boost the general economy. The tax incentive was first introduced to help the industry recover from the effects of the 9/11 attacks. An industry study found that the incentive contributed to a 43 percent increase in sales and another $2 billion in sales when it was implemented again in 2003.[121]

Obama's rhetoric infuriated the jet industry. Aircraft Owners and Pilots Association President Craig Fuller said that Obama's remarks had cast a pall over the entire aviation industry, deterring many potential buyers from acquiring planes. "The industry has suffered terribly in the last two and a half years and it has just started to recover," said Fuller. "Most of the signs were starting to look good. We are so angry as an industry and we have all come together to try to bring a more fair and balanced description to the debate." Similarly, the General Aviation Manufacturers Association and the International Association of Machinists and Aerospace Workers (IAMAW) sent the president an outraged letter. "Words have consequences and, in this industry, a few misguided words can put at risk even the ever-so-modest recovery we have experienced," said IAMAW International President Tom Buffenbarger. "What this industry and its workforce requires is more time to recover, a chance to book more orders and the opportunity to recall more workers."[122]

James K. Coyne, head of the National Air Transportation Association, blasted Obama just a day after he had expediently visited a major American aircraft manufacturing plant for a photo-op to promote job growth. "It is perplexing why the president continues to bash an industry that is responsible for thousands of manufacturing, maintenance and service jobs," said Coyne. "The president's comments before a national audience could weaken consumer confidence in general aviation utilization at a time when economic indicators are demonstrating that the community is finally starting to recover from the recession."[123]

Similarly, Hawker Beechcraft CEO Bill Boisture denounced the administration's "irresponsible" targeting of the private aircraft industry, claiming the assault, both in terms of user fees and fiscal proposals, had

damaged customer confidence and contributed to as much as 25 percent
of the industry's layoffs and workforce reductions.[124]

Hypocritically, the president often avails himself of the full perk of
flying in the most private of public jets—Air Force One. He has reportedly
flown Air Force One more than any other president in a comparable time
period and, if waste were his concern, why do his wife, their family, and
their entourage often fly in separate jets, greatly increasing the cost to
taxpayers? Indeed, just as he was in high dudgeon over this tax break,
the first lady was jetting to Aspen to raise funds from the very fat cats
her husband was demonizing.[125]

Nebraska senator Mike Johanns warned that the president's attacks
on jet owners and manufacturers could have a chilling effect on the
aviation industry—which provides some 1.2 million jobs and pours $150
billion into the economy every year. Indeed, while Obama wanted to
create the impression he was targeting the wealthy, he was obviously
indifferent to the fact that repealing the tax deduction and singling out
the aviation industry could have wider repercussions. "[Obama] demonizes general aviation users," noted Congressman Mike Pompeo. "He calls
them corporate fat cat jet owners at every turn. But it's not impacting the
folks who use those as business tools. It's impacting the people who build
these airplanes. His rhetoric kills sales of American manufactured goods,
and with them the jobs that are created when those airplanes are built."[126]

But liberals either don't know or don't care as much about the economy
and the workers they purport to champion as they do the "righteous"
cause of demonizing the "wealthy." When they imposed a 10 percent
luxury tax on yachts and other high-priced items a generation ago, they
derisively scoffed at the potential negative consequences. Well, yacht owners reacted by purchasing their recreational assets offshore, creating a
devastating impact on the boating industry in Florida and other coastal
states, and destroying the jobs of some twenty-five thousand workers in
the industry. Government expenses for unemployment benefits for these
workers greatly exceeded any revenues generated by the tax,[127] without
even factoring in the lost revenues from potential purchases sabotaged by
the tax.

And as Craig Fuller observed, "There are only 15,000 private jets in America. Even if they tax them all at $10 million apiece—of course his proposal does not come close—it wouldn't make a dent in the deficit."[128] This episode shows just how willing Obama is to harm the U.S. economy and U.S. business owners and workers for the sake of political gain and ideological fealty.

BANKS DON'T HAVE AN INHERENT RIGHT TO PROFIT

When the Bank of America decided to impose a $5 monthly fee on its debit card customers, President Obama appeared outraged. Always willing to weigh in on matters outside the purview of his office, he retorted that banks "don't have some inherent right just to, you know, get a certain amount of profit." This was reminiscent of a comment made by Jared Bernstein, Vice President Joe Biden's chief economic advisor, about the Bush tax cuts—that "the millionaires and billionaires, frankly don't need the extra cash."[129] It obviously didn't occur to Obama that the market could better determine the wisdom of this decision than he could. To Obama, the bank simply had no right to defray its administrative costs with fees. Rather it was surely gouging consumers—an "abuse of Wall Street," as he described it.[130]

Despite Obama's demagoguery about evil "fat-cat" bankers and his full-throated endorsement of the Dodd-Frank financial regulatory scheme, the largest banks are bigger than they were when he took office and are nearing the level of profits they were making before the financial crisis of 2008.[131] And speaking of fat-cat bankers and the executive bonuses they received that so incensed Obama, he was conspicuously silent about the enormous compensation packages paid to executives at the two largest bailout recipients—Fannie Mae and Freddie Mac.[132]

"NOT PARTICULARLY INTERESTED IN BUSINESS"

Obama's steadfast denials of his anti-business inclination fall flat in the face of so much evidence and so much rhetoric. In a September 2010 town hall meeting where he was hoping to shore up his pro-business credentials before the mid-term elections, he ran into a buzzsaw even from his own supporters. *The Hill* reported that the Business Cable Network had carefully selected the audience and that it was "largely deferential to Obama," but questions from Obama voters "provided the most revealing glimpse yet into why the president and his Democratic allies are facing a potential disaster in November." One disgruntled African-American woman exclaimed, "I'm exhausted of defending you, defending your administration, defending the mantle of change that I voted for, and deeply disappointed with where we are right now. I have been told that I voted for a man who said he was going to change things in a meaningful way for the middle class. I'm one of those people. And I'm waiting, sir. I don't feel it yet."[133]

Other questioners challenged Obama on his anti-business hostility. Instead of dealing with the specifics, he defensively argued that he had turned the economy around so that businesses that were in trouble when he took office "now are profitable; the financial markets are stabilized." Incredibly, despite his rhetoric, his pro-union actions against employers, his increased regulations, his finance reform bill, and his proposals to increase business taxes, Obama said, "I think that if you look at what we've done over the last two years, it's very hard to find evidence of anything that we've done that is designed to squash business as opposed to promote business."[134]

It wasn't just Obama voters who acknowledged his lack of sympathy for business. New York mayor Michael Bloomberg, a liberal Republican and frequent Obama supporter, admitted that Obama was no close friend of business, and that anyone paying attention during the 2008 presidential campaign couldn't have missed that. In urging support for Obama, Bloomberg ironically outed him as anti-business. "Obama never said he would be anything other than what he is now," said Bloomberg. "He is a liberal guy, very pro-union, not particularly interested in business." Somewhat incoherently, after noting that many Obama supporters had expected Obama to scale down his anti-business positions, Bloomberg said he had "more respect for him for not changing."[135]

STUNNING HYPOCRISY

Timothy P. Carney, columnist for the *Examiner*, argues that the anti-business charge leveled against Obama isn't precisely accurate. A better description, says Carney, is that he's anti-free market, because he is more than happy to join forces with Big Business when it suits him. "His idea of being friendly to business," writes Carney, "means more government subsidies and corporate-government cooperation."[136]

Obama indeed colludes with well-placed friends in Big Business. Take for example Jeff Immelt, head of General Electric. Despite all his populist bashing of big corporations, Obama appeared with Immelt in Schenectady to boast about GE's imminent sale of a power plant in Samalkot, India. This was hardly a victory for the free market because, as Carney notes, "Obama's Export-Import Bank is providing at least $400 million in subsidized financing to grease the skids." Overall, Carney observes, GE "marches in sync with government, pocketing subsidies, profiting from regulation, and lobbying for more of both."[137]

Immelt, for his part, is just as committed to his government sugar-daddy. "The global economy, and capitalism, will be 'reset' in several important ways," he wrote in a February 2009 letter to GE shareholders shortly after Obama's inauguration. "The interaction between government and business will change forever. In a reset economy, the government will be a regulator, and also an industry policy champion, a financier, and a key partner."[138]

Immelt further explained this emerging Big Government–Big Business dynamic in an op-ed accepting his appointment as an advisor for the Obama administration. "We need a coordinated commitment among business, labor and government to expand our manufacturing base and increase exports," he wrote. "Government should incentivize this investment in innovation.... Government can help business invest in our shared future." Immelt no doubt earned a pat on the head from Obama when he stumped for his benefactor's energy agenda: "A sound and competitive tax system and a partnership between business and government on education and innovation in areas where American can lead, such as clean energy, are essential to sustainable growth."[139] *Voila*, business surrenders to the notion that business can't succeed without government incentives, support, and cooperation.

Of course, there's another reason Obama wants Big Business "partners" like Immelt: in exchange for government subsidies, tax credits, bailouts, and regulations that hurt their smaller competitors, they help advance Obama's policy goals—a dynamic reminiscent of the corporatist economic policies underlying fascism.

Thus, GE is integrally involved in a number of industries promoted by Obama's so-called "industrial policy." For example, Immelt marches in lockstep with Obama's green agenda. This may not be particularly profitable, but it keeps Immelt and his company in Obama's good graces, and besides, any losses can potentially be offset, in part or in full, by Immelt getting his cut of the $100 billion-plus subsidies and tax credits the government provides for green technology.

Consider GE's solar power efforts. Obama obviously prioritizes solar power, as shown in chapter eight, and so it was no surprise when GE announced in April 2011 that it would open the largest solar panel production concern in the United States. This complements GE's position as America's largest producer of wind turbines, which just happens to be another Obama hobbyhorse.[140]

The relationship, sadly, is even deeper. The Obama administration and GE both promote cap-and-trade; GE conveniently opened an embryonic stem-cell business after Obama provided subsidies for such research; and as Obama stumped for railway subsidies, GE hired Linda Daschle, wife of the former South Dakota senator and a strong ally of Obama as a rail lobbyist. "Look at any major Obama policy initiative—healthcare reform, climate-change regulation, embryonic stem-cell research, infrastructure stimulus, electrical transmission smart-grids—and you'll find GE has set up shop, angling for a way to pocket government handouts, gain business through mandates, or profit from government regulation," says the Cato Institute's Daniel Ikenson.[141]

Obama's choice of Immelt as his business BFF is stunningly hypocritical. In 2010, 60 percent of GE's $14.2 billion profits were derived from overseas operations and the remaining $5.1 billion from its business in the United States. Moreover, GE paid precisely zero corporate taxes

that year.[142] Interestingly, we haven't heard Obama complaining about
GE or Immelt when he rails against millionaires and corporate greed.
Nor did we hear Obama object to his buddy conducting so much of his
business overseas, even though Obama often claims American jobs are
his top priority.

"ANOTHER HEAD-FAKE IN THE
DIRECTION OF CAPITALISM"

To try to defuse growing criticism from business, on January 31,
2011, Obama announced the "Startup America" initiative. Again,
Obama revealed his unwavering belief in business's dependence on government to succeed, and his naïveté about business and job creation,
indicating that all that was required for new businesses to sprout was
for him to give a rhetorical pep talk to America, telling prospective business creators to get off their duffs and jump into the market. The White
House website reported, "Startup America is the White House initiative
to celebrate, inspire, and accelerate high-growth entrepreneurship
throughout the nation."[143]

With the White House calling for the government and private sector
to work in partnership on the project, "leaders in the private sector"
obediently launched a "Startup America Partnership" to join "together
to fuel innovative, high-growth U.S. startups."[144] On its website the
group stated, "For an entrepreneurial ecosystem to be successful and
drive job growth, several elements must either exist or be developed."
Unsurprisingly, it listed among those elements the importance of "government serving as convener, but not the leader. Government must make
a deep, long-term commitment to focus on new, young companies."
Another element listed was a commitment to "engage with local, state
and federal government representatives as partners and conveners."[145]

As the Heritage Foundation reported, "This 'coordinated public/
private effort' appears to be just another head-fake in the direction of
capitalism with the intention of growing more government." In analyzing the program's goals, Heritage concluded that the entire effort is
another opportunity for the government to pick more winners and losers.

The government would "strengthen commercialization," i.e., use tax-payer funds to take market share away from private banks and venture capitalists; it would "expand entrepreneurship education and mentorship programs that empower more Americans not just to get a job, but to create jobs" (which is fine in theory, but the government cannot create jobs, except perhaps those that consume more taxes than they generate); and it would "expand collaborations between large companies and start-ups," which the government has no business doing.[146] In short, it's just another government spending program that doesn't increase demand for goods and services but merely redistributes demand and resources within the economy.

OBAMA'S WAR AGAINST SMALL BUSINESS

While Obama maintains a quid-pro-quo relationship with certain corporate cronies, his agenda has been devastating for small businesses, the primary drivers of job creation and economic growth. Small businesses create 70 percent of new jobs in America, but Obama has targeted them across the board, making many small business owners, as well as business and political analysts, wonder whether he's doing so on purpose or through an ideologically based learning disability.

For example, Obama wants to remove the cap on FICA taxes, which would amount to an enormous tax increase on, among others, small business owners, and which would destroy many of those businesses and the jobs they provide. Obama forced through Obamacare, which will increase taxes and other small business burdens. His financial regulation bill would make it much more difficult for small business owners to raise capital without jumping through government hoops. And finally, Obama has accommodated a climate that encourages employees to sue small businesses and others under various pretexts, just as he has steadfastly resisted even modest efforts at tort reform. All these factors and others are making it increasingly difficult for the entrepreneurial risk takers to create and expand businesses and increase employment.

In another potential blow to small business, the administration, in line with its continual focus on identity politics, got behind legislation that would require American businesses to provide the government information about the comparative salaries to employees based on sex, race, and national origin. The Paycheck Fairness Act, which has been reintroduced in Congress after previously passing the House but stalling in the Senate, includes expansive workplace rules, such as training female employees how to better negotiate pay and benefits, and also calls for the establishment of a database for American workers in both the public and private sectors.

The National Association of Manufacturers contends that while purporting to prevent race and gender discrimination, the bill could outlaw many benign, legitimate practices employers use to set employee pay rates.[147] The Heritage Foundation's labor policy expert James Sherk claims the law "could transfer billions of dollars from employers to trial lawyers, bankrupting businesses and costing jobs." Under the law, says Sherk, a woman earning less than a more experienced man could insist that her employer provide her training and thereafter pay her the same wage as her male counterpart. It would invite extensive lawsuits, including class action suits, and would result in the government injecting itself into the daily operations of businesses that it knows nothing about.[148]

In 2012, apparently wanting to appear more small business- and corporate-friendly leading up to the election, Obama rhetorically proposed reducing the corporate tax rate from 35 percent to 28 percent, which sounded inviting on the surface. But he would exclude from this proposal specific industries he opposes, such as oil and gas, insurance, and small aircraft manufacturers, whose "loopholes" he would close. Meanwhile, he would lavish upon industries he favors—green energy concerns—various tax incentives and lower rates. The Heritage Foundation pointed out the absurdity of the administration, with this ostensible proposal to cut taxes, planning on raising $250 billion in revenues over ten years.[149]

About a year after his deceptive announcement that he would streamline the regulatory process, Obama tried it again. In January 2012, in another effort to project himself as business-friendly, he pressed Congress to give him authority to consolidate six agencies that deal with trade and business development "to make it easier to do business in America." As

Investors Business Daily's editors noted, his idea misses the point, which is that businesses aren't complaining about duplication among multiple agencies, but about having to deal with the federal government at all.[150] This mirage would do nothing to relax the onerous regulatory structure Obama has exacerbated for the last three years.

As usual, Obama talks a good game about helping American business, but his policies betray an abiding ideological hostility to them; he seems to resent his inability to control them like an executive branch agency. To his chagrin, despite all his coercive regulations and his cultivation of numerous Big Business dependents, business still frequently acts independently of his will. Far too many businesses still won't hire new workers just for his idea of the common good, and far too many won't shift their production in accordance with his industrial planning. His frustration with this state of affairs fuels his attacks on business as well as on the GOP. But ultimately, simply lashing out isn't enough to achieve the fundamental transformation he wants to effect. He'll need to exert even more control over the economy to do that—and unhindered by election concerns, that's what Americans can expect if he wins another term in office.

CHAPTER TEN

THE WAR ON AMERICA'S NATIONAL SECURITY

Obama's foreign policy flows from his belief that America has been too nationalistic, aggressive, imperialistic, exploitive, and arrogant in world affairs. That worldview explains why he bounces around the world apologizing for our past "sins," why he wants to scale down our War on Terror, believing we've brought on ourselves much of the Islamists' wrath, and why he approaches foreign policy in a way that seems maddeningly inconsistent. It's why he's obsessed, in his way, with improving our image around the world. It's why he has jumped at the chance to intervene in foreign conflicts, even internal ones, when we have no compelling national security interest in doing so, or when such intervention is contrary to our national interests, and why he sometimes resists interventions when our national interest is more compelling.

"SERIOUS RESERVATIONS"

Obama's leftist foreign policy is exemplified in his vow to close down the Guantanamo Bay detention center, a promise he made without first conducting due diligence as to the feasibility of doing so. On his second day in office, he dramatically issued an executive order to shutter the facility within a year. He later learned the hard way that it simply could not be done. He eventually backed down amid opposition from Congress and the public to the astronomical costs and national security implications of closing Guantanamo, but he reiterated his ambition to close the facility some day—showing that there's no embarrassing a liberal with self-professed good intentions.

Obama followed the same careless pattern in his commitment to try international terrorists in American domestic courts, and he achieved the same pathetic results when the government got al-Qaeda terrorist Ahmed Ghailani convicted on only one of 285 charges for the 1998 African embassy bombings.[1] Without acknowledging any egg on his face, Obama announced in March 2011 that the government would resume using military commissions to prosecute terrorists held at Guantanamo Bay, though he remained committed to closing the detention center.[2]

And for all his previous posturing over Bush-era policies providing for the unlimited detentions of terrorism suspects, he reversed course here, too; in March 2011 he tacitly conceded the government's authority to such detentions by issuing an executive order calling for periodic reviews of these cases, reneging on his 2009 promise to work with Congress on the issue.[3]

Even though his order was an about-face, Republicans objected to Obama granting more rights to terrorists and imposing more obstacles to prosecuting them. "The Gitmo detainees already enjoy unlimited access to attorneys and are able to take full advantage of the federal courts," noted Congressman Tom Rooney, a former Army JAG Corps member. "We do not need to create yet another layer of review so that their lawyers can drag their cases through endless litigating during this time of war."[4]

To the chagrin of his leftist base, Obama conceded total defeat on the unlimited detention issue on January 2, 2012, when he signed the

National Defense Authorization Act, which formalized our right to imprison terrorism suspects indefinitely without charge or trial. Obama claimed he signed the bill "despite having serious reservations with certain provisions that regulate the detention, interrogation and prosecution of suspected terrorists."[5]

Despite Obama's bluster about secret detentions, the administration secretly detained Ahmed Abdulkadir Warsame, a Somali terror suspect, for two months on a U.S. Navy ship and, without formal charges or affording him an attorney, extensively interrogated him. Perhaps the administration wanted to have it both ways, avoiding the use of Guantanamo but hypocritically denying Warsame a lawyer and withholding his rights to habeas corpus on a Navy ship at sea. Then, showing total policy incoherence, the administration transported Warsame to New York for trial in a civilian criminal court. "The administration has purposefully imported a terrorist in the US and is providing him all the rights of US citizens in court," observed Senator Mitch McConnell.[6]

Maybe Obama had his way in the end over Guantanamo; while he may not have succeeded in shutting it down, his administration treated its detainees to a $750,000 taxpayer funded soccer field. The U.S. military created the field—part of a new recreation yard—at Camp 6, which holds some 80 percent of the facility's 171 prisoners. Soon the prisoners would also get a walking trail and exercise equipment.[7]

"I WILL MAKE IT MY BUSINESS TO IMPEACH HIM"

Mainstream conservatives typically oppose America's involvement in foreign conflicts unless a strategic national security interest is at stake. Reasonable people may disagree as to what constitutes such an interest, e.g., in Iraq, but that is the driving principle. Even so-called Neoconservatives, who more readily advocate military force to spread democracy, do so on the basis of that principle.

President Obama, on the other hand, subscribes to a much more ambiguous foreign policy vision, often appearing to favor U.S. military intervention even when no national security interest is in play. His policy sometimes seems more directed at catering to the wishes of the international community and the United Nations than safeguarding American interests. Sadly, America's security interests are the last thing the international community wants to protect.

Just as he chafes under constitutional limits to his domestic authority, Obama seems to lament that the Constitution does not vest the president with unfettered power over foreign policy. At one point he bemoaned that it would be much easier to be president of China. As one official explained, "No one is scrutinizing Hu Jintao's words in Tahrir Square."[8]

When Congress frustrates his foreign policy agenda, Obama often circumvents it administratively, through executive orders, or just by outright ignoring it and behaving as though he occupies the sole seat of power in Washington. In marked contrast to President George W. Bush, who ordered the invasion of Iraq only after it was authorized by Congress, Obama initiated military action against Libya without so much as consulting Congress, much less getting its approval. This snub was all the more remarkable in that Obama went through strenuous efforts to secure the endorsement of the Arab League and the UN for the Libya operation—suggesting he values their approval above that of Congress or the American people.

Shockingly, the administration later admitted this is, in fact, its guiding philosophy. Secretary of Defense Leon Panetta, in a March 2012 hearing before the Armed Services Committee about possible U.S. military action in Syria, declared, "Our goal would be to seek international permission, and we would come to the Congress and inform you, and determine how best to approach this, determine whether or not we would want to get permission from the Congress."[9]

Obama's unauthorized Libyan action was all the more outrageous considering Vice President Joe Biden had threatened in 2007 that if President Bush "takes this nation to war in Iran without congressional approval, I will make it my business to impeach him."[10] Obama himself, in a 2007 interview with the *Boston Globe*, declared, "The president does not have power under the Constitution to unilaterally authorize a military attack in a situation that does not involve stopping an actual or imminent threat to the nation." Around the same time, his future secretary of state, Hillary Clinton, proclaimed, "I do not believe that the President can take military action—including any kind of strategic bombing—against Iran without congressional authorization."[11]

GADDAFI NEVER THREATENED CIVILIAN MASSACRE

Concerning Libya, the White House couldn't seem to decide when, to what extent, or on whose behalf we should intervene. Former U.S. ambassador to the United Nations John Bolton described Obama's Libya policy as "incoherent" and illustrative of "the failed approach to national security issues characterizing his administration from the outset." His objectives, said Bolton, "have been unclear and contradictory, and they have shifted over time. He started by declaring that the use of force was to protect Libyan civilians—not to topple Col. Gadhafi. Today, however, the obvious military objective is the removal of the Libyan leader but, apparently not to admit it publicly, and to accomplish it slowly and ineffectively."[12]

As Obama's unspecified action in or above Libya got underway, people began to ask whether we were engaged in a war there. The question elicited a laughably evasive answer from the White House, as national security advisor Ben Rhodes declared, "I think what we are doing is enforcing a resolution that has a very clear set of goals, which is protecting the Libyan people, averting a humanitarian crisis, and setting up a no-fly zone. Obviously that involves kinetic military action, particularly on the front end."[13]

Obama claimed intervention in Libya was necessary to prevent a bloodbath in Benghazi and to forestall genocide. Curiously, those factors didn't guide his policy in Iraq; in response to concerns that his efforts to withdraw U.S. troops from Iraq could result in genocide and ethnic cleansing, he retorted, "If that's the criteria by which we are making decisions on the deployment of U.S. forces, then by that argument you would have 300,000 troops in the Congo right now—where millions have been slaughtered as a consequence of ethnic strife—which we haven't done. We would be deploying unilaterally and occupying the

Sudan, which we haven't done. Those of us who care about Darfur don't think it would be a good idea."[14]

Some argued Obama was grossly exaggerating the humanitarian threat in Libya to justify military action. "Despite ubiquitous cellphones equipped with cameras and video, there is no graphic evidence of deliberate massacre," noted Alan J. Kuperman, professor of public affairs at the University of Texas. "Nor did Khadafy ever threaten civilian massacre in Benghazi, as Obama alleged." His "no mercy" warning of March 17 applied only to rebels, said Kuperman, who pointed to a *New York Times* report that Gaddafi promised amnesty for those "who throw their weapons away." Even Human Rights Watch proclaimed that Gaddafi was "not deliberately massacring civilians, but rather narrowly targeting the armed rebels who fight against his government."[15]

Reports later emerged that Obama had been so determined to intervene in Libya that he rejected his top lawyers' legal advice on the operation. The *New York Times*' Charlie Savage found that Obama ignored the warnings of Jeh C. Johnson, the Pentagon general counsel, and Caroline D. Krass, the acting head of the Justice Department's Office of Legal Counsel, that U.S. military participation in the ostensibly NATO-led air war would amount to "hostilities," thus giving Congress a role in the affair via the War Powers Resolution. Incorrigibly, Obama searched for someone to provide legal validation for his action, eventually hearing what he wanted from White House counsel Robert Bauer and State Department legal advisor Harold H. Koh—famous for his advocacy of transnationalism—that the operation fell short of "hostilities."[16]

"A RADICAL REFORMULATION OF 70 YEARS OF AMERICAN FOREIGN POLICY"

Obama was hell-bent on intervening in Libya, and for reasons that didn't immediately meet the eye. In a March 2011 interview with CNN, Doug Feith, under secretary of defense for policy for President George W. Bush, theorized about Obama's motives:

The only way to make the President's behavior comprehensible is to recognize that he has a larger strategic goal than just the outcome of Libya. While the rest of the country is focused on Libya's future, the President is focused on fundamentally changing America's role and standing in the world. Libya, for him, is simply an occasion for undertaking a radical reformulation of 70 years of American foreign policy.

At least since the U.S. entered World War II, there has been a view of the United States as a leading power, a democratic power, a country that acts boldly in its own interests. I think President Obama does not believe that's the role America should play in the world.[17]

Indeed, a senior administration official told a group of outside experts at a White House meeting that in Obama's view, attacking Libya was "the greatest opportunity to realign our interests and our values." Investors. com editors noted that the United States appeared to be doing the UN's bidding in Libya, and that the entire operation perhaps had less to do with Libya than with transforming America's role in the world. They noted remarks by National Review Online's Stanley Kurtz that Obama's national security advisor, Samantha Power, had been looking for a way "'to solidify the principle of *responsibility to protect* [R2P] in international law,' which 'requires a *pure* case of intervention on humanitarian grounds.' Libya may fit perfectly." This, Kurtz said, could partially explain why Obama didn't consult Congress: "he cannot afford to specify broader ideological motivations he knows the public won't buy."[18]

That same week, I had come to a similar conclusion in my syndicated column:

Obama's animating foreign policy passion is that America has been an international bully that needs to be brought down to size. He couldn't wait to confess America's "arrogance" and "dismissiveness" to foreign nations on their soil. He gleefully told the Muslim world in his Cairo speech how wonderful and peaceful Islam is and how much it has contributed to America. He made clear that he doesn't believe in American exceptionalism when he said it is no different from Greek or British exceptionalism.

Though he couldn't have planned for the unforeseen events in Libya, when they happened, a light bulb eventually went off in his head, signaling that this was his moment to practice what he'd been preaching and to demonstrate how America has changed under his leadership. His primary goals are neither to oust Gadhafi nor to rescue the Libyan rebels for humanitarian reasons, for if ousting an evil dictator or protecting his victims were the motivation, he would have intervened in any number of other places.

His apparent vacillation and indecisiveness must be viewed in the context of his overarching goal: to change America's approach from "unilateralism," which it never was, to radical, deferential multilateralism replete with ceding our sovereign decisions to international bodies—and to change our image.[19]

Others discerned the same agenda. In *The National Interest*, David Rieff argued, essentially, that Obama undertook the Libyan mission to further the R2P concept. The philosophy of R2P is that national governments have a duty to prevent large-scale killing and ethnic cleansing within their own borders, but if they are either unable or unwilling to do so, the international community, through the UN, must intervene with or without the consent of the nations involved. Dismissing R2P as a revival of "the old utopian project of abolishing war," Rieff warned that "as Libya shows, war and utopia should not be mixed up. War is too serious, utopia too unserious, for that."[20]

THE KINETIC PIECES ARE INTERMITTENT

On May 17, 2011, the *Washington Post* featured an editorial by Yale law professor Bruce Ackerman and Yale political science professor Oona Hathaway observing that almost sixty days had passed since President Obama informed Congress of his Libya campaign, and that the War Powers Resolution would soon require him either to obtain congressional approval or cease U.S. involvement within thirty days. The authors noted that Obama hadn't even tried to get congressional approval, nor had the Democratic leadership shown any interest.

Interestingly, in his March 21 letter advising Congress of the Libya campaign, Obama cavalierly insisted his action was consistent with the War Powers Resolution. Ackerman and Hathaway expected Obama at least to assert a legal concoction to get around the act's requirements, pretending that we'd ended our involvement under the act because NATO had nominally taken the lead on April 1. But, as they said, "it is sheer fiction to suggest that we are no longer a vital player in NATO's 'Operation Unified Protector,'" especially because "an active-duty American officer remains at the top of NATO's chain of command." The authors concluded, "If nothing happens, history will say that the War Powers Act was condemned to a quiet death by a president who had solemnly pledged, on the campaign trail, to put an end to indiscriminate warmaking."[21]

Sure enough, a few days later Obama sent a letter to congressional leaders telling them the U.S. role in Libya was now so "limited" that it didn't require congressional approval. Yet despite his obvious attempt to downplay the level of U.S. involvement, his explanation of U.S. actions since April 4 didn't sound so limited. These, Obama said, included "non-kinetic support" such as "intelligence, logistical support, and search and rescue assistance"; aerial assistance in suppressing and destroying air defenses; and since April 23, strikes by unmanned aerial vehicles against "a limited set of clearly defined targets."[22]

Ultimately, the administration claimed its Libya actions were "consistent with the War Powers Resolution" because U.S. operations did "not involve sustained fighting or active exchanges of fire with hostile forces." Despite its expressed support for the Libya operation, the *Wall Street Journal* editorial board commented, "That evasion has been ridiculed in Congress, and rightly so."[23] In addition, indications arose that the U.S. role was significantly greater than the administration was admitting. For example, the *Air Force Times* reported on June 30 that "Air Force and Navy aircraft are still flying hundreds of strike missions over Libya despite the administration's claim that American forces are playing only a limited support role in the NATO operation."[24]

Congress, by an almost three-quarters majority, approved a nonbinding resolution to notify Obama that unless he explained his unauthorized action in Libya, he would face consequences. "He has a chance to get this right," said House Speaker John Boehner. "If he doesn't,

Congress will exercise its constitutional authority and make it right."
Obama speciously argued that he had complied with the War Powers
Resolution because he had supposedly consulted with Congress—never
mind that the act requires congressional *approval*.[25] John Bolton mar-
veled at Obama's disinterest in explaining or defending his actions, a
failure by which Obama "risked a self-inflicted political wound that could
have undermined our national security policy in many other international
arenas."[26]

Senator John McCain, who had supported Obama's Libya policy,
strongly criticized his high-handed refusal to seek congressional
approval. "I think what the president did was he brought this whole
issue to a head now because of this, really, incredible interpretation that
we are not necessarily—that the War Powers Act does not apply to our
activities in Libya," said McCain, adding unequivocally: "We are
engaged in a conflict."[27]

A "MASSIVE HUMILIATION
FOR THE WESTERN ALLIANCE"

The administration continued its hapless, uncertain approach to the
Libyan intervention as the conflict was winding down. After joining
China in abstaining from the vote on the UN resolution authorizing
action in Libya, Russia denounced the operation from the sidelines. And
when the Kremlin attempted to insinuate itself as mediator of the conflict,
Obama, never encountering an insult to American prestige he hasn't
welcomed, accepted the overture.

John Bolton noted the obvious—that affording a "swaggering, international bully boy" like Russia a big role in mediating the conflict and
in shaping post-Gaddafi Libya would amount to a "massive humiliation
for the Western alliance." Of further concern to Bolton and many others,
neither America nor its NATO allies had done anything to strengthen
pro-Western voices in Libya and help them come to power instead of
some new rogue regime.[28]

Stanley Kurtz suggested a rationale for Obama's inexplicable policy:
R2P. "Obama's willingness to cede so much to the Russians reflects the
fact that he is far less interested in achieving and enforcing regime change

in Libya, than in using this intervention to advance the utopian plans of his hyper-internationalist advisers," Kurtz said. By ceding Russia de facto control over Libyan oil and gas resources, Kurtz argued, Obama would avoid sending in U.S. troops while "bolster[ing] the development of a post-American world order—with an R2P-enforcing U.N. exercising a larger military role." While that would enhance Russia's ability to bully Europe, Obama, according to Kurtz, was "less concerned about those sorts of strategic considerations than about advancing the vision of a world policed by a U.N. freed of U.S. domination."[29]

THOUSANDS OF SURFACE-TO-AIR MISSILES DISAPPEAR

It's hard to conceive that the administration helped to oust the Libyan regime without any plan for preventing terrorists from seizing its weapons. But at the end of September, ABC News reported that after Gaddafi's downfall, Libya descended into lawlessness as fighters—including some from al-Qaeda—poured into the country. "Amid this lawlessness, thousands of Libyan surface-to-air missiles that could potentially shoot down civilian aircraft disappeared," ABC reported. The White House said it would expand a program to secure and destroy Libya's huge stockpile of these missiles, but at the time the U.S. State Department had only one official on the ground in Libya, along with five contractors who were experts in "explosive ordinance disposal."[30]

ABC News reported that U.S. officials and security experts were concerned that missing heat-seeking missiles could end up in terrorists' hands. Peter Bouckaert of Human Rights Watch said he'd seen people driving off with truckloads of missiles from weapons facilities when he visited Libya in March 2011, and then again in September. "Every time I arrive at one of these weapons facilities, the first thing we notice going missing is the surface-to-air missiles," he explained. "I myself could have removed several hundred if I wanted to, and people can literally drive up with pickup trucks or even 18 wheelers and take away whatever they want.... In Libya, we're talking about something on the order of 20,000 surface-to-air missiles. This is one of the greatest stockpiles of these weapons that has ever gone on the loose." Chillingly, Richard Clarke, former White House counterterrorism advisor, said, "I think the probability of al Qaeda being able to smuggle some of the stinger-like missiles out of Libya is probably pretty high."[31]

Less than a month later, ABC News reported that some of these missing missiles had turned up near the Israeli border. The *Washington Post* said many of the stolen missiles had been sold in Egyptian black markets and that their price had dropped from $10,000 to $4,000 due to the abundant supply. Most of the missiles were shoulder-fired, had a range of two miles, and would pose a threat to Israeli helicopter and planes on either side of the Israel-Gaza border.[32]

It wasn't until mid-October 2011 that the administration began a campaign to track down these missiles, sending fourteen contractors with military backgrounds to Libya and planning on sending dozens more. Meanwhile, Libyan rebel groups and civilians had carried off an unknown number of these weapons. As the *Washington Post's* Mary Beth Sheridan reported, one rebel fighter, Essam Abu Bakr, said he watched groups of rebels throw "crates of grenades and missiles into trucks 'as though they were sacks of sugar.' 'I'm worried,' he said. 'Loose weapons are everywhere.'"[33]

It was hardly comforting to discover that these Obama administration-backed rebel forces ransacked entire villages, leaving ghost towns in their wake, and administering brutal beatings. "They chased us with guns and knives," testified one victim. "They brought me to a house and beat me with electrical cable to make me confess I worked for Gaddafi, even though I told them I never carried a gun."[34] The rebels also slaughtered some fifty-three Gaddafi supporters and buried them in a mass grave in Gaddafi's hometown.[35]

"WE LED THIS THING"

Quite contrary to the administration's assurances that it was supporting democratic forces, Libya's post-Gaddafi interim leader, Mustafa Abdul Jalil, declared that Libyan laws in the future would have Sharia—strict Islamic law—as their "basic source." Proving he meant business, he immediately lifted a law banning polygamy because it conflicted with Sharia, and also announced that future bank regulations would ban the charging of interest, as mandated by Sharia.[36] In Benghazi, where the Libyan revolution erupted, al-Qaeda planted its flag alongside the Libyan rebel flag atop the city courthouse.[37]

The opportunistic Obama administration, ignoring all these horror stories, changed its tune once Gaddafi had been ousted. After previously downplaying the U.S. role to avoid triggering the War Powers Resolution, the administration began to boast that it had been leading the operation all along. Although some administration supporters had described the U.S. role as "leading from behind," Susan Rice, the U.S. ambassador to the United Nations, called that a "whacked out phrase." "We led this thing," she bluntly declared. "We put teeth in this mandate."

This must have been news to the British and French, who had been frustrated by the administration's vacillation back in March, when they couldn't get Obama to join them in a resolution to establish a no-fly zone over Libya. But the administration wasn't satisfied with support merely from our European allies; it wasn't until the Arab League got behind the no-fly zone that it began taking an active role. Displaying utter incoherence, the administration explained that it based our Libyan action on the UN mandate calling for the protection of civilians, which it "did not conflate" with "regime change as part of the military mission." As writer Marc Thiessen trenchantly summarized, "Got that? We did not lead from behind, we led. But our goal was never to help the overthrow of Qaddafi. But now that he's gone we're claiming credit. Now *that's* 'whacked out.'"[38]

"A NATIONWIDE UPRISING AGAINST MUBARAK DOES NOT EXIST"

President Obama also tried out his R2P approach in Egypt, meandering through mazes of indecision as he contemplated whether to support the overthrow of our longtime ally, President Hosni Mubarak.

In January 2011 a mob of Egyptians took to Cairo's Tahrir Square, demanding Mubarak step down. After initially supporting Mubarak, President Obama seemingly shifted course, expressing dismay at Mubarak's refusal to step down and chiding the Egyptian government for failing to put forward a "credible, concrete and unequivocal path to

democracy." But Mubarak defied Obama's calls to resign, provoking a
cutting observation from Britain's *Guardian*: "Mubarak's response offers
further evidence of the US's slow decline from its status as superpower to
a position where it is unable to decisively influence events in Egypt, in spite
of that country being one of the biggest recipients of US military aid." The
paper also ridiculed the administration's vacillation, saying it had "shifted
from solidly supporting Mubarak, to suggesting he should go now, only
to back him at the weekend to remain in office until the autumn—a decision that secretary of state Hillary Clinton reversed hours later when she
threw US support behind [Egyptian Vice President] Suleiman."[39]

As Obama slowly settled on a policy of encouraging Mubarak to
leave, a fundamental question lurked beneath the heady events: Did the
Egyptian people themselves want to oust Mubarak? Certainly a mob in
Cairo's streets was clamoring for it, yet it was unclear to what extent that
sentiment spread past Tahrir Square. Two Ukrainian bloggers who were
passing through Egypt wrote, "We visited Egypt and studied the situation
in detail, on the ground. Having talked with hundreds of residents of
Cairo and other Egyptian cities, we came to a definite conclusion: *a
nationwide uprising against Mubarak does not exist.*" Most of the Egyptian people, according to the bloggers, did not support the anti-Mubarak
factions, whose rebellion, the Ukrainians argued, was limited to just one
area of Cairo.[40]

"PERHAPS THE STUPIDEST STATEMENT... IN U.S. INTERNATIONAL HISTORY"

Why would Obama support the overthrow of Mubarak when this
would likely bring to power the Muslim Brotherhood, an anti-American
group of Islamic fundamentalists seeking to create a worldwide Islamic
caliphate? Perhaps it was because Obama didn't have a particularly
negative view of the Brotherhood, an 84-year-old organization that,
according to the *New York Times*, "virtually invented Islamism."[41]
Although the Brotherhood's entire *raison d'etre* is to spread Islamism,
Obama's director of national intelligence, James Clapper, told the House
Intelligence Committee, "The term Muslim Brotherhood is an umbrella

term for a variety of movements; in the case of Egypt, a very heteroge-
neous group, largely secular, which has eschewed violence and has
decried al Qaeda as a perversion of Islam."[42]

In damage control mode, the administration later tried to "clarify"
Clapper's inexplicable distortion, releasing a statement that read, in part,
"To clarify Director Clapper's point, in Egypt the Muslim Brotherhood
makes efforts to work through a political system that has been, under
Mubarak's rule, one that is largely secular in its orientation. He is well
aware that the Muslim Brotherhood is not a secular organization."[43]

It's hard to see how the administration could credibly claim this was
a clarification as opposed to an outright retraction. In any case, the statement hardly satisfied administration critics. John Bolton called Clapper's
comment "perhaps the stupidest statement made by any administration
in U.S. international history."[44] British reporter Nile Gardiner commented, "Clapper's remarks were a bizarre whitewash of the organization, and yet another embarrassing gaffe by an Administration that
increasingly specializes in them."[45] Denouncing Clapper's "willful stupidity," *National Review* terrorism expert Andrew McCarthy wrote, "This
is the Muslim Brotherhood whose motto brays that the Koran is the law
and jihad is its way. The MB whose Palestinian branch, the terrorist
organization Hamas, was created for the specific purpose of destroying
Israel—the goal its charter says is a religious obligation. It is the organization dedicated to the establishment of Islamicized societies and, ultimately, a global caliphate. It is an organization whose leadership says
al-Qaeda's emir, Osama bin Laden, is an honorable jihad warrior who
was 'close to Allah on high' in 'resisting the occupation.'"[46]

It was later reported that U.S. officials met with members of the
Muslim Brotherhood's political party once Mubarak was ousted. The
administration denied this was a break from previous U.S. policy,
though in the past such contacts were limited to actual members of the
parliament.[47]

In November, reports surfaced that the U.S. State Department was
training anti-Western Islamist political parties in Egypt in polling, con-
stituent services, and electoral preparations. William Taylor, the State
Department's director of its new office for Middle East Transitions,

responded to the reports with a classic non-denial denial. "We don't do party support. What we do is party training.... And we do it to whoever comes," he said. "Sometimes," he added, "Islamist parties show up, sometimes they don't. But it has been provided on a nonpartisan basis, not to individual parties"—as if providing support indiscriminately excused them from supporting anti-American groups.[48] This perversion was no surprise to those familiar with this administration's leftist ideology. Indeed, Taylor said the United States would be "satisfied" if fair parliamentary elections resulted in a victory for the Muslim Brotherhood—which is exactly what happened in Egypt, as the Brotherhood and the even more radical Salafist sect later won a combined 70 percent of the seats in parliament.[49]

Naturally, the Brotherhood's victory only encouraged the Obama administration to step up its "engagement" efforts. In April 2012, the administration hosted a Muslim Brotherhood delegation in Washington that met with White House staffers and national security officials.[50] According to the Investigative Project on Terrorism, to smooth its entry into America, the State Department prohibited U.S. customs officials from subjecting the Brotherhood delegation to standard inspection checks for visitors from Egypt, and even prevented the secondary inspection that would have been standard for one Brotherhood member implicated in a child pornography investigation.[51] As Andrew McCarthy reported, shortly after the delegation's visit, the Obama administration announced it would give $1.5 billion in aid to the new Muslim Brotherhood-dominated Egyptian government, representing $1.3 billion in military assistance and an additional $200 million in economic aid.[52] Obama would do so despite congressional opposition.[53]

As his administration dutifully set about whitewashing the Muslim Brotherhood, Obama seemed unconcerned by the rising persecution of Christians in Arab Spring nations. For example, when Egyptian soldiers massacred Coptic Christians protesting the burning of a church, the White House issued a statement reeking of moral equivalence. Declining actually to condemn the massacre, which it only referred to in vague terms, it called for restraint from both the victims and the perpetrators. "The President is deeply concerned about the violence in Egypt that has led to a tragic loss of life among demonstrators and security forces," said the statement. "Now is a time for restraint on all sides so that Egyptians can move forward together to forge a strong and united Egypt."[54]

THE ARAB SPRING: "AN UNSHACKLING OF ISLAM"

As it was warming up to the Muslim Brotherhood, the administration backed off its previous support for the Egyptian military. The problem was that after Mubarak's overthrow, Egypt's military rulers faced a choice of either holding quick elections, which the highly organized Brotherhood would surely dominate, or postponing elections and prolonging the transitional period, raising the likelihood that the military would seek to retain power for itself. Fearing the military could become abusive, the White House in November 2011 urged it to relinquish control "as soon as possible." This was in stark contrast to Secretary of State Hillary Clinton's praise for the military just two months before as an "institution of stability and continuity."[55]

Whether you gauge Obama's Egypt policy by the country's progress toward a stable democratic society, its attitude toward the United States, or its intentions toward Israel, it has been a major failure. Notwithstanding his call for Egypt's regime to step aside, Obama, in his new FY2013 budget, proposed more money for Egypt at the very time ascendant Muslim Brotherhood leaders were becoming more belligerent toward Israel and even threatening to attack the Jewish state. Hosni Mubarak may have been a repressive leader, but for three decades he was friendly to the United States, kept the peace with Israel, and helped maintain stability in the region. But by helping to empower Islamist revolutionaries under the pretense that they are democratic forces, Obama has jeopardized regional stability as well as Israel's security.

In another indication of the failure of Obama's diplomacy, in January 2012 the Egyptian government criminally charged forty-three NGO workers, including at least sixteen Americans, with illegally using foreign funds to stir unrest in Egypt. Some of the accused had already left the country or found shelter in the U.S. embassy, but the others were detained, including Sam LaHood, son of Obama's transportation secretary

Ray LaHood. In what seemed to be a personal insult to Obama, LaHood was arrested one day after Obama had contacted Mohammed Hussein Tantawi, the head of Egypt's regime, to urge him to permit NGOs such as LaHood to operate freely.[56] Finally, after being held for more than a month, on March 1, 2012, the detained Americans were allowed to leave Egypt upon putting up bail in excess of $300,000 each.[57]

Before their release, in response to congressional warnings that the United States would cut off aid to Egypt unless the detainees were let go, Egypt's Muslim Brotherhood sent the United States a clear message: "What was acceptable before the revolution is no longer." If we suspend the aid, they warned, Egypt would sever its peace treaty with Israel. "We have been told that fear of losing U.S. aid will constrain Egypt," noted Middle East expert Barry Rubin. "But we are now seeing that this simply isn't true. What happens when the Egyptian government helps Hamas fight Israel?"[58]

It's astonishing that this administration could have pretended the Muslim Brotherhood would usher in a more democratic, peaceful, or America-friendly Egypt. As Investors.com reported, Obama was aware of the Brotherhood's propensities while he was engaging with them, including their threats to revoke Egypt's peace treaty with Israel. He was also aware, as revealed by embassy cables and other intelligence, that Egyptians were highly sympathetic to the Brotherhood and its belligerence toward Israel. And Obama certainly knew it after the Brotherhood dominated Egypt's parliamentary elections, yet still asked Congress for $800 million more in his budget to prop up the "Arab Spring" countries. As Investors.com editors wrote, "The real scandal is that Obama appears to have engineered the Brotherhood's ascendancy. It's no coincidence he invited the Brotherhood to his 2009 Cairo speech over the objections of Mubarak, who had outlawed the group."[59]

The administration's outreach to Islamists was not confined to Egypt. In March 2012 in Tunisia—another "Arab Spring" country where Islamists have filled the vacuum left by an ousted autocrat—thousands of secular Tunisians demonstrated against Obama's close cooperation with the Islamists of the ruling Ennahda party. "People here are against

the United States helping Ennahda," said Tunisian journalist Ashraf
Ayadi. "All Americans who come here are against the Islamists, but the
American government is supporting them. I wish we had a good, modern, respectful Islamic party. I'm a Muslim and I'm proud of it, but I'm
not proud of this party."[60]

As the so-called Arab Spring spread through Tunisia, Egypt, Yemen,
Bahrain, Libya, and Syria, dewy-eyed western optimists had high hopes
for a radical democratic explosion in the Middle East. Obama mostly
welcomed these rebellions, calling for Mubarak's resignation in Egypt
and providing military assistance to the rebels in Libya, blind to indications that the uprisings would likely empower rulers even more repressive, Islamist, and anti-American than their predecessors.

"The Arab Spring is an unshackling of Islam, not an outbreak of
fervor for freedom in the Western sense," observed Andy McCarthy. The
Islamists, he noted, may well use democracy as a train to take them to
their destination, which "is the implementation of sharia." That, said
McCarthy, is "the undeniable trend in Egyptian society" and "in such
basket cases as Libya, where each day brings new evidence that today's
governing 'rebels' include yesterday's al-Qaeda jihadists, and in Yemen."
While Obama and the European Union are deluded into believing democratic elections will bring peace, stability, and more "progressive" societies, added McCarthy, once these Islamist regimes are in power, "they are
sure to make virulent anti-Americanism their official policy and to contribute materially to the pan-Islamic goal of destroying Israel."[61]

Obama's solicitous policy toward the Islamists of the Arab Spring
complements his markedly ingratiating attitude toward Muslims in general, an approach he introduced, in grand fashion, with his fawning Cairo
speech of June 2009. This attitude runs through his whole administration,
including his national security officials. Deputy National Security Advisor
for Homeland Security and Counterterrorism John Brennan described
violent extremists as victims of "political, economic and social forces,"
and said that "jihad is a holy struggle, a legitimate tenet of Islam, meaning to purify oneself or one's community," though he admitted "there is
nothing holy or legitimate about murdering innocent men, women and

children."[62] In a speech on national security at NYU in February 2010, Brennan wistfully praised Islam for the "tolerance and diversity which define [it]," and said he "came to see Islam not as it is often misrepresented, but for what it is ... a faith of peace and tolerance and great diversity." He even used the Arabic term "Al Quds" for Jerusalem.[63]

Indeed Obama and his administration constantly go to great pains to show their deference and admiration for Islam. These displays include:

- Obama launching into an impassioned paean to the "great religion" of Islam, whose adherents, he said, overwhelmingly believe in "peace and justice and fairness and tolerance," when asked by a student in Mumbai about jihad. The city had been the site of a jihadist massacre just two years earlier in which more than a hundred people were killed.[64]
- Obama drawing a link in his Passover message of April 2011 between the suffering of Jews in Egypt and the Muslim uprisings in the Middle East and North Africa.[65]
- The Justice Department scuttling numerous terror-related prosecutions, reportedly outraging some of the prosecutors and FBI agents involved.[66]
- The administration granting U.S. citizenship to three people convicted of crimes in terrorism-related cases.[67]
- Obama revoking the ban on photos of coffins of U.S. soldiers, but refusing to publish the Osama bin Laden death photos for fear of offending Muslims.[68]
- The administration sanitizing all references to "radical Islam" and the "War on Terror" from our national security documents.[69]

Perhaps most disturbingly, the Obama administration collaborated with the Organization of Islamic Cooperation (OIC) to combat "Islamophobia" and supported implementing a UN resolution against religious "stereotyping" specifically as applied to Islam. Nina Shea, in National Review Online, noted, "With the United States providing this new world stage for presenting grievances of 'Islamophobia' against the West, the OIC rallied around the initiative as the propaganda windfall that it is." It reasserted demands for global blasphemy laws, said Shea, and "has made plain its aim to ... pressure Western governments to regulate speech on behalf of Islam."[70]

The administration's relentless PR campaign to win the hearts and minds of Muslims prompted Senator Joe Lieberman to warn, "The administration's fear of offending Muslims will hurt the U.S. war against terrorism." The administration, said Lieberman, "still refuses to call our enemy in this war by its proper name: violent Islamist extremism. To call our enemy 'violent extremism' is so general and vague that it ultimately has no meaning."[71] To Lieberman's point, Vice President Joe Biden, in an interview with Les Gelb of *Newsweek/The Daily Beast*, insisted, "Look the Taliban per se is not our enemy. That's critical. There is not a single statement that the president has ever made in any of our policy assertions that the Taliban is our enemy because it threatens U.S. interests."[72]

"THE HEIGHT OF IRRESPONSIBILITY"

Obama apparently doesn't realize or care that he is not advancing democracy or any other legitimate foreign policy goals through his constant criticism of his own country. He indulges Muslim grievances and implies we are bigoted against the entire religion—that with our tactics in intelligence gathering, detention, rendition, and the like, we have behaved in ways justifying our declining image in the world.

The administration's America-flogging reached new heights with a bizarre utterance from Vice President Joe Biden during his visit to Iraq in November 2011, just as we were irresponsibly withdrawing from that country so quickly that we didn't even renew a treaty to maintain a residual force for training and security purposes. "We're not claiming victory," declared Biden. "What we're claiming here is that we've done our job—ending the war we did not start, to end it in a responsible way, [and] to bring Americans home."

With Biden's statement, the administration, again, consciously made a stark break from pre-Obama America, as if to say that the America that initially invaded Iraq is not the America they represent. "The most outrageous thing about this statement is Biden's conceit that he and Obama are 'ending the war we did not start,'" Max Boot aptly observed. "Obama and Biden are the two most senior elected officials of the U.S. government. The U.S. government as a whole made a decision to intervene in Iraq, and it is the height of irresponsibility for one administration to think it can abandon with impunity the commitments made by its predecessor, whatever it may think of those commitments." What made Biden's assertion even more preposterous was that "Biden himself was part of the majority in both Houses who voted to go to war."[73]

The administration has habitually sent these reckless signals to the world, such as when we were contemplating military intervention in Libya. At that time, Secretary of State Hillary Clinton faced questions from the House Foreign Affairs Committee about why we were not at least threatening to use force to protect our own citizens from danger arising from the Libyan turmoil. Amazingly, Clinton told the committee that the administration didn't want to raise "alarm bells around the region and the world that we were about to invade for oil. If you follow, as we follow, all of the websites that are looking at what's happening in the Middle East, you see a constant drumbeat that the United States is going to invade Libya to take over the oil—and we can't let that happen." Apparently feeling the need to assure Congress and the world, Clinton declared, "Well, we are not going to do that."[74]

Thus, the administration based certain important national security decisions on crackpot allegations found on foreign and leftist websites that the United States invades countries to steal their oil.

When it's not indulging anti-American sentiments, the Obama administration seems to feel driven to create them. For example, in Mumbai, India, in November 2010, Obama gratuitously portrayed his countrymen as ignorant, prejudiced rubes. "I want to be honest," he told his audience. "There are many Americans whose only experience with trade and globalization has been a shuttered factory or a job that was shipped overseas.

And there still exists a caricature of India as a land of call centers and back offices that cost American jobs. That's a real perception."[75]

"U.S. FAVORABLE RATINGS ACROSS THE ARAB WORLD HAVE PLUMMETED"

Obama has prioritized improving U.S. relations with the Muslim world, seeming to believe that a mixture of flattery, self-criticism of the United States, support for Arab Spring Islamists, and his own magnetic personality will do the trick. From his pandering speech in Cairo to his disgraceful fecklessness on the Ground Zero Mosque, Obama has begged Muslims to believe that he, personally, has ushered in a new era of good will between the United States and the Islamic world. Yet his strategy hasn't borne fruit.

Opinion polls not only show no uptick in Muslims' approval of the United States under Obama, but a decline. As famed pollster Zogby International reported, "After improving with the election of Barack Obama in 2008, U.S. favorable ratings across the Arab world have plummeted. In most countries they are lower than at the end of the Bush administration, and lower than Iran's favorable ratings (except in Saudi Arabia)." Among the main reasons cited as "obstacles to peace and stability in the Middle East" are "U.S. interference in the Arab world," precisely what Obama promised to correct.

Zogby further reported that "President Obama's favorable ratings across the Arab World are 10% or less," which is remarkable in view of his pained efforts to ingratiate himself in the Middle East. As Michael Prell observed in the *Washington Times*, "After he promised to restore America's international reputation, not only does the Arab world hate America more under Mr. Obama than it did under President George W. Bush, it even hates Mr. Obama personally, more than it detested the swaggering unilateralist cowboy from Texas."[76]

Furthermore, the administration's approach to the Middle East peace process—largely consisting of pressuring Israel to stop building settlements and even to halt construction of new apartments in certain parts of its capital city of Jerusalem—has been a complete bust, as the Palestinian Authority refuses even to negotiate directly with the Jewish state until it meets Obama's ill-conceived demands.

Recall that the Democratic establishment and President Obama routinely derided the alleged warmongering of President Bush, and the mainstream media published an almost daily casualty count in Iraq. But in 2010, U.S. deaths in Afghanistan rose 57 percent from 2009 and were triple those of 2008. Indeed, total deaths in that country in 2010 exceeded the number of deaths for the previous seven years of the war combined. In light of all that killing, it's no wonder that in Afghanistan, as in most of the rest of the Muslim world, President Obama has failed to make the United States more popular: only 43 percent of Afghans viewed us favorably at the beginning of 2011, compared to 83 percent in 2005.[77]

Aside from his failure to win popular acclaim abroad, Obama has failed to endear himself to foreign leaders, despite his vaunted willingness to talk with America's enemies. Although his many overtures to Iran have met with ridicule and the mullahs continue developing nuclear capabilities, he and his administration still pander like a smitten suitor; American diplomats drew attention in September 2010 when they declined to join Canadian diplomats in walking out during a speech by Iranian President Mahmoud Ahmadinejad at the UN.[78]

In Iraq, despite having proudly boasted of opposing the U.S. invasion from the outset, Obama's diplomatic magic has also backfired. When Obama and Vice President Biden presumptuously urged President Jalal Talabani to resign and allow Iyad Allawi to replace him, they came up empty-handed, embarrassing themselves and harming our relations with our new ally in the process.[79] Likewise in Pakistan; Army General Martin E. Dempsey, chairman of the Joint Chiefs of Staff, told the British media, "[The average Pakistani who] doesn't know the United States, doesn't read about the United States or just watches something on television about the United States, at that level, [the relations] are probably the worst they've ever been." And, he said, the relationship between the U.S. government and the Pakistani government is "on about as rocky a road as I've seen."[80]

Despite multiple overtures, Obama is also continually rebuffed by Venezuelan dictator Hugo Chavez, who even rejected Obama's designated ambassador to Caracas.[81] In addition, Chavez has announced he would host a founding conference of the Community of Latin American and Caribbean States (CELAC). Claiming the gathering would "change the history of the continent," Chavez made it clear against whom the conclave was aimed. "For centuries, they've imposed on us whatever the North [e.g., the United States] felt like imposing on us!" the dictator thundered. "The time of the South has arrived!" As the *Latin American Herald Tribune* noted, the conference is intended to counteract the Organization of American States, a regional grouping that, unlike CELAC, includes the United States.[82]

Meanwhile, Obama continues to alienate our stalwart ally Israel, seeming to view the prospect of an Israeli pre-emptive strike on Iran's nuclear weapons program as a bigger threat than the program itself.[83] Moreover, not only has he pressured the Israelis to make even more unreciprocated concessions to the Palestinians, he also gratuitously insulted Israeli prime minister Benjamin Netanyahu; after French president Nicolas Sarkozy called Netanyahu a liar during a G20 summit in November 2011, Obama, not realizing their conversation was being captured on microphone, replied, "You are sick of him, but I have to work with him every day."[84]

Ironically, Obama hasn't even managed to capitalize on his mistreatment of Israel to improve relations with the Palestinian Authority. To the contrary, after adopting Obama's own conditions for re-starting talks with Israel, the PA abandoned negotiations and instead, ignoring the administration's pleas, sought statehood recognition directly from the United Nations.

ELSEWHERE AROUND THE GLOBE

Even outside the Middle East, Obama has mangled foreign policy across the board. While placating our enemies, Obama has often been thoughtlessly offensive to our allies, particularly Great Britain. The UK

Telegraph's Nile Gardiner wrote a piece in 2010 highlighting "President Obama's top ten insults against Britain," and he updated the list in 2011 and in 2012. Included among the slights were "siding with Argentina over the Falklands," "calling France America's strongest ally," "downgrading the special relationship" between the U.S. and Britain, "supporting a federal Europe and undercutting British sovereignty," "betraying Britain to appease Moscow over the New START Treaty," "placing a 'boot on the throat' of BP," "throwing Churchill out of the Oval Office," "DVDs for the Prime Minister," "insulting words from the State Department," and "undermining British influence in NATO."[85]

"During the Bush presidency relations with Japan, China, India, Mexico, Colombia, Poland, the Czech Republic, and Great Britain (to name just a few countries) were better than they have been during the Obama years," observes writer Peter Wehner. He also notes that our relations with France and Germany have chilled under Obama, since both nations' leaders are skeptical about Obama's commitment to stop Iran's nuclear weapons program, and both view the United States as less than a reliable partner in the Eurozone crisis.[86]

Wehner catalogued Obama's many failed campaign promises on foreign policy, concluding, "What one finds are extravagant promises, from a stronger and more sustained partnership with Pakistan, Afghanistan, Japan, India, and China … to ending our dependence on foreign oil, to deepening our engagement to help resolve the Arab-Israeli conflict, to closing Guantanamo Bay; to meeting (without preconditions) Fidel Castro, Hugo Chavez, and Mahmoud Ahmadinejad during Obama's first year in office; to renewed respect for America in the Muslim world; to rapid economic growth in order to maintain our military superiority."[87]

Heritage Foundation foreign policy experts also note that the Obama Doctrine—"one in which the White House engaged with enemies and undercut allies, apologized for American exceptionalism, and favored the 'soft power' of treaties and international organizations" in order to recast America's image—has yielded "disastrous results." Syria, they say, is another example. Hoping to engage Bashar al-Assad, Obama soft-peddled his criticism of Assad's violent crackdown on anti-government protestors. After that, "Syria ordered the attack on the U.S. embassy in

Damascus, threatened the U.S. ambassador, and to date has killed more than 7,500 Syrians who are standing against the autocratic government."[88]

Consider also the administration's policy toward one small country: Honduras. As recounted in *Crimes Against Liberty*, the Obama administration worked to undermine the democratically and lawfully elected government in Honduras and supported the lawless dictator Manuel Zelaya, who was eventually exiled from his own country after attempting to illegally extend his term in office. The administration's bizarre support for Zelaya against the expressed will of the Honduran people, Congress, and Supreme Court was wholly inconsistent with its professed support for democracy, though not with its strange affinity for leftist dictators. Only after it was clear that the Honduran people would not yield to the administration's bullying did it begin to change course. Finally, the administration belatedly voiced approval of Honduras's democratically elected president, Porfirio Lobo.[89]

But it soon became apparent that Obama's team had not really given up on Zelaya. Congresswoman Ileana Ros-Lehtinen, chairwoman of the House Foreign Affairs Committee, revealed that the administration was engaging in backchannel efforts to pressure President Lobo to drop a case against Zelaya for misappropriating government funds and falsifying documents, and to allow Zelaya to return to Honduras from exile in the Dominican Republic. In a letter to Arturo Valenzuela, the assistant secretary of state for western hemisphere affairs, Ros-Lehtinen wrote, "I am gravely concerned by reports I have received regarding efforts by U.S. officials to pressure the Government of Honduras to absolve former President Manuel Zelaya of the criminal charges he faces in that country and ask, within all applicable rules and guidelines, that if these reports are accurate, the State Department immediately cease exerting such undue influence over duly elected Honduran government officials acting in accordance with Honduran law."[90]

The administration was unmoved, hailing a later agreement backed by Venezuela that allowed Zelaya to return to Honduras without being prosecuted and with the freedom to engage in politics. "Hugo Chavez's handprints are all over this deal," Ros-Lehtinen declared, warning that the accord opened the door for Chavez to work with Zelaya to undermine

Honduran democracy. "It is regrettable and incomprehensible that Honduras continues to be bullied into indulging the incessant demands of Manuel Zelaya and his ALBA cohorts."[91]

U.S. Secretary of State Hillary Clinton not only called the signing of the agreement a "great day" for the Honduran people, she praised the Chavez regime for helping to realize it. As if claiming vindication for the administration's original support for Zelaya, Clinton issued a statement saying, "Thanks to the help of the Colombian and Venezuelan governments, this agreement paves the way for the reintegration of Honduras to the Organization of American States and gives Honduras the opportunity to pursue national reconciliation and end its isolation from the international community." Chavez, as is his wont, praised the agreement as "an example of the value of the resistance of the people."[92]

So what explains Obama's support for Zelaya? Two released WikiLeaks cables from the U.S. embassy in Tegucigalpa, Honduras, suggested that the administration backed him despite being fully aware that he was a threat to Honduran democracy. In a cable, Charles Ford, U.S. ambassador to Honduras, told his successor Hugo Llorens, "Ever the rebellious teenager, Zelaya's principal goal in office is to enrich himself and his family while leaving a public legacy as a martyr who tried to do good but was thwarted at every turn by powerful, unnamed interests.... His erratic behavior appears most evident when he deliberately stirs street action in protest against his own government policy—only to resolve the issue (teacher complaints, transportation grievances, etc.) at the last moment." Ford noted that Zelaya had a "sinister" side and that he was surrounded by "a few close advisors with ties to both Venezuela and Cuba and organized crime." Ford also plainly indicated that Zelaya could not be trusted, saying, "I am unable to brief Zelaya on sensitive law enforcement and counter-narcotics actions due [to] my concern that this would put the lives of U.S. officials in jeopardy."[93]

The *Wall Street Journal*'s Mary O'Grady theorized that the released cables suggest Obama supported the lawless Zelaya regime as a means to improve U.S. relations with Venezuelan dictator Hugo Chavez. "The U.S. knew Mr. Zelaya was a threat to democratic Honduras but had decided the country should tolerate his constitutional violations in the interest of realpolitik," wrote O'Grady. "Practically speaking, Hugo Chavez was the man to please."[94]

THE "RESET" WITH RUSSIA

Shortly after he was elected president, Obama promised to "reset U.S.-Russia relations." The reset policy, unsurprisingly, has consisted of a series of U.S. concessions to Russia apparently geared toward trying to generate goodwill from the Kremlin. But the Russians have not shown any willingness to reciprocate, and why would they? Obama seems content to respond to their intransigence with ever-more concessions and even to adopt their narrative on bilateral issues.

Consider, for example, the prisoner swap that the Obama administration undertook with Russia in July 2010. In exchange for the United States freeing the Anna Chapman spy ring and sending them back to Russia, the Kremlin sent to the West four accused espionage agents. However, not all of the Kremlin's prisoners were actually spies. For example, Igor Sutyagin was a researcher for the USA Canada Institute who had been in detention awaiting trial for over four years and then in prison for six years following his railroaded conviction. He had even been acquitted by a lower court, but was convicted by a higher court in Russia's notoriously corrupt judicial system, a trial Amnesty International denounced for being politically motivated. Yet instead of referring to Sutyagin as a political prisoner, the Obama administration accepted Russia's narrative in characterizing the deal as a spy swap.[95]

Some have rightfully criticized this transaction as an illustration of the erroneous thinking behind Obama's reset policy and, by extension, Obama's entire approach to foreign policy. "The only thing releasing all of these deep-cover Russian intelligence officers within a matter of days is going to teach Prime Minister Vladimir Putin, an old KGB officer, is that Obama is a pushover—overly focused on making sure not to offend Russia," observed CNN's Gene Coyle. "Aside from sending the wrong political message, the quick swap also tells the leadership of the Russian government and the SVR, its intelligence service, that there is really no downside to being caught carrying out espionage in America."[96]

The hasty prisoner exchange was bad enough, but there is no better example of Obama's relentless pandering to Russia than on the issue of arms control. On that topic, Obama has displayed unfettered enthusiasm for placating Russian demands even though, as former U.S. arms control official Paula DeSutter argues, the Russians "have violated every agreement we have ever had with them."[97]

This record casts a troubling light on our recent New START deal with Russia. The deal earned the cautious support of a number of conservatives, anxious to secure some kind of nuclear agreement with Russia and presumably weary of appearing to oppose Obama on every issue. Those reluctant supporters should have become suspicious when Obama tried to get the treaty ratified during the Senate's lame-duck session in late 2010. He finally succeeded in getting it approved, effective February 2011.

In his typical crisis-mode style, Obama presented ratification as a matter of utmost urgency. He attempted to persuade Republican Senator Jon Kyl to withdraw his opposition by promising to spend an additional $4 billion on nuclear programs. But Kyl, realizing the promise was illusory—and indeed, Kyl later noted that Obama's revised spending plans effectively eliminated that funding—didn't take the bait.[98] He and other opponents were concerned by the severe restrictions the agreement would place on U.S. missile defense and by the treaty's weak verification measures. As Heritage Foundation nuclear arms and foreign policy experts noted, the treaty's preamble is a vague "Trojan Horse" that links strategic offensive and defensive weapons and would allow the Russians to withdraw if they perceive the United States to be expanding its ballistic missile defenses.[99]

While Russia had less negotiating leverage than the United States, the terms of the treaty gave it a decided advantage—permitting it to expand its nuclear arsenal while we agreed to downsize ours. Opponents concluded the treaty would leave Russia with a clear advantage in tactical nuclear weapons while gaining the United States little in exchange. And the deal was not just disadvantageous with respect to Russia; opponents also believed it was imprudent to engage in substantial disarmament at a time when rogue nations and terrorists could be getting closer to acquiring nuclear capabilities and other dangerous regimes already possess them.

In his anxiousness for Russia to agree to New START, Obama even agreed to share with the Russians sensitive information concerning the UK's Trident submarines, which are an integral component of Britain's strategic deterrent—this, despite Britain's objections and the opinion of defense analysts that it would undermine Britain's policy of strategic ambiguity about the size of its nuclear arsenal. Duncan Lennox, editor of *Jane's Strategic Weapons Systems*, said that Russia wants "to find out whether Britain has more missiles than we say we have, and having the unique identifiers might help them."[100]

This was not the administration's first major concession to the Russians. On the seventieth anniversary of the Soviet invasion of Poland, it slapped Poland and the Czech Republic in the face by rolling over to Russian demands that we scrap Third Site missile defense plans in those countries. According to leaked WikiLeaks cables, Obama cancelled the anti-missile shield mainly in hopes of earning Russia's support for UN sanctions against Iran.[101]

Showing it was hardly satiated by the concessions in the New START treaty, in March 2011, Russia made the preposterous demand that it be provided "red button" rights to a new, scaled-down missile defense system the United States has proposed for Europe, essentially insisting on a joint role in operating our own system. "We insist on only one thing," Russia's deputy prime minister Sergei Ivanov told Hillary Clinton, speaking about the missile system. "That we are an equal part of it. In practical terms, that means that our office will sit for example in Brussels and agree on a red-button push to launch an interceptor missile, regardless of whether the missile is launched from Poland, Russia or the UK."[102]

With this, Obama officials finally encountered a demand so outrageous that they rejected it. In November 2011, vindicating the prior warnings of the Heritage Foundation, Russian president Dmitry Medvedev threatened to withdraw Russia from the New START treaty if the United States proceeded with the anti-missile system, even threatening to deploy short-range missiles aimed at U.S. missile defenses sites in

Europe. This dire warning, it should be noted, concerned a *defensive* missile shield focused on a threat from Iran, not Russia.[103]

But it turns out Russia had nothing to worry about. In another accidental "hot mic" incident, Obama told Russian president Dmitri Medvedev on March 26, 2012, "On all these issues, but particularly missile defense, this can be solved, but it's important for him [Russian prime minister Vladimir Putin] to give me space.... This is my last election. After my election, I have more flexibility."[104] So Obama wants the Kremlin to know that more "flexibility" is on the way, but since Americans will oppose it, he needs to wait until after his presumed reelection.

Obama gave Medvedev this assurance about a month after more news emerged sure to please the Kremlin: the Obama administration was weighing options to unilaterally cut the U.S. nuclear arsenal by up to 80 percent. At the height of the Cold War during the 1980s, our nuclear arms peaked with some 12,000 strategic warheads. Our numbers have since dropped below 5,000 in 2003, and our current treaty limit is 1,550 deployed strategic warheads. According to the Associated Press, Obama is considering three options: reducing the number of our deployed strategic nuclear weapons to 1,000–1,100, to 700–800, or to 300–400. That last option would reduce us to levels we haven't had since 1950, during the early phase of the Cold War.[105]

Obama has not only compromised our missile defenses with New START and those of our allies around the globe, he would also curtail deployment of additional ground-based interceptors (GBIs) at Fort Greely in Alaska and Vandenberg Air Force Base in California—and he has already nixed ready-to-deploy missile defenses with the cancelation of the Air Force's Airborne Laser program whereby converted 747s with high-intensity lasers could destroy enemy missiles in their "vulnerable boost phase."[106]

All these concessions on arms control come on top of potentially devastating cuts to our conventional forces. At the beginning of 2012, Obama announced a new military strategy to include $487 billion in cuts over the next decade. Our military troop strength will be cut by 27,000 for the Army and 20,000 for the Marines, while our naval strength has already fallen from 429 ships in 1991 to 287 today.[107] "This budget strategy is a road map of American decline," columnist Charles Kraut-hammer argued. "It is going to reduce our capacity. It does exactly what the president had said he was not going to do, which is it will adapt our capacity and our strategies to fit a budget.... It will make it extremely hard to carry on the role we have for 70 years."[108]

"A BACK DOOR" TO LIMITING MISSILE DEFENSE

Although Russia hasn't been capable of rivaling the United States in space militarization—which is why the Kremlin has been determined ever since the Reagan era to keep us from developing our own space assets—we face increasing competition from China. According to investigative journalist Omri Ceren, Beijing has "no interest in even pretending to reciprocate limitations on space development."[109] That is especially problematic considering the Obama administration is bent on foregoing our pursuit of space militarization irrespective of China's activity. Eli Lake, an expert in geopolitics for the *Washington Times*, reported that the Obama administration is trying to establish international rules for space launches and satellite operations that skeptics warn will compromise our ability to deploy military systems to shield satellites from space weaponry being developed by China and other nations.[110]

While the administration has so far been resistant to sign treaties with Russia or China limiting space weaponry, it has signaled a willingness to enter into agreements aimed at reducing space debris that could collide into satellites, including acceptance of the European Union's draft Code of Conduct for Outer Space Activities. The administration insists this would not compromise our national interests in space or limit our research. Yet some fear it could unintentionally limit our deployment and development of satellites that track orbital debris and other satellites. Peter Marquez, former National Security Council director of space policy for President George W. Bush and for President Obama, said it could also lead other states to set limits on U.S. defenses in space. Additionally, "it leaves open the door... for the United States to be forced to disclose the nature of its intelligence collection activities and capabilities from orbit."[111]

Others, such as Rick Fisher, a senior fellow at the International Assessment and Strategy Center, are concerned that such deals do not adequately account for the Chinese threat to U.S. satellites. "One gets the impression from this document [a U.S.-French agreement to share space debris data] that the Obama administration simply wants to ignore the Chinese threat in hopes it will just go away," said Fisher. "There is apparently no consideration for developing U.S. active defenses for space that would more effectively deter China."[112]

Republican officials are also dubious about the administration's stated willingness to adopt the EU code of conduct for outer space activities. In a letter to Secretary of State Hillary Clinton, thirty-seven Republican senators wrote, "We are deeply concerned that the administration sign the United States on to a multilateral commitment with a multitude of potentially highly damaging implications for sensitive military and intelligence programs (current, planned or otherwise) as well as a tremendous amount of commercial activity." The senators pressed for an explanation as to what impact the code of conduct would have on "the research and development, testing and deployment of a kinetic defensive system in outer space that is capable of defeating an anti-satellite weapon, such as the one tested by the People's Republic of China in 2007."[113]

The concern is that given his approach to arms control, Obama is moving forward with these seemingly innocuous agreements that could in fact severely restrict our anti-satellite weapon (ASAT) capabilities in lieu of entering into formal agreements that would require Senate approval. As one congressional staffer said, "There is a suspicion that this is a slippery slope to arms control for space-based weapons, anti-satellite weapons and a back door to potentially limiting missile defense."[114]

These developments should be of significant concern since China appears to be advancing its space arms and defense technology programs. In 2006, China reportedly used an ASAT that effectively blinded a U.S. satellite, and in 2007, used one to destroy one of their own satellites. These incidents, among others, prompted then-Defense Secretary Robert Gates to conclude that China's pursuit of ASATs was designed to enhance their power and marginalize ours. More worrisome, especially in view of our exploding national debt and increasingly vulnerable position with China as one of our principal creditors, is China's clear unwillingness to recipro- cate any commitments we might make to limit space arms exploration. While the State Department has been negotiating with the EU on language in the Code of Conduct, and the United States and Russia are at least discussing the prospect of framing some mutual understanding on space- based activities, China has reportedly declined even to discuss the issue.[115]

Further, in 2010 alone, China launched fifteen satellites, marking the first time since the Cold War that any nation has equaled the number of American launches.[116] And in November 2011, the China National Space Administration achieved an unmanned satellite rendezvous and docking with a prototype space station module. This docking marks a key step toward China's goal of launching and operating a manned space station in Low-Earth Orbit.

While China is rapidly enhancing its space capabilities, President Obama has unilaterally dismantled ours. The U.S. shuttle program is finished without a successor in the wings. Experts have noted that China will probably have a fully operational space lab, and possibly a space station, in earth's orbit by 2020 —the same year when our International Space Station could be decommissioned, which would leave China with the sole capability of hosting a permanent human presence in space, thus posing a serious threat to America's national security.[117]

ARMING THE WORLD

Even as he disarms America, Obama is accepting or even promoting the spread of military weapons, military-related technology, and nuclear power throughout the world. For example, it's a little-known fact that the Obama administration is selling huge amounts of weaponry to for- eign governments, not all of them reliable U.S. allies. Indeed, the admin- istration is revamping arms export rules to relax oversight of U.S. arms sales. Author Peter Schweizer points to the "stunning statistic" that the Department of Defense last year informed Congress of its plans to sell some $103 billion in weapons to overseas buyers, when the average yearly sales between 1995 and 2005 were $13 billion. Presently, almost half our arm sales are to the volatile Middle East. Schweizer speculates that Obama is increasing arms sales to stimulate the U.S. economy, which he calls "a cynical and dangerous approach to arms sales," given the increased risk such sales involve.[118]

Jeff Abramson, deputy director of the Arms Control Association, calls these sales "an Obama arms bazaar." The centerpiece of this bazaar shocked many observers: in 2010, the Obama administration struck a mammoth, $60 billion arms deal with Saudi Arabia. The deal, the single largest arms sale to a foreign nation in our history, would equip the Saudis with a fully modernized and powerful air force.[119]

In addition to arming certain foreign countries to the teeth, Obama made it clear he has no objection to Venezuela developing nuclear energy. In October 2010, following dictator Hugo Chavez's consummation of a deal with Russia to build Venezuela's first nuclear power plant, Obama said, "Our attitude is that Venezuela has rights to peacefully develop nuclear power." Even Russian president Dmitry Medvedev was probably surprised that a U.S. president would be so easily persuaded of the benign intent both of Russia's presence in Venezuela and of the development of nuclear power there; Venezuela, after all, is an oil powerhouse that—like Iran—hardly needs nuclear energy for peaceful purposes. Venezuela has also purchased more than $4 billion of weapons from Russia and agreed to allow Russia more access to its oil fields.

Furthermore, the same week Obama selected General Electric CEO Jeffrey Immelt to serve as his top outside economic advisor,[120] GE announced it would sign a joint-venture agreement under which it would share its most advanced airplane electronics with China's state-owned Aviation Industry Corp. of China. The deal prohibits the use of this technology for military purposes, but as Investors.com editorial writers noted, "China's disrespect for intellectual property rights is legendary," as is its "ability to hack into and retrieve information from computer systems worldwide."[121]

That same week, Obama announced an agreement with China to increase cooperation on nuclear security. The deal involves the formation of a jointly financed nuclear security center in China, which would provide training to improve security at nuclear facilities and accounting of nuclear materials. It also calls for the sharing of nuclear detection technology, though most of that technology and expertise will be provided by the United States.[122]

China was eager to benefit from our technology, but they have shown no interest in sitting down to arms reduction talks, which is unsurprising, since Obama's enthusiasm for reducing our nuclear arsenal gives them little incentive to bargain. When Defense Secretary Gates invited the Chinese to arms talks in January 2011 while in Beijing, they said they'd consider it. John Tkacik, a China expert and former State Department official, interpreted this response to mean, "Don't call us, we'll call you." He added, "For the past 20 years, we've given the Chinese information briefings and tours of our military facilities without demanding any reciprocity. And, as a result, we haven't gotten any reciprocity."[123]

"THE MILITARY BALANCE IS UNDOUBTEDLY SHIFTING"

Meanwhile, China is aggressively enhancing its arms capabilities. Its own government reports show that it is continuing with its pattern of double digit defense spending increases, with a jump of 11.2 percent in 2012.[124] It is deploying the Dong Feng 21D, a mobile missile capable of destroying aircraft carriers; has launched its own aircraft carrier; and is flight testing the J-20, a fifth-generation stealth fighter. But the United States, notwithstanding the ongoing War on Terror and its overseas commitments, is drawing down its own capabilities irrespective of any international arms deals, largely due to the Democrats' spending priorities and their ambivalence toward America's global military supremacy.

In 2009, America's air dominance was significantly diminished when it terminated the F-22 Raptor, replacing it with the F-35 Lightning, which is behind in production and riddled with cost overruns. Defense Secretary Gates had capped the U.S. F-22 program at 187 aircraft—instead of the planned 332—on the assumption that China would be slow to deploy advanced fourth-generation fighters and that Russia wouldn't produce a fifth-generation aircraft until the distant future.

But it's already clear that the administration miscalculated, to the United States' detriment. The Chinese Air Force has since purchased from

Russia 176 fourth-generation fighters comprising one hundred advanced SU-30s and 76 SU-27s. China has now deployed more than three hundred other fourth-generation fighters and is helping to finance Russia's development of the T-50, a fifth-generation fighter, which supposedly incorporates stealth technology.

All this severely undermines Gates's rationale for prematurely scrapping the Raptor. Obama and the Left's insistence on reckless defense cuts, instead of tightening our domestic spending belt, is also ominous for the F-35 Lightning, with which the administration is replacing the Raptor. These cuts could reduce the size and scope of the already-strained F-35 program, which would put enormous pressure on the already-strained F-22 Raptors' workload.[125]

Contrary to their bitter resistance to the smallest cuts in domestic spending, President Obama and his Democratic colleagues in Congress seem eager to make major defense cuts—in keeping with their view that the key to diplomacy is proving to the rest of the world how peaceful we are. The Budget Control Act of 2011 established the so-called Supercommittee to find $1.2 trillion in cuts (meaning reductions in spending, not actual cuts) lest an automatic sequester trigger mandatory cuts in domestic and military spending, in equal measure. The Democrats thus forced a deal whereby the defense budget would be reduced dollar for dollar with the domestic budget, though defense only constitutes 20 percent of the budget.[126]

It's not as though we are so far ahead of other powers militarily that we can afford to trim away some perceived surplus. Australian military analysts and Rand Coproration have conducted wargaming to assess the likely outcome of war between the United States and China over the disputed Taiwan Strait. Rand produced an extensive simulation projecting that although the United States would enjoy a six to one kill ratio over Chinese aircraft, we would nevertheless lose the conflict. Even if every U.S. missile destroyed an opponent, enough attackers would survive to destroy our tankers, as well as our command and control and intelligence-gathering aircraft. Andrew Davies, program director for operations and capabilities for the Australian Strategic Policy Institute, told *Aviation Week*, "The silver-bullet platforms are fantastic ... where a small number of them can completely overwhelm a relatively small power." But against China, a small, high-tech force might not be so formidable, he warns.[127]

Of course, our difficulties will mount the more China ramps up and we scale down. "I would say that the military balance is undoubtedly shifting as China's military expands faster than other regional nations," says Admiral Robert Willard, chief of U.S. Pacific Command. This is not mere alarmism, but a warning for us to reverse this trend before it reaches a dangerous point. As Max Boot cautions, it's not that China will attack us tomorrow, but "the risk of conflict goes up when China has less respect for our deterrent capacity. And with the Obama administration and many lawmakers pushing for even steeper defense cuts than those already announced, China's estimation of our deterrent capacity can only go down."[128]

Likewise, Lieutenant General David Deptula, once the top intelligence officer in the U.S. Air Force and also an F-15 pilot, warns that "for the first time, our claim to air supremacy is in jeopardy." America, he says, is "dangerously ill-prepared to stop the gap-closing efforts of China and Russia." He estimates that within a decade, Russia and China will have airframes compatible to the F-22. Not only are they catching up to us on that aircraft, the latest production of which we have now canceled, but the majority of our front line combat aircraft is aging without replacements, he said. Making matters worse, there is "a global revolution to modernize air defense systems," and Russia and China are building and deploying better surface-to-air missile systems that could eventually overwhelm our fighter aircraft. Deptula cautions, "When taken in total, our potential adversaries can create a nearly impenetrable box that our legacy fighters cannot enter, thus denying us our air supremacy."[129] This combination of factors along with others, he says, makes Gates's sanguinity "foolish at best."[130]

★ ★ ★

During his short time in office, President Obama has shown a disturbing lack of concern for our national security based on his flawed ideology and his much greater interest in advancing his domestic agenda.

His misguided priorities and their destructive consequences were starkly
revealed in reports that Department of Energy inspector general Gregory
Friedman discovered that the rush to distribute $3.5 billion in stimulus
funds to the DOE's Smart Grid Investment Grant Program (SGIG) may
have compromised, rather than enhanced, our national security. "The
issues we found were due, in part, to the accelerated planning, development, and deployment approach adopted by the SGIG program," the
IG's report said. "We also found that the Department was so focused on
quickly disbursing Recovery Act funds that it had not ensured personnel
received adequate grants management training. Without improvements,
there remains a risk that the goals and objectives of the Smart Grid program may not be fully realized."[131]

Indeed, Obama's reckless approach to national security is strikingly
evident in his slashing of our military strength across the board, an unprecedented policy during wartime. As the *Telegraph*'s James Corum argues,
although Obama presents many of these reductions as cost-cutting moves,
his real agenda is doubtless to downsize America's dominant military role
in the world.[132] Obama adheres to the leftist worldview that America is
often a harmful, bellicose force in the world because of, among other
things, its opposition to the "progressive" global agenda. The leftists'
theory, being discredited in real time before our very eyes, is that if the
United States disarms, other nations will follow suit.

To the contrary, Obama's unilateral initiatives have only emboldened
our enemies and rivals. Meanwhile, as Islamists ascend to power via the
Arab Spring uprisings, his administration panders to the Muslim Brotherhood and even whitewashes their Islamist agenda, again displaying the
naïve conviction that foreign governments and political parties will act
according to our goodwill gestures instead of their own interests. The
Brotherhood, for its part, is perfectly open about where its interests lie:
in creating a worldwide Islamic caliphate. No U.S. engagement campaigns
or outreach efforts will change that. So they'll continue to pocket Obama's
aid packages and partake in his political training programs, but he should
not be surprised when they continue to make good on their vow that
"what was acceptable before the revolution is no longer."

CHAPTER ELEVEN

THE WAR ON GUNS: OPERATION FAST & FURIOUS

W ithin weeks of Obama's inauguration in January 2009, Secretary of State Hillary Clinton and Attorney General Eric
Holder began falsely claiming that 90 percent of the guns
used in crimes committed by Mexican drug cartels were sold in American
gun stores. Their intent was to drum up support for reinstituting the
Clinton-era assault weapons ban, a failed law that had resulted in more
of the banned weapons being purchased than ever before. This law also
led to increased sales of existing high capacity magazines, which the ban
did not cover, and to handgun manufacturers producing a whole new
generation of powerful subcompact centerfire pistols, with new companies arising to cater to the market.[1]

Though the Obama administration withdrew its demand to reinstate
the ban, it persisted with the 90 percent fable.[2] It also shifted law enforcement resources to border states to combat the supposed gun trafficking
problem, "blitzing" Houston and the southern half of Texas in April 2009

with a temporary army of one hundred additional inspectors and investigators, with plans to permanently expand those forces later.[3] Further, the
administration demonized American gun dealers to the point that the
National Rifle Association alerted its members to the scapegoating.

Against that background in the autumn of 2009, the Bureau of Alcohol, Tobacco, Firearms and Explosives (ATF), under the umbrella of the
Justice Department, initiated Operation Fast and Furious, a secret gunwalking program whereby ATF agents allowed straw purchasers to buy
guns while under surveillance, with the ostensible goal of tracing them
into the hands of Mexican cartel leaders and weapons traffickers on the
southwestern border and in Mexico. "Allowing loads of weapons that
we knew to be destined for criminals, this was the plan," Special Agent
John Dodson of the ATF Phoenix field division later explained. "It was
so mandated."[4] The idea, according to findings from a House Oversight
Committee report, was "to wait and watch, in the hope that law enforcement could identify other members of a trafficking network and build a
large, complex conspiracy case. This shift in strategy was known and
authorized at the highest levels of the Justice Department."[5]

The ill-conceived program was a total bust that climaxed in the murder of U.S. Border Patrol Agent Brian Terry; AK-47s were found at the
crime scene that had been knowingly sold under Fast and Furious. An
assault on police in Maricopa, Arizona, was also traced to automatic
weapons from the operation. Most of the 2,000-plus guns involved in
Fast and Furious were lost and, reportedly, hundreds turned up at Mexican crime scenes.[6] Two hundred people were killed or wounded in
Mexico with Fast and Furious weapons,[7] and at least eleven violent
crimes occurred in the United States involving fifty-seven Fast and Furious
weapons.[8] This gruesome outcome was by no means unforeseeable. As
Special Agent Larry Alt testified to Congress, "You can't allow thousands
of guns to go south of the border without an expectation that they are
going to be recovered eventually in crimes and people are going to die."[9]

After several ATF whistleblowers alerted Congress that Fast and
Furious weapons were found at the scene of Agent Terry's murder, congressional hearings ensued and certain top officials behind the operation

were removed from their positions. Despite vehement complaints from Mexico and pressure from Congress, however, the administration didn't bother to offer any explanation for the operation and stubbornly refused to apologize.[10]

Congress turned up the heat, as investigators formally requested that the Obama administration turn over copies of "all records" involving: three specific White House national security officials in connection with the Fast and Furious Operation; other ATF gun cases in Phoenix; and all communications between the White House and the ATF field office in Arizona. While White House staffers had briefed Congress on the operation as early as April 2010, they mentioned nothing about the gunwalking tactics in play. For its part, the administration denied that anyone at the White House knew the operation was allowing gunwalking into Mexico.[11]

Casting doubt on the White House's claim, Bill Newell, the ATF agent in charge of the Phoenix office, told Congress he had discussed the operation with Kevin O'Reilly, the White House National Security director for America.[12] Newell was reportedly in close contact with O'Reilly and was seeking White House assistance to convince the Mexican government to let ATF agents recover U.S. guns across the border.[13] Other White House staff who may have known about the operation include National Security staff members who received information from O'Reilly on Phoenix gun trafficking cases, and Assistant to the President for Homeland Security John Brennan, who led a high-level discussion in Phoenix on gun trafficking in June 2010.[14]

"THIS DEATH MIGHT NOT HAVE OCCURRED HAD IT NOT BEEN FOR RECKLESS DECISIONS"

When Congress began investigating Fast and Furious, it quickly realized the Department of Justice would not be cooperative. At a congressional hearing in early May 2011, Darrell Issa, chairman of the House Oversight and Government Reform Committee, criticized Attorney General Eric Holder for refusing to answer questions or comply with subpoenas for documents concerning who approved Fast and Furious. "We're not looking at straw buyers, Mr. Attorney General," said Issa. "We're looking at you. We're looking at you, we're looking at your key people who knew or should've known about this." Holder indignantly replied, "The notion that somehow or another that this Justice Department is responsible for those deaths, that assertion is offensive." Issa persisted, "What if it's accurate, Mr. Attorney General? What am I going to tell Agent Terry's mother about how he died at the hands of a gun that was videotaped as it was being sold to a straw purchaser fully expecting it to end up in the hands of drug cartels?"[15]

A key point of dispute was that Obama and Holder wanted the investigation of Fast and Furious to be conducted internally by the Department of Justice's Office of the Inspector General, while congressional investigators, alleging a lack of DOJ cooperation from the outset, wanted a broad outside investigation. As Issa declared,

> The Justice Department hasn't said how and why two rifles purportedly being tracked and monitored by federal law enforcement officials as part of Operation Fast and Furious ended up in the hands of Agent Terry's killers. It angers me to think that this death might not have occurred had it not been for reckless decisions made by officials at the Department of Justice who authorized and supported an operation that knowingly puts guns in the hands of criminals. For these officials to imagine that this operation would result in anything other than a tragic outcome was naïve and negligent.[16]

"I HAVE NOT TRIED TO EQUATE THE TWO"

Invoking its default "Blame Bush" meme, the administration and its backers attempted to dodge accountability for Fast and Furious by suggesting that the operation was just an extension of a Bush-era program called Wide Receiver—as if that would justify an ill-conceived gunwalking operation that ended in the murder of a U.S. agent. In any case, the two are hardly comparable. Wide Receiver was a small-scale operation involving about one-quarter the amount of guns implicated in Fast and Furious.[17]

What's more, in Wide Receiver, the ATF tried to track guns sold to straw purchasers—even fitting some with electronic tracking devices—and when some guns went missing, the operation was quickly shut down. By contrast, there was no attempt at all to track the weapons sold in Fast and Furious, and agents who tried to follow the purchasers were inexplicably ordered to stand down. The operation continued as more and more guns disappeared into Mexico, only ending after Fast and Furious guns were used in the high-profile Terry killing, and reportedly after ATF officials mistakenly believed its weapons were also used in Jared Loughner's mass shooting in Tucson.[18]

Furthermore, while grilling Eric Holder in a Senate Judiciary Committee hearing, Senator John Cornyn showed that Wide Receiver was coordinated with Mexican authorities, who were deliberately kept in the dark about Fast and Furious. In fact, despite its vast scope, Fast and Furious was kept under such tight wraps that even ATF Attaché to Mexico Darren Gil was kept out of the loop; and when Gil discovered the operation and complained that running it without telling Mexican authorities was tantamount to an act of war, he was reportedly pressured to retire. Challenged by Cornyn, Holder himself acknowledged crucial distinctions between Wide Receiver and Fast and Furious, saying, "I have not tried to equate the two."[19]

FAST AND FURIOUS REQUIRED AGENTS TO ABANDON THEIR TRAINING

At a House Oversight Committee hearing in June 2011, four ATF agents gave testimony that contradicted Department of Justice spokesman Ronald Weich's claim—made in a February 4, 2011, letter to a member of Congress—that the DOJ did not approve the program. The agents testified that Assistant U.S. Attorney Emory Hurley, an Obama appointee, "orchestrated" the operation. ATF Phoenix field office

supervisor Peter Forcelli further alleged, "I have read documents that
indicate that [Hurley's] boss, U.S. Attorney Dennis Burke, also agreed
with the direction of the case."[20]

Forcelli was referring to an order, instituted shortly after Obama was
inaugurated, mandating that Phoenix ATF agents monitor, but not stop,
gun sales to suspected gun traffickers, breaking with long-established
agency practice. Agents told the committee that Phoenix ATF supervisor
David Voth "was jovial, if not giddy, but just delighted" when Fast and
Furious guns were subsequently recovered at multiple Mexican drug
busts. Issa released emails showing that ATF acting director Kenneth
Melson arranged to watch live feeds from ATF cameras in the gun stores
involved in the operation. Issa's panel also released documents indicating
the operation was well-known and vigorously supported at the highest
levels of the ATF.[21]

On June 14, 2011, the House Oversight Committee released its
shocking findings about Fast and Furious. Here are some highlights:

- "ATF agents are trained to 'follow the gun' and interdict
  weapons whenever possible. Operation Fast and Furious
  required agents to abandon this training."
- "Agents knew that given the large numbers of weapons
  being trafficked to Mexico, tragic results were a near
  certainty."
- "Agents [are] expected to interdict weapons, yet were told
  to stand down and 'just surveil.' Agents therefore did not
  act. They watched straw purchasers buy hundreds of
  weapons illegally and transfer those weapons to unknown
  third parties and stash houses."
- "Operation Fast and Furious contributed to the increasing
  violence and deaths in Mexico. This result was regarded
  with giddy optimism by ATF supervisors hoping that guns
  recovered at crime scenes in Mexico would provide the
  nexus to straw purchasers in Phoenix."
- "Every time a law enforcement official in Arizona was
  assaulted or shot by a firearm, ATF agents in Group VII

had great anxiety that guns used to perpetrate the crimes may trace back to Operation Fast and Furious."

- "Despite mounting evidence to the contrary, DOJ continues to deny that Operation Fast and Furious was ill-conceived and had deadly consequences." (The DOJ later modified this ludicrous and indefensible position.)[22]

Even after the panel released its report, astounding revelations about Fast and Furious continued to emerge. During testimony before Issa's panel on July 4, ATF Acting Director Ken Melson said that the operation included more federal agencies than previously revealed, and that DOJ officials muzzled the ATF as they sought to contain the fallout following Brian Terry's death.[23]

"LITERALLY, MY MOUTH FELL OPEN"

Despite the ghastly toll of the botched operation, the ATF and DOJ steadfastly refused to hold anyone accountable. In fact, in mid-August 2011, the ATF promoted three of its officials intimately involved in Fast and Furious, assigning them to new management positions at ATF headquarters in Washington, D.C. They were William D. Newell and David Voth, both supervisors in the Phoenix office overseeing the operation, and the deputy director of operations for the west, William G. McMahon.

One ATF deputy assistant director, Steve Martin, stated that McMahon had ignored his urgings in January 2010 to halt Fast and Furious. "I asked Mr. McMahon, I said, 'what's your plan?'" Martin reported. "Hearing none, I don't know if they had one." Despite his admission that he'd made mistakes in Fast and Furious, McMahon was promoted— ironically—to deputy assistant director of the ATF's Office of Professional Responsibility and Security Operations—the division that investigates employee misconduct.[24] Newell also admitted to making mistakes in Fast and Furious, though he claimed his agents never allowed guns to "walk." The denial angered numerous agents who knew better. "Literally, my mouth fell open," said Agent Larry Alt, who worked under Newell. "I am not being figurative about this. I couldn't believe it."[25]

As for agent Voth, who supervised the agents working on Fast and Furious, he had dismissed agents' concerns about the illegal gun purchases and gunwalking, reportedly insisting the bureau was "watching the right people."[26]

Other key figures in Fast and Furious transferred or retired without facing any consequences. At the end of August 2011, Ken Melson stepped down from his position as ATF acting director and was transferred to the DOJ's Office of Legal Affairs as a senior forensic science advisor. Melson had claimed he'd only learned about Fast and Furious after it was shut down, but Assistant Attorney General Ronald Weich insisted Melson knew about it almost from the beginning.[27] Additionally, the U.S. attorney for Arizona, Dennis Burke, resigned. Notably, statements from Holder and Burke didn't tie these moves to Fast and Furious, though both alluded to distractions affecting federal prosecutors in Arizona.[28]

COVER-UP AND RETALIATION

In the meantime, several ATF agents claimed the agency had retaliated against them for shedding light on the abuses of Fast and Furious. The House Oversight Committee found that Special Agent John Dodson was removed from Phoenix Group VII in the summer of 2010 for complaining to ATF supervisors about the operation.[29] Likewise, Vince Cefalu, a Tucson-based agent who had been with the agency for twenty-four years, said he was served with termination papers in June 2011. "Aside from Jay Dobyns," said Cefalu, "I don't know of anyone that's been more vocal about ATF mismanagement than me. That's why this is happening." He added, "Simply put, we knowingly let hundreds of guns and dozens of identified bad guys go across the border."[30] Although some other agents attributed Cefalu's dismissal to personality clashes, he was adamant that "it was my willingness to expose [Fast and Furious] and support other people to come forward."[31]

In addition, Peter J. Forcelli, group supervisor, ATF, alleged that the U.S. Attorney's Office for the District of Arizona and the DOJ Office of Deputy Attorney General retaliated against him for his remarks before the House Oversight Committee, to whom he testified, "I believe that these firearms will continue to turn up at crime scenes, on both sides of the border, for years to come." According to Forcelli's attorney,

> It now appears to GS Forcelli that a pattern of conduct has emerged designed to attack GS Forcelli's credibility.... Clearly, the USAO is clumsily attempting to paint a picture that GS Forcelli's testimony and conduct resulted from a "personal issue" between AUSA Hurley and himself, rather than hold AUSA Hurley accountable for missteps in several of his cases.... GS Forcelli would respectfully request that the actions of certain members of the Department of Justice be investigated inasmuch as said actions seem to flout the power of Congress to oversee and reform the workings of our great Nation's government.[32]

THE LETTER "CONTAINS INACCURACIES"

During congressional hearings, Democrat committee members generally sided with the Obama administration, showing a reluctance to ask hard questions and trying to deflect attention from Fast and Furious to Operation Wide Receiver. They even tried to leverage the scandal to promote gun control legislation.

Democratic congressman Elijah Cummings heralded this campaign during Darrell Issa's June 15 hearing on Fast and Furious. "No legitimate examination of this issue will be complete without analyzing our nation's gun laws, which allow tens of thousands of assault weapons to flood into Mexico from the United States every year, including fifty caliber sniper rifles, multiple AK variants and scores of others," Cummings argued. "When Mexican President Calderon addressed Congress in May, he pleaded for us to stop fueling a full-scale drug war with military-grade assault rifles."[33]

This may have set a new record for Democratic chutzpah, given that Fast and Furious—not lax gun laws—allowed these deadly weapons to reach Mexico and "fueled" the drug war there—all behind the backs of the Mexican authorities. Regardless, a few weeks after the hearing,

Cummings released a report—cleverly titled "Outgunned"—arguing that stricter gun control laws are needed to help fight organized crime at the border.[34]

Meanwhile, there were growing indications of DOJ stonewalling and even a possible cover-up surrounding Fast and Furious. In testimony before the Senate Judiciary Committee on November 8, Eric Holder told Senator Grassley that after he received two letters from Grassley back in January requesting information about gunwalking tactics, he'd asked his "staff to look into this." Deputy Assistant Attorney General Jason Weinstein drafted a response to Grassley, which was reviewed by Assistant Attorney General Lanny Breuer. On February 4, 2011, Assistant Attorney General Ronald Weich signed off on the letter, which stated that "ATF makes every effort to interdict weapons that have been purchased illegally and prevent their transportation to Mexico."

Of course, in both Wide Receiver and Fast and Furious, that was entirely false. What's more, an email from Anthony Garcia, a DOJ employee assigned to Mexico City, to Adam Lurie of that same date, February 4, 2011, showed that Lanny Breuer was actually advocating a gunwalking scheme to Mexican authorities, who were unaware gunwalking was already occurring through Fast and Furious.[35] So, while gunwalking was already happening, and while he was advocating gunwalking to Mexican officials, Breuer was involved in preparing a letter stating that the ATF does no such thing.

Breuer said he wasn't sure whether he'd seen the draft of the Weich letter. But when internal emails were released in December, they showed that Breuer had been well informed about it. Even more incriminating was the revelation that Breuer had received both drafts of the letter as well as the final version and even forwarded them to his personal gmail account.[36] On December 2, Deputy Attorney General Cole formally withdrew the Weich letter, saying it "contains inaccuracies."

Senator Grassley had harsh words about this episode.

> Assistant Attorney General Lanny Breuer admitted one week
> ago in this room that the department's letter to me in February

was absolutely false. Think about that for a second. It's bad enough that the head of the Criminal Division admits that the department's letter to me was false. It gets worse, though. He admitted that he knew all along that it was false. Although he could not recall whether he helped edit it, he knew it was false because he was aware of a previous gunwalking operation called Wide Receiver. Yet he remained silent for nine months as the public controversy over gunwalking grew. He was aware that Congress had been misled and yet made no effort to correct the department's official denial. I am eager to hear whether the Attorney General thinks that is acceptable and what he intends to do about it.[37]

At a hearing on December 8, 2011, Congressman Trey Gowdy asked Eric Holder to admit that at least four senior DOJ officials knew or should have known Weich's letter was "demonstrably false" and "materially false" at the time it was delivered. Gowdy told Holder he couldn't believe these officials had just recently learned the ten-month-old letter was inaccurate and pressed as to why they hadn't withdrawn or corrected it earlier. "When law enforcement officers lie to lawyers, they go to jail; when they lie to Congress, they get promoted," Gowdy observed. He asked Holder, "What consequences can we expect [for these false statements]?" Holder refused to admit the statements were demonstrably or materially false, saying that would be getting into "the realm" of legal conclusions; rather, they "contained inaccuracies."[38] At a later hearing on February 2, 2012, Holder held fast to his story, saying "Nobody at Justice has lied."[39]

HOLDER: LYING OR WOEFULLY INATTENTIVE?

As Holder continued to plead ignorance, congressional investigators tried to determine exactly what he knew about the operation and when he knew it. Back in May 2011, Holder had told the House Judiciary Committee he had only known about Fast and Furious "for a couple of weeks."

This would imply that after Brian Terry was killed on December 15, 2010, months went by before Holder discovered that guns walked via Fast and Furious were found at the scene—even though email records indicate that fact was immediately known within the DOJ; in fact, Arizona U.S. Attorney Dennis Burke informed DOJ deputy Monty Wilkinson about that fact the very day Terry was killed. Other memos later surfaced that were addressed to Holder and described the specifics of Fast and Furious. Holder claimed he had neither read the memos nor been informed of their content by his staff.[40]

CNN's Anderson Cooper, discussing the matter with reporter Drew Griffin, remarked, "No one seems to know, who authorized this thing? Border Agent Brian Terry, Drew, was murdered back in December 2010. Considering that ATF was part of the Justice Department, does anyone buy that Holder wasn't aware of the program?" Griffin responded, "I've been on the phone talking to some of these ATF agents today, I've talked to them over the weekend, and it's really hard for them to imagine that Holder wasn't at least briefed about it; this was a major operation, Anderson." Drew added, "To the boots on the ground it's unimaginable that high up people in the Department of Justice, including Holder, didn't know about it."[41]

When a reporter asked President Obama about Fast and Furious and about Attorney General Holder's role in the operation, Obama took Holder at his word. "As you know, my Attorney General has made clear he certainly would not have ordered gun running to be able to pass through into Mexico," said Obama. "The investigation is still pending and I'm not going to comment on a pending investigation. It wouldn't be appropriate for me to comment if it is not completed."[42]

Congressman Issa was disappointed by Obama's comments. "There was no sign of urgency to provide answers or explain why no one at the Justice Department has accepted responsibility for authorizing an illegal gunwalking operation six months after Border Patrol Agent Brian Terry's murder," said Issa. "The American people expect more from the President than unsubstantiated assertions that the Attorney General didn't know about this reckless program and no explanation about who authorized it."[43]

"NO ONE AT JUSTICE DEPARTMENT HEADQUARTERS HAS FACED ANY MEANINGFUL CONSEQUENCES"

Congressman Issa, in an op-ed for *USA Today* in December 2011, summarized what his Oversight Committee had learned. He said that almost a year after Border Agent Terry was murdered, the DOJ had spent more time and resources trying to protect the careers of its officials who had been aware of the operation than in holding to account those responsible for it. The operation, Issa said, was the brainchild of the Phoenix field office of the ATF, which is under the DOJ, and began in November 2009 as a result of Justice officials deciding to focus their resources on Mexican drug cartels rather than low-level straw buyers. The idea was that these guns would be purchased by straw buyers and eventually make their way into the hands of drug cartels, whose members could then be identified *after* crimes had been committed and the guns were recovered there and traced to their points of purchase. The operation wasn't terminated until after Agent Terry's murder.

Even though the DOJ knew and approved of the operation, Issa argued, Holder had refused to accept responsibility. He claimed he did not know about Fast and Furious until a few weeks prior to May 3, 2011, though he was sent numerous memos about it, which he claimed he did not read. Holder's senior managers, it was clear, were completely apprised of the operation and did not end it. Specifically, Acting Deputy Attorney General Gary Grindler was given a detailed briefing on the operation on March 12, 2010. Grindler's handwritten notes showed that he was informed about tactical details of the operation and that certain named individuals were purchasing hundreds of weapons for Mexican cartels. Notwithstanding this, Issa noted, Grindler was later elevated to be Holder's chief of staff.

Furthermore, Issa continued, Lanny Breuer, assistant attorney general in charge of the Criminal Division, apologized for certain aspects of the operation but had retained his job. Assistant Attorney General Ronald Weich withdrew a letter he had sent to Congress because it contained false information—and he wasn't removed from his position, either. And ATF Director Ken Melson had said that the DOJ was focused on covering for

its political appointees. "Surprisingly, no one at Justice Department headquarters has faced any meaningful consequences," Issa wrote. "While
replacing the entire ATF leadership structure and causing the U.S. attorney
for Arizona to tender his resignation, Holder has consistently used a con-
current investigation by the inspector general to prevent him from acting
against senior officials close to him."[44]

In an interview with ABC News in October 2011, Obama
acknowledged Fast and Furious was a mistake and vowed that "people who screwed up will be held accountable."[45] But there is no indication
he's exercised any leadership to uncover the facts, and indeed, he has
blindly supported Attorney General Eric Holder.

As Fox News reported in November 2011, the record does not bear
out Obama's promise to hold the wrongdoers accountable. Fox News'
William La Jeunesse corroborated Issa's contention that those accountable have been protected and even promoted. "Those in charge of the
botched operation," wrote La Jeunesse, "have been reassigned or promoted, their pensions intact. But many of those who blew the whistle
face isolation, retaliation and transfer."[46]

As La Jeunesse recounted, the following people whose hands were all
over the operation have appeared to benefit as a result, but in any event
have not been punished:

- ATF Chief Ken Melson is working as an advisor in the
  Office of Legal Affairs.
- Acting Deputy Director Billy Hoover is the special agent
  in charge of the D.C. office.
- Deputy Director for Field Operations William McMahon
  is the second in command at the ATF's Office of Internal
  Affairs.
- Special Agent in Charge of Phoenix Bill Newell was
  promoted to the Office of Management in Washington.
- Phoenix Deputy Chief George Gillette was promoted to
  Washington as ATF's liaison to the U.S. Marshal's
  Service.

- Group Supervisor David Voth has now been elevated to be chief of the ATF Tobacco Division, supervising more employees than he did in Phoenix.[47]

According to Special Agent Jay Dobyns, "These guys are protected. They're insulated. They're all part of a club." The only people who were punished, said Dobyns, are those who exposed the operation and told the truth about it. La Jeunesse's sources say these whistle-blowers can't be fired but "are in a kind of purgatory. On the other hand, they can be transferred but face the problems of relocating on their own."[48]

As such, Field Agent John Dodson, whose whistleblowing helped to ensure the Terry family would learn the truth about the operation, was "isolated, marginalized and referred to as a 'nut job,' 'wing-nut' and 'disgruntled.'" ATF command said that "contact with Dodson was detrimental to any ATF career." Dobson, who had sole custody of his two teenagers and was behind on his house mortgage, transferred to South Carolina after being prohibited from working in Phoenix.[49]

Other whistleblowers met a similar fate. Agent Larry Alt was transferred to Florida, Agent Peter Forcelli, noted above, was demoted to a desk job, Agent James Casa was transferred to Florida, Agent Carlos Canino was moved to Tucson, Agent Jose Wall was moved to Phoenix, and Agent Darren Gil has retired.[50]

This was predictable, given Holder's response when Issa asked him in February 2012 whether he would ever hold anyone accountable for the operation "because you haven't done any so far, as far as we can tell." Holder replied that he was prepared to hold people accountable right now—*the whistleblowers, those who revealed contents of Fast and Furious wiretap applications that showed the operation's transgressions.*[51]

"ACTIVELY ENGAGED IN A COVER-UP"

When Holder continued to stonewall subpoenas and other information requests, Darrell Issa sent a letter threatening to hold him in contempt of Congress and alleging the DOJ had "misrepresented facts and misled Congress." The DOJ's ignoring of the subpoenas, wrote Issa, "lead[s] us to conclude that the department is actively engaged in a cover-up. If the department continues to obstruct the congressional inquiry by not providing documents and information, this committee will have no alternative but to move forward with proceedings to hold you in contempt of Congress."[52]

In testimony to the House Judiciary Committee, Holder claimed that Justice employees were working "tirelessly to identify, locate and provide relevant information" to Congress, "all while preserving the integrity of the ongoing criminal investigations and prosecutions." Holder insisted that the documents show DOJ personnel were relying on information they'd received from supervisors in Arizona, though some of the information later turned out to be "inaccurate."[53]

But in the Senate, Grassley wasn't satisfied, noting that Justice had yet to explain why it was withholding seventy-four thousand pages it had given to the DOJ inspector general but not to Congress. Grassley remarked that he couldn't take anything from Justice at face value, since Holder initially denied gunwalking had ever occurred before later admitting it had, and since Lanny Breuer was less than honest about the topic. "He [Breuer] stood mute as this administration fought tooth and nail to keep any of this information from coming out for a year," said Grassley. "It will take a lot more than a knee-jerk defense from their political allies in Congress to restore public trust in the leadership of the Justice Department."[54]

Luckily for Holder, he had help from his Democratic colleagues. Continuing their counteroffensive, Democrats on the House Oversight Committee began running interference for him in anticipation of his testimony at a House Oversight Committee hearing on February 2, 2012. Just a few days before the hearing, Congressman Cummings filed a 95-page report claiming top DOJ officials did not authorize Fast and Furious. Though copious evidence indicated otherwise, Cummings's report blamed "rogue" officials in the ATF Phoenix Field Division. The essential point was that this was purely a local operation, completely outside the knowledge of anyone important in the ATF or DOJ.

The main problem with this argument was that wiretaps for Fast and Furious were, according to CBS News, authorized by the second-in-command at Justice, Lanny Breuer.[55] Because wiretap applications must be scrupulously detailed and reviewed, it is highly unlikely Breuer would be ignorant of the specifics of the operation, including the gun-walking tactics.[56]

With this in mind, during a congressional hearing, Congressman Gowdy asked Holder to acknowledge that wiretap applications in general are voluminous, long, and factual predicates. Holder agreed they were, but when asked about wiretap applications for Fast and Furious, he said he couldn't discuss them, and later admitted he hadn't even read them—an astounding admission considering the gravity of the investigation. When Gowdy could not get Holder to admit Breuer had reviewed the wiretap applications, he challenged Holder to deny that some other DOJ official would have had to review them. Holder dodged the question.[57]

Gowdy expressed incredulity that Holder would deny Breuer had knowledge of Fast and Furious when Breuer had admitted it in emails. Holder said he was relying only on what Breuer had testified to—which is hard to believe. Nevertheless, if true, it's inexcusable that Holder didn't bother to ask Breuer directly about such a fundamental issue. In any case, Holder has access to the documents and was obligated especially after all these months, to know what's in them.

CONNECTING THE DOTS

The act of putting thousands of weapons in the hands of Mexican drug cartels with no attempt to track them is so inconceivable that many have wondered what exactly Fast and Furious was designed to accomplish. There is widespread speculation that the Obama administration hoped that if enough Fast and Furious guns surfaced in Mexico, it would help pressure Congress to enact more stringent gun control laws. The administration denies this allegation, and the Democratic report on the operation said "no evidence" had surfaced to support the charge.

Yet an email from Assistant Director in Charge of Field Operations Mark Chait related, "Internal ATF emails seem to suggest that ATF agents were counseled to highlight a link between criminals and certain semi-automatic weapons in order to bolster a case for a rule like the one the DOJ announced yesterday." In another email, Chait wrote, "Bill—can you see if these guns were all purchased from the same FfL and at one time. We are looking at anecdotal cases to support a demand letter on long gun multiple sales."[58] Thus, at a minimum, we can voice a reasonable suspicion that Fast and Furious was conceived, at least in part, as a gun control vehicle.

Even CNN's Anderson Cooper seemed incredulous that the government designed a program ostensibly to trace gun purchases to Mexican cartels and make arrests when the ATF agents had no way of knowing where the guns would end up—and that Mexican agents, who would be the ones to make the arrests, weren't even told about the operation at all. "So," said Cooper, "a program meant to stop gun smuggling actually put weapons into criminals' hands in Mexico."[59]

John Hayward, writing in *Human Events* in June 2011, raised the intriguing possibility that the *Washington Post* had run a piece in December 2011 that inadvertently disclosed indications that Fast and Furious was in fact meant to help build the case for tighter gun control laws. In the story, the *Post* reported on U.S. gun dealers with "the most traces for firearms recovered by police." It gave "the names of the dealers, all from border states, with the most traces from guns recovered in Mexico over the past two years." Hayward explained that the purpose of the story was to criticize a 2003 law that shields the government's gun tracking database from the public, and also to suggest that many guns sold by these dealers were traveling across the border and being used in Mexican crimes. This law, according to the *Post*, was passed due to pressure from the dastardly gun lobby.

Interestingly, Hayward points out, the *Post* probably got its data from an ATF leaker, since this very law would have prevented the paper from obtaining the information legally. Hayward also pointed out that two of the gun dealers the *Post* highlighted had been recruited by the ATF in

Operation Fast and Furious. The ATF reportedly instructed these shops to "keep selling" guns to drug cartel front men.

Hayward's theory is that the ATF was feeding information to the press about American guns going into Mexico to build the administration's case for tighter gun laws. Meanwhile, it was manipulating those very gun sales the *Post* was reporting on—and one of those guns ended up being used in the murder of Brian Terry the day after the *Post* story appeared. Hayward concluded:

> Connect the dots: a story that almost certainly required information leaked by the ATF, in a paper noted for its friendliness to the Administration, was used to build the case that lax American gun control laws are contributing to Mexican gun crimes, when the ATF was secretly running a program that deliberately pushed American guns into the hands of Mexican cartels, without any serious plan to track them, until they were used in the commission of crimes. Now, take an educated guess what the true purpose of Operation Fast & Furious was.[60]

Undoubtedly, Obama and his liberal cabal are ardent opponents of gun rights. Obama and Attorney General Eric Holder have long been proponents of the misnamed assault weapons ban. As with so many other issues where he can't muster popular or legislative support, Obama attempts to implement his policies through executive or administrative maneuvers. For example, the administration planned to implement new gun control regulations disguised as "gun safety measures." The measures, according to White House spokesman Jay Carney, would be designed to prevent "another Tucson."

While the White House, as of this writing, has not yet implemented these rules, it did issue regulations applicable to gun shops close to the U.S.-Mexican border, probably hoping to deflect attention from Fast and Furious. The Justice Department invoked a "new reporting measure—tailored to focus only on multiple sales of these types of rifles (semi-automatics greater than .22 caliber with the ability to accept a detachable magazine) to the same person within a five-day period." The "targeted information requests" applied to Arizona, California, New Mexico, and Texas.[61]

"A SERIOUS LACK OF INQUISITIVENESS"

The day before the February 2, 2012, hearing of the House Oversight Committee, committee staff for Chairman Darell Issa and Senator Charles Grassley issued a report detailing Main Justice's involvement in Operation Fast and Furious. According to the report, DOJ headquarters had been passing blame for the operation on to the U.S. Attorney's Office for the District of Arizona and the ATF, despite the fact that both were under the DOJ's domain. Main Justice, said the report, "had much greater knowledge of, and involvement in, Fast and Furious than it has previously acknowledged."[62]

The report discussed emails which showed that Acting ATF Director Kenneth Melson had informed Assistant Attorney General Lanny Breuer that they wanted to take a "different approach" to seizing guns going to Mexico and that Breuer said it was a "terrific idea." But Deputy Attorney General James Cole wrote Issa denying the claim that Breuer wanted the Phoenix division to be involved in gunwalking. The report concluded that the DOJ was "managing the congressional investigation in order to protect the political appointees at the department."[63]

During his testimony at the February hearing, Holder sarcastically alluded to the fact that he'd been summoned before Congress on Fast and Furious six times. Chairman Issa reminded him that not all those appearances were directly related to Fast and Furious, and that the investigation would have gone more quickly if he had been more cooperative. Before the hearing, the House Oversight Committee released a graphic called "Fortress Holder" to illustrate Holder's stonewalling. The image shows, among other things, that over the past year, congressional investigators and the American people had been denied access to 92 percent of the documents related to Fast and Furious, 68 percent of subpoenaed document categories related to the operation, and forty-eight accounts from DOJ officials involved in the operation.[64]

According to the committee report, ATF officials said their goal from the beginning was to go after the people at the top of the gun trafficking operation, not the low-level straw purchasers. That, supposedly, is why they didn't confront those purchasers or interdict guns—they were focused on dismantling the entire cartel organizations. While the ATF said they were dealing with a very complex gun trafficking operation, the committee said, "In reality... the network was not complex.... It actually included a small cadre of about forty straw purchasers—only five of whom purchased 70 percent of the weapons—one ringleader (Manuel Celis-Acosta), and two cartel associates who were the link to the Sinaloa Cartel. The whole point of Fast and Furious ... was to identify this ringleader and these two cartel associates."[65]

As it turns out, federal law enforcement officials had already identified the ringleader by December 2009. Also around that time, the operation had expanded to include fifteen interconnected straw purchasers known to have bought five hundred firearms. The report makes clear that the ATF well understood that these gun sales—which the ATF allowed to proceed—were going to violent criminals. The ATF, based on DEA wiretap intercepts, had sufficient probable cause to make arrests as early as 2009, or at least to use other investigative techniques to disrupt the purchases and seize the weapons.

But the ATF chose not to act or to arrest Celis-Acosta. Instead, according to the committee report, the ATF wanted to get its own wiretaps and build up its own case. This decision "ensured that Fast and Furious lasted nearly a year longer, with 1,500 more guns being purchased—including the guns bought by Jaime Avila in January 2010 that were found at the murder scene of Border Patrol Agent Brian Terry." It wasn't until the ATF finally brought in Celis-Acosta in January 2011 that it learned the identities of the two cartel associates.

It was later discovered that other branches of the DOJ had already been aware of the two associates because their names often appeared in DEA logs provided to the ATF as early as December 2009. But the ATF missed the names because it failed to review this information.

Additionally, the DEA and FBI had jointly opened a separate investigation specifically targeting the two men. Thus, by January 2010, both agencies had collected abundant information on them. Yet the ATF, unaware of that, "spent the next year engaging in the reckless tactics of Fast and Furious in attempting to identify them." Adding insult to injury, the FBI made the two men informants, preventing their indictment. The upshot was "that the entire goal of Fast and Furious—to target these two individuals and bring them to justice—was a failure." The ATF apparently disputed that the two were untouchable.[66]

Consistent with its posture throughout the investigation, the DOJ barely demonstrated any concern for the egregious absence of information-sharing among its three subsidiary entities—the ATF, DEA, and FBI. Upon being apprised of this situation, the deputy attorney general merely remarked, "We will look into it."[67] Fortunately, it was not only Republicans who were alarmed by the DOJ's misdeeds. Concerned about the lack of interagency coordination along the border and the miscommunication between law enforcement agencies concerning Fast and Furious, Senator Joe Lieberman, an independent, directed staff of the Senate Homeland Security and Government Affairs Committee, which he chairs, to examine the situation.[68]

The committee report explained the acquisition of wiretap affidavits that eventually led to the authorization of seven federal wiretaps. The affidavits established the necessity for wiretaps by detailing—with specificity—why other investigative techniques were insufficient. What was appalling was that no one in either ATF leadership or any political appointees at Main Justice admitted to having reviewed the affidavits, even though someone among them had to have read them to approve their issuance. As the committee observed, "Because of the Wiretap Affidavits, the Criminal Division at Main Justice was in a position to know as much about Fast and Furious as ATF. Both Justice Department and ATF leaders in Washington, D.C. claimed that they were unaware of the gunwalking that occurred during Fast and Furious, yet both could have and should have reviewed the Wiretap Affidavits."[69] This is precisely the point Congressman Gowdy was pressing Eric Holder to admit during the February 2012 hearing.

Moreover, the ATF was directly aware of the purchase of weapons when they occurred, because agents were monitoring feeds from cameras inside the stores of cooperating gun dealers. Indeed, ATF Agent Dodson, during a March 3, 2011, CBS News interview, showed footage of ATF agents watching known straw purchasers leave a gun store and load their new weapons into their vehicles. The committee report stated that Deputy Assistant Attorney General Jason Weinstein and his Criminal Division should have known, based on the wiretap affidavits, that the ATF agents were witnessing, monitoring, and recording the purchases and illegal transfers of the weapons. They also should have known that in some cases these weapons were being recovered in Mexico within a day of their purchase.

Weinstein testified that he was unaware of the detailed information in the affidavits because his general practice was only to review the summary memos, not the affidavits themselves. But Weinstein did admit he reviewed what he thought were three of the Fast and Furious wiretaps, saying he found nothing in them that concerned him. Nothing, he said, gave him "any reason to suspect that guns were walking in that case in Fast and Furious." And if he had encountered such information, he "would have reacted very strongly to it." The committee report said it is now clear why Eric Holder and Lanny Breuer were so adamant in their testimony to explain that the Criminal Division reviews the wiretap affidavits only to see if they are legally sufficient, and not to evaluate the appropriateness of tactics. "That distinction," said the report, "is essential in order to avoid responsibility for knowing of the tactics described in the Wiretap Affidavits."[70]

This typified the DOJ's attitude toward the entire investigation—showing a "serious lack of inquisitiveness when it came to discovering details about Operation Fast and Furious," and obstructing the committee's investigation at every turn. Ken Melson's testimony that Justice was managing the investigation to protect its political appointees turned out, according to the committee report, to be "prophetic." The department "has blamed everyone except for its political appointees for Fast and Furious. This includes the U.S. Attorney's Office in Arizona, the ATF Phoenix Field Division, and even ATF Headquarters."[71]

In its conclusion, the committee said that the ATF blames Main Justice for encouraging Fast and Furious while the DOJ blames the ATF and Arizona's U.S. Attorney's Office. Meanwhile, the DOJ officials in a position to stop the operation blame their staffs for not bringing the critical issues to their attention. Additionally, U.S. Attorney's Office personnel have either taken the Fifth Amendment in refusing to testify before Congress or have been prohibited by the DOJ from talking to Congress altogether. As Melson testified, the Department is clearly "circling the wagons to protect its political appointees."

And we can never forget the real victims here. As the committee report stated, "The family of Brian Terry, the families of countless citizens of Mexico slain by weapons purchased through Fast and Furious, and the American people deserve to know the truth."[72]

The Obama administration has gone to great lengths to distance itself from Fast and Furious. Yet the operation shows many hallmarks of Obama's governance, from its excessive secrecy to the incompetence of its execution to the refusal of anyone to take responsibility. We still don't know at what level of the administration this operation was ultimately approved—and Attorney General Holder seems determined that we never find out. Regardless, Operation Fast and Furious testifies to a federal government that, while itself is out of control, demands ever more control over *our* guns, *our* economy, and *our* everyday lives.

CHAPTER TWELVE

THE WAR ON THE DIGNITY
OF HIS OFFICE

Three years into Obama's presidency, widespread criticism has done nothing to temper his unbounded narcissism. According to *Fox Nation*, as of the beginning of August 2010, "Obama [had] spoken some form of 'I' or 'me' more than 16,000 official times since he took office." In his defense, his self-image may be distorted by the fawning and pandering that surrounds him daily, including from our hapless vice president. "This guy has a backbone like a ramrod," said Biden, in one of his many panegyrics to his boss, adding that Obama also possesses "a brain bigger than his skull and he's got a heart to match both."[1] And as his first term comes to an end, Obama still can't resist placing himself in the cultural limelight, appearing on pop-culture television programs ranging from *The Daily Show* to *Mythbusters*.

"WE KNOW WHAT'S RIGHT"

When Obama scheduled his joint session of Congress to campaign for his jobs bill at the same time as a Republican presidential debate, one would have assumed the dispute would end once he rescheduled. Instead, Obama was infuriated that the GOP had forced him to back down. "It is a big deal that the House said 'no' to the president from our end," said a White House source, according to *Politico*. The source continued, "This confirms what we all know: They will do anything in the House to muck us up."[2]

But was the anger justified? Who walked on whom here? *Politico* said the White House was well aware Obama's speech would conflict with the Republican debate, which had been planned well in advance, but it insisted on acting like the aggrieved party. Treating the Republican debate as a non-event and Obama's speech—another predictable, monotonous presidential sales job—as singularly paramount to the nation, the White House source insisted that the "debate was one that was going on a cable station. It was not sacrosanct. We knew they would push it back and then there would be a GOP debate totally trashing the president. So it wasn't all an upside for us."[3]

So, the White House deliberately scheduled over the Republican debate and arrogantly presumed the GOP would automatically reschedule. Continuing in this adolescent posture, Obama sent an email to his supporters with the subject line "Frustrated." His message read, "It's been a long time since Congress was focused on what the American people need them to be focused on. I know that you're frustrated by that. I am too." Obama said he was advancing "a set of bipartisan proposals to help grow the economy and create jobs" and was "asking lawmakers to look past short-term politics and take action on that plan." Even *Politico* acknowledged Obama's non-presidential tone, saying it "was, perhaps, not the friendliest message, but the White House was not in a friendly mood."[4]

WHEN THINGS AREN'T GOING RIGHT, FOLKS ARE GOING TO DIRECT ATTENTION AT YOU

Just a year before, President Obama had assured us that he, too, despite his lavish presidential lifestyle, could relate to the plight of struggling Americans during our economic downturn, as he and the first lady took a hit in the financial meltdown. "We're just not that far removed from what most Americans are going through," Obama told ABC News. "I mean it was only a few years ago when we had high credit card balances, we had two little kids that we were trying to figure out how to save enough for college, we were still thinking about our own retirement and looking at our retirement accounts and wondering, are we going to be able to get enough assets in there to make sure we're protected." At the time of the interview, his disclosure forms revealed he had a net worth of some $7.7 million.[5]

A few weeks later, still fully me-directed, Obama lamented that he was not given the credit he deserves. And "here's the reason," he explained to CBS News: "We've gone through the worst economic downturn since the Great Depression. No other depression comes close. When people have gone through that much trauma, people have every right to be scared, to be angry, to be frustrated. And I don't expect the American people to be satisfied when we're only half of the way back." He added, "One of the things when you're President is, folks are gonna, you know, direct attention—when things aren't going right for them—at *you*."[6] That's Obama—ever the victim.

When asked by CBS how he would grade his performance in office, Obama modestly replied, "When I look back on what we've accomplished in the last 18 months, preventing the country sinking into a Great Depression, two economists, including John McCain's economist from the campaign, estimated that if we hadn't made the decisions we've made, you would have had an additional eight million people unemployed, and we would be in a Great Depression. So, saving the economy, stabilizing the financial market, saving the auto industry, oh, and by the way, passing health care, I'd say that's a pretty good track record."[7]

Of course, today's dismal unemployment numbers speak to a less-than-successful economic track record. But not to worry—according to Obama adviser David Plouffe, Americans won't be judging him on such trivial criteria. "The average American does not view the economy through the prism of GDP or unemployment rates or even monthly jobs numbers," said Plouffe. "People won't vote based on the unemployment rate, they're going to vote based on: 'How do I feel about my own situation? Do I believe the president makes decisions based on me and my family?'"[8]

Vice President Biden wholeheartedly agreed with Plouffe's analysis, arguing that voters would understand Obama "inherited a God-awful circumstance that wasn't our responsibility. That doesn't in any way diminish the genuine suffering of a hell of a lot of Americans. But I think everything gets down to a choice.... Don't compare me to the almighty, compare me to the alternative."[9]

At a press conference a few days later, Obama offered a revealing glimpse of what he really thinks about the people he represents. When a reporter noted that only 24 percent of Americans believed the debt ceiling should be raised, Obama haughtily responded, "Let me distinguish between professional politicians and the public at large. You, know, the public is not paying close attention to the ins and outs of how a Treasury auction goes. They shouldn't. They're worrying about their family; they're worrying about their jobs. They're worrying about their neighborhood. They have got a lot of other things on their plate. We're paid to worry about it."[10]

Actually, no, they are paid *to do something about it*—not to mention that Americans understand that the looming national debt affects all these matters Obama identifies as the people's proper concerns. But the White House thinks Americans shouldn't bother learning about trifling, esoteric things like debt ceilings. When a reporter at a White House press conference asked Press Secretary Jay Carney why the administration was pressing to raise the debt ceiling in the face of public opposition, Carney retorted, "I think it's easy to understand why most Americans don't have a lot of time to focus on 'What is a debt ceiling?' I mean, honestly, did anybody in this room—before they had to cover issues like this—have any idea what a debt ceiling was? Any understanding of the fact that a vote by Congress to increase our ability to borrow was simply a vote to allow the United States to pay the bills it incurred in the past?" If the pollsters would just talk down to the people's level they would support the administration's position, Carney assured him. "I think every American—certainly a vast majority of Americans, would accept the principle, if asked, that the United States should pay its bills, just like they're asked to pay their bills."[11]

THE OBAMAS HAVEN'T DISAPPOINTED AMERICANS. "WE DISAPPOINTED THEM"

An additional year and a half of hard knocks and failures couldn't disabuse Obama of his glowing self-assessment. In December 2011, during a *60 Minutes* interview, he blithely ranked himself as the nation's fourth best president. "The issue here is not gonna be a list of accomplishments," he argued. "As you said yourself, Steve, you know, I would put our legislative and foreign policy accomplishments in our first two years against any president—with the possible exceptions of Johnson, FDR, and Lincoln—just in terms of what we've gotten done in modern history. But, you know, but when it comes to the economy, we've got a lot more work to do. And we're gonna keep at it."[12]

Obama's comparing himself to historical figures wasn't an isolated occurrence. At a campaign appearance a few months later, while discussing the hard work he was doing to bring change to America, he invoked a few other notables who made similar, herculean efforts at change. "Around the world, Gandhi, Nelson Mandela, what they did was hard," declared Obama. "It takes time. It takes more than a single term. It takes more than a single president. It takes more than a single individual."[13]

Columnist Michael Barone described Obama as "profoundly aloof," noting that while his admirers used to compare him to great presidents, "no one seriously compares him with Lincoln or FDR anymore." A more appropriate comparison, said Barone, was "Chauncey Gardiner, the character played by Peter Sellers in the 1979 movie *Being There*. As you may remember, Gardiner is a clueless gardener who is mistaken for a Washington eminence and becomes a presidential adviser. Asked if you can stimulate growth through temporary incentives, Gardiner says, 'As long as the roots are not severed, all is well and all will be well in the garden.'" After citing a few other Gardiner quotes, Barone remarked, "Kind of reminds you of Obama's approach to the federal budget, doesn't it?"[14]

Even some on the Left feel Obama's self-confidence has morphed into churlish arrogance. Uber-liberal *New York Times* columnist Maureen Dowd, after attending an Obama fundraiser at the Apollo in Harlem, wrote, "For eight seconds, we saw the president we had craved for three years: cool, joyous, funny, connected"—and after that fleeting moment, things went downhill. It's not just that Dowd belatedly realized Obama was bereft of messianic qualities; she seemed to acknowledge he is an empty shell. Hitting as hard as any conservative commentator, Dowd wrote, "The man who became famous with a speech declaring that we were one America, not opposing teams of red and blue states, presides over an America more riven by blue and red than ever. The man who came to Washington on a wave of euphoria has had a presidency with all the joy of a root canal."[15]

Dowd was particularly disdainful of Obama's lament that he is only seen as "cool and aloof" because he stays at home with his daughters instead of going "to a lot of Washington parties." Dowd said that Reagan didn't socialize with the press either, "but he knew that to transcend, you can't condescend." Dowd cited Jodi Kantor's new book, *The Obamas*, in which Kantor paints a portrait of "the first couple" as people who feel aggrieved and misunderstood and who, in Dowd's words, "do believe in American exceptionalism—their own, and they feel overassaulted and underappreciated." Dowd said that the Obamas, in their own minds, haven't disappointed Americans. "We disappointed them." The pair, according to Dowd, actually believe the admonition of presidential advisor Valerie Jarrett that Barack Obama is "just too talented to do what ordinary people do."[16]

"THEY TALK ABOUT ME LIKE A DOG"

Obama's frustration is compounded by his inability to please even his own fickle base. His angst trickles down to his spokesmen, who vicariously reflect his narcissism. Then-White House press secretary Robert Gibbs said of the discontented leftists, "I hear these people saying he's like George Bush. Those people ought to be drug tested. I mean, it's crazy." Unwittingly conceding his base's end game, Gibbs declared, "They will be satisfied when we have Canadian healthcare and we've eliminated the Pentagon. That's not a reality." Note that Gibbs didn't say such policies were objectionable, only that they weren't realistic goals.

To Obama and his staff, it's always all about *him*. President George W. Bush never responded to criticism with that kind of self-absorption, but Obama and his team can't contain themselves. For them, it's personal. As *The Hill* noted, "The lack of appreciation or recognition for what Obama has accomplished has left Gibbs and others in furious disbelief."[17] In another telling comment, during a self-pitying speech in Milwaukee, Obama complained that his critics "talk about me like a dog." In this very speech, incidentally, Obama, as usual, talked about former president George W. Bush like he's a dog.[18]

A few months later, Louisiana governor Bobby Jindal said that at a meeting with Obama during the Gulf oil spill, the president had warned Jindal not to criticize him on TV. Jindal said it was obvious Obama was more concerned about being castigated over the spill than actually fixing the problem.[19]

Likewise, after Arizona governor Jan Brewer published a book in which she claimed Obama had acted arrogantly toward her, he confronted her on the airport tarmac as she greeted him when he visited Arizona. Brewer later said Obama "was a little disturbed about my book" and "a bit thin-skinned."[20] Obama downplayed the confrontation and implied Brewer had fabricated his tone. He tried to write it off as Republican party politics when, "laughing and aloof"—according to *Politico*—he told ABC News, "What I've discovered is they think it's always good publicity for a Republican if they're in an argument with me. But this was really not a big deal."[21] Obama's description was not consistent with video footage of the incident or with press descriptions of it.

"OBAMA HAS NOT CONNECTED EMOTIONALLY WITH VOTERS"

Obama is a cool customer, curiously detached and unable to empathize with people who are struggling—which makes his professed ideology of compassion notably incongruent. "Unlike former President Clinton, who famously felt the pain of voters during a recession, Obama has not connected emotionally with voters over their worries and fears," notes *The Hill*.[22]

That doesn't keep Obama from pretending to identify with the downtrodden. In a backyard meeting in Fairfax, Virginia, he told those assembled he would stand with them in the hot sun and "feel their pain." But a few verbal bones didn't convince anyone, including the usual Democratic supporters. "The problem is that he doesn't seem like he's always trying to be empathetic," said one Democratic strategist. "They have been missing the need for the emotional connection people need in times like this—but they've needed it for two years."[23]

Obama not only doesn't empathize with Americans, he looks down on them. Just as he implied Americans were too dense or disengaged to understand his healthcare plan or the debt ceiling, he suggested that disaffected Democratic and independent voters moving toward the GOP were succumbing to fear and turning away from science and facts—as if a firm grasp on reality would lead rational people, inexorably, to support his policies. "People out there are still hurting very badly, and they are still scared," said Obama. "And so part of the reason that our politics seems so tough right now, and facts and science and argument does not seem to be winning the day all the time, is because we're hard-wired not to always think clearly when we're scared."[24] In his comments he failed to mention a few salient "facts," including our unprecedented deficits and exploding debt.

When former George W. Bush speechwriter Michael Gerson criticized Obama's condescending remarks, Obama advisor David Axelrod defensively insisted that Obama is not a snob.[25] But even liberal blogger Mickey Kaus wasn't buying it. "Clinton reacted to his 1994 midterm loss by acknowledging his opponents' strongest arguments and pursuing a balanced budget and welfare reform," Kaus noted. "Obama seems more inclined to just tough it out until the economy recovers and the scared, confused voters become unscared and see the light. Meanwhile, he'll spend his time in a protective cocoon."[26]

Even when stumping for Washington senator Patty Murray, Obama couldn't resist basking in self-adulation; when a female reporter shouted out that we have "the best president on earth," Obama replied, "Well, I won't say that, but we got a pretty good president."[27]

Despite being surrounded by such sycophancy, however, Obama seems upset that people don't worship him as much as they used to. "No I don't think there's a sense that I've been successful," he told Colorado's

9News. "I think people feel that Washington still is dysfunctional." But this isn't his fault, you see, it's because people confuse him with the federal government. "I think people still feel that overall Washington is about a lot of politics and special interests and big money, but that ordinary people's voices too often aren't represented and so my hope is that we are going to continue to work to rebuilding a sense of trust in government."[28]

But if Americans are not as prone to praising him as they once were, Obama will always fill the breach himself. At the presentation of the Nobel Peace Prize to Liu Xiabo, a Chinese political prisoner, in Oslo in December 2010, Obama began by talking about his favorite topic: "One year ago, I was humbled to receive the Nobel Peace Prize—an award that speaks to our highest aspirations, and that has been claimed by giants of history and courageous advocates who have sacrificed for freedom and justice." After thus recognizing himself as a "giant of history," he said, with obvious false modesty, that Liu Xiaobo "is far more deserving of this award than I." Strangely, Obama snuck in another gratuitous reference to himself at the end of the speech, saying, "I regret that Mr. Liu and his wife are denied the opportunity to attend the ceremony that Michelle and I attended last year."[29]

But that's probably not any more revealing of his self-absorption than Obama's choice of children's book to read to second-graders in Arlington, Virginia: *Of Thee I Sing*, written by... Barack Obama.[30]

"ALL HE DID WAS SIGN OFF ON INITIATIVES OTHER, BETTER MEN HAD ORIGINATED"

Obama even frames the advancement of his agenda in terms of personal accomplishment and personal consequences. In pressing congressmen to vote for his tax bill, he reminded them that his presidency was on the line. Congressman Peter DeFazio told CNN's Eliot Spitzer, "The White House is putting on tremendous pressure... the president is making phone calls saying this is the end of his presidency if he doesn't get this." The White House squarely denied Obama had made the statement, but why would DeFazio, a fellow Democrat, concoct such a story?

Indeed, Obama reportedly used similar language during the healthcare debate, telling wavering Democrats that if they refused to pass the bill, it could put his presidency on the line and stall the liberal agenda for decades.[31]

After Obama gave a speech in Tucson to memorialize the victims of the Jared Loughner shootings, White House press secretary Robert Gibbs told the media that Obama felt good after the speech—as if Obama's feelings were the issue. Continuing with his post-mortem on Obama's performance, Gibbs said, "I think he's gone through thinking about this as somebody who knew the congresswoman. And I think he's gone through this, as I'm sure many of you guys have, as a parent or a sibling might—if you read some of the stories that—about the victims that are still very, very hard to read. And I think he's been thinking about this on a lot of different levels."[32]

Yes, the agony of that speech must have been unbearable for Obama. But not to worry, because any hardship he may have endured was cured with a little self-help during his State of the Union speech a few weeks later, when he referred to himself some fifty-five times, proving that he was still master of the art of self-reference.

But nowhere was the stoutness of Obama's narcissism on clearer display than in his exuberance at the death of Osama bin Laden. It quickly became clear he would parlay the bin Laden killing to remake his image as a kick-butt commander in chief. He promptly embarked on what some described as a "bragging tour," in which he repeatedly took credit for bin Laden's death. As he related the events, Obama often recited some of the history leading up to the raid on bin Laden's compound, describing actions that occurred during the Bush administration with the collective "we," without mentioning, much less crediting, Bush for any of it. When he arrived at the point in the narrative where he became president, he conveniently switched to the first person, as if to suggest he personally brought bin Laden to justice.

Novelist Stephen Hunter had choice words to describe Obama's grotesquely self-congratulatory remarks:

> Any joy one might feel in the intelligence of our analysts and
> the bravery of our door kickers was significantly diminished

by Obama's malignant narcissism.... Then there were his tasteless claims of personal leadership, his over-emphasis on "I" and "at my direction." Clearly, all he did was sign off on initiatives other, better men had originated. He was ungenerous to Bush, who had to deal with this thing in real time under more pressure than any president has faced since Pearl Harbor and wasn't helped by the treachery of the Democratic Party, as exemplified by then Senator Obama. Clearly, we staged from Afghanistan. We were able to stage from Afghanistan because of Bush and the intel that led to the kill was just as obviously developed over years of effort, begun by Bush.[33]

"AN ISOLATED MAN TRAPPED IN A COLLAPSING PRESIDENCY"

During the debate over the debt ceiling, Obama seamlessly shifted from denouncing Congress to congratulating himself on the bin Laden operation. "They're in one week, they're out one week," Obama said about Congress. "And then they're saying, 'Obama has got to step in. You need to be here.' I've been here. I've been doing Afghanistan and bin Laden and the Greek crisis. You stay here. Let's get it done."[34]

But the president's triumphalism over the bin Laden raid didn't defuse criticism that he was failing to show leadership in the budget negotiations. Obama said he was "amused" by the charge, adding, "Let me tell you something: right after we finished dealing with the government shutdown, averting a government shutdown, I called the leaders here together. I said we have to get this done"—as if he can just issue an edict, snap his fingers, and decree a deal into existence, reminiscent of his memorable order concerning the Gulf oil spill: "Just plug the damn hole."[35] Meanwhile, he applied a wholly different standard to congressional leaders, saying a deal was up to them and "they need to do their job.... Now's the time to go ahead and make the tough choices, that's why they're called leaders."[36]

This Obama dog and pony show was bizarre considering that, in other contexts, Obama had said the exact opposite. "There is nothing wrong with our country," he said during a speech at a plant in Holland,

Michigan. "There is something wrong with our politics. The last thing we need is Congress spending more time arguing in D.C. What I figure is they need to spend more time out here listening to you and hearing how fed up you are. That's why I'm here."[37]

Obama's chiding was even more ludicrous in light of his own arrogant detachment in dealing with the specifics of the economy, budgets, and the national debt. Even Democrats were appalled when Obama chose not to attend a White House meeting with members of his own debt commission, whom he had convened in an insincere political stunt, and whose recommendations he largely ignored. "He should have at least dropped by," said one Democratic member of the commission. A Democratic aide said that panel members were miffed and privately believed Obama opted out of the meeting to avoid embarrassment because he'd just endorsed $900 billion more in deficit spending.[38]

As his term progressed, more and more people began to notice how isolated Obama was even from his own staff. As columnist Michael Goodwin wrote, "President Obama has become a lone wolf, a stranger to his own government. He talks mostly, and sometimes only, to friend and adviser Valerie Jarrett and to David Axelrod, his political strategist." Everyone else, according to Goodwin, including Obama's cabinet members, has little face time with Obama except for brief meetings disguised as photo-ops. Additionally, quite contrary to his projected public image, Obama is said to have short workdays, knocking off around 4:00 p.m. Goodwin says, "If the reports are accurate, and I believe they are, they paint a picture of an isolated man trapped in a collapsing presidency."[39]

OBAMA PLAYED MORE GOLF IN TWO YEARS THAN BUSH DID IN EIGHT

Obama paints himself as an indefatigable public servant despite his lavish lifestyle in office, his perennial partying with star-studded entertainment at the White House, and his frequent, extravagant vacations and golf outings. Indeed, the person lecturing Congress for not staying in Washington to do their jobs is the same one who took a seventeen-day, $4 million taxpayer-funded luxury vacation in Hawaii which, as British columnist Nile Gardiner pointed out, cost nearly one hundred times the average annual salary of an American worker.[40] Just a few weeks after their seventeen-day vacation, Michelle Obama took her daughters on another ski trip to Colorado—at an exclusive resort in Aspen.[41]

Obama seems indifferent to his hypocrisy, the stark contrast between his constant finger-wagging against the "rich" and his own luxurious exploits. It's as though he has granted himself a personal exemption, a sort of presidential immunity concerning his taxpayer-subsidized lifestyle. So long as he rails against achievers, it doesn't matter that he is one or that he lives a life every bit as lavish as the wealthiest of those he derides—except that he doesn't do it with his own money.

While Obama is berating America's fat-cat bankers and corporatist raiders, his White House sends out photos of a casually dressed Obama with his feet propped high on the people's desk, seemingly unconcerned about the cratering economy and staggering debt. While he directs public money into failed green energy ventures that wouldn't get the first investment dime from the free market and lectures Americans about conservation, he gallivants about in a near twenty-car motorcade of gas-guzzling SUVs and limousines, stopping traffic wherever he goes and subjecting everyone to his aversion to punctuality.

He seems utterly oblivious to the disastrous optics of playing golf the day after he voiced his deep empathy for the victims of the tsunami in Japan, and getting in another round on the links instead of honoring his commitment to attend the Polish president's funeral. He obviously saw nothing untoward in the first lady's sojourn to Europe with her buds while he exhorted Americans to spend their vacations in the oil-spilled Gulf, presumably to help fool others into believing there was nothing to see there, that his policies hadn't made a mess of things, and that all was back to normal.[42]

It's his world, which is why he didn't have to consult Congress before initiating military strikes against Libya or bother to fill the people in on his action, while his entire family and some friends left on yet another junket—this time to South America. It's his world, which is why, after an Easter event at the White House in 2011, the administration released a single photo of Obama watching a child play a game with an egg, but released a slew of pictures spotlighting Obama dribbling a basketball for fawning onlookers.[43] It's his world, which is why the following Easter, he played basketball with NBA players and members of the Harlem Globetrotters using a basketball emblazoned with his own portrait.[44]

It would be one thing for Obama to indulge himself occasionally on the taxpayer dime, but every other week we read about his personal profligacy. How many times did he or Michelle and company fly back to Chicago and elsewhere, or hop a flight to New York City for dinner? How many times did they fly to Martha's Vineyard and live like royalty?[45]

This is a man who played golf eight times in the first eleven weeks of the Gulf oil spill. The aloof, tone-deaf White House staff praised this indolence, with Deputy Press Secretary Bill Burton declaring that Obama's golf outings do "us all good as American citizens. I don't think that there's a person in this country that doesn't think that their president ought to have a little time to clear his mind." A little time? During his first seventeen months in office, Obama played golf thirty-nine times. In other words, he played almost every weekend that it was warm enough to play in Washington or whichever exotic location he happened to be in at the time.[46] By October 2010, Obama had played fifty-two rounds of golf.[47]

While the Left relentlessly ridiculed President George W. Bush for ignoring his job responsibilities in favor of golf, they have barely mentioned Obama's trips to the links. Yet Obama played more golf in less than two years in office than Bush did during his entire eight years.[48] Whereas the press depicted Bush as derelict in his duties, Obama was making judicious use of his downtime to refuel and equip himself to utilize the brain that Joe Biden said was too big for his skull. Nor was Bush credited for ultimately foregoing golf in order to show respect for the families of wounded and fallen soldiers. Obama, by contrast, rarely lets a tragedy get between him and the course.

BO GETS HIS OWN JET

While Obama is unsparing in his vacationing, no one takes a backseat to the first lady when it comes to taxpayer-funded junkets. At a time when congressional Democrats refused to fund visits of Republican congressmen to tour the Gulf oil spill,[49] Obama dispatched Michelle to the scene, though she had no official position and no authority to do anything in connection with the disaster.[50] When she arrived—after stopping in Kansas City to speak to the NAACP about Americans' eating habits and racial problems—she donned her hat as Gulf tour director, saying, "There are still thousands of miles of beaches not touched by the spill. There are still opportunities to experience these beautiful beaches."[51]

Meanwhile, White House press secretary Robert Gibbs was caught flat-footed when CBS's Chip Reid asked him why the Obamas were not vacationing "down there if they are encouraging others to do so." A floundering Gibbs responded, "I think the First Lady's message is that the Gulf is a beautiful place."[52] A few days later, the Obamas jetted to the plush Mount Desert Island, which has been described as "a coastal haven in Maine for old-money Republicans" and "the summer play-ground for the Astors, the Rockefellers and the Morgans," to see the sights and eat lobster.[53] According to a local paper, the Obamas flew their dog to Maine separately in a small jet.[54]

Apparently in response to criticism, the Obamas decided to take their next vacation on the Gulf Coast, in Panama City. Michelle announced, "One of the best ways that fellow Americans can help is to come on down here and spend some money." (She didn't offer any advice as to where they might find that money in this economy.) This would be just the latest vacation since the oil spill, the others being in Asheville, Chicago, and Bar Harbor.[55]

The first family planned another vacation in early August in the posh southern Spanish resort city of Marbella, "a prime holiday destination favored by the rich and famous."[56] Although Obama apparently intended to visit King Juan Carlos and Queen Sofi, reports seemed to indicate this was an excuse to justify the trip rather than a primary reason for it.[57] And despite initial reports, only First Lady Michelle Obama ended up traveling to Spain, accompanied by "long-time family friends," and stayed at the luxurious, five-star Villa Padierna, where all activities on the trip were closed to the press.[58]

There was usually no indication that the Obamas financed these trips themselves. Indeed, as the UK *Daily Mail* reported about Michelle's trip to Spain, "Whether or not the taxpaying American will be paying for meals, they will definitely be footing the bill for the First Lady's 68-strong security detail, her personal staff—and the use of presidential Air Force

Two.... The use of Air Force Two, the Air Force Version of a 757, comes in at 91,900 pounds [around $145,000] for the round trip. This does not include time on the ground."[59] Including all expenses, the *Daily Mail* reported, Michelle's "lavish break in Spain with 40 friends... could easily cost U.S. taxpayers a staggering 50,000 pounds [$79,000] a day.... And her critics will be further annoyed when they learn that the president's wife had a Spanish beach closed off today so that she, her daughter and their entourage could go for a swim."[60]

When the media put a little (*very* little) heat on White House press secretary Robert Gibbs to discuss "the appearance" of the trip, Gibbs responded, "The first lady is on a private trip. She is a private citizen and is the mother of a daughter on a private trip. And I think I'd leave it at that."[61] When a journalist likened Michelle to Marie Antoinette, the White House did a little damage control, protesting that the first lady had gone to Spain to spend time with her best friend, who had lost her father.[62]

Around July 2010, the Obamas took a total of four vacations in a month's time: Bar Harbor, Marbella, Florida, and—of course—Martha's Vineyard, where the family stayed ten days, renting a $20 million estate at an estimated cost of between $35,000 and $50,000 a week. They went on a total of eight vacations by the end of the summer of 2010.[63] While the Obamas were at Martha's Vineyard, according to the Drudge Report, workers at the White House were busy installing new carpets, drapes, painting, and other furnishings in the Oval Office. This appeared particularly insensitive and wasteful given the economic climate at the time.

Eventually, the Obamas' lavishness became the butt of jokes on late-night TV. "He'll have plenty of time for vacations after his one term is up," quipped David Letterman.[64]

AS MUCH POMP AS THE PHARAOHS AND LUDICROUS ROMAN EMPERORS

The granddaddy of all presidential vacations came in October 2010, when the Obamas, as if operating on the scale of the great kings of Ancient Persia, booked eight hundred luxury hotel rooms in Mumbai, including 547 rooms and all the banquet halls at the Taj Mahal hotel, 125 rooms at the Taj President in Cuffe Parade, and between eighty and ninety rooms at the ITC Grand Hyatt. In addition, forty aircraft, including two jets, and forty-five cars, six of them armored, were part of Obama's convoy.[65] It was set to be the biggest trip by any U.S. president in terms of protocol and logistics.[66] Thirty-four U.S. naval ships would be deployed alongside Indian ships to guard the coast outside the hotel. The total cost for Obama's extravagant trip would be an astounding $200 million—per day.[67]

Security teams employed extraordinary measures not just for the main trip, but also for Obama's side tour of the Mani Bhavan Gandhi museum. U.S. military engineers erected a bomb-proof, over-ground, air-conditioned tunnel replete with close-circuit TV cameras and heavily armed guards for his tour. "Probably not since the days of the Pharaohs or the more ludicrous Roman Emperors has a head of state traveled in such pomp and expensive grandeur as the President of the United States of America," observed Britain's *Daily Mail*. "While lesser mortals—the Pope, Queen Elizabeth and so on—are usually happy to let their hosts handle most of the security and transport arrangements when they venture beyond their home shores, the United States creates a mini-America on the move to ensure that nothing is left to chance."[68] It seemed Obama had finally fulfilled his vow to transform America's image abroad.

Perhaps Obama was trying to disprove *Forbes* magazine's recent assessment that Chinese President Hu Jintao, not he, was the most powerful man in the world.[69] But if presidential air travel were any measure, Obama was still quite powerful, for the National Taxpayers Union Foundation published a report showing Obama had set new records for presidential travel costs—far higher than any previously reported.

The U.S. military estimates that it costs $181,757 per hour to operate Air Force One. This cost and accompanying expenses have been amplified for President Obama, who spent more days abroad in his first two years than any other president. "It's astonishing," said the study's author, Demian Brady. "It's far higher than any other ... the figure that's been reported on. It's very surprising, and of course it's just a fraction of the overall cost involved with presidential travel."[70] While the administration disputed some of the cost estimates for his Mumbai trip and others, it would not reveal the actual accounting, as if the public had no right to know.

According to Byron York of the *Examiner*, Obama, as of the beginning of 2011, had spent 339 of his 712 days in office—almost 48 percent—outside Washington. Yet Obama's alter ego, presidential advisor Valerie Jarrett, claimed on *Meet the Press* that Obama's "biggest regret" was that the economic crisis had forced him to "spend almost every waking hour in Washington focusing very hard on solving that crisis," and had prevented him from traveling around to meet everyday Americans. Jarrett quoted Obama as saying, "I really want to figure out a way where I can spend more time outside of Washington listening and learning and engaging the American people."

But if Obama is not seeing enough of Americans, they are certainly seeing plenty of him; in his 712 days in office, York noted, he had only failed to make a public appearance or statement of some sort on forty-five of them.[71] And all these figures, mind you, were established before Obama was to kick his presidential re-election campaign into gear.

"WITH WASHINGTON IN A DEEP FREEZE, OBAMA EXTENDS STAY IN OAHU"

In accordance with his new tradition, Obama took his family and friends to Hawaii again for his Christmas vacation in 2010, in a plush home that rents for $3,500 a night and $75,000 monthly.[72] As usual, the trip incurred enormous costs. Mrs. Obama's early flight to Hawaii cost $63,000; Obama's round-trip flight cost some $1 million. Housing for Secret Service and Seals cost $16,800. There was $134,400 in hotel costs for twenty-four White House staff, excluding meals and other room costs, plus $250,000 in estimated costs for police overtime and $10,000 for ambulance service, for a total cost of $1,474,200. And this did not include expenses for office rental, security upgrades, additional phone lines, car rentals and fuel for White House staff, surveillance prior to his trip, and travel costs for Secret Service and White House staff traveling in advance.

While the White House dismissed these as the ordinary course of business for presidential trips (and again refused to disclose the actual records), the *Hawaii Reporter* observed, "They could have chosen a less expensive and more secure place to stay such as a beachfront home on the Kaneohe Marine Corp Air Station—just a two-minute drive away from the Kailuana Place property where they are now. The president visits the military base daily to workout, bowl with his kids or enjoy the more private beach there. He also could have stayed at a home 15 minutes away on the beach fronting Bellows Air Force Base as President Bill Clinton did." Instead, Obama and his friends chose three luxury beachfront locations, including the $3,500 per day rental home that is "7,000 square feet, with 5 bedrooms, 5 ½ bathrooms, a media room with surround sound, and master-chef-ready kitchen, a secluded lagoon style pool with tropical waterfalls and a lavish island spa."[73]

Obama ended up extending his stay for several days, which caught the notice—again—of the foreign press. Under the headline "Wish you were here? President spends $1.5m on his holiday in Hawaii … while the rest of America faces a bleak New Year," the *Daily Mail* reported, "President Obama has splashed out more than $1.5 million on a sunshine break in Hawaii while many Americans are still struggling in the aftermath of the economic meltdown. With Washington in a deep freeze, Mr. Obama yesterday extended his stay on Oahu until next Monday."[74]

Perhaps Obama wouldn't be criticized as much for his extravagance and self-indulgence if he didn't visit the finest places without regard to or concern for costs to the taxpayer, much less the optics. But it was as if he were trying to make a statement that he and his family were presidential royalty who could do exactly as they pleased, irrespective of America's economic condition, which could explain why he insisted on going to visit a childhood friend in Hawaii, accompanied by a ten-vehicle, twenty-man motorcade.[75]

Obama might have more credibility if he didn't flash $100 bills from his pocket on routine trips to the ice cream stand, which is hardly a suitable image for a president who trucks in class warfare. His professed concerns about income disparities among Americans might ring truer if he didn't let slip, for example, his opinion that the White House press secretary's annual salary of $172,000 was "relatively modest pay."[76] It might seem that he is truly a man of the people if he didn't avail himself and his family of special favors, as when the private school his daughters are attending had its icy sidewalks salted, while the sidewalks of the public school across the street remained uncleared.[77]

People might be more inclined to believe Obama is sincere if he didn't preside over such outrages as serving $199 bottles of wine at White House state dinners.[78] Obama might seem less hypocritical if he weren't hobnobbing and partying with friends and big-shot journalists at a bash for outgoing White House advisor David Axelrod while Egypt was about to be swept up by revolution.[79] If Obama weren't actually brewing his own beer—"White House Honey Ale"—for his own enjoyment, and conspicuously serving it to guests at his frequent White House parties, people might believe he could relate to their difficult circumstances.[80]

"THE MOST GOLF-MAD OF ALL THE PRESIDENTS IN HISTORY"

In February 2011, the first lady took her daughters and friends on another vacation—a ski trip to Vail, Colorado.[81] Their choice of digs, the Sebastian Hotel on Vail Mountain, features rooms ranging from $650 to $2,400 per night. While there, setting aside her usual hectoring about Americans' unhealthy eating habits, Michelle Obama feasted on ancho-chile short ribs at a restaurant beside her luxury ski hotel. Adding to the irony was a recent presidential plea to the American people to live more frugally. "If you're a family trying to cut back," advised Obama, "you might skip going out to dinner, or you might put off a vacation."[82]

Around this time—early March 2011—the president racked up his sixtieth golf outing,[83] the equivalent of two months' recreating on the links. But Obama did take a brief respite from golf when he taped his NCAA picks for airing on ESPN.[84] Obama publicized the ESPN picks in his schedule while the media were simultaneously reporting that Japan had ordered 140,000 of its people to stay indoors to protect themselves from the radiation leak caused by a 9.0-magnitude earthquake and the resulting tsunami that killed some ten thousand people.

The bracket picks followed a night of heavy campaigning with Democratic donors at the St. Regis Hotel.[85] At a press conference NBC News' Mike Viqueira asked Press Secretary Jay Carney, "Is it entirely appropriate for the president to be addressing a crisis of this gravity as he's standing before a whiteboard talking about the basketball tournament?" Without skipping a beat, Carney replied, "There are crises all the time, for every president. And again, this one is happening halfway around the world, and it is severe, and it is important, and it is the focus of a great deal of the president's attention, as are the events in the Middle East, as are the agenda items that he is pursuing to grow the economy." Carney even bragged that Obama, during his bracket frolic on ESPN, had magnanimously urged Americans to donate to the Japanese earthquake victims. "So, yes," said an unapologetic Carney, "I do think it was appropriate."[86]

Obama got back to his golf hobby in short order, however, and by the time the Seals raided bin Laden's compound in May, he had racked up five straight weeks without missing a weekend golf outing, making it a total of sixty-six such outings since his inauguration.[87] He was even playing golf as U.S. special forces prepared to kill bin Laden, a revelation that prompted the UK *Telegraph* to note, "President Obama, it turns out, is by far the most golf-mad of all the Presidents in history."[88] And golf is not the only activity Obama does to excess at taxpayer expense. According to a study by Brendan Doherty, a U.S. Naval Academy assistant professor and expert on presidential travel, as of mid-November 2011, President Obama had visited swing states "on official business" more times in a shorter time-span than either George W. Bush or Bill Clinton. In other words, he campaigns on the taxpayers' dime more than previous presidents did.[89]

In May, Obama opted out of participating in a yearly commemorative service for the families of fallen law enforcement officers. Instead, he played another round of golf with White House aides and friends. This was the second slight against law enforcement that week, as earlier he had hosted controversial rapper "Common" (a.k.a. Lonnie Rashid Lynn, Jr.), whose repertoire includes a song lionizing a convicted cop killer.[90] That incident earned Obama a letter from the Fraternal Order of Police's National President expressing the "profound disappointment" of the organization "over the invitation to a rapper whose body of work includes violent, anti-police lyrics." The letter reminded the White House that National Police Week was a time to honor law enforcement officers for their service and sacrifice.[91]

"FIVE DAYS OF PARTIES, TOASTS AND SIGHTSEEING"

Within a few weeks, Obama had racked up his seventieth golf trip, which he made right after squeezing in a tribute to fallen Americans during a visit to Arlington Cemetery.[92] And a few days later, on June 4, it was reported that he got in his seventy-first round, with his tenth consecutive weekend of golf.[93] Amazingly, his record-breaking streak wasn't over. With his wife off on an African safari of sorts, he achieved his thirteenth weekend in a row before the end of June, with his seventy-fourth outing.[94] But after his seventy-fifth trip, the poor guy had to miss seven weeks in a row and only got in his seventy-sixth round in August 2011, though he planned to make up for the golf fast during his upcoming vacation.[95]

And so he did, even to the point that when he received a call about an earthquake striking Washington, D.C., he kept on playing. As the *Washington Times*' Emily Miller tweeted, "Obama is still playing golf. Not even an act of God can stop him from getting at least 9 holes in today."[96] Before the vacation was over, Obama played his eightieth round, having played all three island courses, just as he did during his vacations the two previous years.[97] By December 26, 2011, Obama had golfed ninety times—equivalent to three months of golfing in less than three years in office.[98]

It took a long time, but eventually the press began to take notice of the Obamas' luxurious lifestyle. The *Hawaii Reporter* noted in August that the Obama family's "pricey vacations are gaining international attention." The *Reporter* cited the *London Daily Mail*, "one of the top news sources in Europe," as highlighting the outrage of Michelle Obama taking a separate jet to arrive four hours early. But that—according to the publication—"is the least of their extravagances.... White House sources today claimed that the First Lady has spent $10 million of U.S. taxpayers' money on vacations alone in the past year."[99] Still, the mainstream media are generally reticent to discuss the Obamas' heavy vacation schedule. This can largely be attributed to their liberal bias, though it can't hurt that the administration wines and dines them. In September 2011, Obama invited one anchor from every network to have lunch at the White House—at taxpayer expense.[100]

Conservatives, however, took more of an interest in Obama's detachment from his duties of office. On Sean Hannity's show, the *Wall Street Journal*'s Stephen Moore observed, "Yes, look, there had been three big crises in the last few months. First, we have the big budget crisis, we saw what happened to the president's budget; it was simply a punt. Then we have the speech the president gave last week on energy policy. I mean, we've got $100 a barrel oil now, Sean. And what did he say? More green energy, more of the same, no change in policy. And ... I think it has been kind of callus to see the president this time, you know, an emergency around the world, to be playing golf and filling out his NCAA [brackets]."

Dana Perino, press secretary to President George W. Bush, added to the list Obama's indecision on Libya. "And what he decides to engage on versus not engage on, it's a moving target, impossible to tell what he actually wants to get across," said Perino. "On Libya, for example, there's still deliberating about a no-fly zone. I mean, at some [point] you either are going to try to help the rebels or you're not, let's just decide and move on."[101]

A few days later, Obama and his family went on a trip that the *Los Angeles Times*' Andrew Malcolm described as "five days of parties, toasts and sightseeing across South America." While he was on what he billed as a diplomatic and trade mission, Obama was under fire for having launched attacks on Libya without congressional approval or consultation. Meanwhile, Vice President Joe Biden had just returned from a fundraising trip to Florida, where he visited the New York Yankees training camp, receiving a cap and jacket, and indulged in photo-ops.

"IT'S HELL. I CAN'T STAND IT"

For her part, Michelle Obama, when not cajoling Americans to eat wood shavings, was self-consciously becoming a style leader, hardly discouraging the media's incessant focus on her wardrobe. *Shine* reported, "Over the past few years, Michelle Obama has generated about $2.7 billion for the fashion industry, just by getting dressed." The report revealed how closely "style guru" Ikram Goldman had worked with Mrs. Obama.[102] While some say she dresses modestly, Michelle apparently enjoys her image as a fashion icon and is unafraid to carry a $1,000 Reed Krakoff two-tone ribboned handbag.[103]

Despite all the attention and fawning press coverage, reports surfaced that Michelle Obama, though luxuriating at taxpayer expense, was not happy in her position as first lady. Carla Bruni, wife of French President Nicolas Sarkozy, in her newly released biography, revealed that Michelle told her that being first lady is "hell. I can't stand it."[104]

Michelle later took a little heat for her high-end fashion choices, wearing $2,000 sundresses and other expensive items. As one critic observed, "She claims to be a champion of the poor and a fellow bargain shopper, but yet, here she is, sporting a dress that no unemployed American can afford."[105]

But the liberal media were not in any rush to expose the Obamas' hypocrisy, and there was scant press mention of the grandiose jewelry Michelle was wearing at a DNC fundraiser in New York in September. According to a report linked by the Drudge Report, she wore "Katie's Lotus cuff priced at $15,000 with 2.9 carats of diamonds, her Gothic cuff at $15,350 with 2.17 carats in diamonds and the Quatrefoil bracelet at $11,800 with 1.73 carats in diamonds."[106]

That $42,000 display of wealth skipped most media attention, but the media establishment was not so quiet when she showed up on the season debut of *Extreme Makeover: Home Edition*, an appearance that provoked ABC News anchor Josh Elliott to rave about what a "cool lady" Michelle Obama is.[107]

Michelle wasn't shy about making fashion something the taxpayers should support. In September 2011, Mrs. Obama joined with TV's Tim

Gunn to honor the nation's top designers at the White House, celebrating innovations from fashion to floor-cleaning products. Straining to shoehorn the production into a public service template, Mrs. Obama said, "Good design is good citizenship."[108]

ABC wasn't the only network swooning over Mrs. Obama. The *Today Show* devoted a segment to showcasing her trip to a Target store in Alexandria, Virginia, showing a series of photos of the event. Capitol Hill correspondent Kelly O'Donnell could barely contain her adoration. "Check this out," she said. "Behind those dark glasses, tucked under that Nike cap, one of the world's most famous women. Yes, that is the First Lady of the United States at Target." Other reporters joined in, praising Mrs. Obama for this media stunt designed to appear that she could relate to ordinary people during tough economic times. "It's great PR for them," commented *Huffington Post* senior politics editor Howard Fineman, "because they can say, 'Look, on this trip and others, we know what's going on outside the gates of the White House.'"[109]

"A BETTER PLANE" AND "A BIGGER ENTOURAGE"

As the first lady alternated between showing off $2,000 dresses and slumming at Target, Barack Obama continued trying to identify with the suffering everyman, stoking class warfare's flames everywhere he went. At a Democratic fundraiser in Boston at the Museum of Fine Arts, he bragged about his record, notwithstanding his failure to make a dent in the sluggish economy despite wasting trillions of dollars on bogus stimulus spending, and even apologized to leftists in attendance for not having spent enough and for going along with some proposed spending "cuts." Obama said that America should not be about the "haves and the have-nots. That's not the America that I envision for Malia and Sasha. And so we're going to have a lot of work to do."[110]

The next day, Obama returned to the White House to host yet another party, this one during midweek, to watch the Chicago Bulls with some of his pals in Congress.[111] He also undermined his common-man shtick during a speech, ostensibly about the tough economic times, at a plant in North Carolina, which he opened by boasting that he had "a better plane" and traveled "with a bigger entourage" than he had when he'd visited the plant some three years ago as a presidential candidate.[112] It's understandable that big money and hefty benefits would be on Obama's mind. At a fundraiser disguised as his fiftieth birthday party in Chicago, tickets sold for as much as $35,800 per couple, with the donations going to Obama's 2012 reelection campaign and the Democratic National Committee.[113]

In June 2011, Michelle Obama took her children, her mother, and friends to South Africa and Botswana at an estimated taxpayer cost of between $700,000 and $800,000.[114] The stated purpose of her trip was "youth leadership, education, health and wellness," which was a controversial allocation of federal funds given the nation's difficult economic times and the federal debt. U.S. Embassy spokeswoman Elizabeth Trudeau allowed that the trip was somewhat of a personal pilgrimage for Michelle Obama.

Because the White House again refused to disclose an itemized listing of the expenses associated with the first lady's trip,[115] on August 19, Judicial Watch filed a Freedom of Information action against the U.S. Air Force to obtain financial records. According to Judicial Watch's website, the military aircraft and crew alone cost at least $424,142. The passenger manifest revealed that the Obama daughters were listed as "senior staff." "This trip was as much an opportunity for the Obama family to go on a safari as it was a trip to conduct government business," declared Judicial Watch President Tom Fitton. "This junket wasted tax dollars and the resources of our overextended military. No wonder we had to pry loose this information."[116]

This back and forth between the White House and Judicial Watch turned into its own news item. *U.S. News & World Report*'s Washington Whispers section reported, "A fight has broken out between the White House, its defenders and a conservative public watchdog group over first lady Michelle Obama's travel costs and how they are calculated." The White House was in a snit over Judicial Watch's tabulation of the costs, but Fitton insisted his numbers were accurate.[117]

"THERE'S NO SUCH THING
AS A PRESIDENTIAL VACATION"

In a Friday document dump, the White House, hoping to avoid the week's news cycle, released figures on its staff salaries. Obama pays twenty-one of his staffers the maximum allowable amount of $172,000 a year and a third of all White House employees make at least $100,000.[118] Despite the struggling economy, more than half the employees received a raise, by an average of 8 percent.[119]

In July, it was reported that the Obamas would be taking another vacation to Martha's Vineyard. The *Boston Herald*'s Margery Eagan, a self-described Obama fan, noted that a new Marist Poll showed that 55 percent of American adults would not take a summer vacation in 2011. "The 'staycation' of 2009," she wrote, "has morphed into the 'Naycation' of 2011. But Obama, who's got us panicked over his debt-ceiling stalemate, will soon be off—again—to Blue Heron Farm, Martha's Vineyard. Check out the pictures of this 'farm' online. You practically drool. It looks like the centerfold of 'Town and Country,' the magazine for aspiring zillionaires. But unless Obama fixes this fiscal disaster—now—he can't go. He should have a staycay like the rest of us."[120]

Again, people were buzzing about the projected price tag, including the mainstream media, some of whom noted that while the Obamas were paying for some of the costs, there would be serious taxpayer funds used for Secret Service and staff housing on the property.[121] The trip was eleven days long and cost taxpayers millions of dollars because of the "dozens of U.S. Secret Service agents, communications officials, top aides, drivers, and U.S. Coast Guard personnel." *U.S. News & World Report* noted that the vacation "comes at an awkward time because of the economic turmoil roiling the nation and Wall Street. Surveys show that a growing number of Americans can't afford even small vacations."[122]

Yet in August it was reported that Michelle Obama had spent forty-two days on vacation in the past year—one out of every nine days—the cost of which was mostly footed by American taxpayers. Her trips included jaunts to Panama City, Martha's Vineyard, Hawaii, South Africa, Latin America, Vail, and Corvallis, Oregon.[123] This was before the eleven-day Martha's Vineyard vacation, which would bring the grand total to fifty-three days. On top of this, as in a previous trip to Hawaii, Mrs. Obama took a separate flight to Martha's Vineyard just so she could arrive with her kids four hours earlier than the president, at an additional cost to taxpayers of thousands of dollars.[124]

While some defended the president's need for downtime, others noted that it wasn't just the vacation itself that was objectionable, but that Obama had promised that during this time he would be "meeting every day" with congressional leaders until they reached a budget deal. He had also scolded Republicans for "walking out of the room" and had assured the nation he had exercised leadership on the issue.

Obama just could not be shamed no matter how luxuriously he recreated while America's economy floundered. ABC News' Jake Tapper asked Press Secretary Carney about the impression Obama's eleven-day vacation might have on the American people, and why, if he was demanding that Congress take these negotiations seriously, he could indulge in "the R&R?" Carney replied, "I don't think Americans out there would begrudge the notion that the President would spend some time with his family." Besides, he continued, "there is no such thing as a presidential vacation. The Presidency travels with you. He will be in constant communication and get regular briefings from his national security team as well as his economic team."[125] This is especially interesting coming from Carney, who once denounced President George W. Bush's working vacations as photo-ops.[126]

With the recent S&P downgrading of America's credit rating, the congressional impasse over the debt, and the volatility of the stock market, some criticized Obama for going on another vacation. "Perception is reality and they've got some bad reality," commented Dana Perino. Even veteran Democratic strategist Bob Shrum said, "The Congress and the president shouldn't be on vacation while tens of millions of Americans are on forced vacations in the form of unemployment."[127]

But in the end, it seemed that no amount of self-indulgence, taxpayer expense, or unnecessary security hassles could keep President Obama from doing precisely what he pleased, precisely when he pleased. The UK *Telegraph* reported that while in Los Angeles in September, Obama wanted to get his workout in. One reporter described what she saw. "'Go on—who is it?' I asked the workmen stapling thick black plastic over the windows of the hotel gym to which I belong.... A stroll down the street told me what they wouldn't. A 40-strong motorcade comprised of blacked-out SUVs, Cadillacs and two armored limousines was parked outside the building. SWAT teams lined the rooftops—their black balaclavas just visible in the sunlight—and above, a Vietnam-style helicopter presence was starting up. President Obama had come to stay."

But not overnight, mind you. He was only in L.A. for twelve hours on a fundraising junket. As the *Telegraph*'s headline read, "Only Barack Obama would bring a SWAT team with him to the gym: No one is allowed near US President Barack Obama when he visits a downtown Los Angeles gym for a workout."[128]

It was only natural, one supposes, that Obama would seek to impress his foreign counterparts with his luxurious lifestyle. On March 14, 2012, Obama and his guest, British Prime Minister David Cameron, flew on Air Force One from Washington, D.C., to Dayton, Ohio, and back to watch an NCAA tournament game between Mississippi Valley State and Western Kentucky. Nile Gardiner of the UK *Telegraph* calculated the cost just for the use of the presidential plane at $478,000. This, said Gardiner, was "symbolic of a big government mentality in Washington that has led to the largest budget deficits since World War Two." Although one might expect a Brit like Gardiner would appreciate the extravagant attention Obama bestowed on the British prime minister, he saw it for what it was. "The trip to Ohio," said Gardiner, "looks very much like an election year visit to a crucial swing state, with David Cameron being cynically used as a campaign prop."[129]

Meanwhile, as Obama was adamantly resisting meaningful spending cuts and holding out for higher taxes, his Office of Government Ethics showed just how out of touch his administration was and how it applied one rule for itself—extravagance—while urging austerity for the rest of us. Judicial Watch reported that this agency was planning a taxpayer-funded conference at a luxurious golf and spa resort in Orlando, Florida.

The federal government would fly hundreds of its employees—whose job description, ironically, is to promote high ethical standards in government—from Washington, D.C., to Florida.[130]

Perhaps the most maddening aspect of Obama's cavalier lifestyle is that it all comes at the expense of the taxpayers to whom Obama preaches the virtue of frugality. He and the first lady jet in style from city to city and country to country, scolding the wealthy for not paying their fair share and for offending all of us with their private jets. We the people, it seems, are expected to simply accept our fate—which, on our current trajectory, is national insolvency—and not ask why the same man who stirs our resentment against more wealthy Americans enjoys a lifestyle on par with European royalty—all financed by our own hard work. Obama himself need not worry about our future debt crisis, since he'll be collecting a generous presidential pension. For the sake of the rest of us, we should get him collecting that pension four years early.

CONCLUSION

In 2012, as the GOP presidential primary contests were unfolding and many Republicans voiced dissatisfaction with the field of candidates, a surprising number of conservatives began to rationalize that our most important goal in November was to win both houses of Congress. If we were to succeed in doing that, they argued, we could stop Obama's agenda and prevent further damage until the 2016 election, when we would no longer have to contend with the bizarre phenomenon of a president whose personal approval ratings remain much higher than those of his policies.

I am skeptical of the conventional wisdom that Obama is still personally popular. Even if some Americans remain duped by his faux charisma, they have seen how he has behaved in office: the bullying, the class warfare, the demonization of opponents, the narcissism, the rigid dogmatism. I was and remain confident that Obama is eminently beatable as long as Republicans don't repeat their mistake of soft-peddling Obama's disastrous record and the danger he represents to the republic, and as long as they aren't cowered into diluting their agenda and abandoning their platform—a decidedly conservative platform—on the mistaken assumption that the only way to defeat him is to cater to so-called centrists.

If there were ever a time in our history that conservatism should be a winning message, it is now, after the nation has suffered from nearly four years of unbridled liberalism. Unlike today's mainstream liberalism, mainstream conservatism is not extremism, and Republicans must quit apologizing for it and running from it. If Republicans soften their message too much, they will demoralize their base and reduce voter intensity, which will be devastating if we are to overcome the inevitable electoral chicanery that we'll see in 2012 from Team Obama's nationwide, coordinated community organizing effort.

The way to win this election is to accentuate and emphasize the stark contrasts between the conservative agenda—a true blueprint for hope, optimism, and national resurrection—and Obama's actual, abysmal record. We've not had a president since Jimmy Carter who has performed so poorly on the economy, foreign policy, and social issues. More important is our runaway national debt; no U.S. president has ever been so willing to push America over the financial cliff as Obama's doing now.

No matter what went on before, no matter how much each party may have contributed to the accumulation of our national debt, Obama has shifted our deficit spending and debt trajectory into hyper-speed, and he and his entire party defiantly refuse to reverse this horrifying trend. They offer no constructive solutions and no semblance of a plan even to stop the fiscal bleeding, much less restructure entitlements to avert the impending disaster. Instead, they demagogue and stir up angst and distrust between people on the basis of race, gender, and, most notably, economic "class." Obama and his Democrats attack the productive and successful, the corporations and the banks, though nothing constructive can come from his broadsides except, from his perspective, a sufficient diversion from his egregious record, without which he can't possibly win re-election.

Whatever we do, we cannot buy into the false notion that a GOP House and Senate will be sufficient to hold us over until 2016. The country, as scrupulously documented in these pages, is on autopilot to bankruptcy. We have only a short window to restructure our entitlements—according to Paul Ryan, between two and three years. So Obama's reelection would ensure that we remain on that course. Not only would a Republican Congress be virtually powerless to reverse Obama's bankrupting policies, but he would see his reelection as a green light to do further end-runs around Congress by ramping up his mischief through renegade administrative agencies that would doubtless be even more defiant and unaccountable in his second term.

Moreover, if you think Obama was radical during his first four years, then wait until he is reelected and has four whole years when he doesn't have to worry about the voters. Just contemplate his agenda to date: his assault on the Constitution, the rule of law, the American idea, and his numerous apologies for America; his attack on the free market and American businesses, corporations, and the U.S. Chamber of Commerce; his appointment of radical czars and liberal activist judges; his $868 billion corrupt and wasteful stimulus bill; his annual deficits consistently in excess of $1 trillion; his reckless path toward doubling the national debt in two terms and his obstruction of entitlement reform; his miserable economy and sky-high unemployment record, his S&P credit downgrade; his mistreatment of our allies and pandering to our enemies; his reprehensible treatment of Israel; his high-handed, unconstitutional invocations of military action without congressional consultation, much less approval; his conversion of the War on Terror into a law enforcement matter; his insulting and semantic redefinition of war to "overseas contingency operations" and "kinetic military actions"; his unconscionable assistance to the Muslim Brotherhood in Egypt; his government's takeover of GM and Chrysler and his restructuring of its loans by lawlessly subordinating the rights of secured creditors to his unsecured union allies; his war against the states on immigration enforcement, abortion funding, and traditional marriage; his EPA's end-runs around Congress and its imposition of draconian rules on American citizens; his unilateral forgiveness and restructuring of mortgage indebtedness; his federal takeover of student loans; his gutting of the military and our national defenses; his support of Big Labor; his NLRB's attack on businesses; his public efforts to intimidate the Supreme Court; his empowering of ACORN and all its corruption; his commandeering of one-seventh of the nation's economy and thwarting the people's will in cramming Obamacare down our throats; his atrocious Dodd-Frank financial bill; his war on oil drilling, the Keystone XL pipeline, and the rest of the conventional domestic energy pantheon; his corrupt federal funding of Solyndra and other green energy debacles; his grossly politicized Department of Justice with its abominable Fast and Furious operation and subsequent cover-up and its racialist application of voter intimidation laws; his war on religious liberty and the right to life; his slander of insurance companies, banks, oil companies, private jet owners, and America itself; his arrogant lack of transparency; his endless rote speeches; his bullying, divisiveness, race-, gender-, and class-warfare; and the myriad other items documented in this book and in *Crimes Against Liberty*.

Next, consider what else Obama might have accomplished had the GOP Congress not stood in his way: cap-and-trade; another $50 billion stimulus bill for high-speed rail; his $447 billion American Jobs Act; capital gains tax hikes; other income tax hikes during his perpetually sluggish economy; and many other spending schemes stopped dead in their tracks—for starters.

Finally, try to imagine what types of overreaches he would attempt if he were re-elected. I have no doubt that if he wins in November, America will be destined to pass the point of no return in its headlong rush to Grecian-style bankruptcy, European socialism on steroids, national weakness, and the end of American freedom as we know it. It will be little comfort to be vindicated in these predictions, because that would mean that our generation had squandered the glorious legacy of freedom bequeathed to us by our parents and grandparents, and that we would have stolen from our children and grandchildren this same wondrous legacy.

It is still not too late to save America and restore her to a path of greatness, of robust liberty, and of economic prosperity. But I fear it is not hyperbole to suggest that it very well may be too late if we don't end this madness in November 2012 by voting Barack Obama out of office. God bless all you patriots fighting for the survival and continued greatness of this nation. God bless the most wonderful Constitution "ever struck off at a given time by the brain and purpose of man," and God bless this American Republic.

ACKNOWLEDGMENTS

Again, I must first thank everyone at Regnery Publishing, with whom I continue to enjoy a tremendous working relationship and whose professionalism and competence make the entire book-writing experience enjoyable instead of drudgery. I especially want to thank Marji Ross and Jeff Carneal for their ongoing support and confidence and for their wisdom in all aspects of the publishing business. I am also indebted to Harry Crocker for his friendship, mentorship, counsel, and enthusiasm for every project in which I've been involved. A sincere thank you goes out to Mary Beth Baker for her proofreading prowess and to the entire Regnery design team, notably Henry Pereira.

For this book as well as its forerunner, *Crimes Against Liberty*, I owe particular gratitude to my primary editor, Jack Langer, for his insight and invaluable ideas, his total accessibility, his work ethic and punctuality, and his unique editing skills which seem to be particularly suited to my writing strengths, and, more importantly, weaknesses. Many thanks as always to my buddy Greg Mueller and his team at Creative Response Concepts for quarterbacking the promotion and marketing of this book along with the excellent marketing staff at Regnery.

I also wish to thank the Heritage Foundation team for their scholarship and writings, and extend a special thanks to Mike Brownfield for clarification on certain articles. Thanks also to John Fleming for providing high resolution charts for this book.

Thanks also to my friend Connie Hair, who works with my friend Congressman Louie Gohmert. Congressman Gohmert graciously arranged for my phone conversations with Congressmen Trey Gowdy and Darrell Issa, who each talked with me in separate, long phone conversations fielding every question I had about Operation Fast and Furious. Thank you also to Katie Pavlich for discussing certain issues about the operation; Katie has just published a fabulous and comprehensive book on this scandal, *Fast and Furious*, to which I devote a mere chapter in this book, that is must reading for those who want to learn the full story of this sordid series of events.

I also thank Conor Sweeney, chief of staff for Congressman Paul Ryan, who patiently walked me through the key differences between Congressman Ryan's original Path to Prosperity and his revised version, as well as other related subjects. His explanations were invaluable. I must also thank my friend Ben Domenech, whose friendship with Conor got me in that door. If you get a chance, check out Ben's "The Transom," an excellent morning daily summary of the relevant news items including his trenchant analysis.

Thanks also to blogger and radio host Ed Morrissey for promptly and graciously answering a number of questions I had about a couple of fine posts he'd written on HotAir.com concerning Obama's green energy spending.

Thanks also to my very good friend Andy McCarthy for his friendship, support, and input on certain national security and terrorism issues on which I required edification for chapter ten.

I'd also like to thank Steven Ertelt for his fine reporting on life issues and his willingness to answer certain questions I had about some of these issues.

As in my previous books I must repeat that I am honored by my friendship with two indispensable forces of nature and incredible talents for the conservative movement and for America: Sean Hannity and Mark Levin. I am forever appreciative of their loyalty and reliability, and their support on my books and countless other things.

Once again I must thank my brother Rush for personally inspiring me, for opening up doors for me directly and indirectly, for leading the charge for American conservatives, and for truly making an immeasurable and positive impact on this nation and the preservation of its Constitution and freedom tradition. It's amazing how often and unfairly he is maligned by people who have never heard his show and instead rely on the vicious slander of others whose antipathy is based on his unparalleled effectiveness as a communicator of the conservative message. On the other hand, no one has a more loyal fan base of people who recognize and appreciate his unique talent, political insight, and his broadcasting and comedic genius.

NOTES

INTRODUCTION

1. Peter Baker, "Obama Making Plans to Use Executive Power," *New York Times*, February 12, 2010.
2. "Obama: Next Two Years Will Be About Implementation Rather than Constant Legislation," Freedom's Lighthouse, August 30, 2010.
3. "How Is President Obama Abusing Presidential Power?" AskHeritage.org, January 6, 2012.
4. "Obama: 'I Have an Obligation As President To Do What I Can Without' Congress," *RealClearPolitics*, January 5, 2012.
5. Lurita Doan, "Obama Proposes New Czar," Townhall.com, September 19, 2011.
6. Joe Schoffstall, "Obama Never Had Contact With Half Dozen Cabinet Officials in First Two Years," MRCTV.org, January 25, 2011.
7. Lurita Doan, "Expansive Role of White House Staffers Undermines Good Government," Townhall.com, October 17, 2011.

8.   Amanda Carey, "Authority given to head of new Consumer Financial Protection Bureau may be unconstitutional," Daily Caller, August 6, 2010.

9.   Rick Moran, "Obama Will Avoid Senate Confirmation Process for Warren Posting," *American Thinker*, September 16, 2010.

10.   Bruce Ackerman, "Obama, Warren and the Imperial Presidency," *Wall Street Journal*, September 22, 2010.

11.   Deborah Solomon and Maya Jackson Randall, "Bank Challenger Picked to Run Consumer Agency," *Wall Street Journal*, July 18, 2011.

12.   Constantine von Hoffman, "Is Obama's appointment of Cordray Illegal?" CBS News, January 5, 2012.

13.   "Senators Demand Accountability For CFPB," The Republic Senate Leader Board, December 6, 2011.

14.   C. Boyden Gray, "Dodd-Frank, the real threat to the Constitution," *Washington Post*, December 31, 2010.

15.   Ibid.

16.   Ibid.

17.   Peter J. Wallison, "Obamacare for the Financial Industry," *Weekly Standard*, April 9, 2012.

18.   Peter Schroeder, "Obama Says He Can Stop Bank of America from Making 'a Certain Amount of Profit,'" *Fox Nation*, Fox News, October 4, 2011.

19.   Steven Ertelt, "NIH Tells Some Embryonic Stem Cell Researchers to Ignore Judge's Ruling," LifeNews.com, September 1, 2010.

20.   Bonner Cohen, Ph.D., "Salazar's Wild Lands Policy Sends Shockwaves Across the West," Committee for a Constructive Tomorrow, January 18, 2011.

21.   Michelle Malkin, "Another Obama Stealth Land Grab: Salazar and the NLCS," MichelleMalkin.com, November 22, 2010.

22.   Rovin, "Obama Administration Passes Dream Act by Executive Memo," HotAir.com, June 26, 2011.

23.   Lynn Sweet, "Obama's La Raza Speech. Plugs Dream Act. Transcript," *Chicago Sun-Times*, July 25, 2011.

24.   Brian Bennett, "Obama Proposes New Rule for Immigrant Families," *Los Angeles Times*, March 30, 2012.

25.   Erik Wasson, "Obama to Launch Summer-Jobs Initiative," *The Hill*, January 5, 2012.

26.   Debra J. Saunders, "Obama Tries to Obstruct Executions," *San Francisco Chronicle*, April 17, 2011.

27.   Erica Werner, "Obama Expected to Boost 'Gun Safety' by Executive Order," CNS News, July 8, 2011.

28. Mark Duell, "Did White House Pressure Air Force General to Help Democrat Donor's Firm Over GPS Worries?" *Daily Mail*, September 16, 2011.

29. Peter Flaherty, "LightSquared Scandal Explodes," National Legal and Policy Center, September 16, 2011.

30. Chester E. Finn, Jr., "The Unilateral Repeal of NCLB and the 2012 Election," *The Corner*, National Review Online, September 23, 2011.

31. Ramsey Cox, "Obama Announces Waiver Plan for States on No Child Left Behind Requirements," *The Hill*, September 23, 2011.

32. Mike Brownfield, "Morning Bell: White House Rules by Fiat Once Again," *The Foundry*, Heritage Foundation, August 9, 2011.

33. "Obama Tells Advisers to Find How To Approve Stimulus Projects 'Without Additional Congressional Authorization,'" *RealClearPolitics*, October 11, 2011.

34. Susan Jones, "The Heck with the Senate: Obama Skips 'Advise and Consent' in Naming 3 New Members of National Labor Relations Board," CNS News, January 5, 2012.

35. Jessica Yellin, "Help for 'Responsible' Underwater Homeowners," CNN, October 24, 2011.

36. Charlie Martin, "College Loan Deal: Worse Than You Think," *PJ Media*, October 26, 2011; Mike Shedlock, "Obama Student Loan Bubble About to Blow," Townhall Finance, February 12, 2012; and Chris Stirewalt, "Obama Taps Taxpayers for Student Stimulus," Fox News, October 26, 2011.

37. Mark Tapscott, "Obama's OMB Ignores Document Subpoena; Upton/Stearns House Panel Says Monday Morning or Else," *Examiner*, July 2011.

38. Philip Klein, "White House Rejects Subpoena Request for Solyndra Docs," *Examiner*, November 4, 2011.

39. Jonathan Strong, "President Obama Snubs Issa on First Major Document Deadline," Daily Caller, February 1, 2011.

40. Jeannie DeAngelis, "Laws Are for the Little People," *American Thinker*, July 3, 2011.

41. Neil Munro, "Fed Instructs Teachers to Facebook Creep Students," Daily Caller, March 16, 2011.

42. "Z Street's Legal Battle Continues Against the IRS," *Weekly Standard*, November 22, 2010.

43. "U.S. Agency Breaks Promise, Opts for No-Bid Contract," *USA Today*, January 22, 2011.

44. Justin Sink, "Obama Adviser Jarrett Defends Church Pulpit Criticism of GOP," *The Hill*, January 17, 2012.

45. PLF Press Release, "Historic Supreme Court Ruling Allows the Sacketts to Fight EPA Takeover of Their Land," Pacific Legal Foundation, March 21, 2012; and "Obama's Tyrannical EPA Goons Get Shot Down By Supreme Court In Idaho Couple's 'Wetlands' Case," *The Freedom Post*, March 21, 2012.

46. "Attorneys General Join Forces to Call Into Account Illegal Obama Administration Violations," *Tea Party Tribune*, March 5, 2012.

CHAPTER ONE

1. Mike Brownfield, "Morning Bell: What is the American Idea?" *The Foundry*, Heritage Foundation, October 27, 2011.

2. Mary Bruce, "White House Defends Apology To Afghanistan; Criticism from Newt Gingrich, Sarah Palin," ABC News, February 23, 2012.

3. "Obama Says His Apology Over Koran Burnings Calmed Anti-US Violence in Afghanistan," Fox News, March 1, 2012.

4. Kyodo, "Obama Hiroshima trip discouraged in '09: Wikileaks cable," *Japan Times*, September 28, 2011.

5. Justin McCurry, "John Roos is first U.S. representative to attend Hiroshima memorial ceremony in Japan," *The Guardian*, August 6, 2010.

6. Kyodo, "Obama Hiroshima trip discouraged in '09: Wikileaks cable," *Japan Times*.

7. Charles Hurt, "Bam AWOL on Vets Day," *New York Post*, November 11, 2010.

8. Eve Zibel, "President Obama Discusses Immigration and Reform Plans in El Salvador," Fox News, March 22, 2011.

9. "Obama's Spiritual Advisor Trashes US in UK," Breitbart TV, December 11, 2010.

10. Jeannie DeAngelis, "He can't resist: Obama bashes Founders on the 4th of July," *American Thinker*, July 6, 2010.

11. Hazel Trice Edney, "First Lady Obama Tells NAACP not to rest," *Madison Times*, July 15, 2010.

12. "Obama: 'Mexicans' Were Here 'Long Before America Was Even An Idea,'" *RealClearPolitics* Video, September 21, 2010.

13. "Obama Praises Indian Chief Who Defeated U.S. General," *Fox Nation*, Fox News, November 15, 2010.

14. Erica Werner, "Back in Iowa, Obama Says USA Must up Its Game," Associated Press, June 28, 2011.
15. Gary Bauer, "Obama's Malaise Speech?" *We Are Politics*, October 28, 2011.
16. Corbett B. Daly, "Obama Says U.S. 'had gotten a little soft' before he took office," CBS News *Political Hotsheet*, September 30, 2011.
17. Jeff Poor, "Krauthammer rips Obama's 'ill-concealed contempt' for Americans: 'It's unseemly,'" Daily Caller, November 14, 2011.
18. Joel Gehrke, "Obama: My kids will succeed, even if USA doesn't," *Examiner*, December 1, 2011.
19. Juliette Kayyem, "Let US see Al Jazeera," *Boston Globe*, February 14, 2011.
20. Ibid.
21. Ed Lasky, "Obama administration official urges cable companies to carry Al-Jazeera," *American Thinker*, February 14, 2011.
22. "Report of the United States of America Submitted to the U.N. High Commissioner for Human Rights," State.gov, undated.
23. Editorial, "Letting crooks and illegals vote," *Washington Times*, January 7, 2010.
24. Wendy Wright, "What Obama Thinks of America," *American Thinker*, January 6, 2011.
25. Ibid.
26. Matt Loffman, "US Cites AZ Immigration Law During Human Rights Talks with China, Conservatives Call It An Apology," ABC News, May 17, 2010.
27. Governor Janice K. Brewer, "Letter to the Honorable Hillary Rodham Clinton, Re: Protest of State Department Report to the United Nations Human Rights Council," Janbrewer.com, August 27, 2010; Governor Janice K. Brewer, "Governor Brewer Condemns U.S. State Department Report to UN Human Rights Council," Janbrewer.com, August 27, 2010.
28. Jonathan S. Tobin, "U.S. Pays Salaries to Palestinian Terrorists," *Contentions, Commentary*, July 26, 2011.
29. Michael Rubin, "State Department Funds Anti-American Propaganda," *Contentions, Commentary*, August 16, 2011.
30. Mel Frykberg, "Palestinians Prepare for Massive Uprising," *IPS News*, July 29, 2011.
31. Neil MacFarquhar, "Peacekeepers' Sex Scandals Linger, On Screen and Off," *New York Times*, September 7, 2011.
32. Penny Starr, "Hillary Clinton: United Nations Is 'Single Most Important Global Institution,'" CNS News, September 8, 2010.

33.   Patrick Goodenhough, "Ban Ki-Moon and U.N. Human Rights Council Face Critical Scrutiny," CNS News, January 26, 2011.

34.   Patrick Goodenhough, "House Foreign Affairs Chairman: U.S. Must Withdraw from U.N. Human Rights Council," CNS News, March 22, 2011.

35.   George Russell, "Budget-Cutting Process Reveals U.S. Overpaid UN by Millions for Its Share of Peacekeeping Expenses," Fox News, April 15, 2011.

36.   Patrick Goodenough, "We Must Pay Our U.N. Bills, Obama Administration Insists," CNS News, June 16, 2011.

37.   Office of the Spokesman, "The United States Joins the International Renewable Energy Agency (IRENA)," U.S. Department of State, March 4, 2011.

38.   Marjorie Ann Browne, *United Nations System Funding: Congressional Issues*, Congressional Research Service, January 14, 2011.

39.   *Statute of the International Renewable Energy Agency (IRENA)*, Conference on the Establishment of the International Renewable Energy Agency, January 26, 2009.

40.   Greg Pollowitz, "Sec. Chu Uses Taxpayer Dollars For Multi-Billion-Dollar Spanish Company," National Review Online, August 23, 2011.

41.   Matthew Boyle, "Obama to speak at NC company shipping jobs to Costa Rica," Daily Caller, September 13, 2011.

42.   Ibid.

43.   Amanda Carey, "Obama discusses jobs at company shifting focus to China," Daily Caller, June 12, 2011.

44.   Patrice Hill, "'Green' jobs no longer golden in stimulus," *Washington Times*, September 9, 2010.

45.   Patrick Thibodeau, "Xerox CEO, an Obama appointee, may send jobs to Indian firm," *Computerworld*, May 23, 2011.

46.   Penny Starr, "U.S. Transportation Secretary: I Told My Daughter to Buy Japanese Car," CNS News, February 9, 2011.

47.   Timothy P. Carney, "U.S. taxpayers guarantee $2.1b loan to German firms," *Examiner*, April 20, 2011.

48.   Shaun McKinnon, "U.S. funds, Arizona effort help Mexico trucks pollute less," *Arizona Republic*, April 11, 2011.

49.   Dylan Stableford, "President Obama's Budget Proposal Doesn't Cut Funds to NPR," *The Wrap*, February 14, 2011.

50.   "Your tax dollars now funding the BBC in addition to NPR," *The PJ Tatler*, March 21, 2011.

51. Editors, "Too Few Of Us Still Believe Our Culture Is Superior," Investors. com, November 21, 2011.

52. "First ever national Spanish spelling bee to be held," Associated Press, July 9, 2011.

53. Editors, "Too Few Of Us Still Believe Our Culture is Superior," Investors. com, November 21, 2001.

54. Devin Dwyer, "Obama Administration Curtails Deportations of Non-Criminal Immigrants," ABC News, August 18, 2011.

55. Tom Fitton, "NCLR Funding Skyrockets After Obama Hires Its VP," *Judicial Watch*, June 20, 2011.

56. Lynn Sweet, "Obama's La Raza Speech. Plugs Dream Act. Transcript," *Chicago Sun-Times*, July 25, 2011.

57. Mark Krikorian, "Yes, He Did! Yes, He Did!" National Review Online, August 19, 2011.

58. "Academia Semillas Del Pueblo (Seeds of the People Academy): Training the Next Generation of Mexican Revolutionaries with American Tax Dollars?" A Judicial Watch Special Report, Judicial Watch, 2006.

59. Ibid.

60. Ibid.

61. Tom Fitton, "NCLR Funding Skyrockets After Obama Hires Its VP," Judicial Watch.

62. Michelle Mondo and Allan Turner, "Despite Obama bid, Mexican executed for Texas teen's death," *Houston Chronicle*, July 8, 2011.

63. John G. Winder, "Obama and the U.N. Trying to Delay Texas' Execution of Humberto Leal," *Cypress Times*, July 4, 2011.

64. Ibid.

65. Ibid.

66. Michelle Mondo and Allan Turner, "Despite Obama bid, Mexican executed for Texas teen's death," *Houston Chronicle*.

67. Humberto Fontova, "State Dept. Official Hails Che Guevara as Symbol of Freedom," Townhall.com, November 21, 2011. See also Josh Halliday, "Hillary Clinton adviser compares internet to Che Guevara," *The Guardian*, June 22, 2011.

68. Humberto Fontova, "Fantasies of Nuclear War," Frontpagemag.com, July 26, 2010.

69. "Navy Officially Names New Ship After Cesar Chavez," 10News.com, May 16, 2011.

70. John Rossomando, "Commerce nominee appears to endorse world government in video, Republicans say," Daily Caller, June 7, 2011.

71. Cliff Kincaid, "Obama Endorses Global Taxes on Eve of U.N. Summit," Accuracy in Media, September 16, 2010.

72. Ibid.

CHAPTER TWO

1.   M. Alex Johnson, "Barack Obama elected 44th president," MSNBC, November 5, 2008.

2.   "Obama Tells Republicans to 'Sit in Back,'" Fox News, October 25, 2010.

3.   "Obama on Tea Partiers: 'You Would Think They'd Be Saying Thank You,'" *RealClearPolitics* Video, April 16, 2010.

4.   Greg Halvorson, "Obama calls Republicans 'hostage takers,'" *Canada Free Press*, December 7, 2010.

5.   "Transcript of President Barack Obama with Univision," *Los Angeles Times*, October 25, 2010.

6.   Christi Parsons, "Obama's speech to high school also a subtle jobs bill pitch," *Los Angeles Times*, September 29, 2011.

7.   Devin Dwyer, "At Ohio Rally, Obama Says Jobs Plan 'Isn't About Giving Me a Win,'" ABC News, September 13, 2011.

8.   President Barack Obama, "Remarks By the President at DNC Finance Event in Atlanta, Georgia," WhiteHouse.gov, August 2, 2010.

9.   Mark Knoller, "Obama Casts Republicans as Slurpee Sippers," CBS News *Political Hotsheet*, October 8, 2010.

10. President Barack Obama, "Remarks By the President at DNC Finance Event: in Atlanta, Georgia," WhiteHouse.gov.

11. "Obama: 'Republicans Messed Up So Bad' That Millions Are Still Out of Work," *RealClearPolitics*, October 10, 2010.

12. "Obama on GOP: 'The Empire Is Striking Back,'" *RealClearPolitics*, October 17, 2010.

13. "Obama brands Republicans as radicals," Agence France-Presse, October 22, 2010.

14. "Obama: Republicans Will Have to Learn to Get Along With Me," Fox News, October 13, 2010.

15. Matt Negrin, "Obama: GOP agenda is, 'defeat me,'" *Politico*, November 2, 2010.

16. "Obama: Republicans Will Have to Learn to Get Along With Me," Fox News.

17. Meredith Jessup, "Obama Rallies With MoveOn.org Day After Election Upsets," *The Blaze*, November 3, 2010.

18. "Obama Appeals for 'Common Ground' After Democrats Lose House," Fox News, November 3, 2010.

19. Ibid.

20. Josh Gerstein, "Obama turns up the rhetoric," *Politico*, February 5, 2009.

21. Helene Cooper and Jeff Zeleny, "Obama Calls for a New Era of Civility in U.S. Politics," *New York Times*, January 12, 2011.

22. "Did Sarah Palin's Target Map Play [a] Role in Giffords Shooting?" The Atlantic Wire, January 10, 2011.

23. Jonathon Martin, Ben Smith, and Alexander Burns, "Violence and politics merge," *Politico*, January 9, 2011.

24. Conn Carroll, "Combative Obama blames debt crisis on Congress," *Examiner*, June 29, 2011.

25. Ibid.

26. "Carney: Obama Telling People To Tweet GOPers Is A 'Bipartisan Message,'" *RealClearPolitics*, July 29, 2011.

27. Jonathan M. Seidl, "Politico: Biden Likens Tea Party Republicans to 'Terrorists,'" *The Blaze*, August 1, 2011.

28. Jonathan Allen and John Bresnahan, "Sources: Joe Biden likened tea partiers to terrorists," *Politico*, August 1, 2011.

29. Neil Munro, "Obama defaults to economic blame game," Daily Caller, June 7, 2011.

30. Nile Gardiner, "Even in China, Joe Biden couldn't resist using the Tea Party as a political punching-bag," *Telegraph*, August 22, 2011.

31. Helene Cooper, "Obama Urges Voters to Scold Republicans," *New York Times*, August 11, 2011.

32. Sam Youngman, "Obama: 'Last thing we need,' is for Congress to return to DC," *The Hill*, August 11, 2011.

33. "Obama to Frustrated Voters: Tell Congress to Start Delivering," Fox News, August 13, 2011.

34. Keither Koffler, "Michelle: GOP Would Curb Freedom of Speech, Religion," *White House Dossier*, October 28, 2011.

35. Mary Bruce, "Hoffa On Tea Party: 'Let's Take These Sons Of Bitches Out!'" ABC News *Political Punch*, September 5, 2011.

36. Doyle McManus, "Obama's new tone," *Los Angeles Times*, September 8, 2011.

37. John Matthews, "WMAL Exclusive; Listen – Obama's New Rule for Political Civility," WMAL.com, September 7, 2011.

38. Neil Munro, "White House releases talking points to liberals ahead of speech," Daily Caller, September 8, 2011.

39.   Ben Smith and Jonathan Martin, "Obama plan: Destroy Romney,"
      Politico, August 9, 2011.

40.   Tim Graham, "Obama Adviser Says 'He Will Have to Kill Romney,'"
      NewsBusters, August 9, 2011.

41.   Jeff Poor, "Garofalo: Herman Cain a paid prop to 'deflect' charges of GOP
      racism," Daily Caller, August 18, 2011.

42.   "Obama Team Sharpens Attacks on Republican Field, Defends President,"
      Fox News, August 14, 2011.

43.   President Barack Obama, "Remarks by the President at the Human Rights
      Campaign's Annual National Dinner," WhiteHouse.gov, October 1, 2011.

44.   "Obama schedules jobs speech on the same night as GOP debate,"
      Houston Chronicle, August 31, 2011.

45.   Colby Hall, "Jay Carney: White House Not Interested in Bickering; Just
      Wants to Create Jobs," *Mediate*, September 1, 2011.

46.   Michael O'Brien, "WH official: Obama struggling in polls because voters
      don't know GOP opponents," *The Hill*, September 1, 2011.

47.   Jim Provance, "Ohio on front lines of labor fight," *Toledo Blade*,
      September 5, 2011.

48.   Jonathan Capehart, "Andre Carson was wrong to invoke lynching,"
      Washington Post, September 6, 2011.

49.   Ed Henry, "Obama Conversation With Tea Partier Gets Heated," Fox
      News, August 15, 2011.

50.   Laura MacInnis, "Obama accuses Congress of holding back recovery,"
      Reuters, August 20, 2011.

51.   Fred Lucas, "Obama Suggests Republicans Want a 'Race to the Bottom,'"
      CNS News, September 9, 2011.

52.   Abby Phillip, "Obama: GOP leaders 'don't get it,'" *Politico*, July 3, 2010.

53.   Lori Ziganto, "NBC News Race Card Play Rejected at Tea Party,"
      RedState.com, April 16, 2010.

54.   Rick, "Were racial slurs hurled at John Lewis and his entourage by Tea
      Party members?" *Wizbang Blog*, March 21, 2010; and "Tea Party
      Protestors Dispute Reports of Slurs, Spitting Against Dem Lawmakers,"
      March 22, 2010.

55.   "NAACP Resolution Calls on Tea Party to Repudiate 'Racist Elements' in
      Movement," Fox News, July 14, 2010; and Lynn Sweet, "Michelle Obama
      in NAACP speech, compares crusade against obesity to civil rights battles.
      Transcript," *Chicago Sun-Times*, July 13, 2010.

56.   Kenneth T. Walsh, "Obama Says Race a Key Component in Tea Party
      Protests," *U.S. News & World Report*, March 2, 2011.

57. Joe Newby, "Jim Wallis says Fox News 'assassin of Obama's religion,'" Examiner.com, November 27, 2010.

58. Charlie Savage, "Under Partisan Fire, Holder Soldiers On," *New York Times*, December 17, 2011.

59. John Newby, "Dem. Congressman blames Fast and Furious on NRA, Tea Party, Senate," Examiner.com, December 9, 2011.

60. David French, "A Broad-Based IRS Assault on the Tea Party?" *The Corner*, National Review Online, March 2, 2012.

61. "Obama's Team Crosses the Rhetorical Line," *The Foundry*, Heritage Foundation, September 1, 2009.

62. Jeffrey T. Kuhner, "Is Obama fomenting a race war?" *Washington Times*, April 30, 2010.

63. Transcript, "Transcript of President Barack Obama with Univision," *Los Angeles Times*, October 25, 2010.

64. Andrew Restuccia, "Michelle Obama urges Latino community to pressure GOP to back immigration bill," *The Hill*, February 12, 2011.

65. Lynn Sweet, "Obama black radio blitz in Chicago, Philadelphia, Milwaukee, Florida, Ohio," *Chicago Sun-Times*, October 19, 2010.

66. John, "Obama Says 'Other Side' Trying to 'Hijack Democracy,' Bring 'Hand to Hand Combat,'" *Verum Serum*, October 8, 2010.

67. Michael A. Memoli, "GOP takeover of Congress would mean 'hand-to-hand combat,' Obama warns," *Los Angeles Times*, October 7, 2010.

68. Peter Wallsten, "Obama to Blacks: Vote Like I'm on the Ballot," *Wall Street Journal*, October 26, 2010.

69. "Biden: 'If We Lose, We're Going To Play Hell,'" *RealClearPolitics* Video, October 8, 2010.

70. "Obama: Republicans Counting on Blacks Staying Home," *RealClearPolitics*, October 11, 2010.

71. "Obama rallies minority voters, says Latinos feel 'under assault,'" MyFoxOrlando.com, November 2, 2010.

72. Sam Youngman, "At campaign event Biden mentions rape in criticizing Republicans," *The Hill*, March 18, 2011.

73. Jon Cohen and Peyton M. Craighill, "About a third of Americans say Obama's presidency has improved race relations," *Washington Post* Behind the Numbers, January 17, 2011.

74. Suzanne Murray, "Morgan Freeman Says Obama Has Made America More Racist," TheStir.CafeMom.com, September 24, 2011.

75. Jeffrey T. Kuhner, "Is Obama Fomenting a Race War?" *Washington Times*.

76. John Roberts, "African-American Middle Class Eroding As Unemployment Rate Soars," Fox News, July 28, 2011.

77. Jon Ward, "Dunn acts as Obama attack dog on mosque, says GOP 'solidifying its reputation for intolerance,'" Daily Caller, August 17, 2010.

78. Ibid.

79. David Limbaugh, *Crimes Against Liberty* (Washington, D.C.: Regnery, 2010), 188.

80. Daniel Strauss, "@BarackObama urging users to tweet Republicans on debt ceiling," *The Hill*, July 29, 2011.

81. Rob Bluey, "White House uses Twitter to bully critics," Daily Caller, July 6, 2011.

82. Ed Morrissey, "WH tweeting at gnats; Update: White House responds," HotAir.com, July 6, 2011.

83. Sam Stein, "White House Beefs Up Online Rapid Response," *Huffington Post*, July 23, 2011.

84. "Inside Media Matters: Sources, memos reveal erratic behavior, close coordination with White House and news organizations," Daily Caller, February 2, 2012

85. Ibid.

86. Ibid.

87. Neil Munro, "Obama spokesman asks GOP to 'put country before party' hours after Obama implored Americans not to question each others' patriotism," Daily Caller, October 16, 2011.

88. "Obama: GOP Wants 'Dirtier Air, Dirtier Water, Less People With Health Insurance,'" *RealClearPolitics*, October 17, 2011.

89. Keith Koffler, "Obama launches cultural warfare," *Politico*, October 16, 2011.

90. Ibid.

91. Stephen Clark, "Obama Official: GOP Budget Would Kill 70,000 Kids," Fox News, April 1, 2011.

92. Daniel Halper, "Geithner: 'Privilege of Being an American' Is Why Rich Need Higher Taxes," *The Weekly Standard* blog, February 24, 2012.

93. Jason Horowitz, "For David Plouffe, a top Obama adviser, a new strategy and old doubts," *Washington Post*, September 27, 2011.

94. Ibid.

95. David Nakamura and Paul Kane, "President Obama goes on the attack, to Democrats' delight," *Washington Post*, October 4, 2011.

96. Ibid.

97. Carol E. Lee, "Obama to GOP: 'We Don't Have Time for Games,'" Washington Wire, *Wall Street Journal*, April 5, 2011.

98. Stephanie Kirchgaessner, "Obama tells Congress to act like 'grown ups,'" *Financial Times*, April 5, 2011.

99. Emily Esfahani Smith, "Obama Tells Congressional Leaders To 'Act Like Grownups' On Budget," *The Blaze*, April 5, 2011.

100. Tyler Burden, "The Petulant Teleprompter: Obama 'Abruptly' Walks Out Of Debt Negotiations," *Zero Hedge*, July 13, 2011.

101. Carol E. Lee, "Obama to GOP: 'We Don't Have Time for Games,'" *Wall Street Journal*.

102. Chris Stirewalt, "Obama-Boehner Fight Gets Ugly," Fox News, April 6, 2011.

103. Jonathan Strong, "Obama chats with Boehner by phone for three minutes before flying to Philly," Daily Caller, April 6, 2011.

104. "Geithner: Republicans Will Be to Blame if US Defaults," MoneyNews.com, April 14, 2011.

105. "Carney: Obama Agrees GOP Approach To Budget Is 'Immoral,'" *RealClearPolitics*, June 27, 2011.

106. Perry Bacon Jr., "Obama's budget speech has partisan tone," *Washington Post*, April 13, 2011.

107. Ibid.

108. Ibid.

109. Allahpundit, "Paul Ryan rips Obama's speech: 'Rather than building bridges, he's poisoning wells,'" HotAir.com, April 13, 2011.

110. Mira Oberman, "Republicans Will Make US 'Third World' Nation: Obama," Agence France-Presse, April 15, 2011.

111. Michael O'Brien, "White House says it 'forced Republicans to back down' in debt fight," *The Hill*, August 4, 2011.

112. "Obama Reflects on Debt Fight: Didn't Need This 'Manufactured Crisis,'" *RealClearPolitics*, August 2, 2011.

113. Steven T. Dennis, "Debt Deal Emerging With Rightward Tilt," *Roll Call*, August 1, 2011.

114. Jonathan Allen and John Bresnahan, "Sources: Joe Biden likened tea partiers to terrorists," *Politico*.

115. Jeff Poor, "Maxine Waters: 'The tea party can go straight to hell,'" Daily Caller, August 21, 2011.

116. Julie Pace, "Obama Calls GOP Medicare, Spending Plan 'Radical,'" AOLNews.com, April 20, 2011.

117. Ben Geman, "Obama jabs 'climate change deniers,'" *The Hill*, April 21, 2011.

118. President Barack Obama, "Obama: Let's reclaim the post-9/11 unity," *USA Today*, September 8, 2011.

119. "Obama Says Americans reject Tea Party ideas," Breitbart.com, September 12, 2011.

120. Devin Dwyer, "At Ohio Rally, Obama Says Jobs Plan 'Isn't About Giving Me a Win,'" ABC News, September 13, 2011.

121. Jason Horowitz, "For David Plouffe, a top Obama adviser, a new strategy and old doubts," *Washington Post*, September 27, 2011.

122. Jackie Calmes, "At Fund-Raisers, Obama Refers to Audiences at G.O.P. Debates," *New York Times*, September 26, 2011.

123. Sam Youngman, "Obama Mocks Perry, Republican debates," *The Hill*, September 26, 2011.

124. Jason Horowitz, "For David Plouffe, a Top Obama adviser, a new strategy and old doubts," *Washington Post*.

125. Jordan Fabian, "Boehner responds to Obama's 'hot mic' Jab," *The Hill*, April 15, 2011.

126. Peter Wehner, "Obama the Divider," *Contentions, Commentary*, October 7, 2011.

127. "Obama Adviser: Shutdown Looms as GOP Bends to Will of Tea Party," Fox News, September 25, 2011.

128. Erica Werner, "Obama Says GOP Would 'Cripple' America," CBS News, September 25, 2011.

129. Shannon Travis, "Analysis: Obama's second year is the most polarizing since Eisenhower," CNN *Political Ticker*, February 4, 2011.

CHAPTER THREE

1. "Combative Obama warns Supreme Court on health care," Agence France Presse, April 2, 2012.

2. Mike Riggs, "Updated: White House asked California paper to take out unflattering remark about first lady," Daily Caller, May 3, 2011.

3. Allahpundit, "Report: White House asked small California paper to remove negative remarks about First Lady," HotAir.com, May 3, 2011.

4. Rob Bluey, "White House uses Twitter to bully critics," Daily Caller, July 6, 2011.

5. Phil Bronstein, "Update: Chronicle responds after Obama Administration punishes reporter for using multimedia, then claims they didn't," SFGate. com, April 28, 2011.

6. Ibid.

7. Macon Phillips, "Change has Come to WhiteHouse.gov," WhiteHouse. gov, January 20, 2009, http://www.whitehouse.gov/blog/change_has_come_to_whitehouse-gov.

8. Rob Bluey, "White House Uses Twitter to Bully Critics," Daily Caller.

9. "President Obama Goes on the Attack Against Oil Companies," Fox News, undated.

10. Michael Riley, "A New Agency Will Go After Oil Royalties," *Bloomberg Businessweek*, October 28, 2010.

11. Ibid.

12. Tait Trussell, "Oil Producers Bullied," FrontPageMag.com, November 23, 2010; and Michael Riley, "Oil Royalty Agency Threatens Fines in Wake of Spill and Corruption Scandal," Bloomberg, October 28, 2010.

13. Ken Thomas, "Biden warns Republicans on debt-ceiling talks," *Washington Times*, June 26, 2011.

14. Jim McElhatton, "Wage initiative stymies labor nominee," *Washington Times*, August 28, 2009.

15. Carl Horowitz, "Labor Department Solicitor Adopts Plan to Bully Employers," National Legal and Policy Center, December 9, 2010.

16. Ibid.

17. John Fund, "Government By Executive Order," *Wall Street Journal*, December 3, 2010.

18. Ibid.

19. Ibid.

20. John Bellows, "Just the Facts: S&P's $2 Trillion Mistake," U.S. Department of the Treasury, August 6, 2011.

21. Richard Adams, "US attacks S&P's 'credibility and integrity' over debt downgrade," *The Guardian* Richard Adams's Blog, August 7, 2011; and "Obama administration official: S&P move 'a facts-be-damned decision,'" CNN, August 8, 2011.

22. Jeannette Neumann and Aaron Lucchetti, "S&P President Says Firm Was 'Objective' in Its Analysis," *Wall Street Journal*, August 7, 2011.

23. "Obama administration official: S&P move 'a facts-be-damned decision,'" CNN.

24. Matt Schneider, "Bob Schieffer To David Axelrod On Downgrade: 'Are You Saying The President Bears No Responsibility?'" Mediate.com, August 7, 2011.

25. Kara Scannell, "SEC Makes S&P Downgrade Inquiries," CNBC, August 12, 2011.

26. Jeff Mason, "Biden: more US stimulus needed, business mad at S&P," Reuters, August 26, 2011.

27. Elizabeth Flock, "Attack Watch, new Obama campaign site to 'fight smears,' becomes laughing stock of conservatives," *Washington Post*, September 14, 2011.

28. Ibid.

29. Howard Fischer, "Horne: Obama wants illegal immigrants to vote in Arizona," *East Valley Tribune*, June 7, 2011.

30. Jonah Goldberg, "Proof of Life," *The Daily*, March 18, 2012.

31. David Fredosso, "DOJ goes after tea partiers, leaves club-wielding Black Panthers alone," *Examiner*, October 18, 2010.

32. Ibid.

33. J. Christian Adams, *Injustice: Exposing the Racial Agenda of the Obama Justice Department* (Washington, DC: Regnery, 2011), 103. (Hereinafter *Injustice*.)

34. Laura Johnston, "Cuyahoga County Board of Elections told to print bilingual ballots or be sued," *Cleveland Plain Dealer*, August 10, 2010; "Justice Department Announces Agreement With Cuyahoga County, Ohio, Board Of Elections On Protecting The Rights Of Spanish-Speaking Puerto Rican Voters," Department of Justice press release, September 1, 2010; and "Editorial: Dead in Ohio, but still voting," *Washington Times*, September 2, 2010.

35. "Editorial: Dead in Ohio, but still voting," *Washington Times*.

36. Ibid.

37. J. Christian Adams, "Eric Holder Probing State Voter ID Laws," *PJ Tatler*, July 27, 2011.

38. J. Christian Adams, *Injustice*, p. 3.

39. "GOP Disputes Obama's Claim That Border Security Has Improved," Fox News, May 10, 2011.

40. "Holder Floats Possibility of Racial Profiling Suit Against Arizona," Fox News, July 11, 2010.

41. Penny Starr, "Arizona Sheriff: 'Our Own Government Has Become Our Enemy,'" CNS News, August 1, 2010.

42. "Department of Justice Challenges Alabama Immigration Law," Department of Justice press release, August 1, 2011.

43. Bridget Johnson, "Issa: Justice Lawsuit against Arizona is a 'misuse of the Supremacy Clause,'" *The Hill*, July 11, 2010.

44. "Justice Department Asks Appeals Court to Block Alabama's Immigration Law," Fox News, October 7, 2011.

45. Ibid.

46. Ibid.

47. Katie Pavlich, "Which State is Getting Sued by the Obama Justice Department Now? South Carolina," Townhall.com, November 1, 2011.

48. Scott Rasmussen, "67% Say States Should Be Able to Enforce Immigration Laws If Feds Are Not," *Rasmussen Reports*, February 18, 2011; and Scott Rasmussen, "60% Think Federal Government Encourages Illegal Immigration," *Rasmussen Reports*, December 16, 2011.

49. Kent Faulk, "Updated: U.S. Justice Department files court challenge to Alabama's new immigration law," *Birmingham News*, August 1, 2011.

50. Neil Munro, "Obama's inspectors scour Alabama for immigration law abuses," Daily Caller, October 14, 2011.

51. Ibid.

52. Katie Pavlich, "Which State is Getting Sued by the Obama Justice Department Now? South Carolina," Townhall.com.

53. Mara Sacchetti, "R.I. troopers embrace firm immigration role," Boston.com, July 6, 2010.

54. "White House Denies Flood Assistance," KOCO.com, July 3, 2010.

55. Jay Nordlinger, "Re 'To Be a Republican Lawmaker in Madison,'" *The Corner*, National Review Online, February 17, 2011.

56. "Jay Sorgi, "Capitol Chaos: Sen. Fitzgerald Claims Democrats Using Delay For Recall Efforts," 620wtmj.com, March 8, 2011; and "Team Obama Directly Working to Recall Wisconsin Republicans," Americans for Tax Reform, March 8, 2011.

CHAPTER FOUR

1. Steven Ertelt, "Biden to China: 'Not Second-Guessing' One-Child Policy," LifeNews.com, August 22, 2011.

2. Charlie Spiering, "WH: Biden finds China one-child policy 'repugnant,'" *Examiner*, August 23, 2011.

3.   Steven Ertelt, "Clinton Can't Say if Obama Asked Hu About Forced Abortions," LifeNews.com, March 3, 2011.

4.   Tim Graham, "Obama Announces 'Bilateral Talks' With Lady Gaga on Gays," *NewsBusters*, October 2, 2011.

5.   Patrick Ryan, "Education Dept. Blocks Reporters from LGBT 'Youth Summit' Sessions for Teens," CNS News, June 7, 2011.

6.   Nirvi Shah, "Duncan Warns Schools on Banning Gay-Straight Clubs," *Education Week*, June 14, 2011.

7.   Dave Blount, "Big Government Comes Out of the Closet at Federal LGBT Youth Summit," *Right Wing News*, June 7, 2011.

8.   Penny Starr, "Obama Administration Youth Summit: Gov't 'Has Finally Come Out of the Closet,'" CNS News, June 6, 2011.

9.   Jeff Zeleny, "Obama Signs Hate Crimes Bill," *New York Times*, October 28, 2009; and Kathleen Gilbert, "Obama admin introduces gay rights declaration at UN," LifeSiteNews.com, March 22, 2011.

10.   Glenn Thrush, "LGBT memo—Clinton, Obama target bias," *Politico*, December 6, 2011.

11.   Igor Volsky, "White House Press Secretary Challenged On Obama's 1996 Gay Marriage Questionnaire," ThinkProgress.org, June 20, 2011.

12.   Chris Johnson, "Pressure mounts on Obama to back marriage," *Washington Blade*, June 22, 2011; and Greg Sargent, "Obama's position on gay marriage: still evolving," *Washington Post*, June 20, 2011.

13.   "Obama On Gay Marriage Position: 'I'm Still Working On It,'" *Huffington Post*, October 3, 2011.

14.   Helene Cooper, "Obama to Support Repeal of Defense of Marriage Act," *New York Times*, July 19, 2011.

15.   Jim Meyers and David A. Patten, "Boehner: Obama Wrong on Defense of Marriage Act," *Newsmax*, November 9, 2011.

16.   "Family Research Council Sues Obama Justice Department for Documents Regarding Decision Not to Defend Defense of Marriage Act," press release, *Judicial Watch*, August 31, 2011.

17.   Ibid.

18.   "North Carolina Bishops Criticize Obama Statement on Marriage Amendment," *Catholic World News*, March 23, 2012.

19.   Terence P. Jeffrey, "Archbishop Warns Obama: You'll Cause 'Conflict Between Church and State of Enormous Proportions,'" CNS News, September 29, 2011.

20. Targeted News Service, "Obama Official Tells 100s of Youth: We're Recruiting Homosexuals to Adopt Kids," *Targeted News Service*, June 12, 2011.

21. Terence P. Jeffrey, "Archbishop Warns Obama: You'll Cause 'Conflict Between Church and State of Enormous Proportions,'" CNS News.

22. Thomas Messner, "Yet Another Attack on Marriage," *The Foundry*, Heritage Foundation, November 2, 2011.

23. "Bishops Call on Faithful to Oppose Bill That Would Repeal DOMA," *National Catholic Register*, November 2, 2011.

24. Terence P. Jeffrey, "Archbishop Warns Obama: You'll Cause 'Conflict Between Church and State of Enormous Proportions,'" CNS News.

25. Thomas Messner, "The Price of Prop 8," Heritage Foundation, October 22, 2009.

26. Thomas Messner, "Same-Sex Marriage and the Threat to Religious Liberty," Heritage Foundation, October 30, 2008.

27. Nathan Black, "Christian Consultant Fired by Bank of America Over Gay Marriage Book," *Christian Post*, September 4, 2011.

28. "Fact Sheet: Willock v. Elane Photography," Alliance Defense Fund, http://oldsite.alliancedefensefund.org/userdocs/ElanePhotoFactSheet.pdf.

29. Thomas Messner, "From Culture Wars to Conscience Wars: Emerging Threats to Conscience," Heritage Foundation, April 13, 2011.

30. "Big Victory for Religious Hiring in a World Vision Case," Institutional Religious Freedom Alliance, August 29, 2010.

31. "Same-Sex Marriage and State Anti-Discrimination Laws," Becket Fund for Religious Liberty Issues Brief, January 2009.

32. Terence P. Jeffrey, "DOJ: Feds Can Tell Church Who Its Ministers Will Be," CNS News, October 12, 2011.

33. Charles C. Haynes, "At the High Court, High Stakes for Religious Freedom," *St. Petersburg Progress-Index*, October 18, 2011.

34. Editorial Board, "The Supreme Court and the 'Ministerial Exception,'" *Christian Science Monitor*, October 3, 2011.

35. Warren Richey, "Supreme Court justices find government line in church-state case 'amazing,'" *Christian Science Monitor*, October 5, 2011.

36. "Supreme Court Sides with Church 9-0 in Landmark First Amendment Ruling," The Becket Fund for Religious Liberty, January 11, 2012.

37. Tom Bowman, "Marine Leaders Would Prefer Gay Troops Not Tell," NPR.org, November 29, 2010.

38. Jim Kouri, "Military commanders oppose openly gay military policy," Examiner.com, August 27, 2010, http://www.examiner.com/law-

Notes

enforcement-in-national/military-commanders-oppose-openly-gay-military-policy.

39. Elaine Donnelly, "DoD Inspector General Exposes Improper Activities to Repeal the Law re Gays in the Military (Don't Ask, Don't Tell)," Center for Military Readiness, June 2011.

40. Ibid.

41. William Dunham, "Obama hails end of U.S. military restrictions on gays," Reuters, September 20, 2011.

42. Robert Ritchie, "Aborted Fetal Cell Lines Used to Test Food Products," The American Society for the Defense of Tradition, Family and Property, March 31, 2011.

43. Julie Rovner and Jenny Gold, "Obama Lifts Limit On Funding Stem Cell Research," NPR, March 10, 2009.

44. Shelby Lin Erdman, "Judge stops federal funding of embryonic stem cell research," CNN, August 23, 2010.

45. "Arguments Against Embryonic Stem Cell Research," The American Policy Roundtable, 2007; and Steven Ertelt, "Judge Dismisses Suit Against Obama Embryonic Stem Cell Funding," LifeNews.com, July 27, 2011.

46. Steven Ertelt, "Appeals Court Allows Obama to Fund Embryonic Stem Cell Research During Suit," LifeNews.com, September 9, 2010.

47. Ibid.

48. Steven Ertelt, "President Obama Also Kills Bush Executive Order for Adult Stem Cell Research," LifeNews.com, March 10, 2009.

49. Charles Babington and Darlene Superville, "Obama Tells Questioner He's 'Christian by Choice,'" Associated Press, September 28, 2010.

50. Christine C., "Obama: Freedom of Choice Act 'Not Highest Legislative Priority,'" *Our Bodies Ourselves*, April 30, 2009.

51. Gary Bauer, "Bishops Battling Big Government," American Values Email Alert, November 15, 2011; and Representative Chris Smith, "President Obama denies trafficking victims grant to Catholic Bishops over abortion," *Catholic Philly*, December 5, 2011.

52. Mary, "On the 39th Anniversary of Roe v. Wade," BarackObama.com, January 22, 2012.

53. Steven Ertelt, "President Barack Obama's Pro-Abortion Record: A Pro-Life Compilation," LifeNews.com, November 7, 2010.

54. Steven Ertelt, "Abortion Advocates Didn't Expect Obama Transition Team to Publish Memo," LifeNews.com, December 10, 2008.

55. Steven Ertelt, "Pro-Abortion Groups Issue 55-Page Marching Orders for Barack Obama Admin," LifeNews.com, December 10, 2008.

56. Jake Tapper, "Obama Overturns 'Mexico City Policy' Implemented by Reagan," ABC News, January 23, 2009.

57. Steven Ertelt, "Obama Administration Promotes Pro-Abortion Agenda at UN Women's Meeting," LifeNews.com, March 11, 2009; and "Barack Obama Forces Taxpayers to Fund, Promote Worldwide Abortions," LifeNews.com, January 1, 2009.

58. "Access to Health Care Under CEDAW = Abortion Rights," EagleForum.org, August 15, 2002.

59. Jeanne Monahan, "Abortion, the United Nations, and CEDAW," Family Research Council Blog, March 15, 2010.

60. "Senate Hearing on Women and Arab Spring Includes Discussion of CEDAW," *Ms. Magazine*, November 4, 2011.

61. Steven Ertelt, "Obama Policy Resulted in 300 Tax-Funded Abortions in D.C.," LifeNews.com, July 7, 2011.

62. Patrick O'Connor, "Historic Win Close After Bart Stupak Deal," *Politico*, March 21, 2010.

63. Family Research Council, "Executive Order Will In No Way Prevent Federal Funding of Elective Abortion," PRNewswire.com, March 21, 2010.

64. Michael James, "Obama Administration Clarifies Rules on Abortion Funding in Health Care Legislation," ABC News, July 14, 2010.

65. Kathryn Jean Lopez, "Obamacare Covers Abortion in Pennsylvania – and in New Mexico, Too," National Review Online, July 14, 2010.

66. Steven Ertelt, "Obama Admin Authorized Abortion Funding in Third State Under Health Care Law," LifeNews.com, July 16, 2010.

67. Jason Millman, "Health Secretary Sebelius: 'There is no taxpayer funding for abortion,'" *The Hill*, January 21, 2011.

68. Kathryn Jean Lopez, "Obamacare in Kenya?" National Review Online, July 12, 2010; and "Obama Lauds Passage of Kenyan Constitution As Critics Slam Its Abortion Rights Stand," Fox News, August 5, 2010.

69. Jeff Sagnip and Steven Ertelt, "Probe: Obama Admin Broke Law to Push Abortion in Kenya," LifeNews.com, November 16, 2011.

70. "State Department Rebuffs Watchdog's Advice Following Abortion Flap Over Kenya Constitution," Fox News, November 15, 2011.

71. Ryan Jaslow, "Abortion tied to sharp decline in women's mental health," CBS News, September 1, 2011; Priscilla K. Coleman, "Abortion and

mental health: quantitative synthesis and analysis of research published 1995–2009," *British Journal of Psychiatry*, (2011); "Abortion Risks: A list of major psychological complications related to abortion," AfterAbortion.org, February 23, 2011; "Peer review: aborted women suffer mental anguish and worse," *No Apologies,* September 5, 2011; and Steve Doughty, "Women who have abortions 'face double the risk of mental health problems,'" *Daily Mail*, September 1, 2011.

72. Tina Korbe, "Obama DOJ Takes Elderly Pro-Life Sidewalk Counselor to Court," HotAir.com, July 21, 2011.

73. James Henderson, Sr. and Jordan Sekulow, "Obama Admin's Targeting of Pro-Lifers Shows Pro-Abortion Bias," LifeNews.com, November 9, 2011.

74. Terence P. Jeffrey, "Boehner-Obama Deal Permits Funding for Group That Does 910 Abortions Per Day," CNS News, April 9, 2011.

75. Jill Stanek, "Breaking News: Planned Parenthood recruits abortion volunteers thru Obama's Serve.gov" JillStanek.com, October 20, 2009.

76. Erik Wasson, "Obama threatens appropriators with veto," *The Hill*, October 20, 2011.

77. Steven Ertelt, "Obama Admin Defunds Planned Parenthood Funding in Indiana," LifeNews.com, June 17, 2011.

78. Caroline May, "White House protects abortion provider, allows cuts to community health centers," Daily Caller, April 13, 2011.

79. Steven Ertelt, "Obama Admin Ignores Planned Parenthood Sex Trafficking Videos," LifeNews.com, March 2, 2011.

80. Steven Ertelt, "Obama Admin Demands New Hampshire Restore Planned Parenthood $," LifeNews.com, July 21, 2011.

81. "Obama to bypass Governor and Council to directly fund Planned Parenthood," *New Hampshire Union Leader*, September 8, 2011.

82. Steven Ertelt, "Komen's Karen Handel Resigns After Planned Parenthood Dispute," LifeNews.com, February 7, 2012.

83. Ben Johnson, "Planned Parenthood guilty of tens of millions of dollars in fraud charge whistleblowers, report," LifeSiteNews.com, February 16, 2012.

84. David Schmidt, "Planned Parenthood Pushes Bill Forcing Mandatory Abortion Coverage on Pro-Lifers," LiveAction.org, February 11, 2012.

85. Matthew Clark, "Planned Parenthood: All About Abortion, All the Time," LifeNews.com, December 12, 2011; and Steven Ertelt, "Alaska Court Holds Hearing on Abortion-Parental Notification," LifeNews.com, September 8, 2011.

86. Chuck Donavan, "The Vanderbilt Abortion Decision: How Obama Can Better Protect Civil Rights," *The Foundry,* Heritage Foundation, January 19, 2011.

87. Ibid.

88. "Transcript: Obama's Notre Dame Speech," *Chicago Tribune*, May 17, 2009.

89. Steven Ertelt, "President Obama Starts Process of Removing Doctors' Protections on Abortions," LifeNews.com, February 27, 2009.

90. Steven Ertelt, "Obama Takes Next Step to Scrap Protections for Pro-Life Doctors on Abortion," LifeNews.com, March 6, 2009.

91. Steven Ertelt, "Obama Misleads on Federal Abortion Conscience Clause in Health Care Speech," LifeNews.com, September 10, 2009.

92. Steven Ertelt, "Congressmen Challenge President Obama on Abortion-Conscience Clause Promise," LifeNews.com, May 19, 2009.

93. Steven Ertelt, "Obama Admin Working to Rescind Conscience Rights on Abortion," LifeNews.com, December 14, 2010.

94. The concern over these so-called contraceptive drugs was hardly manufactured hysteria by pro-life advocates. On June 17, 2010, the Obama administration, via an FDA advisory committee approved the new abortion drug ulipristal, to be sold in the United States under the name "Ella," which some euphemistically labeled a "morning after pill." The Advisory Committee for Reproductive Health Drugs approved what others call an "early abortion drug" by unanimous vote. The panel, by adopting the clever rhetorical device of redefining the beginning of pregnancy from conception to implantation, said that women could use the drug to prevent pregnancy when taken up to five days after intercourse. This formulation allowed the panel to disregard that the drug actually kills a human being. It's not contraception; it's abortion. In their seeming zeal to approve the drug, the panel apparently couldn't be sure—because the drug sponsor wasn't even sure—whether Ella could cause birth defects, or what might happen to pregnant women who take it. Despite that gap in knowledge, the committee strongly recommended not giving women a pregnancy test, according to Wendy Wright, president of Concerned Women for America. "The committee voted to deceive women," said Wright. Advocates of the drug said the FDA would likely make it prescription only, but proponents of the Plan B drug said the same thing, which didn't keep abortion activists from high-pressure lobbying for it to be sold over the counter, nor from pushing for sales of the drug to minors without a doctor visit or parental consent or notification.

95. Steven Ertelt, "Obama Admin Weakens Protections for Pro-Life Medical Workers," LifeNews.com, February 18, 2011.

96. Ibid.

97. Steven Ertelt, "Groups: Obama Admin Decision Violates Catholic Conscience Rights," LifeNews.com, August 1, 2011.

98. Ibid.

99. Kathleen Gilbert, "Sebelius reiterates Obama: birth control mandate pays for itself because fewer babies are born," LifeSiteNews.com, March 2, 2012.

100. Steven Ertelt, "Groups: Obama Admin Decision Violates Catholic Conscience Rights," LifeNews.com, August 1, 2011.

101. Sarah Torre, "House Panel Hears How HHS Mandate Tramples on Conscience Rights," Heritage Foundation *The Foundry*, November 3, 2011.

102. "HHS: Obamacare Requires Coverage of Abortion Drugs," *ACLJ*, January 23, 2012.

103. John McCormack, "More on Obama's Phony Compromise," *Weekly Standard*, February 11, 2012.

104. Steven Ertelt, "Cardinal: Catholic Hospitals May Close in Two Years Under Mandate," LifeNews.com, February 27, 2012.

105. Steven Ertelt, "Obama's HHS Mandate Sparks Nationwide Pro-Life Protests," LifeNews.com, February 27, 2012.

106. "Abstinence and Sex Education" Avert.org, 2010.

107. Shannan Martin, Robert Rector, and Melissa G. Pardue, "Comprehensive Sex Education vs. Authentic Abstinence: A Study of Competing Curricula," Heritage Foundation, August 10, 2004.

108. Budget of the United States Government, FY 2007, GOP.gov.

109. Ewen MacAskill, "Obama to scrap funding for abstinence-only programmes," *The Guardian*, May 8, 2009.

110. Steven Ertelt, "Obama, Congress Cut Funding for 176 Abstinence Programs Despite New Study," LifeNews.com, August 26, 2010.

111. Ibid.

112. Sharon Jayson, "Obama budget cuts funds for abstinence-only sex education," *USA Today*, May 11, 2009.

113. Michael McAuliff, "President Obama's budget cuts funding for abstinence-only sex education programs," *New York Daily News*, May 8, 2009.

114. "Abstinence Works! Studies Validating the Efficacy of Abstinence Education," National Abstinence Education Association, April 12, 2007.

115. Christine Kim and Robert Rector, "Executive Summary: Evidence on the Effectiveness of Abstinence Education: An Update," Heritage Foundation, February 19, 2010.

116. Steven Ertelt, "Obama Admin Relents, Posts Pro-Abstinence Education Study After Complaints," LifeNews.com, August 24, 2010.

117. Shannan Martin, Robert Rector, and Melissa G. Pardue, "Comprehensive Sex Education vs. Authentic Abstinence, A Study of Competing Curricula," Heritage Foundation, 2004.

118. "Obama Supports Kindergarten Sex Ed," Fox News Radio, July 13, 2010. The entire plan can be read here: http://www.helena.k12.mt.us/images/documents/curriculum/HealthCurriculum/K12FinalHealth.pdf.

119. A'Melody Lee, "Sex Ed for Kindergartners 'Right Thing to Do,' Says Obama," ABC News, July 18, 2007.

120. Kiki Bradley, "Twelve-Anti-Family Gifts from Congress," *The Foundry*, Heritage Foundation, December 25, 2009.

121. Ibid.

122. Daniel Doherty, "Thomas Sowell Blasts Liberal Professor Derrick Bell," Townhall.com, March 10, 2012.

123. Madeleine Morganstern, "CNN Host Loses It Over Obama Harvard Vid, Calls White Supremacist Aspect of Critical Race Theory 'A Complete Misreading,'" *The Blaze*, March 8, 2012.

124. Mythcos Holt, "Revealed: The Radical Racial Ideas of the Prof. Obama Raves About in New Harvard Video," *The Blaze*, March 7, 2012.

125. See the video here: http://www.youtube.com/watch?v=tz3qShugQ9I&fe ature_player_embedded.

126. La Shawn Barber, "Washington Times on Thomas Perez," American Civil Rights Institute, September 29, 2009.

127. Jennifer Haberkorn, "Exclusive: Panel sees race bias in health care bill," *Washington Times*, August 11, 2009.

128. "Amid Controversy Over Obama's Green Jobs Adviser, GOP Renews Criticism of White House Czars," Fox News, September 5, 2009.

129. Seton Motley, "Audio: FCC's Diversity Czar: 'White People' Need to be Forced to 'Step Down' 'So Someone Else Can Have Power,'" *NewsBusters*, September 23, 2009.

130. Alexander Burns and Josh Gerstein, "White House to Sonia Sotomayor critics: Be 'careful,'" *Politico*, May 27, 2009.

131. Joe Dejka, "OPS Busy 8,000 diversity manuals," *Omaha World-Herald*, July 10, 2011.

132. Kevin Bogardus, "Vilsack looks to finalize black farmers' settlement," *The Hill*, November 29, 2010.

133. Krissah Thompson, "USDA Secretary Vilsack says agency will adopt recommendations on diversity," *Washington Post*, May 11, 2011.

134. Roger Clegg, "Obama Issue Executive Order on 'Diversity,'" National Review Online, August 19, 2011.

135. William Tate, "Race Played Role in Obama Car Dealer Closures," *American Thinker*, July 22, 2010.

136. Paul Sperry, "DOJ Begins Bank Witch Hunt; New Lax Credit Cycle; Administration Pushes Loans to Minorities – Job Status Not an Issue," *Investors Business Daily*, July 11, 2011.

137. Roger Clegg, "Obama Administration Files Brief Supporting Racial Preferences in University Admissions," *The Corner*, National Review Online, March 15, 2010.

138. Morgen, "White House Initiates Budget Push Centered Around Identity Politics," *Verum Serum*, February 16, 2011.

139. Hazel Trice Edney, "White House Outlines Tax Benefits for Black Families," *The Louisiana Weekly*, December 28, 2010.

140. "Former Justice Department Lawyer Accuses Holder of Dropping New Black Panther Case for Racial Reasons," Fox News, June 30, 2010.

141. J. Christian Adams, *Injustice*.

142. Andrew C. McCarthy, "Breitbart: Obama Appeared and Marched with New Black Panther Party in 2007 – Photos Included," *The Corner*, National Review Online, October 3, 2011.

143. Hans A. Von Spakovsky, "Stop the Presses: Shutting Down the Civil Rights Commission's Investigation of DOJ," PJ Media, February 15, 2011.

144. J. Christian Adams, *Injustice*.

145. Hans A. von Spakovsky, "Stop the Presses: Shutting Down the Civil Rights Commission's Investigation of DOJ."

146. "Editorial: Black Panther case: Red Hot," *Washington Times*, September 24, 2010.

CHAPTER FIVE

1. Matt Cover, "Flashback: Obama in 2008: Adding $4 Trillion in National Debt 'Unpatriotic,'" CNS News, August 24, 2011.

2. Ed Gillespie, "Myths & Facts About the Real Bush Record," *RealClearPolitics*, December 22, 2008.

3. Dr. Tim Renz, "Tax Truth," *Dr. Tim's Moment of Clarity*, November 25, 2011.
4. Jim Hoft, "Ya Think?... Obama Says He Will Be Judged in 2012 Over the Economy," *Gateway Pundit*, August 21, 2011.
5. Mike Brownfield, "Stimulus Three Years Later: Obamanomics Has Failed," *The Foundry*, Heritage Foundation, February 17, 2012.
6. J.D. Foster, "Obama's November Jobs Deficit One More Reason to Extend Bush Tax Cuts," *The Foundry*, Heritage Foundation, December 3, 2010.
7. Timothy Conley and Bill Dupor, "The American Recovery and Reinvestment Act: Public Sector Jobs Saved, Private Sector Jobs Forestalled," report updated May 17, 2011, web.econ.ohio-state.edu/dupor/arra10_may11.pdf.
8. Jeffrey H. Anderson, "Obama's Economists : 'Stimulus' Has Cost $278,000 per Job," *Weekly Standard*, July 3, 2011.
9. Peter Suderman, "CBO on the Stimulus: 'A net negative effect on the growth of GDP over 10 years,'" Reason.com, November 17, 2011.
10. *Understanding and Responding to Persistently High Unemployment*, Congressional Budget Office, February 2012.
11. Brian Riedl, "Why the Stimulus Failed," *The Corner*, National Review Online, September 7, 2009.
12. James Sherk, "Delayed Recovery Historically Slow," Heritage Foundation, February 14, 2012.
13. Ibid.
14. Annalyn Censky, "Black Unemployment: Highest in 27 years," CNN *Money*, September 2, 2011.
15. Terence P. Jeffrey, "Obama Calls for More Redistribution of Wealth, Declaring: 'I Am My Brother's Keeper," CNS News, April 2, 2012.
16. Justin Hart, "Does Obama [Hate] Poor People," *I Hart Politics*, September 13, 2011.
17. Heidi Shierholz, "Labor Force Participation Skewing Unemployment Numbers," *US News & World Report*, March 13, 2012.
18. James Sherk, "Delayed Recovery Historically Slow."
19. Ibid.
20. Devin Dwyer, "Your Money: Billions in Stimulus Funds Paid to Tax Delinquent Contractors," ABC News, May 24, 2011.
21. Senator Tom Coburn, M.D., and Senator John McCain, "Summertime Blues, 100 Stimulus Projects that Give Taxpayers the Blues," Senate.gov, August 2010.
22. "Where Did All the Money Go," GOP.com, February 17, 2012.

23. Shikha Dalmia, "Treasury Admits What Everybody Already Knew: Taxpayer Losses On GM Bailout Are Going to be Massive," Reason.com, November 17, 2011.

24. Matt Cover, "True Cost of Fannie, Freddie Bailouts: $317 Billion, CBO Says," CNS News, June 6, 2011.

25. Tim Mak, "Austan Goolsbee Flunks 'Cash For Clunkers,'" *Politico*, October 20, 2011.

26. Doug Powers, "California High Speed Rail Project Triples in Projected Cost, Won't Be Ready for 22 Years," MichelleMalkin.com, November 1, 2011.

27. Emily Goff and Romina Boccia, "Infrastructure Spending Would Not Create Jobs," in Mike Brownfield, "Reaction Roundup: Heritage Responds to Obama's 2013 Budget Proposal," Heritage Foundation, February 13, 2012 (hereafter "Reaction Roundup"); Ronald Utt, "More Transportation Spending: False Promises of Prosperity and Job Creation," Heritage Foundation, April 2, 2008; Brian Riedl, "Why Government Spending Does Not Stimulate Economic Growth: Answering the Critics," Heritage Foundation, January 5, 2010.

28. John Hayward, "International Study Confirms Government Spending Crushes the Economy," *Human Events*, December 15, 2011.

29. Bob Beauprez, "February: Worst Monthly Deficit in History," Townhall.com, March 11, 2012.

30. Mike Brownfield and Emily Goff, "The Truth about Obama's Budget Deficits, in Pictures," *The Foundry*, Heritage Foundation, July 28, 2011.

31. Jeff Poor, "Krauthammer calls Obama budget 'worthy of Greece,' 'truly scandalous,'" Daily Caller, February 13, 2012.

32. David Freddoso, "Obama's budget includes 'Death Star' savings," *Examiner*, February 13, 2012.

33. Editors, "Obama's 2013 Budget: A Monument To Irresponsibility," Investors.com, IBD Editorials, February 13, 2012.

34. J. D. Foster, "What Would Obama Do? Insights from His Budget," in "Reaction Roundup," Heritage Foundation, February 13, 2012.

35. "The Daily History of the Debt Results," TreasuryDirect.gov.

36. "President's Budget Charts Path to Debt and Decline," House Budget Committee and Senate Budget Committee Republican Summary of President's FY2013 Budget, February 13, 2012.

37. Patrick Louis Knudsen, "President Obama's Budget Proposal: Running on Empty," in "Reaction Roundup," Heritage Foundation, February 13, 2012.

38. David Jackson, "Obama jokes about 'shovel-ready projects,'" *USA Today*, June 13, 2011.

39. Patrick Louis Knudsen, "President Obama's Budget Proposal Running on Empty," in "Reaction Roundup," Heritage Foundation, February 13, 2012.

40. Lindsey Burke, "Budget Further Grows Bureaucracy at Department of Education," in "Reaction Roundup," Heritage Foundation, February 13, 2012.

41. Lindsey Burke, "Morning Bell: Top 10 Education Stories of 2011," Heritage Foundation *The Foundry*, December 27, 2011.

42. Curtis Dubay, "Obama's Budget: A Barrage of Economy-Slowing Tax Hikes," in "Reaction Roundup," Heritage Foundation, February 13, 2012.

43. J. D. Foster, "Obama's Budget Sings a Golden Oldie: 'Do You Believe in Magic?'" in "Reaction Roundup," Heritage Foundation, February 13, 2012.

44. Andrew Restuccia, "Energy's IG: Goal of stimulus law unrealistic," *The Hill*, November 2, 2011.

45. Nicolas Loris, "Obama's Energy Budget: The Antithesis of a Market-Driven Energy Economy," in "Reaction Roundup," Heritage Foundation, February 13, 2012.

46. Nicolas Loris, "Obama's Energy Budget: The Antithesis of a Market-Driven Energy Economy."

47. Terence P. Jeffrey, "Gallup: Uninsured Have Increased Under Obama and Since Obamacare Was Enacted," CNS News, September 6, 2011.

48. David Limbaugh, *Crimes Against Liberty*.

49. Alana Goodman, "ObamaCare Gross Cost Expected to Double," *Commentary*, March 14, 2012.

50. Ibid.

51. Julian Pecquet, "CBO Report Says Healthcare Law Could Cause as Many as 20M to Lose Coverage," *The Hill*, March 15, 2012.

52. "Firms to cut health plans as reform starts: survey," *MarketWatch*, June 6, 2011.

53. "The Health Care Reform Survey 2011-2012," Willis, 2012.

54. Sam Baker, "Republican probes $111 billion in jump in cost of healthcare law," *The Hill*, March 2, 2012.

55. "The Uncertainty of ObamaCare Is Causing Small Business to Flat-Line," GOP.com, February 15, 2012.

56.   Reed Abelson, Gardiner Harris, and Robert Pear, "Whatever Court Rules, Major Changes in Health Care Likely to Last," *New York Times*, November 14, 2011.

57.   "The Future of Health Care, a National Survey of Physicians," The Doctors Company Market Research, February 29, 2012.

58.   Gina Kolata, "Considering When It Might Be Best Not to Know About Cancer," *New York Times*, October 29, 2011.

59.   Glenn Reynolds, "Early Cancer Detection: Suddenly, It's Not Good for You After all," Instapundit.com, October 31, 2011.

60.   Grover Norquist, "The Five Tax Hikes in Obamacare That Most Hurt Seniors," Daily Caller, March 18, 2012.

61.   Alison Meyer, "Chart of the Week: Obamacare's 17 New Taxes," *The Foundry*, Heritage Foundation, March 25, 2012.

62.   Michelle Malkin, "Taxing medical progress to death," *Human Events*, February 17, 2012.

63.   Gerald Prante, "Would 'Obamacare' (Health Care Reform) Tax the Sale of Your Home? Probably Not," Tax Foundation, *Tax Policy Blog*, September 24, 2010.

64.   Grover Norquist, "The Five Tax Hikes in Obamacare That Most Hurt Seniors."

65.   Kathryn Nix, "The President's Budget on Health Care: Too Little, Too Late, Totally Wrong Direction," in "Reaction Roundup," Heritage Foundation, February 13, 2012.

66.   Sam Baker, "House panel votes to ax health law's cost-cutting board," *The Hill*, March 6, 2012.

67.   J.D. Foster, Ph.D., "Premium Support Is Incremental, Not Radical Medicare Reform," Heritage Foundation, February 7, 2012.

68.   Michelle Malkin, "The $4 Billion Obamacare Slush Fund for Progressives," Townhall.com, February 24, 2012.

69.   Ibid.

70.   Joel Gehrke, "WH backs away from Obamacare as economic plus," *Examiner*, March 19, 2012.

71.   "How long are the Obamacare regulations? 5x the length of the Obamacare statutes," *Obamacare Watcher*, February 29, 2012.

72.   Sam Baker, "HHS finalizes over 1,200 waivers under healthcare reform law," *The Hill*, January 6, 2012.

73.   Administrator, "List of health reform waivers keeps growing," *The Hill*, April 2, 2011.

74. Michael Barone, "Obama skirts rule of law to reward pals, punish foes," *Examiner*, May 2011.

75. Matthew Boyle, "Nearly 20 percent of new Obamacare waivers are gourmet restaurants, nightclubs, fancy hotels in Nancy Pelosi's district," Daily Caller, May 17, 2011.

76. Baker, "HHS finalizes over 1,200 waivers under healthcare reform law."

77. "5-4 Ruling Against ObamaCare a Likely Scenario," David Horowitz Freedom Center, March 28, 2012.

78. See Obama's remarks at http://www.youtube.com/watch?v=AAmtNCtdWeo.

79. John Hayward, "White House Budget Director Destroys ObamaCare's Supreme Court Defense," *Human Events*, February 15, 2012.

80. NRO Staff, "Krauthammer's Take," National Review Online, July 12, 2011.

81. Mike Brownfield, "Reaction Roundup: Heritage Responds to Obama's 2013 Budget Proposal," *The Foundry*, Heritage Foundation, February 13, 2012.

82. James J. Carafano, Ph.D. and Alison Acosta Fraser, "Senate Initiative Would Block Blow to Military Readiness," Heritage Foundation Web Memo on National Security and Defense; and Baker Spring, "Obama's Budget Shortchanges America's Vital National Security," in "Reaction Roundup," Heritage Foundation, February 13, 2012.

83. Michaela Bendikova, "President's 2013 Budget Guts Military," in "Reaction Roundup," Heritage Foundation, February 13, 2012.

CHAPTER SIX

1. Congressman Paul Ryan, "A Roadmap for America's Future, Roadmap Plan 2.0," House Budget Committee, Republicans.

2. John Hayward, "White House Budget Director Destroys Obamacare's Supreme Court Defense," *Human Events*, February 15, 2012.

3. *Fiscal Year 2013 Analytical Perspectives, Budget of the U.S. Government*, Office of Management and Budget, February 2013.

4. Representative Paul D. Ryan, Chairman, "Rep. Paul D. Ryan Holds a Hearing on FY2013 Revenue and Economic Policy Proposals," 2012 *CQ Transcriptions*, February 16, 2012.

5. Ibid.

6. Ibid.

7. Senator Kent Conrad, Chairman, "Sen. Kent Conrad Holds a Hearing on FY2013 Budget and Revenue Proposals," 2012 *CQ Transcriptions*, February 16, 2012.

440   *Notes*

8.   Ibid.
9.   James Pethokoukis, "U.S. debt crisis might be on fast track," Reuters, July 7, 2011.
10.   Chairman Paul Ryan, *The Path to Prosperity, Restoring America's Promise*, House Committee on the Budget, April 5, 2011. I obtained updated and revised information directly from the congressman's staff for which I am very grateful.
11.   Chairman Paul Ryan, *The Path to Prosperity, A Blueprint for American Renewal, Fiscal Year 2013 Budget Resolution*, House Budget Committee, 2013.
12.   Ibid.
13.   U.S. Congressman Paul Ryan, "Charts and Graphs," A Roadmap for America's Future, The Budget Committee Republicans, 2013.
14.   "CBO Director: Trillion-Dollar Deficits Risk 'Fiscal Crisis' in U.S.," Fox News, January 27, 2011.
15.   "Obama to Push for New Spending as GOP Demands Deep Budget Cuts," Fox News, January 22, 2011.
16.   Charles Krauthammer, "The Elmendorf Rule," *Washington Post*, July 8, 2011.
17.   Erik Wasson, "Obama budget falls far short of debt commission savings plan," *The Hill*, February 13, 2011.
18.   Conn Carroll, "Obama's Fake Budget Spending Cuts," *The Foundry*, Heritage Foundation, February 14, 2011.
19.   Andrew Stiles, "Obama's Spending Spree: By the Numbers," National Review Online, February 14, 2011.
20.   Guy Benson, "Obama Defends Budget Proposal, Lies Repeatedly," Townhall.com, February 15, 2011.
21.   David Limbaugh, "Responsible Adults Cannot Ignore These Numbers," DavidLimbaugh.com, February 18, 2011.
22.   Summary Tables FY2012, http://www.whitehouse.gov/sites/default/files/omb/budget/fy2012/assets/tables.pdf#page=3.
23.   Tim Nerenz, "Tax Truth," *Moment of Clarity* blog, November 25, 2011.
24.   Brian Riedl, "Obama Budget Adds $80,000 per Household to National Debt," *The Foundry*, Heritage Foundation, March 23, 2011.
25.   Fred Lucas, "Obama Budget Nominee Admits Current Budgets Higher than Bush Debt," CNS News, March 23, 2011.
26.   Ibid.
27.   President Barack Obama, "Remarks of President Barack Obama – As Prepared for Delivery," *Wall Street Journal*, April 13, 2011.

28. Karl Rove, "Obama Versus Bush on Spending," *Wall Street Journal*, January 21, 2010.

29. Editors, "The Presidential Divider," *Wall Street Journal*, April 14, 2011.

30. "CBO: President's Speech Not A Serious Budget Plan," House Budget Committee, video uploaded to YouTube.com, June 23, 2011.

31. Alexander Bolton, "President's budget sinks, 97-0," *The Hill*, May 25, 2011.

32. "Mega-FAIL: Obama's Budget Goes Down In Flames, Defeated 414-0 In House…" *Weasel Zippers* blog, March 29, 2012.

33. Paul Ryan, Chairman, "Actions Speak Louder Than Words," House Committee on the Budget, HBC Publications, July 15, 2011.

34. Philip Klein, "Transcript: WH spokesman struggles to explain why Obama hasn't released detailed plan," *Examiner*, July 2011.

35. John R. Parkinson, "House Passes Paul Ryan Budget Proposal in Partisan Vote," ABC News, April 15, 2011.

36. David Rogers, "Senate votes down Paul Ryan budget plan, 57-40," *Politico*, May 25, 2011.

37. Chairman Jim Jordan, "Cut, Cap, and Balance," Republican Study Committee, June 2011; and Brian Darling, "Cut, Cap, and Balance," *The Foundry*, Heritage Foundation, June 6, 2011.

38. John Hayward, "Against the ATM Scourge," *Human Events*, June 14, 2011.

39. Editors, "Editorial: Did Bo (Obama's Dog) Eat The Recovery?" Investors.com, August 16, 2011.

40. President Barack Obama, "Press Conference by the President," the White House, Office of the Press Secretary, June 29, 2011.

41. Sam Youngman and Alicia M. Cohn, "Obama: Public is 'sold' on tax increases in a debt-ceiling deal," *The Hill*, July 15, 2011.

42. Russell Berman, "House GOP passes ill-fated 'cut, cap, and balance' legislation," *The Hill*, July 19, 2011; and Ed Morrissey, "Breaking: GOP passes Cut, Cap, & Balance Act," HotAir.com, July 19, 2011.

43. Sam Youngman, "Obama officially threatens to veto Republicans 'cut, cap, and balance' bill," *The Hill*, July 18, 2011.

44. Scott Wong, "Senate rejects 'Cut, Cap, Balance,'" *Politico*, July 22, 2011.

45. George Will, "Congress stands its ground," *Washington Post*, July 25, 2011.

46. Neil Munro, "Obama defaults to economic blame game," Daily Caller, June 7, 2011.

47. Jeffrey H. Anderson, "Obama Threatens to Withhold Social Security Checks," *Weekly Standard* blog, July 12, 2011.

48. Richard Rubin and Andrew Zajac, "Corporate Jet Tax Gets Six Obama Mentions, $3 Billion Estimate," Bloomberg, June 30, 2011.

49. Katherine Mangu-Ward, "Obama Uses Bully Pulpit to Demand End of Political Rhetoric," *Reason*, July 5, 2011.

50. Charles Krauthammer, "The Elmendorf Rule," *Washington Post*.

51. "Carney: Economy Has 'Vastly Improved' Since Obama Was Sworn In," *RealClearPolitics* Video, July 21, 2011.

52. Fred Lucas, "Economist Who Said Unemployment Wouldn't Top 8% Now Says it Won't Go Below 8% Before 2012 Ends," CNS News, August 16, 2011.

53. "US Rating Downgrade: S&P's Beers says risks on downside for future US rating," Reuters, August 7, 2011.

54. President Barack Obama, "Transcript of Obama's Remarks on S&P Downgrade," *Wall Street Journal*, August 8, 2011.

55. Michelle Malkin, "Austerity Hilarity," National Review Online, August 3, 2011.

56. Jim Kuhnhenn, "Obama on tour: 'I make no apologies for being reasonable," *Chicago Sun-Times*, August 16, 2011.

57. Ed Morrissey, "New Obama metric: 'Jobs supported,'" HotAir.com, October 13, 2011.

58. Sam Youngman, "Push for President Obama's jobs bill illustrates the art of beating a dead horse," *The Hill*, October 5, 2011.

59. John Brandt, "Senate Dems Change Rules, Enraging Republicans and Postponing Vote on China Currency," Fox News, October 6, 2011.

60. John Kartch, "Obama Inches Closer to a Value Added Tax," Fox News, April 22, 2010.

61. "Obama's Re-Election Budget," transcript of The Journal Editorial Report, *Wall Street Journal*, February 20, 2012.

62. "Obama Gives Oregon, $5M 'Bonus' For Boosting Food Stamp Rolls..." *Fox Nation*, September 29, 2011.

63. "Fox Attacks Obama For Food Stamp Awards That Date To The Bush Administration," Media Matters For America, October 2, 2011.

64. William Beach and Patrick Tyrrell, "The 2012 Index of Dependence on Government," Heritage Foundation, February 8, 2012.

65. Phil Izzo, "Some 15% of U.S. Uses Food Stamps," *Wall Street Journal* Real Time Economics Blog, November 1, 2011.

66. Rob Bluey, "Chart of the Week: 1 in 5 Americans Are Dependent on Government," *The Scribe*, Heritage Foundation, February 12, 2012.
67. William Beach and Patrick Tyrrell, "The 2012 Index of Dependence on Government," Heritage Foundation, February 8, 2012.
68. Ibid.
69. "Carney: Unemployment Benefits Could Create Up to 1 Million Jobs," *RealClearPolitics*, August 10, 2011.
70. "Obama Ag Secretary Vilsack: Food Stamps Are A 'Stimulus,'" *RealClearPolitics*, August 16, 2011.
71. Editors, "'Osawatomie Obama' launches assault on facts and history," *Examiner*, December 8, 2011.
72. Rosalind S. Helderman and Paul Kane, "House approves $3.5 trillion budget plan proposed by Paul Ryan," *Washington Post*, March 29, 2012.
73. "Obama: Reagan could not survive in 'radical' GOP," Townhall.com, April 3, 2012.

CHAPTER SEVEN

1. See the exchange at http://www.youtube.com/watch?v=5M1WlV7vafk.
2. See Obama delivering these remarks at http://www.youtube.com/watch?v=fpAyan1fXCE.
3. Victor Davis Hanson, "Are Sky-High Gas Prices Good?" National Review Online, April 28, 2011.
4. Philip Elliott, "Barbour: Obama Favors Higher Gas Prices," *Washington Times*, March 2, 2011; and Peter Ferrara, "Obama's War on Oil," *American Spectator*, May 4, 2011.
5. Jonathan Fahey, "Chu Energy Advisory Board Has No Oil, Gas, Electricity Execs," *Forbes*, August 10, 2010.
6. Terence P. Jeffrey, "Obama's Transportation Secretary Says He Wants to 'Coerce People Out of Their Cars,'" CNS News, May 25, 2009.
7. Peter Ferrara, "Obama's War on Oil," *American Spectator*, May 4, 2011.
8. Siobhan Hughes, "Plugs Ordered on Idle Wells," *Wall Street Journal*, September 16, 2010.
9. Congressman Dan Boren, "Boren: President Obama Uninformed about Oil and Gas Industry," Boren.House.Gov, April 26, 2011.
10. Darlene Superville, "Obama on High Gas Prices: Get Used to Them," *Fox Nation*, April 6, 2011.
11. Darlene Superville, "President Obama pitches green energy in Bucks Co.," 6abc Action News, April 7, 2011.

12. Dr. M., "The Gulf Of Mexico Oil Spill: A Timeline," *Deep Sea News*, April 29, 2010.

13. "How the White House Public Relations Campaign on the Oil Spill is Harming the Actual Clean-up," staff report, U.S. House of Representatives Committee on Oversight and Government Reform, July 1, 2010, http://oversight.house.gov/report/how-the-white-house-public-relations-campaign-on-the-oil-spill-is-harming-the-actual-clean-up/.

14. President Barack Obama, "Remarks by the President on the Gulf Oil Spill," Whitehouse.gov, May 27, 2010.

15. Ibid.

16. Mark Tapscott, "Remember the flap over foreign ships and the Deepwater Horizon cleanup?" *Examiner*, June 24, 2011.

17. "Top Six Obama Mistruths From National Energy Address," Americans For Tax Reform, June 16, 2010.

18. Ben Geman, "New report slams White House spill response," *The Hill*, July 1, 2010.

19. "How the White House Public Relations Campaign on the Oil Spill is Harming the Actual Clean-up," U.S. House of Representatives Committee on Oversight and Government Reform.

20. Ibid.

21. Senator James M. Inhofe, *Failure of Leadership: President Obama and the Flawed Federal Response to the BP Disaster*, United States Senate, August 2010.

22. Joe Palazzolo, "Holder: Disclosure of Oil Spill Probe Was 'Appropriate,'" *Main Justice*, July 11, 2010.

23. Editors, "The odd responses of the Attorney General to the oil spill," *Washington Post*, July 2, 2010.

24. Joe Palazzolo, "Holder: Disclosure of Oil Spill Probe Was 'Appropriate'," *Main Justice*.

25. Carol E. Lee, "White House sends 2012 rescue team to Florida," *Politico*, July 25, 2010.

26. "Poll: By a Whopping 54%-33% Margin Louisiana Voters Think Bush Did a Better Job With Katrina Than Obama With Gulf Oil Spill," *Weasel Zippers* blog, August 27, 2010.

27. "President: I'll 'make sure we get the job done,'" MSNBC.msn.com, August 29, 2010.

28. Sean J. Miller, "Obama: New Orleans making a comeback under my administration," *The Hill*, August 29, 2010.

29. Stephen Power, "Judge Overturns Drilling Ban," *Wall Street Journal*, June 22, 2010; John M. Broder, "Obama Asks Court to Reinstate Ban on Deepwater Drilling," *New York Times*, July 7, 2010; and Michelle Malkin, "Another ass-kicking; 5th Circuit rejects White House drilling ban appeal," MichelleMalkin.com, July 8, 2010.

30. Stephen Power, "Judge Overturns Drilling Ban," *Wall Street Journal*.

31. Josh Gerstein, "Axelrod: Rigs' exit from Gulf 'not optimal,'" *Politico*, July 11, 2010.

32. Ibid.

33. John M. Broder, "U.S. Issues Revised Offshore Drilling Ban," *New York Times*, July 12, 2010.

34. "Louisiana: Oil Moratorium Halting Much Drilling," Breitbart.com, July 22, 2010.

35. "Carville Slams Obama Administration on Moratorium," Breitbart TV, July 15, 2010.

36. Robyn Walensky, "Finance Expert: President Obama's Drilling Moratorium Devastates The Economy In The Gulf Coast Region," WGNO ABC26.com, July 19, 2010.

37. Bob McCarty, "Offshore Drilling Moratorium Would Cost United States 175,000 Jobs Per Year Through 2035," BigGovernment.com, July 27, 2010.

38. Justin Gillis, "Oil in Gulf Poses Only Slight Risk, New U.S. Report Says," *New York Times*, August 4, 2010.

39. Richard Fausset, "BP says it's closer to oil containment," *Los Angeles Times*, July 12, 2012.

40. Darrell Issa, "NOAA Scientist: Release of Oil Spill Report done by White House Not NOAA," *Canada Free Press*, August 19, 2010.

41. MacAoidh, "Obama Says Moratorium Doesn't Really Hurt Anybody; Louisiana Seethes With Indignation," *The Hay Ride*, September 16, 2010.

42. Stephen Power and Leslie Eaton, "Administration Risked 23,000 Jobs With Oil Drilling Ban, Documents Show," *Wall Street Journal*, August 21, 2010.

43. Andrew Malcolm, "Obama quicker to claim credit for BP oil well-sealing," *Los Angeles Times*, September 20, 2010.

44. Matt Cover, "Exclusive: U.S. Government Loaned Mexican Government More Than $1 Billion to Drill Oil in Gulf of Mexico Last Year; Has $1 Billion More Planned For This Year," CNS News, September 7, 2010.

45. President Barack Obama, "Remarks By the President at CEO Business Summit in Brasilia, Brazil," the White House, Office of the Press Secretary, March 19, 2011.
46. "Lawmakers, Executives Slam Obama for Boosting Brazil's Offshore Drilling," Fox News, March 23, 2011.
47. Ibid.
48. Carlos Batista, "Cuba to Drill Five New Oil Wells by 2013," Agence France Presse, April 5, 2011.
49. Nick Snow, "Interior Department toughens regulation of offshore drilling," *Oil and Gas Journal*, September 30, 2010.
50. Ibid.
51. Conn Carroll, "Oil imports spike as Obama oil ban decreases domestic production," *Examiner*, April 27, 2011.
52. Nick Snow, "Interior Department Toughens Regulation of Offshore Drilling," *Oil and Gas Journal*.
53. Nicolas Loris, "Obama Administration Admits New Drilling Rules Will Kill Jobs," *The Foundry*, Heritage Foundation, October 11, 2010.
54. Steve Maley, "Energy Policy Outrage: 'OPEC Has Plenty of Oil,'" RedState.com, October 28, 2010.
55. Dan Berman, "White House may have withheld spill info," *Politico*, October 7, 2010.
56. Ben Geman, "OMB denies report it may have suppressed data during BP spill," *The Hill*, October 6, 2010.
57. Mark Hemingway, "Inspector General investigating Department of Interior report falsely claiming experts endorsed offshore drilling ban," *Examiner*, July 24, 2010.
58. Dan Berman, "Interior Inspector General: White House skewed drilling-ban report," *Politico*, November 9, 2010, and "White House altered report justifying drilling ban," MSNBC.MSN.com, November 10, 2010.
59. Rory Cooper, "10 Things You Need to Know About High Gas Prices and Obama's Oil Policy," *The Foundry*, Heritage Foundation, February 23, 2011; and Conn Carroll, "Obama's Offshore Ban Already Cutting Domestic Energy Supply," *The Foundry*, Heritage Foundation, January 3, 2011.
60. John M. Broder and Clifford Krauss, "U.S. Drops Bid to Explore Oil in Eastern Gulf," *New York Times*, December 1, 2010.
61. Jazz Shaw, "The Full Cost of the Drilling Moratorium," HotAir.com, December 4, 2010.

62. "Expert: Seven-year Moratorium on Gulf Oil Drilling an Unwise Decision," *Eureka Alert*, December 13, 2010.
63. Juliet Eilperin, "Obama administration reimposes offshore oil drilling ban," *Washington Post*, December 1, 2010.
64. Rory Cooper, "10 Things You Need to Know About High Gas Prices and Obama's Oil Policy," *The Foundry*, Heritage Foundation.
65. "Update 1-Factbox-Deepwater Rigs Moved Out of the Gulf of Mexico," Reuters, January 27, 2011.
66. Darren Goode, "Bill Clinton: Drilling delays 'ridiculous,'" *Politico*, March 11, 2011.
67. Sean Higgins, "Obama Blames Oil Companies for Lack of Drilling," Investors.com, March 11, 2011.
68. Jennifer A. Dlouhy, "U.S. releases oil from stockpiles to aid economy," *San Francisco Chronicle*, June 24, 2011.
69. Rachelle Younglai, "Treasury's Geithner: Oil release not political move," Reuters, June 24, 2011.
70. Patti Domm, "Oil Prices Climb Back to Pre-Reserve Release Levels," CNBC.com, July 5, 2011.
71. "Restarting 'The engine': Securing American jobs, investment, and energy security," IHS Global Insight and IHS CERA Report, August 2011.
72. "House Report: Obama's Gulf Oil Slowdown Costing 230,000 Jobs!" *YID With LID*, July 21, 2011.
73. Jim Adams, "Obama's Interior Chokehold on America," *American Thinker*, September 27, 2011.
74. Curry W. Smith, "GPI+ — Gulf Permit Index – As of November 22," Greater New Orleans Inc., November 22, 2011.
75. Rob Bluey, "Obama Administration Approving Only 35 Percent of Gulf Drilling Plans," *The Foundry*, Heritage Foundation, November 24, 2011.
76. Pierre Bertrand, "Gulf Oil Drilling Moratorium, 'Permitatorium' to Cost Nation $24B, Industry Says," *International Business Times*, January 11, 2012.
77. Paul Foy, "Salazar defends pulling oil leases," *Deseret News*, July 14, 2010.
78. Michelle Malkin, "Why does Ken Salazar hate our economy? Update: Western Energy Alliance calls for reinstating oil leases," MichelleMalkin.com, July 20, 2010.
79. Editors, "Energy Needs Left High And Dry," Investors.com, July 15, 2010.
80. Joel Gehrke, "Obama USDA Delays Shale Drilling, Up to 200k Jobs," *Examiner*, November 18, 2011.

81.   Editors, "Will the EPA Choke Oil Shale Production," Investors.com, November 30, 2011.

82.   Alan Boyle, "It's Not Fracking's Fault, Study Says," MSNBC.MSN.com, February 16, 2012.

83.   Joel Gehrke, "Obama USDA delays shale drilling, up to 200k jobs," *Examiner*, November 18, 2011.

84.   Steve Maley, "President Obama, Dr. Chu and Their Fracking Whopper," RedState.com, February 11, 2012.

85.   "VP Joe Biden: Fracking Can Cause Earthquakes," *The Right Scoop*, April 3, 2012.

86.   John M. Broder and Dan Frosch, "U.S. Delays Decision on Pipeline Until After Election," *New York Times*, November 11, 2011.

87.   Nicolas Loris, "Obama Delays Keystone Pipeline: Delays Jobs and Energy, Too," *The Foundry*, Heritage Foundation, November 10, 2011.

88.   Nicolas Loris, "Canada: U.S. Delaying Pipelines Means We'll Go Elsewhere," *The Foundry*, Heritage Foundation, November 15, 2011.

89.   John M. Broder and Dan Frosch, "U.S. Delays Decision on Pipeline Until After Election," *New York Times*.

90.   Elana Schor, "Canada-U.S. Oil Pipeline Poses Few Environmental Risks – State Dept.," *New York Times*, August 26, 2011.

91.   Manu Raju, "Obama lobbying Dems over Keystone XL pipeline," *Politico*, March 7, 2012.

92.   John M. Broder and Dan Frosch, "U.S. Delays Decision on Pipeline Until After Election," *New York Times*.

93.   Mike Brownfield, "Morning Bell: How President Obama Killed Thousands of Jobs," *The Foundry*, Heritage Foundation, November 14, 2011.

94.   David Kreutzer, "Where Will the Oil Go?" *National Journal*, May 24, 2011.

95.   John M. Broder and Dan Frosch, "U.S. Delays Decision on Pipeline Until After Election," *New York Times*.

96.   Nicolas Loris, "Unnecessary Keystone XL Pipeline Delay Obstructs Energy, Jobs," Heritage Foundation, December 13, 2011; and Afshin Honarvar et al., *Economic Impacts of New Oil Sands Projects in Alberta (2010–2035)*, Canadian Energy Research Institute (CERI), June 2011, http://www.ceri.ca/images/stories/2011-08-24_CERI_Study_125_Section_1.pdf (December 8, 2011).

97.   Joel Gehrke, "Obama: More jobs in jobless benefits than Keystone," *Examiner*, December 8, 2011.

98.   Lisa Mascaro, "Obama threatens payroll tax veto over Keystone provision," *Los Angeles Times*, December 7, 2011.

99. Hubert Tate, "Welspun announces company cutbacks," Fox16.com, December 13, 2011.

100. Katie Boyd, "Editorial Backlash Against President Obama's Job-Destroying Keystone Decision Continues," Speaker John Boehner's Blog, January 20, 2012.

101. *U.S. Supply Forecast and Potential Jobs and Economic Impacts (2012-2030)*, Wood Mackenzie Energy Consulting, September 7, 2011.

102. Fred Lucas, "Obama's Claim of Increasing Drilling Not Accurate, Say Energy Analysts," CNS News, February 23, 2012.

103. Lachlan Markay, "Fact Check: 10 Dubious Claims from Obama's State of the Union," *The Foundry*, Heritage Foundation, January 25, 2010.

104. Nicolas Loris, "High Gas Prices: Obama's Half-Truths vs. Reality," Heritage Foundation, February 23, 2012; and Bureau of Labor Statistics, "Local Area Unemployment Statistics," http://www.bls.gov/web/laus/laumstrk.htm.

105. Amy Harder, "Obama's Fuzzy Oil Production Math," *National Journal*, March 17, 2011.

106. Mead Grever, "Federal Judge Throws Out Obama Drilling Rules," Seattlepi.com, August 13, 2011.

107. David Kreutzer, Ph.D. "Quit Repeating Nonsensical Oil Statistics!" *The Foundry*, Heritage Foundation, March 31, 2011.

108. Lachlan Markay, "Fact Check: 10 Dubious Claims from Obama's State of the Union," *The Foundry*, Heritage Foundation, January 25, 2010.

109. Ibid.

110. Nicolas Loris, "High Gas Prices: Obama's Half-Truths vs. Reality," Heritage Foundation.

111. Ibid.

112. David Kreutzer, Ph.D. "Quit Repeating Nonsensical Oil Statistics!"

CHAPTER EIGHT

1. Mike Brownfield, "Morning Bell: The Nuclear Option for Powering America," Heritage Foundation, March 12, 2012.

2. "Editorial: Obama appeals to a higher power," *Washington Times*, July 20, 2010; and Hannah Northey, "GAO: Death of Yucca Mountain Caused by Political Maneuvering," *New York Times*, May 10, 2011.

3. Hannah Northey, "GAO: Death of Yucca Mountain Caused by Political Maneuvering," *New York Times*.

4.   C. J. Ciaramella, "Obama's new fuel standards to add $2,000 to car prices," Daily Caller, November 16, 2011.

5.   Ibid.; and Josh Mitchell and Sharon Terlep, "Your Mileage May Vary," *Wall Street Journal*, June 27, 2011.

6.   C. J. Ciaramella, "Obama's new fuel standards to add $2,000 to car prices," Daily Caller.

7.   Ibid.

8.   Josh Mitchell and Sharon Terlep, "Your Mileage May Vary," *Wall Street Journal*.

9.   Sam Kazman, "Why Your New Car Doesn't Have a Spare Tire," *Wall Street Journal*, June 26, 2011.

10. Holman W. Jenkins, Jr., "Overcaffeinated CAFÉ," *Wall Street Journal*, July 6, 2011.

11. John Merline, "EPA Funds Green Groups That Sue The Agency To Expand," Investors.com, July 6, 2011.

12. Juliet Eilperin, "EPA proposes stricter controls on water pollution," *Washington Post*, April 27, 2011.

13. "Transcript: Obama's State Of The Union Address," NPR, January 25, 2011.

14. Carol D. Leonnig, Joe Stephens, and Alice Crites, "Obama's focus on visiting clean-tech companies raises questions," *Washington Post*, June 25, 2011.

15. Ibid.

16. Russ Choma, "Renewable energy money still going abroad, despite criticism from Congress," Investigative Reporting Workshop, February 8, 2010.

17. "Top Six Obama Mistruths From National Energy Address," Americans For Tax Reform, June 16, 2010.

18. Ibid.

19. Ibid.

20. Vanessa Ho, "Seattle's 'green jobs' program a bust," KOMONews.com, August 17, 2011.

21. "Top Six Obama Mistruths From National Energy Address," Americans For Tax Reform.

22. Elizabeth MacDonald, "The Treasury Bank Behind Solyndra – And Mortgage Bailouts," *Fox Business*, October 6, 2011.

23. Ed Morrissey, "Obama: Let's spend $2 billion to create 5100 jobs," HotAir.com, July 3, 2010.

24. Tina Korbe, "Report: Stimulus-backed solar company lays off 70 percent of workforce," HotAir.com, February 29, 2012.

25. Richard Pollock, "Another DOE Loan Scandal: Are We Bailing Out *Spain's* Solar Collapse?" *PJ Media*, November 10, 2011.

26. "Political Entrepreneurship: The Case of Abengoa," Institute for Energy Research, September 7, 2011.

27. Joe Stephens and Carol D. Leonnig, "Solyndra solar company fails after getting controversial federal loan guarantees," *Washington Post*, August 31, 2011.

28. Ibid.

29. "Vice President Biden Announces Finalized $535 Million Loan Guarantee for Solyndra," Energy.gov, September 4, 2009.

30. Joe Stephens and Carol D. Leonnig, "Solyndra: Politics infused Obama energy programs," *Washington Post*, December 25, 2011.

31. Lachlan Markay, "Morning Bell: Solyndra Scandal Ends Green Jobs Myth," *The Foundry*, Heritage Foundation, September 16, 2011.

32. Eric Lipton and John M. Broder, "In Rush to Assist a Solar Company, U.S. Missed Signs," *New York Times*, September 22, 2011.

33. Carol D. Leonnig and Joe Stephens, "Obama was advised against visiting Solyndra after financial warnings," *Washington Post*, October 3, 2011.

34. Ibid.

35. Joe Stephens and Carol D. Leonnig, "Solyndra: Politics infused Obama green energy programs," *Washington Post*.

36. Ibid.

37. Lachlan Markay, "Morning Bell: Solyndra Scandal Ends Green Jobs Myth," *The Foundry*, Heritage Foundation.

38. Joe Stephens and Carol D. Leonnig, "Solyndra: Politics infused Obama green energy programs," *Washington Post*.

39. Carol D. Leonnig and Joe Stephens, "Obama was advised against visiting Solyndra after financial warnings," *Washington Post*.

40. Joe Stephens and Carol D. Leonnig, "Solyndra solar company fails after getting controversial federal loan guarantees," *Washington Post*.

41. Mark Matthews, "Solyndra execs quiet; former employees speak out," ABCLocal.go.com, September 23, 2011.

42. Thomas Catan and Deborah Solomon, "FBI Raids Solar-Panel Maker," *Wall Street Journal*, September 9, 2011.

43. Joe Stephens and Carol D. Leonnig, "Solyndra solar company fails after getting controversial federal loan guarantees," *Washington Post*.

44. Carol D. Leonnig, Joe Stephens, and Alice Crites, "Obama's focus on visiting clean-tech companies raises questions," *Washington Post*.

45. Carol D. Leonnig and Joe Stephens, "Obama was advised against visiting Solyndra after financial warnings," *Washington Post*.

46. Joe Stephens and Carol D. Leonnig, "Solyndra solar company fails after getting controversial federal loan guarantees," *Washington Post*.

47. "Bush Admin. Voted AGAINST Solyndra Loan," Fox News, September 14, 2011.

48. "Department of Energy Finalizes Partial Loan Guarantee for $852 Million Loan to Support California Concentrating Solar Plant," Energy.gov, August 26, 2011.

49. Katie Pavlich, "Another Taxpayer Funded $825 Million Solar Loan Going to Waste," Townhall.com, February 14, 2012.

50. Joe Stephens and Carol D. Leonnig, "Solyndra solar company fails after getting controversial federal loan guarantees," *Washington Post*.

51. "Memorandum: The Solyndra Story," The Committee on Energy and Commerce, September 14, 2011.

52. Joe Stephens and Carol D. Leonnig, "Solyndra Loan: White House pressed on review of solar company now under investigation," *Washington Post*, September 13, 2011.

53. Amanda Carey, "Solyndra officials made numerous trips to the White House, logs show," Daily Caller, September 8, 2011.

54. Lachlan Markay, "Energy Department rewrote the law to aid Solyndra," *Examiner*, October 20, 2011.

55. Lachlan Markay, "Solyndra to Auction Assets, But Taxpayers Won't See a Dime," *The Foundry*, Heritage Foundation, October 21, 2011.

56. Ericka Andersen, "Morning Bell: The Solyndra Legacies," *The Foundry*, Heritage Foundation, September 30, 2011.

57. Carol D. Leonnig and Joe Stephens, "Solyndra: Energy Dept. pushed firm to keep layoffs quiet until after midterms," *Washington Post*, November 15, 2011.

58. Ed Morrissey, "Blockbuster: Obama administration pressured Solyndra to delay layoffs for political gain," HotAir.com, November 15, 2011.

59. "Solyndra Not Sole Firm to Hit Rock Bottom Despite Stimulus Funding," Fox News, September 15, 2011.

60. Steve Hargreaves, "Solar power bankruptcies loom as prices collapse," CNN *Money*, November 30, 2011.

61. Erika Andersen, "Morning Bell: The Solyndra Legacies," *The Foundry*, Heritage Foundation.

62. Ibid.

63. Lachlan Markay, "Report: 80% of DOE Green Energy Loans Went to Obama Backers," *The Foundry*, Heritage Foundation, November 14, 2011.

64. *Export-Import Bank: Reaching New Targets for Environmentally Beneficial Exports Presents Major Challenges for Bank*, Report to Congressional Committees, United States Government Accountability Office, July 2010.

65. Doug Ross, "Schweizer's New Book: 80% of Energy Department's 'Green Loan' Program Went to Obama's Backers," *Doug Ross Journal*, November 13, 2011.

66. Ronnie Greene and Matthew Mosk, "Skipping safeguards, officials rushed benefit to a politically-connected energy company," *iWatch News*, May 24, 2011.

67. Joe Stephens and Carol D. Leonnig, "Solyndra solar company fails after getting controversial federal loan guarantees," *Washington Post*.

68. Michael Graham, "Another 'Green Jobs' Fiasco for Obama/Patrick?" *The Natural Truth, MichaelGraham.com*, April 3, 2012; "Some clean-energy firms found U.S. loan-guarantee program a bad bet," *Washington Post*, September 26, 2011; and Paul Chesser, "Taxpayer-Funded Green Job Losses Easy as A123," National Legal and Policy Center, December 2, 2011.

69. Aaron Glantz, "Number of Green Jobs Fails to Live Up to Promises," *New York Times*, August 18, 2011.

70. Carol D. Leonnig and Steven Mufson, "Obama green-tech program that backed Solyndra struggles to create jobs," *Washington Post*, September 14, 2011.

71. Dr. Milton R. Wolf, "Wolf: Energy Obamanomics: No green jobs and plenty of red ink," *Washington Times*, August 23, 2011.

72. Byron York, "Key Dems: Obama's 'green jobs' plan a bust," *Examiner*, August 19, 2011.

73. Aaron Glantz, "Number of Green Jobs Fails to Live Up to Promises," *New York Times*.

74. Ibid.

75. Yuliya Chernova, "Dark Times Fall on Solar Sector," *Wall Street Journal*, December 27, 2011.

76. P. J. Gladnick, "Audio: Obama Tells SF Chronicle He Will Bankrupt Coal Industry," *Newsbusters*, November 2, 2008.

77. Frederic J. Frommer, "Coal miners rally for mountain marring," *Washington Times*, September 15, 2010.

78. Thomas Pyle, "EPA's Propose Ozone Regulation Could Cost $1 Trillion," *U.S. News & World Report*, August 25, 2011.

79. John Engler, "The Latest Job Killer From the EPA," *Wall Street Journal*, July 26, 2011.

80. Mark Drajem, "Obama Asks EPA to Withdraw Ozone Rules," Bloomberg, September 2, 2011; and Ben Geman and Erik Wasson, "Obama shelves EPA smog rule in huge defeat for environmental groups," *The Hill*, September 9, 2011

81. Christine Hall, "President Postpones Trillion-Dollar Ozone Rule Until After 2012 Presidential Election," Competitive Enterprise Institute, September 2, 2011.

82. Conn Carroll, "Flood of new EPA rules could drown economic growth," *Examiner*, August 29, 2011.

83. Matthew Boyle, "EPA regulation forces closure of Texas energy facilities, eliminates 500 jobs," Daily Caller, September 12, 2011.

84. Juliet Eilperin, "EPA to impose first greenhouse gas limits on power plants," *Washington Post*, March 26, 2012.

85. Editorial, "Lisa Jackson's Freudian Slip," *Wall Street Journal*, November 22, 2011.

CHAPTER NINE

1. Jeff Mason, "Obama urges companies to hire, studies housing moves," Reuters, May 12, 2011.

2. Eamon Javers, "The Obama Cabinet is a CEO black hole," *Politico*, February 20, 2009.

3. D. Mark Renaud and Robert L. Walker, "'Good government' rules that aren't," *Washington Post*, September 28, 2011.

4. "Obama NLRB Delays (Doesn't Cancel) Requiring Businesses to Post Union Posters," NLRB, LaborUnionReport.com, October 6, 2011.

5. "Obama's NLRB's War on Workers and Job Creators Continues," LaborUnionReport.com, August 31, 2011.

6. "NLRB Sues Arizona & South Dakota Over Secret-Ballot Amendments," LaborUnionReport.com, April 25, 2011.

7. Jazz Shaw, "Senate bill targets NLRB creation of 'micro' unions," HotAir.com, November 16, 2011.

8. "Help Halt the NLRB's Assault on America's Union-Free Employees and Companies," *The Liberty Watch*, December 5, 2011.

9. NLRB Watch, "The Union-Controlled NLRB issues complaint against Boeing for transferring work to a non-union facility," LaborUnionReport.com, April 20, 2011.

10. Joe Weisenthal, "Suddenly, The White House Claims It's Pro-Growth And Pro-Business," *Business Insider*, July 7, 2010.

11. Dennis Jacobe, "Gov't Regulations at Top of Small-Business Owners' Problem List," Gallup.com, October 24, 2011.

12. Fareed Zakaria, "Obama's CEO problem – and ours," *Washington Post*, July 5, 2010.

13. Steven Pearlstein, "Obama vs. big business: The battle everyone can lose," *Washington Post*, July 7, 2010.

14. Lloyd Grove, "The Elite Turn Against Obama," *Daily Beast*, July 7, 2010.

15. Jon Ward, "Lack of jobs increasingly blamed on uncertainty created by Obama's policies," Daily Caller, July 7, 2010.

16. Ken Sweet, "3M CEO slams Obama as 'anti-business,'" CNN *Money*, February 28, 2011.

17. Susan Feyder, "3M's CEO says Obama is driving firms away," *Star Tribune*, March 1, 2011.

18. Jon Ward, "Lack of jobs increasingly blamed on uncertainty created by Obama's policies," Daily Caller.

19. "Wynn Resorts' CEO Discusses Q2 2011 Results – Earnings Call Transcript," SeekingAlpha.com, July 18, 2011.

20. Ibid.

21. Albert R. Hunt, "Obama Get's a Bum Rap With Anti-Business Charge," *BusinessWeek*, July 4, 2010.

22. "Obama: 'Nothing More Important' Than A Government Job," *RealClearPolitics* Video, May 12, 2011.

23. Terence P. Jeffrey, "Geithner: Taxes on 'Small Business' Must Rise So Government Doesn't 'Shrink,'" CNS News, June 23, 2011.

24. David Jackson, "Obama backs debt collection via cellphone," *USA Today* The Oval, October 4, 2011.

25. Jon Ward, "Obama as anti-business moves into mainstream discussion," Daily Caller, July 8, 2010.

26. "Remarks by the President on the Economy in Osawatomie, Kansas," WhiteHouse.gov, December 6, 2011.

27. Mike Brownfield, "Morning Bell: The Last Incarnation of Barack Obama," *The Foundry*, Heritage Foundation, December 7, 2011.

28. "Who Pays Income Taxes?" The National Taxpayers Union, 2011.

29.   Editors, "The Buffett Alternative Tax," *Wall Street Journal*, September 20, 2011.

30.   "JP Morgan CEO Jamie Dimon: Stop Bashing the Rich," Associated Press and Reuters, December 7, 2011.

31.   Mike Brownfield, "State of the Union 2012: Heritage Reaction Roundup," *The Foundry*, Heritage Foundation, January 24, 2012.

32.   "Obama Adviser: Shutdown Looms as GOP Bends to Will of Tea Party," Fox News, September 25, 2011. As Obama's adviser David Plouffe said, "The American people are screaming out, saying it's unfair that the wealthiest, the largest corporations who can afford the best attorneys, the best accountants, take advantage of these special tax treatments that the lobbyists have—along with lawmakers—have cooked into the books here."

33.   Mike Brownfield, "Morning Bell: Buffett Rule 101," *The Foundry*, Heritage Foundation, April 11, 2012; Ashe Schow, "Note to Pres. Obama: The Rich Don't Pay Less Than Their Secretaries," *Heritage Action for America*, September 20, 2011; and Thomas Cloud, "Boehner: Obama Should Contribute 10% More of His Income to the Government," CNSNews, April 17, 2012.

34.   Mike Brownfield, "Morning Bell: Buffett Rule 101," *The Foundry*, Heritage Foundation, April 11, 2012.

35.   Douglas H. Shulman, Rosemary D. Marcus, M. Susan Boehner, and David P. Paris, "Individual Income Tax Returns 2009," Publication 1304 (Rev. 07-2011), IRS.gov, 2009; and Mark Perry, "Fact-Checking the Buffett Rule: The Math Doesn't Add Up," The Enterprise Blog, September 21, 2011.

36.   Ashe Schow, "Note to Pres. Obama: The Rich Don't Pay Less Than Their Secretaries," Heritage Action for America.

37.   Bernie Becker, "Tax Break for Charitable Giving Targeted," *The Hill*, March 27, 2011.

38.   Michael Tomasky, "Obama Finally Seizes the Moment in His Kansas Speech," *The Daily Beast*, December 7, 2011.

39.   Ron Fournier, "No TR: The Limits of Obama's Bully Pulpit," *National Journal*, December 6, 2011.

40.   Editors, "Obama's Middle Class Speech Falls Short of a Cure," *USA Today*, December 7, 2011.

41.   Editors, "Rightly targeting income inequality," *Washington Post*, December 7, 2011.

42. Rea Hederman, Jr. and James Sherk, "Heritage Employment Report: April Jobs Report Shows Showers, not Flowers," Heritage Foundation, May 6, 2011.

43. Robert Costa, "Haley Pressures Obama, '12 Field on NLRB," *The Corner*, National Review Online, April 25, 2011.

44. Ibid.

45. Doug McKelway, "Senate Republicans Threaten to Fight NLRB Nominations Over Boeing Complaint," Fox News, May 5, 2011.

46. Mike Brownfield, "Morning Bell: Obama's Attack on Private Industry," *The Foundry*, Heritage Foundation, May 9, 2011.

47. Keith Lang, "Issa: NLRB Withdrawal a 'Victory,' but Investigation Will Continue," *The Hill*, December 9, 2011.

48. Ibid.

49. Steven Greenhouse, "Labor Board Drops Case Against Boeing," *New York Times*, December 9, 2011.

50. Tina Korbe, "NLRB finalizes rule to establish ambush elections," HotAir. com, December 21, 2011.

51. Andrew Stiles, "Obama and the Regulators," National Review Online, August 25, 2011.

52. Hans A. von Spakovsky and James Sherk, "The New NLRB: Boeing is Just the Beginning," National Review Online, May 16, 2011.

53. Ibid.

54. Matthew Boyle, "Obama's Department of Labor forces unionization," Daily Caller, January 18, 2011.

55. Matthew Boyle, "Obama uses 'green' emissions standards to push truckers into Teamsters Union," Daily Caller, January 26, 2011.

56. James P. Hoffa, "The Ports Challenge," *Huffington Post*, March 1, 2010.

57. President Barack Obama, "Op-ed: Toward a 21st-Century Regulatory System," *Wall Street Journal*, January 18, 2011.

58. Ibid.

59. Erik Wasson, "White House Unveils Plans to Trim Regs, Save at Least $10 Billion," *The Hill*, August 23, 2011.

60. Katie Boyd, "Chamber: White House Review Won't 'Make Any Impact on the Overall Regulatory Burdens' Facing Job Creators," Speaker of the House John Boehner *Speaker Alert*, August 23, 2011.

61. Erik Wasson, "White House Unveils Plans to Trim Regs, Save at Least $10 Billion," *The Hill*.

62. John Merline, "Regulation Business, Jobs Booming Under Obama," *Investors Business Daily*, August 15, 2011.

63.   Mark Drajem and Catherine Dodge, "Obama Wrote 5% Fewer Rules
      Than Bush While Costing Business," Bloomberg, October 25, 2011, http://
      www.bloomberg.com/news/2011-10-25/obama-wrote-5-fewer-rules-than-
      bush-while-costing-business.html.

64.   James L. Gattuso and Diane Katz, "Red Tape Rising: A 2011 Mid-Year
      Report on Regulation," Heritage Foundation *Backgrounder* No. 2586,
      July 25, 2011, http://www.heritage.org/research/reports/2011/07/red-tape-
      rising-a-2011-mid-year-report.

65.   Ibid.

66.   Ibid.

67.   James Gattuso, "Obama's Red Tape: Tsunami or Ripple?" Heritage
      Foundation *Web Memo*, November 8, 2011.

68.   Curtis W. Copeland and Maeve P. Carey, "REINS Act: Number and Types
      of 'Major Rules' in Recent Years," Congressional Research Service,
      February 24, 2011.

69.   James Gattuso and Diane Katz, "Red Tape Rising: Obama-Rea Regulation
      at the Three-Year Mark," Heritage Foundation, March 13, 2012.

70.   Ibid.

71.   Senator John Barrasso, M.D., "Red Tape Review, Regulations by the
      Numbers for 2011," Senate Republican Conference, December 2, 2011.

72.   John Merline, "Regulation Business, Jobs Booming Under Obama,"
      Investors Business Daily.

73.   Senator John Barrasso, "Barrasso: Regulatory overreach smothering
      economy," *Washington Times*, August 22, 2011.

74.   Paul Bedard, "Report: Obama Administration Added $9.5 Billion in Red
      Tape in July," *US News & World Report*, August 3, 2011.

75.   "EPA Boiler Emission Rules Could Cost $20 Billion and 800,000 Jobs,"
      The Foundry, Heritage Foundation, November 1, 2010; and James L.
      Gattuso, Diane Katz, and Stephen A. Keen, "Red Tape Rising: Obama's
      Torrent of New Regulation," *Backgrounder* No. 2482, Heritage
      Foundation.

76.   Diane Katz, "President Obama's Regulatory Bait-and-Switch," *The
      Foundry*, Heritage Foundation, August 24, 2011.

77.   Katie Boyd, "Chamber: White House Review Won't 'Make Any Impact
      on the Overall Regulatory Burdens' Facing Job Creators," Speaker of the
      House John Boehner *Speaker Alert*.

78.   Philip Klein, "Obamacare Menu Regs Eat Into Small-Business Profits,"
      Examiner, August 8, 2011.

79.   Ibid.

80. Alan Rappeport, "Coca-Cola Chief Criticizes US Tax Rules," *Financial Times*, September 26, 2011.

81. Clarence Otis Jr., "What's stopping job creation? Too much regulation," CNN, December 6, 2011.

82. John Merline, "Regulation Business, Jobs Booming Under Obama," *Investors Business Daily*.

83. "Executive Summary: Economic Freedom of the World: 2011 Annual Report," Freetheworld.com, 2011.

84. Mike Brownfield, "Morning Bell: Tangled Up in Washington's Red Tape," *The Foundry*, Heritage Foundation, July 27, 2011.

85. Jessica Estepa, "GOP Media Goes Guerilla," *Roll Call*, September 12, 2011; and Elisabeth Meinecke, "GOP Releases 5 Job Destroying Regulations Proposed By the Obama Administration," Townhall.com, September 22, 2011.

86. T. Randolph Beard, Ph.D., George S. Ford, Ph.D., Hyeongwoo Kim, Ph.D., and Lawrence J. Spiwak, Esq., "Regulatory Expenditures, Economic Growth and Jobs: An Empirical Study," Phoenix Center for Advanced Legal and Economic Public Policy Studies, April 2011.

87. Phil Kerpen, "The REINS Act Ends Unchecked Bureaucratic Power," *The Hill* Congress Blog, December 2, 2012.

88. Senator Marco Rubio, "Reining in the Feds," National Review Online, December 7, 2011.

89. Peter Schiff, "Prepared Testimony Before the House Oversight and Government Reform Subcommittee on Regulatory Affairs, Stimulus Oversight and Government Spending, Hearing on Take Two: The President's Proposal to Stimulate the Economy and Create Jobs," *Financial Markets Regulatory Wire*, September 13, 2011.

90. James Gattuso, "Joblessness and Regulation: The 'Mass Layoff' Fallacy," Heritage.org, November 21, 2011; and Editors, "Democrat Denial Of Impact Of Regulations On Economy Holds Back Robust U.S. Recovery," *IBD* Editorials, November 21, 2011.

91. James Gattuso, "Joblessness and Regulation: The 'Mass Layoff' Fallacy," Heritage.org.

92. John Merline, "Regulation Business, Jobs Booming Under Obama," *Investors Business Daily*.

93. "Obama Dismisses Farmer's Concerns About Regulations: 'Don't Always Believe What You Hear,'" *Fox Nation*, Fox News, August 17, 2011.

94. Ashe Schow, "Beware Dust," *Heritage Action*, December 8, 2011.

95. "Cole Votes to Block EPA Farm Dust Regulations," Cole.house.gov, December 8, 2011.

96. Peter Wallsten and Jia Lynn Yang, "White House's Daley seeks balance in outreach meeting with manufacturers," *Washington Post*, June 16, 2011.

97. John Merline, "Home Depot Co-Founder: Obama Is Choking Recovery," Investors.com, July 20, 2011.

98. Tim Devaney, "Consumer electronics chief: Obama regulators lack business experience," *Washington Times*, October 17, 2011.

99. John Merline, "Regulation Business, Jobs Booming Under Obama," *Investors Business Daily*.

100. David Limbaugh, *Crimes Against Liberty* (Washington, D.C.: Regnery Publishing, 2010), p. 96.

101. Jon Ward, "War between Chamber of Commerce and White House spills into open," Daily Caller, July 14, 2010.

102. President Barack Obama, "Remarks of President Barack Obama to the Chamber of Commerce," White House Documents and Publications, February 7, 2011.

103. Ibid.

104. Matt Negrin and MR Lee, "Obama pleads with businesses," *Politico*, January 7, 2011.

105. President Barack Obama, "Remarks of President Barack Obama to the Chamber of Commerce."

106. Tahman Bradley, "D'oh! Caterpillar CEO Contradicts President on Whether Stimulus Will Allow Him to Re-Hire Laid Off Workers," ABCNews.go.com, February 12, 1009.

107. Greg Hengler, "CEO of Caterpillar Gives President Obama an 'F' on Job Creation," Townhall.com, December 13, 2011.

108. President Barack Obama, "Remarks of President Barack Obama Weekly Address August 21, 2010," CNN *Political Ticker*, August 21, 2010.

109. Jessica Rettig, "Senate Republicans Block DISCLOSE Act," *U.S. News & World Report*, July 27, 2010.

110. Michael O'Brien, "Obama Needles GOP for Allowing 'Corporate Takeover' of U.S. Campaigns," *The Hill*, September 17, 2010.

111. Jenny Schlesinger, "J'Accuse! President Obama Says Chamber of Commerce Using Foreign Funds to Influence US Elections," ABC News, October 7, 2010.

112. Matthew Murray, "U.S. Chamber Tangles With Obama Over Foreign Influences," *Roll Call*, September 18, 2010.

113. "CBS 'Face the Nation', Host: Bob Schieffer," interview of David Axelrod, Federal News Service, October 10, 2010.

114. Walter Alarkon, "Axelrod: Chamber Must Prove Foreign Money Allegations False," *The Hill*, October 10, 2010.

115. Eric Lichtblau, "Topic of Foreign Money in U.S. Races Hits Hustings," *New York Times*, October 8, 2010.

116. Ibid.

117. Meredith Shiner, "Chamber of Commerce to Joe Biden: 'Not a single cent,'" *Politico*, October 11, 2010.

118. Michelle Malkin, "Newly Nativist Democrats and Their Own Foreign Money," MichelleMalkin.com, October 11, 2010.

119. Peter Nicholas, "White House Accused of Urging Businesses to Quit Chamber of Commerce," *Los Angeles Times*, December 2, 2010.

120. Kingsley Guy, "Rich Target: Obama's Jet-Owner Bashing Isn't Smart," *Sun Sentinel*, July 17, 2011.

121. Lachlan Markay, "Obama Blasts Private Jet Tax Breaks Included in His Own Stimulus," *The Foundry*, Heritage Foundation, June 29, 2011.

122. Caroline May, "Jet Industry Furious at Obama," Daily Caller, July 6, 2011.

123. Ibid.

124. Alton K. Marsh, "Hawker Beechcraft CEO Takes On Obama Administration," AOPA Online, October 9, 2011.

125. Caroline May, "Jet Industry Furious at Obama," Daily Caller; and Charles C. W. Cooke, "Even the *West Wing* Rejected Obama's 'Private Jet' Meme," National Review Online, July 26, 2011.

126. Pete Kasperowicz, "GOP: Obama's Anti-corporate Jet Talk is Killing Aviation," *The Hill*, September 21, 2011.

127. Kingsley Guy, "Rich Target: Obama's Jet-Owner Bashing Isn't Smart," *Sun Sentinel*.

128. Caroline May, "Jet Industry Furious at Obama," Daily Caller.

129. "WH's Bernstein: Millionaires 'Don't Need the Extra Cash,'" *RealClearPolitics* Video, September 14, 2010.

130. Victoria McGrane, "Partisan Fight Flares Over New Bank Fees," *Wall Street Journal*, October 5, 2011.

131. Zachary A. Goldfarb, "Wall Street's resurgent prosperity frustrates its claims, and Obama's," *Washington Post*, November 6, 2011.

132. Ed Morrissey, "The stunning silence from the White House on GSE bonuses," HotAir.com, November 16, 2011.

133. Sam Youngman, "Obama Defends Business Record," *The Hill*, September 20, 2010.

134. Ibid.

135. Jon Ward, "Bloomberg: Obama 'not particularly interested in business,'" Daily Caller, September 30, 2010.

136. Timothy P. Carney, "Immelt, Daley, and Obama's antipathy to free markets," *Examiner*, January 23, 2011.

137. Ibid.

138. Rachel Layne, "GE Boss Issues Mea Culpa as Shares Fall: Conglomerate's Image 'Tarnished,' Immelt Admits," *Ottawa Citizen*, March 4, 2009.

139. Jeffrey R. Immelt, "How to keep America competitive," *Washington Post*, January 21, 2011.

140. Daniel Ikenson, "GE and Obama: A Betrothal at the Altar of Industrial Policy," *Cato @ Liberty*, April 8, 2011.

141. Ibid.

142. David Kocieniewski, "G.E.'s Strategies Let It Avoid Taxes Altogether," *New York Times*, March 24, 2011.

143. "Startup America," WhiteHouse.gov, January 31, 2011.

144. Ibid.

145. "What is a Startup Region?" Startup America Partnership, About Startup Regions.

146. Jim Roberts, "Obama's 'Startup America' Initiative: Stalling Entrepreneurs," *The Foundry*, Heritage Foundation, March 3, 2011.

147. Penny Starr, "White House Backs Bill to Collect Employee Pay Information from Businesses," CNS News, July 21, 2010.

148. James Sherk, "The Paycheck Fairness Act: Heritage Foundation 2010 Labor Boot Camp," Heritage Foundation, January 14, 2010.

149. Mike Brownfield, "Morning Bell: Obama's Crony Capitalist Trap Door," *The Foundry*, Heritage Foundation, February 23, 2012.

150. Editors, "Businesses Need Relief From Obama, Not Gov't Reorg," Investors.com, January 12, 2012.

CHAPTER TEN

1.   Editors, "Editorial: Obama & U.S. global decline: Year Two," *Washington Times*, January 2, 2011.

2.   CNN Wire Staff, "Obama says military commissions for Guantanamo detainees will resume," CNN *Political Ticker*, March 7, 2011.

3.   Ibid.

4.	Emily Miller, "Congressional GOP Push Back Against Obama's New Gitmo Policy," *Human Events*, March 8, 2011.

5.	Erik Kain, "President Obama Signed the National Defense Authorization Act – Now What?" *Forbes*, January 2, 2012; Sheldon Richman, "Congress, Obama Codify Indefinite Detention," Reason.com, December 28, 2011; and Matt Taibbi, "Indefinite Detention of American Citizens: Coming Soon to Battlefield U.S.A." RollingStone.com, December 9, 2011.

6.	Ed Pilkington, "Obama under fire over detention of terror suspect on US navy ship," *Guardian*, July 6, 2011.

7.	Mark Duell, "Guantanamo prisoners treated to $750,000 revamped soccer field courtesy of taxpayer," *Daily Mail*, February 29, 2012.

8.	Mark Landler and Helene Cooper, "Obama Seeks a Course of Pragmatism in the Middle East," *New York Times*, March 10, 2011.

9.	Kate Hicks, "Panetta: We'd Seek 'International Approval,' Not Congress', to Act in Syria," TownHall.com, March 8, 2012.

10.	"Editorial: What is U.S. National Interest In Libya?" Investors.com, March 23, 2011.

11.	Glenn Kessler, "On Libya, where you stand depends on where you sit," *Washington Post* The Fact Checker, March 29, 2011.

12.	John R. Bolton, "War-powers crisis, Obama's Libyan debacle could undercut U.S. credibility elsewhere," *Washington Times*, June 6, 2011.

13.	Byron York, "White House: Libya Fight Is Not War, "It's 'Kinetic Military Action,'" *Examiner*, March, 2011.

14.	Jonah Goldberg, "Obama's Biggest Flip," *The Corner*, National Review Online, March 29, 2011.

15.	Alan J. Kuperman, "False Pretenses for War in Libya," Boston.com, April 14, 2011; David D. Kirkpatrick and Kareem Fahim, "Qaddafi Warns of Assault on Benghazi as U.N. Vote Nears," *New York Times*, March 17, 2011.

16.	Charlie Savage, "2 Top Lawyers Lost to Obama in Libya War Policy Debate," *New York Times*, June 17, 2011.

17.	Amar C. Bakshi, "Doug Feith: The President wants to cut America down to size," CNN *World*, March 23, 2011.

18.	"Editorial: What Is U.S. National Interest In Libya?" Investors.com.

19.	David Limbaugh, "Obama's Libya: Completing His Remaking of America," DavidLimbaugh.com, March 24, 2011.

20.	David Rieff, "Saints Go Marching In," *The National Interest*, June 21, 2011.

21.	Bruce Ackerman and Oona Hathaway, "Death of the War Powers Act?" *Washington Post*, May 17, 2011.

22. Jake Tapper, "White House on War Powers Deadline: 'Limited' US Role in Libya Means No Need to Get Congressional Authorization," ABC News *Political Punch*, May 20, 2011.
23. Editors, "Leading Libya From Behind," *Wall Street Journal*, June 18, 2011.
24. Dave Majumdar, "AFRICOM: AF, Navy still flying Libya missions," *Air Force Times*, June 30, 2011.
25. Stephen Dinan, "Bipartisan Congress rebuffs Obama on Libya mission," *Washington Times*, June 3, 2011.
26. John R. Bolton, "War-powers crisis, Obama's Libyan debacle could undercut U.S. credibility elsewhere," *Washington Times*.
27. David M. Drucker and Jessica Brady, "McCain Scolds White House on Libya," *Roll Call*, June 16, 2011.
28. John Bolton, "Why is Obama giving Libya to the Russians?" Reuters, July 19, 2011.
29. Stanley Kurtz, "Obama Hands Libya to Russia?" *The Corner*, National Review Online, July 20, 2011.
30. Brian Ross, "Nightmare in Libya: Thousands of Surface-to-Air Missiles Unaccounted For," ABC News, September 27, 2011.
31. Ibid.
32. Lama Hasan, "Missing Libya Missiles Find Their Way to Gaza Border," ABC News, October 13, 2011.
33. Mary Beth Sheridan, "U.S. launches campaign to track down Libyan missiles," *Washington Post*, October 13, 2011.
34. Brian Rohan, "Displaced black Libyans tell of beatings, expulsion at gunpoint," Reuters, October 17, 2011.
35. Karin Laub and Kim Gamel, "Rights Group Finds Mass Grave in Gadhafi Hometown," Associated Press, October 24, 2011.
36. Richard Spencer, "Libya's liberation: interim ruler unveils more radical than expected plans for Islamic law," *Telegraph*, October 23, 2011.
37. Sherif Elhelwa, "Al Qaeda Plants Its Flag In Libya," Vice.com, October 28, 2011.
38. Marc Thiessen, "Leaving behind 'leading from behind'?" *The American*, November 1, 2011.
39. Ewen MacAskill, "Barack Obama impatient for credible transition in Egypt," *Guardian*, February 11, 2011.
40. JR Nyquist, "Egypt and the Muslim Brotherhood," *Financial Sense*, February 11, 2011.
41. David D. Kirkpatrick, "Islamists Win 70% of Seats in the Egyptian Parliament," *New York Times*, January 21, 2012

42. "Obama Administration Corrects Clapper's Claim That Muslim Brotherhood Is 'Secular,'" *Fox News*, February 10, 2011.

43. Ibid.

44. Devonia Smith, "James Bolton on Egypt: Mob rule is not democracy – stability is urgent need," *Examiner*, February 10, 2011.

45. Nile Gardiner, "The Muslim Brotherhood gets a PR makeover from the Obama administration," *Telegraph*, February 11, 2011.

46. Andrew C. McCarthy, "There's Willful Blindness, and Then There's Willful Stupidity," *The Corner*, National Review Online, February 10, 2011.

47. Edmund Blair, "U.S. met with Egypt Islamists: U.S. diplomat," Reuters, October 2, 2011.

48. Josh Rogin, "State Department training Islamic political parties in Egypt," *Foreign Policy* The Cable, November 3, 2011.

49. "Washington Hints It Would Not Object to Brotherhood Win in Egypt," Agence France Presse, November 4, 2011.

50. Byron Tau, "Muslim Brotherhood delegation meets with White House officials," *Politico*, April 4, 2012.

51. Steven Emerson, "IPT Exclusive: State Department Barred Inspection of Muslim Brotherhood Delegation," The Investigative Project on Terrorism *IPT News*, April 9, 2012.

52. Andrew McCarthy, "Report: Obama State Department Barred Inspection of Muslim Brotherhood Delegation," *The Corner*, National Review Online, April 11, 2012; and Jim Hoft, "Screw Democracy!... Obama Administration Will Give Muslim Brotherhood $1.5 Billion in US Aid," Gateway Pundit, March 22, 2012.

53. Awr Hawkins, "Obama Bypasses Congress, Gives $1.5 Billion to Muslim Brotherhood," Breitbart.com, March 21, 2012.

54. Keith Koffler, "Obama Calls for Restraint by Egypt's Christians," *White House Dossier*, October 13, 2011.

55. "Major change in U.S. tone on Egypt," CNN, November 26, 2011.

56. "Day 68 of Egyptian Hostage Crisis: Americans Go on Trial," *Atlas Shrugs*, February 26, 2012.

57. "Egypt 'lifts' travel ban on US NGO workers," BBC, March 1, 2012.

58. Editors, "Obama's Chickens Come Home To Roost in Egypt," Investors.com, February 14, 2012.

59. Ibid.

60. Michael J. Totten, "US Criticized by Tunisian Secularists for Backing Islamists," *World Affairs*, March 21, 2012.

61. Andrew C. McCarthy, "Islam Is Islam, And That's It," National Review Online, January 23, 2012.
62. Scott McKay, "Exclusive: John Brennan Thinks Jihad is a 'Legitimate Tenet of Islam,'" *Family Security Matters*, May 28, 2010.
63. William Mayer, "John Brennan's 'Al Quds' NYU Address – Providing Aid and Comfort to Islamists," PipelineNews.org, May 25, 2010.
64. "Obama regrets distortion of Islam to justify violence – Copyright The Times of India," YouTube.com, November 7, 2010; and Erick Stakelbeck, *The Terrorist Next Door* (Washington, D.C.: Regnery, 2011), 195–96.
65. "Obama, the Interpreter of the Message of the Passover," *Arutz Sheva*, April 18, 2011.
66. "(PJM Exclusive) Holder's DOJ Scuttled More Terror-Related Prosecutions," PJ Media, April 28, 2011.
67. Edwin Mora, "Three Convicted in Terror-Related Cases Later Granted U.S. Citizenship by Obama Administration," CNS News, April 29, 2011.
68. John J. Miller, "Photo Finish," *The Corner*, National Review Online, May 5, 2011.
69. "Whom Are We At War With?" *The Foundry*, Heritage Foundation, September 22, 2010.
70. Nina Shea, "The Administration Takes on 'Islamophobia,'" National Review Online, September 1, 2011.
71. Jordy Yager, "Lieberman: Obama's concern with offending Muslims is hurting the war effort," *The Hill*, September 1, 2011.
72. Leslie H. Gelb, "Joe Biden On Iraq, Iran, China and the Taliban," *The Daily Beast*, December 19, 2011; and Ben Smith, "'The Taliban is not our enemy,'" *Politico*, December 19, 2011.
73. Max Boot, "Biden's Appalling Statement on Iraq," Contentions, *Commentary*, December 1, 2011.
74. Witness Secretary of State Hillary Rodham Clinton, Hearing of the House Committee on Foreign Affairs, Subject: Assessing U.S. Foreign Policy Priorities and Needs Amidst Economic Challenges, Federal News Service, March 1, 2001; and Rush Limbaugh, "Mrs. Clinton Assures the World: America Won't Steal Libya's Oil," *The Rush Limbaugh Show*, March 2, 2011.
75. President Barack Obama, "Remarks by the President to U.S.-India Business Council and Entrepreneurship Summit," WhiteHouse.gov, November 8, 2010.

76. Michael Prell, "Prell: Obama made them hate us," *Washington Times*, August 19, 2011.
77. "Editorial: Obama & U.S. global decline: Year Two," *Washington Times*.
78. News Staff, "Harper Tells UN to Focus on Child, Maternal Health," CTV News, December 1, 2010; and Jim Hoft, "Canadians Walk Out on Ahmadinejad at UN – US Officials Stay Put," *The Gateway Pundit*, September 21, 2010.
79. "Editorial: Obama & U.S. global decline: Year Two," *Washington Times*.
80. Joel Gehrke, "General: Worst U.S. image in Pakistan ever," *Examiner*, November 28, 2011.
81. Staff Writers, "Obama Backs Venezuela's Right to Nuclear Energy," *Nuclear Power Daily*, October 19, 2010.
82. Ray Walser, "Hugo Chavez: The End of the Inter-American System," *The Foundry*, Heritage Foundation, December 1, 2011; and Editors of VenEconomy, "Yet Another Parallel Organization Joins the List," *Latin American Herald Tribune*," December 2, 2011.
83. "Containing Israel on Iran," *Wall Street Journal*, February 21, 2012.
84. "White House Silent on Conversation With French President Insulting Israeli Prime Minister," Fox News, November 8, 2011.
85. Nile Gardiner, "President Obama's top ten insults against Britain – 2011 edition," *Telegraph*, May 24, 2011.
86. Peter Wehner, "U.S. Relations Have Soured Worldwide," Contentions, *Commentary*, November 29, 2011.
87. Ibid.
88. "Obama Doctrine Failure" *The Foundry*, Heritage Foundation, February 27, 2012.
89. Alberto de la Cruz, "Obama Admin Lobbying Honduras To Allow Zelaya Back In? Are you Kidding?" PJ Media, January 20, 2011.
90. Ileana Ros-Lehtinen, "Ros-Lehtinen Concerned by Reported State Department Pressure on Honduras to Absolve Zelaya," U.S. House Committee on Foreign Affairs, January 6, 2011.
91. Patrick Goodenough, "Obama on Wrong Side of Honduras Dispute, GOP Lawmaker Warns," CNS News, May 24, 2011.
92. Ibid.
93. Mary Anastasia O'Grady, "WikiLeaks, Honduras and the U.S.," *Wall Street Journal*, December 20, 2010.
94. Ibid.
95. Transcript, "Rahm Emanuel: Obama 'Fully Informed' on Spy Swap Plan," PBS *News Hour*, July 8, 2010; and Ellie Velinska, "Igor Sutyagin is not a

spy. He is a KGB political prisoner," *Big Bureaucracy*, July 8, 2010. White House chief of staff Rahm Emanuel did not object to PBS's Jim Lehrer characterizing the deal as a "spy swap."

96. Gene Coyle, "Spy swap was a mistake," CNN, July 9, 2010.

97. The Honorable Paula DeSutter, "Verification and the New START Treaty," Heritage Foundation, July 12, 2010.

98. Daniel Horowitz, "Obama's Un-American Nuclear Weapons Policy," RedState.com, February 17, 2012.

99. Ariel Cohen, Ph.D., Baker Spring, and Michaela Bendikova, "Reset Regret: Obama's Cold War-Style Arms Control Undermines U.S.-Russian Relations," Heritage Foundation, June 20, 2011.

100. Matthew Moore, Gordon Rayner, and Christopher Hope, "WikiLeaks cables: US agrees to tell Russia Britain's nuclear secrets," *Telegraph*, February 4, 2011.

101. "WikiLeaks: Pres. Obama Traded Missile Shield for Russian Support," *Fox Nation*, November 29, 2010.

102. Andrew Osborn, "Russia Wants 'Red Button' Rights for US Missile Defense System," *Telegraph*, November 28, 2011.

103. "Russia threatens U.S. missile shield," Associated Press, November 23, 2011; "Moscow may quit START over US deploying missile shield in Europe," May 16, 2011, at http://rt.com/politics/nato-missile-defense-medvedev/; and Ariel Cohen, "Will Russian Missile Defense Hysteria Torpedo the 'Reset'?" *The Foundry*, Heritage Foundation, November 29, 2011.

104. J. David Goodman, "Microphone Catches a Candid Obama," *New York Times*, March 26, 2012.

105. Katie Pavlich, "Obama Wants to Cut U.S. Nukes by 80 Percent," Townhall.com, February 15, 2012.

106. Editors, "Disarming America: Obama Betrays Reagan's Dream," Investors.com, March 16, 2012.

107. Editors, "China Spurns Defense Secretary Gates," Investors.com, January 11, 2011; and Tom Vanden Brook, Jim Michaels and Aamer Madhani, "Obama unveils strategy for slimmed-down military," *USA Today*, January 6, 2012.

108. Jeff Poor, "Krauthammer: Obama military reforms a 'road map of American decline,'" Daily Caller, January 5, 2012.

109. Omri Ceren, "Obama Administration Unilaterally Limiting U.S. Space Development, Ceding to China," *Contentions*, *Commentary*, March 3, 2011.

110. Eli Lake, "Report calls for restraints in space activity," *Washington Times*, February 7, 2011.

111. Ibid.

112. Ibid.

113. Ibid.

114. Omri Ceren, "Obama's New Anti-Satellite Weapons Push to Cede Space to the Chinese," Contentions, *Commentary*, January 28, 2011.

115. Ibid.

116. Conn Carroll, "Morning Bell: Dragon Week," *The Foundry*, Heritage Foundation, January 18, 2011.

117. Congressman Pete Olson, "Guest Blog: China's Space Program Threatens U.S. National Security," *The Foundry*, Heritage Foundation, November 14, 2011.

118. Peter Schweizer, "Why is Obama Arming the World?" *Big Peace*, March 8, 2011.

119. Matthew Mosk, "Critics Slam Obama Administration for 'Hiding' Massive Saudi Arms Deal," ABC News, November 19, 2010; and Mina Kimes, "America's hottest export: Weapons – Full version," CNN *Money*, February 24, 2011.

120. Shahien Nasiripour, "Obama Picks Jeffrey Immelt, GE CEO, To Run New Jobs-Focused Panel As GE Sends Jobs Overseas, Pays Little In Taxes," *Huffington Post*, May 25, 2011.

121. Editors, "Trading Away Secrets," Investors.com, January 19, 2011.

122. Peter Barnes and the Associated Press, "U.S., China Announce $45 Billion Business Deal," Fox News, January 19, 2011.

123. Editors, "China Spurns Defense Secretary Gates," Investors.com.

124. Chris Buckley, "China boosts defense budget 11 percent after U.S. 'pivot,'" Reuters, March 4, 2012.

125. Daniel Goure, Ph.D., "Sale Of Russian Fighters To China Undermines Gates Decision On F-22," *Defense Professionals News*, November 22, 2010.

126. James Corum, "US defence cuts are not about saving money – they are about changing America's strategic role," *Telegraph*, January 12, 2011.

127. David A. Fulghum, "Chinese Air Force Could Overwhelm," *Aviation Week*, January 7, 2011.

128. Max Boot, "War Games Show U.S. Cannot Afford Defense Cutbacks," *Contentions*, *Commentary*, January 10, 2011.

129. Kevin Baron, "Exiting AF Flag Officer Intel Chief: No US Air Superiority," *Stars and Stripes*, September 15, 2010.

130. Jim Emerson, "Letter to President Barack Obama, Sen. Jim Webb and Sen. Mark Warner: Is U.S. Air Superiority Ending? Top USAF General Says 'Yes,' Gates Says 'No'," Congress.org, September 25, 2010.

131. Paul Chesser, "Did DOE Rush to Give Away Stimulus Compromise National Security?" National Legal and Policy Center, January 30, 2012.

132. James Corum, "US defense cuts are not about saving money – they are about changing America's strategic role," *Telegraph*, January 12, 2011.

CHAPTER ELEVEN

1.   Bob Owens, "Gunwalker: From Obama's Inauguration to Issa's Report," PJ Media, June 20, 2011.

2.   Michael Isikoff, "A Self-Inflicted Gun Wound," *The Daily Beast*, March 24, 2009.

3.   Dane Schiller, "U.S. border czar confronts disturbing Mexico discovery," *Houston Chronicle*, April 14, 2009.

4.   Katie Pavlich, "Obama Administration to Implement More Gun Control Without Congress," Townhall.com, July 8, 2011.

5.   Joint Staff Report, "The Department of Justice's Operation Fast and Furious: Account of ATF Agents," United States House of Representatives Committee on Oversight and Government Reform, June 14, 2011.

6.   Richard A. Serrano, "Congress expands Fast and Furious probe to White House," *Los Angeles Times*, September 9, 2011.

7.   Katie Pavlich, "Attorney General in Mexico: 200 Murders Result of Operation Fast and Furious," Townhall.com, September 20, 2011; and Tina Korbe, "Mark Steyn: Why the lack of MSM outrage at 'dead Mexicans'?" HotAir.com, October 7, 2011.

8.   Richard A. Serrano, "Firearms from ATF sting linked to 11 more violent crimes in U.S.," *Los Angeles Times*, August 17, 2011.

9.   Editorial, "Operation Fast and Furious Should End Holder Tenure," *Examiner*, June 16, 2011.

10. Ken Ellingwood, Richard A. Serrano, and Tracy Wilkinson, "Mexico still waiting for answers on Fast and Furious program," *Los Angeles Times*, September 19, 2011.

11. Richard A. Serrano, "Congress expands Fast and Furious probe to White House," *Los Angeles Times*, September 9, 2011.

12. Sharyl Attkisson, "ATF manager says he shared Fast and Furious Info with White Hose," CBS News, July 26, 2011.

13. Richard A. Serrano, "White House received emails about Fast and Furious gun-trafficking operation," *Los Angeles Times*, September 2, 2011.

14. "Key Players and Places," Committee on Oversight and Government Reform, Operation Fast and Furious.

15. William La Jeunesse, "Friction Grows Between Lawmakers and DOJ Over 'Project Gunrunner' Probe," Fox News, May 4, 2011.

16. Matthew Boyle, "DOJ deflects gunrunner, Fast and Furious blame to local officials," Daily Caller, May 10, 2011.

17. John Hayward "No, Operation Wide Receiver Does Not Excuse Obama Or Holder," *Human Events*, October 7, 2011.

18. Ibid.

19. Ed Morrissey, "Video: Cornyn blows up 'Bush did it too' on Fast and Furious," HotAir.com, November 10, 2011; and Andrew C. McCarthy, "Fast & Furious Was... Bush's Fault," *The Corner*, National Review Online, November 8, 2011.

20. Editorial, "Operation Fast and Furious Should End Holder Tenure," *Examiner*.

21. Ibid.

22. "The Department of Justice's Operation Fast and Furious: Accounts of ATF Agents," Joint Staff Report, United States House of Representatives Committee on Oversight and Government Reform, June 14, 2011.

23. Paul Bedard, "Fast & Furious Was Much Broader, Issa Charges," *U.S. News & World Report* Washington Whispers, July 6, 2011.

24. Richard A. Serrano, "ATF promotes supervisors in controversial gun operation," *Los Angeles Times*, August 16, 2011.

25. Ibid.

26. Ibid.

27. Bob Owens, "ATF Whistleblower: Gunwalker Officials Being Shielded," PJ Media, August 19, 2011.

28. Jennifer Epstein and Josh Gerstein, "Ken Melson, acting ATF chief, steps down," *Politico*, August 30, 2011.

29. "The Department of Justice's Operation Fast and Furious: Accounts of ATF Agents," Joint Staff Report, United States House of Representatives Committee on Oversight and Government Reform.

30. Maxim Lott, "'Project Gunrunner' Whistleblower Says ATF Sent Him Termination Notice," Fox News, June 27, 2011.

31. Ibid.

32. David Codrea, "Federal LEO Advocacy Group Charges Retaliation for Gunwalker Testimony," *Examiner*, September 5, 2011; and Luciano Cerasi, Associate General Counsel, Federal Law Enforcement Officers Association, "Letter to Sen. Charles Grassley and Rep. Darrell Issa," August 31, 2011.

33. Katie Pavlich, "Dems Call for More Gun Control in Light of Operation Fast and Furious," Townhall.com, June 30, 2011.

34. Seung Min Kim, "'Fast and Furious' inquiry broadens," *Politico*, June 30, 2011.

35. Committee Staff for Chairman Darrell Issa and Senator Charles Grassley, Ranking Member, Senate Judiciary Committee, "Memorandum: Re: Main Justice: Extensive Involvement in Operation Fast and Furious," House Committee on Oversight and Government Reform, February 1, 2012.

36. Ronald Kolb, "Connecting the Dots on Fast and Furious," *American Thinker*, March 2, 2012.

37. News Release, "Grassley Presses Holder on Gunwalking Allowed by Justice Department," Federal News Service, November 8, 2011.

38. "Gowdy Questions AG Holder on Key Players Involved with Fast & Furious," YouTube.com, December 8, 2011.

39. Ibid.

40. Katie Pavlich, "Democrats Fully Engaged in Fast and Furious Coverup," Townhall.com, January 31, 2012.

41. Anderson Cooper, "AC360 Follow: Congress Wants Answers on ATF Operation," AC360Blogs.CNN.com, June 22, 2011.

42. Katie Pavlich, "Obama Still Denies Holder Authorized Operation Fast and Furious," Townhall.com, June 29, 2011.

43. Ibid.

44. Darrell Issa, "Issa: Holder protecting staff over 'Fast and Furious,'" *USA Today*, December 7, 2011.

45. Devin Dwyer, "Obama on 'Fast and Furious': 'People Who Have Screwed Up Will Be Held Accountable,'" ABC News, October 18, 2011.

46. William La Jeunesse, "'Fast and Furious' Whistleblowers Struggle Six Months After Testifying Against ATF Program," Fox News, November 30, 2011.

47. Ibid.

48. Ibid.

49. Ibid.
50. Ibid.
51. Ed Morrissey, "Holder to Issa: I'll hold people accountable... for whistleblowing," HotAir.com, February 2, 2012.
52. William La Jeunesse, "Issa Threatens Contempt Proceeding Against Holder if Justice Fails to Comply with Fast and Furious Subpoenas," Fox News, January 31, 2012.
53. Ibid.
54. Ibid.
55. Sharyl Attkisson, "DOJ's Breuer authorized wiretap in ATF Fast and Furious case," CBS News, May 4, 2011.
56. Katie Pavlich, "Democrats Fully Engaged in Fast and Furious Coverup," Townhall.com.
57. "Gowdy to AG Holder: Wiretaps for Operation Fast & Furious and Hierarchy of Key DOJ Players," YouTube.com.
58. Katie Pavlich, "Democrats Fully Engaged in Fast and Furious Coverup," Townhall.com.
59. Anderson Cooper, "AC360 Follow: Congress Wants Answers on ATF Operation," AC360Blogs.CNN.com.
60. John Hayward, "The Truth About Gunwalker," *Human Events*, June 24, 2011.
61. Deputy Attorney General James Cole, "Statement of Deputy Attorney General James Cole Regarding Information Requests for Multiple Sales of Semi-Automatic Rifles with Detachable Magazines," United States Department of Justice, July 11, 2011.
62. William La Jeunesse and Laura Prabucki, "GOP Report: Justice Officials Were on Top of Fast and Furious," Fox News, February 2, 2012.
63. Ibid.
64. "Fortress Holder: A Year of Justice Department Stonewalling, Visualized," Committee on Oversight and Government Reform, February 2012.
65. Committee Staff for Chairman Darrell Issa and Senator Charles Grassley, Ranking Member, Senate Judiciary Committee, "Memorandum: Re: Main Justice: Extensive Involvement in Operation Fast and Furious," House Committee on Oversight and Government Reform.
66. Ibid.
67. Ibid.
68. Matthew Boyle, "Lieberman Directs Staff to Examine Fast and Furious Coordination," Daily Caller, December 22, 2011.

69. Committee Staff for Chairman Darrell Issa and Senator Charles Grassley, "Memorandum: Re: Main Justice: Extensive Involvement in Operation Fast and Furious," House Committee on Oversight and Government Reform.
70. Ibid.
71. Ibid.
72. Ibid.

CHAPTER TWELVE

1. "Biden: Obama Has a 'Brain Bigger Than His Skull,'" *RealClearPolitics*, October 15, 2010.
2. Roger Simon, "W.H. furious over speech delay," *Politico*, September 4, 2011.
3. Ibid.
4. Ibid.
5. "Obama: My Finances Have Suffered Too," Breitbart TV, July 27, 2010.
6. "Obama: We don't get enough credit for success," CBS News, August 1, 2010.
7. Ibid.
8. Ian Swanson, "Top Obama adviser says unemployment won't be key in 2012," *The Hill*, July 7, 2011.
9. Michael A. Memoli, "Biden: Second Obama term possible even with high unemployment," *Los Angeles Times*, August 22, 2011.
10. Eric Scheiner, "Obama: 'Professional Politicians' Understand Debt Crisis Better Than 'The Public,'" CNS News, July 11, 2011.
11. Matt Cover, "White House: 'Americans Don't Have a Lot of Time to Focus on 'What is a Debt Ceiling?'" CNS News, July 13, 2011.
12. "Obama: Fourth Best President in History Due to Foreign Policy Achievements," *RealClearPolitics*, December 17, 2011.
13. "Obama Likens Himself To Gandhi And Nelson Mandela," *RealClearPolitics*, March 2, 2012.
14. Michael Barone, "Like Chauncey Gardiner, Obama is Profoundly Aloof," *Examiner*, June 25, 2011.
15. Maureen Dowd, "Showtime at the Apollo," *New York Times*, January 21, 2012.
16. Ibid.

17. Sam Youngman, "White House unloads anger over criticism from 'professional left,'" *The Hill*, August 10, 2010.
18. Alexander Mooney, "Obama: They talk about me like a dog," CNN *Political Ticker*, September 6, 2010.
19. "Jindal: Obama Told Us Not to Criticize Him on TV," *The Right Scoop*, November 22, 2010.
20. "Arizona Gov. Jan Brewer, Obama have intense exchange on tarmac," *Chicago Sun-Times*, January 26, 2012.
21. Carrie Budoff Brown, "Obama's tarmac tiff with Jan Brewer: the president fights back," *Politico*, January 27, 2012.
22. Sam Youngman, "President Obama seeks his inner Bill Clinton and feels voters' pain," *The Hill*, September 13, 2010.
23. Ibid.
24. "Obama: Voters 'Scared,' Not Thinking Clearly About Election," Fox News, October 18, 2010.
25. David Jackson, "Obama Aide Axelrod: The president is not a snob," *USA Today*, October 20, 2010.
26. Mickey Kaus, "Obama Clings Again! Blames 'Scared' Voters," *The Daily Beast*, October 17, 2010.
27. Allahpundit, "Obama: You know who's a pretty good president? *Me*," HotAir.com, October 21, 2010.
28. "Obama: 'I Don't Think There's A Sense That I've Been Successful,'" *RealClearPolitics*, December 14, 2010.
29. Byron York, "Obama Honors Nobel Winner with Statement about Himself," *Examiner*, December 10, 2010.
30. Matt Negrin, "Obama reads his book to kids," *Politico*, December 17, 2010.
31. Jordan Fabian, "Obama tells lawmakers not passing tax deal could end presidency, Dem says," *The Hill*, December 15, 2010.
32. Matt Negrin, "After speech, Obama feels good," *Politico*, January 13, 2011.
33. Scott Johnson, "Osama Bin Gone: Stephen Hunter Comments," *Powerline* blog, May 2, 2011.
34. Sara Just, "Obama Scolds Congress, Says Malia and Sasha Are More Disciplined," ABC News, June 29, 2011.
35. Major Garrett, "Obama Patience Wears Thin as BP Struggles to Contain Oil Spill," Fox News, May 25, 2010.
36. "Obama 'Amused' When People Say He Should Be Involved in Debt Talks," *RealClearPolitics*, June 29, 2011.

37. Sam Youngman, "Obama: 'Last thing we need' is for Congress to return to DC," *The Hill*, August 11, 2011.

38. "Obama skips debt commission meeting," CNN, December 9, 2010.

39. Michael Goodwin, "Aimless Obama walks alone," *New York Post*, October 9, 2011.

40. Nile Gardiner, "Barack Obama, the most arrogant US president in decades," *Telegraph*, January 5, 2012.

41. Hannah Roberts, "Well it has been a whole month! Just weeks after 17-day Hawaii vacation Michelle hits the slopes with daughters on Aspen ski trip," *Daily Mail*, February 20, 2012.

42. Andrew Malcolm, "The increasingly odd political optics of Barack Obama," *Los Angeles Times*, April 26, 2011.

43. Ibid.

44. Jake Tapper, "Hoopster In Chief Has Own Image on Ball," ABC News, April 9, 2012.

45. Keith Koffler, "Obamas Share Sacrifice at Pricey Vineyard Restaurant," *White House Dossier*, August 19, 2011.

46. Jon Ward, "White House says Obama's golf outings 'do us all good,'" Daily Caller, June 21, 2010.

47. Administrator, "Obama hits links for 52nd golf day," *The Hill*, October 9, 2010.

48. Toby Harnden, "Barack Obama plays golf eight more times than George W. Bush," *The UK Telegraph*, April 19, 2010.

49. Jake Sherman, "Oil spill visits get partisan," *Politico*, July 1, 2010.

50. "Michelle Obama to visit Florida to view effects of Gulf oil spill," *NOLA*, July 7, 2010.

51. "Michelle Obama in Panama City, Fla; 'There Are Still 1000s of Miles of Beaches Not Touched By the Spill,'" *Alabama Press Register*, July 12, 2010.

52. "Gibbs Explains Why Obamas Won't Vacation in Gulf," *RealClearPolitics*, July 13, 2010.

53. Melissa Grace, "President Obama, wife Michelle and kids to see sights, eat lobster in Bar Harbor, Maine," *New York Daily News*, July 16, 2010.

54. Rebekah Metzler, "White House Wanderers Tour Acadia," *Morning Sentinel*, July 17, 2010.

55. "Obamas Will Vacation on Gulf Coast," MSNBC.com, July 22, 2010.

56. "Obama to holiday in southern Spain: reports," Expatica.com, July 25, 2010.

57. "Barack Obama to Stay in Marbella," TypicallySpanish.com, July 25, 2010.

58. Jordan Fabian, "Michelle Obama to make private visit to Spain during president's birthday," *The Hill*, July 26, 2010.

59. Mail Foreign Service, "Spanish police close public beach for Michelle Obama's 250,000 pound Spanish holiday," *UK Mail*, August 6, 2010.

60. Ibid.

61. Lynn Sweet, "Michelle Obama at luxury Spanish resort: Gibbs asked about 'the appearance' of trip," *Chicago Sun-Times*, August 5, 2010.

62. Holly Bailey, "First Lady Went to Spain to Spend Time with Grieving Friend," *Yahoo! News*, August 10, 2010.

63. Exurban Jon, "Obamas take 4 vacations in 1 month," ExurbanLeague.com, July 26, 2010; Jake Tapper, "What Does a President Do on a Rainy Vacation Day?" ABC News, August 23, 2010; and Lynn Sweet, "Michelle Obama at luxury Spanish resort: Gibbs asked about 'the appearance' of trip," *Chicago Sun-Times*.

64. "Letterman: Obama Will 'Have Plenty of Time for Vacations After His One Term is Up,'" *But As For Me News*, August 25, 2010.

65. Somendra Sharma, "800 Luxury Hotel Rooms Booked for Obama's Visit to Mumbai," *DNA India*, October 22, 2010.

66. Saurabh Shukla, "Obama's Trip to be Biggest Ever," *India Today*, October 27, 2010.

67. "34 Warships Sent from US for Obama Visit," *NDTV*, November 4, 2010; and "US to Spend $200 mn a Day on Obama's Mumbai Visit," *NDTV*, November 3, 2010.

68. "Bomb-proof tunnel with air-conditioning: Obama's security go to extraordinary measures for his tour of the Gandhi Museum," *Daily Mail*, November 6, 2010.

69. "More bad news, Mr. President… Obama is no longer the 'world's most powerful man,'" *Daily Mail*, November 5, 2010.

70. "Military Pegs Hourly Air Force One Cost at $181G, as Obama Sets Travel Record," Fox News, November 24, 2010.

71. Byron York, "Obama Spends Nearly Half His Presidency Outside Washington, Plans to Travel More," *Examiner*, January 1, 2011.

72. "Photos of President Barack Obama's Hawaii Vacation Home," *Aloha Update*, December 23, 2010.

73. Malia Zimmerman, "Obama's Million Dollar Hawaiian Vacation: Cost to Taxpayers Detailed," *Hawaii Reporter*, December 28, 2010.

74.   David Gardner, "Wish you were here? President spends $1.5m on his holiday in Hawaii… while the rest of America faces a bleak New Year," *Daily Mail*, December 30, 2010.

75.   "All the President's Men: Obama given a 20-MAN motorcade to visit childhood friend in Hawaii (no wonder his Christmas holiday is costing the country $1.5m)," *Daily Mail*, January 1, 2011.

76.   James Warren, "No Pity for Robert Gibbs and His 'Modest' Salary," *The Atlantic*, January 6, 2011.

77.   Vince Coglianese, "Ice cleared from outside Obama's daughters' school, but not from public school across the street," Daily Caller, January 20, 2011.

78.   Jim Hoft, "Sacrifice Is For the Little People… Obama White House Serves $399 Bottles of Wine at State Dinner," *Gateway Pundit*, January 20, 2011.

79.   Keith Koffler, "While Cairo Burns, Obama Parties," *White House Dossier*, January 30, 2011.

80.   "Keeping busy, Mr. President? Obama heads out for his 60th game of golf since reaching the White House…as he also takes up brewing his own beer," *Daily Mail*, March 7, 2011.

81.   Ed O'Keefe, "Michelle Obama, with Malia and Sasha, skiing in Colorado this weekend," *Washington Post*, February 19, 2011.

82.   David Gardner, "So Much for the diet: anti-obesity crusader Michelle Obama feasts on ribs during pricey vacation," *Daily Mail*, February 22, 2011.

83.   Keith Koffler, "Golf is Back! Obama's 60th Outing as President," *White House Dossier*, March 5, 2011.

84.   Mike Allen, "Obama taping NCAA brackets today for ESPN," *Politico*, March 15, 2011.

85.   Jim Geraghty, "While Japan Burns, Obama Fills Out His Bracket," National Review Online, March 15, 2011.

86.   Julie Mason, "W.H. responds to bracket gripes," *Politico*, March 16, 2011.

87.   Keith Koffler, "Obama Golfs for Fifth Weekend in a Row," *White House Dossier*, May 1, 2011.

88.   Harry Mount, "Obama played golf as US special forces prepared to kill bin Laden," *UK Telegraph*, May 2, 2011.

89.   Tina Korbe, "Confirmed: President Obama campaigns on the taxpayer's dime more than previous presidents," HotAir.com, November 28, 2011.

90.   Anneke E. Green, "Green: Obama hits the links rather than honor police dead," *Washington Times*, May 15, 2011.

91.   "National President Canterbury Sent a Letter Expressing the 'Profound Disappointment' of the Fraternal Order of Police," Fraternal Order of Police, May 11, 2011.

92. "Golfer-in-Chief," *Weasel Zippers*, May 30, 2011.

93. Keith Koffler, "Obama Makes it Ten Weekends in a Row," *White House Dossier*, June 4, 2011.

94. Keith Koffler, "Obama Out Golfing for 13th Weekend in a Row," *White House Dossier*, June 25, 2011.

95. "Our Long National Nightmare Is Over: Obama Makes It Back To The Golf Course After Seven-Week Lull...," *Weasel Zippers*, August 13, 2011.

96. David Nakamura, "Obama plays through on golf course during earthquake, inspires critics," *Washington Post*, August 24, 2011.

97. "Golfer-in Chief Plays 80th Golf Game Since Taking Office," *Bluegrass Pundit*, August 25, 2011.

98. Keith Koffler, "Obama Golf for 90th Time as President," *White House Dossier*, December 26, 2011.

99. Malia Zimmerman, "Obama Family's Pricey Vacations Are Gaining International Attention," *Hawaii Reporter*, August 26, 2011.

100. Greta Van Susteren, "Anchors Get Schmoozed by President Obama – Lunch at the White House Tomorrow!" *Gretawire*, September 7, 2011.

101. "Transcript: Obama Finds Times for NCAA Bracket, Golf Amid Global Turmoil," *Sean Hannity Show*, March 15, 2011.

102. Piper Weiss, "Michelle Obama's Style Dream Team," *Shine*, March 3, 2011.

103. Keith Koffler, "Michelle Obama Sports a $1,000 Handbag," *White House Dossier*, March 10, 2011.

104. Peter Allen, "'It's hell. I can't stand it.' Carla Bruni reveals what Michelle Obama really thinks of being First Lady," *Daily Mail*, September 16, 2010.

105. "Michelle Obama's Pricey Vacation Wardrobe," ABC News, December 29, 2011.

106. "Moochtastic! Queen Michelle Flashes Her $42,150 Diamond Cuffs," *Weasel Zippers*, September 22, 2011.

107. Tim Graham, "ABC News Promotes 'Cool Lady' Michelle Obama on ABC Home-Rehab Show," *NewsBusters*, September 26, 2011.

108. Brett Zongker, "Michelle Obama honors top designers at White House," Bloomberg *Businessweek*, September 13, 2011.

109. Kyle Drennen, "NBC's 'Today' Swoons Over Michelle Obama Shopping at Target," *NewsBusters*, September 30, 2011.

110. "Boston fundraiser," Politico 44, *Politico*, March 8, 2011.

111. Andrew Malcolm, "Another Obama White House party, this one a midweek soiree to watch Da Bulls," *Los Angeles Times*, March 9, 2011.

112. Mark Finkelstein, "In Speech On Tough Times For Americans, Obama Brags 'I Have Better Plane' And 'Bigger Entourage' Than Three Years Ago," *NewsBusters*, June 13, 2011.
113. Scott Paulson, "Barack Obama's 50th Birthday Bash," *The Chicago Conservative Examiner*, July 14, 2011.
114. "Michelle Obama's 'Goodwill Tour' of Africa Cost U.S. Taxpayers Up to $800,000," *Daily Mail*, June 28, 2011.
115. Keith Koffler, "Mrs. Obama's South Africa Trip Cost Taxpayers Over $500,000," *White House Dossier*, June 28, 2011.
116. "Judicial Watch Obtains Documents Detailing the Cost to Taxpayers for Michelle Obama's Family Trip to Africa," Judicial Watch, October 4, 2011.
117. Paul Bedard, "Fight Erupts Over First Lady's Travel Costs," *U.S. News & World Report*, October 5, 2011.
118. Charles Riley, "141 White House Staffers Make Six Figures," CNN *Money*, July 1, 2011.
119. "It Pays to Work at the White House: Most Staffers Got a Hefty Raise Last Year... and You Didn't," *Daily Mail*, July 7, 2011.
120. Jazz Shaw, "Obamas heading to Blue Heron," HotAir, July 19, 2011.
121. Ibid.
122. Paul Bedard, "Obama's Vineyard Vacation Will Cost Taxpayers Millions," *US News & World Report*, August 11, 2011.
123. Keith Koffler, "Michelle Obama Spent 42 Days on Vacation this Past Year," *White House Dossier*, August 12, 2011.
124. "Obama gets into the swing of things on his Martha's Vineyard vacation... after increasing his personal debt ceiling with rare sighting of the First credit card," *Daily Mail*, August 20, 2011.
125. "Carney Defends Obama Vacay To Martha's Vineyard; 'No Such Thing As A Presidential Vacation,'" *RealClearPolitics*, August 10, 2011.
126. David Nakamura, "White House's Jay Carney once called Bush's working vacation strategy a 'photo op,'" *Washington Post*, August 16, 2011.
127. Alex Spillius, "Barack Obama faces calls to cancel summer holiday," *Telegraph*, August 12, 2011.
128. Celia Walden, "Only Barack Obama would bring a SWAT team with him to the gym," *Telegraph*, September 29, 2011.
129. Nile Gardiner, "Cameron US visit: President Obama adds $478,000 to the US national debt with Ohio basketball jaunt," *Telegraph*, March 14, 2012.
130. "Government Ethics Conference At Lavish Golf Resort," Judicial Watch, July 22, 2011.

INDEX

60 Minutes, 2, 373

A

A123 Systems, 256
ABC News, 57, 182, 250, 315–16,
    371, 375, 392, 396
Abengoa Bioenergy Biomass of
    Kansas LLC, 26
abortion
    abortifacients, 117, 119
    Barack Obama and, 93, 106,
        112–15
    forced abortions, 94, 107
    international right to, 106–7
    making rare, 105–8, 111
    making safe, 105
    Obamacare and, 109–10
    objections to, 94, 111, 117–19
    partial-birth abortion, 106–7
    Planned Parenthood and, 105–7,
        111–15
    as preventive care, 118

as profitable industry, 112
state laws and, 107
taxpayer funding and, 106–7,
    110, 124, 132, 401
United Nations and, 107–8
Abramson, Jeff, 340,
Academia Semillas Del Pueblo, 31
Accuracy in Media, 35
Ackerman, Bruce, 3, 312–313,
Adams, J. Christian, 86, 131
Advanced Energy Manufacturing
    Tax Credit, 27
Afghanistan
    Obama and, 10, 43, 328, 330,
        379
    war in, 146, 149, 151, 153, 173,
        181
African Americans, 16, 20, 52, 58,
    129–30, 257, 298
Ahmadinejad, Mahmoud, 328, 330
Air Force, 102, 164, 313, 336, 343,
    394

Air Force One, 296, 385, 397
Air Force Times, 313
Al Jazeera, 19, 35
Alabama, 130
  Gulf oil spill and, 215
  immigration laws of, 88–90
al-Assad, Bashar, 330
Alexander, Ryan, 248
Allawi, Iyad, 328
al-Qaeda, 306, 315, 317, 319, 323
Alt, Larry, 346, 351, 359
American Atheists Inc., 101
American Center for Law and
  Justice, 54
American Civil Liberties Union
  (ACLU), 87–88
American Enterprise Institute, 5, 23,
  223, 260
American Federation of State,
  County and Municipal
  Employees (AFCSME), 196
American Human Rights Council,
  20
American Idea, 14, 269, 401
"American Jobs Act," 2, 26
American Petroleum Institute, 78,
  217, 224, 227, 231
American Principles Project, 78,
  217, 224, 227, 231
American Recovery and
  Reinvestment Act (ARRA), 137
American sovereignty, 23
American Thinker, 19
Americans for Tax Reform, 160,
  242
Americans United for Separation of
  Church and State, 101
Americans with Disabilities Act, 100
Amnesty International, 333
Amos, James, 103
anti-satellite weapons (ASAT), 338
anti-Semitism, 53

Arab League, 308, 317
Arab Spring, 108, 320–27, 344
Argonne National Laboratory, 228
Arizona, 28, 244, 254, 375
  Operation Fast and Furious and,
    346–47, 350, 352, 360, 364,
    367–68
  safety of, 87–88
  S.B. 1070 and, 22–23, 87–90
  Tucson shooting, 41–43
  voter ID laws of, 84
Arizona Department of
  Environmental Quality, 28
Arlington Cemetery, 390
Arms Control Association, 640
Army, 102, 119, 164, 227, 306, 328,
  336
Asia-Pacific-Economic Cooperation,
  18
Asian-Americans, 21, 129
Atlantic Wire, 42
AttackWatch.com, 83–84
Australian Strategic Policy Institute,
  342
Aviation Industry Corp. of China,
  340
Aviation Week, 342
Avila, Jaime, 365
Axelrod, David, 58, 83, 216, 218,
  292, 376, 380, 388
Ayadi, Ashraf, 322
Ayuda Inc., 32

B

Babeu, Paul, 87
Bachman, Mark, 254
Baisden, Michael, 56
Bakr, Essam Abu, 316
Bank of America, 99, 297
Bank of China, 133
Barnes, Melody, 106, 121
Barone, Michael, 162–63, 373

BBC World Service, 28
Beck, Glenn, 60
Becket Fund for Religious Liberty, 100–2
Beechcraft, Hawker, 295
Beijing, 337, 341
Being There, 373
Belford, Janet, 119
Bell, Derrick, 125–26
Bellows, John, 82
Benghazi, 309–10, 317
Benioff, Marc, 70
Bernstein, Jared, 194, 268, 297
Biden, Joe, 10, 44–45, 50, 56, 67, 78, 83, 93–94, 146, 191, 229, 243, 246, 248, 252, 293, 297, 308, 325–28, 369, 372, 382, 391
Big Labor, 264–65, 275, 401
bin Laden, Osama, 19, 43, 319, 324, 378–79, 389
Bipartisan Budget Commission. *See* Committee for a Responsible Federal Budget
Bipartisan Debt Commission. *See* National Committee on Fiscal Responsibility and Reform
Bird, Jeremy, 84
birth control, 107, 110, 118–19. *See also* contraception
Black Liberation Theology, 125
Bloomberg, Michael, 298
Blue Chip, 155
Boehner, John, 40, 64, 66, 96, 104, 110, 203, 314
Boeing, 163, 265, 272–76
BOEMRE, 221
Boisture, Bill, 295
Bolton, John, 309, 314, 319
Boot, Max, 326, 343
border patrol, 87, 346, 356, 365
Boren, Dan, 210
Boston, 76, 393

Boston Globe, 19, 91, 308
Boston Herald, 76, 395
Botswana, 394
Bouckaert, Peter, 315
Bowie State University, 39
BP, 78, 211–20, 224–25, 330
Brady, Demian, 385
Brazil, 220
Breitbart, Andrew, 125–26
Brennan, John, 323–24, 347
Breuer, Lanny, 354–57, 360–61, 364, 367
Brewer, Jan, 22–23, 375
Britain, 15, 45, 318, 329–30, 335, 385
Britain's Foreign Service, 29
British Petroleum, *see* BP
Broglio, Timothy, 119
Bronstein, Phil, 77
Brown, Jerry, 257
Brown, Scott, 40
Brownfield, Mike, 8, 149, 406
Brune, Michael, 261
Bruni, Carla, 392
Bryson, John, 34
Buckley, George, 266
Budd Falen Law Offices, 240
Budget Control Act, 164, 177, 195, 342
Buffenbarger, Tom, 295
Buffett Rule, 269–72
Buffett, Warren, 269
Burbidge, Michael, 97
Bureau of Alcohol, Tobacco, Firearms and Explosives (ATF), 346–60, 362–67
Burke, Dennis, 350–52, 356
Burns, Ursula, 27
Burton, Bill, 382
Bush administration, 4, 10, 19, 25, 56, 81, 115, 121, 198, 228, 250–51, 327, 378

Bush, George W., 38, 234, 374, 389
  Barack Obama blaming of, 12,
    44–45, 48, 147, 165, 187,
    191, 193, 272, 348, 375
  business and, 81
  conscience rights protections of,
    115–17
  deficits under, 133–34, 148–49,
    152, 175, 184
  golf and, 382
  Hurricane Katrina and, 215
  international relations and, 330
  as leader, 72
  media and, 328
  Muslim world and, 327
  Operation Wide Receiver and,
    348–49
  Osama bin Laden death and,
    378–79
  personal approval ratings of, 74
  regulatory costs of, 278–79
  stem cell research and, 103–4
  tax cuts of, 67, 134, 272, 294,
    297
  terrorist detentions and, 306
  unemployment under, 141
  war in Iraq and, 308, 328
  welfare and, 124
  working vacations of, 396
Bushee, Ward, 77
business
  big businesses, 64, 265, 299–300,
    304
  hiring and, 7, 139–40, 144, 158–
    59, 201, 263, 284–85, 289–90
  outsourcing jobs and, 26–28,
    229, 242–43, 274, 300–1, 326
  small businesses, 18, 64, 158–59,
    243, 260, 263, 256, 267, 280,
    285, 302–4
  taxes on, 18, 78–79, 154,177,
    263, 270, 300–1, 303, 402

C

CAGW, *see* Citizens Against
  Government Waste
Cain, Herman, 48
Calderón, Felipe, 353
California, 70, 73, 76, 97, 146, 227,
  245, 248, 251, 253, 257–58, 336,
  364
Cameron, David, 397
Camp, Dave, 158
Campbell, David, 261
Canino, Carlos, 359
Cannon, Frank, 113
Cantor, Eric, 64–65, 104, 278
Capitol Hill, 41, 56, 68, 108, 186,
  259, 393
Carl's Jr., 280
Carney, Jay, 43–44, 49–50, 67, 76,
  96, 190, 194, 201, 203, 299, 363,
  372, 389, 396
Carson, Andre, 50
Carter, James ("Jimmy"), 400
Carville, James, 217
Casey, George, 102
Cash for Clunkers, 146, 165
Castro, Fidel, 34, 330
Catholic Church
  employee contraceptive coverage
    mandate and, 118–20
  pro-life position of, 105
  support of traditional marriage,
    98
CBO. *See* Congressional Budget
  Office
CBS News, 67, 214, 292, 361, 367,
  371, 383
CEDAW. *See* Committee on the
  Elimination of Discrimination
  Against Women
Cefalu, Vince, 352
CELAC. *See* Community of Latin
  American and Caribbean States

Celis-Acosta, Manuel, 365
Center for American Progress, 61
Center for Immigration Studies, 31, 90
Center for Military Readiness, 102
Centers for Disease Control, 32
Cenzon-DeCarlo, Catherine, 115–16
Ceren, Omri, 337
Chait, Mark, 362
Chambers, John, 82
Channell-Allen, Gina, 76
Chao, Elaine, 81
Chapman, Anna, 333
Chavez, Hugo, 329–33, 340
Chicago, 55, 72, 76, 92, 120, 163, 186, 293, 382–83, 393–94
China, 28, 308, 314, 330
    American debt and, 133
    clean energy jobs and, 242
    competition and, 337
    human rights and, 22, 24
    Joe Biden trip to, 45, 93
    military of, 161, 337–39, 13
    one-child policy of, 94, 107, 124
    outsourcing of American jobs to, 27, 281
China National Space Administration, 339
Christian Medical Association, 117
Chrysler, 128, 253, 264, 401
Chu, Steven, 26, 208–9, 238, 246, 251, 294
Church Amendment, 115–16
Cisco Systems, 99
Citizens Against Government Waste (CAGW), 25
Citizens United v. Federal Election Commission, 290–91
CKE Restaurants, 280
Clapper, James, 318
Clarke, Richard, 315
Clean Air Transport Rule, 260

Clean Water Act, 241
Cleaver, Emanuel, 69, 257
Clinton, Bill, 225, 387, 389
Clinton, Hillary, 24, 94, 106, 108, 309, 318, 321, 326, 332, 335, 338, 345
CNN, 57, 62, 74, 281, 310, 333, 356, 362, 377
Coast Guard, 164, 212–13, 395
Coates, Christopher, 132
Coburn, Tom, 144–45
Coca-Cola, 281
Code of Conduct for Outer Space Activities, 337–39
Cole, James, 364
Cole, Tom, 287
Columbine High School, 126–27
Commission on the Status of Women, 107
Committee on the Elimination of Discrimination Against Women (CEDAW), 108
"Common." *See* Lynn, Lonnie Rashid, Jr.
Community College Career Fund, 154
Community of Latin American and Caribbean States (CELAC), 329
Competitive Enterprise Institute, 223, 260
Comprehensive Review Working Group (CRWG), 102
Congressional Budget Office (CBO), 137–38, 143, 151, 155, 157, 167, 174, 179, 183, 189
Conley, Timothy, 136
Consumer Energy Alliance, 222
contraception, 117–18, 120–21. *See also* birth control
Conway, James, 102
Cook Medical, 159
Cooper, Anderson, 356, 362

Cooper, Rory, 223–24
Corinthians, book of, 101
Cornyn, John, 349
Corporate Average Fuel Economy (CAFE) standards, 239–40
Corum, James, 344
Council of Economic Advisors, 137
Council on Foreign Relations, 24
Coyle, Gene, 333
Coyne, James K., 295
Cree LED light company, 27
Crimes Against Liberty, 1, 2, 4, 11, 37, 83, 197, 209, 253, 264, 331, 402
CRWG. *See* Comprehensive Review Working Group
Cuba, 22, 24, 221, 332
Cuban Missile Crisis, 33
Cummings, Elijah, 353–54, 360
Custer, General George, 17
Cut, Cap, and Balance Act, 190, 192
Cuyahoga County, 85

D
Daily Beast, 272, 325
Daily Caller, 48, 58, 61, 62, 77
Daily Mail, 384–87, 390
Daily Show, The, 369
Daley, William M., 287
Dalmia, Shikha, 145
Damascus, 331
Dannenfelser, Marjorie, 114
Darden Restaurants, 281
Daschle, Linda, 300
Daschle, Tom, 106
Davies, Andrew, 342
Davis-Bacon, 243
de Rugy, Veronique, 147
debt
  burden, 170, 172, 178
  China and, 339
  credit rating and, 195

debt ceiling, 66, 69, 150, 190–91, 193–96, 372, 376, 379, 395
  national debt, 133, 139, 147, 152, 174, 176, 180, 182–83, 372, 380, 400–1
  Obama budget and, 270
  per household, 183–86, 244
Declaration of Independence, 17
Deepwater Horizon, 210, 218, 222
DeFazio, Peter, 377
Defense of Marriage Act (DOMA), 96
deficit, 43–46, 57, 68, 73, 78, 133–35, 147–53, 155, 157, 169–97, 297, 376, 380, 397, 400–1
Delta, 275
DeMint, Jim, 274
Democratic National Committee Communications, 292
Democratic party, 47, 85, 93, 225, 274, 379
Dempsey, Martin E., 328
Deptula, David, 343
DeSoto Solar Center, 243
DeSutter, Paula, 334
Diffey, James, 226
Dimon, Jamie, 270
DiNardo, Daniel, 118
Disclose Act, 291
Dobbs, Lou, 62
Dodson, John, 346, 352, 359, 367
Doherty, Brendan, 250, 389
DOJ. *See* U.S. Department of Justice
Dolan, Timothy, 97–99
DOMA. *See* Defense of Marriage Act
Domestic Policy Council, 106
Domino's Pizza, 280
Dong Feng 21D, 341
"Don't Ask, Don't Tell," 102
Donnelly, Elaine, 102–3
Donovan, Chuck, 116
Dowd, Maureen, 373–74

Doyle, Mike, 44
Dream Act, 7, 30, 55
Dreams from My Father, 125
Drudge Report, 384, 392
Drug Enforcement Administration
(DEA), 365–66
Duncan, Arne, 95
Dunn, Anita, 58–61
Dupor, Bill, 136

E

e pluribus unum, 29, 129
Eagan, Margery, 395
Earnest, Josh, 62
Ebell, Myron, 260
Economic Policy Institute, 58
Eder, Kevin, 60
El Salvador, 15
Ella, 117
Elliott, Josh, 392
Elmendorf, Douglas, 137, 180, 187
Emanuel, Rahm, 2, 69, 106, 257
Emily's List, 106
Emir of Qatar, 19
"Employee Free Choice Act," 275
employment, 101, 115, 128, 132–
39, 143, 228, 286, 302. *See also*
jobs, unemployment
energy
American consumption of, 156,
209, 233–36, 258
American resources, 156, 220,
232, 235–36
green energy, 26, 155–56, 165,
208, 236, 237, 241–42, 245,
247, 249, 254–55, 259, 262,
303, 381, 391, 402, 406
sources, 156–57, 208, 233, 237–
62
Energy Advisory Board, 209
Engler, John, 260
Ennahda, 322

entitlements
Barack Obama and, 183–84,
187, 201–2
debt and, 83
Obamacare as entitlement, 168
reform, 45–46, 70, 165, 167,
170, 180–81
restructuring of, 12, 82, 173,
176, 203, 400–1
tax revenues and, 152–55
entrepreneurs, 13, 144, 301–2
Environmental Protection Agency
(EPA), 11, 28, 188–89, 229–30,
239–40, 259–62, 277–78, 284,
286–87, 401
Enzi, Mike, 79
Equal Employment Opportunity
Commission, 100
equal opportunity, 13, 20, 204, 268
ESPN, 388–89
Establishment Clause, 101
Euro Pacific Capital, Inc., 284
European Central Bank (ECB), 147
European Union, 323
Evergreen Solar, 254

F

Face the Nation, 83, 214, 292
Facebook, 10, 59, 70
Falk, Richard, 25
Family Research Council, 94, 97,
103, 109
Fannie Mae, 145, 177, 297
FDA. *See* U.S. Food and Drug
Administration
Federal Emergency Agency's
Disaster Relief Fund, 73
Federal Register, 116
Feith, Doug, 310
Feldman, Martine L. C., 215
Ferguson, Stephen, 159
Fineman, Howard, 393

First Amendment, 5, 54, 101, 127
Fisher, Rick, 338
Fitton, Tom, 97, 394
Fitzgerald, Scott, 92
Fleischer, Ari, 40
Florida, 46, 55, 90, 215, 246, 296, 359, 384, 391, 398
Forbes, 385
Forcelli, Peter, 350–53, 359
Ford, Charles, 332
Form T-1, 81
Fort Greely, 336
Foster, J. D., 134, 155, 161
Founding Fathers, 16
Fournier, Ron, 272
Fox News, 15, 18, 53, 58, 197, 216, 358
Fox News Sunday, 216
Freddie Mac, 145, 177, 297
Free Exercise Clause, 101
freedom, 33, 51, 377
    American tradition of, 2, 13, 407
    Arab Spring and, 323
    Barack Obama budget and, 161
    end of, 402
    freedom of speech, 127
    new birth of, 16
    religious freedom, 98–99, 101–2, 118–19
    reproductive freedom, 105
Freedom of Choice Act, 105, 107
Freedom House, 24
Freedom of Information Act (FOIA), 97, 122, 394
Freeman, Morgan, 57
French, Cameron, 97
French, David, 54
Freudenthal, Nancy, 234
Friedman, Gregory, 155, 156, 255, 344
Fuller, Craig, 295, 297
Fund, John, 80

G

Gaddafi, Muammar, 310, 314, 316–17
Gallagher, Maggie, 98
Gallup, 74, 157, 158, 265
GAO. *See* Government Accountability Office
Gardiner, Chauncey, 373
Gardiner, Nile, 45, 319, 330, 373, 381, 397
Garrett, Scott, 163, 168
Gates, Robert, 338, 341–43
Gattuso, James, 279, 285
Geithner, Timothy, 64, 66, 169–73, 180, 225, 265, 267
Gelb, Les, 325
General Motors (GM), 128, 145, 264, 401
Genesis Solar Energy Project, 251
George, Francis, 120
Georgia, 54, 238
Gerard, Jack, 217, 224, 231
Gerson, Michael, 376
Gerstein, Josh, 41
Ghailani, Ahmed, 306
Gibbs, Robert, 127, 215, 374–75, 378, 383–84
Giffords, Gabrielle, 41–43
Gigot, Paul, 197
Gil, Darren, 349, 359
Gillespie, Ed, 292
Gingrich, Newt, 14, 197
Global Poverty Act, 35
globalism, 34, 326
GM. *See* General Motors
Godfrey, Rob, 89
Goff, Emily, 149
Goldberg, Jonah, 85
Golden Gate Bridge, 17
Goldman, Ikram, 392
Goldwater, Barry, 126
Goodrich, Luke, 101
Goodwin, Michael, 380

Goolsbee, Austan, 145–46, 197
Got Green, 243
Gould, Gregory J., 78
Government Accountability Office (GAO), 111, 144, 238, 243, 255–56, 279
Government Affairs Committee, 366
Gowdy, Trey, 355, 361, 366, 406
Graham, Tim, 48
Grant Park, 37
Grassley, Charles, 354, 360
Great Depression, 39, 58, 137–38, 194, 195, 371
Great Society, 195, 198
Greek crisis, 43, 379
green energy, 26, 155–56, 165, 208, 236–37, 241–49, 254–59, 262, 303, 381, 391, 402, 406
green jobs, 27, 244, 256–68
Greenwich, Howard, 244
Grid Investment Grant Program (SGIG), 344
Griffin, Drew, 356
Grindler, Gary, 357
Ground Zero, 58, 327
ground-based interceptors (GBIs), 36
Guantanamo Bay, 22, 306, 307, 330
Guardian, 318
Guevara, Che, 33
Gulf Economic Survival Team, 226
Gulf oil spill, 78, 191, 214, 215, 224, 242, 375, 379, 382
gun control, 8, 353, 354, 361–63
Gunn, Tim, 393
gunwalking, 53, 346–66
Gutierrez, Luis, 70

H
Haiti, 23–24
Haley, Nikki, 273

Halperin, Mark, 77
Hamas, 23, 319, 322
Hami, Sheeraz, 14
Handel, Karen, 114
Hanna, Colin, 34
Hannity, Sean, 406
Hanson, Victor Davis, 208
Hardee's, 280
Harlem, 373, 382
Harper, Steven, 230
Harvey, Steve, 39
Harwood, John, 197, 207
Hathaway, Oona, 312–13
Hawaii, 18, 380, 386–87, 396
Hawaii Reporter, 390
Hawkins, Kristan, 114
Hayward, John, 362–63
HCL Technologies, 28
Health and Human Services (HHS), 95, 106, 110, 113–15, 122
healthcare, 72, 90, 107–18, 124, 126, 155, 157–67, 207, 266–67, 300, 374, 376, 378
Heiss, Scott, 256
Heritage Foundation, 116, 121–22, 134, 135, 139, 141, 148, 152, 198, 229, 233, 235, 269, 279, 301, 303, 330, 334–35, 406
"Heroes Day," 15
HHS. *See* Health and Human Services
Higginbottom, Heather, 184–85
Hiroshima, 14–15
Hispanic Caucus, 16 Hoffa, Jimmy, 46–49, 277
Holder, Eric, 53–54, 86–91, 97, 128–31, 214, 345–68
Hollywood, 57
Holt, David, 222
Honduras, 331–32
Hoover, Billy, 358
Hope Forum UK, 15

Horne, Tom, 84
Hosanna-Tabor Evangelical School, 100
HotAir, 76, 406
House Appropriations State and Foreign Ops, 63
House Budget Committee, 135, 148, 151, 152, 163, 168
House Committee on Oversight and Government Reform, 212, 284, 347
House Energy and Commerce Subcommittee on Health, 119
Houston Votes, 85
Hsu, Norman, 293
Hu Jintao, 94, 308, 385
Huffington Post, 60, 277, 393
Human Events, 362
human rights, 21–24, 94, 107
Human Rights Campaign, 49
Human Rights Watch, 310, 315
Hunter, Duncan D., 33
Hunter, Stephen, 378
Hurley, Emory, 349, 353
Hurricane Katrina, 215
Hyde Amendment, 107
Hyde, Pam, 95

I

IHS Global Insight's U.S. Regional Economic Group, 227
Ikenson, Daniel, 300
Immelt, Jeffrey ("Jeff"), 290, 299–301, 340
immigration
    enforcement, 91, 401
    illegal immigration, 7, 30, 32, 87–90
    Obama policy of, 6–7, 15, 30–31
    reform of, 55
    S.B. 1070, 22–23, 87, 90

    voting and, 84, 86
Immigration and Customs Enforcement (ICE), 7, 91
Independent Payment Advisory Board (IPAB), 160–61
individualism, 13
Inhofe, James, 213
Injustice, 86, 131
Innovate Conference, 33
Institute on Energy Research (IER), 233–34
Institute for Marriage and Public Policy, 98
"intangible drilling costs" (IDCs), 210
Inter Press Service (IPS), 23
Intergovernmental Affairs, 32
Internal Revenue Service (IRS), 10, 54, 163, 270–71
International Association of Machinists and Aerospace Workers (IAMAW), 295
International Planned Parenthood Federation, 107
International Renewable Energy Agency (IRENA), 25–26
Investigative Project on Terrorism, 320
Investors Business Daily, 128, 225, 228, 304
Investors.com, 30, 311, 322, 340
IPAB. *See* Independent Payment Advisory Board
Iraq, 34, 74, 146, 149, 151, 153, 173, 181, 307–9, 325–28
IRS, *see* Internal Revenue Service
Islam
    America and, 15, 327
    Arab Spring and, 321–25, 344
    jihad, 323–24
    Islamic law, 316

"Islamophobia," 324–25
mockery of, 24
as peaceful, 311, 322–24
radical components, 324
Sharia and, 316
War on Terror and, 305
worldwide Islamic caliphate goal, 318–19
Israel, 23
Barack Obama and, 10, 327–30, 401
Egypt and, 321–23
Hamas and, 319
Libyan weapons and, 316
UN Human Rights Council and, 24–25
Issa, Darrell
Arizona immigration law and, 88
CAFE standards and, 239
Gulf oil spill and, 212–13, 218
National Labor Relations Board (NLRB) and, 274–75
Operation Fast and Furious and, 347–51, 353, 356–60, 364
Solyndra scandal and, 10
Ivanov, Sergei, 335
Ivory Coast, 24

J

Jackson, Lisa, 229, 259–61
Jalil, Mustafa Abdul, 316
Jane's Strategic Weapons Systems, 335
Japan Times, 14
Jarrett, Valerie, 3, 10, 61, 288, 294, 374, 380, 386
Jealous, Todd, 53
Jefferies and Co., 254
Jenkins, Holman, 240
Jennings, Kevin, 95
Jim Crow, 16

Jindal, Bobby, 217, 219, 375
jobs, *see also* employment, unemployment
green jobs, 27, 126, 244, 256–59
job creation, 27, 64, 144, 159, 181, 232, 257, 266, 273, 275, 277, 281, 284–85, 287, 289, 301–2
outsourcing of, 27–28, 229, 274, 326
shovel-ready jobs, 69, 146, 152, 156, 231–32
Johanns, Mike, 296
Johnsen, Dawn, 106
Johnson, Douglas, 108
Johnson, Hank, 54
Johnson, Jeh C., 310
Johnson, Lyndon B. (LBJ), 195
Jones Act, 212
Jones, Brad, 247
Jones, Van, 126
Josten, Bruce, 292
Journal Editorial Report, 197
JPMorgan Chase, 270
Judicial Watch, 32, 97, 197, 394, 398
Jugis, Peter, 97

K

Kagan, Elena, 101
Kailuana Place, 387
Kaiser Health, 162
Kaiser, Mark, 209
Kaneohe Marine Corp Air Station, 387
Kantor, Jodi, 374
Karzai, Hamid, 14
Katz, Diane, 260, 279, 280
Kaus, Mickey, 376
Kayyem, Juliette, 19
Kennedy, John F. (JFK), 134, 241, 288

Kent, Muhtar, 281
Kenya, 110–11
Kessler, Glenn, 202
Keynesian theory of economics, 51, 138, 139, 146, 180, 201
Keystone XL pipeline, 150, 230–36, 402
Kim, Christine, 121–22
Kindt, John W., 224
King Jr., Martin Luther, 10, 125
King, Loretta, 132
Kish, Dan, 233
Kmiec, Doug, 105
Koffler, Keith, 63, 77
Koh, Harold H., 34, 310
Koran, 14, 319
Kovacs, Bill, 278
Krass, Caroline D., 310
Krauthammer, Charles, 7, 18, 150, 164, 194, 337
Kreutzer, David, 231, 235
Krikorian, Mark, 31, 90
Kruger, Leondra, 101
Kuhner, Jeff, 57
Kuperman, Alan J., 310
Kurtz, Stanley, 311, 314–15
KVEG radio, 56
Kyl, Jon, 87, 334

L
La Jeunesse, William, 358
LaHood, Ray, 28, 209, 321
LaHood, Sam, 321
Lake, Eli, 337
Lambrew, Jeanne, 106
Lasky, Ed, 19
Latin American Herald Tribune, 329
Latinos, 38, 55–56, 129
Leahy, Patrick, 32
Leal, Humberto, 32–33
Lee, Jesse, 59–60

Lehr, Bill, 218
Lehrich, Matt, 76
Leistikow, Dan, 250
Lennox, Duncan, 335
Lesbian, Gay, Bisexual, Transgender (LGBT) Youth Summit, 94
Let Freedom Ring, 34
Lew, Jacob, 185
Lewis, John, 52–53
Libya, 22, 24, 226, 308–23, 326, 381, 391
Lieberman, Joe, 325, 366
Lincoln, Abraham, 16, 39, 373
Liu Xiaobo, 377
Live Action organization, 113
Llorens, Hugo, 332
Lloyd, Mark, 127
Lobo, Porfirio, 331
Locke, Gary, 293
Lockwood, Rob, 26
London Daily Mail, 390
Loris, Nicolas ("Nick"), 156, 227, 229, 232
Los Angeles Times, 38, 220, 293, 391
Loughner, Jared, 41, 378
Louisiana Department of National Resources, 216
Louisiana State University, 209
Luminant, 261
Lurie, Adam, 354
Lynch, Peter, 249
Lynn, Lonnie Rashid, Jr. ("Common"), 389

M
Machaceck, Rick, 91
Macroeconomic Advisers, 173–74
Malament, Charlie, 280
Malcolm, Andrew, 220, 391
Maley, Steve, 222

Malkin, Michelle, 6, 161–62, 195, 293

Maloney, Carolyn, 121

Mani Bhavan Gandhi museum, 385

Marcus, Bernie, 287

Marie Stopes International, 107

Marine One, 76

Marines, 34, 102, 102, 387

Marinucci, Carla, 77

Marquez, Peter, 337

marriage
  Defense of Marriage Act (DOMA) and, 96–98
  Respect for Marriage Act, 96
  same-sex marriage, 21, 93, 95–96, 98–100
  sex education and, 121–23
  traditional marriage, 97–99, 401

Martha's Vineyard, 51, 382, 384, 395–96

Martin, Steve, 351

Mason, Joe, 217

McCain, John, 145, 314

McCarthy, Andrew ("Andy"), 131, 319–23, 406

McCaul, Michael, 87

McCluskey, Tom, 94

McConnell, Mitch, 4, 64, 259, 291, 307

McCormick, Katie, 76

McGinn, Mike, 243

McKinsey Quarterly, 158

McMahon, William G., 351, 358

McMorris, Cathy, 282

McVeigh, Timothy, 41

Meckler, Laura, 201

Medal of Honor, 34

media, 19, 33, 42, 116, 127, 131, 174, 285, 388
  Barack Obama and, 64, 72, 191, 203, 378, 391, 395
  liberalism of, 47, 52, 60, 102, 114, 392
  Michelle Obama and, 392–93, 395
  right-wing, 15–16, 61

Media Matters, 61–62

Media Watch, 23

Medical Savings Account, 197

Medicare, 45, 48, 50, 67, 68, 153, 157, 161, 164, 167–78, 186–87, 203

Medvedev, Dmitry, 335–36, 340

Meet the Press, 386

Melson, Kenneth ("Ken"), 350–52, 357–58, 364–68

Merkel, Angela, 44

Messner, Thomas, 99–100

Mexico, 6, 17, 28–31, 87, 90, 99, 107, 109, 110, 124, 212, 220–28, 235, 266, 330, 346–68

Michigan, 45, 47, 100, 129, 239, 257, 380

Middle East, 10, 26, 208, 226, 229, 319, 322–29, 340, 389

Millennium Development Goals (MDGs), 34–35

Miller, Emily, 390

Missouri, 86

Mitchell, Steve, 255

"Monterrey Consensus," 35

Moore, Stephen, 391

Moran, Ellen, 106

Morgan, Piers, 57

Morgenthau, Henry, 138

Morici, Peter, 27

Morrissey, Ed, 60, 196, 245, 254, 406

Mount Desert Island, 383

Mount Sinai Hospital, 115

Mount St. Helens, 145

MoveOn.org, 40

MSNBC, 58, 62, 76, 77

Mubarak, Hosni, 317–23
Mullen, Mike, 102
Muñoz, Cecilia, 32
Murray, Patty, 376
Muslim Brotherhood
  Barack Obama and, 344, 401
  in Egypt, 318–22
  worldwide Islamic caliphate and,
    318
Muslims, 59, 323–27
Mythbusters, 369

N

NAACP, 16, 53, 383
NAAQS, *see* National Ambient Air
  Quality Standards
Nagasaki, 14
NARAL, 106, 115
National Abstinence Education
  Association, 121
National Academy of Engineers, 223
National Ambient Air Quality
  Standards (NAAQS), 286–87
National Council of La Raza, 30
national debt, 43, 133, 139, 147,
  152, 174, 176, 180–85, 193, 195,
  244, 270, 339, 372, 380, 400–1.
  See also debt
National Defense Authorization Act,
  307
National Hispanic Cultural Center, 29
National Interest, 312
National Journal, 270, 272
National Labor Relations Board, 9,
  18, 273
National Legal and Policy Center, 8,
  80
National Oceanic and Atmospheric
  Administration (NOAA), 218, 222
National Police Week, 390
National Policy Center, 80

National Public Radio (NPR), 28
National Review, 85, 92, 319, 323
National Review Online, 54, 110,
  131, 311, 324
National Rifle Association (NRA),
  54, 346
National Right to Life Committee,
  108, 110
national security, 1, 12, 70, 103,
  164, 187, 204, 236, 242, 305–
  314, 320–26, 339, 343, 344, 347,
  396, 406
National Taxpayers Union
  Foundation, 385
Navy, 33–34, 98, 164, 307, 313
NBC News, 2, 52, 71, 389
Neal, Tim, 274
Nemazee, Hasan, 293
Netanyahu, Benjamin, 329
New Black Panther Party, 85, 112,
  130–31
New Deal, 138, 152, 195
New Mexico Civil Rights
  Commission, 99
New START, 330, 334–36
New Testament, 101
New York, 33, 66, 79, 80, 115, 270,
  277, 298, 307, 382, 391–92
New York Times, 23, 41, 53, 72,
  159, 224, 230, 246, 257, 293,
  310, 373
Newell, Richard, 234
Newell, William D. ("Bill"), 347,
  351, 358
NewsBusters, 48
Newsweek, 265, 325
NOAA, *see* National Oceanic and
  Atmospheric Administration
Nobel Peace Prize, 377
Noem, Kristi, 286
Nordlinger, Jay, 92

Norquist, Grover, 160
North Carolina, 26–27, 71, 90, 97,
    145, 152, 242, 394
Notre Dame, 105, 116
Nuclear Regulatory Commission
    (NRC), 237–38
Nyholm, Allison, 78

O

Obama, Barack
    abortion and, 93, 105–6, 112–15
    as anti-business president, 79–82,
        263, 265–67, 288, 294, 297–
        99
    apologies for America of, 14–15,
        132, 330, 401
    approval ratings of, 74, 327, 399
    Arab Spring support of, 320,
        322–23, 327, 344
    bipartisanship of, 11, 18, 37,
        43–45, 47–48, 50, 61, 75,
        186, 201, 370
    blaming American people, 17–18
    blaming ATMs, 191
    blaming Bush, 12, 44–45, 48,
        147, 165, 187, 191, 193, 249–
        50, 272, 348, 375
    blaming business, 17
    blaming oil companies, 225
    blaming Republicans, 39, 52, 66,
        82–83, 150, 195–96, 203
    budgets of, 146, 148–49, 151–
        52, 156–57, 164, 168, 176,
        181–82, 184, 187–88, 203,
        321, 380
    Cairo speech of, 311, 322–23
    and Congress, 43, 191, 193, 306,
        314, 379–80, 396
    Dodd-Frank bill and, 3–5, 264,
        278–80, 297, 402

domestic energy production and,
    70, 157, 177, 210, 218, 220,
    225, 232–34, 238, 241–44,
    402
Egypt and, 317–24, 388, 401
Fast and Furious and, 356, 358
foreign policy of, 33, 100, 305–8,
    310–12, 325, 329–30, 333,
    373, 400
as fourth best president, 373
golf habit of, 381–82, 388–91
green energy and, 26, 155–56,
    165, 236, 237, 241–42, 245,
    247, 249, 255, 259, 262, 303,
    381, 391, 402
Gulf oil spill and, 78–79, 191,
    211, 214–15, 224, 242, 375,
    379, 382
gun control and, 8, 353–54, 361–
    63
Israel and, 10, 321–23, 327,
    329–30, 401
Libya and, 308–17, 323, 326,
    381, 391
lifestyle of, 370, 380–81, 390,
    397–98
middle class and, 47, 58, 71, 73,
    268, 272, 289, 298
Muslim world and, 311, 323–25,
    327–28, 330
narcissism of, 369, 374, 378–79,
    399
national debt and, 43, 52–54,
    133, 147, 152, 180, 182–86,
    270, 372, 380, 400–1
national security and, 1, 70, 103,
    164, 178, 187, 204, 236, 242,
    305–44, 347, 396
Nobel Peace Prize and, 377
Obamacare and, 3, 40, 54, 64,
    75–76, 109–10, 116, 153–54,

157–60, 162–64, 168, 278, 280, 302, 402

public appearances of, 267, 386

reelection and, 49, 51, 71, 83, 134, 214, 230, 248, 260, 336, 386, 394, 400–2

the rich and, 16, 38, 48–49, 64, 172, 175, 178, 186, 194, 197, 269–70, 272, 294, 296, 398

shovel-ready jobs and, 69, 146, 152, 156, 231

Supreme Court and, 32–33, 46, 75, 105, 127, 290–91, 331, 401

taxes and, 78, 150, 153–55, 163,176–78, 184, 190–92, 195–97, 202, 209, 263, 302, 397, 402

tea party and, 38, 44, 47, 52–54, 57, 70–71, 73

use of Air Force One, 296, 385, 397

vacations of, 51, 380–84, 386–91, 395–96

women and, 55–57, 116

Obama, Malia, 18, 393

Obama, Michelle, 76, 377

debt debates and, 46

debut on *Extreme Makeover: Home Edition*, 392

Gulf oil spill and, 382–83

immigration and, 55

as style leader, 392–94

tea party and, 53

vacations of, 381–84, 388, 390, 395

view of America, 16

Obama, Sasha, 18, 393

Obamacare, 293, 402

abortion funding and, 109–10

class warfare and, 64

conscience protections and, 116–17, 119

Constitution and, 75

cost of, 153–54, 157–62, 168, 177, 302

discriminatory medical system and, 21

Dodd-Frank bill and, 3, 5

individual mandate of, 11, 75, 163–64

public reception of, 21, 76

regulations and, 279–80

tea party and, 54

waivers and, 162–63, 284

Obamas, The, 374

Oberhelman, Doug, 290

Occupational Safety and Health Administration (OSHA), 80–81, 276

Occupy Wall Street, 16, 64

O'Donnell, Kelly, 52, 393

Of Thee I Sing: A Letter to My Daughters, 17, 377

Office of Civil Rights (OCR), 115

Office of Management and Budget, 9, 163, 168, 222, 245, 251

Office of Natural Resources Revenue, 78

Office of Navy Chaplains, 98

O'Grady, Mary, 332–33

Ohio, 3, 39, 50, 55, 64, 71, 73, 86, 228, 229, 259, 397

Ohio Oil and Gas Energy Education Program, 229

oil, 207–36

American reserves of, 220, 234–36

"Big Oil," 38, 47–48, 78, 157

domestic production of, 70, 208, 210, 216–18, 220, 222, 232, 234

foreign oil, 70, 210, 221, 236, 239, 330
offshore drilling, 209, 211, 213, 217, 220–24, 228
oil shale, 228–29, 235
OPEC and, 222
rising prices of, 70
world production of, 221, 236
Oklahoma, 41–42, 91, 230, 256
Omnibus Appropriations bill, 123
Operation Fast and Furious, 53, 246–68, 406
Operation Wide Receiver, 348–49, 353, 355
O'Reilly, Kevin, 347
Organization of Islamic Cooperation (OIC), 324–25
Organizing for America, 54
Otis, Jr., Clarence, 281
Oval Office, 14, 330, 384
Owens, Jim, 290

P

Palin, Sarah, 42
Panetta, Leon, 165, 308
parachurches, 100
Path to Prosperity, 167–79, 186, 190, 406
Path to Prosperity 2.0, 167, 173, 176–78
Patient Protection and Affordable Care Act. *See* Obamacare
Pawlenty, Tim, 48
Pearl Harbor, 15, 379
Pearlstein, Steven, 265
Pell Grant, 67, 154, 181
Pelosi, Nancy, 60, 108, 163, 255
Pelosi, Ronald, 255
PEMEX, 220
Pennsylvania, 44, 92, 109, 110, 229, 259
Peralta, Rafael, 34

Perez, Thomas, 126
Perich, Cheryl, 100–1
Perino, Dana, 391, 396
Perkins, Tony, 103, 109
Perry, Rick, 64, 72
Peters, Ralph, 126
Pethokoukis, James, 173–74
Petrowsky, Joe, 221
Pfeiffer, Dan, 47, 50, 58, 60
Phoenix Center for Advanced Legal and Economic Public Policy Studies, 283
Pichel, Jessie, 254
Pinal County, 87
Plan B, 177
Planned Parenthood, 105–15, 124
Pleasanton Weekly, 76
Plouffe, David, 71–73, 371–72
Politico, 41, 44, 48, 63, 263, 370, 375
Pollak, Joel, 126
Pompeo, Mike, 296
Portman, Ervin, 27
Postell, Darryl, 52
Power, Samantha, 311
Prell, Michael, 327
President's Export Council, 27
Presley, Elvis, 196
Priebus, Rence, 38, 71
"primary balance," 185
private property, 13
protests, 14, 38, 52, 53, 77, 94, 112, 120, 228, 251, 259, 320, 330, 332, 384
Psaki, Jen, 61
Puget Sound Sage, 244
Putin, Vladimir, 333

Q

Qatar, 19

R

Race to the Top, 154
racism, 21, 48, 52–55, 57, 74, 125–27, 129, 132
Rasmussen, 89
Reagan Presidential Library, 49
Reason, 145
recession, 58, 134, 139–41, 143–44, 289, 295, 375
Reconquista movement, 31
Rector, Robert, 121–22
Redpoint Ventures, 247
Regulations from the Executive in Need of Scrutiny Act (REINS Act), 284
Reid, Chip, 67, 383
Reid, Harry, 109, 192, 267, 285–86
Reilly, Patrick, 118
religious liberty, 12, 58, 98–101, 120, 402
Repeal Act, 103
Republican National Committee, 38, 71
Republican party, 39, 45, 50–51, 55–56, 65,70, 196, 272, 292, 304, 370, 375–76
Respect for Marriage Act, 96
responsibility to protect (R2P), 311–12, 315, 317
Retta, Dick, 111–12
Reuters, 173, 225
Reynolds, Karen, 114
Rhode Island, 91
Rhodes, Ben, 309
Rhodes, Ryan, 50
Rice, Susan, 317
Rieff, David, 312
Ries, J. Scott, 117–18
Roberts, John (Chief Justice), 101
Roberts, John (reporter), 58
Rockefeller, John D., 259
Roe v. Wade, 105

Rohrabacher, Dana, 94
Romney, Mitt, 48, 50, 76
Rooney, Tom, 306
Roos, John V., 15
Roosevelt, Franklin, 21
Roosevelt, Theodore ("Teddy"), 202, 268
Rose, Lila, 113
Ros-Lehtinen, Ileana, 24, 331
Ross, Alec, 33
Rubin, Barry, 322
Rubin, Michael, 23
Rubio, Marco, 284
Rumsfeld, Donald, 19
Rusco, Franklin, 256
Russia, 24, 164, 281, 314–15, 333–37, 339–43
Ryan, Paul, 14, 46, 68, 167–69, 180–81, 186–88, 190, 192, 202, 204, 401

S

Safeway, 41
Salazar, Ken, 6, 209, 215–16, 221–24, 228, 234
SalesForce.com, 70
same-sex marriage, *see also* marriage, 21, 93, 95–96, 99–100
San Francisco Chronicle, 77
Sarkozy, Nicolas, 329, 392
Sauceda, Adria, 32–33
Saudi Arabia, 24, 220, 235–36, 327, 340
Save the Children U.K., 24
S.B. 1070, 22–23, 87, 90
Scalia, Antonin, 101
Schatz, Tom, 25
Schieffer, Bob, 83, 292
Schiff, Peter, 284–85
Schweizer, Peter, 255, 339–40
Sebelius, Kathleen, 95, 110, 118

Second Amendment, 8, 54
Securities and Exchange
    Commission (SEC), 4, 83, 278
Seidenberg, Ivan, 266
Sellers, Peter, 373
Senate Finance Committee, 35
Senate Health, Education, Labor
    and Pensions Committee, 79
Senate Homeland Security and
    Government Affairs Committee,
    366
Sensenbrenner, Jim, 116
Service Employees International
    Union (SEIU), 196, 274
Sessions, Jeff, 172–73, 184–85
sex education, 120–24
Shabazz, Malik Zulu, 131
Shah, Rajiv, 63
Shapiro, Gary, 288
Sharia, 316–17, 323
Sharma, Deven, 82–83
Sharpton, Al, 56, 66
Shea, Nina, 324–25
Sherk, James, 139, 276, 303
Shrum, Bob, 72, 396
Siljander Amendment, 111
Sinaloa Cartel, 365
Sitting Bull, 17
Slurpee, 39
Smith, Chris, 111, 116
Smith, Lamar, 7
Smith, M. Patricia, 79–80, 277
Smith, Wesley J., 104
SNAP. *See* Supplemental Nutrition
    Assistance Program
social media, 59–60
Social Security, 48, 50, 68, 153, 160,
    168, 177, 187, 189, 193–94
Solar Trust of America, The, 256
Solis, Hilda, 32, 80
Solyndra, 9–10, 28, 156, 242, 245–
    58, 262, 402

Sotomayor, Sonia, 127
South Carolina, 84, 89, 273, 359
South Korea, 27, 265
Sowell, Thomas, 125
Spain, 26–27, 381, 383–84
Spalding, Matthew, 269
SpectraWatt, 254
Sperling, Gene, 82
Sri Lanka, 24
St. Hilaire, Daniel, 114
Standard and Poor's (S&P), 82–83,
    195, 396, 401
Star Wars, 39
Starrett, Doug, 287
Stearns, Cliff, 252
stem cell research
    adult stem cell research, 104
    embryonic stem cell research, 6,
        93, 103–4, 300
Stephanopoulos, George, 163
Stevens, Clark, 250
Stilley, Randy, 225
stimulus, 9, 27, 38, 41, 46, 51,
    64–65, 71, 127, 134–39, 144–47,
    150, 152, 165, 188–89, 194,
    196, 201, 242–44, 246–47, 254,
    256–57, 290, 294, 300, 344,
    393, 401–2
Strait of Hormuz, 164
Strategic Petroleum Reserve, 225
Students for Life, 114
Stupak, Bart, 109
Sullivan, Andrew, 42
Summers, Larry, 247
"Summertime Blues," 145
SunShot, 156
Sunstein, Cass, 59, 278
Supplemental Nutrition Assistance
    Program (SNAP), 197–98, 201
Susan G. Komen for the Cure, 114
Sutyagin, Igor, 333
Swoboda, Chuck, 27

Syria, 308, 323, 330–31

T

Taiwan Strait, 342
Taj Mahal hotel, 385
Talabani, Jalal, 328
Tantawi, Mohammed Hussein, 322
Tapper, Jake, 182, 396
Target, 393
taxes
    Bush cuts, 67, 134, 272, 294, 297
    capital gains taxes, 78, 154, 160,
        263, 270, 402
    corporate taxes, 18, 300, 303
    income taxes, 154, 176–77, 199,
        263, 269–71, 282, 402
    middle class and, 47, 73
    Value-Added Tax (VAT), 197
    on the wealthy, 48–49, 172, 175,
        186, 194, 272
Taylor, William, 319–20
tea party, 38, 45, 47, 49, 70, 73, 85
    as racist, 50, 52–54, 57
    "teabaggers" reference to, 53
    tea party downgrade, 82–83
    as terrorists, 44
    vast majority of Americans and,
        71
Telegraph, 330, 344, 389, 397
Tennessee, 86, 259
terrorist prisoners, 23
Terry, Brian, 346, 348–49, 351,
    356–57, 359, 363, 365, 368
Texas, 11, 85, 87, 91, 114, 230, 233,
    261, 327, 345, 364
Thiessen, Marc, 317
Throw Them All Out, 255
Tkacik, John, 341
Today Show, 191, 393
Todd, Don, 276
Toledo, Ohio, 50
Tomasky, Michael, 272

Toumpas, Nick, 114
transnationalism, 34, 310
transparency, 77, 81, 239, 252, 256,
    274, 278, 284, 291, 402
Travis, Shannon, 74
Trident submarines, 335
Trudeau, Elizabeth, 394
Tucson shooting, 41–42, 349, 363,
    378
Turek, Frank, 99
Twitter, v, 59–60, 84

U

UN Development Program, 23
unemployment, *see also*
    employment, jobs, 17, 20, 52, 58,
        130, 134–35, 137–39, 141–42,
        144, 146, 194–95, 201, 230,
        232–33, 236, 259, 279, 285–86,
        296, 371, 392, 396, 401
unions, 18, 27, 47, 56, 79, 81–82,
    85, 91–92, 162–63, 196, 212,
    253, 264–65, 273–77, 298, 401
    card check legislation and, 81,
        264–65, 275
    Obamacare and, 162–63
    right-to-work states and, 265, 273
United Nations, 20, 22–26, 32,
    34–35, 95, 107–8, 124, 308–9,
    311–12, 314, 317, 324, 328–29,
    335
United Nations Human Rights
    Council (HRC), 20, 24–25
United Nations Population Fund
    (UNFPA), 107, 124
United States of America
    capitalism and, 30, 202
    Constitution of, 1–2, 5, 20, 22,
        88, 192, 282, 308, 401–3
    credit rating of, 82, 195, 396
    economy of, 133–65, 232, 234,
        242, 260, 289–90, 297, 340

freedom and, 2, 13, 16, 51, 402
future of, 16, 68, 92, 167–205, 242, 246, 274
pre-Obama, 20, 326
security of, 1, 12, 70, 103, 164–65, 178, 204, 236, 305–44
socialism and, 283, 402
in the United Nations, 20, 22, 34–35, 95, 107, 308, 317, 329
world standing of, 29, 305, 311, 325, 344
United States Supreme Court, 5, 11, 32–33, 46, 75, 100–1, 105, 127, 129, 157, 163, 290–91, 331, 401
University of Arizona, 41
University of Illinois, 224
University of Maryland, 27
University of Michigan law school, 129
University of North Carolina, 145
University of Texas, 129, 310
University of Texas at Austin, 229
University of Virginia, 274
Univision, 55
Upton, Fred, 162, 238, 251–52
USA Today, 70, 272, 357
USCCB Committee on Pro Life Activities, 118
U.S. Census Bureau, 142
U.S. Conference of Catholic Bishops, 97–98, 118–19
U.S. Congress
2010 midterm elections and, 253
Barack Obama and, 43–44, 46–48, 191, 192–93, 379–80
as coequal branch of government, 192–93
debt-ceiling debates of, 69, 190–91, 195–97
partisanship in, 45–47
Republicans in, 2, 45–46, 204, 282, 401–2

U.S. Department of Agriculture, 98, 127, 189, 197–98, 201, 228
U.S. Department of Education, 10, 29, 32, 94–95, 98, 129, 154, 189
U.S. Department of Energy, 2, 26–28, 155–56, 237, 244–45, 249–56, 280, 344
U.S. Department of Homeland Security, 7, 10, 19, 189, 323, 347
U.S. Department of Housing and Urban Development, 32
U.S. Department of the Interior, 5–6, 78, 189, 209, 215–17, 221–26, 234
U.S. Department of Justice (DOJ), 32, 84–90, 97, 100–1, 104–6, 111–13, 126, 129–32, 189, 230, 310, 324, 346–49, 351–58, 360–68, 402
U.S. Department of Labor, 32, 79–81, 135, 140, 189, 258, 276
U.S. Department of State, 22–23, 33–34, 108, 111, 189, 230–31, 310, 315, 319–20, 330–31, 339, 341
U.S. Food and Drug Administration (FDA), 8, 118
U.S. News & World Report, 394–95
USNS *Cesar Chavez*, 33–34
U.S. Treasury, 3–5, 64, 66, 82, 134, 138, 145, 169, 171, 173-74, 189, 225, 245, 253–54, 265, 267, 271, 372
Utah, 228, 282

V

Valenzuela, Arturo, 331
Value Added Tax (VAT), 197
Vandenberg Air Force Base, 336
VAWA, *see* Violence Against Women Act

Venezuela, 23, 236, 329, 331–32, 340
Verizon, 266
Verveer, Malanne, 108
Veterans Day, 15
Vienna Convention on Consular Relations, 32
Villaraigosa, Antonio, 277
Vilsack, Tom, 127–28, 201
Violence Against Women Act (VAWA), 56
Viqueira, Mike, 389
Virginia, 8, 71, 90, 212, 259, 375, 377, 393
Vitter, David, 34, 220
von Spakovsky, Hans A., 131, 276
voter ID legislation, 84–87
voter intimidation, 112, 130–32, 402
voter registration, 20, 86, 132
Voth, David, 350–52, 359

W

"wage watch" program, 79–80
Walker, Scott
Wall, Jose, 359
Wall Street Journal, 80, 82, 187, 197–98, 201, 240, 258, 269, 277, 313, 332, 391
Wallis, Jim, 15, 53
Wallison, Peter J., 5
War Powers Resolution, 310, 312–14, 317
War on Terror, 21, 305, 324, 341, 401
Warsame, Ahmed Abdulkadir, 307
Warsh, Kevin, 266
Washington (state), 145, 273, 376
Washington Archdiocese, 119
Washington Athletic Club, 243
Washington Examiner, 299, 386

Washington Post, 57, 64–65, 67–68, 103, 202, 214, 242, 247, 249, 252–53, 257, 265, 272, 312, 316, 362–63
Washington Times, 86, 238, 327, 337, 390
Waters, Maxine, 70, 257
Wayne National Forest, 228
Webb, Jim, 259
Webb, Jo Ann, 94, 359
Wehner, Peter, 73, 330
Weich, Ronald, 349, 352,354–55, 357
Weinstein, Jason, 354, 367
Welspun Tubular Company, 232
West Virginia, 259
WestStar Precision, 26
Wheeler, David K., 114
White House, 3–4, 7–8, 10, 16, 40, 42–44, 48–50, 52–53, 58–62, 65–67, 69, 71, 73, 76–79, 82–83, 91, 94, 98, 106, 110, 112, 116, 121, 127, 130, 137, 173, 190, 192, 194, 196, 201–3, 211, 213–16, 218, 222–23, 226, 239, 242–43, 245, 247, 250-52, 254, 265, 268, 273, 276, 287–88, 292–94, 301, 309–11, 315, 320–21, 330, 347, 363, 370, 372, 374, 377–78, 380–84, 386–91, 393–95
White House Council of Economic Advisers, 82
Whitfield, Ed, 241
WikiLeaks, 14, 332, 335
Will, George, 192–93, 209
Willard, Robert, 343
Williams, Brian, 2, 215
Willis Group, 158
Wiretap Affidavits, 366–67
Wisconsin, 91–92, 116, 242
Woo, Michael, 243
Wood Mackenzie, 232

Woodhouse, Brad, 48
world economy, 45
World Service, 28–29
World Vision, 100
Wright, Jeremiah, 47, 125–26
Wynn Resorts, 266
Wynn, Steve, 266–67

X
Xavier University, 215
Xerox, 27

Y
Yabunaka, Mitoji, 14

Yahoo!, 250
Yale Law School, 34, 312
Yemen, 323
York, Byron, 386
Youngman, Sam, 196
YouTube, 145

Z
Zakaria, Fareed, 265
Zelaya, Manuel, 331–32
Zients, Jeffrey, 163, 168–69
Zimbabwe, 23–24
Zogby International, 327
Zuckerman, Mortimer, 265